W9-CSK-929

Fodor's

New
3RD EDITION

Israel

" "When it comes to information on regional history, what to see and do, and shopping, these guides are exhaustive."

—*USAir Magazine*

"Valuable because of their comprehensiveness."
—*Minneapolis Star-Tribune*

"Fodor's always delivers high quality...thoughtfully presented...thorough."

—*Houston Post*

"An excellent choice for those who want everything under one cover."

—*Washington Post* "

Fodor's Travel Publications, Inc.
New York • Toronto • London • Sydney • Auckland
http://www.fodors.com/

Fodor's Israel

Editor: Linda Cabasin

Area Editors: Judy Stacey Goldman, Lisa Perlman, Mike Rogoff, Miriam Feinberg Vamosh

Ediitorial Contributors: Robert Andrews, Bob Blake, David Brown, Audra Epstein, Natasha Lesser, Anastasia Mills, Tracy Patruno, Heidi Sarna, Helayne Schiff, Mary Ellen Schultz, M.T. Schwartzman (Gold Guide editor), Barbara Sofer, Dinah Spritzer, Karen Wolman

Creative Director: Fabrizio La Rocca

Associate Art Director: Guido Caroti

Photo Researcher: Jolie Novak

Cartographer: David Lindroth

Cover Photograph: Sarah Stone/Tony Stone Images

Text Design: Between the Covers

Copyright

Special Sales

Fodor's Travel Publications are available at special discounts for bulk purchases for sales promotions or premiums. Special editions, including personalized covers, excerpts of existing guides, and corporate imprints, can be created in large quantities for special needs. For more information, contact your local bookseller or write to Special Markets, Fodor's Travel Publications, 201 East 50th Street, New York, NY 10022. Inquiries from Canada should be directed to your local Canadian bookseller or sent to Random House of Canada, Ltd., Marketing Dept., 1265 Aerowood Drive, Mississauga, Ontario L4W 1B9. Inquiries from the United Kingdom should be sent to Fodor's Travel Publications, 20 Vauxhall Bridge Road, London SW1V 2SA, England.

PRINTED IN THE UNITED STATES OF AMERICA

10 9 8 7 6 5 4 3 2 1

CONTENTS

Maps

ON THE ROAD WITH FODOR'S

WE'RE ALWAYS THRILLED to get letters from readers, especially one like this:

It took us an hour to decide what book to buy and we now know we picked the best one. Your book was wonderful, easy to follow, very accurate, and good on pointing out eating places, informal as well as formal. When we saw other people using your book, we would look at each other and smile.

Our editors and writers are deeply committed to making every Fodor's guide "the best one"—not only accurate but always charming, brimming with sound recommendations and solid ideas, right on the mark in describing restaurants and hotels, and full of fascinating facts that make you view what you've traveled to see in a rich new light.

About Our Writers

Our success in achieving our goals—and in helping to make your trip the best of all possible vacations—is a credit to the hard work of our extraordinary writers.

Judy Stacey Goldman was born in Montréal and has lived in Israel, where she is now a professional tour guide, for 24 years. She has coauthored three books about Jerusalem and Tel Aviv and is currently preparing a new book on Jerusalem. Her territory for Fodor's includes the Northern Coast and Western Galilee chapter, as well as Eilat and the Negev.

Lisa Perlman, a native of Australia, wrote her way through Japan and France before moving to Israel in 1986. She specializes in environmental issues and is a former editor of the *Jerusalem Post*'s Tel Aviv weekly, *Metro.* Look for her insights in the Gold Guide and in chapters on Tel Aviv and the Upper Galilee and the Golan.

Mike Rogoff, a professional tour guide and writer, has been exploring and studying the byways of Israel since he moved there from his native South Africa in 1970. His calling—to excite visitors of all persuasions about his new/old land—became a profession when he discovered that peo-

ple would actually pay him for doing what he loved best. Mike lives in Jerusalem and is a recipient of the Israel government's Guide of the Year award. He has contributed to *Fodor's Israel* since 1985; look for his byline in the Jerusalem, Around Jerusalem, and Lower Galilee chapters.

Miriam Feinberg Vamosh wrote the new side trip to Petra in Jordan and updated the Sinai excursion. She is a New Jersey native who has lived in Israel since 1969. A veteran tour guide, Miriam is senior editor of *Eretz* magazine, Israel's English-language geographic bimonthly.

Fodor's editor **Linda Cabasin** has hiked in the Galilee, walked the walls of the Old City in Jerusalem, and snorkeled in Eilat. She's planning her next trip to Israel with her family.

New This Year

This year we've reformatted our guides to make them easier to use. Each chapter of *Fodor's Israel* begins with brand-new recommended itineraries to help you decide what to see in the time you have; a section called When to Tour points out the optimal time of day, day of the week, and season for your journey. You may also notice our fresh graphics, new in 1996. More readable and more helpful than ever? We think so—and we hope you do, too.

To make this edition even more helpful, Mike Rogoff has expanded the sightseeing information on central and West Jerusalem, and Lisa Perlman has added a tour of Neve Tzedek, a historic neighborhood in Tel Aviv. Miriam Feinberg Vamosh wrote a new side trip to Petra in Jordan. The open borders between Israel and its neighbor make it easy for travelers to make the short trip to see the awesome remains of the ancient Nabatean city.

On the Web

Also check out Fodor's Web site (http://www.fodors.com/), where you'll find travel information on major destinations around the world and an ever-changing array of travel-savvy interactive features.

How to Use This Book

Organization

Up front is the **Gold Guide.** Its first section, **Important Contacts A to Z,** gives addresses and telephone numbers of organizations and companies that offer destination-related services and detailed information and publications. **Smart Travel Tips A to Z,** the Gold Guide's second section, gives specific information on how to accomplish what you need to in Israel as well as tips on savvy traveling. Both sections are in alphabetical order by topic.

Chapters in *Fodor's Israel* are arranged regionally, beginning with Jerusalem and its environs and Tel Aviv. The next three chapters cover Israel's northern coast and areas of the Galilee and the Golan. The book then moves south to Eilat and the Negev; it concludes with side trips to the Sinai and Petra.

Each **city chapter** begins with an Exploring section, which is subdivided by neighborhood; each subsection recommends a walking or driving tour and lists sights in alphabetical order. Each **regional chapter** is divided by geographical area; within each area, towns are covered in logical geographical order, and attractive stretches of road and minor points of interest between them are indicated by the designation *En Route*. Throughout, Off the Beaten Path sights appear after the places from which they are most easily accessible. And within town sections, all restaurants and lodgings are grouped together.

To help you decide what to visit in the time you have, all chapters begin with **recommended itineraries**; you can mix and match those from several chapters to create a complete vacation. The **A to Z section** that ends all chapters covers getting there, getting around, and helpful contacts and resources.

At the end of the book you'll find a **Chronology** and **Further Reading.** The chronology covers thousands of years of history in a few pages; Further Reading has pretrip reading, both fiction and nonfiction, to enrich your visit to Israel.

Icons and Symbols

★   Our special recommendations
✕   Restaurant
🏠   Lodging establishment
✕🏠 Lodging establishment whose restaurant warrants a detour
🐤   Good for kids (rubber duckie)
☞   Sends you to another section of the guide for more information
✉   Address
☎   Telephone number
☉   Opening and closing times
💰   Admission prices (those we give apply only to adults; substantially reduced fees are almost always available for children, students, and senior citizens)

Numbers in white and black circles that appear on the maps, in the margins, and within the tours correspond to one another.

Dining and Lodging

The restaurants and lodgings we list are the cream of the crop in each price range. Price charts appear in the Pleasures and Pastimes section that follows each chapter introduction.

Hotel Facilities

We always list the facilities that are available—but we don't specify whether they cost extra: When pricing accommodations, always ask what's included.

Restaurant Reservations and Dress Codes

Reservations are always a good idea; we note only when they're essential or when they are not accepted. Book as far ahead as you can, and reconfirm when you get to town. Unless otherwise noted, the restaurants listed are open daily for lunch and dinner. We mention dress only when men are required to wear a jacket or a jacket and tie. Look for an overview of local habits under Dining in Smart Travel Tips A to Z and in the Pleasures and Pastimes section that follows each chapter introduction.

Credit Cards

The following abbreviations are used: **AE,** American Express; **DC,** Diners Club; **MC,** MasterCard; and **V,** Visa.

Please Write to Us

You can use this book in the confidence that all prices and opening times are based on information supplied to us at press time; Fodor's cannot accept responsibility for any errors. Time inevitably brings changes, so always confirm information when it matters—especially if you're making a detour to visit a specific place. In addition, when making reservations be sure

IX

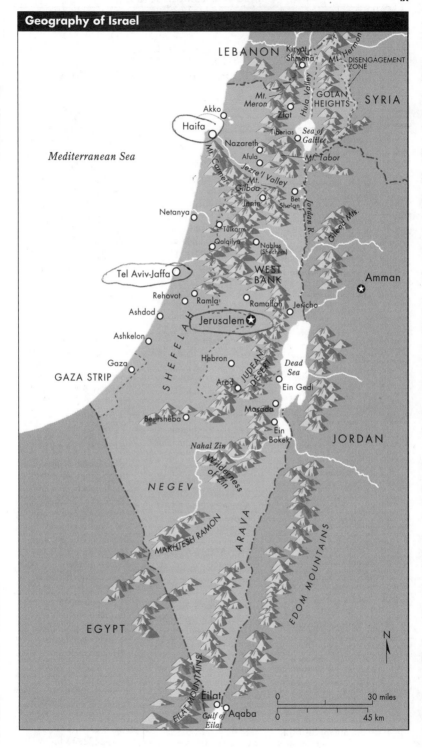

Geography of Israel

LEBANON

Kiryat Shmona

Mt. Hermon

DISENGAGEMENT ZONE

GOLAN HEIGHTS

SYRIA

Mt. Meron

Akko

Haifa

Zfat

Hula Valley

Tiberias

Sea of Galilee

Nazareth

Afula

Mt. Tabor

Mediterranean Sea

Mt. Carmel

Jezre'il Valley

Mt. Gilboa

Jenin

Bet Shean

Jordan R.

Gilead Mts.

Netanya

Tulkarm

Qalqiliya

Nablus (Shechem)

WEST BANK

Amman

Tel Aviv-Jaffa

Rehovot

Ramla

Ramallah

Jericho

Ashdod

Jerusalem

Ashkelon

SHEFELAH

Hebron

JUDEAN DESERT

Dead Sea

Gaza

GAZA STRIP

Arad

Ein Gedi

Beersheba

Masada

Ein Bokek

JORDAN

Nahal Zin

Wilderness of Zin

NEGEV

MAKHTESH RAMON

ARAVA

EDOM MOUNTAINS

EGYPT

N

EILAT MOUNTAINS

Eilat

Aqaba

Gulf of Eilat

30 miles

45 km

IMPORTANT CONTACTS A TO Z

An Alphabetical Listing of Publications, Organizations, & Companies That Will Help You Before, During, & After Your Trip

A

AIR TRAVEL

The main gateway to Israel is **Ben-Gurion International Airport** (☎ 03/971–2484), which is about halfway between Jerusalem and Tel Aviv. Charter flights from the United States sometimes land at **Ovda Airport** (☎ 07/637–5880) or **Eilat Airport** (☎ 07/637–1311 or 07/637–2614), in southern Israel.

CARRIERS

Carriers from the United States include **El Al Israel Airlines** (☎ 212/768–9200 or 800/223–6700, with nonstop service from a number of cities; in Canada ☎ 514/875–8900 or 416/804–9779), **Delta** (☎ 800/241–4141), **Tower** (☎ 718/553–8500 or 800/221–2500), **TWA** (☎ 800/892–4141), and **World Airways** (☎ 800/967–5350). **CSA/Czech Airlines** (☎ 212/682–5833) has flights to Tel Aviv requiring an overnight stay in Prague, but the airline pays for two meals and accommodations.

Carriers from Canada include **Air Canada** (☎ 800/776–3000 from the U.S., 800/268–7240 from Toronto, 800/361–8620 from Montreal, 800/663–3721 from Vancouver), and **El Al Israel Airlines** (☎ 212/768–9200 or 800/223–6700; in Canada ☎ 514/875–8900 or 416/804–9779).

FROM THE U.K.

Carriers from the United Kingdom include **British Airways** (☎ 0181/897–4000 or 0345/222–111 outside London) and **El Al Israel Airlines** (☎ 0171/957–4100).

COMPLAINTS

To register complaints about charter and scheduled airlines, contact the U.S. Department of Transportation's **Aviation Consumer Protection Division** (⌧ C-75, Washington, DC 20590, ☎ 202/366–2220). Complaints about lost baggage or ticketing problems and safety concerns may also be logged with the **Federal Aviation Administration (FAA) Consumer Hotline** (☎ 800/322–7873).

CONSOLIDATORS

For the names of reputable air-ticket consolidators, contact the **United States Air Consolidators Association** (⌧ 925 L St., Suite 220, Sacramento, CA 95814, ☎ 916/441–4166, ℻ 916/441–3520). For discount air-ticketing agencies, *see* Discounts & Deals, *below.*

PUBLICATIONS

For general information about charter carriers, ask for the Department of Transportation's free brochure **"Plane Talk: Public Charter Flights"** (⌧ Aviation Consumer Protection Division, C-75, Washington, DC 20590, ☎ 202/366–2220). The Department of Transportation also publishes a 58-page booklet, **"Fly Rights,"** available from the Consumer Information Center (⌧ Supt. of Documents, Dept. 136C, Pueblo, CO 81009; $1.75).

For other tips and hints, consult the Consumers Union's monthly **"Consumer Reports Travel Letter"** (⌧ Box 53629, Boulder, CO 80322, ☎ 800/234–1970; $39 1st year).

WITHIN ISRAEL

Arkia Israeli Airlines has flights from Jerusalem and Tel Aviv (Sde Dov Airport) to Eilat and Rosh Pina, and from Tel Aviv to Haifa, Masada (Bar Yehuda), Mitzpe Ramon, Gush Katif, and the Dead Sea (Ein Yahav). There is also service from Haifa to Jerusalem, Eilat, and the Dead Sea. Children fly for half price. Tour packages sometimes offer better deals on these flights. For reservations contact the Arkia reservations center (⌧ Sde Dov Airport, Box 39301, Tel Aviv 61392, ☎ 03/690–2222, ℻ 03/699–1390). There are Arkia offices in Jerusalem (⌧ Clal Center, ☎ 02/623–

4855, FAX 02/623–5758), Eilat (✉ Shalom Center, ☎ 07/637–3388, FAX 07/637–3370), and Haifa (✉ 84 Ha'atzmaut Blvd., ☎ 04/864–3371, FAX 04/866–3097), among other cities.

B

BETTER BUSINESS BUREAU

For local contacts in the hometown of a tour operator you may be considering, consult the **Council of Better Business Bureaus** (✉ 4200 Wilson Blvd., Suite 800, Arlington, VA 22203, ☎ 703/276–0100, FAX 703/525–8277).

BUS TRAVEL

The **Egged** cooperative (☎ 03/537–5555) handles all the country's bus routes except those in metropolitan Tel Aviv, where the Dan company (☎ 03/639–4444) operates.

For city bus information call Egged in Jerusalem (☎ 02/530–4704) or Haifa (☎ 04/854–9250) or Tel Aviv (☎ 03/537–5555).

C

CAR RENTAL

The major car-rental companies represented in Israel are **Alamo** (☎ 800/327–9633; in the U.K., 0800/272–2000), **Avis** (☎ 800/331–1084; in Canada, 800/879–2847), **Budget** (☎ 800/527–0700; in the U.K., 0800/181181), **Dollar** (☎ 800/800–4000; in the U.K., 0990/565656, where it is known as Eurodollar), **Hertz** (☎ 800/654–3001; in Canada, 800/263–0600; in the U.K., 0345/555888), and **National InterRent** (sometimes known as Europcar InterRent outside North America; ☎ 800/227–3876; in the U.K., 0345/222–525). Rates in Israel begin at $68 a day and $259 a week for an economy car with unlimited mileage; some companies require a minimum of three weeks' rental in high season. There is no tax on car rentals in Israel.

RENTAL WHOLESALERS

Contact the **Kemwel Group** (☎ 914/835–5555 or 800/678–0678).

CHILDREN & TRAVEL

FLYING

Look into **"Flying with Baby"** (✉ Third Street Press, Box 261250, Littleton, CO 80163, ☎ 303/595–5959; $4.95 includes shipping), cowritten by a flight attendant. **"Kids and Teens in Flight,"** free from the U.S. Department of Transportation's Aviation Consumer Protection Division (✉ C-75, Washington, DC 20590, ☎ 202/366–2220), offers tips on children flying alone. Every two years the February issue of *Family Travel Times* (☞ Know-How, *below*) details children's services on three dozen airlines. **"Flying Alone, Handy Advice for Kids Traveling Solo"** is available free from the American Automobile Association (AAA; send SASE: ✉ Flying Alone, Mail Stop 800, 1000 AAA Dr., Heathrow, FL 32746).

KNOW-HOW

Family Travel Times, published quarterly by Travel with Your Children (TWYCH; ✉ 40 5th Ave., New York, NY 10011, ☎ 212/477–5524; $40 per year), covers destinations, types of vacations, and modes of travel.

LODGING

The **Hilton** hotels (☎ 800/445–8667; in the U.K., ☎ 0181/780–1155) in Jerusalem and Tel Aviv offer a family plan, an organized youth camp during the summer months, and/or an all-day children's program. The **Dan** hotels (☎ 212/752–6120; in the U.K., 0171/439–9893) offer the Family Advantage plan and usually have recreation programs during vacations. **Ramada** hotels in Jerusalem and Tel Aviv offer a family plan, as do the **Radisson Moriah** hotels (☎ 800/221–0203) in Jerusalem, Tel Aviv, the Dead Sea, Eilat, and Tiberias, which also have children's programs during school vacations.

PEN PALS

Young tourists who would like to make contact with Israeli children before their visit should write to Etty Moskowitz, **Pen Pals in Israel**, ICCY, Box 8009, Jerusalem, 93107.

TOUR OPERATORS

Contact **Grandtravel** (✉ 6900 Wisconsin Ave., Suite 706, Chevy Chase, MD 20815, ☎ 301/986–0790 or 800/247–7651), which has tours for people traveling with grandchildren ages 7–17.

If you're outdoorsy, look into family-oriented programs run by the **American Museum of Natural History** (✉ 79th St. and Central Park W, New York, NY 10024, ☎ 212/769–5700 or 800/462–8687).

CUSTOMS

IN THE U.S.

The **U.S. Customs Service** (✉ Box 7407, Washington, DC 20044, ☎ 202/927–6724) can answer questions on duty-free limits and publishes a helpful brochure, "Know Before You Go." For information on registering foreign-made articles, call 202/927–0540 or write U.S. Customs Service, Resource Management, 1301 Constitution Avenue NW, Washington, DC 20229.

COMPLAINTS➤ Note the inspector's badge number and write to the commissioner's office (✉ 1301 Constitution Ave. NW, Washington, DC 20229).

CANADIANS

Contact **Revenue Canada** (✉ 2265 St. Laurent Blvd. S, Ottawa, Ontario K1G 4K3, ☎ 613/993–0534) for a copy of the free brochure **"I Declare/Je Déclare"** and for details on duty-free limits. For recorded information (within Canada only), call 800/461–9999.

U.K. CITIZENS

HM Customs and Excise (✉ Dorset House, Stamford St., London SE1 9NG, ☎ 0171/202–4227) can answer

questions about U.K. customs regulations and publishes a free pamphlet, **"A Guide for Travellers,"** detailing standard procedures and import rules.

D

DISABILITIES & ACCESSIBILITY

COMPLAINTS

To register complaints under the provisions of the Americans with Disabilities Act, contact the U.S. Department of Justice's **Disability Rights Section** (✉ Box 66738, Washington, DC 20035, ☎ 202/514–0301 or 800/514–0301, FAX 202/307–1198, TTY 202/514–0383 or 800/514–0383). For airline-related problems, contact the U.S. Department of Transportation's **Aviation Consumer Protection Division** (☞ Air Travel, *above*). For complaints about surface transportation, contact the Department of Transportation's **Civil Rights Office** (✉ 400 7th St. SW, Room 10215, Washington, DC 20590, ☎ 202/366–4648).

LOCAL INFORMATION

Contact the **Roof Association of Organizations of Persons with Disabilities** (✉ 55 Hamasger St., Tel Aviv 67217, ☎ 03/561–8557); **MILBAT–The Israeli Center for Technical Aids and Transportation** (✉ Tel Hashomer, Tel Aviv 52621, ☎ 03/530–3739); and **ILAN–The Israeli Foundation for Handicapped Children** (✉ 9 Gordon St., Tel Aviv 63458, ☎ 03/524–8141). To obtain a

copy of **Access in Israel,** a guide to accessible sights and accommodations in Israel, contact the **Pauline Hephaistos Survey Projects** (✉ 39 Bradley Gardens, West Ealing, London W13 8HE, England). The **Jerusalem Action Committee** (☎ 02/563–9839) offers advice on special problems.

Travelers who need assistance with guide dogs can contact Orna and Noah Braun (✉ Kfar Yedidye, ☎ 09/332544). In Jerusalem, the mikvah (ritual bath) in the Baka neighborhood has special facilities for visitors with disabilities (☎ 02/671–7597).

ORGANIZATIONS

TRAVELERS WITH HEARING IMPAIRMENTS➤ The **American Academy of Otolaryngology** (✉ 1 Prince St., Alexandria, VA 22314, ☎ 703/836–4444, FAX 703/683–5100, TTY 703/519–1585) publishes a brochure, "Travel Tips for Hearing Impaired People."

TRAVELERS WITH MOBILITY PROBLEMS➤ Contact **Mobility International USA** (✉ Box 10767, Eugene, OR 97440, ☎ and TTY 541/343–1284, FAX 541/343–6812), the U.S. branch of a Belgium-based organization (☞ *below*) with affiliates in 30 countries; **MossRehab Hospital Travel Information Service** (☎ 215/456–9600, TTY 215/456–9602), a telephone information resource for travelers with physical disabilities; the **Society for the Advancement of Travel for the Handicapped** (✉ 347

5th Ave., Suite 610, New York, NY 10016, ☎ 212/447–7284, FAX 212/725–8253; membership $45); and **Travelin' Talk** (✉ Box 3534, Clarksville, TN 37043, ☎ 615/552–6670, FAX 615/552–1182), which provides local contacts worldwide for travelers with disabilities.

TRAVELERS WITH VISION IMPAIRMENTS➤ Contact the **American Council of the Blind** (✉ 1155 15th St. NW, Suite 720, Washington, DC 20005, ☎ 202/467–5081, FAX 202/467–5085) for a list of travelers' resources or the **American Foundation for the Blind** (✉ 11 Penn Plaza, Suite 300, New York, NY 10001, ☎ 212/502–7600 or 800/232–5463, TTY 212/502–7662), which provides general advice and publishes "Access to Art" ($19.95), a directory of museums that accommodate travelers with vision impairments.

IN THE U.K.

Contact the **Royal Association for Disability and Rehabilitation** (RADAR; ✉ 12 City Forum, 250 City Rd., London EC1V 8AF, ☎ 0171/250–3222) or **Mobility International** (✉ Rue de Manchester 25, B-1080 Brussels, Belgium, ☎ 00–322–410–6297, FAX 00–322–410–6874), an international travel-information clearinghouse for people with disabilities.

PUBLICATIONS

Several publications for travelers with disabilities are available from the **Consumer Information Center** (✉ Box 100, Pueblo, CO 81009, ☎ 719/948–3334). Call or write for its free catalog of current titles. The Society for the Advancement of Travel for the Handicapped (☞ Organizations, *above*) publishes the quarterly magazine **"Access to Travel"** ($13 for a 1-year subscription).

The 500-page **Travelin' Talk Directory** (✉ Box 3534, Clarksville, TN 37043, ☎ 615/552–6670, FAX 615/552–1182; $35) lists people and organizations who help travelers with disabilities. For travel agents worldwide, consult the **Directory of Travel Agencies for the Disabled** (✉ Twin Peaks Press, Box 129, Vancouver, WA 98666, ☎ 360/694–2462 or 800/637–2256, FAX 360/696–3210; $19.95 plus $3 shipping).

TRAVEL AGENCIES, TOUR OPERATORS

The Americans with Disabilities Act requires all travel firms to serve the needs of all travelers. That said, you should note that some agencies and operators specialize in making travel arrangements for individuals and groups with disabilities, among them **Access Adventures** (✉ 206 Chestnut Ridge Rd., Rochester, NY 14624, ☎ 716/889–9096), run by a former physical-rehab counselor.

TRAVELERS WITH MOBILITY PROBLEMS➤ Contact **Accessible Journeys** (✉ 35 W. Sellers Ave., Ridley Park, PA 19078, ☎ 610/521–0339 or 800/846–4537, FAX 610/521–6959), an escorted-tour operator exclusively for travelers with mobility impairments; **Hinsdale Travel Service** (✉ 201 E. Ogden Ave., Suite 100, Hinsdale, IL 60521, ☎ 630/325–1335), a travel agency that benefits from the advice of wheelchair traveler Janice Perkins; and **Wheelchair Journeys** (✉ 16979 Redmond Way, Redmond, WA 98052, ☎ 206/885–2210 or 800/313–4751), which can handle arrangements worldwide.

TRAVELERS WITH DEVELOPMENTAL DISABILITIES➤ Contact the nonprofit **New Directions** (✉ 5276 Hollister Ave., Suite 207, Santa Barbara, CA 93111, ☎ 805/967–2841).

TRAVEL GEAR

The **Magellan's** catalog (☎ 800/962–4943, FAX 805/568–5406) includes a section devoted to products designed for travelers with disabilities.

DISCOUNTS & DEALS

AIRFARES

For the lowest airfares to Israel, call 800/FLY–4–LESS.

CLUBS

Contact **Entertainment Travel Editions** (✉ Box 1068, Trumbull, CT 06611, ☎ 800/445–4137; $28–$53, depending on destination), **Great American Traveler** (✉ Box 27965, Salt Lake City, UT 84127, ☎ 800/548–2812; $49.95 per year), **Moment's Notice Discount Travel Club** (✉ 7301 New Utrecht Ave., Brooklyn, NY 11204,

THE GOLD GUIDE / IMPORTANT CONTACTS

☎ 718/234–6295; $25 per year, single or family), **Privilege Card International** (✉ 3391 Peachtree Rd. NE, Suite 110, Atlanta, GA 30326, ☎ 404/262–0222 or 800/236–9732; $74.95 per year), **Travelers Advantage** (✉ CUC Travel Service, 49 Music Sq. W, Nashville, TN 37203, ☎ 800/548–1116 or 800/648–4037; $49 per year, single or family), or **Worldwide Discount Travel Club** (✉ 1674 Meridian Ave., Miami Beach, FL 33139, ☎ 305/534–2082; $50 per year for family, $40 single).

PASSES

See Bus Travel *in* Smart Travel Tips A to Z.

STUDENTS

Members of Hostelling International–American Youth Hostels (☞ Students, *below*) are eligible for discounts on car rentals, admissions to attractions, and other selected travel expenses.

PUBLICATIONS

Consult *The Frugal Globetrotter,* by Bruce Northam (✉ Fulcrum Publishing, 350 Indiana St., Suite 350, Golden, CO 80401, ☎ 800/992–2908; $16.95 plus $4 shipping). For publications that tell how to find the lowest prices on plane tickets, *see* Air Travel, *above.*

DRIVING

AUTO CLUBS

The local representative of AAA and of the British AA in Israel is **Memsi** (in Tel Aviv, ☎ 03/564–1133 for visitor information; in Jerusalem, ☎ 02/625–0661). Car-rental companies usually provide road service.

E

EGYPT & JORDAN

For information about traveling to these countries, *see* Chapter 9.

G

GAY & LESBIAN TRAVEL

ORGANIZATIONS

The **International Gay Travel Association** (✉ Box 4974, Key West, FL 33041, ☎ 800/448–8550, FAX 305/296–6633), a consortium of more than 1,000 travel companies, can supply names of gay-friendly travel agents, tour operators, and accommodations.

PUBLICATIONS

The 16-page monthly newsletter **"Out & About"** (✉ 8 W. 19th St., Suite 401, New York, NY 10011, ☎ 212/645–6922 or 800/929–2268, FAX 800/929–2215; $49 for 10 issues and quarterly calendar) covers gay-friendly resorts, hotels, cruise lines, and airlines.

TOUR OPERATORS

Toto Tours (✉ 1326 W. Albion Ave., Suite 3W, Chicago, IL 60626, ☎ 773/274–8686 or 800/565–1241, FAX 773/274–8695) offers group tours to worldwide destinations.

TRAVEL AGENCIES

The largest agencies serving gay travelers are **Advance Travel** (✉ 10700 Northwest Fwy., Suite 160, Houston, TX 77092, ☎ 713/682–2002 or 800/292–0500), **Club Travel** (✉ 8739 Santa Monica Blvd., W. Hollywood, CA 90069, ☎ 310/358–2200 or 800/429–8747), **Islanders/Kennedy Travel** (✉ 183 W. 10th St., New York, NY 10014, ☎ 212/242–3222 or 800/988–1181), **Now Voyager** (✉ 4406 18th St., San Francisco, CA 94114, ☎ 415/626–1169 or 800/255–6951), and **Yellowbrick Road** (✉ 1500 W. Balmoral Ave., Chicago, IL 60640, ☎ 773/561–1800 or 800/642–2488). **Skylink Women's Travel** (✉ 2460 W. 3rd St., Suite 215, Santa Rosa, CA 95401, ☎ 707/570–0105 or 800/225–5759) serves lesbian travelers.

H

HEALTH

FINDING A DOCTOR

For its members, the **International Association for Medical Assistance to Travellers** (IAMAT, membership free; ✉ 417 Center St., Lewiston, NY 14092, ☎ 716/754–4883; ✉ 40 Regal Rd., Guelph, Ontario N1K 1B5, ☎ 519/836–0102; ✉ 1287 St. Clair Ave. W, Toronto, Ontario M6E 1B8, ☎ 416/652–0137; ✉ 57 Voirets, 1212 Grand-Lancy, Geneva, Switzerland, no phone) publishes a worldwide directory of English-speaking physicians meeting IAMAT standards.

MEDICAL ASSISTANCE COMPANIES

The following companies are concerned primarily with emergency medical assistance, although they may provide some insurance as part of their coverage. For a list of full-service travel insurance companies, *see* Insurance, *below.*

Contact **International SOS Assistance** (✉ Box 11568, Philadelphia, PA 19116, ☎ 215/244–1500 or 800/523–8930; ✉ Box 466, Pl. Bonaventure, Montréal, Québec H5A 1C1, ☎ 514/874–7674 or 800/363–0263; ✉ 7 Old Lodge Pl., St. Margarets, Twickenham TW1 1RQ, England, ☎ 0181/744–0033), **Medex Assistance Corporation** (✉ Box 5375, Timonium, MD 21094, ☎ 410/453–6300 or 800/537–2029), **Near Travel Services** (✉ Box 1339, Calumet City, IL 60409, ☎ 708/868–6700 or 800/654–6700), **Traveler's Emergency Network** (✉ 1133 15th St. NW, Suite 400, Washington, DC 20005, ☎ 202/828–5894 or 800/275–4836, FAX 202/828–5896), **TravMed** (✉ Box 5375, Timonium, MD 21094, ☎ 410/453–6380 or 800/732–5309), or **Worldwide Assistance Services** (✉ 1133 15th St. NW, Suite 400, Washington, DC 20005, ☎ 202/331–1609 or 800/821–2828, FAX 202/828–5896).

I
INSURANCE

IN CANADA

Contact **Mutual of Omaha** (✉ Travel Division, 500 University Ave., Toronto, Ontario M5G 1V8, ☎ 800/465–0267 in Canada or 416/598–4083).

IN THE U.S.

Travel insurance covering baggage, health, and trip cancellation or interruptions is available from **Access America** (✉ 6600 W. Broad St., Richmond, VA 23230, ☎ 804/285–3300 or 800/334–7525), **Carefree Travel Insurance** (✉ Box 9366, 100 Garden City Plaza, Garden City, NY 11530, ☎ 516/294–0220 or 800/323–3149), **Tele-Trip** (✉ Mutual of Omaha Plaza, Box 31716, Omaha, NE 68131, ☎ 800/228–9792), **Travel Guard International** (✉ 1145 Clark St., Stevens Point, WI 54481, ☎ 715/345–0505 or 800/826–1300), **Travel Insured International** (✉ Box 280568, East Hartford, CT 06128, ☎ 203/528–7663 or 800/243–3174), and **Wallach & Company** (✉ 107 W. Federal St., Box 480, Middleburg, VA 22117, ☎ 540/687–3166 or 800/237–6615).

IN THE U.K.

The **Association of British Insurers** (✉ 51 Gresham St., London EC2V 7HQ, ☎ 0171/600–3333) gives advice by phone and publishes the free pamphlet **"Holiday Insurance and Motoring Abroad,"** which sets out typical policy provisions and costs.

L
LODGING

APARTMENT & VILLA RENTAL

Among the companies to contact are **Europa-Let/Tropical Inn-Let, Inc.** (✉ 92 N. Main St., Ashland, OR 97520, ☎ 541/482–5806 or 800/462–4486, FAX 541/482–0660), **Hometours International** (✉ Box 11503, Knoxville, TN 37939, ☎ 423/690–8484 or 800/367–4668), and **Property Rentals International** (✉ 1008 Mansfield Crossing Rd., Richmond, VA 23236, ☎ 804/378–6054 or 800/220–3332, FAX 804/379–2073).

CAMPING

Most Israeli campsites offer water, bathrooms, showers, first aid, telephones, cabins for rent and often have mobile homes set on blocks. Some even have swimming pools or are near beaches. They are all guarded and lighted at night. Advance reservations are recommended for July, August, and Jewish holidays. Information is available from the **Israel Government Tourist Office** (☞ Visitor Information, *below.*).

HOME EXCHANGE

Some of the principal clearinghouses are **HomeLink International/Vacation Exchange Club** (✉ Box 650, Key West, FL 33041, ☎ 305/294–1448 or 800/638–3841, FAX 305/294–1148; $78 per year), which sends members five annual directories, with a listing in one, plus updates; and **Loan-a-Home** (✉ 2 Park La., Apt. 6E, Mount Vernon, NY 10552, ☎ 914/664–7640; $40–$50 per year), which specializes in long-term exchanges.

KIBBUTZ GUEST HOUSES

For more information, contact the **Kibbutz Hotels Chain** (✉ 90 Ben Yehuda St., Box 3193,

THE GOLD GUIDE / IMPORTANT CONTACTS

Tel Aviv 61031, Israel, ☎ 03/524–6161, FAX 03/527–8088; ✉ 60 E. 42nd St., Suite 620, New York, NY 10165, ☎ 212/697–5116; ✉ Israel Hotel Reservation Center, 20 S. Van Brunt St., Englewood, NJ 07631, ☎ 201/816–0830 or 800/522–6401).

YOUTH HOSTELS

Contact the **Israel Youth Hostel Association** (✉ Binyenei Ha'Ooma, Congress Center, Box 1075, Jerusalem 91009, ☎ 02/655–8420, FAX 02/655–8430; 36 Bnei Dan, Tel Aviv 61021, ☎ 03/544–1748, FAX 03/544–1030), which offers several bargain travel packages.

M
MONEY MATTERS

ATMS

For specific foreign **Cirrus** locations, call 800/424–7787; for foreign **Plus** locations, consult the Plus directory at your local bank.

CURRENCY EXCHANGE

If your bank doesn't exchange currency, contact **Thomas Cook Currency Services** (☎ 800/287–7362 for locations). **Ruesch International** (☎ 800/424–2923 for locations) can also provide you with foreign banknotes before you leave home and publishes a number of useful brochures, including a "Foreign Currency Guide" and "Foreign Exchange Tips."

WIRING FUNDS

Funds can be wired via **MoneyGram℠** (for locations and informa-tion in the U.S. and Canada, ☎ 800/926–9400) or **Western Union** (for agent locations or to send money using MasterCard or Visa, ☎ 800/325–6000; in Canada, 800/321–2923; in the U.K., 0800/833833; or visit the Western Union office at the nearest major post office).

N
NATURE RESERVES & PARKS

For such a small, arid country, Israel has many parks and nature reserves. A full list of parks, including those with camping facilities, can be obtained from the **Jewish National Fund** (JNF; ✉ Corner of Keren Kayemet and Keren Hayesod Sts., Box 283, Jerusalem 91002, ☎ 02/670–7411). The JNF also runs summer camping programs for families (☎ 02/625–8210). For information on nature reserves, contact the **Nature Reserves Au-thority** (✉ 78 Yirmi-yahu St., Jerusalem 94467, ☎ 02/500–5444). For about NIS 45 ($15) you can pur-chase a pass valid for entry to all 13 reserves in Israel for one month.

The Green Card, priced at around NIS 51 ($17), allows unlimited entry for 14 days to any of the 40 parks and historical sites adminis-tered by the **National Parks Authority** (✉ 35 Jabo St., Ramat Gan 52511, ☎ 03/576–6834). Cards can be purchased from the National Parks Au-thority or at the follow-ing sites: Herodion, Masada, Megiddo, Bet She'an, Hammat Tiberias, Tel Hatzor, Qumran, Ovdat, Bet Alfa, Zippori, Bet She'arim, Korazim, and Caesarea.

P
PACKING

For strategies on pack-ing light, get a copy of **The Packing Book,** by Judith Gilford (✉ Ten Speed Press, Box 7123, Berkeley, CA 94707, ☎ 510/559–1600 or 800/841–2665, FAX 510/524–4588; $7.95 plus $3.50 shipping).

PASSPORTS & VISAS

IN THE U.S.

For fees, documentation requirements, and other information, call the State Department's **Office of Passport Services** information line (☎ 202/647–0518).

CANADIANS

For fees, documentation requirements, and other information, call the Ministry of Foreign Affairs and Interna-tional Trade's **Passport Office** (☎ 819/994–3500 or 800/567–6868).

U.K. CITIZENS

For fees, documentation requirements, and to request an emergency passport, call the **Lon-don Passport Office** (☎ 0990/210410).

PHOTO HELP

The **Kodak Information Center** (☎ 800/242–2424) answers con-sumer questions about film and photography. The **Kodak Guide to Shooting Great Travel**

Pictures (available in bookstores; or contact Fodor's Travel Publications, ☎ 800/533–6478; $16.50 plus $4 shipping) explains how to take expert travel photographs.

S

SAFETY

"Trouble-Free Travel," from the AAA, is a booklet of tips for protecting yourself and your belongings when away from home. Send a stamped, self-addressed, legal-size envelope to Trouble-Free Travel (✉ Mail Stop 75, 1000 AAA Dr., Heathrow, FL 32746).

SENIOR CITIZENS

CLUBS

Sears's **Mature Outlook** (✉ Box 10448, Des Moines, IA 50306, ☎ 800/336–6330; annual membership $14.95) includes a lifestyle/travel magazine and membership in ITC-50, a travel club that offers discounts of up to 50% at participating hotels and restaurants (☞ Discounts & Deals *in* Smart Travel Tips A to Z).

EDUCATIONAL TRAVEL

The nonprofit **Elderhostel** (✉ 75 Federal St., 3rd floor, Boston, MA 02110, ☎ 617/426–7788), for people 55 and older, has offered inexpensive study programs since 1975. Courses cover everything from marine science to Greek mythology and cowboy poetry. Costs for two- to three-week international trips—including room, board, and transportation from the United

States—range from $1,800 to $4,500.

ORGANIZATIONS

Contact the **American Association of Retired Persons** (AARP; ✉ 601 E St. NW, Washington, DC 20049, ☎ 202/434–2277; annual dues $8 per person or couple). Its Purchase Privilege Program secures discounts for members on lodging, car rentals, and sightseeing.

SPORTS

GOLF

Israel's only golf course, the **Caesarea Golf Club** (✉ Box 1010, Caesarea 38900, ☎ 06/366–1172), on the northern coast, is open seven days a week. Tourists can obtain special memberships, and the clubs rents all equipment.

PARACHUTING, GLIDING, & AEROMODELING

Parachuting, hang gliding, and aeromodeling (manipulating model airplanes) can be arranged through the **Aero Club of Israel** (✉ 67 Hayarkon St., Tel Aviv 63903, ☎ 03/517–5038).

SKIING

Israel's only ski resort sits on Mt. Hermon (☎ 06/698–1337) and offers gentle as well as steep slopes. There is a rental shop and a ski school in season.

TENNIS

Tennis centers are located throughout the country. There are nominal court fees, and you should reserve in advance. Ask for the **National Tennis Center** in your area (✉ Central office: Box 51, Ramat

Hasharon 47100, ☎ 03/645–6666).

WATER SPORTS

Scuba diving and snorkeling are popular in Eilat and various Mediterranean beaches. Information is available from the **Israeli Diving Federation** (✉ Box 3404, Tel Aviv 61033, ☎ 03/523–6436). Divers must present an advanced open-water license or a junior scuba-diver license, or take a course. Windsurfing and waterskiing are offered at various beaches, but not at hotels.

STUDENTS

GROUPS

A major tour operator specializing in student travel is **AESU Travel** (✉ 2 Hamill Rd., Suite 248, Baltimore, MD 21210-1807, ☎ 410/323–4416 or 800/638–7640).

HOSTELING

In the United States, contact **Hostelling International–American Youth Hostels** (✉ 733 15th St. NW, Suite 840, Washington, DC 20005, ☎ 202/783–6161, FAX 202/783–6171); in Canada, **Hostelling International–Canada** (✉ 205 Catherine St., Suite 400, Ottawa, Ontario K2P 1C3, ☎ 613/237–7884); and in the United Kingdom, the **Youth Hostel Association of England and Wales** (✉ Trevelyan House, 8 St. Stephen's Hill, St. Albans, Hertfordshire AL1 2DY, ☎ 01727/855215 or 01727/845047). Membership ($25 in the U.S.; C$26.75 in Canada; £9.30 in the U.K.) gives you access to 5,000

THE GOLD GUIDE / IMPORTANT CONTACTS

hostels in 77 countries that charge $5–$40 per person per night.

ORGANIZATIONS

A major contact is the **Council on International Educational Exchange** (Mail orders only: ✉ CIEE, 205 E. 42nd St., 16th floor, New York, NY 10017, ☎ 212/822–2600, FAX 212/822–2699). The **Educational Travel Centre** (✉ 438 N. Frances St., Madison, WI 53703, ☎ 608/256–5551 or 800/747–5551, FAX 608/256–2042) offers rail passes and low-cost airline tickets, mostly for flights that depart from Chicago.

In Canada, also contact **Travel Cuts** (✉ 187 College St., Toronto, Ontario M5T 1P7, ☎ 416/979–2406 or 800/667–2887).

The **Israel Student Travel Association** (ISSTA; ✉ 128 Ben Yehuda St., Tel Aviv 63401, ☎ 03/521–4444) has 12 branches, most of them on university campuses throughout Israel. Other main offices are in Tel Aviv (✉ 50 Dizengoff St., 64332, ☎ 03/525–0037), Jerusalem (✉ 31 Hanevi'im St., 95103, ☎ 02/625–7257), and Haifa (✉ 29 Nordau St., 33121, ☎ 04/866–9139). ISSTA offers discounted tours, car rentals, hotels, and flights. Students from abroad often take advantage of ISSTA's international travel programs.

T
TELEPHONES

The international country code for Israel is

972. For local access numbers for calls abroad, contact **AT&T** USADirect (☎ 800/874–4000), **MCI** Call USA (☎ 800/444–4444), or **Sprint** Express (☎ 800/793–1153).

TOUR OPERATORS

Among the companies that sell tours and packages to Israel, the following are nationally known, have a proven reputation, and offer plenty of options.

GROUP TOURS

SUPER-DELUXE➤ **Abercrombie & Kent** (✉ 1520 Kensington Rd., Oak Brook, IL 60521-2141, ☎ 708/954–2944 or 800/323–7308, FAX 708/954–3324) and **Travcoa** (✉ Box 2630, 2350 S.E. Bristol St., Newport Beach, CA 92660, ☎ 714/476–2800 or 800/992–2003, FAX 714/476–2538).

DELUXE➤ **Globus** (✉ 5301 S. Federal Circle, Littleton, CO 80123, ☎ 303/797–2800 or 800/221–0090, FAX 303/795–0962) and **Maupintour** (✉ Box 807, 1515 St. Andrews Dr., Lawrence, KS 66047, ☎ 913/843–1211 or 800/255–4266, FAX 913/843–8351).

FIRST-CLASS➤ **Brendan Tours** (✉ 15137 Califa St., Van Nuys, CA 91411, ☎ 818/785–9696 or 800/421–8446, FAX 818/902–9876), **Central Holidays** (✉ 206 Central Ave., Jersey City, NJ 07307, ☎ 201/798–5777 or 800/935–5000), **Collette Tours** (✉ 162 Middle St., Pawtucket, RI 02860, ☎ 401/728–3805 or 800/832–4656, FAX 401/728–1380), **General Tours** (✉ 53 Summer

St., Keene, NH 03431, ☎ 603/357–5033 or 800/221–2216, FAX 603/357–4548), **Insight International Tours** (✉ 745 Atlantic Ave., #720, Boston, MA 02111, ☎ 617/482–2000 or 800/582–8380, FAX 617/482–2884 or 800/622–5015), **Isram Tours and Travel** (✉ 630 3rd Ave., New York, NY 10117, ☎ 212/661–1193), and **Trafalgar Tours** (✉ 11 E. 26th St., New York, NY 10010, ☎ 212/689–8977 or 800/854–0103, FAX 800/457–6644).

BUDGET➤ **Cosmos** (☞ Globus, *above*).

PACKAGES

Independent vacation packages that include round-trip airfare and hotel accommodations are available from major airlines and tour operators. Among U.S. carriers, contact **Delta Dream Vacations** (☎ 800/872–7786). Leading tour operators include **Central Holidays Tours** (☞ Group Tours, *above*) and **General Tours** (☞ Group Tours, *above*).

FROM THE U.K.

Contact **Longwood Travel & Holidays** (✉ 182 Longwood Gardens, Ilford, Essex IG5 0EW, ☎ 0181/551–4494). **Superstar** (✉ 185 Regent St., London W1R 8EU, ☎ 0345/125–84781 or 0171/437–9277) and **Pullman** (✉ 31 Belgrave Rd., London SW1V 1RB, ☎ 0171/630–5111) also offer accommodations in kibbutzim.

THEME TRIPS

Travel Contacts (✉ Box 173, Camberley, GU15

1YE England, ☎ 011/
44/1/27667–7217, FAX
011/44/1/2766–3477),
which represents over
160 tour operators, can
satisfy just about any
special interest in Israel.

ADVENTURE➤ Action-
packed tours of Israel
are sold by **Adventure
Center** (✉ 1311 63rd
St., #200, Emeryville,
CA 94608, ☎ 510/
654–1879 or 800/227–
8747, FAX 510/654–
4200).

BICYCLING➤ For a
biking and hiking
expedition through
Israel and Turkey, try
Butterfield & Robinson
(✉ 70 Bond St.,
Toronto, Ontario M5B
1X3, ☎ 416/864–1354
or 800/387–1147).

ARCHAEOLOGY➤ **Ar-
chaeological Tours**
(✉ 271 Madison Ave.,
New York, NY 10016,
☎ 212/986–3054,
FAX 212/370–1561)
explores Israel's rich
history.

HISTORY➤ History
buffs should contact
Herodot Travel (✉ 775
E. Blithedale, Box 234,
Mill Valley, CA 94941,
☎ FAX 415/381–4031).

JUDAISM➤ Jewish life in
Israel can be experi-
enced on trips with the
**American Jewish
Congress** (✉ 15 E. 84th
St., New York, NY
10028, ☎ 212/879–
4588 or 800/221–
4694). The **B'nai B'rith
Center for Jewish Iden-
tity** (✉ 1640 Rhode
Island Ave. NW, Wash-
ington, DC 20036, ☎
202/857–6577 or 800/
500–6533) has travel
programs with a Jewish
orientation.

LEARNING VACATIONS➤
For educational pro-
grams contact **Earth-**

watch (✉ Box 403, 680
Mt. Auburn St., Water-
town, MA 02272, ☎
617/926–8200 or 800/
776–0188, FAX 617/
926–8532), which
recruits volunteers to
serve in its EarthCorps
as short-term assistants
to scientists on research
expeditions, and **Smith-
sonian Study Tours and
Seminars** (✉ 1100
Jefferson Dr. SW, Room
3045, MRC 702, Wash-
ington, DC 20560, ☎
202/357–4700, FAX 202/
633–9250).

NATURAL HISTORY➤
The **Society for the
Protection of Nature in
Israel (SPNI) Nature
Trails** (✉ 89 5th Ave.,
Suite 800, New York,
NY 10008, ☎ 212/
645–8732 or 212/398–
6750 for information
about membership,
which includes tour
discounts) has a range
of tours to help you
encounter nature in
Israel. **Questers** (✉ 381
Park Ave. S, New York,
NY 10016, ☎ 212/
251–0444 or 800/468–
8668, FAX 212/251–
0890) explores the wild
side of Israel in the
company of expert
guides.

SCUBA DIVING➤ Dive
packages are available
from **Rothschild Dive
Safaris** (✉ 900 West
End Ave., #1B, New
York, NY 10025-3525,
☎ 212/662–4858 or
800/359–0747, FAX 212/
749–6172).

SINGLES AND YOUNG
ADULTS➤ Travelers 18–
35 looking to join a
group should try **Contiki
Holidays** (✉ 300 Plaza
Alicante, #900, Garden
Grove, CA 92640,
☎ 714/740–0808 or
800/266–8454, FAX 714/
740–0818).

WALKING/HIKING➤
For walking and hiking
tours in Israel, contact
Adventure Center (☞
Adventure, *above*),
Backroads (✉ 1516
5th St., Berkeley, CA
94710-1740, ☎ 510/
577–1555 or 800/462–
2848, FAX 510/527–
1444), and **Wilderness
Travel** (✉ 801 Allston
Way, Berkeley, CA
94710, ☎ 510/548–
0420 or 800/368–2794,
FAX 510/548–0347).

**GUIDE-DRIVEN
LIMOUSINES**

Modern, air-condi-
tioned limousines and
minibuses driven by
expert guides are often
available at prices lower
than those of taxis. This
is a good value for a
family or group of five
to seven passengers. At
press time costs are
$265 a day (nine hours)
for up to three passen-
gers, $300 for four to
seven passengers, and
$350 for 9–11 passen-
gers. Rates are based on
200 km (120 mi) of
travel a day, averaged
out over the entire tour,
and nine hours a day of
touring. An additional
$55–$70 per night
(depending on location)
is charged for the
driver's expenses if he
or she sleeps away from
home base. Half-day
tours are also available.
Companies specializing
in guide/driver services
include **Eshkolot Tours**
(✉ 36 Keren Hayesod
St., Jerusalem, ☎ 02/
563–5555 or 02/566–
5555, FAX 02/563–
2101); and **Twelve
Tribes** (✉ 29 Hamered
St., Tel Aviv, ☎ 03/
510–1911, FAX 03/510–
1943, or at Ben-Gurion
Airport, ☎ 03/973–
1780).

ORGANIZATIONS

The **National Tour Association** (NTA; ⊠ 546 E. Main St., Lexington, KY 40508, ☎ 606/226–4444 or 800/755–8687) and the **United States Tour Operators Association** (USTOA; ⊠ 211 E. 51st St., Suite 12B, New York, NY 10022, ☎ 212/750–7371) can provide lists of members and information on booking tours.

PUBLICATIONS

Contact the USTOA (☞ Organizations, *above*) for its **"Smart Traveler's Planning Kit."** Pamphlets in the kit include the "Worldwide Tour and Vacation Package Finder," "How to Select a Tour or Vacation Package," and information on the organization's consumer protection plan. Also get copy of the Better Business Bureau's **"Tips on Travel Packages"** (⊠ Publication 24-195, 4200 Wilson Blvd., Arlington, VA 22203; $2).

TRAIN TRAVEL

Although train travel is not as important in Israel as in other countries, there are routes between Jerusalem and Tel Aviv and from Tel Aviv north to Haifa and Nahariya. For information, contact the **Central Station** (also known as Arlosoroff) in Tel Aviv at 03/693–7515.

TRAVEL AGENCIES

For names of reputable agencies in your area, contact the **American Society of Travel Agents** (ASTA; ⊠ 1101 King St., Suite 200, Alexandria, VA 22314, ☎ 703/739–2782), the

Association of Canadian Travel Agents (⊠ Suite 201, 1729 Bank St., Ottawa, Ontario K1V 7Z5, ☎ 613/521–0474, FAX 613/521–0805), or the **Association of British Travel Agents** (⊠ 55–57 Newman St., London W1P 4AH England, ☎ 0171/637–2444, FAX 0171/637–0713).

TRAVEL GEAR

For travel apparel, appliances, personal-care items, and other travel necessities, get a free catalog from **Magellan's** (☎ 800/962–4943, FAX 805/568–5406), **Orvis Travel** (☎ 800/541–3541, FAX 540/343–7053), or **TravelSmith** (☎ 800/950–1600, FAX 415/455–0554).

ELECTRICAL CONVERTERS

Send a self-addressed, stamped envelope to the **Franzus Company** (⊠ Customer Service, Dept. B50, Murtha Industrial Park, Box 142, Beacon Falls, CT 06403, ☎ 203/723–6664) for a copy of the free brochure "Foreign Electricity Is No Deep, Dark Secret."

U

U.S. GOVERNMENT TRAVEL BRIEFINGS

The U.S. Department of State's American Citizens Services office (⊠ Room 4811, Washington, DC 20520; enclose SASE) issues **Consular Information Sheets** on all foreign countries. These cover issues such as crime, security, political climate, and health risks as well as listing embassy locations, entry require-

ments, currency regulations, and providing other useful information. For the latest information, stop in at any U.S. passport office, consulate, or embassy; call the interactive hot line (☎ 202/647–5225, FAX 202/647–3000); or with your PC's modem, tap into the department's computer bulletin board (☎ 202/647–9225).

V

VISITOR INFORMATION

IN THE U.S.

Contact the **Israel Government Tourist Offices:** ⊠ 800 2nd Ave., 16th floor, New York, NY 10017, ☎ 212/499–5650, FAX 212/499–5645; ⊠ 5 S. Wabash Ave., Chicago, IL 60603, ☎ 312/782–4306, FAX 312/782–1243; ⊠ 5151 Belt Line Rd., Suite 1280, Dallas, TX 75240, ☎ 800/472–6364 or 214/991–9097, FAX 214/392–3251; ⊠ 6380 Wilshire Blvd., Suite 1700, Los Angeles, CA 90048, ☎ 213/658–7462, ext. 03, FAX 213/658–6543. For on-line information, try the IGTO Web site at http://www.infotour.co.il.

IN CANADA

Contact the **Israel Government Tourist Office** (⊠ 180 Bloor St. W, Toronto, Ontario M5S 2V6, ☎ 416/964–3784, FAX 416/964–2420).

IN THE U.K.

Contact the **Israel Government Tourist Office** (⊠ 18 Great Marlborough St., London W1V 1AF, ☎ 0171/434–3651).

W
WEATHER

For current conditions and forecasts, plus the local time and helpful travel tips, call the **Weather Channel Connection** (☏ 900/932– 8437; 95¢ per minute) from a Touch-Tone phone.

The *International Traveler's Weather Guide* (✉ Weather Press, Box 660606, Sacramento, CA 95866, ☏ 916/ 974–0201 or 800/972– 0201; $10.95 includes shipping), written by two meteorologists, provides month-by-month information on temperature, humidity, and precipitation in more than 175 cities worldwide.

THE GOLD GUIDE / IMPORTANT CONTACTS

SMART TRAVEL TIPS A TO Z

Basic Information on Traveling in Israel & Savvy Tips to Make Your Trip a Breeze

A
AIR TRAVEL

If time is an issue, **always look for nonstop flights,** which require no change of plane. If possible, **avoid connecting flights,** which stop at least once and can involve a change of plane, even though the flight number remains the same; if the first leg is late, the second waits.

For better service, **fly smaller or regional carriers,** which often have higher passenger satisfaction ratings. Sometimes they have such in-flight amenities as leather seats or greater legroom, and they often have better food.

CUTTING COSTS

Look for deals in the Sunday travel section of most newspapers.

MAJOR AIRLINES➤ The least-expensive airfares from the major airlines are priced for round-trip travel and are subject to restrictions. Usually, you must **book in advance and buy the ticket within 24 hours** to get cheaper fares, and you may have to **stay over a Saturday night.** The lowest fare is subject to availability, and only a small percentage of the plane's total seats is sold at that price. It's smart to **call a number of airlines, and when you are quoted a good price, book it on the spot**—the same fare may not be available on

the same flight the next day. Airlines generally allow you to change your return date for a $25 to $50 fee. If you don't use your ticket, you can apply the cost toward the purchase of a new ticket, again for a small charge. However, most low-fare tickets are nonrefundable. To get the lowest airfare, **check different routings.** If your destination has more than one gateway, **compare prices to different airports.**

FROM THE U.K.➤ To save money on flights, **look into an APEX or Super-Pex ticket.** APEX tickets must be booked in advance and have certain restrictions. Super-PEX tickets can be purchased right at the airport.

CONSOLIDATORS➤ Consolidators buy tickets for scheduled flights at reduced rates from the airlines, then sell them at prices below the lowest available from the airlines directly—usually without advance restrictions. Sometimes you can even get your money back if you need to return the ticket. Carefully read the fine print detailing penalties for changes and cancellations. If you doubt the reliability of a consolidator, **confirm your reservation with the airline.**

ALOFT

AIRLINE FOOD➤ If you hate airline food, **ask for special meals when**

booking. These can be vegetarian, low-cholesterol, or kosher, for example; commonly prepared to order in smaller quantities than standard fare, they can be tastier.

JET LAG➤ To avoid this syndrome, which occurs when travel disrupts your body's natural cycles, try to maintain a normal routine. At night, **get some sleep.** By day, move about the cabin to **stretch your legs, eat light meals, and drink water—not alcohol.**

SMOKING➤ Smoking is not allowed on flights of six hours or less within the continental United States. Smoking is also prohibited on flights within Canada. For U.S. flights longer than six hours or international flights, **contact your carrier regarding its smoking policy.** Some carriers have prohibited smoking throughout their system; others allow smoking only on certain routes or even certain departures of that route.

B
BEACHES

Israel's Mediterranean coastline has many public beaches, which usually offer changing facilities and bathrooms for a modest fee. It is advisable to **swim only at designated areas, where lifeguards are on duty.** A flag system indicates how dangerous the waves and undertow are: A black flag means that conditions are rough, and swimming is not allowed; a red flag means moderate waves, swim with discretion; a white flag indicates a calm sea.

Women often sunbathe topless on the beaches in Eilat. At the other extreme, many beaches offer sections for women and men who prefer to bathe separately for reasons of modesty. Some Mediterranean beaches and most beaches on the Dead Sea and the Sea of Galilee are stony. Be sure to **wear rubber beach shoes,** especially when swimming amid the spiky coral reefs of the Red Sea.

BUS TRAVEL

You can get almost anywhere in Israel by bus, and the Central Bus Station is a fixture in most towns. Ask for the *tahana merkazit,* and anyone will direct you. The Egged cooperative handles all the country's bus routes except those in metropolitan Tel Aviv, where the Dan company also operates. Rates are relatively low, and timetables are accurate. You do not need exact change on city buses. If you get on a bus at a highway stop, you can pay the driver. **Keep in mind that public transportation generally stops for Shabbat** (the Jewish sabbath, which lasts from late Friday afternoon to Saturday evening), although some lines run minibuses in Tel Aviv, and Haifa, with a large Arab population, also has some service. It is advisable to **reserve seats in advance on buses from the major cities to Eilat and the Dead Sea.**

DISCOUNT PASSES

Egged offers a variety of bus passes. The Israbus Pass, payable in shekels and available only at Egged Tours offices in Israel, allows tourists unlimited travel. A one-week pass costs NIS 219 ($73); two weeks, NIS 349 ($116); three weeks, NIS 425 ($142); four weeks, NIS 480 ($160). You must **present your passport at the time of purchase.** Within each city you can **purchase a multi-ride ticket,** or *kartisia* (10% reduction of bulk tickets of 10 or 20 rides), and monthly tickets (unlimited service within the month) at nearly any city bus station or on the bus. These are particularly good for children and senior citizens, who get large discounts.

BUSINESS HOURS

For information about national and religious holidays in Israel and their effect on various businesses and services, *see* National and Religious Holidays *in* Chapter 1. The weekly observance of Shabbat has a different impact on different parts of the country: Businesses in Jewish Israel close, but non-kosher restaurants will be open in more secular cities such as Tel Aviv.

Businesses are often open by 8:30 in Israel and shops a little later (9–10); neighborhood grocery stores often open as early as 6. Some businesses still close for siesta for two or three hours between 1 and 4. Most stores do not close before 7 PM. Supermarkets are often open later, and in large cities, there are all-night supermarkets. Arab-owned stores usually open at 8 and close late afternoon.

Stores are closed Friday afternoon; some eateries and kiosks remain open. Some supermarkets are open Saturday night. Museums don't have a fixed closing day, and, although hours are usually 10–6, you must call.

Although hours can differ among banks, almost all open by 8:30. Most close from 12:30 to 4 and then reopen until 5:30, but some stay open longer, and in large cities there are branches open in the evening. Banks are closed on Saturday except in Muslim areas, where they're closed Friday. In Christian areas they're open Saturday morning and closed Sunday.

C
CAMERAS, CAMCORDERS, & COMPUTERS

IN TRANSIT

Always **keep your film, tape, or disks out of the sun;** never put these on the dashboard of a car. Carry an extra supply of batteries and **be prepared to turn on your camera, camcorder, or laptop computer for security personnel** to prove that it's real.

X RAYS

Always **ask for hand inspection at security.** Such requests are virtually always honored at

THE GOLD GUIDE / SMART TRAVEL TIPS

U.S. airports and are usually accommodated abroad. Photographic film becomes clouded after successive exposure to airport X-ray machines. Videotape and computer disks are not harmed by X rays, but **keep your tapes and disks away from metal detectors.**

CUSTOMS

Before departing, **register your foreign-made camera or laptop with U.S. Customs.** If your equipment is U.S.-made, call the consulate of the country you'll be visiting to find out whether it should be registered with local customs upon arrival.

CAR RENTAL

CUTTING COSTS

To get the best deal, **book through a travel agent who is willing to shop around.** Ask your agent to **look for fly-drive packages,** which also save you money, and **ask if local taxes are included** in the rental or fly-drive price. These can be as high as 20% in some destinations. Don't forget to find out about required deposits, cancellation penalties, drop-off charges, and the cost of any required insurance coverage.

Also **ask your travel agent about a company's customer-service record.** How has it responded to late plane arrivals and vehicle mishaps? Are there often lines at the rental counter, and—if you're traveling during a holiday period—does a confirmed reservation guarantee you a car?

Always **find out what equipment is standard**

at your destination before specifying what you want; automatic transmission and air-conditioning are usually optional—and very expensive.

Be sure to **look into wholesalers**—companies that do not own their own fleets but rent in bulk from those that do and often offer better rates than traditional car-rental operations. Prices are best during off-peak periods; you must pay for rentals booked through wholesalers before you leave the United States.

INSURANCE

When driving a rented car, you are generally responsible for any damage to or loss of the rental vehicle, as well as any property damage or personal injury that you cause. Before you rent, **see what coverage you already have** under the terms of your personal auto-insurance policy and credit cards.

If you do not have auto insurance or an umbrella insurance policy that covers damage to third parties, it's highly recommended you purchase coverage from your car rental company, known as collison- or loss-damage waiver (CDW or LDW), that eliminates your liability for damage to the car.

LICENSE REQUIREMENTS

In Israel your own driver's license is acceptable, but an International Driver's Permit is a good idea; it's available from the American or Canadian automobile associa-

tions, or in the United Kingdom, from the AA or RAC.

SURCHARGES

Before you pick up a car in one city and leave it in another, **ask about drop-off charges or one-way service fees,** which can be substantial. Note, too, that some rental agencies charge extra if you return the car before the time specified on your contract. To avoid a hefty refueling fee, **fill the tank just before you turn in the car**—but be aware that gas stations near the rental outlet may overcharge.

CHILDREN & TRAVEL

Israel welcomes young tourists, and baby supplies are easily available. Children travel half price on domestic flights and on trains. Many tourist sites offer excellent programs that children will enjoy. Remember that children dehydrate faster than adults, so **bring along a canteen for each child.** Sunscreen and sun hats are also essential.

When traveling with children, **plan ahead** and **involve your youngsters** as you outline your trip. When packing, **include a supply of things to keep them busy** en route. On sightseeing days, try to **schedule activities of special interest to your children,** like a trip to a zoo or a playground. If you **plan your itinerary around seasonal festivals,** you'll never lack for things to do. In addition, **check local newspapers for special**

events mounted by public libraries, museums, and parks, and for other child-centered activities.

BABY-SITTING

For recommended local sitters, **check with your hotel desk.**

DRIVING

If you are renting a car, don't forget to **arrange for a car seat when you reserve.** Sometimes they're free.

FLYING

As a general rule, children under two not occupying a seat fly at greatly reduced fares and occasionally for free. If your children are two or older **ask about special children's fares.** Age limits for these fares vary among carriers. Rules also vary regarding unaccompanied minors, so again: Check with your airline.

BAGGAGE➤ In general, the adult baggage allowance applies to children paying half or more of the adult fare. If you are traveling with an infant, **ask about carry-on allowances** before departure. In general, for infants charged 10% of the adult fare, you are allowed one carry-on bag and a collapsible stroller, which may have to be checked; you may be limited to less if the flight is full.

SAFETY SEATS➤ According to the FAA, it's a good idea to **use safety seats aloft** for children weighing less than 40 pounds. Airline policies vary. U.S. carriers allow FAA-approved models but usually require that you buy a ticket, even if

your child would otherwise ride free, since the seats must be strapped into regular seats. However, some U.S. and foreign-flag airlines may require you to hold your baby during take-off and landing—defeating the seat's purpose. Other foreign carriers may not allow infant seats at all or may charge a child, not infant, fare for their use.

FACILITIES➤ When making your reservation, **request children's meals or freestanding bassinets** if you need them; the latter are available only to those seated at the bulkhead, where there's enough legroom. If you don't need a bassinet, **think twice before requesting bulkhead seats**—the only storage space for in-flight necessities is in inconveniently distant overhead bins.

LODGING

Hotel policy varies greatly on pricing for children. In most luxury hotels, children under 12 sharing a hotel room with adults either stay free or receive a discount rate. Be sure to **ask about the cutoff age.** Children's discounts are often less generous at kibbutz guest houses. Many hotels, especially in resorts such as Eilat, feature entertainment that appeals to children and activities such as arts and crafts or field trips.

CUSTOMS & DUTIES

To speed your clearance through customs, **keep receipts for all your purchases abroad** and

be ready to show the inspector what you've bought. If you feel you've been incorrectly or unfairly charged a duty, you can **appeal assessments in dispute.** First ask to see a supervisor. If you are still unsatisfied, **write to the port director** at your point of entry, sending your customs receipt and any other appropriate documentation. The address will be listed on your receipt. If you still don't get satisfaction, you can take your case to customs headquarters in Washington.

IN ISRAEL

Those over 17 may import duty-free into Israel: 250 cigarettes or 250 grams of tobacco products; 2 liters of wine and 1 liter of spirits; ¼ liter of eau de cologne or perfume; and gifts totaling no more than $125 in value. Fresh meats may not be imported.

Nonresidents may bring any amount of foreign currency and shekels into Israel, but may not take out more foreign currency than they brought in. You should **save your bank receipts.** You can reconvert up to $5,000 worth of shekels. In addition, up to $500 worth of shekels can be reconverted at the airport bank on departure (without receipts).

A large deposit is sometimes required at Israeli customs to bring expensive and/or professional-quality video and computer equipment into the country. This is to ensure that it is not being imported for resale. The deposit is refundable in the original currency on departure and can be paid in cash, in traveler's checks, or by Visa credit card.

IN THE U.S.

You may bring home $400 worth of foreign goods duty-free if you've been out of the country for at least 48 hours and haven't already used the $400 allowance, or any part of it, in the past 30 days.

Travelers 21 or older may bring back 1 liter of alcohol, duty-free, provided the beverage laws of the state through which they reenter the United States allow it. In addition, regardless of their age, they are allowed 100 non-Cuban cigars and 200 cigarettes. Antiques, which the U.S. Customs Service defines as objects more than 100 years old, are duty-free. Original works of art done entirely by hand are also duty-free. These include, but are not limited to, paintings, drawings, and sculptures.

Travelers may mail packages, duty-free, valued at up to $200 to themselves and up to $100 to others, with a limit of one parcel per addressee per day (and no alcohol or tobacco products or perfume valued at more than $5); on the outside, the package must be labeled as being either for personal use or an unsolicited gift, and a list of its contents and their retail value must be attached. Mailed items do not affect your duty-free allowance on your return.

IN CANADA

If you've been out of Canada for at least seven days, you may bring in C$500 worth of goods duty-free. If you've been away for fewer than seven days but for more than 48 hours, the duty-free allowance drops to C$200; if your trip lasts between 24 and 48 hours, the allowance is C$50. You cannot pool allowances with family members. Goods claimed under the C$500 exemption may follow you by mail; those claimed under the lesser exemptions must accompany you.

Alcohol and tobacco products may be included in the seven-day and 48-hour exemptions but not in the 24-hour exemption. If you meet the age requirements of the province or territory through which you reenter Canada, you may bring in, duty-free, 1.14 liters (40 imperial ounces) of wine or liquor *or* 24 12-ounce cans or bottles of beer or ale. If you are 16 or older, you may bring in, duty-free, 200 cigarettes, 50 cigars or cigarillos, and 400 tobacco sticks or 400 grams of manufactured tobacco. Alcohol and tobacco must accompany you on your return.

An unlimited number of gifts with a value of up to C$60 each may be mailed to Canada duty-free. These do not affect your duty-free allowance on your return. Label the package "Unsolicited Gift—Value Under $60." Alcohol and tobacco are excluded.

IN THE U.K.

From countries outside the European Union, including Israel, you may import, duty-free, 200 cigarettes, 100 cigarillos, 50 cigars, or 250 grams of tobacco; 1 liter of spirits or 2 liters of fortified or sparkling wine or liqueurs; 2 liters of still table wine; 60 milliliters of perfume; 250 milliliters of toilet water; plus £136 worth of other goods, including gifts and souvenirs.

D

DINING

Israel is not a must-do stop on a gastronomic world tour, and yet some of the best tastes and tantalizing aromas can be found here. This is, after all, the Middle East: Fresh grilled fish and a plate of hummus and warmed pita bread come to mind, but today you can also taste any national cuisine you desire—Italian, Indian, Chinese, Turkish, Indonesian, Hungarian—even American! And whereas previously, "kosher" meant unvaried, today kosher restaurants have to compete with a growing number of nonkosher restaurants (that, among other differences, serve seafood and also serve milk and meat together), and thus the variety is becoming larger. Moreover, with street stalls and ice cream stores all over the place, you can be sure you won't go hungry in Israel.

In the hotels, the day begins with a huge buffet-style breakfast that includes a variety of breads and rolls, eggs, oatmeal, excellent yogurt, cheeses, vegetable and fish salads, and Western-style breakfast foods like cornflakes and granola. Every city and small town has modestly priced soup-salad-and-grilled-meat restaurants that open in mid-morning. Many restaurants offer business-lunch specials or fixed-price menus, but à la carte menus are most common. A service charge (*sherut* in Hebrew) of 10%–15% is sometimes charged and should be noted separately on your bill.

When used in reference to food, the word *Oriental* (a translation of the Hebrew for "eastern") means Middle Eastern cuisine, not Asian cuisines such as Thai or Chinese.

Israelis like Western-style fast food such as hamburgers and pizza, but more traditional favorites are falafel served with salad and condiments in a pita pocket, *shwarma* (grilled meat), cheese, and *borekas* (phyllodough turnovers with spinach or potato filling). Many falafel stands have salad bars where you can fill the pita yourself. Supermarkets, particularly in the large cities, have long, eclectic counters of take-out food—everything from fried eggplant to chocolate croissants.

DISABILITIES & ACCESSIBILITY

Facilities in Israel for people with disabilities still lag behind those of many Western countries. Crowded, hilly streets and steps can make it difficult to get around without a companion, and adapted minibuses and rental cars are hard to come by. However, new hotels are required to provide facilities for guests with disabilities, and improvements are being made at several tourist sights.

When discussing accessibility with an operator or reservationist, **ask hard questions.** Are there any stairs, inside *or* out? Are there grab bars next to the toilet *and* in the shower/tub? How wide is the doorway to the room? To the bathroom? For the most extensive facilities, meeting the latest legal specifications, **opt for newer accommodations,** which more often have been designed with access in mind. Older properties or ships must usually be retrofitted and may offer more limited facilities as a result. Be sure to **discuss your needs before booking.**

DISCOUNTS & DEALS

You shouldn't have to pay for a discount. In fact, you may already be eligible for all kinds of savings. Here are some time-honored strategies for getting the best deal.

LOOK IN YOUR WALLET

When you **use your credit card to make travel purchases,** you may get free travel-accident insurance, collision damage insurance, or medical or legal assistance, depending on the card and bank that issued it. American Express, Visa, and MasterCard provide one or more of these services, so **get a copy of your card's travel benefits.** If you are a member of AAA or an oil-company-sponsored road-assistance plan, always **ask hotel or car-rental reservationists for auto-club discounts.** Some clubs offer additional discounts on tours, cruises, or admission to attractions. And don't forget that auto-club membership entitles you to free maps and trip-planning services.

SENIOR CITIZENS & STUDENTS

As a senior-citizen traveler, you may be eligible for special rates, but you should mention your senior-citizen status up front. If you're a student or under age 26, you can also get discounts, especially if you have an official ID card (☞ Senior-Citizen Discounts *and* Students on the Road, *below*).

DIAL FOR DOLLARS

To save money, **look into "1-800" discount reservations services,** which often have lower rates. These services use their buying power to get a better price on hotels, airline tickets, and sometimes even car rentals. When booking a room, always **call the hotel's local toll-free number** (if one is available) rather than the central reservations number—you'll often get a better price. Ask the reservationist about special packages or corporate rates, which are usually available even if you're not traveling on business.

JOIN A CLUB?

Discount clubs can be a legitimate source of savings, but you must use the participating hotels and visit the participating attractions in order to realize any benefits. Remember, too, that you have to pay a fee to join, so **determine if you'll save enough to warrant your membership fee.** Before booking with a club, **make sure the hotel or other supplier isn't offering a better deal.**

GET A GUARANTEE

When shopping for the best deal on hotels and car rentals, **look for guaranteed exchange rates,** which protect you against a falling dollar. With your rate locked in, you won't pay more, even if the price goes up in the local currency.

DRIVING

The Hebrew word for a native-born Israeli is sabra, which literally means the prickly cactus with sweet fruit inside. You'll meet the sweet Israeli should you get lost or have automotive difficulties—helping hands are quick to arrive—but behind the wheel, Israelis are prickly, very aggressive, and honk their horns far more than their Western counterparts. Try not to take it personally.

Highways are basically in good shape, except in some rural areas. Try to **avoid entering and leaving the main cities at rush hours** (7:30 AM–8:30 AM and 4 PM–6 PM), when roads are absolutely jammed. Roads are marked with international traffic symbols, and because signs are often in Hebrew only, it's smart to **write down the road numbers before setting out.** Good maps in English are available at bookstores and through the Israel Government Tourist Office (IGTO).

It's a good idea to **carry extra water—for your car and for yourself—while driving any time of year.** Every winter there are several days of flash flooding in the desert; if it's raining, try to find a police officer or call the IGTO to ask about road and weather conditions.

Service stations are more or less full service, but many drivers save time by filling their own tank. Many rental cars now use unleaded gas. At press time, a liter of high-test gasoline costs about 90¢ ($3.60 a gallon). City gas stations stay open into the evening, and quite a few are open around the clock. Many are closed on Saturday (Shabbat) and religious holidays, beginning late the previous afternoon. More but not all highway gas stations are open all night, and almost all are open on Saturday and holidays.

Israel is slowly assigning numbers to its roads and highways (north–south even, east–west odd), but most people still know them simply by the towns they connect, for example, the Tiberias–Nazareth Road. Intersections and turnoffs are referred to similarly: for example, the Eilat Junction. In addition, interurban signs for sights such as parks and historic places are being changed from orange to brown.

E

EGYPT & JORDAN

For information about traveling to these countries, see Chapter 9.

ETIQUETTE

Etiquette is not a word that ranks high on the Israeli vocabulary list. In this very informal society, there are many traditions but few rules. Having said that, both Jewish and Arabic cultures have their own sets of rules and etiquette, which should be taken into account. Visitors (women in particular) to ultra-Orthodox Jewish quarters, such as Bnei Brak, near Tel Aviv, and the Jerusalem neighborhood of Mea Shearim, should **wear modest dress.** Local women keep their knees and elbows covered, and they do not wear pants; married women keep their heads covered as well (keep a scarf handy). Tourists wandering the streets will feel more comfortable if they keep this in mind, and it is essential for anyone who desires to enter a synagogue or other important religious institutions (again, women in particular, though head covering for men will also be appreciated). Very religious Jews, who wear black garb, do not shake hands or mingle socially with members of the opposite sex.

Guests in Muslim households insult their hosts if they will not accept a drink (usually strong coffee or a soft drink is offered). Muslims do not drink alcohol, so a gift of wine is inappropriate. Like religious Jews, Muslims do not eat pork. **When entering mosques, remove your shoes.** Women should cover their hair. Shaking hands or picking up food with the left hand is considered impolite.

H

HEALTH

It's safe in Israel to drink tap water and eat fresh produce after it has been washed, but **take care when buying cooked products from outdoor food stands**; in some cases, the food may have been sitting unrefrigerated for a long time.

A sun hat is a must, and **carry a canteen or bottled water** (available even in the most remote places) to guard against dehydration.

I

INSURANCE

Travel insurance can protect your monetary investment, replace your luggage and its contents, or provide for medical coverage should you fall ill during your trip. Most tour operators, travel agents, and insurance agents sell specialized health-and-accident, flight, trip-cancellation, and luggage insurance as well as comprehensive policies with some or all of these coverages. Comprehensive policies may also reimburse you

for delays due to weather—an important consideration if you're traveling during the winter months. Some health-insurance policies do not cover preexisting conditions, but waivers may be available in specific cases. Coverage is sold by the companies listed in Important Contacts A to Z; these companies act as the policy's administrators. The actual insurance is usually underwritten by a well-known name, such as The Travelers or Continental Insurance.

Before you make any purchase, **review your existing health and homeowner's policies** to find out whether they cover expenses incurred while traveling.

BAGGAGE

Airline liability for baggage is limited to $1,250 per person on domestic flights. On international flights, it amounts to $9.07 per pound or $20 per kilogram for checked baggage (roughly $640 per 70-pound bag) and $400 per passenger for unchecked baggage. Insurance for losses exceeding the terms of your airline ticket can be bought directly from the airline at check-in for about $10 per $1,000 of coverage; note that it excludes a rather extensive list of items, as shown on your airline ticket.

COMPREHENSIVE

Comprehensive insurance policies include all the coverages described above plus some that may not be available in more specific policies. If you have purchased an expensive vacation,

especially one that involves travel abroad, comprehensive insurance is a must; **look for policies that include trip delay insurance,** which will protect you in the event that weather problems cause you to miss your flight, tour, or cruise. A few insurers will also sell you a waiver for preexisting medical conditions. Some companies that offer both features are Access America, Carefree Travel, Travel Insured International, and TravelGuard (☞ Insurance *in* Important Contacts A to Z).

FLIGHT

You should **think twice before buying flight insurance.** Often purchased as a last-minute impulse at the airport, it pays a lump sum when a plane crashes, either to a beneficiary if the insured dies or sometimes to a surviving passenger who loses his or her eyesight or a limb. Supplementing the airlines' coverage described in the limits-of-liability paragraphs on your ticket, it's expensive and basically unnecessary. Charging an airline ticket to a major credit card often automatically provides you with coverage that may also extend to travel by bus, train, and ship.

HEALTH

Medicare generally does not cover health-care costs outside the United States; nor do many privately issued policies. If your own health-insurance policy does not cover you outside the United States, **consider buying supplemental medical cover-**

age. It can reimburse you for $1,000–$150,000 worth of medical and/or dental expenses incurred as a result of an accident or illness during a trip. These policies also may include a personal-accident, or death-and-dismemberment, provision, which pays a lump sum ranging from $15,000 to $500,000 to your beneficiaries if you die or to you if you lose one or more limbs or your eyesight, and a medical-assistance provision, which may either reimburse you for the cost of referrals, evacuation or repatriation, and other services, or automatically enroll you as a member of a particular medical-assistance company (☞ Health *in* Important Contacts A to Z).

U.K. TRAVELERS

You can buy an annual travel-insurance policy valid for most vacations during the year in which it's purchased. If you are pregnant or have a preexisting medical condition, make sure you're covered before buying such a policy.

TRIP

Without insurance, you will lose all or most of your money if you cancel your trip, regardless of the reason. Especially if your airline ticket, cruise, or package tour is nonrefundable and cannot be changed, it's essential that you **buy trip-cancellation-and-interruption insurance.** When considering how much coverage you need, look for a policy that will cover the cost of your trip plus the nondiscounted price of a one-way airline ticket should you need to return home early. Read the fine print carefully, especially sections that define "family member" and "preexisting medical conditions." Also **consider default or bankruptcy insurance,** which protects you against a supplier's failure to deliver. Be aware, however, that if you buy such a policy from a travel agency, tour operator, airline, or cruise line, it may not cover default by the firm in question.

L
LANGUAGE

Hebrew has a unique history: The language of the Bible was long dormant, used only for reading the Holy Scriptures and prayers, writing religious works and poetry, and as the Jewish lingua franca to communicate with compatriots in other countries. A revival begun a century ago has given it a whole new life. If Abraham, Isaac, and Jacob came back today, they'd have to take *ulpan* classes just like new immigrants. English has also had an impact on Hebrew to the extent that you will hear not only official words like bank, *telefon* and *lefaksess* (to fax), but also slang such as *ledaskess* (to discuss) and *heppening* (happening, event). Arabic is Israel's other official language, spoken by Arabs as well as many Jews (especially those with origins in Arab lands). In this country of immigrants, mistakes and a variety of accents are tolerated cheerfully.

In fact, so many different languages are spoken by polyglot Israelis that you might be able to try out French, Spanish, Italian, or, particularly in recent years, Russian. All Israeli schoolchildren study English and speak it with a range of fluency.

Israelis use a lot of hand gestures when they talk. A common gesture that sometimes annoys foreigners is turning a palm and pressing the thumb and forefinger together to mean "wait a minute." Rest assured that this gesture has no negative connotations. Just as harmless in intention is the Israeli who says he "doesn't believe you" when he means something is unbelievably wonderful. Few Israelis differentiate between bus stop and bus station (because one Hebrew word covers both), so if you want the central bus station, make sure you ask for it (tahana merkazit). Different systems of transliteration have produced widely inconsistent spellings: So is that Golan town Katzrin or Qazrin?

You can hear news in English on Reshet Alef, the "A" station of Kol Yisrael at 7 AM, 1 PM, 5 PM, and 8 PM. There's an English news broadcast on TV Channel One (Ha'arutz Harishon) Sunday through Thursday at 6:15 PM, Friday at 4:30 PM, and Saturday at 4:20 PM. Movies are almost always shown in their original languages with Hebrew subtitles. You can pick up a copy of the *Jerusalem Post*,

Israel's only English-language daily (Sunday through Friday) newspaper and the semimonthly news magazine the *Jerusalem Report* at most newsstands. The *International Herald Tribune* is sold at many newsstands, many hotels, and at airports. Stores carry a wide range of English titles.

LODGING

Nearly all hotel rooms in Israel have private bathrooms with a combined shower/tub. A buffet breakfast, often very sumptuous, is almost always included in the room rate (☞ Dining, *above*). You can expect a swimming pool, a health club, and tennis courts in the best hotels; with rare exceptions in the major cities, most hotels have parking facilities. Although the government's star ratings of hotels have officially been abolished, people still talk of "five-star hotels" as the top category of hotel.

APARTMENT & VILLA RENTAL

If you want a home base that's roomy enough for a family and comes with cooking facilities, **consider taking a furnished rental.** This can also save you money, but not always—some rentals are luxury properties (economical only when your party is large). Home-exchange directories list rentals—often second homes owned by prospective house swappers—and some services search for a house or apartment for you (even a castle if that's your fancy) and handle the paperwork.

Some send an illustrated catalog; others send photographs only of specific properties, sometimes at a charge; up-front registration fees may apply.

BED-AND-BREAKFASTS

B&Bs have opened at many of the country's kibbutzim. Typically, a tourist can rent a simple room and eat meals in the kibbutz dining room. Most kibbutzim have large lawns, swimming pools (often open only in summer), and athletic facilities, and offer lectures and tours of the settlement. Private home owners are also increasingly opening their doors to guests.

CHRISTIAN HOSPICES

Christian hospices (meaning hostelries, not a facility for the ill) provide lodging and sometimes meals. These are mainly in Jerusalem and the Galilee. Some are real bargains, others merely reasonable, and their facilities range from spare to luxurious. Preference is given to pilgrimage groups, but when space is available, almost all will accept secular tourists. A full listing of hospices is available from the Israel Government Tourist Office.

HOLIDAY VILLAGES

Holiday villages can range from the near primitive to quite luxurious. Commonly they offer simple facilities, usually sleeping from four to six persons in a unit, with basic cooking facilities in each unit. Some villages have full kitchens and even

televisions. Most holiday villages have a grocery store on the grounds. The rooms vary from huts and trailers to little houses. Such villages, often near beaches or in resort areas, are relatively inexpensive.

HOME EXCHANGE

If you would like to find a house, an apartment, or some other type of vacation property to exchange for your own while on holiday, **become a member of a home-exchange organization,** which will send you its updated listings of available exchanges for a year and will include your own listing in at least one of them. Arrangements for the actual exchange are made by the two parties involved, not by the organization.

KIBBUTZ GUEST HOUSES

Kibbutz guest houses, which have been a popular lodging in Israel for years, are similar to motels; guests are taken in as a source of extra income for the kibbutz and are not involved in its social life (with the possible exception of having meals in the communal dining room). Unlike motels, though, these offer rustic, quiet settings, and usually have pools and athletic activities.

YOUTH HOSTELS

Youth hostels in Israel have improved in recent years. Many of the 31 hostels in Israel provide family rooms with private baths. Most are air-conditioned, some have communal cooking facilities, and all provide meals. It is worthwhile to come equipped with a valid HI (Hostelling International, formerly the International Youth Hostel Association) membership card—otherwise, the attractive, modern hostels charge guest-house prices, but even without one, the hostels are a good deal.

M
MAIL

Israel's mail service has improved dramatically in recent years. The post office handles regular and express letters, sends and receives faxes, takes bill payments, sells phone tokens and telephone cards, and offers quick delivery service. Nearly every neighborhood has a post office, identified by a racing deer, and English is almost always spoken. The main branches are usually open from 8 to 6 or 7, and small offices are usually open Sunday–Tuesday and Thursday 8–12:30 and 3:30–6, Wednesday 8–1:30, and Friday 8–noon. In Muslim cities and in Gaza the post office is closed Friday; in Christian towns it's closed Sunday; and in Jericho it's closed Saturday. You must **bring identification if you want to send packages.**

A regular letter within Israel costs about 30¢. An air letter to the United States or Europe costs about 45¢. If you bring a letter to the post office before 10 AM, same-day delivery is guaranteed for about NIS 9 ($3) within the city, NIS 16 ($5.30) out of town. A letter of 20 grams or less to Europe costs about NIS 1.60 (50¢), and postage is about NIS 1.90 (60¢) to the United States. An airmail postcard to anywhere in the world requires an NIS 1.20 (40¢) stamp. Mail abroad takes 5 to 10 days. The first page of a fax costs about NIS 6 ($2) within Israel, NIS 18 ($6) to the United States.

In most big cities, yellow mailboxes are for mail being sent within the same city, and red boxes are for all other mail.

In mailing addresses, the abbreviation M.P. stands for Mobile Post (M.P. Gilboa, for example). You'll see this as part of addresses in more rural areas.

RECEIVING MAIL

Tourists who want to receive mail at a local post office should have it addressed to "Post Restante" along with the name of the particular town. Such mail will be held for pickup for up to three months, and the service is free. American Express offices in the big cities also receive and hold mail free for card members; for a list of foreign American Express offices, call 212/477–5700 in New York City or 800/525–4800.

MEDICAL
ASSISTANCE

No one plans to get sick while traveling, but it happens, so **consider signing up with a medical assistance company.** These outfits provide referrals, emergency evacuation or repatriation, 24-hour telephone hot lines for medical consultation, cash for emergencies, and other personal and legal assistance. They also dispatch medical personnel and arrange for the relay of medical records. Coverage varies by plan, so **read the fine print carefully.**

MONEY &
EXPENSES

Israel's monetary unit is the shekel, abbreviated NIS. There are 100 agorot to the shekel. The silver-color one-shekel coin is about the size of an American dime, but thicker. Smaller-value bronze coins are the half-shekel and the 10-agorot coin (both of which are larger than the shekel), and the less-used 5-agorot coin. There is also a 5-shekel coin (silver in color), about the size of an American quarter, and a similar-size 10-shekel coin (bronze center, silver-color rim). Paper bills come in 20-, 50-, 100-, and 200-shekel denominations.

Israeli currency fluctuates against the U.S. dollar, so exact rates vary daily. At press time (fall 1996), the exchange rate was about 3.2 shekels to the dollar. Because of the frequent fluctuations, prices quoted throughout the book are listed both in shekels and in their approximate equivalent in U.S. dollars. Because paying bills at hotels, car-rental firms, and special tourist shops in foreign currency eliminates the value-added tax (VAT), price charts in the dining and lodging sections of the book are in U.S. dollars.

ATMS

CASH ADVANCES➤ Before leaving home, **make sure your credit cards have been programmed for ATM use in Israel.** Note that with few exceptions, Discover is accepted only in the United States. Local bank cards often do not work overseas either; **ask your bank about a MasterCard/Cirrus or Visa debit card,** which works like a bank card but can be used at any ATM displaying a MasterCard/Cirrus or Visa logo.

TRANSACTION FEES➤ Although fees charged for ATM transactions may be higher abroad than at home, Cirrus and Plus exchange rates are excellent, because they are based on wholesale rates offered only by major banks.

COSTS

Israel is a moderately priced country compared to Western Europe, but it is more expensive than many of its Mediterranean neighbors. Tourist costs, calculated in dollars, are little affected by inflation. Prices are much the same all over the country. To save money, **try the excellent prepared food from supermarkets (buy local brands), take public transportation, eat your main meal at lunch, avoid ordering drinks (ask for water), eat inexpensive local foods such as falafel one meal a day,** and **stay at hotels with kitchen facilities and guest houses.** Plane fares are lowest in winter.

SAMPLE PRICES➤ Cup of coffee, $2; falafel, $1.80; beer at a bar, $3; canned soft drink, $1–$2; hamburger at a fast-food restaurant, $3; 2-kilometer (1-mile) taxi ride, about $3.50; movie, $6.

EXCHANGING CURRENCY

For the most favorable rates, **change money at banks.** You won't do as well at exchange booths in airports or rail and bus stations, in hotels, in restaurants, or in stores, although you may find their hours more convenient. To avoid lines at airport exchange booths, **get a small amount of the local currency before you leave home.**

TAXES

VAT➤ A value-added tax (which at press time was 17%) is charged on all purchases and transactions except tourists' hotel bills and car rentals paid in foreign currency (cash, traveler's checks, foreign credit cards). You are entitled at your point of departure to a refund of this tax on purchases made in foreign currency of more than $50 on one invoice, but it is not mandatory, and not all stores are organized with VAT return forms. Stores so organized display TAXVAT signs and give 5% discounts. If you charge meals and other services to your room at a hotel, there is no VAT if you pay with foreign currency; the refund does not apply elsewhere. Keep your receipts and ask for a cash refund at Ben-Gurion Airport or Haifa Port (there is a special Bank Leumi desk set up for this in the duty-free area); if you leave from other departure points, the VAT refund will be sent to your home address. You are expected to be able to produce the purchases on which you claim a VAT refund. Allow time for this procedure when you plan your departure. The Ministry of Tourism publishes a useful booklet, "Made in Israel," that is free at Ben-Gurion International Airport or at an Israel Government Tourist Office (☞ Visitor Information *in* Important Contacts A to Z.

TRAVELER'S CHECKS

Whether or not to buy traveler's checks depends on where you are headed; **take cash to rural areas and small towns, traveler's checks to cities.** The most widely recognized checks are issued by American Express, Citicorp, Thomas Cook, and Visa. These are sold by major commercial banks for 1%–3% of the checks' face value—it pays to **shop around.** Both American Express and Thomas Cook issue checks that can be countersigned and used by either you or your traveling companion. So you won't be left with excess foreign currency, **buy a few checks in small denominations** to cash toward the end of your trip. Before leaving home, **contact your issuer for information on where to cash your** checks without incurring a transaction fee. Record the serial numbers of all your checks and keep this listing in a separate place, crossing off the numbers of checks you have cashed.

WIRING MONEY

For a fee of 3%–10%, depending on the amount of the transaction, you can have money sent to you from home through Money-Gram[SM] or Western Union (☞ Money Matters *in* Important Contacts A to Z). The transferred funds and the service fee can be charged to a Master-Card or Visa account.

P

PACKING FOR
ISRAEL

Israel is a casual country where comfort comes before fashion. Rarely will you need more than an afternoon dress or sports jacket to feel comfortable at any event. Most restaurants do not require a jacket and tie. For touring in the hot summer months, **wear cool, easy-care clothing.** If you are coming from May through September, you won't need a coat, but you should **take a sun hat.** Take one sweater for cool nights, particularly in the hilly areas. Women should **bring modest dress for touring in religious neighborhoods,** and many religious sites forbid shorts and sleeveless shirts for both men and women. Bring long pants to protect your legs and a spare pair of walking shoes for adventure travel. A raincoat with a zip-out lining is ideal for October to April, when the weather can get cold enough for snow (and is as likely to be warm enough in the south for outdoor swimming). Rain boots may also be a useful accessory in winter; **pack a bathing suit for all seasons.**

Take plenty of sunscreen, insect repellent, a water canteen, and sunglasses, as well as the aforementioned sun hat that completely shades your face and neck. Bring an extra pair of eyeglasses or contact lenses in your carry-on luggage, and if you have a health problem, **pack enough medication** to last the trip or have your doctor write you a prescription using the drug's generic name, because brand names vary from country to country (you'll then need a duplicate prescription from a local doctor). It's important that you **don't put prescription drugs or valuables in luggage to be checked,** for they could go astray. To avoid problems with customs officials, carry medications in the original packaging. Also, don't forget the addresses of offices that handle refunds of lost traveler's checks.

ELECTRICITY

To use your U.S.-purchased electric-powered equipment, **bring a converter and an adapter.** The electrical current in Israel is 220 volts, 50 cycles alternating current (AC); wall outlets take Continental-type plugs, with two round prongs.

If your appliances are dual-voltage, you'll need only an adapter. Hotels sometimes have 110-volt outlets for low-wattage appliances near the sink, marked FOR SHAVERS ONLY; don't use them for high-wattage appliances like blow-dryers. If your laptop computer is older, carry a converter; new laptops operate equally well on 110 and 220 volts, so you need only an adapter.

LUGGAGE

Airline baggage allowances depend on the airline, the route, and the class of your ticket; ask in advance. In general, on domestic flights and on international flights between the United States and foreign destinations, you are entitled to check two bags. A third piece may be brought on board, but it must fit easily under the seat in front of you or in the overhead compartment. In the United States, the FAA gives airlines broad latitude regarding carry-on allowances, and they tend to tailor them to different aircraft and operational conditions. Charges for excess, oversize, or overweight pieces vary.

If you are flying between two foreign destinations, note that baggage allowances may be determined not by piece but by weight—generally 88 pounds (40 kilograms) in first class, 66 pounds (30 kilograms) in business class, and 44 pounds (20 kilograms) in economy. If your flight between two cities abroad *connects* with your transatlantic or transpacific flight, the piece method still applies.

SAFEGUARDING YOUR LUGGAGE➤ Before leaving home, **itemize your bags' contents** and their worth and label them with your name, address, and phone number. (If you use your home address, cover it so that potential thieves can't see it readily.) Inside each bag, **pack a copy of your itinerary.** At check-in, **make sure each bag is correctly tagged** with the destination airport's three-letter code. If your bags arrive damaged— or fail to arrive at all— file a written report with the airline before leaving the airport.

PASSPORTS & VISAS

If you don't already have one, **get a passport.** It is advisable that you **leave one photocopy of your passport's data page** with someone at home and keep another with you, separated from your passport, while traveling. If you lose your passport, promptly call the nearest embassy or consulate and the local police; having the data page information can speed replacement.

In Israel, three-month tourist visas are issued free of charge at the point of entry when a valid passport is presented. At press time, there are still some countries (particularly in the Middle East) that refuse to admit travelers whose passports carry an Israeli visa entry stamp. If you are concerned about having an Israeli stamp or visa in your passport, you can ask the customs officer at your point of entry to issue a tourist visa on a separate piece of paper to keep with your passport; or you can apply for a second passport and include a letter with the application that explains you need it to travel to Israel. Be advised that it is not unheard of for Israeli customs officers to stamp passports despite requests not to do so; if you plan to travel repeatedly between Israel and those Arab states still hostile to Israel, a second passport is advisable.

IN THE U.S.

All U.S. citizens, even infants, need only a valid passport to enter Israel for stays of up to 90 days. Application forms for both first-time and renewal passports are available at any of the 13 U.S. Passport Agency offices and at some post offices and courthouses. Passports are usually mailed within four weeks; allow five weeks or more in spring and summer.

CANADIANS

You need only a valid passport to enter Israel for stays of up to 90 days. Passport application forms are available at 28 regional passport offices, as well as post offices and travel agencies. Whether for a first or a renewal passport, you must apply in person. Children under 16 may be included on a parent's passport but must have their own to travel alone. Passports are valid for five years and are usually mailed within two to three weeks of application.

U.K. CITIZENS

Citizens of the United Kingdom need only a valid passport to enter Israel for stays of up to 90 days. Applications for new and renewal passports are available from main post offices and at the passport offices in Belfast, Glasgow, Liverpool, London, Newport, and Peterborough. You may apply in person at all passport offices, or by mail to all except the London office. Children under 16 may travel on an accompanying parent's passport. All passports are valid for 10 years. Allow a month for processing.

S SECURITY

Security checks on airlines flying to Israel are stringent. **Be prepared for what might sound like personal questions** about your itinerary, packing habits, and desire to travel to Israel. Remember that the staff is concerned with protecting you. Once you are in Israel, **expect to have your handbags searched** as a matter of course when you enter department stores, places of entertainment, museums, and public buildings. These checks are generally fast and courteous.

Traveling throughout most of Israel is safe and comfortable. You'll see Jews and Arabs peacefully coexisting in the major cities. **Take a common-sense ap-**

proach to driving or **walking in isolated areas at night,** yet even the downtown areas of major cities are comfortable enough for walking alone at all hours.

Over the years scenes on TV screens and in newspapers have often created both consternation and confusion as to what areas are affected by political tension. The Golan Heights area is as safe as anywhere else in Israel. Jerusalem's Old City is thronged during the day and almost deserted at night, but almost everything is closed then anyway. The Arab neighborhoods of East Jerusalem have been less hospitable in recent years than they were, but the daytime visitor should not encounter any problems. In the West Bank, Bethlehem and Jericho are still much visited, though many will choose to go on an organized tour or with a guide who is familiar with the area. Changing political realities elsewhere in the West Bank have put many towns, like Hebron, outside tourist itineraries. Even public buses traveling in these areas have reinforced glass to protect them against stone throwing. Do not drive your own car through these areas. Avoid the Gaza Strip entirely. There are standard security checks along the roads to the West Bank, but these routes are closed off only in periods of particular political tension.

SENIOR-CITIZEN DISCOUNTS

To qualify for age-related discounts, **mention your senior-citizen status up front** when booking hotel reservations, not when checking out, and before you're seated in restaurants, not when paying the bill. The same would be true for discounts at parks and museums. Note that discounts may be limited to certain menus, days, or hours. When renting a car, **ask about promotional car-rental discounts**—they can net even lower costs than your senior-citizen discount.

SHOPPING

The Ministry of Tourism publishes a guide to shopping in Israel, with frequent updates on special discounts for tourists. It is available at Israel Government Tourist Offices (☞ Visitor Information *in* Important Contacts A to Z).

Jewelry, gems, and locally cut diamonds are considered good buys in Israel. The large cities have many reputable jewelry outlets. Ethnic items such as embroidered skullcaps (*kippot*, or yarmulkes), tie-dyed scarves, spice boxes, blown glass, Hanukkah lights, and the like are popular gifts.

Israeli clothing is not inexpensive, but the high-fashion designs, particularly in bathing suits and leather goods, often appeal to visitors. Tel Aviv is the fashion center.

Jerusalem is a good place to look for antiques and Judaica (Jewish religious items). The downtown area known as Arts and Crafts Lane, the Cardo in the Jewish Quarter of the Old City, and the neighborhood called Mea She'arim have a large selection. Christian objects are also plentiful in Jerusalem, especially in the Old City. If you are shopping in an outdoor market (except a food market), stall owners expect you to bargain.

STUDENTS ON THE ROAD

To save money, **look into deals available through student-oriented travel agencies.** To qualify, you'll need to have a bona fide student ID card. Members of international student groups are also eligible (☞ Students *in* Important Contacts A to Z).

T
TAXIS

Taxis are plentiful and relatively inexpensive and can be reached by phone. On the whole, drivers are cheerful. According to law, every driver must use the meter unless you hire him for the day or to make a trip out of town, for which there are also set rates. You can **ask your hotel staff for an estimate of the cost of your journey** in case you are pressed to agree to take the taxi for a set price. In such a case, **agree on the price before you begin the journey** and assume he has already built in a tip. In the event of a serious problem with the driver, report his cab number (on the illuminated plastic sign on the roof) or his license plate number to the Ministry of Tourism or the Ministry of Transport. Note that rates are legitimately 25% higher after 9 PM and any time public transportation is not running (on Shabbat, for example).

Certain shared taxis or minivans run fixed routes, such as from Tel Aviv to Haifa or from the airport to Jerusalem, leaving when they're full. Such a taxi is called a *sherut* (as opposed to special, the term used for a private cab). There are fixed rates for these routes, generally slightly more expensive than bus rates, and they leave when they're full. Some sheruts can be booked in advance.

TELEPHONES

The telephone company in Israel is called Bezek. It still has a monopoly on regular services within the country, but it now has competitors for international calls and cellular phone services. Israel has changed over to a digital telephone system, and almost all telephone numbers have been or will be changed. Many have added a digit. This book has incorporated as many of these changes as possible. **Double-check a number if you don't get an answer.**

Toll-free numbers in Israel begin with 177. For local and out-of-town directory assistance, dial 144 (which charges four phone units for the service). When calling an out-of-town number in Israel, **be sure to dial the zero that begins every area code.** Public telephones operate with a magnetic telephone card (telecard), available in units of 20 (NIS 12, or $4) or 50 (NIS 25, or $8.10) and sold at post offices, many newsstands and kiosks, some hotel reception desks, and the occasional special vending machine. On the public telephones the number you are dialing appears on a digital readout; to its right is the number of units remaining on your card.

COUNTRY CODE

The international country code for dialing Israel from abroad is 972. You also need the city or regional area code, such as 2 for Jerusalem. In this case you do not have to dial a zero before the area code.

LONG DISTANCE

You can make international calls using a telecard from a public phone. A call from Israel when discount rates are in effect costs about 13 units per minute. Large cities have central phone agencies usually near or at main post offices where you make your phone call and pay upon completion.

By dialing Israel's toll-free number (177) and the number of your long-distance service, you can link up directly to an operator in your home country (☞ Telephones *in* Important Contacts A to Z for numbers). This service can be operated from public telephones without a telecard and often from your hotel room (begin by getting an outside line, of course).

However, in many hotels you may find it impossible to dial the access number. The hotel operator may also refuse to make the connection. Instead, the hotel will charge you a premium rate—as much as 400% more than a calling card—for calls placed from your hotel room. To avoid such price gouging, **travel with more than one company's long-distance calling card**—a hotel may block Sprint but not MCI. If the hotel operator claims you cannot use any phone card, **ask to be connected to an international operator,** who will help you to access your phone card. You can also dial the international operator yourself. If none of this works, try calling your phone company collect in the United States.

OPERATORS & INFORMATION

Dial 144 for information. If the operator doesn't speak English or can't find your number, you can ask for a *mefakahat* (supervisor) to help you with the number. You can reach an international operator at 188.

TIPPING

There are no hard and fast rules on tipping in Israel. Although taxi drivers do not expect tips, a gratuity for good service is in order. If you have negotiated a price, assume the tip has been built in. If the service has not been included on a restaurant bill, 10% is expected—round up if the service was particularly good, down if it was dismal. Hotel bellboys are tipped a lump sum of NIS 5–NIS 10 ($1.70–$3.30), not per bag. Tipping is customary for guides, tour bus drivers, and chauffeurs. Bus groups typically tip the guide $4–$5 per person per touring day, and half that for the driver. Private guides normally get tipped $20–$25 a day from the whole party. A small tip is expected by both the person who washes your hair and the beautician—except if one of them owns the salon. Leave NIS 2 for bathroom and coatroom attendants.

TOUR OPERATORS

A package or tour to Israel can make your vacation less expensive and more hassle-free. Firms that sell tours and packages reserve airline seats, hotel rooms, and rental cars in bulk and pass some of the savings on to you. In addition, the best operators have local representatives available to help you at your destination.

A GOOD DEAL?

The more your package or tour includes, the better you can predict the ultimate cost of your vacation. Make sure you know exactly what is covered, and **beware of hidden costs.** Are taxes, tips, and service charges included? Transfers and baggage handling? Entertainment and excursions?

Most packages and tours are rated deluxe, first-class superior, first class, tourist, or budget. The key difference is usually accommodations. If the package or tour you are considering is priced lower than in your wildest dreams, **be skeptical.** Also, **make sure your travel agent knows the accommodations** and other services. Ask about the hotel's location, room size, beds, and whether it has a pool, room service, or programs for children, if you care about these. Has your agent been there in person or sent others you can contact?

BUYER BEWARE

Each year a number of consumers are stranded or lose their money when operators—even very large ones with excellent reputations—go out of business. To avoid becoming one of them, take the time to **check out the operator**—find out how long the company has been in business and ask several agents about its reputation. Next, **don't book unless the firm has a consumer-protection program.** Members of the USTOA and the NTA are required to set aside funds for the sole purpose of covering your payments and travel arrangements in case of default. Non-member operators may instead carry insurance; look for the details in the operator's brochure—and for the name of an underwriter with a solid reputation. Note: When it comes to tour operators, **don't trust escrow accounts.** Although there are laws governing those of charter-flight operators,

no governmental body prevents tour operators from raiding the till.

Next, **contact your local Better Business Bureau and the attorney general's offices** in both your own state and the operator's: Have any complaints been filed? Finally, **pay with a major credit card.** Then you can cancel payment, provided you can document your complaint. Always **consider trip-cancellation insurance** (☞ Insurance, *above*).

BIG VS. SMALL➤ Operators that handle several hundred thousand travelers per year can use their purchasing power to give you a good price. Their high volume may also indicate financial stability. But some small companies provide more personalized service; because they tend to specialize, they may also be more knowledgeable about a given area.

USING AN AGENT

Travel agents are excellent resources. In fact, large operators accept bookings made only through travel agents. But it's good to **collect brochures from several agencies** because some agents' suggestions may be skewed by promotional relationships with tour and package firms that reward them for volume sales. If you have a special interest, **find an agent with expertise in that area;** ASTA can provide leads in the United States. (Don't rely solely on your agent, though; agents may be unaware of small-niche operators, and some special-interest travel companies only sell direct.)

SINGLE TRAVELERS

Prices are usually quoted per person, based on two sharing a room. If traveling solo, you may be required to pay the full double-occupancy rate. Some operators eliminate this surcharge if you agree to be matched up with a roommate of the same sex, even if one is not found by departure time.

The train ride from Jerusalem to Tel Aviv is slow and extremely picturesque. It takes about 1½ hours and costs NIS 15 ($5). Trains leave twice a day in each direction. Trains are much more frequent between Tel Aviv and Haifa, running almost hourly. Express trains take an hour to make the trip; local trains, about 1½ hours; the cost is NIS 16.50 ($5.50). There are also trains to Nahariya, and tickets cost NIS 25 ($8.30). You can **find up-to-date schedules in English** at all train stations.

TRAVEL GEAR

Travel catalogs specialize in useful items that can **save space when packing** and make life on the road more convenient. Compact alarm clocks, travel irons, travel wallets, and personal-care kits are among the most common items you'll find. They also carry dual-voltage appliances, currency converters and

foreign-language phrase books. Some catalogs even carry miniature coffeemakers and water purifiers.

U

U.S. GOVERNMENT

The U.S. government can be an excellent source of travel information. Some of this is free, and some is available for a nominal charge. When planning your trip, **find out what government materials are available.** For just a couple of dollars, you can get a variety of publications from the Consumer Information Center in Pueblo, Colorado. Free consumer information also is available from individual government agencies, such as the Department of Transportation or the U.S. Customs Service. For specific titles, *see* Publications *under* the appropriate entry *in* Important Contacts A to Z.

W

WHEN TO GO

There's no bad time to visit Israel. There are no rainy days at all from May through September, but some visitors prefer risking rain and coming in the cooler, less expensive season of November through March. In the winter months, snow falls occasionally in the northern and central hills. In the months of April, May, September, and October, the weather is generally sunny but not uncom-

fortably hot. March and April have the added attraction of a lush countryside splashed with banks of vivid wildflowers.

During school holidays, particularly in July and August, Israelis themselves take vacations. Accommodations and attractions are crowded and surcharges are often added to hotel rates. Hotel prices jump during the Passover and Sukkoth holiday periods (early April and late September–early October, respectively), and services and commerce are sharply curtailed; many Israelis simply go away for Passover. Reservations should be booked at least four months in advance and plane reservations six months to a year in advance for this busy week. Some hotels require full board for the week of Passover.

CLIMATE

Temperatures along the Mediterranean coast are similar to those of Tel Aviv. Hill cities and towns have climates more like that of Jerusalem. Temperatures at the Dead Sea and in Eilat can get very high and stay very warm at night; in the Negev Desert, on the other hand, the higher altitudes causes a significant drop in nighttime temperatures. The following are average daily maximum and minimum temperatures for Tel Aviv, Jerusalem, and Eilat.

Climate in Israel

EILAT

Jan.	70F	21C	May	95F	35C	Sept.	97F	36C
	49	9		70	76			24
Feb.	74F	23C	June	100F	38C	Oct.	92F	33C
	52	11		76	24		68	20
Mar.	79F	26C	July	102F	39C	Nov.	81F	27C
	58	14		77	25		61	16
Apr.	86F	30C	Aug.	102F	39C	Dec.	72F	22C
	65	18		77	25		52	11

JERUSALEM

Jan.	52F	11C	May	77F	25C	Sept.	81F	27C
	45	7		59	15		65	18
Feb.	58F	14C	June	81F	27C	Oct.	77F	25C
	45	7		65	18		61	16
Mar.	61F	16C	July	83F	28C	Nov.	67F	19C
	49	9		67	19		54	12
Apr.	68F	20C	Aug.	83F	28C	Dec.	56F	13C
	54	12		67	19		47	8

TEL AVIV

Jan.	63F	17C	May	70F	21C	Sept.	85F	29C
	49	9		61	16		70	21
Feb.	65F	18C	June	81F	27C	Oct.	81F	27C
	50	10		68	20		65	18
Mar.	68F	20C	July	85F	29C	Nov.	74F	23C
	52	11		72	22		58	14
Apr.	74F	23C	Aug.	85F	29C	Dec.	67F	19C
	58	14		72	22		52	11

1 Destination: Israel

SMALL COUNTRY, BIG HISTORY

SRAEL IS A LAND of pastel land-scapes and primary-color people; a land where the beauty of nature is subtle, but the natives often are not. The sometimes rambunctious Israeli affability may envelop you as soon as you board your flight to Tel Aviv, especially if you're flying El Al, Israel's national carrier. The cries of recognition and the chatter of passengers exchanging stories about their trips and their duty-free purchases recall first days back at school after summer vacations. Some passengers greet El Al touchdowns on Holy Land soil with spontaneous applause. They are the sentimental tourists; the red-blooded Israelis are already on their feet collecting their bags, despite pleas from the cabin staff.

This Israeli feistiness can come across as assertive, intrusive, even aggressive; the fighter-pilot style of driving you see on Israeli roads is the best example. On the other hand, many claim that this attitude helped Israel tame the land and successfully defend it. The related lack of inhibition leads to quickly made and genuinely warm human contacts that come as a refreshing surprise to many visitors from more reserved cultures.

Ever since the days of Abraham's tent, hospitality has been a deeply ingrained tradition in this part of the world; if an Israeli even casually invites you home for coffee or a meal, he or she probably expects that you'll accept the invitation. Do. Even the Ministry of Tourism has free programs in some cities that match you with an Israeli family for an evening of coffee, cake, and conversation. There is no better way to dive into the culture, and you will likely acquire instant expertise on local politics, ethnic differences, food, the cost of buying a house, and how much your host earns. Be prepared for similar questions about *your* life; there are fewer conversational taboos in Israel than in most English-speaking countries. An oft-quoted example is that of the Israeli company rep sent abroad who was advised to avoid discussing politics, religion, and sex in social situations. "What *else* is there to talk about?" asked the astonished Israeli.

The key to understanding Israel is that it was created as the modern reincarnation of an ancient Jewish state. Israel was the "Promised Land" of Abraham and Moses, the Israelite kingdom of David and Solomon, and home to Jesus of Nazareth and the Jewish Talmudic sages. Although the Jewish presence in the country has been unbroken for over 3,000 years, several massive exiles—first by the Babylonians in 586 BC and then by the Romans in AD 70—created a diaspora, a dispersion of the Jewish people throughout the world.

The Jewish attachment to the ancient homeland weaves through the entire fabric of Jewish history and religious tradition. For 2,000 years, wherever they lived, Jews daily turned their faces toward Jerusalem in prayer. The Jewish liturgy is saturated with prayers for the restoration of "Zion and Jerusalem." Over the centuries, many Jews trickled back to Eretz Yisrael (the Land of Israel); others looked forward to fulfilling their dream of return in some future—many felt imminent—messianic age. An 18th-century story tells of a certain Rabbi Yitzhak of Berdichev in Poland who sent out invitations to his daughter's wedding: "It will take place next Tuesday in the Holy City of Jerusalem. If, God forbid, the Messiah has not arrived by then, it will take place in the village square."

Not all were prepared to wait for divine assistance. During the late 19th century, Zionism was founded as a political movement to give a framework and an impetus to bringing the Jewish people home to Israel. Some early Zionist leaders, like founding father Theodore Herzl, believed that the urgent priority was a Jewish haven safe from persecution, wherever that haven might be. Argentina was suggested, and Great Britain offered Uganda. In the light of their historical and emotional links to the land of Israel, most Jews rejected such suggestions as bizarre. British statesman Arthur James (later Earl) Balfour was perplexed and asked Zionist leader Chaim Weizmann to explain the Jewish refusal. "Mr. Balfour," Dr. Weizmann responded, "if I were to offer you Paris instead of London, would you accept it?" "Of course not," Balfour replied, "London is our capital." "Precisely," said Weizmann, "and Jerusalem was *our* capital when London was still a marsh!"

The establishment of the state of Israel was not met with universal rejoicing. To the Arab world, it was anathema, an alien implant in a Muslim Middle East. To many ultra-Orthodox Jews, it was an arrogant preempting of God's divine plan; and, to make matters worse, the new state was blatantly secular, despite its concessions to religious interests. This internal battle over the character of the Jewish state, together with the implacable hostility of Israel's neighbors, which has resulted in a half century of almost constant conflict, have been the two main issues engaging the country since its birth.

About 83% of Israel's 5.5 million citizens are Jewish, some proudly tracing their family roots many generations in local soil; others are first, second, or third generation *olim* (immigrants) from more than 100 countries. The first modern pioneers arrived from Russia in 1882, purchased land, and set about developing it with romantic zeal. A decade or two later, inspired by the socialist ideas then current in Eastern Europe, a much larger wave founded the first kibbutzim, which are collective villages or communes. In time, these fiercely idealistic farmers became something of a moral elite, having little financial power, but providing a greatly disproportionate percentage of the country's political leadership, military officer cadre, and intelligentsia. "We are workers," they liked to say, "but not working class!" The kibbutz movement today still makes its voice heard and its economic presence felt, but it is no longer the dominant force it once was. A more ambitious younger generation has increasingly eschewed the communal lifestyle in favor of the attractions of the big city.

Although most who immigrated before Israel's independence in 1948 were Ashkenazi Jews whose background was Central or Eastern European, the big waves of immigration in the first decade of statehood were of Sephardim, who came from the Arab lands of North Africa and the Middle East. Israel's Jewish population—

600,000 at the time of its independence—doubled within 3½ years, and tripled within 10! For a long time, the visible differences between the haves and have-nots seemed to break down along the lines of the more established and better-educated Ashkenazim and the poorer unskilled Sephardim. Resentment may still simmer in some disadvantaged neighborhoods, and some stereotypes may still survive, but generally both the distinction and the prejudices have subsided.

ISRAEL WAS FOUNDED just three years after the end of World War II, in which the Nazis annihilated fully a third of the world's Jewish population. The new state's first order of business was to provide a haven for the scattered remnants of the shattered European communities, and the 1949 Law of Return recognized the right of any Jew to Israeli citizenship. Immigration and immigrant absorption became national priorities, warranting a full government ministry. Absorption centers were eventually established to give new immigrants an orientation period and teach them Hebrew in the renowned immersion method known as the *ulpan.*

While generally very successful, the system's resources and creativity have been sorely taxed in recent years. Between 1989 and 1992, Israel absorbed over half a million new immigrants from the former Soviet Union, increasing the population by a full 10%! The initial urgent housing problem has been solved, but unemployment and underemployment linger, and only a minority of the often well-trained immigrant professionals work in their own fields. The 14,400 Ethiopian Jews airlifted to Israel in just one day in May 1991 posed a radically different challenge: how to help them bridge a centuries-wide cultural and technological gap to cope with a modern society.

The vast majority of Israel's 1 million non-Jewish minority are Muslim Arabs, with about 60,000 Christian Arabs, 80,000 Druze, and a similar number of Bedouin (nominally Muslim Arabs, but a community apart). All are citizens, equal under the law, who vote for and may be voted into the Knesset, the Israeli parliament. (Not included are the almost 2 million *Pales-*

tinian Arabs of the partly autonomous West Bank and the autonomous Gaza Strip, who are not Israeli citizens.)

The Muslims in Israel are mainstream Sunnis, regarded as both politically and religiously moderate by the standards of the region. Recent years have seen some radicalization of the community's youth, however, and with it a tendency to identify politically with the Palestinian liberation movement or religiously with the Islamic fundamentalism currently sweeping the Middle East.

Of the Christian Arabs, most belong to the Greek Catholic, Greek Orthodox, or Roman Catholic churches; a handful of tiny Eastern denominations and a few Protestant groups account for the rest. The Western Christian community is minuscule and with few exceptions consists of clergy and temporary sojourners, such as diplomats and foreign professionals on assignment.

The Druze, though Arabic-speaking, are a separate and secret religion that broke from Islam about 1,000 years ago. Larger kindred communities exist in long-hostile Syria and Lebanon, but Israeli Druze have solidly identified with Israel, and the community's young men are routinely drafted into the Israeli army. The Arab community is not liable for military service in order to avoid the possibility of a battlefield confrontation with kinsmen from neighboring countries.

There is no firm separation of religion and state in Israel; and matters of personal status—marriage, divorce, adoption, burial, inheritance—are the preserve of the religious authorities of the community concerned. For this reason there is no civil marriage. If one partner does not convert to the faith of the other, the couple must marry abroad. Within the Jewish community, such functions fall under the supervision of the Orthodox chief rabbinate, much to the chagrin of members of the tiny but growing Conservative and Reform movements (many of whom are American expatriates) and of the large number of nonobservant Jews.

The confrontation between secular Israelis and the hard-line ultra-Orthodox has escalated over the years, as the religious community tries to impose on what it considers an apostate citizenry its vision of how a Jewish state should behave. Hot issues include debating the Orthodox definition of what a Jew is (born of a Jewish mother or converted by strict Orthodox procedures) for the purpose of Israeli citizenship and public observance of the Sabbath and of dietary laws. For many nonreligious Israelis, already irked by what they consider religious coercion, it just rubs salt in the wound that many ultra-Orthodox Jewish men have been able avoid of military service on the grounds of continuing religious studies.

SRAEL PRIDES ITSELF on being the only true democracy in the Middle East, and it sometimes seems bent on politically tearing itself apart in the process. This is how the system works (or doesn't): Once every four years, prior to national elections, every party publishes a list of its candidates for the 120-member Knesset. There are no constituencies or voting districts; each party that breaks the minimum threshold of 1.5% of the *national* vote gets in, winning the same percentage of seats as its *proportion* of nationwide votes (hence "proportional representation").

The good news is that the system is intensely democratic. A relatively small grouping of like-minded voters *countrywide* (currently about 30,000) can elect an M.K. (Member of the Knesset) to represent its views. The largest party able to gain a parliamentary majority through a coalition with other parties becomes the government. The bad news is that the system creates a proliferation of small parties, whose support the government needs in order to rule. Since no party has ever won enough seats to rule alone, Israeli governments have always been based on compromise, with small parties exerting a degree of political influence quite out of proportion to their actual size. Any attempts to change the system have been doomed to failure, because the small parties, which stand to lose if the system is changed, are precisely those on whose support the *current* government depends. Classic Catch-22.

Traditionally the leader of the victorious large party became prime minister, but beginning with the general elections of May 1996, the prime minister is now elected directly on a separate ballot. The move was designed to reduce the influence of the small parties by giving the PM a popular mandate, but the innovation may have complicated the system rather than improved it. In the 1996 elections many voters split their vote, supporting one of the two big-party candidates as PM, but casting their *party vote* in favor of the small party that most closely represented their views. The parliamentary strength of the big parties, Labor and Likud, declined dramatically as a result, with a proportionate rise in the power of the small parties.

ISRAEL IS JUST OVER 400 KM (under 300 mi) long, from Metulla on the northern border with Lebanon to the southern resort city of Eilat on the Red Sea. It's 100 km (63 mi) at its widest, across the Negev Desert, and as little as 50 km (31 mi) at its narrowest, across the Galilee—making Israel merely the size of Wales or just larger than Massachusetts. The American writer Mark Twain was astonished by the smallness of the Holy Land when he visited in 1867. He had envisioned, he wrote, "a country as large as the United States. . . . I suppose it was because I could not conceive of a small country having so large a history."

Mark Twain's astonishment is instructive: In Israel the past is more ever-present than almost anywhere else on earth. There is something about the place that seeps into one's soul. For the Jewish visitor, it is a feeling of coming home, of getting back to one's roots. For the Christian pilgrim, it is the awe of retracing Jesus' footsteps in the Scripture's actual landscape, where the Bible takes on new meaning and will never be read the same way again.

Indeed, the country's biblical past has made names like Jerusalem, the Galilee, and the Jordan River household words for almost half the human race. Many a pilgrim has reached Israel expecting a Jerusalem preserved as an uncommercialized shrine, a Galilee of donkey traffic and tiny fishing boats, a river Jordan "deep and wide." The reality hits as you find the ancient names on store billboards and on the signposts of fast, modern highways. And you discover that Jerusalem is a modern national capital of 600,000 inhabitants; Galilee is the name of a pro-fessional basketball team; and Jericho, Joshua's first target 33 centuries ago, is now a Palestinian autonomous zone.

The past is far from forgotten, however. Archaeology is almost a national sport (though less for today's video-game generation than for its parents), and an unusual find in any of the many ongoing excavations is sure to make the prime-time news. There are prehistoric settlement sites over a million years old; the world's oldest walled town at Jericho; echoes of the biblical patriarchs; and evidence of the kings of Israel. You can stand on the Temple Mount steps that Jesus almost certainly climbed or marvel at an ancient wooden boat by the Sea of Galilee. There is a lot of *old* stuff in the country, but here it has to be more than, say, 1,500 years old to be called *ancient*.

Despite its small size, Israel offers an astonishing diversity of climate and terrain. Drive east from Tel Aviv via Jerusalem to the Dead Sea, and in 1½ hours you pass from classic Mediterranean white beaches and orange groves, through olive-draped hills and up rugged pine-wooded mountains, and then plunge almost 4,000 feet down the other side, through wild barren desert, to the subtropical oasis of Jericho and the Dead Sea at the lowest point on the planet.

Half of Israel is desert, but don't think in terms of endless sand dunes. Awesome canyons slice through the Judean Desert to the Dead Sea, a few with sweet waterfalls and brilliant shocks of greenery. The Negev highlands, south of Beersheva, are punctuated by three huge erosion craters, the only such formations in the world. The city of Eilat sits on the coral-reefed Red Sea against a backdrop of jagged granite peaks and desert moonscapes. And in the spring, after the meager winter rains, the deserts burst into often unexpected bloom, the hard landscapes softened by a fuzz of grass and multicolored wildflowers. For the even slightly adventurous visitor, a desert excursion—by foot, Jeep, or camel—is not quickly forgotten.

The northern and western part of the country is a complete antidote to the desert. True, it's also hot in the summer and somewhat parched in the rainless season from May through October, but it's a land of good winter rains, some springs and streams, miles of Mediterranean beaches, extensive irrigated fields and orchards, mountainsides of evergreen forests, lush nature reserves, and the freshwater "Sea" of Galilee.

Despite its heritage and location—think of it as Eastern Mediterranean rather than Middle Eastern—Israel is as European as it is Levantine. Scientifically, the country is at the forefront of agriculture, electronics, computer technology, lasers, medicine, and biotechnology. Seven universities, some world renowned, set exceptional standards. Although Israel's health system is groaning under the weight of financial deficits, and hospital conditions sometimes reflect this, the high medical standards do not seem to have been compromised. Doctors on call for your hotel will speak English and likely be on par with physicians back home.

Violent crime is extremely low in Israel. Politically motivated violence is infrequent and, despite occasional outrages, has typically occurred in areas at the center of the conflict with the Palestinians (like the West Bank) and that are not recommended tourist destinations anyway. You *will* see automatic weapons on the street, obviously in the hands of uniformed security personnel, but also sometimes over the shoulder of a young off-duty soldier in civvies. The Israeli Defense Force is a people's army: Almost everybody serves, and a national serviceman or servicewoman, once issued a weapon, is *wedded* to it for the duration. The criminal misuse of army-issue firearms is very, very rare.

There are many large towns in Israel, but only three major cities. Jerusalem, the capital and spiritual center, lies 60 km (38 mi) inland, at an elevation of 2,500 feet, and is a limestone blend of the ancient and the modern. Tel Aviv, on the Mediterranean coast, is unlovely but lively—the country's commercial and entertainment center, the city that never sleeps. Two out of every five Israelis live within its metropolitan area. Haifa, 100 km (63 mi) north of Tel Aviv, sprawls up the slopes of Mt. Carmel, offering sweeping views and one of the country's two main ports and industrial areas.

Urban life, at least in the metropolis, has changed dramatically over the years. Greater affluence and a sharp sense of international fashion and style have produced a consumerism not unlike that of North America or Western Europe. You see it in the delis and supermarkets, the boutiques and home furnishing stores. The increased popularity of eating out as an evening activity has created a clientele with more sophisticated expectations, and a large number of great restaurants and local fine wines is the result. A good climate and fine beaches have spawned a burgeoning leisure industry as well. Add all of this to the physical attractions, historical fascination, and religious impact of the country, and you have one of the most intriguing destinations around.

—Mike Rogoff

WHAT'S WHERE

Around Jerusalem

This is less a unified region than a variety of eclectic options for which you can use Jerusalem as a base. The most spectacular is the Judean Desert east of Jerusalem, a land of baked rock cliffs and lush oases; of the briny Dead Sea, in which you cannot help but float; and of the broodingly unassailable ancient palace-fortress of Masada. West, toward the Mediterranean coast, are evergreen forests, an exquisite stalactite cave and mazes of man-made ones, and the dueling ground of David and Goliath. Precious to the Christian pilgrim is Bethlehem, just south of Jerusalem, where Jesus was born.

Eilat and the Negev

Most visitors fly into or whiz down to the sun-and-fun city of Eilat, on the Red Sea. Its beaches, tropical reefs for snorkeling or scuba diving, nightspots, and restaurants make it the quintessential winter escape. But if you have the time to take it slow and your soul expands in the quiet vastness of desert landscapes, explore the Negev proper. You will find craters and canyons, the footprints of dead civilizations, and the brilliant achievements of new ones trying to "make the desert bloom." Get off the beaten path: It's an experience you will not easily forget.

Jerusalem

For some, Jerusalem is a place where the past and the future meet and merge; for others, romantic illusions splinter on the concrete of a modern city. The city is both history and today's headlines, both spiritual and decidedly temporal. It is holy to Jews, Christians, and Muslims—each in a unique way—and the age-browned limestone walls and prayer-encrusted shrines of the Old City bear witness to centuries of often competing devotions. Modern Jerusalem, the capital of Israel, has all the bustle and press of a city of half a million souls, but its airy views, stone architecture, museums, and markets make it an absorbing area to visit.

Lower Galilee

Travel with a Bible in hand: Gideon and Deborah both fought here; King Saul died here; Solomon built; Elijah ranted. Jesus grew up in the hill country of Nazareth and spent most of his ministry around the lovely Sea of Galilee. This serious area of antiquities and churches and mosaics is not as well known for its beautiful panoramas and recreation spots and good food. The Lower Galilee is a year-round destination, but in March and April, when wildflowers blanket the hillsides and touch the fields with brilliance, it is at its best.

Northern Coast and Western Galilee

This region is custom-made for the pampered explorer. You can wend your way up the Mediterranean coast, never too far from a good hotel, a good beach, and a good restaurant. The city of Haifa, Israel's third-largest, is the region's center of gravity, and it alone, along with the rugged Mt. Carmel over which it sprawls, is worth a chunk of time. Classic itinerary items are the Roman city of Caesarea and the Crusader town of Akko, both in the process of reexcavation and restoration. Getting off the beaten track in the Western Galilee is a rewarding experience in which wild natural beauty and traces of the long past make a dreamy mix.

Tel Aviv

It's brash and unlovely, but it has the sea—and it's where the action is. A cosmopolitan center of commerce, entertainment, and fashion, Tel Aviv likes to bill itself as "the city that never stops." Fine sandy beaches, a pleasure-boat marina, restaurants, pubs, and clubs aplenty, culture on tap any day of the week—all this makes Tel Avivians see little reason to go elsewhere. On the aesthetic side are Old Jaffa, a landscaped blend of greenery and revived stone buildings; early 20th-century neighborhoods now being renovated and gentrified; the European International Style of the 1930s and '40s, which still survives in the streets of Tel Aviv; and the clean lines of tall modern buildings that make a statement about a city on the move.

Upper Galilee and the Golan

Here you'll find what is arguably the finest scenery in Israel. Hike to a waterfall, boat on the Jordan, ski, go birdwatching, explore a medieval castle, eat some trout, taste wine on the Golan, wrap yourself in Jewish mysticism in the mountain city of Zfat (Safed), and use high vantage points to better understand "the situation" between Israel and its northern neighbors. It is a region in which to recharge your batteries and be as active or as indolent as you choose.

Beyond Israel

Visitors to Israel can easily get a taste of two neighboring countries. The Sinai in Egypt attracts both adventurous travelers who want to trek or dive in its awesome beauty and pilgrims seeking biblical sights, such as St. Catherine's Monastery and Mt. Sinai. From Eilat, you can travel in luxury or join a Jeep safari. Israelis and visitors alike are flocking to nearby Jordan to see Petra, the rose red remains of an ancient Nabatean city carved into sandstone. Its gigantic buildings are treasures even in an area studded with impressive antiquities.

PLEASURES AND PASTIMES

Antiquities

For some, ancient sites are a chore that must be endured. For others, such sites make palpable the clash of ancient arms, the roar of long-dead crowds, and the boom of silent orators. In Israel this is even more true. Not everyone comes here with Bible in hand, but a vast majority of visitors have at least a childhood familiarity with the names that punctuate the country's history. Jerusalem, Beersheva, Bethlehem, the Jordan River, Armageddon are as much concepts as map references. To walk in the footsteps of Abraham, King David, and Jesus of Nazareth is to relive chunks of the history of Western civilization. And where stone remains of the past can be connected—whether scientifically or by tradition—to the very wellsprings of religious faith or cultural identity, the experience is often exultant.

Beaches

Fans of beaches have their choice of an appealing variety of shorelines. The Mediterranean coast has many fine sandy public beaches. The Red Sea beaches at Eilat are of two kinds: the sandy, on the North Shore, for sun worshipers, and the pebbly, near the coral reefs. Dead Sea beaches and the freshwater Sea of Galilee beaches tend to be rocky. You'll float in the supersalty waters of the Dead Sea, a unique experience.

Culture

Classical music is the country's long suit, with several good orchestras—most notably the famous Israel Philharmonic—and many smaller ensembles. Many recent Russian immigrants have made their mark here, and young homegrown virtuosos seem to be keeping up the tradition of Israeli superstars like Itzhak Perlman, Pinchas Zuckerman, Daniel Barenboim, and Shlomo Mintz, all of whom periodically reappear on Israeli stages. Opera's revival in Tel Aviv—new location, new company—recalls the days over 30 years ago when a young tenor named Placido Domingo got his start there.

Jazz and blues are popular, and excellent summer festivals have gained international recognition, though they're largely dependent on foreign artists. The local pop scene tends to be of the softer type, but superstars from abroad help heat it up. Middle Eastern sounds remain very popular, and fusion variations that incorporate Western musical elements have won adherents. Even folk music is alive and well, both the native Israeli and the "Anglo" variety.

There is very little English-language theater, but quite a few Hebrew productions provide simultaneous translation. Dance—particularly modern—can be very good. Watch out especially for the renowned Bat Sheva company.

Dining

The culinary scene in Israel has undergone a revolution in the last decade or so. Middle East specialties immediately come to mind: a *meze* (appetizer) of well-flavored salads with warmed pita bread, some fresh grilled fish, or a skewer of shish kebabs. But soaring tourism and a new generation of Israelis with more money have created a demand for a higher level and wider range of specialty restaurants. Add to that the rainbow of cultural influences that is part of the fabric of Israeli society and the year-round availability of extremely good local produce, and the food scene will come as less of a surprise. Fine steaks or tasty quiches, the dishes of France and Italy, of China and India, and even (perish the comparison!) international fast-food chains—it's all here, though obviously more so in the big cities (with Tel Aviv in the lead) than in the country.

Museums

Throughout Israel, museums help bring alive the past for visitors. Local museums tell the story of a particular site or display archaeological artifacts found there. There are regional museums that do much the same thing, often with the addition of the area's natural history. And there are national museums, where the art of museology is far more in evidence. Among these are historical or ethnographical museums like the Diaspora and Eretz Israel museums, both in Tel Aviv, or Yad Vashem, the Holocaust museum and memorial, in Jerusalem. Consider all of the above, of course, but allow time for Jerusalem's marvelously eclectic and world-renowned Israel Museum, a repository of much of the nation's finest art and archaeological treasures.

Outdoor Activities

Israel has become known to adventurous travelers as a destination for everything from desert treks to scuba diving. Many Israelis are avid hikers, and the country has several thousand miles of officially marked hiking trails. In addition, parks and nature reserves dot the country. In the process of development is a long route called the Israel Trail, running the length of the country, from the village of Metulla, on the northern border with Lebanon, to Eilat, on the Red Sea, in the south. Cliff rappelling has developed a following, with the precipices of the Judean and Negev deserts the choice sites.

Scuba diving and snorkeling are popular amid the world-renown coral reefs of Eilat and off the Mediterranean beaches of Ashkelon, Tel Aviv, Hadera, Caesarea, Haifa, Akko, and Nahariya.

Visitors can take advantage of pools and gyms, tennis and squash courts, sailboats and Windsurfers, scuba equipment and Para-Sails, horses, and canoes. You can trek the Negev by Jeep or camel. In the early spring, you could conceivably water-ski on the Sea of Galilee and snow-ski on Mt. Hermon on the same day.

NEW AND NOTEWORTHY

Jerusalem

It has been 3,000 years since King David made Jerusalem his capital, and the celebration of that milestone was the centerpiece of events in the city throughout 1996. Several projects launched to coincide with the trimillennium promise to change the face of archaeological sites in Jerusalem. An ambitious **park** is being developed, which will stretch from the Garden of Gethsemane at the foot of the Mount of Olives down to the Kidron Valley; it will also embrace the historical sites of the City of David and stretch up the Hinnom Valley to the west. The most immediate results are an **observation point** near the Old City's southeastern corner, with a panorama of the Kidron Valley; and a cleaning up and guarding of the famous **Hezekiah's Tunnel,** under the City of David. Eventually the park will provide explanations of newly renovated archaeological sites en route, as well services such as refreshment stands.

Another high-visibility project is the re-excavation and restoration of the **Ophel Archaeological Garden** (better known as the Western and Southern Wall Excavations), just inside the Old City's Dung Gate. What has come to light are vast underground sewage tunnels and enormously evocative sections of one of Jerusalem's main streets from 2,000 years ago. Currently being prepared for public access, the site will offer frozen-in-time evidence of the destruction of the city by the Romans in AD 70. On the same site, the scanty remains of 8th-century AD Arab palaces have not been overlooked: In them will be small gardens reproducing the style and range of plants thought to be grown at that time.

One contribution to solving Jerusalem's shortage of hotel rooms is the new **Hilton Hotel**—in an advanced stage of construction at press time—part of the new Mamilla complex, near but outside the Jaffa Gate. Other proposed hotel-building plans of recent years have yet to get off the ground.

With Jerusalem 3000 behind it, the city is bracing itself for two more celebratory years—1998, Israel's 50th birthday, and the year 2000, the Christian bimillennium—though no details of events were available at press time.

Around Jerusalem

The long-awaited second **cable-car system** is underway at **Masada,** the great ancient citadel near the Dead Sea. Expected to be completed by late 1997 or early 1998, it will whisk 80 visitors at a time to its upper station on the summit (the present system ends 90 steps below the top). By almost tripling the present cable-car capacity, the new system will provide a long-term solution to peak-season delays. Also planned is a sophisticated **visitor center,** with visual and audiovisual aids.

Currently, no new developments are planned for the labyrinthine chalk-cave complexes at Maresha, part of the **Bet Guvrin National Park,** southwest of Jerusalem; but the excavation and restoration of the nearby Roman **amphitheater** continues apace and is expected to be open to the public in the near future.

Tel Aviv

Driving in the city is becoming increasingly difficult because of the number of cars on the road and a lack of parking. But if you can wait 20 years, you may be able to ride an **electric rail system** linking Tel Aviv with the surrounding suburbs. This quiet, nonpolluting system will replace the buses now in use. Meanwhile, **intercity roads** are being improved: The Ayalon Highway (Route 1), for example, is being widened to ease congestion on Tel Aviv's access roads.

One of the biggest problems for visitors to Tel Aviv is a shortage of reasonably priced accommodations. With any luck, this is going to change—albeit slowly—over the coming years. Several thousand additional hotel rooms are planned for the city by the year 2000. Many of these, city officials state, will be much more budget priced than the average hotel today.

Four marked **walking tours** were introduced in 1995; they are called the Orange (Tapuz) Routes. Although they can also be done as driving tours, walking is preferred. The routes cover numerous points of historic and cultural interest in the city. Maps are available from the Tel Aviv Tourist Information Office in the Central Bus Station.

Something is also being done to promote the city's **architectural history:** City Hall says it wants to make Tel Aviv "the world's largest open-air International Style museum." One thousand buildings designed in International Style and dating from the 1930s and '40s are slated for restoration. Although these buildings' characteristic straight lines and simple forms can still be seen, their whitewash is blackened, and plastic shutters and ugly air-conditioners have become their dominant visual elements. Progress is slow because money for the massive project is hard to come by, but the city's change in attitude toward preservation and restoration is a step in the right direction.

Lower Galilee

Nazareth is coming of age as a tourism city, if the Mifneh (Turnaround) '97 project is anything to go by. Inspired by predictions of an upsurge in pilgrimage to mark the bimillennium of the Christian era (2000), the city and the Ministry of Tourism are investing huge sums in **infrastructure and face-lifting.** Road resurfacing and flower beds are the most immediate results, and the renovation of the old market off Casa Nova Street is nearing completion. Parking areas and public bathroom facilities are being planned; and the city's hotels—old, new, and still-to-be—should provide 2,000 rooms by the year 2000.

Nazareth has always celebrated **Christmas** with parades, fireworks, and choral singing; but the Israel Ministry of Tourism is giving these events even greater support since Bethlehem came under Palestinian autonomous control in December 1995. Nazareth's own international Christmas choir assembly seems set to rival the longer-established event in Bethlehem.

The ancient city of **Zippori,** west of Nazareth, has become famous (and a national park) mostly because of the fine **mosaic floors** unearthed there. Apart from the famous "Mona Lisa" floor, the restored "Nile" mosaic is soon to be reopened; and the poorly preserved but intriguing synagogue floor, at press time on display at the Israel Museum, is also due to return home.

Upper Galilee

The range of accommodations in this region is constantly expanding, with a recent emphasis on the great outdoors. Among the new entrants are **vegetarian inns** that offer health-and-beauty packages and **sports-oriented vacations** centered around activities such as horseback riding and kayaking.

Eilat, the Negev, and Petra

Peace is upon Israel, at least in some directions, making **Eilat** a convenient departure point for trips to neighboring Jordan (for many years diving and sightseeing trips to the Egyptian **Sinai** have also departed from Eilat). The main attraction is the ancient pink-hued stone city of **Petra,** the capital of the Nabatean kingdom, which some 2,000 years ago controlled a lucrative perfume-and-spice route. A link road between the Indo-Chinese markets and the Mediterranean world led from Transjordan through Israel's Negev Desert and on to the coastal city of Gaza. One of the stops along the way was **Avdat,** which may be explored today.

It's a pleasure to report that the management of Eilat's newer **hotels** have taken into consideration the sensitivities of visitors not in love with loud music and nightly entertainment in the lobby. New hotels have been built with two lobbies—local jargon calls the one without entertainment the "quiet lobby."

Hotels in **Eilat** and **Ein Bokek** get bigger and plusher by the minute. The Dan Eilat has 600 rooms, and its lobby is furnished with individual groupings of futuristic furniture in bold colors. The luxurious 600-room Hyatt Regency has opened in Ein Bokek, at the Dead Sea, with the largest spa in the region. Under construction around the Dead Sea are a deluxe Hilton and a couple of smaller hotels.

FODOR'S CHOICE

Quintessentially Israeli

☆ **The Western (Wailing) Wall on Monday and Thursday mornings, Jerusalem.** Festivities welcome the newly bar mitzvahed into the adult Jewish community.

☆ **The Machaneh Yehuda market on Thursday and Friday, Jerusalem.** In the pre-Shabbat shopping frenzy, look for treasures among stalls piled with produce and hand-crafted goods.

☆ **Nahalat Binyamin street market and Sheinkin Street, Friday afternoon, Tel Aviv.** Hang out at a café and enjoy music and local color.

☆ **Bargaining at the Arab *souk* (outdoor market), Akko.** Middle Eastern flavors and aromas create a feast for the senses.

☆ **Saturday lunch in Caesarea.** You can eat by the Crusader city and gaze at the Mediterranean.

☆ **A visit to a nature reserve, Upper Galilee.** Take in the wildflowers at the Tel Dan or Hermon River (Banias) nature reserves.

☆ *Kabbalat Shabbat* **at the Dolphin Reef tent pub, Eilat.** Late on Friday afternoons, people gather to greet the Sabbath.

Biblical Highlights and Holy Places

☆ **Western (Wailing) Wall, Jerusalem.** The most important existing Jewish shrine, this stone wall was part of the retaining wall of the Temple Mount.

☆ **Calvary, Jerusalem.** Different theories claim either the Church of the Holy Sepulcher or the Garden Tomb to be the site of Jesus' crucifixion.

☆ **Dome of the Rock and El-Aqsa Mosque, Jerusalem.** Muslims identify these buildings with events central to the teachings of Islam.

☆ **Warren's Shaft and Hezekiah's Tunnel, Jerusalem.** These underground structures once brought water to the ancient City of David.

☆ **Via Dolorosa, Jerusalem.** The 14 Stations of the Cross mark the path believed to have been Jesus' last journey.

☆ **Church of the Nativity, Bethlehem.** Israel's oldest church encompasses the cave in which Jesus is said to have been born.

☆ **Carmelite Monastery, Muhraka.** Near this site, Elijah defeated the priests of Ba'al in the struggle against paganism.

☆ **Baha'i Shrine, Haifa.** Topped by a golden dome, the mausoleum of a central figure in the Baha'i faith sits amid the shrine's magnificent gardens.

☆ **Mt. Tabor, Lower Galilee.** Both the biblical victory of the prophetess-judge Deborah and the Church of the Transfiguration add religious significance to this site.

☆ **Church of the Annunciation, Nazareth.** Here, Roman Catholics believe, the angel Gabriel announced the upcoming birth of Jesus to the Virgin Mary.

☆ **Mount of Beatitudes, Lower Galilee.** The site of the Sermon on the Mount offers peaceful views of the Sea of Galilee.

☆ **Tel Dan Nature Reserve, Upper Galilee.** Joshua led the Israelites through this area to victory against the Canaanites.

☆ **Tel Beer Sheva, the Negev.** Atop the hill of biblical Beersheva is the well some consider to be Abraham's Well.

Archaeological Gems

☆ **The archaeology wing of the Israel Museum, Jerusalem.** Artifacts from the past brilliantly illuminate the area's long history.

☆ **Herodian Quarter/Wohl Archaeological Museum, Jerusalem.** Study ancient interior design through the remains of Second Temple–period mansions.

☆ **Herod's Palace/Fortress of Masada.** This lasting expression of King Herod's taste for opulence is also the site of the Jews' last stand against the Romans.

☆ **Tel Maresha and Bet Guvrin, west of Jerusalem.** Take a walking tour through the man-made caves that served as storerooms, cisterns, and quarries during the Hellenistic period.

⭐**Crusader City, Akko.** A stroll through this area—both above and below ground—captures a sense of Akko's past glory.

⭐**Herodian port and Crusader city, Caesarea.** Walls enclose the remains of some of Herod's elaborate buildings and Crusader fortifications set along the seashore.

⭐**Zippori, Lower Galilee.** Recently excavated mosaic floors and elaborate water systems recall Jewish life in the Roman period.

⭐**Bet She'an, Lower Galilee.** The remains of what was the great Roman-Byzantine city of Scythopolis are Israel's latest and most impressive find.

⭐**Avdat, the Negev.** The ancient ruins of this hilltop city were left by the Nabateans, Romans, and Byzantines.

Dining

⭐**Le Tsriff, Jerusalem.** Locals flock to this backstreet gem for entrées such as meat and vegetable pies in perfect crusts. $$

⭐**Little Italy, Jerusalem.** Choose from a wide range of meatless Italian fare, from fish-and-pasta dishes to pizza. $$

⭐**Mul-Yam, Tel Aviv.** Dine on imported oysters and seafood in an attractive setting at the old port. $$$$

⭐**Shipudei Hatikva, Tel Aviv.** This simply decorated, family-style eatery serves wonderful grilled meats. $

⭐**The Pine Club Restaurant, Mt. Carmel.** Local ingredients help create a memorable experience in French dining. $$$$

⭐**Shuni Castle, Shuni.** The chef's inventive dishes mix well with wine from neighboring vineyards. $$$

⭐**Abu Christo, Akko.** This family-run fish restaurant serves the catch of the day, grilled or fried, in a relaxed waterfront setting. $$

⭐**Pagoda** and **The House, Tiberias.** While both establishments specialize in excellent pork- and shellfish-free Chinese and Thai food, the Pagoda keeps kosher. $$–$$$

⭐**Auberge Shulamit, Rosh Pina.** Home-smoked meats and sophisticated fish dishes draw crowds to this charming inn. $$$$

⭐**The Last Refuge, Eilat.** Huge salads and seasonal fish and seafood are served with style at this Coral Beach eatery. $$$

Lodging

⭐**American Colony, Jerusalem.** Guest rooms are modest, but this 19th-century limestone oasis draws visitors because of its ambience and service. $$$$

⭐**Lev Yerushalayim, Jerusalem.** Well-done suite accommodations with kitchenettes provide convenience in the city center. $$$

⭐**Ramat Rachel, Jerusalem.** Great views and superb facilities give this rustic kibbutz hotel a resort feel; it's also 15 minutes from downtown. $$$

⭐**Dan Tel Aviv.** A welcoming atmosphere and personal touches set the tone at this landmark establishment. $$$$

⭐**Sheraton Tel Aviv Hotel and Towers.** A well-designed lobby, comfortable rooms, and plenty to do make the Sheraton a haven. $$$$

⭐**Dan Panorama, Haifa.** Nearby shopping and dining enhance this sparkling hotel. $$$

⭐**Galei Kinneret, Tiberias.** This lakeside establishment with attractive grounds has drawn many distinguished visitors. $$$$

⭐**Church of Scotland Centre, Tiberias.** A private beach and stone buildings with porches and high-ceilinged rooms are appealing features. $$

⭐**Rimon Inn, Zfat.** Stone walls and a mountain setting add to the rustic mood of this well-equipped inn. $$$$

⭐**Dan Eilat, Eilat.** This strikingly modern luxury hotel—the city's newest—has an array of facilities. $$$$

GREAT ITINERARIES

Highlights of the Holy Land

Jerusalem is a city in which history wraps its mantle around the present. Abraham brought Isaac to Mt. Moriah. King David made the city his capital, and his son, King Solomon, built the First Temple there. Conqueror after conqueror battled for this city, but Jerusalem transcends its martial past, and you'll be struck by its beauty and its spiritual quality.

In contrast, Tel Aviv is a new city, the fulfillment of modern pioneers who believed a metropolis could rise atop sand dunes. Jerusalem is a busy city and can even be a bit frenetic when people hurry in the streets to prepare for the Sabbath. But the rest of the time the city seems provincial, compared to fast-paced, modern Tel Aviv, home of fashion and commerce.

Tiberias is a small city perched on the Sea of Galilee, a perfect base for seeing the Galilee and Golan.

By booking hotel rooms in these three cities, you can see most of Israel in a short time and do a minimum of packing and unpacking.

Duration

8 days

The Main Route

3 NIGHTS: OLD AND NEW JERUSALEM➤ Wear good walking shoes for Old City tours. Begin with a visit to the Tower of David Museum, just inside Jaffa Gate in the Old City, which recounts the history of Jerusalem. Spend an evening at a folklore show. Have dinner at an ethnic restaurant. Local specialties are *kubeh* soup (a rich vegetable soup with semolina-stuffed meatballs), Jerusalem mixed grill, and hummus. Have coffee or onion soup on Ben Yehuda Street and enjoy the atmosphere of a street fair. For the fourth day, book a full-day tour to the Dead Sea and Masada with a tour company or a private guide. Return to Jerusalem for dinner.

2 NIGHTS: TEL AVIV➤ Frequent buses make the trip between Jerusalem and Tel Aviv in less than an hour. Military vehicles from the War of Independence have been left on the roadside as memorials to the days when the city was under siege. Farther along, the bus passes through the Ayalon Valley, named in the Bible as the site where the sun stood still in the heavens for Joshua.

In Tel Aviv, make sure to window-shop on Dizengoff Street and visit the Diaspora Museum. Shop at the outdoor Carmel Market. Have dinner at a beachside restaurant or eat authentic falafel. Catch local per-

formers at a Jaffa nightclub or hear the Israel Philharmonic Orchestra at the Mann Auditorium.

2 NIGHTS: TIBERIAS➤ Around the Sea of Galilee on the first day, see the Mount of Beatitudes, the synagogue at Capernaum, the Hammat Gader hot springs in the remains of the Roman baths, Israel's oldest kibbutz, and Tabgha, said to be where Jesus multiplied the loaves and the fishes. Swim or go boating in the lake. Have dinner on the wharf; the local specialty is St. Peter's fish (*amnoon* in Hebrew). On the second day, take a daylong excursion to the Upper Galilee and the Golan Heights to see sights like the old Syrian bunkers, the Banias Waterfall, ancient Gamla, the town of Katzrin, the Mt. Hermon ski resort, and Nimrod's Castle. Return to Tiberias via Zfat, a city of mystics and artists, and take a nighttime cruise across the Sea of Galilee.

On the eighth and last day of the tour, return to the airport via Rosh Hanikra, and Haifa. In Haifa, ride by cable car to the top of Mt. Carmel for the view.

Getting Around

Pick up a rental car at Ben-Gurion Airport and drive to Jerusalem. From Jerusalem to Tel Aviv, leave Jerusalem from the same main westbound exit, near the Central Bus Station, and follow signs for Route 1, past the Ben-Gurion Airport, into Tel Aviv. Leave Tel Aviv by the Ayalon Bypass and the Haifa Road (Route 2), drive north along the coast, and turn east onto Route 65 (look for power station chimneys on your left) toward Afula to reach Tiberias.

You can also do this itinerary by bus. Buses leave the airport every half hour for Jerusalem; buses from North Tel Aviv (Arlozorov Street; Bus 480) and from the new Central Bus Station (Bus 405) leave every 10–15 minutes. There are also frequent buses to Tiberias from the Central Bus Station in Tel Aviv.

Information

Chapters 2, 3, 4, 6, and 7.

Action Tour

The weather is so good in Israel that outdoor adventure lovers can always find plenty to do. The only limits are your energy and, sometimes, the heat. Drink a lot of fluids and watch out for the sun. Israelis are great hikers. Trails are well marked, and you can add day hikes to any of the suggested activities below.

Duration
11 days

The Main Route
3 NIGHTS: JERUSALEM➤ Park outside Jaffa Gate and walk along the walls of the Old City. Join a walking tour through the archaeological tunnels under the Western Wall. Eat in an ethnic restaurant and attend a folklore show. On the second day, visit key West Jerusalem sites, including Yad Vashem, the Knesset, the Chagall windows at Hadassah Hospital, and the Israel Museum. Return to the Old City for a moonlight tour.

On the third day, take a donkey ride or a vigorous walking tour through the Judean Hills. Visit a kibbutz, the Sorek Stalactite Cave, and the man-made caverns of Maresha/Bet Guvrin.

2 NIGHTS: DEAD SEA AREA➤ Visit Masada (by way of the steep Snake Path, if you're fit) and hike in the Ein Gedi Nature Reserve for the day, then stay overnight on the shore of the Dead Sea at a kibbutz guest house, a hotel at Ein Bokek, or at the SPNI field school at Ein Gedi. The next day, go cliff rappelling at Metzukei Dragot, near Kibbutz Shalem. Soothe your skin in the local mud baths. Take a night jeep tour of the area.

2 NIGHTS: EILAT➤ Take a one-day camel tour into the breathtaking hills around Eilat; swim with the dolphins and snorkel at a superb coral beach. Take a self-driven jeep tour or go for a desert hike in the magnificent Red Canyon and in Ein Netifim.

1 NIGHT: TEL AVIV➤ Rest up in Tel Aviv with a stroll on the boardwalk. Rent a sailboat at the marina.

2 NIGHTS: TIBERIAS➤ You can hike and horseback ride in the Golan Heights, or depending on the weather, ski on Mt. Hermon or take an inner-tube or kayak ride down the Jordan River. Try parasailing on the Sea of Galilee.

Getting Around
To do this itinerary, pick up a rental car at Ben-Gurion Airport and follow signs east to Jerusalem. You can park at one of the lots adjacent to the Old City. As an alternative, take a bus from the airport; they leave every half hour or, from Tel Aviv to Jerusalem, every 10–15 minutes.

Information
Chapters 2, 3, 4, 6, and 8.

Archaeology Tour

Israel is an archaeology lover's dream, with a wide variety of fascinating sites within a small geographical area. Visitors may want to consider joining a dig for part of the time. Most prehistoric sites are in the Lower Galilee and along the northern coast, and Jerusalem is a treasure trove of ancient sites from all periods of history. Following the archaeologists' trails will take you around most of the country.

Duration
8–10 days

The Main Route
4 NIGHTS: JERUSALEM WITH DAY TRIPS➤ Plan on at least two days in the Old City and two days in museums. Some essential sites for archaeology buffs in Jerusalem are the City of David (including Warren's Shaft and Hezekiah's Tunnel), the Ophel Archaeological Garden, the Pools of Bethesda, the Jewish Quarter (including the Herodian Mansions and Burnt House, the Broad Wall, and the Cardo), and the Western Wall tunnel. Visit the Tower of David Museum, the Israel Museum (where the Dead Sea Scrolls are displayed, as well as countless other ancient artifacts), the Bible Lands Museum, and the Rockefeller Museum. Have dinner at the Cardo Culinaria (✉ Jewish Quarter, Old City, ☎ 02/589–4155), a restaurant modeled after a Roman *triclineum*, a dining establishment of 2,000 years ago.

Make a day trip to the Qumran caves, where the Dead Sea Scrolls were found; the Chalcolithic temple at Ein Gedi (a considerable climb); and the great desert fortress at Masada (where the sound-and-light program makes a perfect evening). Also visit the Bet Guvrin caves, southwest of Jerusalem.

2 NIGHTS: TIBERIAS➤ Travel along the Jordan Valley to Bet She'an and on to the Crusader castle Belvoir and to Hammat Gader, with its excavated Roman baths,

hot springs, and pools. Leave time to bathe in the hot pools and visit the site's alligator farm. Travel to the Golan Heights town of Katzrin to visit its small but fascinating museum. Don't miss the gates and high place of Tel Dan, the water system of Hazor, the ancient synagogues of Capernaum, either Hammat Tiberias or Bet Alfa, the mosaics of Zippori, and the prehistoric museum at Ma'ayan Baruch.

1 NIGHT: NAHARIYA➤ See the mosaics in the church at Givat Katznelson, the Crusader city in Akko, and the ancient city of Megiddo, one of the inspirations for James Michener's *The Source*. Stay either in the resort town of Nahariya or in a coastal kibbutz guest house.

The next day, visit a cluster of sites in the Western Galilee and along the northern coast: Bet She'arim, with its Jewish catacombs dating from the 2nd–4th centuries AD; the healing center and baths at Shuni, near Zichron Ya'akov; and the Roman city and port of Caesarea.

2 NIGHTS: BEERSHEVA AND EILAT➤ If you have two extra days, head south to the Negev to see the biblical city at Tel Beer Sheva (Beersheva) and the ancient copper works of Timna Valley, north of Eilat.

Getting Around

Except in Jerusalem, it's best to rent a car to reach most of the archaeological sites. Buses will get you to many places, but plan carefully to make sure you have return transportation.

Information

Chapters 2, 3, 5, 6, and 8.

NATIONAL AND RELIGIOUS HOLIDAYS

Time is figured in different ways in Israel. The Western Gregorian calendar—the solar year from January to December— is the basis of day-to-day life and commerce, of course, but the school year, for example, which runs from September through June, follows the *Hebrew* lunar calendar (dated to when Creation was believed to have occurred). Thus fall 1997–fall 1998

is the equivalent of the Hebrew year 5758, reckoned from Rosh Hashanah, the Jewish New Year, which usually falls in September. Since the lunar year is 11 days shorter than the solar year, Jewish holidays are out of sync with the Gregorian calendar and fall on different dates (though within the same season) from one year to the next. Jewish religious festivals are observed as national public holidays, when businesses and some museums are closed (on Yom Kippur, the Day of Atonement, *all* sites are closed).

The Muslim calendar is also lunar, but without the compensatory leap-year mechanism of its Hebrew counterpart. Muslim holidays thus drift through the seasons and can fall at any time of the year.

Even the Christian calendar is not uniform: Christmas in Bethlehem is celebrated on different days by the Roman Catholic ("Latin") community, the Greek Orthodox, and the Armenians.

Jewish Holidays

Below is a calendar of holidays as they are observed in Israel. *Remember that Jewish holidays begin at sundown and end at nightfall the following day.* The dates listed for Jewish holidays in 1997 and 1998 are for the day itself, not for the beginning of the holiday on the previous evening. "Not religious" in the text indicates that the holiday might be part of the religious tradition, but few or no public restrictions apply.

SHABBAT (SABBATH)➤ The Day of Rest in Israel is Saturday, the Jewish Sabbath, beginning at sundown Friday and ending at nightfall Saturday. By Friday afternoon, you can feel the country winding down, as most Jewish-owned businesses close until Saturday night or Sunday morning. Religious neighborhoods become frenetic as families do last-minute cooking and cleaning before the Sabbath begins. Devout Jews do not cook, travel, answer the telephone, or use money or writing materials during the Shabbat, which explains the Sabbath ban on photography at Jewish holy sites like the Western Wall. In Jerusalem, where religious influence is strong, the downtown area dies on Friday evening, and some religious neighborhoods are even closed to traffic; in more secular and cosmopolitan Tel Aviv, Haifa, and Eilat, much of the populace spills out onto the streets and into the nightspots.

Kosher restaurants close on the Sabbath, except for the main hotel restaurants, where some menu restrictions apply. Outside Jerusalem you will scarcely be affected: In fact, many restaurants do their best business of the week because non-Jewish Israelis take to the roads. In the holy city, your dining choices are considerably reduced.

In Arab areas, like East Jerusalem and Nazareth, Muslims take time off for the week's most important devotions, on midday Friday, but the visitor will notice this much less than Sunday, when most Christian shopkeepers take the whole day off. Saturday is market day, and the towns buzz with activity.

There is no public intercity transportation on the Sabbath, although the *sherut* taxis drive between the main cities. Urban buses only operate in Nazareth and on a reduced schedule in Haifa. Shabbat is also the busiest day for the nature reserves and national parks—indeed, anywhere the city folk can get away for a day. Keep this in mind for long drives: The highways in the direction of the main cities can be choked with returning weekend traffic on Saturday afternoon.

Sunday, then, is the first day of the regular workweek (in Israel, says the old quip, Monday blues begin on Sunday), and though the country is moving rapidly toward a five-day workweek, the weekend will include *Friday*, already a half day and holy to the country's Muslim minority, and Saturday. The public sector and most corporations already work Sunday through Thursday only, and the schools may soon follow suit.

TU B'SHEVAT➣ Jan. 23, 1997 and Jan. 12, 1998. Not religious. Israelis eat fruit and plant trees on the New Year of Trees, a time when the white- and pink-blossomed almond trees bloom.

PURIM➣ Mar. 23, 1997 and Mar. 12, 1998 (in Jerusalem, one day later). Not religious. For days before Purim, children dress up in costumes. In synagogues and on public television, pious Jews read the Scroll of Esther, the story of the valiant Jewish queen who prevented the massacre of her people in ancient Persia. Street festivals are held in many towns.

PESACH (PASSOVER)➣ Apr. 22–28, 1997 and Apr. 11–17, 1998. First and last days religious; dietary restrictions in force throughout. Passover is preceded by vigorous household spring-cleaning to remove all traces of leavened bread and related products. During the seven-day holiday, no bread is sold in Jewish stores, and the crackerlike matzo replaces bread in most hotels and restaurants. On the first evening of the holiday, Jewish families gather to retell the ancient story of their people's exodus out of Egyptian bondage and to eat a symbolic, festive meal called the seder (Hebrew for "order"). Hotels have communal seders, and the Ministry of Tourism can sometimes arrange for tourists to join with Israeli families celebrating Passover in their homes.

YOM HASHO'AH (HOLOCAUST MEMORIAL DAY)➣ May 4, 1997 and Apr. 23, 1998. Not religious. Special services take place at the Yad Vashem Holocaust Memorial, in Jerusalem, and elsewhere in the country. Entertainment venues are closed, and at 11 AM all stand silent as a siren sounds in memory of the 6 million Jews who were annihilated by the Nazis in World War II.

YOM HAZIKARON (MEMORIAL DAY)➣ May 11, 1997 and Apr. 29, 1998. Not religious. This is a day of mourning for Israel's war dead. Commemorative ceremonies are held around the country, entertainment sites are closed, and at 11 AM a siren sounds in memory of the fallen.

YOM HA'ATZMA'UT (INDEPENDENCE DAY)➣ May 12, 1997 and Apr. 30, 1998. Not religious. A celebration of Israel's independence, in May 1948; the exact date follows the *Hebrew* calendar. Although there are many gala events, fireworks displays, and military parades all over the country, most Israelis go picnicking or swimming. Stores and a few sites are closed, but public transportation runs.

LAG BA'OMER➣ May 25, 1997 and May 14, 1988. Not religious. The 33rd day between Passover and Shavuot marks the end of a string of historic tragedies and the commemoration of the death of Rabbi Shimon Bar Yochai. Kids build bonfires, and the devout make trips to the rabbi's grave in Meron, near Zfat.

SHAVUOT (FEAST OF WEEKS)➣ June 11, 1997 and May 31, 1998. This holiday, seven weeks after Passover, marks the harvest of the first fruits and, according to tradition, is the day on which Moses received the Torah (the law) on Mt. Sinai. Many observant Jews stay up all night studying the Torah. It is customary to eat dairy meals on this one-day holiday.

TISHA B'AV (THE NINTH OF AV)➤ Aug. 12, 1997 and Aug. 2, 1998. Not religious. Among the calamities that (apparently) occurred on this day was the destruction in antiquity of both the First and Second Temples. Observant Jews fast and recite the biblical Book of Lamentations. Entertainment venues and many restaurants are closed.

ROSH HASHANAH (JEWISH NEW YEAR)➤ Oct. 2–3, 1997 and Sept. 21–22, 1998. Yom Kippur and this two-day holiday are collectively known as the High Holy Days. Rosh Hashanah traditionally begins a 10-day period of introspection and repentance. Observant Jews attend rather long synagogue services and eat festive meals, including apples and honey to symbolize the hoped-for sweetness of the new year. Nonobservant Jews often use this holiday break for picnics and for going to the beach.

YOM KIPPUR (DAY OF ATONEMENT)➤ Oct. 11, 1997 and Sept. 30, 1998. This is the most solemn day of the Jewish year. Observant Jews fast, wear white clothing, and avoid leather footwear. There are no radio and television broadcasts. All sites, entertainment venues, and most restaurants are closed. Much of the country comes to a halt, and in towns like Jerusalem the roads are almost entirely empty of traffic other than emergency vehicles. It is a privilege to be invited to somebody's house to "break fast" as the holiday ends at nightfall.

SUKKOTH (FEAST OF TABERNACLES)➤ Oct. 16–23, 1997 and Oct. 5–12, 1998. First and last days religious. Jews build open-roof "huts" or shelters called *sukkot* (singular *sukkah*) on porches and in backyards to remember the makeshift lodgings of the biblical Israelites as they wandered in the desert. The more observant will eat as many of their meals as possible in their sukkah and even sleep there through this period.

Right before the holiday, colorful street markets sell special decorations and the four kinds of "species" that are used in the Sukkoth ceremonies—the *etrog* (citron, like a yellow lime) and the elements that make up the *lulav* (a palm frond and sprigs of willow and myrtle). The first day is observed like the Sabbath, except that food can be cooked. The intervening days are half holidays, and shopkeepers often take vacations. An annual hike to Jerusalem takes place. Many Evangelical Christians come to Israel to celebrate the festival as well, in obedience to the passage in the prophecy of Zechariah 14.

SIMHAT TORAH➤ The last day of the week of Sukkoth (☞ *above*), this holiday marks the end, and the immediate recommencement, of the annual cycle of the reading of the Torah, the Five Books of Moses. The evening and morning synagogue services are characterized by joyful singing and dancing as people carry the Torah scrolls.

HANUKKAH➤ Dec. 24–31, 1997 and Dec. 14–21, 1998. Not religious. A Jewish rebellion in the 2nd century BC renewed Jewish control of Jerusalem. In the recleansed and rededicated Temple, the tradition tells, a vessel was found with enough oil to burn for a day. It miraculously burned for eight days, hence the eight-day holiday marked by the lighting of an increasing number of candles from night to night. Customary foods are potato pancakes (latkes or *levivot*) and a local version of the jelly doughnut called *sufganiah*. The schools are on winter break. Shops, businesses, and services all remain open.

Christian Holidays

For up-to-date holiday information, contact the Israel Government Tourist Office (IGTO) in your country or region, or the Christian Information Service in Jerusalem (☎ 02/628–7647).

EASTER➤ Apr. 27, 1997 and Apr. 12, 1998. The festival celebrates the resurrection of Jesus. The nature and timing of its ceremonies and worship services are colorfully different in each religious tradition represented in the Holy Land—Roman Catholic, Protestant, Greek Orthodox, Armenian Orthodox, Ethiopian, and so on; check the dates for different groups.

CHRISTMAS➤ Except in towns with a large indigenous Christian population, like Nazareth and Bethlehem, Christmas is not the high-visibility holiday in Israel that it is in predominantly Christian countries. The Christmas of the Catholic and Protestant traditions is, of course, celebrated on December 25; but the Greek Orthodox calendar has it pegged on January 7, and the Armenian Orthodox celebrate on January 18. Shuttle buses from Jerusalem bring tourists to Manger Square in Bethlehem on Christmas Eve (December 24) for the annual international choir songfest and the Roman Catholic midnight mass. Information is available from the IGTO.

Muslim Holidays

Muslims observe Friday as their holy day, but there are none of the restrictions and far less of the solemnity that mark either the Jewish Shabbat or the Christian Sabbath. The noontime prayer on Friday is the most important of the week and is typically preceded by a sermon, often broadcast from the loudspeakers of the mosques.

The dates of Muslim holidays vary widely each year because of the lunar calendar.

RAMADAN➤ Dec. 23, 1997 and Jan. 31, 1998. Observant Muslims fast all day and eat in the evening for the duration of this holy period of 40 days. Special festivities lasting several days mark the end of the holiday. Anticipate changes in entrance times to Muslim holy places like the Temple Mount during this period.

FESTIVALS AND SEASONAL EVENTS

More festivals appear each year on the national calendar. Some, like the Israel Festival and the Red Sea Jazz Festival, are international in character, with reliable dates. Some are permanent seasonal features, timed to coincide with the Jewish holidays in spring and fall. Still others are more local "occasionals," where past success makes future scheduling probable but not definite. Most dates were not available at press time; check with the Israel Government Tourist Office (☞ Visitor Information *in* Important Contacts A to Z) for details. Tickets for major events can be purchased in advance at ticket agencies in Israel.

WINTER

Dec.➤ A gala pre-Christmas performance of **Choirs from Around the World** takes place in Jerusalem. Many international choirs perform at the **International Christmas Choir Assembly** in Manger Square, Bethlehem, on Christmas Eve. International choirs sing at Nazareth's **Christmas Parade** and songfest on December 26.

Late Dec.–early Jan.➤ The **Liturgical Festival of Choral Music** is organized by the Jerusalem Symphony Orchestra from the end of December through the beginning of January. The **Classical Music Winter Festival** is a Jerusalem event.

Jan.➤ The **International Marathon** takes place in Tiberias in early January.

SPRING

Mar.➤ The **International Book Fair** opens in Jerusalem mid-month. The **Spring Migration Birdwatchers' Festival** is held in Eilat around the end of the third week. Mid-March is the time for the **Tel Aviv half-marathon.** The **Mt. Tabor Run,** in the Lower Galilee, is scheduled during the third week of the month.

Watch for the revival of the **Tel Aviv minicarnival** to mark the joyous Purim holiday.

Apr.➤ Look for **Rock at the Red Sea,** in Eilat. During **Passover,** when many Israelis are on holiday, the country hums with activities and events. Ask at the local TIO and watch newspapers for details. The **Ein Gev Festival,** on the Sea of Galilee, presents all kinds of music. **Days of Music and Blossoms,** in the Misgav region of Western Galilee, has eclectic offerings. The **International Festival of Sacred Music** is a Nazareth event. **Sounds of Spring,** in Zichron Ya'akov, is worth checking out. The **Haifa Festival of Children's Theater** appeals to families. Tel Aviv hosts a festival called **Spring in the Eretz Israel Museum.** The **National Parks Authority** in Tel Aviv (☎ 03/576-6834) can update you on the varied performances

and activities (many of them great for kids) scheduled during this period at their sites throughout the country.

Late Apr.–early June➤ An **Independence Day Gala Concert** in Jerusalem marks Israel's birthday; April 30, 1998, is its 50th and is sure to be marked by many special events throughout the country.

The international **Israel Festival** of all the performing arts takes place in Jerusalem (May 29–June 15, 1997; May 23–June 13, 1998). This is the country's premier festival: Get tickets to major events well in advance. Haifa hosts a **Blues Festival.** Bet She'an's Roman Theater is the venue for an eclectic festival, with music from opera to pop. The village of **Abu Ghosh,** west of Jerusalem, hosts a **Vocal Music Festival.** You can indulge yourself at the **International Ethnic Food Fair,** in Jaffa's port.

SUMMER

Late June–early July➤ The **International Folklore Festival,** much of which takes place in small villages, draws performers and artists from Israel and abroad. The **Israeli Folk-Dance Festival,** in Karmiel in early July, has ethnic groups from around the world, as well as community dancing. **Jacob's Ladder Folk Festival** (mostly Anglo-American) takes place at Gan Hashelosha (Sachne) the first weekend in July. The late June **Cherry Festival** of Kibbutz Kiryat Anavim, west of Jerusalem, features musical events in natural surroundings and has a cafeteria devoted to cherry-based delicacies.

Jerusalem hosts **U.S. and Canadian Independence Days** the first week in July. The **Food Trail,** in the Western Galilee, is peripatetic enough to digest between tastings. Film buffs should look for the **International Student Film Festival,** in Tel Aviv in early June. The prestigious **International Film Festival** is held in Jerusalem in early July.

LATE JULY–AUG.➤ The **Voice of Music in the Upper Galilee,** on Kibbutz Kfar Blum, is perhaps the year's highlight for chamber music lovers. The **Klezmer Festival,** in Zfat (Safed), showcases Jewish soul music. The regional **Jewish Music Festival,** in the Upper Galilee, showcases a variety of music. In Jerusalem, check out the **Phenomena Festival of Puppet and Visual Theater.** The **Khutzot Hayotzer Arts and Crafts Fair,** in

Jerusalem, has handmade items, and there's nightly entertainment, too. Jerusalem is the site of the **18th Zimriya,** the triennial World Assembly of Choirs; dates are August 10–20, 1998.

The fine **Red Sea Jazz Festival,** in Eilat, has become a respected date on the international calendar. Israeli pop stars are in the limelight at the **Arad Festival,** in the Negev. **Night of Love,** in Tzemach at the southern end of the Sea of Galilee, brings in national pop stars. **Jaffa Nights** offers music, theater, and entertainment in the square of Old Jaffa. The **Wine Festival,** in Binyamina, has wine tasting and performances by singers and dance groups. The **Sea of Galilee Crossing** is a 4-km (2½-mi) swim from Kibbutz Ha'on to Tzemach.

AUTUMN

OCT.➤ The week of the Jewish holiday of **Sukkoth**

can claim almost as busy a calendar as that of Passover in the spring.

The **Israel Fringe Theater Festival,** in Akko, has original Israeli theater productions, street theater, children's shows, and musicals. Rishon Lezion, south of Tel Aviv, has a festival of **Wine and Song.** On Mt. Carmel, Zichron Ya'akov celebrates with a **Wine and Song** festival. **Music in Tabgha,** on the Sea of Galilee, has vocal and chamber music in the Church of the Loaves and Fishes. Tel Aviv has a **Chamber Music Festival.** Haifa holds its **International Film Festival** in the fall. Yehiam in the Western Galilee is the site of the **Renaissance Festival.**

The **Christian Celebration of the Feast of Tabernacles** takes place in Jerusalem.

NOV.➤ Tel Aviv hosts the **International Guitar Festival.**

An **Olive Festival** of crafts and folklore is held in Nazareth and the rural areas west of it.

2 Jerusalem

Revered by the three great religions of Judaism, Christianity, and Islam, Jerusalem has drawn multitudes of pilgrims and plenipotentiaries to its splendid mountain isolation for thousands of years. Yet the city's domes, spires, and ancient walls share the skyline with hypermodern high-rises, and its archaeological treasures vie for attention with great museums, fun shops, and fine restaurants.

By Mike Rogoff

JERUSALEM MAKES A STRONG CLAIM to be unique, however overworked that word may be. A mountainous walled city with a 5,000-year history of continuous habitation, Jerusalem is holy to more than one-third of the world's population.

For Jews, Jerusalem has always been the focal point of devotion and spiritual yearnings and the psychic center of their nationhood. "The world is like a human eye," wrote a Jewish sage in the 1st century AD: "The white is the ocean that girds the earth, the iris is the earth upon which we dwell, the pupil is Jerusalem, and the image therein is the Temple of the Lord."

For two millennia Christians have also venerated Jerusalem as the place where the most momentous events of their faith took place—the death, burial, and resurrection of Jesus of Nazareth. A famous Renaissance map shows the continents of Asia, Africa, and Europe as the leaves of a clover meeting in the holy city, a reality at once spiritual, historical, and (almost) geographically accurate.

Islamic tradition identifies Jerusalem as the *masjad el aksa*, the "farthermost place" from which Muhammad ascended to Heaven for his portentous meeting with God, making it the third-holiest city to Muslims after Mecca and Medina. A Muslim tradition claims that the great rock of Jerusalem's Mt. Moriah, site of the onetime Jewish Second Temple and present Dome of the Rock, is made of stones from the Garden of Eden and that on the Day of Judgment, "the holy Kaaba stone of Mecca will come to Jerusalem to be joined with it."

The first known mention of Jerusalem is in Egyptian "hate texts" of the 20th century BC, although recent archaeological evidence gives the city a founding date at least 1,000 years earlier. Many scholars identify Jerusalem with the Salem of Abraham's time (18th century BC). Joshua defeated the Amorite king of Jerusalem in the mid-13th century BC, but the Israelites were unable to retain possession of the city. It was only King David, in 1000 BC, who took it again, made it his capital, and thus propelled it onto the center stage of history. His son Solomon built the Temple of the Lord, known as the First Temple, giving the city a preeminence it enjoyed until its destruction by the Babylonians in 586 BC.

Returning exiles at the end of the 6th century BC rebuilt the Temple—to become known as the Second Temple—and began the slow process of revival. By the 2nd century BC, Jerusalem was again a vibrant Jewish capital, albeit one with a good dose of Hellenistic cultural influence. Herod the Great (who reigned 37 BC–4 BC) renovated the Second Temple on a magnificent scale and expanded the city into a cosmopolis of world renown. This was the Jerusalem Jesus knew, a city of monumental architecture, teeming—especially during the Jewish pilgrim festivals—with tens of thousands of visitors from elsewhere in the country and from abroad. It was here that the Romans crucified Jesus (circa AD 29) and here, too, that the Great Jewish Revolt against the Roman overlords erupted, ending in AD 70 with the total destruction (once again) of the city and the Temple.

The Roman emperor Hadrian redesigned Jerusalem as the pagan polis of Aelia Capitolina (AD 135), an urban plan that became the basis for the Old City of today. The Byzantines made it a Christian center, with a massive wave of church building (4th–6th centuries AD), until the Arab conquest of AD 638 brought the holy city under Muslim sway. Except during the golden age of the Ummayad dynasty in the late 7th and early 8th centuries, Jerusalem was no more than a provincial town under the Muslim regimes of the early Middle Ages, until the Crusaders stormed it in 1099 and made it the capital of their Latin Kingdom. With the reconquest of Jerusalem by the Muslims, for seven centuries the city again lapsed into a languid provincialism under the Mamluk and Ottoman empires. The British conquest in 1917 thrust the holy city back into the world limelight, as rising rival nationalisms vied to possess it.

Jerusalem was divided by the 1948 war, with Jordan annexing the smaller, predominantly Arab eastern sector (including the Old City); the much larger Jewish western sector became the capital of the State of Israel. The Six-Day War of 1967 reunited the city under Israeli rule, but the concept of an Arab "East" Jerusalem and a Jewish "West" Jerusalem still remains, even though new Jewish neighborhoods in the northeastern and southeastern sections have made the distinction somewhat oversimplified today.

The focal point of any visit to Jerusalem is the walled Old City, a square kilometer of exotic sights, sounds, and smells, its air as thick with chanting as with charcoal smoke, the *souk* (market) redolent with the tang of tamarind and alive with the tinkle of trinkets. Its 40,000 inhabitants—Jewish, Christian, and Muslim—jostling in the cobblestone lanes all carry an air of ownership, at best merely tolerating the "intruders" from other quarters. Devout Jews in black and white scurry from their neighborhoods north and west of the Old City, through the Damascus Gate and the Muslim Quarter, toward the Western (or Wailing) Wall, a holy relic of the Second Temple enclosure. Arab women with baskets of fresh produce on their heads flow across the Western Wall plaza to the Dung Gate and the village of Silwan beyond it. It is not unusual to stand at the Western Wall, surrounded by the burble of devotions, and hear the piercing call to prayer of the muezzin above you, with the more distant bells of the Christian Quarter providing a counterpoint.

Step outside the Old City, and you will discover a vibrant, modern city of a half-million inhabitants—not as cosmopolitan as Tel Aviv, to be sure, but possessing a variety of good restaurants, concert halls, markets, and high-quality stores, as well as quaint neighborhoods that embody an earlier simplicity.

No matter how oblivious they are to the burden of the city's past or to the various grand designs for its future, contemporary Jerusalemites are not untouched by the subtle spirit that infuses the place. Even the irreverent Mark Twain, who visited Jerusalem in 1867, was moved to write: "The thoughts Jerusalem suggests are full of poetry, sublimity, and, more than all, dignity." He may have been a bit carried away, but watch the limestone buildings glow golden in the sunset, and the mystical hold the city has had on people's minds and hearts for millennia becomes almost tangible.

Pleasures and Pastimes

Antiquities

If you thrill to the thought of standing where the ancients once stood, you will be in your element in this city of stored-up memories. From Old Testament walls and water systems to Second Temple streets and stones, the past calls to the attentive soul like a siren to a sailor. Scale models and outstanding local museums such as the Israel Museum and the Bible Lands Museum help give depth and perspective to the experience of exploring the past.

Arts and Crafts

In general, handicrafts in Israel are interesting, with jewelry and Judaica exceptional standouts in design and workmanship. Jerusalem offers many of these, as well as a few fine artists in other specialties: paper cutting, ceramics, weaving, and harp making.

Dining

Although eating out at restaurants has not been "institutionalized" as much in Jerusalem as in the more cosmopolitan Tel Aviv, you still can eat very well in the holy city, and its timeworn stone and unique ambience have created many magical corners for doing so. Jerusalem favors Middle Eastern cuisine and vegetarian meals Italian style or of the quiche-and-salad variety. Less popular are seafood and the more exotic Far East cuisines, though there are some outstanding exceptions. There is a reason for this trend: The high percentage of religious Jews who live in or visit Jerusalem (in contrast, again, with epicurean Tel Aviv) has resulted in a considerable number of kosher restaurants in the city. Drop your preconceptions: "Kosher" does not mean Grandma's traditional Eastern European delicacies (though you will find these, too). It implies a set of culinary restrictions, rather than a specific cuisine: no pork or shrimp, for example; no mixing of meat and milk products; no cooking on the Sabbath. These requirements account for the popularity of dairy-style restaurants and those cuisines, like Middle Eastern, that don't use dairy products anyway. But the quality of meals need not suffer, attested by some of the city's finest eateries that are kosher (and, incidentally, closed for Friday dinner and Saturday lunch in observance of the Jewish Sabbath). Having said that, several *non*kosher restaurants—not all of them pricey—help to keep the flag of haute cuisine bravely flying.

Holy Places

Central to two faiths and holy to a third, Jerusalem is an almost bewildering collage of religious traditions and the shrines that have sanctified them. Even pilgrims of one faith or another tend to take some time to view the shrines of the others. Sites such as the Western Wall, Calvary, Gethsemane, and the Haram esh-Sharif bring the thrill of recognition to ancient history. The devout cannot fail to be moved by the holy city, and its special, if sometimes dissonant, moods and peoplescapes tend to fascinate the unbeliever as well.

Scenic Views

Jerusalem is a city of hills—hard going for cyclists but marvelous for the photographer and the romantic. Quite different views of the Old City are offered by Mt. Scopus and the Mount of Olives (you're facing west, so it's best to go in the morning) and the Haas Promenade to the south. Mt. Scopus also looks east, to the Judean Desert and the Dead Sea; Mt. Herzl looks west; and Nebi Samwil, in the northwest, gives a commanding view in all directions.

EXPLORING JERUSALEM

Jerusalem is built on a series of hills, part of the Judea-Samaria range, and straddles the "watershed," the mountain divide that runs north–south through much of the country. The eastern edge of the city is marked by the high ridge of Mt. Scopus–Mount of Olives, beyond which the arid Judean Desert tumbles down to the Dead Sea. To the west are the Judean Hills, or the Mountains of Judah, many capped by modern farming villages and draped in the new pine forests that have transformed and softened the rugged landscape. North and south of the city—Samaria and Judea, respectively—is the so-called West Bank, since 1967 a contested area administered by Israel and part of the same highlands, geographically and historically, of which Jerusalem has always been a part.

The city has two centers of gravity: the downtown area of West Jerusalem, with its central triangle of Jaffa Road, King George Street, and Ben Yehuda Street; and the Old City farther east. Most restaurants and a good number of the hotels recommended in this chapter are in or near the downtown area. Almost all the rest are farther west, where the modern Jewish neighborhoods share the hills with the best of the city's museums. The squarish, walled Old City is divided into four major residential quarters—Jewish, Christian, Muslim, and Armenian—and entered through seven gates, of which the Jaffa and Dung gates are those most used by tourists.

Since 1987 the nationalist unrest in the Arab community (one-quarter of the city's population) has made East Jerusalem a less welcoming place than it once was. Visitors should exercise some caution in the Arab neighborhoods north of the Damascus Gate and in the Old City's Muslim Quarter.

When all is said and done, however, Jerusalem is a safe city, as Israeli cities are in general. Jerusalem is a fun city to see on foot, and most outlying sites are fairly accessible by public transportation. For many areas of Jerusalem, exploring with a rental car is sometimes more a bother than a boon, and you can spend the money more productively on cabs.

Of the key areas described, Old City: The Classic Sights takes you from the Western (Wailing) Wall to the Church of the Holy Sepulcher and plunges you in at the deep end, with a heady whirl of ancient ruins and the all-important sites of the three religions that call this city holy. The Jewish Quarter tour explores that attractively restored quadrant of the Old City, with its intriguing potpourri of archaeological sites unearthed in the 1970s. The Tower of David and Mt. Zion begins and ends with a museum, as it skirts (or climbs) the Old City walls en route to David's Tomb and the site of Jesus' Last Supper. Old Testament Jerusalem is the theme of the City of David walking tour, exploring a geographically tiny area below and outside the Dung Gate of the Old City. Mainly Christian landmarks are explored under the title Mount of Olives and East Jerusalem, with highlights including Mount of Olives itself and its spectacular view, the Garden of Gethsemane, and the Garden Tomb. Also covered are the Rockefeller Museum, Damascus Gate, and the option of a walk along the Old City ramparts. Swing across town to West Jerusalem, visiting Yad Vashem, Israel's most prominent Holocaust memorial and museum complex, the famous Chagall stained-glass windows at the Hadassah Hospital, the village of Ein Kerem, and a large-scale model of Second Temple–period Jerusalem. Take time off to walk the Center City and visit the magnificent Israel Museum, where the Dead Sea Scrolls (and much else) are displayed. Also on the itinerary are the nearby Knesset, Israel's parliament, and the newer Bible Lands Museum.

Great Itineraries

Most visitors spend only a few days in Jerusalem; but if you have more time or your interest ranges beyond the classic sights, the following suggestions may happily fill your days.

IF YOU HAVE 1 DAY: A GENERAL ORIENTATION

Catch the morning view from atop the Mount of Olives or anytime of day from the Haas Promenade. Enter the Old City through the Dung Gate to visit the Western Wall, El-Aqsa Mosque, and Dome of the Rock.

Exploring Jerusalem *(Boxes Refer to Detail Maps)*

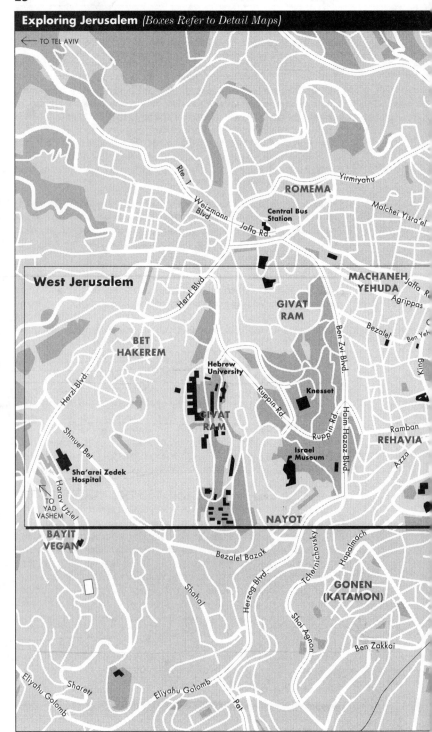

← TO TEL AVIV

ROMEMA

Yirmiyahu

Malchei Yisra'el

Rte. 1

Weizmann Blvd.

Central Bus Station

Jaffa Rd.

MACHANEH YEHUDA

Jaffa Rd

Agrippas

West Jerusalem

Herzl Blvd

GIVAT RAM

Bezalel

Ben Yeh

BET HAKEREM

Hebrew University

Ben Zvi Blvd.

King

Herzl Blvd.

GIVAT RAM

Ruppin Rd.

Knesset

Rupp in Rd.

Haim Hazaz Blvd.

Ramban

REHAVIA

Shmuel Bet

Israel Museum

Azza

Sha'arei Zedek Hospital

Harav Uziel

TO YAD VASHEM

NAYOT

BAYIT VEGAN

Bezalel Bazak

Tchernichovsky

Hapalmach

GONEN (KATAMON)

Shahal

Herzog Blvd.

Shai Agnon

Ben Zakkai

Eliyahu Golomb

Sharett

Eliyahu Golomb

Pat

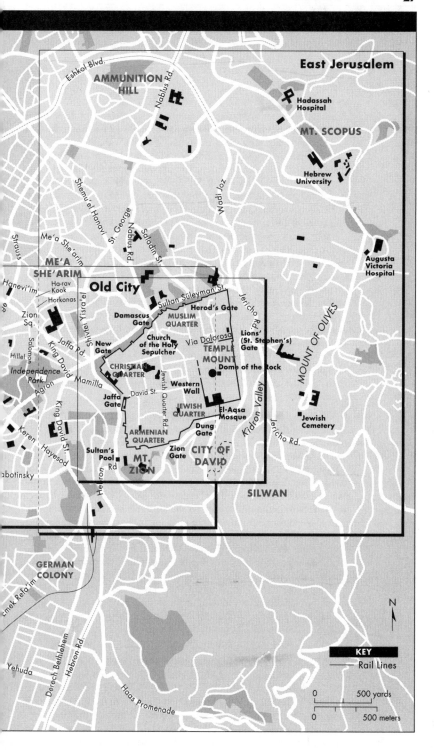

East Jerusalem

AMMUNITION HILL

Eshkol Blvd.

Nablus Rd.

Hadassah Hospital

MT. SCOPUS

Shemu'el Hanavi St.

Wadi Joz

Hebrew University

St. George

Nablus Rd.

Saladin St.

Me'a She'arim

Strauss

Augusta Victoria Hospital

ME'A SHE'ARIM

Shivtei Yisra'el

Old City

MOUNT OF OLIVES

Hanevi'im

Ha-rav Kook

Horkonas

Zion Sq.

Salomon

Jaffa Rd.

Damascus Gate

Sultan Süleyman St.

Herod's Gate

MUSLIM QUARTER

Jericho Rd.

Lions' (St. Stephen's) Gate

Hillel

King David St.

Mamilla

New Gate

Church of the Holy Sepulcher

Via Dolorosa

TEMPLE MOUNT

Dome of the Rock

Independence Park

Agron

CHRISTIAN QUARTER

Jewish Quarter Rd.

David St.

Western Wall

Keren

Hayesod

King David St.

Jaffa Gate

JEWISH QUARTER

El-Aqsa Mosque

Kidron Valley

Jericho Rd.

Jewish Cemetery

abotinsky

Hebron Rd.

ARMENIAN QUARTER

Dung Gate

Sultan's Pool

MT. ZION

Zion Gate

CITY OF DAVID

SILWAN

GERMAN COLONY

Emek Refa'im

N

Yehuda

Derech Bethlehem

Hebron Rd.

Haas Promenade

Return via the Western Wall plaza and ascend to the Jewish Quarter to explore its fascinating archaeological finds. Visit the Church of the Holy Sepulcher en route to the Jaffa Gate. Drive over to West Jerusalem (the New City) to visit the Israel Museum (Dead Sea Scrolls, archaeology, Judaica, and art) or Yad Vashem (a monument and memorial to the Holocaust).

IF YOU HAVE 1 DAY: A CHRISTIAN ORIENTATION

Begin with the view from the Mount of Olives, then walk or drive down to the Garden of Gethsemane with its ancient olive trees. Enter the Old City through the Dung Gate to visit the Western Wall, the holiest Jewish site, and the Muslim shrines, the El-Aqsa Mosque and Dome of the Rock, on the Temple Mount just above it. Join the Via Dolorosa near the serene courtyard of St. Anne's Church and the Pools of Bethesda (site of the healing of the lame man) and follow the Stations of the Cross to the Church of the Holy Sepulcher. If you're Catholic, aim your visit in time to join the Friday afternoon Franciscan walk of the stations. If you're Protestant—and especially, Evangelical—be certain to include the Garden Tomb (check times) in addition to or instead of the Holy Sepulcher. After this, you have four options. Option One: Visit the Room of the Last Supper on Mt. Zion after lunch, and go on to the Church of the Nativity, in Bethlehem (a 15-minute drive; ☞ Bethlehem and the Etzion Bloc *in* Chapter 3). Option Two: Lunch in and explore the archaeological finds of the Jewish Quarter and end at the Room of the Last Supper. Option Three: Lunch near the Jaffa Gate and visit the Tower of David Museum on the history of Jerusalem, also ending the day (time permitting) at the Room of the Last Supper. Option Four: Lunch en route to the Room of the Last Supper, then on to the Israel Museum to see the Dead Sea Scrolls. Check opening times of sites when planning your day.

IF YOU HAVE 2–3 DAYS: A GENERAL ORIENTATION

On the first day, begin with the view from the Mount of Olives. Explore the City of David. Drive around to the Jaffa Gate to visit the Tower of David Museum, covering the history of Jerusalem (try to catch the 11 AM tour). Eat lunch inside Jaffa Gate and follow the Ramparts Walk to Mt. Zion. Explore the Jewish Quarter, ending the day there or at the Western Wall. On the second day, begin at the Israel Museum (note hours). If you're a museum person, spend the morning and have lunch there; if not, spend the remainder of the morning in the downtown area and eat lunch there. After lunch, plunge back into the Old City through the Dung Gate and visit the Western Wall and the Temple Mount (the Muslim shrines: Get up there early because of limited afternoon hours). Stroll the Arab bazaar (the souk) to the Church of the Holy Sepulcher and end at the Jaffa Gate. Begin the third day at Yad Vashem, the Holocaust museum and memorial. Visit the stained-glass Chagall windows at Hadassah Hospital. Have a leisurely lunch in picturesque Ein Kerem and then take in the Church of the Visitation. Take the rest of the afternoon off for a well-earned break at the pool or to do some shopping.

IF YOU HAVE 2–3 DAYS: A CHRISTIAN ORIENTATION

You can afford to relax a bit! On the first day, do the Western Wall, El-Aqsa Mosque, and Dome of the Rock, the Pools of Bethesda and St. Anne's Church, the Ecce Homo Convent (site of the fortress where Jesus was tried), the Via Dolorosa, and the Church of the Holy Sepulcher. In the afternoon, visit Bethlehem (☞ Bethlehem and the Etzion Bloc *in* Chapter 3). On the second day, start with the view from the Mount of Olives (Catholics should add the Pater Noster Convent on the Mount of Olives—with the Lord's Prayer in over 70 languages on ceramic tiles—and Dominus Flevit, halfway down the slope) and walk or drive down to the Garden of Gethsemane. Visit the Room of the Last Supper on Mt. Zion (Catholics should add the Dormition Abbey, where, tradition says, Mary fell into eternal sleep) and enter the Jewish Quarter through Zion Gate. If biblical archaeology speaks to you, consider a walking tour with Archaeological Seminars (☞ Contacts and Resources *in* Jerusalem A to Z, *below*). In the afternoon, visit the Israel Museum or Yad Vashem. Spend the third day on the west side of town (the New City), picking up whichever of the two museums you didn't manage the day before. Visit the biblically inspired Chagall windows at Hadassah Hospital, Ein Kerem; and the Holyland Hotel's scale model of Jerusalem in the days of Jesus, built to a fiftieth of the city's actual size then. Protestants should use this day to visit the Garden Tomb in East Jerusalem. Catholics will want to visit the Church of St. John the Baptist and the Church of the Visitation, in Ein Kerem on the western edge of town.

Numbers in the text correspond to numbers in the margin and on the Exploring the Old City, Exploring East Jerusalem, and Exploring West Jerusalem maps.

Old City: The Classic Sights

Drink in the very essence of Jerusalem as you explore the city's primary religious sites and touch the different cultures that share it. All the holy places described demand modest dress: no shorts and no sleeveless shirts.

A Good Walk

You can begin at the Dung Gate, literally "Refuse Gate" in Hebrew, apparently because of the ancient practice of dumping garbage over the adjacent city walls. Just inside the gate is the **Ophel Archaeological Garden** ①, often known as the Western and Southern Wall Excavations. The most impressive and evocative remains here are those of King Herod the Great's grand structures, ones that Jesus knew well.

It's a few steps to the entrance of the **Western (Wailing) Wall** ② plaza. You can expect a routine check of your bags by security personnel at the entrance to the plaza. This is the most important Jewish shrine today, not because the structure itself is historically sacred, but because of its proximity to the onetime Jewish Temple and that it's the last remnant of the enclosure around that Temple.

Between the Western Wall and the Ophel Archaeological Garden, a ramp ascends to the vast plaza covering the summit of the biblical Mt. Moriah, called the **Temple Mount** by Jews and Christians and Haram esh-Sharif (the Noble Enclosure) by Muslims. The ancient Jewish Temple once stood here, both the "First" of King Solomon, and the "Second." Today the Temple Mount is administered by a Muslim council. Tall cypress trees create shady retreats from the glare of the whitish limestone pavements. Immediately in front of you as you enter the area is the large, black-domed **El-Aqsa Mosque** ③, the third-holiest mosque in the Muslim world. Two hundred yards to the left is the brilliantly golden **Dome of the Rock** ④, the don't-miss site of the area.

As you exit the Temple Mount at its northeastern corner through the al-Asbat Gate, the Lions' (also known as St. Stephen's) Gate is on your right. Stay within the city walls and turn left. Twenty yards on, an unobtrusive dark wooden door on your right opens onto the tranquil courtyard-garden of the **Pools of Bethesda and St. Anne's Church** ⑤. The Pools of Bethesda are the authentic site of the healing described in the New Testament (John 5), and the Romanesque St. Anne's Church offers amazing acoustics.

Exploring the Old City

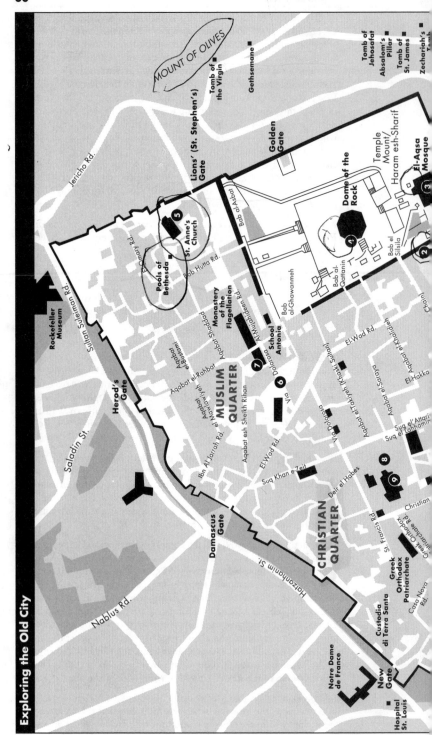

MOUNT OF OLIVES

Tomb of the Virgin

Gethsemane

Tomb of Jehosafat
Absalom's Pillar
Tomb of St. James
Zechariah's Tomb

Lions' (St. Stephen's) Gate

Golden Gate

Temple Mount/ Haram esh-Sharif

El-Aqsa Mosque

Dome of the Rock

Bab al-Asbat

Jericho Rd.

Rockefeller Museum

Sultan Suleiman Rd.

St. Anne's Church

Pools of Bethesda

Dhraar Rd.

Bab Hutta Rd.

Bab al-Qattanin

Bab al-Silsila

Bab al-Ghawanmeh

Chain

Monastery of the Flagellation

Aqabat Shaddad

Aqabat el Bustami

School Antonia

Al Mujahideen Rd.

Dolorosa

Via

El-Wad Rd.

MUSLIM QUARTER

Aqabat el-Rahbat

Herod's Gate

Aqabat el Mawlawiyeh

Aqabat esh Sheikh Rihan

Via Dolorosa

Suq el Takiyeh (Khaki Suhan)

El-Hakka

Aqabat el Satara

El-Hakka

Suq el'Attari
Suq el Lahhamin

Saladin St.

Ibn Al Jarrah Rd.

El-Wad Rd.

Suq Khan e-Zeit

Deir el Habes

Christian

CHRISTIAN QUARTER

Damascus Gate

Holtzenham St.

St. Francis Rd.

Greek Orthodox Patriarchate

Greek Orthodox Patriarchate

Casa Nova Rd.

Christian

Custodia di Terra Santa

Nablus Rd.

New Gate

Notre Dame de France

Hospital St. Louis

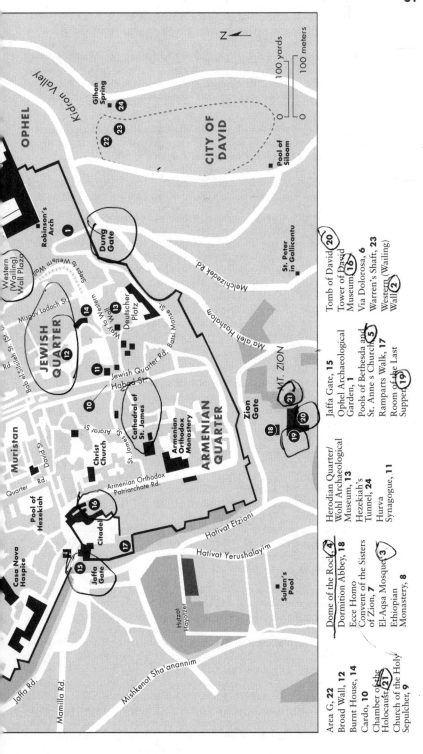

OPHEL

Kidron Valley

Gihon Spring

24

23

22

CITY OF DAVID

Pool of Siloam

Robinson's Arch

1

Dung Gate

Western (Wailing) Wall Plaza

Steps to Western Wall

St. Peter in Gallicantu

Melchizedek Rd.

Mispov Ladach St.

Rd. el-Silsilah St. [St. ...

Western Wall

JEWISH QUARTER

12

14

Deutscher Platz

13

Ma'aleh Hashalom

Bab. el-Silsilah St.

Batsi. Mansf...

Jewish Quarter Rd.

11

Habad St.

10

MT. ZION

Muristan

Pool of Hezekiah

Quarter

David St.

David St.

Ararat St.

Christ Church

St. James St.

Cathedral of St. James

Armenian Orthodox Monastery

Zion Gate

18

21

20

ARMENIAN QUARTER

19

Armenian Orthodox Patriarchate Rd.

Citadel

16

Hativat Elzioni

Casa Nova Hospice

5

15

Jaffa Gate

17

Hativat Yerushalayim

Sultan's Pool

Jaffa Rd.

Mamilla Rd.

Hutzot Hayotzer

Mishkenot Sha'anannim

Area G, 22
Broad Wall, 12
Burnt House, 14
Cardo, 10
Chamber of the Holocaust, 21
Church of the Holy Sepulcher, 9

Dome of the Rock, 4
Dormition Abbey, 18
Ecce Homo Convent of the Sisters of Zion, 7
El-Aqsa Mosque, 3
Ethiopian Monastery, 8

Herodian Quarter/ Wohl Archaeological Museum, 13
Hezekiah's Tunnel, 24
Hurva Synagogue, 11

Jaffa Gate, 15
Ophel Archaeological Garden, 1
Pools of Bethesda and St. Anne's Church, 5
Ramparts Walk, 17
Room of the Last Supper, 19

Tomb of David, 20
Tower of David Museum, 16
Via Dolorosa, 6
Warren's Shaft, 23
Western (Wailing) Wall, 2

N

0 100 yards
0 100 meters

Return to the street and turn right (your back will be to Lions' Gate). About 300 yards up the road, look for a ramp on your left leading to the turquoise-color door of a school. On Friday afternoon at 3, the brown-robed Franciscans begin their procession of the **Via Dolorosa** ⑥ in the school courtyard beyond the door. Chapels along the way are open at that time. (In summer, the procession starts at 4; ask at the Christian Information Center; ☞ Visitor Information *in* Jerusalem A to Z, *below*.)

Just beyond the start of the Via Dolorosa, an arch crosses the street. On the street corner on the right before the arch is the entrance to the **Ecce Homo Convent of the Sisters of Zion** ⑦, with a basement of ancient pavements and cisterns. Just beyond the arch, steps on your right bring you into a small vestibule, separated from the convent's chapel by a glass panel, and with a view of the so-called Ecce Homo Arch.

The Via Dolorosa runs down into El-Wad Road, one of the Old City's important thoroughfares. To the right, the street climbs toward the Damascus Gate; to the left, it passes through the heart of the Muslim Quarter and reaches the Western Wall. It's a sensorial experience to sit at a café sipping cardamom-flavored Turkish coffee and watch the passing parade. Buxom Arab matrons in bright embroidered dresses rub shoulders with black-hatted Hasidic Jews in beards and side curls. Local Muslim kids in the universal uniform of T-shirt, jeans, and sneakers dodge around groups of pious Christian pilgrims almost oblivious to the cacophonous scene.

As you turn left onto El-Wad Road, Station III of the Stations of the Cross is immediately on your left. A few steps beyond it, also on the left, is Station IV, and on the next corner, Station V. The Via Dolorosa turns right and begins its ascent toward Calvary. Halfway up the street, a brown wooden door on your left marks Station VI. At the top of the stepped street is a brown metal door: Station VII. The little chapel contains one of the columns of the Byzantine Cardo, the main street of 6th-century Jerusalem, which ran from the Damascus Gate (off to your right) to today's Jewish Quarter, some 300 yards to your left. Step to the left, then walk 30 yards up the street facing you. You are now at Station VIII, marked by nothing more than an inscribed stone. Return to the main street (Suq Khan e-Zeit) and turn right (left as you reach Station VII from VI). The street is almost impossibly crowded on Saturday, when Arab Jerusalem does its shopping—beware of pickpockets in these quarters! One hundred yards from Station VII, a ramp parallel to the street ascends to your right. Take the ramp and the small lane above it to its end. A column in the Wall represents Station IX.

Step through the open door on your left into the courtyard of the **Ethiopian Monastery** ⑧, also known as Deir es-Sultan, an esoteric enclave of this poor but colorful sect. From the monastery's upper chapel, descend through a lower one and out a small wooden door to the court of the **Church of the Holy Sepulcher** ⑨ (☞ Site map, *below*). Had you continued along Suq Khan e-Zeit without the ascent to the Ethiopian Monastery, a right turn would have brought you more quickly to the Holy Sepulcher. Most Christians venerate this site as that of the death, burial, and resurrection of Jesus; you will find Stations X, XI, XII, XIII, and XIV here (many Protestants believe these events occurred at Skull Hill and the Garden Tomb, north of the Damascus Gate; ☞ Mount of Olives and East Jerusalem, *below*). The present vast structure is 12th-century Crusader, with a plethora of interior structures and decorations added down to this day. Rather bizarrely, the property is shared by four different denominations, which lends the church much of its color.

To get to the Jaffa Gate from the courtyard of the church, ascend to the right as you leave the church, turn left at the main street—Christian Quarter Road—go as far as David Street, and make a right again. You can reach the Jewish Quarter (☞ *below*) by going left from the courtyard, taking an immediate right past the high white-stone Lutheran Church of the Redeemer and continuing as far as David Street, then turning left and taking any of the next three lanes to the right.

TIMING

You need 3–3½ hours for this walk, more if you like to linger. The Via Dolorosa takes no more than 20 minutes, but the full pilgrim procession takes an hour. Add 30–45 minutes to visit the Ophel Archaeological Garden; you can easily pass up this site if pressed for time or have no interest in ancient artifacts. Several sites close for a few hours over lunch. Afternoons are less crowded, but pay attention to the short opening hours of the Temple Mount (Haram esh-Sharif). Some Christian sites are closed on Sunday, the entire Temple Mount is closed on Friday, and photography is forbidden at the Western (Wailing) Wall on Saturday.

Sights to See

★ ❾ **Church of the Holy Sepulcher.** Most Christians believe this is the site where Jesus was crucified by the Romans, buried, and rose from the dead. Belief in the transcendent significance of those events, both personal and universal, is what characterizes the community of believers called Christianity. The first church was built here circa AD 326 by Helena, mother of the Byzantine emperor Constantine the Great, and destroyed by Persian invaders in 614. It was rebuilt almost immediately, destroyed again by the Egyptian caliph El-Hakim in 1009, and once more restored, on a reduced scale, apparently as a cluster of shrines not under one roof. In the 12th century the Crusaders unified the shrines into the present vast structure (which is only two-thirds the length of its Byzantine predecessor). The very antiquity of the tradition argues in favor of its authenticity, many claim; the early Christian community, fiercely committed to the point of martyrdom, would likely have preserved the memory of the site where events on which their entire faith hinged had taken place. The church is outside the city walls of Jesus' day—an important point, for no executions or burials took place within Jerusalem's sacred precincts.

Note the fine stone carving above the Gothic entrance (☞ Site plan, *below*). As you enter the church's dim interior, steep steps to the right take you up to **Golgotha** (the word comes from Aramaic, through Greek), or Calvary (through Latin), meaning "the place of the skull" (Mark 15). The chapel on the right is Roman Catholic and contains **Station X** (where Jesus was stripped of his garments) and **Station XI** (at the front—note the mosaic—where Jesus was nailed to the cross). On the right wall is a mosaic depicting the Old Testament story of Abraham's binding of Isaac—the sacrifice of the son by the father, seen as a symbolic parallel to the death of Jesus himself.

The central chapel—all candlelight, oil lamps, and icons—is Greek Orthodox. Under the altar, and capping the rocky hillock on which you stand, is a bronze disc with a hole, purportedly the place where the cross actually stood and thus **Station XII**, where Jesus died on the cross. The Franciscans indicate the spot between XI and XII, at the icon of Mary, as **Station XIII**, where Jesus' body was taken down. At ground level opposite the entrance is a rectangular, pink stone slab called the

34

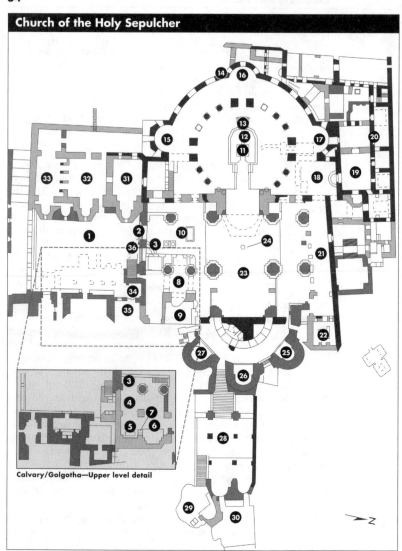

Church of the Holy Sepulcher

Calvary/Golgotha—Upper level detail

Entrance courtyard, **1**
Twelfth-century facade and entrance to church, **2**
Calvary/Golgotha steps, **3**
Station X, **4**
Station XI, **5**
Station XII, **6**
Station XIII, **7**
Chapel of Adam, **8**
Rock of Golgotha, **9**
Stone of Unction, **10**
Chapel of the Angel, **11**

Tomb of Christ (Station XIV), **12**
Coptic Chapel, **13**
Tomb of Joseph of Aramathea, **14**
Southern apse, 4th-century church, **15**
Western apse, 4th-century church, **16**
Northern apse, 4th-century church, **17**
Altar of Mary Magdalene, **18**
Chapel of the Apparition, **19**
Franciscan Convent, **20**

Arches of the Virgin, **21**
Prison of Christ, **22**
Crusader church, **23**
"Center of the World," **24**
Chapel of St. Longinus, **25**
Chapel of the Division of the Raiment, **26**
Chapel of the Mocking, **27**
Chapel of St. Helena, **28**
Chapel of the Holy Cross, **29**

Byzantine wall etching of ship, **30**
Chapel of 40 Martyrs, **31**
Chapel of St. John, **32**
Chapel of St. James, **33**
Chapel of the Franks, **34**
Chapel of St. Michael and exit from Ethiopian Monastery, **35**
Tomb of Philip d'Aubigny, **36**

Stone of Unction, where, it is said, the body of Jesus was cleansed and prepared for burial. Greek pilgrims can often be seen rubbing crosses and clothing on the stone in order to take home scrapings of the sanctity of the site. The tomb itself (**Station XIV**) is in the cavernous, dimly lit rotunda to the left of the entrance, encased in a small, pink marble edifice.

Some 50 feet above you is the great dome that is the landmark of the Christian Quarter. With scaffolding for its repair still in place—the work ground to a halt in the 1980s and has only recently been renewed—the dome became a symbol (and victim) of the denominational rivalry that has beset Holy Land sites in general, and the Holy Sepulcher in particular, for centuries. (Critical structural repairs did take place in the 1970s, however, and the huge, pink stone pillars surrounding the rotunda are the result.) An agreement in 1995 among the Greeks, "Latins" (Roman Catholics), and Armenians on the great dome's interior decoration was hailed as an almost-miraculous breakthrough in ecumenical relations. The Status Quo Agreements, a list of possessions and privileges frozen in the 19th century, are in effect in the church. In the late afternoon, for example, each of the church's four "shareholders"—Greek Orthodox, Latins, Armenians, and Copts (Egyptians)—exercises its right in turn to a procession from Calvary to the tomb, with full-frocked chanting clergy and with censers streaming pungent smoke.

Enter the tomb between the sentinels of giant brass candleholders. The only hint of what it must have been like two millennia ago is the ledge in the inner chamber (now covered with marble) on which the body would have been laid. This detail is reminiscent of hundreds of Jewish tombs found in Jerusalem and elsewhere from the Second Temple period (the time of Jesus).

On the Greek Orthodox Easter, the Holy Fire ceremony takes place here. The church is typically packed with candle-carrying pilgrims tense with excitement. The patriarch enters the tomb, there is a flash of fire seen through its portholes, a messenger emerges with a flaming torch, and within moments the whole church is ablaze with thousands of candles.

Among the church's many chapels, the most interesting is the **Chapel of St. Helena.** From the corridor at the eastern end of the church, steps lead down to a crypt adorned with a fine Armenian mosaic floor and an ancient wall "etching," probably Byzantine, of a ship. Tradition has it that here Helena found the True Cross of Christ circa AD 326. ⊠ *Between Suq Khan e-Zeit and Christian Quarter Rd.,* ☎ *02/627–3314.* 🎫 *Free.* ☉ *Apr.–Sept., daily 5 AM–8 PM; Oct.–Mar., daily 5 AM–7 PM.*

★ ❹ **Dome of the Rock.** The splendid octagonal building is the original one completed in AD 691 over the great rock—the summit of Mt. Moriah—from which the Prophet Muhammad is said to have risen to heaven where he received from God the teachings of the faith. Considering the original builders were immediate heirs of Byzantine artistic traditions, it is hardly surprising that the plan of the shrine resembles that of its contemporaries, like the Byzantine Church of San Vitale in Ravenna, Italy. The exterior glazed ceramic tiles in shades of blue are the result of renovations in the 1950s and '60s, but the marvelous gold dome is a more recent restoration, 80 kilograms (176 pounds) of 24-carat gold electroplated on copper.

The shrine's interior is wondrous. Granite columns support arches, some bearing the original green-and-gold mosaics set in arabesque motifs: In observance of Islamic religious tradition, no human or animal forms appear in the artwork. Although the dome's mosaics were restored in 1027, it is believed the original designs were retained. Some of the Arabic inscriptions in the mosaics are quotations from the Koran; others are dedications. One of the latter originally lauded Abd el-Malik, caliph of the Damascus-based Ummayad dynasty, who built the shrine. Some 140 years later, the caliph of a rival dynasty removed el-Malik's name and replaced it with his own, neglecting, however, to change the date! Notice the outstanding marble slabs that adorn the walls. Without benefit of power tools, medieval stonemasons were able to expose the natural grain of the marble, creating impressive symmetries.

The huge **rock** around which the shrine is built is considered by more than one faith to be the center of the world. Jewish tradition identifies it as the place where Abraham bound and almost sacrificed his son Isaac (Genesis 22). With King David's conquest of Jerusalem in 1000 BC, however, the rock became part of (relatively) indisputable history. Against the warning of his counselors, who said it was arrogant to count the people of Israel (who were supposedly like "the sands of the sea and the stars of the sky"), the triumphant king undertook a national census, thus inviting divine retribution in the form of a plague (II Samuel 24). At the last minute, God stayed the hand of the Angel of Death, who was about to smite Jerusalem. It was on the rock—"the threshing floor of Araunah [or Ornan] the Jebusite"—that David saw the angel, and it was there he erected an altar and burned a repentance offering to the Lord. In the absence of other suitable candidates, modern scholars identify the rock with that threshing floor.

One generation later, David's son Solomon built his temple here. Did the rock become the innermost chamber, the Holy of Holies, of the Temple (meaning the sanctuary is where the Dome of the Rock stands today)? Or did it become the altar in the Court of the Israelites (with the sanctuary a bit to the west)? To this day, Judaism continues to grapple with this question.

At the southwestern corner of the rock, a 10-foot-high ornamented canister is said to contain several hairs of the prophet Muhammad's beard. The reliquary is opened for the Muslim faithful on one day a year during the holy month of Ramadan. A small opening in the marble facade below it allows you to put your hand in and feel the indentation in the rock; the faithful believe it's from the Prophet's foot as he ascended to heaven. A few steps to the right bring you to a marble staircase leading down to a small grotto, perhaps once a water cistern or a grain store in the pre-Davidic days. Legend calls it the Well of Souls, the entrance to the netherworld and the place where the dead pray. An Islamic tradition relates that as Muhammad rose to heaven, the rock tried to follow him and had already left a void (the cave) when the archangel Gabriel intervened to hold it down. *For times and entrance fees, see Temple Mount, below.*

❼ Ecce Homo Convent of the Sisters of Zion. The arch that crosses the Via Dolorosa outside the convent and continues into the present-day Ecce Homo Church was once thought to have been the gate of Herod's Antonia Fortress and thus the spot where the Roman governor Pontius Pilate presented Jesus to the crowd with the words *ecce homo,* "Behold, the man!" Recent scholarship, however, has established that the structure was a triumphal arch built by the Roman emperor Hadrian in the 2nd century AD.

The basement of the convent has two points of interest. The first is an impressive arched reservoir with a barrel-vault roof, apparently built by Hadrian in the moat of Herod's older Antonia Fortress and still filled with clear water. The second is the famous *lithostratos,* or stone pavement, etched with games played by bored Roman legionnaires. One such diversion—the notorious Game of the King—called for the execution of a mock king, a sequence tantalizingly reminiscent of the New Testament description of the treatment of Jesus by the Roman soldiers. Contrary to tradition, however, the pavement of large, foot-worn brown flagstones is not from Jesus' day but was laid down a century later. ⊠ *Via Dolorosa,* ☎ *02/627–7292.* ✉ *NIS 3 ($1).* ☉ *Mon.–Sat. 8:30–12:30 and 2–5.*

❸ **El-Aqsa Mosque.** The name of the mosque—"the Farthermost Place"— comes from the story in the Koran that it was from the nearby rock (☞ Temple Mount, *below*) that Muhammad ascended to heaven to meet with God. At the far (southern) end of this cavernous building, under the landmark copper dome, is the *mihrab,* the niche indicating the direction of prayer toward Mecca. This wall is believed to be the only remnant of the original building created by the Ummayad dynasty in the early 8th century AD. Since then the mosque has been destroyed, usually by earthquake, and rebuilt several times. The rows of square stone columns on the right (west) as you enter date from the 14th century; the round marble ones in the center and on the left are the products of renovations in the 1920s and '30s. Persian rugs are interspersed with modern runners, on which individual prayer mats have been patterned. Undoubtedly the mosque's finest feature is the wonderfully complex set of stained-glass windows under the dome.

In the 12th century, the Templars, one of the Crusader monastic orders, made its headquarters here, taking its name from the ancient site. The place has been the setting for more recent dramas, too. In 1951, King Abdullah of Jordan (the present king Hussein's grandfather) was assassinated in the mosque; and in 1969, a demented arsonist set fire to a priceless wooden *minbar,* or pulpit, in an attempt to destroy the building. West of the mosque is the **Islamic Museum,** displaying some fine stone relief work and carved wood from El-Aqsa's earlier incarnations. *For times and entrance fees,* see *Temple Mount,* below.

❽ **Ethiopian Monastery.** Standing in the monastery's courtyard beneath the medieval bulge of the Church of the Holy Sepulcher, you are literally surrounded by those churches of Christendom that revere the site. An Egyptian Coptic monastery lies close by, next to the ninth of the Stations of the Cross; and around you the skyline is broken by a Russian Orthodox gable, a Lutheran bell tower, and the crosses of Greek Orthodox, Armenian, and Roman Catholic churches.

The robed Ethiopian monks, tall and slender, gentle and shy, live in tiny cells in the rooftop monastery. Their small, dark church is adorned with modern paintings, one of which depicts the visit of the Queen of Sheba to King Solomon. Ethiopian tradition holds that more passed between the two than is related in the Bible (I Kings 10) and that their supposed union produced an heir to the Ethiopian royal house. The unfamiliar script in the paintings is Gehz, the ecclesiastical language of the Ethiopian church. ⊠ *Roof of the Church of the Holy Sepulcher, access from Suq Khan e-Zeit.* ✉ *Free.* ☉ *Daily, daylight hrs.*

❶ **Ophel Archaeological Garden.** Often known as the Western and Southern Wall Excavations, this extensive dig in the 1970s under the direction of archaeologist Benjamin Mazar unearthed very little of Old Testament Jerusalem, but a great deal of the Herodian, Byzantine, and Arab periods. Have a look at an artist's reconstruction of the area on display at the entrance (you can buy your own copy from the attendant) and walk down to the corner of the massive wall facing you. King

Solomon's First Temple on Mt. Moriah was destroyed by the Babylonians in 586 BC. Fifty years later, Jews returning from the Babylonian Exile began building the Second Temple on the same site (where the golden Dome of the Rock now stands). In the 1st century BC, when King Herod the Great rebuilt the Second Temple, he expanded the enclosure around it by constructing a massive retaining wall on the slopes of Mt. Moriah and filling the inside with thousands of tons of rubble, thus producing the huge plaza still known today as the Temple Mount. The great stones near the corner—their well-cut borders characteristic of the Herodian period—are not held together with mortar; their sheer weight gives the structure its stability.

To the right of the corner, in an excavation trench, is the pavement of a Second Temple–period street. Two thousand years ago, the retaining wall would have been more than 50% higher above the street than today, and its foundations, plumbed by British army engineer Charles Warren in 1867, are as deep below you as the present height of the wall is above you. Left of the corner and way above your head is the protrusion known as **Robinson's Arch** (named for the 19th-century American explorer Edward Robinson), which is the beginning of a bridge to the Temple Mount, once reached by a staircase from the commercial area where you now stand.

On the Wall a few yards north of the arch is an upbeat piece of biblical graffiti in Hebrew, written possibly in the 4th century AD by a Jewish pilgrim and filled with messianic dreams: "You shall see, and your heart shall rejoice, and your bones shall flourish like the grass" (Isaiah 66).

Return to the fork in the path and turn left. Fifty yards farther, a small, modern spiral staircase on your left descends below present ground level to an intriguing, partially reconstructed labyrinth of Byzantine dwellings, mosaics and all. You reemerge outside the present city walls. Or go straight, passing through the city wall by a small arched gate. The wide staircase to your left, a good part of it original, once brought hordes of pilgrims through the now-blocked gates of the southern wall of the Temple Mount and into the sacred temple precincts. A prominent archaeologist, interviewed on live TV on these steps, committed himself to this statement: "Ladies and gentlemen, this is the one place in the city I can guarantee you Jesus walked!" The rock-hewn *mikvaot* (plural of *mikveh*), Jewish ritual baths, at the bottom of the steps, are a visual reminder of the purification rites once demanded of Jews before entering the Temple Mount. ⊠ *Dung Gate,* ☎ *02/625–4403.* ▨ *NIS 8 ($2.70); combined ticket including Ramparts Walk and Damascus Gate NIS 20 ($6.70).* ⊙ *Sun.–Thurs. 9–4, Fri. and holiday eves 9–2.*

❺ **Pools of Bethesda and St. Anne's Church.** The transition is sudden and complete from the raucous cobbled streets and persistent vendors to the drooping pepper trees, flower patches, and birdsong of this serene Catholic cloister. The Romanesque Crusader **St. Anne's Church,** built in 1140, was restored in the 19th century, and with its austere and unadorned stone interior, it is one of the finest examples of medieval architecture in the country. According to local tradition, Anne, the mother of the Virgin Mary, was born in the grotto below the site of the church. It is worth waiting for one of the frequent pilgrim groups, who invariably test the church's extraordinarily reverberant acoustics with some hymn singing.

On the facade of the church, above the main door, is an unexpected five-line inscription in Arabic. After Saladin's defeat of the Crusaders in 1187, the church was turned into a *madrasa,* a Muslim house of study, and despite the Christian restoration, the inscription—a dedication to Saladin—has survived.

In the same compound, and just a few steps from the church, are the excavated **Pools of Bethesda,** a large, double public reservoir in use in the 1st century BC and the 1st century AD. The New Testament (John 5) speaks of Jesus miraculously curing a lame man by "a pool, which is called in the Hebrew tongue Bethesda (the Place of Mercy)." The actual bathing pools used by the citizens were the small ones, east of the reservoir, but it was over the big pools that both the Byzantines and the Crusaders built churches, now ruined, to commemorate the miracle. ⊠ Al-Miyahideen Rd., ☎ 02/628–3285. ▧ NIS 3 ($1). ⊗ Mon.–Sat. 8–11:45 and 2–5 (until 6 during daylight saving time).

NEED A BREAK? A little **café,** about 100 yards up the road as you turn right after leaving St. Anne's Church, serves freshly squeezed orange juice, Turkish coffee, and mint tea. It's on the corner of a lane on your left. There are public toilets across the road.

Temple Mount. Some 35 acres in area, the Temple Mount is regarded by some scholars as one of the greatest religious enclosures of the entire ancient world. King Herod the Great (1st century BC) had an immense stone wall built surrounding the hill to retain the rubble used to level off the crest and create the massive plaza. At its center stood Herod's rebuilt Second Temple, a splendid edifice that gained international fame as one of the architectural wonders of its day. That was the Temple Jesus knew. The Romans reduced it to ashes in the summer of AD 70. The Temple Mount today is a Muslim preserve (modest dress is essential), administered by the Waqf, the Supreme Muslim Religious Council.

When the Arab caliph Omar Ibn-Khatib conquered Jerusalem from the Byzantines in AD 638, he found the Temple Mount covered with rubbish and had to clear the site to expose the great rock at its summit. It is related that Omar asked his aide Ka'ab al'Akhbar, a Jew who had converted to Islam, where he should build his mosque. Ka'ab recommended a spot north of the rock, hoping, the tale suggests, that the Muslims, praying south toward Mecca, would thus include the old Temple site in their obeisance. "You dog, Ka'ab," bellowed the caliph. "In your heart you are still a Jew!" Omar's mosque, which he built south of the rock, has not survived, but the splendid gold-dome shrine, completed in AD 691, still stands.

Jerusalem is not mentioned in the Koran, the Muslim holy book, but Muhammad's Night Ride is. Awakened one night by the archangel Gabriel, Muhammad was taken on the fabulous winged horse el-Burak to the *masjad el-aqsa,* the "farthermost place"—hence, the El-Aqsa Mosque (☞ *above*). There he rose to heaven, came face to face with God himself, received the teachings of Islam, and returned home the same night. The tradition evolved that the masjad el-aqsa was none other than Jerusalem, and the great rock the spot from which the Prophet ascended.

The triumphant Arabs of the generation after Muhammad clearly venerated Jerusalem as the city of biblical kings and prophets. Many modern scholars also believe, however, that the feeling of being Johnnys-come-lately in the holy city of rival faiths did not sit well with the new masters of Jerusalem. The masjad el-aqsa tradition and the magnificent Dome of the Rock were designed to proclaim the ascendancy of the "true faith" and the new Arab empire over the rival Byzantine Christians.

The splendid **Dome of the Rock** (☞ *above*) dominates the center of the plaza and, in fact, the entire old cityscape, despite its relatively low elevation.

To the west of the Dome of the Rock is a large *sabil,* a public drinking fountain (now defunct), with an elaborate ornamented stone dome built by the Egypt-based Mamluk rulers in the 14th or 15th century. A large number of the nearby buildings lining the western edge of the Temple Mount are from this period, distinguished by their impressive jigsaws of fitted red, white, and black stone.

Overlooking the plaza at its northwestern corner is a long building, today an elementary school, built on the artificial scarp that once protected Herod's Antonia fortress. The Christian tradition, probably true, identifies the site as the *praetorium* where Jesus was tried.

In the eastern outer wall, facing the Mount of Olives, is the ornate, domed inner **Golden Gate,** or Gate of Mercy, now blocked. The present masonry is Byzantine, though the gate—the Eastern Gate of Christian tradition through which Jesus is believed to have entered the area on Palm Sunday—existed in the Second Temple period. In the Jewish tradition, the long-awaited Messiah will one day enter the city through the same gate. ☎ *02/628–3292 or 02/628–3313. ▢ Combined ticket for El-Aqsa Mosque, Dome of the Rock, and Islamic Museum: NIS 22 ($7.40). Buy tickets to the right of El-Aqsa. Guards will require you to leave shoes, bags, and cameras outside (at your own risk, though theft is rare here); a small purse is usually allowed, but be sure your outfit has pockets just in case. ☉ Sat.–Thurs. 8–11:30 and 12:30– 3. Seasonal changes are made without notice to accommodate changing prayer times; approximate summer hrs are 8–12:30 and 1:30–3. Last entry to area is 30 min before closing.*

❻ Via Dolorosa. The Way of the Cross, as it's more commonly called in English, is the route walked by Jesus carrying his cross from the place of his condemnation by Pontius Pilate to the site of his crucifixion and burial. The present tradition is essentially 12th-century Crusader, but draws as well on older Byzantine beliefs. Some of the incidents represented by the 14 Stations of the Cross are scriptural; some (III, IV, VI, VII, and IX) are not. Many of the stations on the route, which winds through the Muslim and Christian quarters, are marked by tiny chapels opened only during the Franciscan ceremonies. The last five stations are contained within the Church of the Holy Sepulcher. (For walking directions and information, *see* A Good Walk *and* Church of the Holy Sepulcher, *above.*)

Station I. Jesus is tried and condemned by Pontius Pilate.
Station II. Jesus is scourged and given the cross. This station is at the Monastery of the Flagellation; its shaded cloister and cool greenery offer some relief from the noisy street. The Roman pavement within the two chapels dates from the century after Christ. It's open April to September, Monday–Saturday 8–noon and 2–6; October to March, Monday–Saturday 8–noon and 1–5.
Station III. Jesus falls for the first time. (The chapel was built after World War II by soldiers of the Free Polish Forces.)
Station IV. Mary embraces Jesus.
Station V. Simon of Cyrene picks up the cross.
Station VI. A woman wipes the face of Jesus, whose image remains on the cloth. (Her name has come down to us as Veronica, apparently derived from the words *vera* and *icone,* meaning true image.)

Station VII. Jesus falls for the second time. (The little chapel contains one of the columns of the Byzantine Cardo, the main street of 6th-century Jerusalem.)

Station VIII. Jesus addresses the women in the crowd.

Station IX. Jesus falls for the third time.

Station X. Jesus is stripped of his garments.

Station XI. Jesus is nailed to the cross.

Station XII. Jesus dies on the cross.

Station XIII. Jesus is taken down from the cross.

Station XIV. Jesus is buried.

★ ❷ **Western (Wailing) Wall.** The Wall (*Kotel* in Hebrew), the most important *existing* Jewish shrine, was not itself part of the ancient Second Temple, but of King Herod's retaining wall surrounding the Temple Mount (☞ *above*). After the Roman destruction of Jerusalem in AD 70, and especially after the dedication of its pagan successor in 135, the city was off-limits to Jews for generations. Although the general location of the Temple was known (the vicinity of today's Dome of the Rock; ☞ *above*), its precise location was lost. Even when access eventually became possible, Jews avoided ascending the Temple Mount for fear of unwittingly trespassing on the most sacred—and thus forbidden—areas of their ancient sanctuary. With time, the closest remnant of the period took on the aura of the Temple itself. The Western Wall is thus really a holy place "by proxy," and in a sense, it is *through* the stones rather than *to* them that devout Jews pray. It is the tears of generations of such worshipers, grieving for the lost temple, to which its gentile name—the Wailing Wall—refers.

The Western Wall functions under the authority of the rabbinic authorities, with all the trappings of an Orthodox synagogue: a dress code (modest dress; men are required to cover their heads), segregation of men and women in prayer (men on the left), and prohibition of smoking and photography on the Sabbath and religious holidays. The cracks between the massive stones are stuffed with slips of paper bearing petitions, and the swaying and praying of the devout leave no doubt about the powerful hold this place still has on the minds and hearts of many Jews.

On Monday and Thursday mornings, the place bubbles with often colorful bar mitzvah ceremonies, when Jewish families celebrate the coming of age of their 13-year-old sons; but the fervor is greater on Friday evenings just after sunset, when the young men of a nearby yeshiva (Jewish seminary) come dancing and singing down to the Wall to welcome in the "Sabbath bride." But many visitors believe it is only when the crowds have gone (the Wall is floodlit at night and always open), and you share the warm, prayer-drenched stones with just a handful of bearded stalwarts, that the true spirituality of the Western Wall can be felt.

A long **tunnel** beyond the men's side (north of the plaza) was excavated in recent years, exposing ancient arches and chambers and several courses of the Western Wall along almost its entire length. Among the masonry were two stones estimated to weigh an incredible 400 and 540 tons, respectively. The tunnel is open to organized tour groups only. (Call Archaeological Seminars, ☎ 02/627–3515, or Western Wall Heritage, ☎ 02/627–1333, for details.)

Visitors going directly to the Western Wall can take Bus 1, which will deposit you inside the Dung Gate. The wall can also be reached by descending from the Jewish Quarter or from the Street of the Chain, in the Arab souk. ☉ *Daily, 24 hrs.*

Jewish Quarter

When the Crusaders reached Jerusalem in 1099, the Jewish community was concentrated in the northeastern quadrant of the city, which is today the Muslim Quarter of the Old City. The Crusaders' destruction of that quarter and its population was so complete that when the Spanish rabbi Nachmanides, known as the Ramban, reached the city in 1267, he found "only two Jews, brothers, dyers by trade." The men established themselves in the city's southern quadrant—perhaps on Mt. Zion—eventually occupying the medieval building in today's Jewish Quarter that still bears the Ramban's name. The Ramban Synagogue is on Jewish Quarter Road, adjacent to and south of the Hurva. The community slowly revived, then mushroomed with the influx of Sephardic Jews expelled from Spain in 1492, and again with the flow of Ashkenazi Jews from Central and Eastern Europe in the early 18th century. By 1865, more than half the population of Jerusalem was Jewish, most living in the Jewish Quarter in very difficult conditions, some in the Muslim Quarter, and a handful in the new neighborhoods developing beyond the city walls.

During Israel's War of Independence in 1948, the Jewish Quarter was severely damaged, forced to capitulate to Transjordan's (now Jordan's) Arab Legion, evacuated, plundered, and abandoned for a generation. With the reunification of Jerusalem after the Six-Day War of 1967, the restoration of the quarter began in earnest. With so many buildings little more than rubble, Israeli archaeologists were given a unique opportunity to explore the area systematically, and a decade of frenetic excavation in order to keep ahead of construction schedules yielded a harvest of archaeologically important sites. The simultaneous reconstruction of the quarter emphasized the restoration of the old as much as possible, as well as the design of new buildings that would preserve the original architectural flavor of the neighborhood. The result is an eye-pleasing harmony of limestone masonry, arched windows and buttresses, cobblestone alleyways, open archaeological sites, and splashes of greenery, making the Jewish Quarter the Old City's most attractive.

A Good Walk

This walk's starting point, the parking lot of the Jewish Quarter, can be reached from a number of directions. You can follow Armenian Orthodox Patriarchate Road from the Jaffa Gate (700 yards) or enter through the Zion Gate and continue right (200 yards). With your back to the bus stop, cross the lot and enter Jewish Quarter Road (there will be a small supermarket on your right). One hundred yards down the road on your left and some 20 feet below you are the excavated and partly restored remains of the **Cardo** ⑩, the colonnaded main street of 6th-century AD Byzantine Jerusalem.

Some 50 yards farther and on the right is the entrance to the ruined **Hurva Synagogue** ⑪, the great landmark of the Jewish Quarter until it was blown up in 1948. Visual aids are useful in reconstructing its past splendor. The second lane to the right beyond the Hurva Synagogue brings you to the **Broad Wall** ⑫, 23 feet thick and 2,700 years old.

Facing the Broad Wall and with your back to the Cardo, bear right for 50 yards to Hurva Square, the center of the Jewish Quarter. It still offers pleasant shady spots in which to take the weight off your feet and have some refreshment. On the eastern side of the square, take a few steps down the lane some 25 yards, to the right of Tony's Deli, where you'll find the **Herodian Quarter/Wohl Archaeological Museum** ⑬, containing the impressive remains of Second Temple–era mansions.

Once outside the site, you can descend a wide staircase to the Western Wall and the Dung Gate (☞ Old City: The Classic Sights, *above*). To return to Hurva Square, ascend the staircase. Just beyond the top of the steps, on your right, is the 2,000-year-old **Burnt House** ⑭, once a basement industrial workshop and destroyed by fire in the great destruction of AD 70.

TIMING

Allocate two hours to do this walk, though the many good stores and restaurants may tempt you to spend more time. The Herodian Quarter, Burnt House, and all commercial establishments close early Friday afternoon and remain closed Saturday.

Sights to See

⑫ **Broad Wall.** The discovery of this rather modest-looking 23-foot-thick wall was hailed as one of the most important archaeological finds in the Jewish Quarter. It was built in 701 BC by Hezekiah, King of Judah and a contemporary of the prophet Isaiah, to protect the city against an Assyrian invasion (II Chronicles 32). Seemingly attached to the Broad Wall are the scanty foundations of a dwelling, once in an unfortified outer neighborhood, possibly once inhabited by refugees from the devastated northern Kingdom of Israel (721 BC). "And you [Hezekiah] counted the houses of Jerusalem, and you broke down the houses to fortify the Wall" (Isaiah 22). So the concept of eminent domain is not a modern innovation: Hezekiah's city planners expropriated private houses for the more urgently needed city wall.

⑭ **Burnt House.** During the Second Temple period, this was the basement industrial workshop of the priestly Bar Katros family—a fact gleaned from inscribed stone weights discovered on this spot. The evidence of the city's fiery destruction is strongest here, with charred cooking pots and debris giving a vivid sense of the devastation 19 centuries ago. The archaeologists were riveted by the discovery of the skeletal hand and arm of a woman clutching a scorched staircase in a futile attempt to escape the flames. An audiovisual presentation illuminates the period, putting the artifacts in clear context. ☒ *Tiferet Israel St.* ☜ *Combined ticket with Herodian Quarter (☞ below): NIS 12 ($4); Burnt House only: NIS 6 ($2).* ☯ *Sun.–Thurs. 9–4:30, Fri. and holiday eve 9–12:30.*

⑩ **Cardo.** In AD 135, the Roman emperor Hadrian built his town of Aelia Capitolina on the ruins of Jerusalem, an urban plan essentially preserved in the Old City of today. Hadrian's *cardo maximus* (the generic name for the city's main street) began at the strategic Damascus Gate in the north, where sections of it have been unearthed. Originally, it didn't run so far south into today's Jewish Quarter, but with the Christianization of the Roman Empire in the 4th century, access to Mt. Zion and its important Christian sites became a priority, so the main street was eventually extended. The original width—today you see only half—was 73 feet, about the width of an eight-lane highway. Some 20 feet below modern ground level, you can walk among the flagstones and columns of Byzantine Jerusalem in its heyday.

★ ⑬ **Herodian Quarter/Wohl Archaeological Museum.** Excavations in the 1970s exposed the area's most visually arresting site: the remains of mansions from the luxurious Upper City of Second Temple–period Jerusalem. Preserved in the basement of the yeshiva built later over the ruins, the geometrically patterned mosaic floors, colorful frescoes, and costly glassware, stone objects, and ceramics give a peek into domestic life at the top in the days of Herod and Jesus. In the first hall, several small stone cisterns have been identified as private mikvaot; holograms depict their use. A small ascending staircase ends abruptly, a reminder that nothing above ground level survived the Roman devastation of AD 70.

The quality, and even rarity, of some of the goods displayed in the second hall would have been the pride of any aristocratic household in those days: decorated ceramic plates, a ribbed green glass bowl, an imported mottled-alabaster vase. Large stone water jars are just like those described in the New Testament story of the marriage at Cana (John 2; ☞ Nazareth and the Galilee Hills *in* Chapter 6). Rare stone tables recall the dining-room furniture depicted in Roman stone reliefs found in Europe.

Ancient steps bring you down to the last of the three distinct levels, a mansion with an estimated original area of more than 6,000 square feet. None of the upper stories has survived, of course, but the frescoes, half replaced by the later, more fashionable stucco, and the quality of the artifacts found here indicate a standard of living so exceptional that some scholars have suggested this might have been the long-sought palace of the high priest. At the southern end of the fine reception hall is a badly scorched mosaic floor with a charred ceiling beam lying on it. The Upper City held out against the Roman army for a month after the destruction of the Second Temple, but in September of AD 70, "on the eighth day of [the Hebrew month of] Elul," wrote the Jewish historian Josephus in his contemporary account of Jerusalem's last hours, "the sun rose over a city in flames." Precisely 19 centuries later, the victims' compatriots uncovered evidence of destruction so vivid, wrote archaeologist Nahman Avigad, "that we could almost smell the burning and feel the heat of the flames." ☒ *Hakara'im Rd.,* ☏ *02/628–3448.* ☞ *Combined ticket with Burnt House (☞ above): NIS 12 ($4); Herodian Quarter only: NIS 10 ($3.40).* ☉ *Sun.–Thurs. 9–4:30, Fri. 9–12:30.*

⑪ Hurva Synagogue. Ruined walls, alcoves that once housed sacred texts, and a modern arch retracing the old are all that remain of what was once the Jewish Quarter's most prominent building. In 1700, a large group of devout Eastern European (Ashkenazi) Jews arrived in the holy city, led by the venerable Rabbi Yehuda Hehassid (Judah the Pious). The old man died days after their arrival, throwing his followers into despair and leaving them with a problem: With the death of the rabbi, the promised funds from the Old Country never materialized, and the money for building a synagogue had to be borrowed from their Muslim neighbors. By 1720, the loan was still outstanding, and the creditors burned down the synagogue, exiling Ashkenazi Jews from the city for more than a century. In 1862, a new and splendid synagogue was completed on the *hurva* (ruins) of the old. It became the preeminent synagogue of the neighborhood, its high dome a Jewish Quarter landmark until the surrender of the quarter in the War of Independence in 1948 and the destruction of the synagogue by local Arabs.

Tower of David and Mt. Zion

"From Jaffa Gate to Zion Gate" could well be the title for the walk suggested for this area of the city. It takes in a fine museum of the history of Jerusalem, a section of the Ramparts Walk, and a clutch of sites, both Christian and Jewish, on Mt. Zion.

A Good Walk

Begin at the **Jaffa Gate** ⑮, which can be reached by Buses 6, 19, 20, 30, 38, and 99. If you have your own car, look for parking in the Mamilla area opposite the walls (undergoing renovation at press time). Walk to the bottom of the road that leads to Jaffa Gate and pause to look at the **Old City walls** above you. Above your head is the photogenic

Tower of David—actually a Turkish tower and minaret—which has become one of Jerusalem's landmarks.

The road that enters the Jaffa Gate is a mere 100 years old; the gate to your left, which you would enter if you come from the downtown area by way of Jaffa Road, dates to the 16th century. The road immediately bends to the right. Directly ahead is David Street, one of the main streets of the souk, the Arab bazaar (not to be confused with King David Street, in West Jerusalem). Follow the vehicular road (Armenian Orthodox Patriarchate Road). On your left 30 yards after the bend is the entrance to the Anglican Christ Church, a neo-Gothic structure built in the 1840s and the oldest Protestant church in the Middle East. On your right is the platform from which British general Edmund Allenby officially reviewed his victorious troops on December 11, 1917, after the Turkish army had abandoned the city.

Ascend the ramp, cross a moat, and enter the **Tower of David Museum** ⑯, a city history museum that is one of Jerusalem's highlights. From the entrance hall, a winding outside staircase on your right brings you to the roof. Turn left at once to reach the auditorium, where a film is shown, and a second staircase to the top of the great tower. The view in all directions is marvelous, but especially looking east across the Old City to the Temple Mount and Mount of Olives. Return to the roof and follow the red signs marked EXHIBIT.

The exit from the museum puts you outside the Jaffa Gate, where there are two ways to walk to Zion Gate. You can follow the road down to the left, then take an ascending path that hugs the Old City wall. The views across the Hinnom Valley to the Yemin Moshe neighborhood and the New City are splendid. At the southwestern corner of the Old City, turn left and continue 150 yards along the city wall to Zion Gate. You can reach the same point by way of the **Ramparts Walk** ⑰, on top of the walls of the city. As you leave the museum, do not rejoin the road; instead, walk south across the terrace, which only seems like a blind alley. A left at the end brings you to the ticket office for the ramparts. Follow the route—watch the steep steps—and descend at Zion Gate.

Turn right a few steps past Zion Gate and follow the path away from the Old City wall. Bear right at the first fork and turn right at the second. You will be outside the **Dormition Abbey** ⑱; its black conical dome and tall clock tower are prominent landmarks of Mt. Zion. The church preserves the tradition that Mary, mother of Jesus, did not die but fell into "eternal sleep" (hence *dormition*).

Return to the corner on the main path (the second fork) and turn right. Thirty yards on, step through a doorway to your left and climb one flight of steps to the **Room of the Last Supper** ⑲. The room has been enshrined by tradition as the site of Jesus' institution of the Eucharist ("This is my body . . . this is my blood") and of the gathering of the disciples on Pentecost.

Return to the main path and turn left. A few steps and another left turn bring you to a small tranquil courtyard surrounded by flowerpots and a colonnaded corridor, the cloister of a medieval monastery. The arched windows of the Room of the Last Supper are above you, and immediately beneath the cloister in an inner chamber is the traditional **Tomb of David** ⑳, draped in velvet and silver. As you emerge from the tomb, turn left and leave the cloister from the side opposite where you entered. Across the road is the **Chamber of the Holocaust** ㉑, a small but powerful exhibit dedicated to the Jews killed by the Nazis. To return to Zion Gate, turn left as you leave the memorial.

TIMING

Allow 1½–2 hours for the Tower of David Museum and a similar amount of time for the rest of the route.

Sights to See

㉑ Chamber of the Holocaust. This small memorial to the 6 million European Jews annihilated by the Nazis in the Second World War contains artifacts salvaged from the death camps, including items that the Nazis forced Jews to make out of sacred Torah scrolls (the Five Books of Moses). With grim humor, one Jewish tailor fashioned the inscribed parchment into a vest, choosing sections that contained the worst of the biblical curses. Ceremonial plaques commemorate some of the 5,000 Jewish communities wiped out by the Nazis. ⊠ Mt. Zion, ☎ 02/671–5105. ▦ NIS 6 ($2). ۞ Summer: Sun.–Thurs. 8:45–6, Fri. 8:45–3; winter, Sun.–Thurs. 8:45–5, Fri. 8:45–3.

⑱ Dormition Abbey. Black-domed and built of limestone, with ornamented turrets at each "corner" and a tall landmark clock tower, this large German Benedictine church stands on a site given by the Turkish sultan to Kaiser Wilhelm II during the latter's 1898 visit to Jerusalem and dedicated in 1910. The interior is an echo chamber with six small recessed chapels. At the eastern end is a large Byzantine-style apse with a wall mosaic of Jesus and Mary. The mosaic floor is decorated with expanding circles of names of the Trinity, the evangelists, the disciples, the Old Testament prophets, and the signs of the zodiac. In the basement is a cenotaph with the carved-stone figure of Mary in repose, embracing the tradition of her dormition, which holds that she didn't die but fell into eternal sleep. Among the little chapels in the lower level is one donated by the Ivory Coast, whose wooden figures and motifs are inlaid with ivory. A bookstore and pleasant coffee shop are on the premises. ⊠ Mt. Zion, ☎ 02/671–9927. ▦ Free. ۞ Daily 8–noon and 2–6.

⑮ Jaffa Gate. The gate got its name from its westerly orientation, toward the once-important Mediterranean harbor of Jaffa, now part of Tel Aviv. In Arabic, the gate is called Bab el-Halil, the Gate of the Beloved (referring to Abraham, the "Beloved of God" in Muslim tradition), because from here another road strikes south toward Hebron, El-Halil in Arabic, where Abraham is buried. The vehicle entrance was created by the Ottoman Turks in 1898 to accommodate the carriage of the visiting German emperor, Kaiser Wilhelm II. In December 1917 during the First World War, the victorious British general Allenby had a different approach: He and his staff dismounted from their horses in order to enter the holy city with appropriate humility. The older bent gate is attributed by the Arabic inscription outside it to the Ottoman Turkish sultan Suleiman the Magnificent (1536).

On your left as you enter, a Tourist Information Office offers maps and information; next to the office is a tiny recessed terrace fronted by a grille. Between the two tall cypress trees in the recess are two Muslim tombs, said to be those of the architects of Suleiman's city walls. One story says the angry Suleiman had them executed for rebuilding the city walls without encompassing Mt. Zion and the venerated Tomb of David. Another version has it that they met their fate for being too good at their jobs: Suleiman made sure they would never build anything grander for anyone else!

Opposite the Tourist Information Office is a huge stone tower built of well-cut stones reminiscent of those in the Western Wall. It is the last survivor, once called Phatza'el, of the three towers built by King Herod the Great in the 1st century BC. This has become known as the Tower of David, but has as little to do with that biblical king as the photogenic 16th-century Turkish tower, *also* known as the Tower of David, visible from outside Jaffa Gate. Apart from this tower, there are scant remains of Herod's fortress, but in later centuries Crusaders and Muslims continued to fortify this vulnerable spot in the city's defenses, creating the Citadel, as it is still known locally today.

Old City walls. Built between 1536 and 1542 by the Ottoman sultan Suleiman the Magnificent, the walls incorporate clearly visible chunks of the so-called First Wall, some 21 centuries old. In some places, the older stones, distinguished by the chiseled border characteristic of the Hasmonean period, project out of the line of the Turkish wall, tracing the foundations of ancient defense towers.

⑰ Ramparts Walk. From atop the Old City walls, you'll get to play voyeur as you catch glimpses into the gardens, courtyards, and homes of the Armenian Quarter, which occupies the southwestern quadrant of the Old City. As you walk along the narrow stone catwalks and peer through the crenellated shooting niches, you'll also gain some empathy for the medieval soldiers who defended the city. There are a large number of fairly high steps on this route. The railings are secure, but small children should not walk alone.

The northern section of the Ramparts Walk is accessible at two points— the Jaffa Gate and the Damascus Gate—and exits are provided at these as well as the New Gate. There is no connection at the Jaffa Gate between the two sections of the Walk. ☎ *02/625–4403.* 🎫 *NIS 8 ($2.70); combined ticket with Ophel Archaeological Garden and Damascus Gate: NIS 12 ($4).* ⊙ *Sat.–Thurs. 9–4, Fri. and holiday eves 9–2.*

⑲ Room of the Last Supper. According to tradition, it was on this location—*inside* the city walls of 2,000 years ago—that Jesus celebrated the Passover seder with his disciples. The bread and wine consecrated at the Last Supper became the elements of the Christian Eucharist. Alternately known as the Cenacle or the Coenaculum—the "Upper Room" referred to in the Gospels (Mark 14)—the present room is a large, bare medieval chamber with flagstones and Gothic arches, apparently built in the 14th century. A second tradition identifies the same room with the "one place" of 2 Acts, where the disciples of Jesus gathered on Pentecost, seven weeks after his death: "They were all filled with the Holy Spirit and began to speak in other tongues. . . ."

Incongruously, the chamber has the trappings of a mosque as well: stained-glass Arabic inscriptions in the Gothic windows (now newly replaced); one window blocked by an ornate mihrab that indicates the direction of Mecca); two Arabic plaques in the wall; and a Levantine dome. The Muslims were not interested in the Christian tradition of the place, but in the supposed Tomb of David (☞ *below*) on the floor below. ⊠ *Mt. Zion.* 🎫 *Free.* ⊙ *Sat.–Thurs. 8:30–4, Fri. 8:30–1.*

⑳ Tomb of David. The Bible refers to Jerusalem, King David's capital in the 10th century BC, as the "City of David." Medieval Jewish pilgrims erroneously identified the location of that ancient city as the southwestern hill; because the City of David was also called the "Stronghold of Zion" (II Samuel 5), the hill got the name by which it is known today, Mt. Zion. Because the Bible relates that David was buried in the City of David, the tomb of the great king was sought—and supposedly found— here. The real City of David has been excavated to the east of Mt. Zion, but nine centuries of tears and prayers have sanctified this place.

Enter the antechamber behind the blue-painted barred windows (men must cover their heads) and pass onto the tomb itself. The cenotaph, a massive stone tomb marker, is draped with a velvet cloth—changed periodically—typically embroidered with stars of David and inscriptions in Hebrew: "David, King of Israel, lives forever" (meaning his dynasty, from which the Messiah is to come, is eternal) and "If I forget thee, O Jerusalem, may my right hand lose its cunning" (Psalm 137).

On top of the cenotaph are several ornaments that crown Torah scrolls and two beautifully engraved silver canisters, used by Sephardic Jews as containers for the Torah. Behind the cenotaph is an age-blackened stone alcove, thought by scholars to be the oldest remnant of a synagogue in Jerusalem (from about the 5th century AD). In the antechamber opposite the tomb is a mihrab surrounded by green ceramic tiles, which once oriented the Muslim faithful toward Mecca in honor of Nebi Daoud—the prophet David—whom Islam has retroactively beatified. ⊠ *Mt. Zion,* ☎ *02/671–9767.* 🎫 *Free.* ☉ *Sun.–Thurs. 8–5, Fri. 8–2.*

★ ⑯ **Tower of David Museum.** Entered through a gated tower and over a moat, the museum is housed in a series of medieval halls in what is known locally as the Citadel (*Hametzuda* in Hebrew). Confusingly enough, although the name "Tower of David" has traditionally been applied to the 16th-century Turkish minaret at the Citadel's southern edge, other traditions attach it to the massive Herodian tower at the opposite end. Neither claimant has the slightest connection to the biblical King David! The museum tells the city's 5,000-year-old history, not with original artifacts but through a variety of interesting visual and audiovisual aids, including models, maps, holograms, and videos. You can rent an audio guide at the entrance. Be sure to inquire about the next screening of the animated introductory film, which has English subtitles.

The old stones and arches of the site lend an appropriately antique atmosphere to the entire exhibit, whose galleries are organized by historical period around the citadel's central courtyard. Landscaped archaeological remains in the courtyard form an eye-catching but incomprehensible jumble, except for the massive Herodian tower and the Hasmonean First Wall (2nd–1st centuries BC) to which it is attached. Walking the Citadel's ramparts, with sometimes unexpected panoramas glimpsed from odd angles, is worth your time but is certainly a lesser priority. Ask about the occasional temporary exhibitions. On summer evenings, a sound-and-light show in the Citadel creates a magical atmosphere in an area out of sight of the modern city. ⊠ *Jaffa Gate,* ☎ *02/627–4111 or 02/628–3394.* 🎫 *Museum or sound-and-light show: NIS 20 ($6.70); combined ticket to museum and sound-and-light show: NIS 35 ($11.70); electronic tour: NIS 10 ($3.40)* ☉ *Museum: Apr.–Oct., Sun.–Thurs. 9–5, Fri.–Sat. 9–2; Nov.–Mar., Sun.–Thurs. 10–4, Fri.–Sat. 10–2; free guided tour in English Sun.–Fri. at 11; sound-and-light show in English: Apr.–Oct., Mon. and Wed. at 9:30 PM, Sat. at 10:30 PM (call ahead to verify).*

City of David

The City of David is mentioned in the Bible (II Samuel 5) as a synonym for Jerusalem, once King David had conquered it (1000 BC) from the Jebusites and established it as his capital. In the mid-10th century BC, David's son Solomon expanded the city northward and built the Temple of God on Mt. Moriah, where the Dome of the Rock now stands. With time Jerusalem spread farther west and north, but in recent years the name City of David has been revived to describe the city's ancient core.

A Good Walk

Begin at the Dung Gate. If you're driving, you can park your car outside the gate. Walk east on Ophel Road, so the Old City wall is on your left and after it the Ophel Archaeological Garden ☞ Old City: The Classic Sights, *above*). Where the Ophel Road swings left, cross the road *carefully.* The **Kidron Valley** yawns beneath you, and from the lookout terrace you can see ancient funerary monuments below and to your left.

Return to the bend in Ophel Road. This was the northern limit of the City of David and the only side not protected by a valley. The city has been conquered at least 35 times in its 5,000-year history and almost always from the north. Continue south along the paved path that skirts the steep Kidron slope to the excavation site known as **Area G** ㉒, one of the areas dug up between 1978 and 1985 amid great public interest, with the most interesting finds made here. When you're ready to go, leave the site by the gate at the opposite side of the excavations.

From here on, the route is not recommended for visitors who have difficulty with steps. Descend the stairway and follow a small sign on the right to **Warren's Shaft** ㉓, an extraordinary access shaft to the Gihon Spring. It is commonly accepted that this was the way King David's commandos penetrated the city in 1000 BC. The room at the top of the shaft has several useful visual aids.

The main stairway continues down to the Kidron Valley. Under a modern building on the right, a short flight of steps descends to the spring itself. This was the original water supply of ancient Jerusalem and probably the reason the city was first built on this small hill. In 701 BC, in the face of an Assyrian invasion, King Hezekiah had a remarkable water tunnel built, a third of a mile long, to bring the spring water to an inner-city reservoir; it's now called **Hezekiah's Tunnel** ㉔. Walking the tunnel is a memorable experience, but you must bring flashlights or candles and be prepared to walk through water.

The tunnel emerges at a small pool, the "pool of Siloam" in the New Testament story of the healing of the blind man (John 9). Climb the steep road back to the Dung Gate. Bus 1 runs from here to Jaffa Gate and near the city center.

TIMING

Allow two hours for the walk, three if you walk Hezekiah's Tunnel. The tunnel involves 30–40 minutes' walking in knee- to thigh-deep water. Sites are closed Friday afternoon, Saturday, and Jewish religious holidays.

Sights to See

㉒ **Area G.** For more than a century, archaeologists, notably Kathleen Kenyon in the 1960s, have sporadically dug up bits of the City of David. The most thorough expedition, however, was led by the late Israeli archaeologist Yigal Shiloh from 1978 to 1985. In this sector, he confirmed the city wall dated to the 2nd century BC (marked 1, 2, and 3 on the site) but redated the so-called stepped structure (marked 4) to the 10th century BC, the century of Israelite kings David and Solomon. It once supported a palace or fortification; in the 7th century BC, a house (now partially restored on a platform) was built against the structure.

The most intriguing artifacts the dig yielded were 51 bullae, clay seals used for documents, just as hot wax might be used today. All had personal names impressed on them in ancient Hebrew script. All the seals were found in one chamber, suggesting its use as an archive; the name on one of the seals—Gemariah ben Shafan, the Temple secretary in the days of Jeremiah—confirms this. The clay seals were seared into ceramic permanence, apparently from the fire of the Babylonian destruction of Jerusalem in 586 BC. ✉ *Off Ophel Rd.,* ☎ *02/628–8141.* 🎫 *NIS 5 ($1.70) includes Warren's Shaft.* ☉ *Sun.–Thurs. 9–4, Fri. 9–1.*

NEED A
BREAK?

A vine-shaded terrace with a view of the Kidron Valley lies immediately opposite the exit from Area G. The enterprising owner of the spot sells soft drinks, fresh orange juice, and Turkish coffee, which you can sip leisurely at one of the stone tables. The toilet facilities are not great but are the only ones in the area.

(24) **Hezekiah's Tunnel.** Preparing for an imminent assault by the Assyrians on his capital city of Jerusalem, the Judean king Hezekiah rushed to protect his precious water supply by building a tunnel to bring water from the Gihon Spring (in Hebrew, the tunnel is known as the Shilo'ach, or Siloam in English). The invaders had destroyed the northern Kingdom of Israel in 721 BC and exiled most of its population into historical oblivion—the so-called Ten Lost Tribes. Twenty years later, Israel's sister kingdom of Judah in the south revolted against the Assyrian overlords, triggering a devastating, punitive military invasion. The Bible, which describes the siege in three parallel accounts, tells that Hezekiah gave instructions to "stop the water of the springs that were outside the city . . . saying, 'Why should the kings of Assyria come and find much water?' " Racing against time, Hezekiah's men dug a water tunnel a third of a mile long through solid rock, one team starting from the spring and another from the new inner-city reservoir. Miraculously, considering the serpentine course of the tunnel, the two teams met in the middle! The chisel marks, the ancient plaster, and the zigzags near the halfway point (as each team sought each other by sound) bear witness to the project. Again the Bible: And Hezekiah "closed the upper outlet of the waters of Gihon and directed them down to the west side of the city of David" (II Chronicles 32).

Most exciting was an inscription in ancient Hebrew, found in the last century near the exit of the tunnel (and now in a Turkish museum): "This is the story of the boring through. . . ," it began, echoing the biblical account, and "the tunnelers hewed the rock, each man toward his fellow, pickax against pickax. And the water flowed from the spring toward the reservoir for 1,200 cubits [533 meters, or 577 yards]."

Please note the following: There is no lighting in the tunnel, and visitors must come with flashlights or a good supply of candles and matches; the flow of the spring is unpredictable, and thus so is the water level, which can sometimes reach a depth of four feet in places; and the water is very cool, even in summer—this is no place for small children or claustrophobes. Although there are guards at the site, single women here could attract unwanted attention from local youths. ☎ 02/623–1221. 🎫 NIS 6 ($2). 🕐 Sun.–Thurs. 8–4:30, Fri. and holiday eves 8–2; last entry to tunnel 45 min before closing.

Kidron Valley. This valley separates the Old City from the high ridge of the Mount of Olives. Jewish tradition predicts the Messiah will make his appearance here. The cliff face below the village houses on the opposite side of the valley is marked with symmetrical holes, which are mouths of tombs from both the First Temple (Old Testament) and Second Temple (Hellenistic-Roman) periods. From the new lookout terrace across the street from Ophel Road as it swings left, you can look down and to your left at the impressive group of 22-centuries-old funerary monuments. The huge square, stone structure with the conical roof is known as **Absalom's Pillar**; the one crowned by a pyramidal roof, a solid block of stone cut out of the mountain, is called **Zachariah's Tomb**—but neither has anything to do with the Old Testament personalities for whom they are named. Wealthy Jerusalemites in the Second Temple period had themselves entombed at the foot of the Mount of Olives to await the Messiah and the resurrection that would follow.

㉓ **Warren's Shaft.** Charles Warren was an inspired British army engineer who explored Jerusalem in 1867. In the City of David he discovered this spacious, ancient access shaft, which burrowed under the city wall to a point 40 feet above the Gihon Spring in the valley. Water was hauled up the vertical shaft, perhaps by "the lame and the blind" of II Samuel 5. The conventional wisdom until Yigal Shiloh's dig (1978–85) said the shaft was pre-Davidic and was the actual one—called the *tzinnor* (gutter or water shaft) in that same biblical passage—through which David's warriors penetrated the city in 1000 BC. Shiloh disagreed and dated the shaft to the 9th century BC, based on its similarity to water systems of that later period found elsewhere in Israel. Yet nobody quite knows what the word *tzinnor* meant in Old Testament times (the word appears only twice in the Bible), and therefore there *is* room for interpretation; until the traditional explanation has been discredited, it is too good a story to surrender.

As you descend into the bowels of the earth, note the ancient chisel marks on the walls. It is now accepted that a good part of the shaft was a natural fissure reamed out by workmen in antiquity. The bottom of the shaft today is a dry chamber, walled off from the spring in the Israelite (Old Testament) period. ⊠ *Off Ophel Rd.,* ☎ *02/628–8141.* ☞ *NIS 5 ($1.70) includes Area G.* ☉ *Sun.–Thurs. 9–5, Fri. 9–1.*

Mount of Olives and East Jerusalem

The dominant theme of the sights in this area is distinctly Christian, though there's certainly enough to interest the nonpilgrim. The variety of sights, some definitely off the beaten path, makes for an absorbing experience. The walk is long but doable and is possible with a car or by using public transportation. A few words of caution: Pickpockets continue to be a problem on the Mount of Olives viewing area and on the road down to Gethsemane. The walk takes you through East Jerusalem's Arab neighborhoods, areas that Israelis have avoided in recent years because of political tensions. At press time the situation was fairly relaxed, but you are still advised to stick to the main streets and spend your evenings in some other part of town. If you are driving, choose your parking spots carefully since Palestinian nationalist zeal has been known to spill over into old-fashioned vandalism. The Seven Arches Hotel atop the Mount of Olives, the Rockefeller Museum compound, and the American Colony Hotel are recommended.

A Good Drive and Walk

Begin the tour on the **Mount of Olives** ㉕, at the panoramic lookout outside the Seven Arches Hotel. This is the classic picture-postcard view of the Old City. You are looking west across the Kidron Valley. Below you is a huge and ancient Jewish cemetery; around you are the Christian spires and domes that preserve other traditions.

Leave your car near the Seven Arches Hotel and walk some 150 yards back along the approach road to the hotel. In a bay on your right, through a stone gateway, is a round stone structure about 10 feet in diameter called the **Dome of the Ascension,** with rock alleged to bear the footprint of Jesus. Just beyond the dome, the road turns sharply right. Enter the **Pater Noster Convent** ㉖ through a light gray metal door on your right. Here, it is said, Jesus taught his disciples what is known as the Lord's Prayer, now recalled here in dozens of languages on ceramic tiles.

Walk back toward the hotel. If you are on foot, begin the descent from the Mount of Olives via the steps to your right before the parking lot. If you have a car, you can drive on an asphalt road that breaks off to

Exploring East Jerusalem

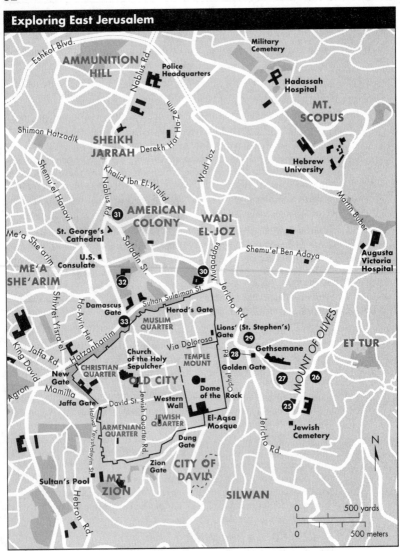

the right just beyond the steps, switches back, and then begins a *very* steep descent. Note: It is *not* a one-way street!

Just down the steps on the left is a courtyard with a burial complex said to be the **Tombs of the Prophets** Haggai and Malachi. Below the tombs, in the Jewish cemetery, is the common grave of 48 Jews killed in the battle for the Jewish Quarter in 1948. Hastily buried at the time within the quarter itself, their remains were disinterred in 1967 and reburied here. Among those buried with military honors were 10-year-old boys killed while running messages between defensive positions in the quarter.

Dominus Flevit ㉗ is a small, modern church halfway down the mountain that recalls Jesus' sorrowful prediction of the destruction of Jerusalem. The courtyard is a place for quietly enjoying the view between waves of tour groups. (Not to be dismissed are the rest rooms, rare on this tour!)

Continue down the hill. The gold onion domes and sculpted white turrets of the Russian **Church of Mary Magdalene,** straight out of a fantasyland, can be seen in tantalizing glimpses over a high wall to the right. At the bottom of the road on the left and marked by the platoon of vendors outside is the **Garden of Gethsemane** ㉘, mentioned in the New Testament as the site of Jesus' arrest. The ancient olive trees and impressive Church of All Nations are the prominent features of the site.

Gethsemane abuts Jericho Road at the foot of the Mount of Olives. The road bends sharply at this point, and to the right a staircase takes you deep into the subterranean Church of the Assumption, better known by the name of the shrine within it—the **Tomb of the Virgin** ㉙, the presumed burial place of Mary. To the right of the entrance is the Franciscan-administered **Grotto of Gethsemane.**

Continuing toward the Old City, the first left takes you to the City of David, Dung Gate, and Mt. Zion. Continue right for this tour, however. Turn left at the traffic light into Sultan Suleiman Street. Immediately on your right is a steep driveway leading up to the **Rockefeller Museum of Archaeology** ㉚, with its landmark octagonal tower. Do not park on the street; parking is permitted within the museum grounds. A good plan is to bring your lunch to to enjoy in the shade of the lovely garden.

Continue along Sultan Suleiman Street and turn right at the post office into Saladin Street. Where Saladin Street meets Nablus Road (about 1½ km, or 1 mi, from the Rockefeller Museum), on the right, are the **Tombs of the Kings** ㉛. If you are driving, turn right at the intersection and again into the second street on the right (a dead-end road) to the American Colony Hotel (☞ Lodging, *below*), where you will find safe parking. If you intend to complete the tour, leave your car here and see the other sights on foot. The immensely impressive tombs, once thought to be of Old Testament vintage, date to the 1st century AD and are the finest example of such catacombs in Israel. You will need a flashlight or several candles.

Continue down Nablus Road, heading back toward the Old City. Almost immediately on your left is the neo-Gothic Anglican St. George's Cathedral, built at the beginning of the century as a copy of New College at Oxford University. Its tower is a landmark of Jerusalem's skyline. Some 500 yards farther, beyond the U.S. Consulate and opposite the bus station, a well-marked narrow lane to the left—Conrad Schick Street—leads to the **Garden Tomb** ㉜. The magnificently landscaped garden is adjacent to a cliff face with distinctly skull-like features. Could this have been "the place of the skull," where Jesus was crucified by the Romans? In the late 19th century, a certain General Gordon thought so, and many Protestant visitors, especially those of Evangelical orientation, agree.

Back on Nablus Road, turn left and continue for 200 yards. You are now at the Old City walls opposite **Damascus Gate** ㉝. The archaeological remains of the Roman period found beneath the gate are worth your time and the small fee.

You now have several options: Return by foot to the American Colony Hotel; take a cab from Damascus Gate to your next destination; walk up Hativat Hatzanhanim Street (outside the Old City, with its walls on your left) toward Jaffa Gate and the New City; walk the Ramparts (☞ Tower of David and Mt. Zion, *above*) to Jaffa Gate; or plunge into the Old City to reach the Via Dolorosa and the Western Wall (left fork inside Damascus Gate) or the Church of the Holy Sepulcher and the Jewish Quarter (right fork).

TIMING

You can easily spend a day on this walk, with a stop for a picnic lunch on the grounds of the Rockefeller Museum. If archaeology is not your thing, you can start early and do most sights in time for a leisurely lunch at the American Colony, with just a bit of sightseeing left for the afternoon. The Mount of Olives is best in early morning, when you can see the Old City with the sun at your back, or at sunset on days with some clouds, when the golden glow can compensate for the glare. Several of the Christian sites are closed on Sunday.

Sights to See

Church of Mary Magdalene. The church, dedicated in 1888, is Russian Orthodox and part of the Garden of Gethsemane tradition. The site is rarely open, but it's worth visiting the icon-decorated interior if you happen to be in the area at the right time. ⊠ *Mt. of Olives,* ☎ *02/628–4371.* ⊡ *NIS 2 (70¢).* ⊘ *Tues. and Thurs. 10–11:30.*

㉝ **Damascus Gate.** The name of the gate gives away its location; it faces north toward Damascus, Syria. Its Hebrew name—Sha'ar Shechem, for the Nablus Gate—delivers the same message. With its tapered carved-stone crenellations and ornamented embrasures, the gate is the most beautiful of the seven still open in the present 16th-century Old City wall. It is also the busiest of them all, the main link between the Old City and the Arab neighborhoods of East Jerusalem.

To the left and below the approach bridge is a surviving arched entrance of the pagan **Roman town** built by Emperor Hadrian in AD 135 on the ruins of its Jewish predecessor. Hadrian's plan to build the town touched off the Jewish Bar Kochba Revolt in AD 132. Excavations just inside the arch (reached by going to the right of Damascus Gate and then left under the bridge) have brought to light an almost entirely intact Roman tower that connects with the Ramparts Walk (a separate ticket; ☞ Tower of David and Mt. Zion, *above*) and is part of an open plaza of the 2nd-century town. A tall column topped by the emperor's statue once dominated the plaza, exactly as depicted in the famous 6th-century mosaic floor map of the city found in Madaba, Jordan. The column served as the point of reference for measuring distances throughout the country, and though it has not survived, the Arabic name for the gate—Bab el-Amud, the Gate of the Column—preserves its memory. ⊠ *Damascus Gate,* ☎ *02/623–1221 or 02/628–5400.* ⊡ *NIS 3.50 ($1.20) for Roman plaza; combined ticket with Ramparts Walk and Ophel Archaeological Garden: NIS 12 ($4).* ⊘ *Sat.–Thurs. 9–4, Fri. 9–2.*

Dome of the Ascension. This building dates from the Crusader period and once opened to the sky. Credulous medieval pilgrims were shown an indentation in the natural rock, said to be the footprint of Jesus as he ascended to heaven, and the tradition stuck. The dome is actually Islamic in style, and curiously, the current caretakers are Muslim. ✉ *Mt. of Olives.* ▣ *Small fee, about NIS 3 ($1).* ☉ *No set hrs; to enter, ring bell.*

㉗ Dominus Flevit. Designed by Antonio Barluzzi and built between 1953 and 1955, the tear-shape church (whose name means "the Lord wept") provides a potentially tranquil haven with a superb view of the Old City. The crowds of pilgrims often make that calm elusive, however. The outstanding feature of the church's simple interior is the picture window facing west, with an iron cross on the altar silhouetted against the Old City and the Dome of the Rock. Although there have been many small archaeological finds here, the tradition that this is the site where Jesus wept over Jerusalem as he prophesied its destruction—"and they shall not leave in thee one stone upon another" (Luke 19)—is apparently no earlier than the Crusader period. ✉ *Mt. of Olives,* ☎ *02/627-4931.* ▣ *Free.* ☉ *Daily 8–noon and 2:30–5.*

㉘ Garden of Gethsemane. The New Testament does not specifically refer to Gethsemane as a garden, but as the "place" where Jesus came with his disciples after the Last Supper, where he prayed and sweated blood (Matthew 26) and where, in the end, he was betrayed and arrested. The name Gethsemane derives from the Aramaic *gat shamna* or the Hebrew *gat shemanim,* both meaning "oil press." The olive tree, which gives this hill its name (Mount of Olives), grew in greater profusion in antiquity than today, its fruit providing precious lamp oil. The "Garden of the Oil Press" still boasts eight enormous, gnarled trees—still productive—that some botanists surmise might be as old as Christianity itself.

Within the garden is the **Church of All Nations,** designed by the architect Antonio Barluzzi and dedicated in 1924. Within each of its interior domes are mosaic symbols of the countries that contributed to its building (the seal of the United States can be seen in the first dome as you enter the church). The windows are glazed with translucent alabaster in somber browns and purples, creating a mystical atmosphere in the dim interior. At the altar is the so-called Rock of the Agony, where Jesus is said to have endured his Passion. The large mosaics depict the events associated with the site. Small windows in the floor show sections of the Byzantine mosaics that inspired those of the contemporary church. ✉ *Jericho Rd.,* ☎ *02/628–3264.* ▣ *Free.* ☉ *Oct.–Mar., daily 8–noon and 2:30–5; Apr.–Sept., 8–noon and 2:30–6.*

★ ㉜ Garden Tomb. The theory identifying this site with Jesus' burial place and Calvary goes back to 1883, when General Charles Gordon (of later Khartoum fame) spent several months in Jerusalem. From his window just inside the Old City walls, he was struck by the skull-like features of a cliff face north of the Damascus Gate. He was convinced that this, not the traditional Calvary in the Church of the Holy Sepulcher (☞ Old City: The Classic Sights, *above*), was "the place of the skull" (Mark 15), where Jesus was crucified. His conviction was infectious, and after his death a fund-raising campaign in England resulted in the purchase of the adjacent site in 1894. An ancient rock-cut tomb uncovered there some years earlier took on new importance because of its proximity to Skull Hill (already becoming known as Gordon's Calvary). Subsequent excavations exposed cisterns and a wine press, features typical of an ancient garden.

The newly formed Garden Tomb Association was jubilant: All the elements of the gospel account of Jesus' death and burial were here. Jesus was buried in the fresh tomb of the wealthy Joseph of Arimathea (Matthew 27), and contemporary archaeologists lent their authority to the identification of the tomb as an upper-class one of the Second Temple period. Recent research has strongly challenged that conclusion, however. The tomb might be from the Old Testament period, making it too old to have been Jesus', since his was one "in which no man had yet been laid." It should be noted that the gentle guardians of the Garden Tomb do not insist on the identification of the site as that of Calvary and the tomb of Christ, but suggest (as their brochure puts it) that "the features of the Garden . . . provide an atmosphere which brings into focus the relevance of the Death and Resurrection of the Lord Jesus Christ." Indeed, the beautifully tended garden of trees, flower beds, and seats for private meditation makes this an island of tranquillity in the hurly-burly of East Jerusalem. ⊠ *Conrad Schick St.,* ☎ *02/627–2745.* ▦ *Free.* ☉ *Mon.–Sat. 8:30–noon and 2–5:30; Sun. service only (nondenominational Protestant in English) at 9.*

Grotto of Gethsemane. The rock ceiling seems to press down on you in this hewn chapel. The Franciscans identify the *Garden* of Gethsemane with Christ's Passion and this spot with his arrest. ⊠ *Jericho Rd.,* ☎ *02/628–3264.* ▦ *Free.* ☉ *Daily 8:30–11:30 and 2:30–4.*

★ ㉕ **Mount of Olives.** The Mount of Olives has been bathed in sanctity—both past and future—since time immemorial. Separating you from the Old City is the Kidron Valley, which continues south for a way before breaking east and beginning its steep descent to the Dead Sea. On the slope below you and spreading off to your left is the very extensive **Jewish cemetery,** the oldest cemetery—of any religion—still in use. For more than 2,000 years, Jews have been buried on the Mount of Olives to await the coming of the Messiah and the resurrection to follow. It's said that elsewhere you die and disintegrate; in Jerusalem you die and mingle! The raised structures over the graves are merely tomb markers, not crypts; burial is still below ground.

In the Old City wall facing you, and just to the right of the golden Dome of the Rock, is the blocked-up, double-arched Gate of Mercy, or Golden Gate. Jewish tradition holds that the Messiah will enter Jerusalem this way; Christian tradition says he already has. To the south of the Dome of the Rock is the black-domed El-Aqsa Mosque, behind which are the stone arches of the Jewish Quarter. Some distance behind the Dome of the Rock is the large, gray dome of the Church of the Holy Sepulcher. To the left of the Old City, the cone-roofed Dormition Abbey and its adjacent tower mark the top of Mt. Zion, today outside the walls but within the city of the Second Temple period.

㉖ **Pater Noster Convent.** The focal point of this Carmelite convent is a grotto, traditionally identified as the place where Jesus taught his disciples the so-called Lord's Prayer: "Our Father [*Pater Noster*], Who art in Heaven . . . " (Mark 11; Luke 11). The site was purchased by the Princess de la Tour d'Auvergne of France in 1868, and the convent built on the site of earlier Byzantine and Crusader structures. The ambitious Basilica of the Sacred Heart, begun here in the 1920s and designed to follow the lines of Constantine's 4th-century Basilica of Eleona, was never completed. Its aisles, open to the sky, are now incongruously lined with pine trees, and its altar is more reminiscent of an Aztec high place than a Catholic church. The princess, entombed in a beautiful marble sarcophagus, lies in state in the cloister, oblivious to the abandonment of the master plan. Ceramic plaques lining the cloister walls quote the Lord's Prayer in more than 70 different languages. A small metal plaque in braille is to the left of the entrance. ⊠ *Mt. of Olives,* ☎ *02/589–4904.* ▣ *Free.* ☉ *Mon.–Sat. 8:30–11:45 and 3–4:45.*

㉚ Rockefeller Museum of Archaeology. Built in the 1930s during the British Mandate, the stone halls of the museum still retain an Old World atmosphere. The chronological presentation of its fine archaeological collection recalls the style of the British Museum; but though it is still not the last word on the art of museology, it has become far more visitor friendly of late. If you have only a passing interest in archaeology, the Israel Museum's finely presented collection will probably suffice (☞ Center City, *below*). The Rockefeller is for the enthusiast.

The finds are all from Israel, dating from prehistoric times to around AD 1700. Among the most important exhibits are cultic masks from Neolithic Jericho, ivories from Canaanite (Bronze Age) Megiddo, the famous Israelite "Lachish Letters" (6th century BC), Herodian inscriptions, and decorative reliefs from Hisham's Palace in Jericho and from the Church of the Holy Sepulcher. ⊠ *Sultan Suleiman St.,* ☎ *02/628–2251.* ▣ *NIS 17 ($6.40); inquire about combined ticket with Israel Museum.* ☉ *Sun.–Thurs. 10–5, Fri.–Sat. 10–2.*

㉛ Tombs of the Kings. These catacombs were explored in the 19th century by the Frenchman Félicien de Saulcy, who accepted the local tradition identifying them with the biblical kings of Judah. Royal tombs they were, but not quite that old. In the 1st century AD, Queen Helene of Adiabene, a country on the border of Persia, converted to Judaism and came to live and die in the holy city. Although she built her palaces in the onetime City of David in the south of the city, she and her descendants were buried here.

Wide, rock-hewn steps descend to rain catchment pools and into a spacious courtyard, all excavated out of solid rock. The entrance to the tombs is across a porch that once boasted two massive stone columns and still has its Hellenistic-style frieze above. The "rolling stone" that once sealed the mouth of the catacombs is still in situ, a graphic example of those described in the New Testament.

The "weeping chamber" immediately inside the low doorway has rock benches for the mourners and tiny triangular niches to hold oil lamps. Other chambers branching off it contain the many alcoves and ledges where the dead, wrapped in shrouds, were laid. ⊠ *Saladin St.* ▣ *Attendant requires small fee.* ☉ *Daily 8:30–5, but hrs are unreliable and site is sometimes closed during opening hrs. Bring a flashlight or candles.*

NEED A BREAK?

The **American Colony Hotel** (⊠ Nablus Rd., ☎ 02/628–5171) is a 19th-century limestone building with cane furniture, Armenian ceramic tiles, and a delightful courtyard. The food is generally very good, and a light lunch or afternoon tea in the cool lobby lounge, poolside restaurant, or on the patio can come as a well-earned break.

Tombs of the Prophets. The tradition that holds these to be the burial places of the prophets Haggai and Malachi is spurious, but the site is interesting in its own right. It is a burial cave from the Byzantine period, about 1,500 years ago. From the round entrance hall, three passages radiate out to meet the two semicircular inner corridors containing the cave's 26 burial niches. ⊠ *Mt. of Olives.*

㉙ Tomb of the Virgin. The Gothic facade of the underground Church of the Assumption, which contains this shrine, clearly dates it to the Crusader era (12th century), but the tradition that this is where the Virgin Mary was interred and then "assumed" into heaven apparently reaches back to the Byzantine period. In an otherwise gloomy church, hung with age-darkened icons and brass lamps, the marble sarcophagus, thought to date from the 12th century, remains illuminated. The Status Quo Agreement in force in the Church of the Holy Sepulcher and Bethlehem's Church of the Nativity pertains here, too: The Greek Orthodox, Armenians, and even Muslims control different parts of the property—the Roman Catholic Franciscans, to their chagrin, do not. ⌧ *Jericho Rd.* 🔳 *Free.* ☉ *Daily 6–11:45 and 2:30–5.*

West Jerusalem

In the nature of things, visitors tend to focus on the historical and religious sights on the eastern side of town; but exploring West Jerusalem, beyond the great interest of individual sights, gives insights into contemporary life in Israel's largest city. These attractions on the western edge of Jerusalem are most easily accessible by car or by a combination of buses, short cab rides, and a little patience.

A Good Drive

Begin at **Yad Vashem** ㉞, the national Holocaust memorial and museum, 700 yards west of Mt. Herzl. Only Bus 99 stops at the site, but Mt. Herzl, a 10-minute walk away, is served by many lines (Buses 18 and 27 run from the city center). The experience of the Holocaust is so deeply seared into the Jewish national psyche that understanding it goes a long way toward understanding the Israelis themselves.

A good plan for seeing this complex site is the following: Walk up the slope to the right of the bookstore near the entrance to the small but riveting Children's Memorial. Continue past the tall aluminum memorial to the Jewish resistance to visit the heavy basalt and concrete Hall of Remembrance. Step down through the carob trees of the Avenue of the Righteous and turn right onto Warsaw Ghetto Square. Here is the entrance to the Historical Museum; the Art Museum is in the same building but can be entered separately. Many impressive sculptures are scattered around the site. From the parking lot a road descends (about 1 km, or ½ mi) to the Valley of the Communities. If you are on foot, a path to the left of Warsaw Ghetto Square (opposite the museum entrance) will lead you down to the valley by a shorter route.

Return toward Herzl Boulevard, but turn left into the large parking lot that abuts it (*before* you reach the traffic lights). This is the entrance to **Mt. Herzl (National Memorial Park)** ㉟, named for Theodor Herzl, the founder of the modern Zionist movement, whose grave is at its summit. The path to the left of the Herzl Museum entrance eventually turns right across a huge plaza (used for state ceremonies) to the unadorned black stone grave marker. To the left (west) of the grave site, a path leads down to a section containing the graves of national leaders, among them assassinated prime minister Yitzhak Rabin.

Continue west for a few yards, descending to the **Mt. Herzl Military Cemetery** ㊱. The paths through the cemetery bear around to the right, so double back to the cemetery entrance and reach Herzl Boulevard 300 yards below the first entrance where you entered Mt. Herzl. An alternative route is to enter the military cemetery directly without going through the park.

One hundred yards down Herzl Boulevard from the entrance to Mt. Herzl, turn right at the next traffic light, into Harav Uziel Street. After 2 km (1¼ mi)—keep bearing left—the road passes the Holyland Hotel, and 150 yards farther is the **Second Temple Period Model** ㊲, a huge

59

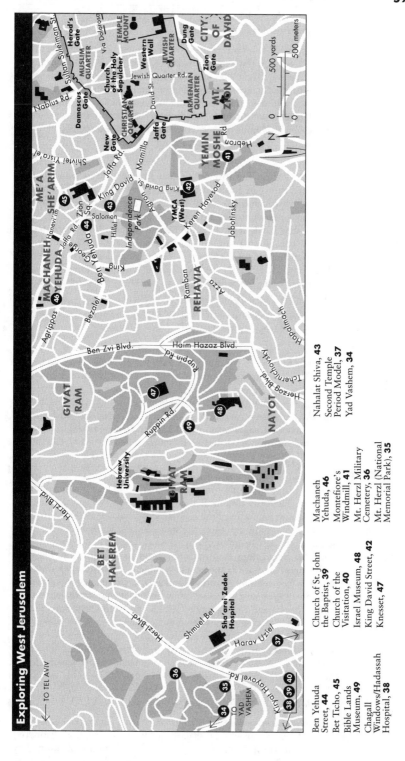

Exploring West Jerusalem

Ben Yehuda
Street, **44**
Bet Ticho, **45**
Bible Lands
Museum, **49**
Chagall
Windows/Hadassah
Hospital, **38**

Church of St. John
the Baptist, **39**
Church of the
Visitation, **40**
Israel Museum, **48**
King David Street, **42**
Knesset, **47**

Machaneh
Yehuda, **46**
Montefiore's
Windmill, **41**
Mt. Herzl Military
Cemetery, **36**
Mt. Herzl (National
Memorial Park), **35**

Nahalat Shiva, **43**
Second Temple
Period Model, **37**
Yad Vashem, **34**

open-air scale model of Jerusalem as it existed 2,000 years ago. Park and take the short path on the left.

If you're driving, return to the intersection with Herzl Boulevard and turn left. Stay on the winding main road, the name of which changes several times: Kiryat Hayovel Road, Hantke Street, and Henrietta Szold Road. The road swings sharply right to Hadassah Hospital. There is a relatively remote parking lot on the hospital grounds and a free shuttle bus to the main buildings. What draws visitors, however, are the world-famous stained-glass **Chagall windows** ⓧ, which adorn the hospital's synagogue. The theme is biblical: Jacob's deathbed blessings on his sons. The effect is magical.

As you leave from the hospital's main entrance, turn right and descend to where the road joins Route 386. Turn right again, reentering Jerusalem through **Ein Kerem.** Dominating the center of the village (on the left, as you approach from the west, from the bottom of the village) is the **Church of St. John the Baptist** ⓧ, its orange tile roof a distinctive local landmark. Opposite the church, a short street takes you to the small Spring of the Virgin. Turn right and climb a steep, stepped street, past a Russian Orthodox monastery, to the impressive Franciscan **Church of the Visitation** ⓧ, said to have been the home of John the Baptist's parents, Zechariah and Elizabeth.

Return to the main road of the village and turn right onto the steep road that emerges at Mt. Herzl.

TIMING

This is a full day of touring, even with the convenience of your own car. Allow two to three hours to do Yad Vashem justice, though the highlights can be seen in a shorter time. It is best to visit the Second Temple Period Model *after* you have become familiar with the Old City of today; 45 minutes is the most you need. Note that Yad Vashem, Mt. Herzl, and the Chagall windows close very early on Friday and are not open on Saturday or on Jewish religious holidays.

Sights to See

ⓧ **Chagall windows/Hadassash Hospital.** Hadassah is one of the two largest general hospitals in the Middle East and is the teaching hospital for Hebrew University's medical and dental schools. When the Hadassah organization approached the Russian-born Jewish painter Marc Chagall in 1959 about designing the stained-glass windows for the synagogue of the new hospital, the artist was delighted and contributed his work for free. Taking his inspiration from Jacob's deathbed blessings on his sons (Genesis 49) and, to a lesser extent, from Moses's valediction to the tribes of Israel (Deuteronomy 33), Chagall created 12 vibrant windows in primary colors, with an arkful of characteristically Chagallian beasts and a scattering of Jewish and esoteric symbols. The innovative techniques of the Reims glassmakers give the wafer-thin windows an astounding illusion of depth in many places. To see the windows, take the tour of the synagogue, which includes a film about the hospital. Buses 19 and 27 serve the hospital. ✉ *Hadassah Hospital, Henrietta Szold Rd., Ein Kerem,* ☎ *02/641–6333.* 🎟 *NIS 5 ($1.70).* ☉ *Guided tours of synagogue: Sun.–Thurs. at 8:30, 9:30, 10:30, 11:30, 12:30, and 2:30; Fri. and holidays at 9:30, 10:30, 11:30.*

ⓧ **Church of St. John the Baptist.** The orange tile roof of this late-17th-century Franciscan church, a large white structure, is a distinctive local landmark in Ein Kerem (☞ *below*). Though not mentioned by name in the New Testament, the village has long been identified as John the Baptist's birthplace, a tradition that apparently goes back to the Byzantine period (5th century AD). The old paintings and glazed tiles in the church make it worth a visit. You can also see the grotto where John the Baptist is said to have been born. ⊠ *Ein Kerem Rd., Ein Kerem,* ☎ *02/641–3639.* 🎫 *Free.* ⊙ *Apr.–Sept., weekdays 8–noon and 2:30–6, Sun. 9–noon and 2:30–5; Oct.–Mar., weekdays 8–noon and 2:30–5, Sun. 9–noon and 2:30–5.*

40 **Church of the Visitation.** Said to have been the home of John the Baptist's parents, Zechariah and Elizabeth, the church is high up the hillside in Ein Kerem (☞ *below*), with a wonderful view of the valley and the surrounding wooded hills. When Mary, pregnant with Jesus, came to visit her pregnant cousin Elizabeth, "the babe leaped in [Elizabeth's] womb" with joy. Mary then pronounced the paean of praise to God known as the Magnificat ("My soul doth magnify the Lord . . . ."—Luke 1). A wall of the courtyard is covered with ceramic tiles quoting the Magnificat in 41 languages. The upper church is adorned with large wall paintings depicting the various mantles with which Mary has been endowed: Mother of God, Refuge of Sinners, Dispenser of All Grace, Help of Christians, and the Immaculate Conception. Other frescoes depict Hebrew women of the Bible also known for their "hymns and canticles," as the Franciscan guide puts it. ⊠ *Ein Kerem,* ☎ *02/641–7291.* 🎫 *Free.* ⊙ *Apr.–Sept., Sun.–Fri. 8–11:45 and 2:30–6; Oct.–Mar., daily 8–11:45 and 2:30–5.*

Ein Kerem. Now part of Jerusalem, this village boasts a mix of its original working-class population along with artists and professionals living in renovated old stone buildings that have become upscale showpieces. Among the notable buildings here are the ☞ **Church of St. John the Baptist** and the ☞ **Church of the Visitation.** Ein Kerem is served by Bus 17.

35 **Mt. Herzl (National Memorial Park).** The simple grave marker of Theodor Herzl, founder of modern Zionism, lies at the top of Mt. Herzl, inscribed in Hebrew only with the name HERZL. The site is beautifully landscaped, with cedars of Lebanon lording it over the native pine and cypress. The **Herzl Museum,** to the left of the entrance, preserves Herzl's Vienna study intact.

In 1894, the Budapest-born Herzl was the Paris correspondent for a Vienna newspaper when the Dreyfus treason trial hit the headlines. The anti-Semitic outbursts that Herzl encountered in cosmopolitan Paris shocked him—Dreyfus, a Jewish officer in the French army, had, in fact, been framed and was later exonerated—and thereafter Herzl devoted himself to the problem of Jewish vulnerability in "foreign" host countries and the need, in his eyes, of creating a Jewish state where Jews could control their own destiny. The result of his activities was the first World Zionist Congress, in Basel, Switzerland, in 1897. That year Herzl wrote in his diary: "If not in five years, then in 50, [a Jewish state] will become reality." Just 50 years later, in November 1947, the United Nations gave its sanction to the idea. Herzl died in 1904, and his remains were brought to Israel in 1949.

To the left (west) of the grave site, a gravel path leads down to a section containing the **graves of national leaders,** among them assassinated prime minister Yitzhak Rabin; his predecessors of the 1960s and '70s, Levi Eshkol and Golda Meir; and Zalman Shazar, Israel's third president. ⊠ *Herzl Blvd.,* ☎ *02/651–1108.* 🎫 *Free.* ⊙ *Park and museum: Apr.–Sept., Sun.–Thurs. 9–6:45, Fri. and holiday eves 9–1; Oct.–Mar., Sun.–Thurs. 9–4:45, Fri. 9–1.*

36 **Mt. Herzl Military Cemetery.** The tranquillity and well-kept greenery of Israel's largest military cemetery almost belie its real purpose. Different sections are reserved for the veterans of the various wars the nation has fought. The large number of identical headstones is a sobering reminder of the price of national independence and security. Officers and privates are buried alongside one another, an Israeli egalitarianism that expresses the idea that lives lost are mourned equally by the nation, regardless of rank. ⊠ *Herzl Blvd.,* ☎ *02/643–7257.* ▣ *Free.* ☉ *Daily 24 hrs.*

㊲ **Second Temple Period Model.** Seven years in the building, the huge open-air model—the size of a tennis court—represents Jerusalem at its largest size in the mid-1st century AD. The scale is 1:50, roughly ¼ inch to the foot. Although built around a concrete core, the miniature structures are faced with the same Jerusalem stone as the originals. The designer of the model, the late Professor Michael Avi-Yonah, was guided by ancient literary descriptions of Jerusalem and modern archaeological finds. Public works, such as the city's fortifications and King Herod's great reconstructed marble temple (the Second Temple), are thought to be substantially accurate, although private buildings are more generic, reflecting the known architectural style of the period. The model is constantly evolving: Where new evidence contradicts old assumptions, elements of the model are changed. A booklet on the site is available from the bookstore; or you can eavesdrop on one of the many guides who escort groups here! Buses 21 and 21A go here from the city center and the Central Bus Station. ⊠ *On grounds of Holyland Hotel,* ☎ *02/643–7777.* ▣ *NIS 15 ($5).* ☉ *Daily 8 AM–10 PM.*

★ **㉞** **Yad Vashem.** It is not by chance that Yad Vashem—the primary national Holocaust memorial and museum—is a mandatory stop on the itineraries of most official guests of the State of Israel. Created in 1953 by an act of the Knesset, it possesses the largest Holocaust archive in the world (over 50 million documents). Through its museum, research, and publication departments and its youth education programs, the institute attempts not merely to document the period but to convey the challenge of understanding the Holocaust, especially to younger generations. The name Yad Vashem—"an everlasting memorial"—comes from the biblical book of Isaiah.

Perhaps the most riveting component of Yad Vashem is the small **Children's Memorial.** Of the 6 million Jews murdered by the Nazis in World War II, fully a quarter were children, a statistic that emphasizes the single-mindedness of the "Final Solution." In trying to do the seemingly impossible—to convey the enormity of the crime without numbing the visitor's emotions or losing sight of the victims' individuality—architect Moshe Safdie found an ingenious solution. Five candles and some 500 mirrors create an infinity of living flames in the dark interior (there are guide rails and no steps), while recorded narrators intone the names, ages, and countries of origin of known victims. The effect is electrifying.

The **Avenue of the Righteous,** which encircles the site, contains some 5,500 trees bearing plaques with the names of gentiles in Europe who risked and sometimes lost their lives trying to save Jews from the Nazis. Raoul Wallenberg, King Christian X of Denmark, Corrie ten Boom, and Oskar Schindler are among the more famous honored here. The **Hall of Remembrance** is a heavy basalt and concrete building that houses an eternal flame; the names of the death camps are inscribed on the floor.

The **Historical Museum,** entered from Warsaw Ghetto Square, is the centerpiece of Yad Vashem. Through artifacts, photographs, videos, recordings, and explanations in English, it documents the period from Hitler's rise to power in 1933 through the following 12 nightmare years to the postwar turmoil that precipitated the birth of Israel. In the same building is the **Art Museum,** a simultaneously beautiful and heart-wrenching display of art and sculpture by Jewish artists—known and unknown, adults and children—who either perished in the Holocaust although their work miraculously survived or who survived the period and expressed their experiences through their art.

The **Valley of the Communities** was a project of individual Holocaust survivors and survivors' organizations. Walls of enormous rough-hewn limestone boulders create a series of canyons, each representing a region of Nazi Europe, laid out geographically. The names of 5,000 destroyed Jewish communities are inscribed in the stone, with the largest letters emphasizing particularly important communities in prewar Europe.

An information booth is next to the bookstore at the entrance. Photography is permitted in the Historical Museum, but not in the Children's Memorial and the Art Museum. There is a cafeteria next to the parking lot. ⊠ *Near Herzl Blvd.,* ☎ *02/675–1611.* ▣ *Free.* ☉ *Sun.–Thurs. 9–4:45, Fri. and holiday eves 9–1:45.*

Center City

New Jerusalem's downtown and near-downtown areas are a mix of old neighborhoods and new limestone edifices, of monuments and markets, of landscapes and peoplescapes. Add the readily accessible (by doable walk or a quick bus or cab ride) Givat Ram district, with the Israel Museum, the Bible Lands Museum, and the Knesset, and you have an absorbing day's sightseeing.

A Good Walk and Drive

Begin in the **Yemin Moshe** neighborhood at the famous **Montefiore's Windmill** ㊶, named for the Anglo-Jewish benefactor who built it in the mid-19th century. The restored carriage in which Moses Montefiore once traveled the country was on display here until it was torched by vandals some years ago. The one you see now is an exact replica. Walk to the edge of the patio adjacent to the windmill. Immediately below you is the long roof of **Mishkenot She'ananim,** the first settlement outside the walls of Jerusalem, built by Montefiore in 1860. Today it is a prestigious guest house for visiting artists, writers, and musicians.

Separating you from Mt. Zion and the Old City is the deep **Hinnom Valley,** mentioned in the Bible (Joshua 15) as the border between the Israelite tribes of Judah (to the south) and Benjamin (to the north) and as the site of renewed pagan sacrifices in the 7th century BC. As you face the valley, look right. On a hill just a few hundred yards away is the Scottish Church of St. Andrew. To the left of and below the church, on the bend in the valley known as Ketef Hinnom—the Hinnom Shoulder—an archaeological excavation in the late 1970s discovered a series of tombs. Cut out of the rocky scarp and still visible today, the tombs yielded a treasure trove of finds.

To your left is the prestigious neighborhood of Yemin Moshe, one of the city's most affluent. The top of Yemin Moshe is separated from **King David Street** ㊷ by a small park. Follow the street a short distance to the landmark King David Hotel, a handsome, rectangular limestone building with a back terrace overlooking some well-kept gardens and the Old City walls. Across the street is the imposing YMCA; don't miss an opportunity to ride by elevator to the top of its tower for stunning panoramas of the city.

Turn left onto Abraham Lincoln Street, immediately after the YMCA. From the small intersection a hundred yards beyond it, a narrow pedestrian lane (George Eliot Street) continues in the same direction, emerging at Agron Street, next to the U.S. Consulate-General Building. Cross Agron and enter **Independence Park** (not recommended at night) by way of the road 500 feet to your right.

The park's crossroad emerges at Hillel Street to the north. Immediately across the road is Yoel Moshe Salomon Street and to the right and parallel to it is Yosef Rivlin Street, named after two of the seven founders of **Nahalat Shiva** ㊸, the second neighborhood built outside the city walls, established in 1869. At the other end of Salomon Street is Zion Square, where Jaffa Road, Jerusalem's main thoroughfare, is met by **Ben Yehuda Street** ㊹. If you've had enough for one day, take a stroll up Ben Yehuda (on your left) and visit the shops and cafés of its bustling pedestrian mall.

If you still have strength, time, and patience, cross Jaffa Road at Zion Square and turn left. The first street on the right is Harav Kook, named after Rabbi (*Harav*, in Hebrew) Kook, chief rabbi of Palestine in the British Mandate period. Two hundred yards up the road on the left, a path (clearly signposted in orange) takes you to **Bet Ticho** ㊺, a magnificent limestone edifice that today houses a small art exhibit and a fine restaurant.

Return to Jaffa Road and turn right. Cross the intersection of King George and Strauss streets (a rare example of a *six*-way pedestrian crossing) and keep going. Six hundred yards farther up Jaffa Road, on your left just beyond the high-rise Clal Center, is the entrance to the **Machaneh Yehuda** ㊻ produce market. At the opposite end of Machaneh Yehuda is Agrippas Street. Across the street and through an arch is a small, somewhat neglected park in the turn-of-the-century neighborhood of Ohel Moshe, where you can sit under a tree and munch the goodies you've just bought. A left turn on Agrippas Street, on the other hand, brings you down to King George Street and the city center. Bus 9—make sure you take it in the right direction!—will get you in 10 minutes to Givat Rama, site of the Knesset and both the Israel and Bible Lands museums.

To drive there, take the wide, divided Ruppin Road, running west from the tall white condominium complex known as the Wolfson Buildings (on the edge of the Rehavia neighborhood, opposite Sacher Park). Five hundred yards from Sacher Park, at the first traffic light, turn right. The modern, flattop building on the rise to your right is the **Knesset** ㊼, Israel's parliament. The next turn to the right brings you to the security barrier. You may be able to gain entry and let the guards guide you to the parking lot, or simply park on the street before reaching the barrier. City Bus 9 drops you right at the main gate. Note: You will have to produce your passport for identification and will be asked to check your camera before entering the building.

The world-class **Israel Museum** ㊽ was built in 1965 as a series of glass and white-stone pavilions clinging to a 22-acre hilltop across Ruppin Road from the Knesset; Buses 9, 17, and 24 stop here. A shuttle bus for passengers with disabilities makes runs on request from the main gate to the main entrance 200 yards away. The museum's eclectic collection includes the famous Dead Sea Scrolls and extensive fine art exhibits.

The **Bible Lands Museum** ㊾, across the Israel Museum parking lot, is highly recommended for the archaeology buff and the student of ancient cultures.

TIMING

The route can easily be separated into the walk (2–2½ hours, not counting breaks), and the Givat Ram cluster of the Knesset and the two museums. Except for the first part of the route (up to the YMCA), the walk is pointless on Saturday (the Jewish Sabbath), when the downtown area is dead. Friday is great, but shops close early afternoon. You can *view* the Knesset from the outside any time, but there are tours only Sunday and Thursday morning. Allow at least an hour for the tour, more in summer high season when the lines are longer. The museums are closed Friday afternoon and have shorter hours on Saturday. Visiting during their once-a-week evening hours is a time-effective idea. The eclectic Israel Museum demands from two to six hours; the Bible Lands Museum is pure archaeology, conceptually not simple, and is best done with a local guide.

Sights to See

❹❹ Ben Yehuda Street. Part of the downtown triangle formed with King George Street and Jaffa Road, the street is named after Eliezer Ben Yehuda, who in the late 19th century almost single-handedly revived Hebrew as a modern spoken language. Ben Yehuda has become the nerve center of downtown Jerusalem. The decision some years ago to close Ben Yehuda to vehicular traffic was opposed by some local merchants who feared that changing patterns of pedestrian traffic would adversely affect their business. It was true for a few, but most prospered. The mall is called the Midrachov in Hebrew, a combination of *midracha* (sidewalk) and *rechov* (street). Cafés have tables out on the cobblestones, cheap artsy items like funky jewelry and prints are on display, and buskers are everywhere, offering music old and new, good and indifferent. It's a great place to sip coffee and watch the passing crowd.

❹❺ Bet Ticho. This fine, large stone house was built by Dr A. A. Ticho, a renowned early 20th-century ophthalmologist. He married his cousin, Anna, a trained nurse, who had emigrated Eastern Europe to join him in his pioneering struggle against the endemic scourge of trachoma. Her artistic talent gradually established her reputation as a brilliant chronicler—in charcoal, pen, and brush—of the landscape of Jerusalem's hills. Set among pine trees, off the busy downtown streets, Bet Ticho houses a permanent exhibit of Anna Ticho's works and a very good restaurant serving light fare (☞ Dining, *below*). ⊠ *Ticho Lane,* ☎ *02/624–5068.* 🔳 *Free.* ⊙ *Sun.–Thurs. 10–5, Fri. 10–2.*

❹❾ Bible Lands Museum. The museum's curators have abandoned the traditional method of display, which groups artifacts according to their place of origin (Egyptian, Babylonian, and so on), opting instead for a chronological display. This allows a comparison of objects from the region's different cultures dating from the same period, the better to explore cross-cultural interactions and influences. The museum was the brainchild of Canadian collector Elie Borowski, whose personal collection of ancient artifacts forms its core.

The exhibits cover a time period of more than six millennia, from the prehistoric Neolithic period to that of the Byzantine Empire, and sweep geographically from Afghanistan to Nubia (present-day Sudan). Rare clay vessels, fertility idols, cylinder seals, ivories, and sarcophagi fill the soaring, naturally lit galleries. Look especially for the ancient Egyptian wooden coffin, in a stunning state of preservation. ⊠ *Givat Ram,* ☎ *02/611066.* 🔳 *NIS 20 ($6.70).* ⊙ *Sun.–Tues. and Thurs. 9:30–5:30, Wed. 9:30–9:30 (except Apr.–Oct. and Nov.–Mar. 1:30–9:30), Fri. 9:30–2, Sat. 11–3. Guided tours in English Sun.–Fri. at 10 plus additional tour Wed. at 5:30; no Wed. morning tour Nov.–Mar.*

Hinnom Valley. The valley achieved notoriety in the 7th century BC during the long reign of Menasseh (697–640 BC), son of King Hezekiah. Menasseh was an idolater who "burned his sons as an offering [to the god Moloch] in the valley of the son of Hinnom" (II Chronicles 33). The very name of the valley in Hebrew—Gei Ben Hinnom, contracted to Gehennom or Gehenna—has become a synonym for hell in Hebrew and Yiddish.

At the bend in the valley, below the fortresslike Scottish Church of St. Andrew, Israeli archaeologist Gabriel Barkai discovered in the late 1970s a series of Old Testament–period tombs cut out of the rocky scarp. An unplundered pit came to light that contained "grave goods" like clay vessels and jewelry. The most spectacular finds were two tiny rolled strips of silver designed to be worn around the neck as talismans. When experts finally unrolled the fragile pieces, they discovered the biblical priestly benediction inscribed in the ancient Hebrew script: "The Lord bless you and keep you; the Lord cause his face to shine upon you and be gracious unto you; the Lord give you peace." This text dates to the 7th century BC, four centuries earlier than the Dead Sea Scrolls, and is the oldest biblical passage ever found.

Independence Park. Recently relandscaped, this is a lovely spot for lounging around, throwing Frisbees, or eating a picnic lunch in warm weather. It also holds a Muslim cemetery with several well-preserved tombs, dating to the 13th century. A huge reservoir just below the graves, known as the Mamilla Pool, is probably medieval, though it might have even earlier origins.

★ ㊽ **Israel Museum.** Some of the museum's exhibits, especially the ones devoted to archaeology and Judaica, are among the best of their kind in the world. The most distinctive edifice in the museum complex is the white, domelike Shrine of the Book, which houses the famous **Dead Sea Scrolls,** arguably the most important archaeological find ever made in the region. The first of the 2,000-year-old scrolls was discovered by a Bedouin boy in 1947 in a Judean desert, not far from the Dead Sea. The adventures of these priceless artifacts before they finally came to rest here is the stuff of which Indiana Jones movies are made (☞ Dead Sea Region *in* Chapter 3). The dome of the pavilion in which they are housed was inspired by the shape of the lids of the clay jars in which the first scrolls were found.

The scrolls were written in the Second Temple period by a fundamentalist Jewish sect generally identified as the Essenes. All the archaeological, laboratory, and textual evidence dates the earliest of the scrolls to the late 3rd or early 2nd century BC; none could have been written later than AD 68, the year in which their home community of Qumran was destroyed by the Romans. Written on parchment and in an extraordinary state of preservation because of the exceptional dryness of the Dead Sea region, the scrolls include the oldest Hebrew manuscripts of the Old Testament ever found, authenticating the almost identical Hebrew texts still in use today. Sectarian literature includes "The Rule of the Community" (also known as "The Manual of Discipline"), a constitution of this ascetic group, and "The War of the Sons of Light Against the Sons of Darkness," a blow-by-blow account of a final cataclysmic conflict that would, they believed, presage the messianic age.

The entrance corridor to the Shrine of the Book displays parchment and papyrus letters and documents of a slightly later period, the Bar Kochba Revolt of AD 132–135. With the collapse of the revolt, Jews fled the Roman legionnaires to remote caves in sheer desert canyons, taking with them their most prized possessions, including legal documents such as land deeds and marriage contracts. In the basement of the main hall are some of the objects the Jews escaped with to the desert, among them woolen blankets, prayer shawls, and a glass bowl of stunning perfection, regarded by scholars as one of the finest ever found in the ancient world.

Next to the shrine is the open-air **Billy Rose Sculpture Garden,** donated by the American impresario and designed by the artist Isamu Noguchi as a series of semicircular terraces divided by stone walls. Crunch over the gravel amid works by Daumier, Rodin, Maillol, Moore, Lipchitz, Nadelman, and Picasso, among many others, all seen against a Judean Hills cityscape. It's an art lover's dream setting for a picnic.

In the main building, the **Judaica** section, part of the Jewish Heritage collection, has perhaps the world's greatest collection of Jewish ceremonial art and artifacts. Among the highlights are medieval illuminated Haggadot (Passover texts) and wedding contracts, a huge collection of Sabbath spice boxes and Hanukkah menorahs, the interior of a 17th-century Venetian synagogue brought here virtually intact, and a reconstructed 19th-century German sukkah, a temporary booth associated with the holiday of Sukkoth (mentioned in Tabernacles), decorated inside with stylized scenes of Jerusalem. Recently installed is the almost complete 16th-century Kadavumbagam Synagogue, which served the ancient but now defunct Jewish community of Cochin in India.

Ethnographic exhibits, including dazzling formal costumes and jewelry and everyday objects used in Jewish communities throughout the Middle East, North Africa, and Eastern Europe, separate the Judaica collection from the now much-expanded fine arts section. A modest but good-quality collection of European art includes paintings by Van Dyck, Monet, van Gogh, and Renoir. Period rooms reflecting 18th- and 19th-century European design are an unexpected presence. Most recently opened is the adjacent **Cummings 20th-Century Art Building,** dedicated to modern and contemporary art, from Cézanne, Picasso, and Chagall to Dubuffet, Rothko, and Lipchitz.

The **archaeology wing** in the main building boasts a lucid exhibit of finds made in Israel (and some from elsewhere in the Near East). Visitors are often surprised by Israel's unexpected *pre*-history. Israel lies on the only land bridge between Africa and Asia, and the wealth of important prehistoric finds from across the country on display here is evidence of movement and settlement across it in the misty past. For many visitors, however, the focal point is the biblical (Old Testament) period. Pots from the time of Abraham, a Solomonic gateway, and inscriptions from Isaiah's day are just some of the many artifacts that help to illuminate and add a sense of immediacy to the history of this ancient land. A side hall displays a superb collection of glass, from rainbow-patinated Roman pieces to sleek art deco objects.

There's also a **youth wing,** where delightful hands-on exhibits and workshops encourage children to appreciate art—and a changing variety of other subjects—and try their hand in a do-it-yourself craft workshop. Parents with restless children will be grateful for the outdoor play areas. ⊠ *Givat Ram,* ☎ *02/708873, 708811.* ⊠ *NIS 22 ($7.40).* ☉ *Sun.–Mon. and Wed.–Thurs. 10–5; Tues. 4–10 (Shrine of the Book Tues. 10–10); Fri. 10–2; Sat. 10–4. Many free tours offered; call ahead for details.*

42 **King David Street.** The famous **King David Hotel** (⊠ 23 King David St.; ☞ Lodging, *below*) was built in 1931 as the country's premier hotel and is one of the most luxurious in the Middle East. Its guest book boasts most of the heads of state and other international personalities who have passed through Jerusalem. The interior columns and ceilings were decorated in a style that the artist claimed was representative of the spirit of the ancient Near East—Mesopotamian motifs, to coin a phrase.

The hotel acquired a degree of notoriety in the 1940s as the British military headquarters in Jerusalem in the twilight of the British Mandate. Great Britain had governed Palestine since conquering it from Ottoman Turkey in 1918. In 1939, Britain issued the "White Paper," which severely restricted Jewish immigration (when European Jews were already being persecuted by the Nazis) and banned Jewish land purchases in the country. Despite the outcry this produced, the Palestinian Jewish community (the *Yishuv*) put its opposition to the British on hold when World War II broke out and joined ranks with Allied forces. When the war ended and the hoped-for British support for the Jewish state (as envisioned by the League of Nations back in 1922) failed to materialize, the Jewish underground became active again. The radical Irgun blew up the south wing of the King David Hotel as a military target in July 1946, with considerable loss of life. The Irgun's claim that its advance warning to evacuate the building was ignored by the British is still a matter of controversy. The wing was rebuilt and two extra floors added in the 1950s.

The Jerusalem **YMCA** (⊠ 26 King David St.; ☞ Lodging, *below*) was dedicated in 1933. Its almost palatial white-limestone facade and high, domed bell tower often surprise visitors who associate modest buildings and sport facilities with that international organization. The Y has those, too, of course—as well as an auditorium with excellent acoustics, built with a Levantine-inspired dome and decorative motifs. The tower, serviced by a small elevator, is 150 feet high, giving superb views in all directions; you can take a ride Monday through Saturday between 9:30 and 5 for NIS 2 (70¢).

NEED A BREAK?
The **King David Hotel coffee shop** (⊠ 23 King David St.) is not cheap, but it offers the best cheese blintzes (crepes) around. In good weather, the ambience of the garden patio with a view of the Old City walls is unbeatable. For cold beer and a snack, take a seat on the **YMCA patio** (⊠ 26 King David St.), across the street from the King David.

④⑦ Knesset. Both the name Knesset and the number of seats (120) in this one-chamber assembly were taken from Haknesset Hagedolah, the Great Assembly of the Second Temple period. Visitors may see the building only on a 40-minute guided tour, conducted on Sunday and Thursday, which includes the Knesset session hall and the reception hall with its three enormous, brilliantly colored tapestries designed by artist Marc Chagall on the themes of the Creation, the Exodus, and Jerusalem. On the other days, you can attend open sessions of the Knesset (in Hebrew, of course); call ahead for the session schedule.

"Take two Israelis," runs the old quip, "and you've got three political parties!" The saying is not without truth in a nation where everyone has an opinion and will usually not hesitate to express it. The Knesset reflects this rambunctious spirit, sometimes to the point of despair. Israel's electoral system, known as proportional representation, is a legacy of the dangerous but heady days of Israel's War of Independence in 1948–49. To avoid an acrimonious and divisive election while the fledgling state was still fighting to stay alive, the founding fathers developed a one-body parliamentary system that gave representation to rival ideological factions in proportion to their comparative strength in the country's *pre*-State institutions.

Instead of the winner-takes-all approach of the constituency system, the Israeli system grants any party that wins 1.5% of the *national* vote its first seat in the Knesset. As a result, even fringe parties can have their voices heard. The disadvantage of this system is it spawns a plethora of political parties, making it virtually impossible for one party to get the majority needed to govern. Israeli governments have thus always consisted of a coalition of parties, often a government of compromise. The smaller parties, whose support is critical for the government to keep its ruling majority, have thus been able to extract major political and material concessions for their own party interests, which are often at odds with those of the nation at large. Extensive discussion, public campaigns, demonstrations, and even proposed legislation to change the system have produced one important result. As of the 1996 general elections, the prime minister is no longer simply the leader of a victorious large party, but is elected directly by the voters. Potentially this could produce a deadlock where the successful candidate for prime minister fails to win a parliamentary majority for his party. Already it has produced the unexpected result of strengthening the smaller parties at the expense of the big ones.

Across the road from the Knesset main gate is a 15-foot-high bronze menorah, a seven-branched candelabra, based on the one that once graced the First and Second Temples in Jerusalem, and now the official symbol of the State of Israel. Designed by artist Bruno Elkin and a gift of the British Parliament to the Knesset in 1956, the menorah is decorated with bas-relief depictions of events and personages in Jewish history from biblical times to the modern day. Behind the menorah (enter below the security barrier) is the Wohl Rose Garden, filled with dozens of varieties of roses and plenty of lawns for children to romp on. ⊠ *Givat Ram,* ☎ *02/675–3333.* ▭ *Free.* ☉ *Guided tours Sun. and Thurs. 8:30–2.*

46 **Machaneh Yehuda.** This block-long alley is filled with the brilliant colors of the city's best-quality fruit and vegetables, pickles and cheeses, fresh fish and poultry, and confection stalls and falafel stands. It's riotously busy, especially on Thursday and Friday, when Jewish Jerusalem shops for the Sabbath. ☉ *Sun.–Tues. about 8 AM–sunset (open later on Wed. and Thurs.), Fri. and holiday eve 8–2 hrs before sunset.*

Mishkenot She'ananim. The first neighborhood settlement outside the walls of Jerusalem was built by Moses Montefiore in 1860 with funds donated by the New Orleans philanthropist Yehuda Tura. The idea was to offer small apartments rent-free to destitute Jews who were prepared to abandon the wretched conditions of the Jewish Quarter and begin a new life. People did not rush to the new project at first, for however dismal conditions were within the walls, at least the city gates were shut at night to keep bandits and beasts at bay. Today this splendidly renovated property, with balconies that face the Old City walls, is run by the city-connected Jerusalem Foundation as a retreat for visiting writers, musicians, and artists. ⊠ *Yemin Moshe.*

41 **Montefiore's Windmill.** Moses Montefiore was a prominent and wealthy Jew in the financial circles of 19th-century London, a rare phenomenon at the time. He devoted much of his long life to aiding fellow Jews in distress, wherever they might be. To this end he visited Palestine (as this district of the Ottoman Empire was then known) seven times. The windmill was built in 1857 to provide a source of income for Jews in the new planned neighborhood of Mishkenot She'ananim (☞ *above*), but its location in relation to the prevailing winds was less than brilliant. In any event, the windmill was soon superseded by new-fangled steam-driven rivals. The narrow interior of the attractive, tapered limestone structure has a small photographic exhibit on Montefiore's life and works. ⊠ *Yemin Moshe,* ☎ *02/625–4321.* ▭ *Free.* ☉ *Sun.–Thurs. 10–4, Fri. 10–1.*

❹❸ **Nahalat Shiva.** The name roughly translates as "the Estate of the Seven," for the seven Jewish families that formed an association and established the neighborhood—only the second outside the Old City walls—in 1869. Defying both physical and bureaucratic hostility, they persevered and determined the direction of the growth of the "New City." Salomon Street and its adjacent alleys and courtyards have been renovated as a pedestrian mall and offer the keen photographer and the eager shopper many opportunities. The neighborhood has a profusion of snack and lunch options.

Yemin Moshe. The core of this now-affluent neighborhood is the turn-of-the-century buildings that in the '50s and '60s had become an immigrant slum and were dangerously near the Jordanian sniper positions on the Old City walls across the valley. The reunification of the city after the 1967 Six-Day War changed all that. Developers bought up the area, renovated the old, and built new spacious homes in a compatible style. It's a place to wander in at random. Several artists' galleries are well signposted, the well-known Mishkenot She'ananim French-style restaurant (not part of the original complex) is on your right as you descend the stepped Yemin Moshe Street, and at the southern end of the guest house is a pleasant patio café.

OFF THE
BEATEN PATH

HAAS PROMENADE – Taking in the panorama of Jerusalem from this 1 km (½ mi) promenade is a great way to get your bearings. You'll see the turret of the United Nations Headquarters, once the residence of the British high commissioner for Palestine, crowning one of the highest points in the city. The ridge on which it sits is known in Hebrew as Armon Hanatziv (the Commissioner's Palace). Quite a bit of West Jerusalem is visible off to your left, the downtown area easily distinguished by its high-rises. The Old City, identified by the walls and golden Dome of the Rock, is directly in front of you. To the right of it is the ridge of Mt. Scopus–Mount of Olives, with its three towers (from left to right: Hebrew University, Augusta Victoria Hospital, Russian Church of the Ascension), separated from the Old City by the deep Kidron Valley. Between the Kidron Valley on the east and the Cheesemakers' Valley (now just an asphalt road) on the west is a blade-shape strip of land that Jerusalem occupied for its first 2,000 years—the City of David. To get here, drive south along Hebron Road. About 1¼ km (¾ mi) beyond the Ariel Hotel is a police compound on your left known as the Allenby Camp. Turn left at the next traffic light, following signs to East Talpiot and the Haas Promenade. The parking lot is on the left.

DINING

A brief glossary of restaurant and cooking terms will help you appreciate some of the pleasures of eating out in Jerusalem. When used in reference to food, the word *Oriental* (the translation of the Hebrew *mizrachi*—"eastern") means Middle Eastern cuisine, *not* Far Eastern (such as Chinese, Japanese, or Thai). Dairy restaurants are simply those establishments serving meals without meat; many places serve fish as well. Hummus, one of the ubiquitous dishes in the region, is a creamy paste made from chick-peas, moistened with olive oil and often tahini (a ground sesame–based sauce), and scooped up with pieces of flat pita bread. Eat it at a place that specializes in Middle Eastern dishes; many "Western" establishments serve only a poor imitation. Also look for a Kurdish/Iraqi specialty called *koubeh*, seasoned ground meat formed into small torpedo shapes and deep-fried in a jacket of bulgur (cracked wheat).

Falafel, the region's fast food, consists of deep-fried chickpea balls served in pita pockets and topped by a variety of salads. It is filling, nutritious, and cheap (about NIS 7, or $2.40, for a full portion). About twice that price is *shwarma,* grilled slices of meat (traditionally lamb, but today more commonly turkey) similarly served in pita bread with salads. Both falafel and shwarma are sold at stands; try King George Street, the Ben Yehuda Street open-air mall, the area of the Machaneh Yehuda produce market, or the good cluster of fast-food places on Emek Refa'im Street at the corner of Rachel Imenu, in the German Colony neighborhood. A specialty of the grills at Machaneh Yehuda, on Agrippas Street, is *me'oorav yerushalmi* (Jerusalem mixed grill), a deliciously seasoned meal-in-a-pita of grilled chicken hearts and other organ meats. It's a popular stop after the movies let out.

Dress codes are pretty much nonexistent in Jerusalem's restaurants (or in Israel in general, for that matter). People tend to dress very casually, and jeans would not be inappropriate in most places. The only exceptions might be some of the fancier establishments at deluxe hotels. Even then it's only a matter of degree: Informal dress is quite proper, but a modicum of neatness would be expected. Still, if you have taken the trouble to bring your dressy duds, you will not be out of place so dressed in the more exclusive Jerusalem restaurants. Remember that kosher restaurants will be closed for Friday dinner and Saturday lunch because of the Jewish Sabbath.

CATEGORY	COST*
$$$$	over $35
$$$	$22–$35
$$	$12–$22
$	under $12

per person for a three-course meal, excluding drinks and 10% service charge

Chinese

$$ ✕ Mandarin. This veteran establishment with a cook from Beijing is in an unpretentious second-story location in the heart of the downtown New City. Frosted windows with Chinese motifs keep the sights and sounds of the city at bay, and some decor—a mural of misty mountains, for example—gives a suggestion of what the place is. The food is good, if not exciting; particularly recommended are the fish in ginger and green onions and the beef in oyster sauce. ⊠ *2 Shlomzion Hamalka St.,* ☎ *02/625–2890. AE, DC, MC, V.*

$$ ✕ Sini Ba-Moshava (Chinese Colony). An old stone house with a pleasant courtyard for outside dining holds a restaurant, better known to the locals by its Hebrew name. The owners are a Taiwanese couple: The utterly charming wife runs the dining area while the husband cooks with a sure and creative hand. The crispness of the food—the spring rolls are a good example—testifies to the fact that all dishes are made on the spot. The hot-and-sour soup is excellent; the oxtail soup—a local rarity—is fantastic. The usual long list of main dishes includes duck, chicken, beef, pork, and shrimp, but each dish has its own character, some strong, some more subtle. The slices of meat are thin and tender, the sweet-and-sour chicken (despite the lurid red sauce) is as good as you'll find anywhere, and the unusual beef in chili-garlic sauce is worth trying. ⊠ *48 Emek Refaim St.,* ☎ *02/567–1788. AE, DC, MC, V.*

Eastern European

$$ ✕ **Europa.** The atmosphere is homey and the value good at this unpretentious eatery overlooking Zion Square. Traditional Eastern European Jewish cooking is represented by an excellent gefilte fish and the meat strudel, but the menu's main inspiration is Hungarian. Try schnitzel stuffed with smoked goose; roast goose; stuffed chicken; and goulash soup. A dessert of sweet apple strudel or *palacsinta* (a sweet almond crepe with chocolate sauce) is de rigueur. ⊠ *42 Jaffa Rd., 2nd floor,* ☎ *02/625–8953. DC, MC, V. No dinner Fri. Closed Sat.*

French

$$$$ ✕ **Cow on the Roof.** Impeccable service, and the superb homemade rolls and complimentary tiny appetizer of baked salmon, immediately produce a sense of occasion at the Sheraton Jerusalem Plaza's gourmet restaurant (named after the Chagall painting; a reproduction hangs in the bar). Dining niches and comfortable Louis XV–style high-back chairs add a pleasing salon intimacy. Chef Shalom Kadosh earned his reputation by successfully meeting the challenge of preparing fine traditional dishes despite kosher culinary rules. A recommended appetizer is the napoleon of veal and sweetbreads with eggplant and shitaki mushrooms in a tomato and pepper sauce. For entrées, the steaks are excellent, but the standout is a fillet of red drumfish with eggplant confit. The results are not universally successful—some sauces are a bit heavy-handed, and not all the desserts live up to their visual promise. ⊠ *Sheraton Jerusalem Plaza Hotel, 47 King George St.,* ☎ *02/625–9111. Reservations essential. AE, DC, MC, V. Closed Fri. No lunch Sat.*

$$$–$$$$ ✕ **Le Chateau.** A welcome newcomer in a recently built small stone
★ edifice offers the ambience of a castle amid the greenery and Old World feeling of the Ein Kerem neighborhood. Imagination characterizes the menu, and pride in top-quality ingredients shows in the results. The foie gras, either with cranberries or with a vinaigrette of port wine, thyme, and balsamic vinegar, is sublimely creamy. Among the wide choice of meat, fish, and seafood, try the superb aged fillet steaks and the mussels in a butter-and-herb sauce. Ask about specials not on the menu. Desserts are good but unmemorable. ⊠ *74 Ein Kerem,* ☎ *02/641– 5939. Reservations essential on weekends. AE, DC, MC, V.*

$$$ ✕ **Cézanne.** Housed in a fine old flagstone-floored building, Cézanne has a hearth for the cold and a rear courtyard used in warm weather. These features, along with the art gallery that shares its premises, produce an atmosphere of which the great artist himself might have approved. For starters, try veal brains in a lemon-and-caper sauce, or the excellent salmon carpaccio. There are good steaks with a choice of sauces, but especially recommended are the tender lamb chops, accompanied by a tasty bouquet of braised vegetables. An attractive feature is the Chef's Menu, offering a good three-course meal (with several choices of items) for $20–$25. ⊠ *Artists' House, 12 Shmuel Hanagid St.,* ☎ *02/625–9459. AE, DC, MC, V.*

$$$ ✕ **Chez Simon.** The cooking at this venerable restaurant right downtown is French style filtered through colonial French North African cuisine, with a Moroccan influence especially evident in the appetizers. There are complimentary starters for diners ordering a full dinner, and a salad comes with the main course. Now that the restaurant is kosher, the shrimps are imitation and the *cordon bleu* is cheeseless, but some items are still good. Try the veal *piccata* (in lemon sauce) or the steak Rossini (or, for that matter, any of the other fillet steaks). The owner, Asher, gives Fodor's readers an unrestricted choice of appetizer, main course, and dessert for $27 if they're carrying this book; call ahead to make sure the deal is still on. ⊠ *15 Shammai St., 2nd floor,* ☎ *02/625–5602. AE, DC, MC, V. No dinner Fri., no lunch Sat.*

Grills

$$–$$$ ✕ **El Gaucho.** Red meat is the thing at this Argentine grill in the Nahalat Shiva neighborhood. Housed in a stone building with interior arches and a flagstone floor, El Gaucho adds rustic wooden tables, lattice screens, and artifacts from the Argentinian pampas. Munch an excellent beef empanada while you wait for your steak. Best are the steak entrecôte and the steak chorizo (no relation to the sausage of the same name, also available) with a parsley-based *chimichurri* (herbs with olive oil and vinegar) sauce. The grilled udders and innards are definitely an acquired taste. There is a children's menu and a couple of fish dishes for noncarnivores. ⊠ *22 Rivlin St.,* ☎ *02/624–2227. AE, DC, MC, V. Closed Fri. No lunch Sat.*

$$ ✕ **Gilly's.** This small restaurant at the southern end of Salomon Street in Nahalat Shiva exploded onto the scene a number of years ago with a reputation for excellent steaks at reasonable prices. Unfortunately, popularity and the attendant crowds have taken their toll on the standard of service. It's still a good value but try to avoid it on weekends. You can go with the more common pepper and barbecue sauces or smother your sirloin with the more stylish brandy cream sauce. ⊠ *33 Hillel St. at Salomon St.,* ☎ *02/625–5955. Reservations not accepted. No credit cards. Closed Sun.*

$ ✕ **Burger Ranch.** It's a fast-food place, pure and simple, with the expected variety of hamburgers, hot dogs, chicken combinations, and french fries (known in Israel as chips). The quality is good, but prices are often higher than the equivalent back home. ⊠ *16 King George St.,* ☎ *02/623–3766;* ⊠ *43 Emek Refa'im St.,* ☎ *02/666–2318. MC, V. No dinner Fri., no lunch Sat.*

Italian

$$$ ✕ **Spaghettim.** Tucked away on a side street off one of the downtown arteries is a nonkosher restaurant with a courtyard that's filled with tables in summer. In all seasons the spare but attractive decor welcomes you into an old stone building, tastefully painted in pastel neutrals. Although it's popular among the young set, you can also take the family without breaking the bank. Sauces are grouped in three categories: tomato-, oil-, and cream-based. The *bolognese* sauce is ordinary, but the *arrabbiata* (fiery chili pepper–flavored tomato sauce) is good; the smoked salmon (with optional asparagus), delicious; and the fresh mushrooms (with optional bacon), sublime. Some oil-based sauces tend to be quite spicy. The pasta portions are generous, and two youngsters can easily share one. Friendly and efficient service adds the final welcoming touch. Spaghettim has a no-smoking section. ⊠ *8 Rabbi Akiva St.,* ☎ *02/623–5547 or 02/623–5548. AE, DC, MC, V.*

$$$ ✕ **Valentino's.** The Hyatt Regency opted for a dairy-fish-vegetarian menu in its kosher Italian restaurant. An attractive booth allows diners to see the making and cooking of the house pastas; in fact, the chef prides himself on serving *no* precooked food. Appetizers are unexceptional, but soups are excellent; the fisherman's soup is particularly outstanding. Pasta sauces are equally fine: Try the rigatoni Romano, with mushroom-and-sage cream sauce, and the fettuccine *primavera* tossed with market vegetables. The pièce de résistance is the perfectly grilled sea bass steak, served with a sauce of tomatoes, pine nuts, garlic, and fresh herbs. Desserts are good and inexpensive. A less expensive fixed-price menu is also available. Service is attentive and the atmosphere congenial, but neither the decor nor the piped music adds anything to the character of the place. ⊠ *Hyatt Regency Hotel, 32 Lehi St.,* ☎ *02/533–1234. AE, DC, MC, V. No dinner Fri., no lunch Sat.*

$$ ✕ **Little Italy.** This meatless Italian restaurant is in the center of the King
★   David–Radisson Moriah–Laromme axis of near-downtown hotels, which would probably ensure its popularity even if the food were not as good as it is. New York–trained chef-owner Avi Elkayam creates dishes with flair. The antipasti *misto* (mixed antipasto) is a subtle sonata of tastes and textures. Among the tempting fish-and-pasta combinations, try the fettuccine with fresh salmon, prepared in white wine with fresh mushrooms and herbs. For more conventional fare, there is an extensive variety of very good pizza. Try the homemade gelati. The decor is pleasant but not memorable. ⊠ *38 Keren Hayesod St.,* ☎ *02/561–7638. AE, DC, MC, V. No dinner Fri., no lunch Sat.*

$$ ✕ **Mamma Mia.** A nicely renovated old stone building with a shady courtyard for outside dining is the setting for a restaurant that virtually pioneered the concept of vegetarian Italian food in Jerusalem. For an appetizer, try focaccia with *insalata alla siciliana* (salad of tomato and grated mild feta with a basil dressing). The cannelloni entrées—especially with salmon—are superb, as is the lasagna, or choose from the wide selection of pizza. All pasta is homemade. A refreshing summer offering is spaghetti primavera, with an uncooked sauce of tomatoes, olive oil, and garlic. ⊠ *38 King George St., behind parking lot,* ☎ *02/624–8080. AE, DC, MC, V. No dinner Fri., no lunch Sat.*

Mediterranean

$$$$ ✕ **Ocean.** Chef-owner Eyal Shani prides himself on the quality, and often
★   rarity, of the ingredients on his constantly changing menus, providing a leisurely dining experience with appealing visual aesthetics and subtle flavors . . . and a bill worthy of such a meal (main courses run $36–$40 apiece, with few side dishes included). Two methods of preparing fish are particularly unusual: baked in a *taboon,* a closed earth oven, and grilled over glowing chips of citrus wood. This may be the only place in Jerusalem that serves lobster. Seafood is still the restaurant's main calling card, but several fine lamb dishes have broadened its own self-image and appeal. The desserts don't justify their price. Portions are fashionably small, but the management claims it will serve you seconds rather than have you leave unsatisfied. The restaurant occupies a fine old stone building in Nahalat Shiva; the drawback of its attractive vaulted ceiling and color floor tiles is the noise. ⊠ *7 Rivlin St., opposite Independence Park,* ☎ *02/624–7501. AE, DC, MC, V.*

Mexican

$$–$$$ ✕ **Amigos.** Mexican restaurants are a rarity in Israel, but this one—on the Nahalat Shiva pedestrian mall—would stand proud even in North America. There are sidewalk tables in good weather, and in the evenings the waiters serve to the beat of recorded Latin American music. Sip an arctic-cold margarita (lemon, strawberry, mango, or melon) while you discuss the menu with one of the owners ("If you don't like the food, you don't pay!"). Along with the expected list of burritos and chili con carne (as well as several vegetarian options) are fajitas, the house specialty, a sizzling combination of grilled slices of beef, chicken, and vegetables served with warm tortillas, refried beans, and guacamole (when avocados are in season). There's a $10 lunch menu, and an even cheaper sandwich option. ⊠ *19 Salomon St.,* ☎ *02/623–4177. AE, DC, MC, V. No dinner Fri., no lunch Sat.*

Middle Eastern

$$–$$$ ✕ **Eucalyptus.** The yesteryear traditional cooking of the "Land of Is-
rael" has aroused the passion of owner Moshe Basson, who has ram-
bled across the country quizzing old-timers and searching for wild greens
that few people use anymore. The result is an intriguing experience for
adventurous palates—though there's good, more typical Middle Eastern fare as well. For appetizers, try the unusual (but salty) mixture of
sabanach ("Arab spinach") with *postulaka* or *hobeiza* greens (depending on season) and either the koubeh or almond soup. Stuffed leaves
(grape, cyclamen, and many others) come in both meat and vegetarian versions. Especially recommended among the meat dishes is the mous-
saka, baby eggplants baked with a filling of well-seasoned ground
meat. Collections of early 20th-century artifacts, both rural and urban,
enhance the comfortable atmosphere. ✉ *7 Horkanos St.,* ☎ *02/624–
4331. AE, DC, MC, V. No dinner Fri., no lunch Sat.*

$$ ✕ **Ima.** It's pronounced ee-maah, means "mom," and is named for
Miriam, the owner's Kurdish mother, who still does all the cooking.
This restaurant at the bottom of the Nahla'ot neighborhood, opposite
Sacher Park, serves traditional—and plentiful—Middle Eastern food
that's very good. First courses include a modest *meze* (appetizers) of
some half-dozen salads, such as hummus and *baba ghanoush* (a dip
of eggplant and tahini), as well as the excellent koubeh and stuffed vine
leaves. Try the tangy koubeh soup, full of dumplings: It is almost a meal
in itself. The entrée, which could be *shishlik*, kebabs, or Jerusalem mixed
grill, is accompanied by *majadra* (rice and lentils). ✉ *189 Agrippas St.,*
☎ *02/624–6860. AE, DC, MC, V. No dinner Fri. Closed Sat.*

$–$$ ✕ **Armenian Tavern.** The onetime cistern with medieval arches, a floor
below street level, has been redecorated with fine Armenian wall tiles,
a fountain, wooden furniture, and old-style chandeliers. Good choices
for appetizers are the excellent koubeh; and the *lachmajun*, so-called
Armenian pizza, made with meat and served like a crepe. The best homemade salad is the tahini; some others are blander than the standard
Arab equivalents. The most distinctive entrée is the *khaghoghi* (pronounced cha-ror-i) *derev*, vine leaves wrapped around well-flavored
ground beef. Both the baklava and the coffee (don't call it *Turkish* coffee here!) are first class. ✉ *79 Armenian Patriarchate Rd., Old City,
inside Jaffa Gate,* ☎ *02/627–3854. AE, DC, MC, V. Closed Mon.*

$–$$ ✕ **Mifgash Ha'esh.** Here's a good example of the wisdom of eating where
the locals eat. When the restaurant opened a few years ago in the
Romema industrial zone behind the Central Bus Station, its almost instant reputation for good food and good value began attracting
Jerusalemites from farther afield—and even the occasional tourist.
Customers flock to this eatery for the skewers of grilled meat and for
the house specialty, succulent grilled pieces of marinated chicken. Appetizers include unusually good hummus and koubeh. ✉ *23 Yirmiyahu
St., Romema,* ☎ *02/538–8888 or 02/528–8889. Reservations not accepted. AE, DC, MC, V. No dinner Fri., no lunch Sat.*

Mixed Menu

$$ ✕ **Le Tsriff.** This very Jerusalemite restaurant, on a downtown back street,
★ has a slightly funky, very congenial character. It has cultivated a faith-
ful local clientele, from students to celebrities, establishing its reputa-
tion on savory pies encased in terrific crusts: chicken with nuts and
raisins; veal and prunes; shrimp; and vegetables such as mushrooms,
broccoli, and cauliflower. Pies, soups, and salads are still good, but spe-
cialties now include succulent grilled salmon and scallops, a lovely Roque-
fort sauce to embellish your tender fillet, and delectable shrimps in
tarragon sauce. For starters, try the hot breaded goat cheese and sun-

Jerusalem Dining and Lodging

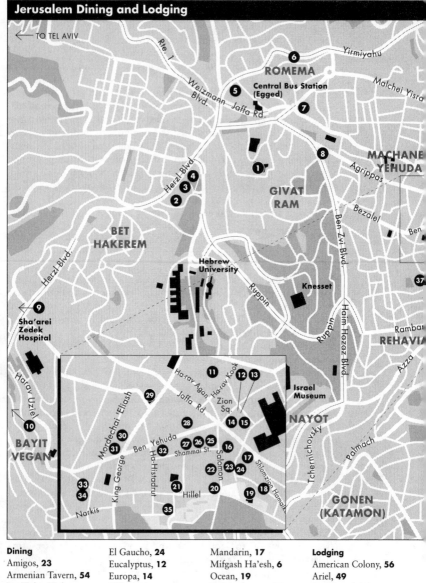

Dining
Amigos, **23**
Armenian Tavern, **54**
Bet Ticho (Ticho House), **11**
Burger Ranch, **31, 52**
Cézanne, **34**
Chez Simon, **27**
Cow on the Roof, **36**
Dag Le Dag, **18**
Darna, **15**

El Gaucho, **24**
Eucalyptus, **12**
Europa, **14**
Gilly's, **20**
Ima, **8**
La Brasa, **16**
Le Chateau, **9**
Le Tsriff, **13, 41**
Little Italy, **45**
Mamma Mia, **37**

Mandarin, **17**
Mifgash Ha'esh, **6**
Ocean, **19**
Off the Square, **22**
Sini Ba-Moshava, **51**
Spaghettim, **35**
Te'enim, **50**
Valentino's, **33**
Village Green, **33**

Lodging
American Colony, **56**
Ariel, **49**
Bet Shmuel, **39**
Caesar, **7**
Christ Church, **55**
Eyal, **26**

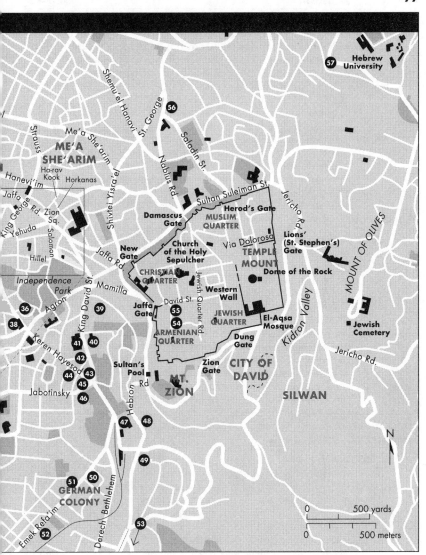

Four Points
Jerusalem, **3**
Holiday Inn Crowne
Plaza, **1**
Hyatt Regency, **57**
Jerusalem Gate, **5**
Jerusalem Inn, **32**
Jerusalem Tower, **21**
Kikar Zion, **25**

King David, **40**
King Solomon, **43**
Kings, **38**
Laromme, **46**
Lev Yerushalayim, **30**
Louise
Waterman-Wise, **10**

Mount Zion, **48**
Palatin, **29**
Park Plaza, **4**
Radisson Moriah
Plaza, **42**
Ramat Rachel, **53**

Renaissance
Jerusalem, **2**
Scottish Hospice, **47**
Sheraton Jerusalem
Plaza, **36**
Windmill, **44**
YMCA (West), **41**
Zion, **28**

dried red peppers or the fine salmon carpaccio. Le Tsriff's second location, in the more formal YMCA (West), has a very similar menu but with this difference: Instead of ordering appetizers à la carte, you automatically receive a wide selection (with bread and mineral water), adding NIS 15 ($5) to the price of the entrées. ⊠ *5 Horkonos St.,* ☎ *02/625–5488 or 02/624–2478;* ⊠ *YMCA (West), 26 King David St.,* ☎ *02/625–7111 or 02/625–3433. AE, DC, MC, V.*

$ ✕ **La Brasa.** This unassuming eatery on the Salomon Street mall, near Zion Square, specializes in grilled chicken but offers other inexpensive options as well. Its prices have gone up a bit, but you can still fill up for under $10, a feature that draws a young, budget-conscious crowd. You can take to the street in good weather at its outdoor tables. ⊠ *7 Salomon St.,* ☎ *02/623–1456. Reservations not accepted. AE, DC, MC, V. No dinner Fri., no lunch Sat.*

Moroccan

$$$$ ✕ **Darna.** In an era of peace, the Moroccan-born owners wanted to re-create the "real" Morocco. The results are delightful: A vaulted beige-painted tunnel deposits you in a corner of Morocco, with an asymmetrical arrangement of different-size rooms, round stone arches, and decorative motifs of wood and copper, pottery, brass, and fabrics. Order à la carte; the set menu is overpriced. The *harira hamra,* a winter meat-and-barley soup redolent of coriander, is great, as is the selection of salads, so different from the local Arabic mezes. Another excellent starter is *pastilla,* thin phyllo pastry stuffed with almonds, cinnamon and Cornish hen; there is a vegetarian version. The couscous is competent, and the various *tagines,* or Moroccan stews, are very good. End the meal with refreshing sweet mint tea and skip the unexceptional desserts. ⊠ *3 Horkonos St.,* ☎ *02/624–5406. DC, MC, V. Closed Fri. No lunch Sat.*

Seafood

$$$ ✕ **Dag Le Dag.** The owners' maxim seems to be seems to be: "Thou shall not leave here hungry." For appetizers, there's a good-value selection of superfresh Middle Eastern salads. Shrimps, mussels, and calamari can be ordered as a first course or an entrée, either cooked simply or with a choice of several nicely blended sauces. Fish selections change with the season, but justly popular are the grouper (known locally as *lokus*), salmon, trout, and larger-than-usual St. Peter's fish (*tilapia*). The restaurant's single long room is short on ambience, but at press time, more atmospheric decor was being planned. ⊠ *14 Shlomzion Hamalka St.,* ☎ *02/625–6278. AE, DC, MC, V.*

Vegetarian and Fish

$$–$$$ ✕ **Bet Ticho (Ticho House).** This is one of downtown Jerusalem's loveli-
★   est and most tranquil nooks. The imposing stone building was built in the 1920s as the home and office of the famous ophthalmologist A. A. Ticho and his even more famous wife, artist Anna Ticho, whose evocative drawings of Jerusalem adorn the place. The lobby and patio of the house (now a national monument) have been turned into a fine restaurant for light meals. House specialties include Anat's salad (an intriguing mix of pasta, soy sauce, fresh mushrooms, cherry tomatoes, and sunflower seeds), salmon paté, fish in fresh ginger sauce, and a light, utterly indulgent ice-cream cake. On Tuesday nights, the restaurant has a wine-and-cheese buffet, to be enjoyed to the sounds of a jazz combo (reservations needed). There is usually a classical chamber music performance on Friday at 11 AM. In good weather, angle for a table on the

patio. ⊠ *7 Harav Kook St.,* ☎ *02/624–4186. Reservations not accepted for outside tables. AE, DC, MC, V. No dinner Fri., no lunch Sat.*

$$ ✗ **Off the Square.** As in most buildings in Nahalat Shiva, the stone walls and arches create much of the restaurant's ambience. There is a lot of courtyard seating in good weather. The large selection is in keeping with this very big eatery, with the focus on fish, soups, salads, vegetable pies (among them whole-wheat options), and pasta. Particularly good are the salmon, the mushroom soup, and the large menu of excellent desserts. The place is child-friendly; there's lots of room for restless kids, and the menu has half portions of many items and such favorites as pizza. ⊠ *6 Salomon St.,* ☎ *02/624–2549. AE, DC, MC, V. No dinner Fri., no lunch Sat.*

$$ ✗ **Te'enim.** The name means "figs," and if you're a "veggiphile"—let alone a card-carrying vegetarian—the association with the Garden of Eden is inescapable. You aren't coming for the decor, which is done in a pleasant café style; but the chef has crafted an international menu of some originality and many delights. Try the excellent green salad, a jungle of seasonal greens under which lurk slices of goat cheese bedecked with roasted almonds and bits of fruits. Some menu items change daily, others (like the good soups) seasonally as well. Permanent ones are pies and baked potatoes, but try the basil-and-Roquefort quiche. ⊠ *21 Emek Refaim St.,* ☎ *02/563–0048. No credit cards. No dinner Fri. Closed Sat.*

$–$$ ✗ **Village Green.** The two downtown locations of this purely vegetarian restaurant are now both self-service: The Bezalel Street location offers a quiet stone courtyard, while in bustling Ben Yehuda Street you get to people-watch as you eat. There is a good variety of soups, quiches, pies, and very fresh salad vegetables, with a choice of great dressings. Several menu items have three prices: to indicate the item only, with a small salad, or with a large salad. The homemade bread is included, and the dessert pies are worth trying. ⊠ *1 Bezalel St.,* ☎ *02/625–1464;* ⊠ *10 Ben Yehuda St.,* ☎ *02/625–2007. Reservations not accepted. AE, DC, MC, V. No dinner Fri., no lunch Sat.*

Cafés

Coffee and cake in one of Jerusalem's several fine cafés is something of a tradition. The selection of sweets includes the gooey, cream-filled pastries many Israelis favor, more sophisticated cheesecakes and pies, and yeast cakes and strudels, a Central European inheritance.

The downtown Midrachov, the open-air mall of Ben Yehuda Street and its side lanes, has several of the venerable hangouts of an earlier era, but a new generation of cafés offers more interest and better quality. **La Riviera** (⊠ 4 Dorot Rishonim St., ☎ 02/624–8347), specializing in croissants, draws the city's expat French for a taste of home. **Bohlinat** (⊠ 6 Dorot Rishonim St., ☎ 02/624–9733) provides an unrushed atmosphere in which to read your Fodor's over a coffee. The self-service **Aroma** (⊠ 18 Hillel St., ☎ 02/625–5365) is brash, young, and almost never closes. The croissants are good, prices are reasonable, and some claim its coffee is the best in town. **Clafouti** (⊠ 2 Hasoreg St., ☎ 02/623–5817), beyond Zion Square, is a *creperie* with a reputation for great coffee as well.

Conus (⊠ 18 King George St., ☎ 02/625–5317), next to the Hamashbir department store, is the outlet for a local maker of excellent Italian-style ice cream and gelati. **Dalia Renaud's Bistro** (⊠ In the lane off 10 Agrippas St., ☎ 02/625–7647) has a lot of atmosphere—arches and flagstones, genteel personal attention—and superb but very pricey cakes (and light meals). The slightly Bohemian atmosphere and shaded patio seating of **Paradiso** (⌧ 4 Narkis St., ☎ 02/623–6393) makes a particularly attractive refuge from the city bustle; try it for light meals, coffee, and exceptional cakes.

Ye Olde English Tea Room (⌧ At Habustan on Raoul Wallenberg St., off 68 Jaffa Rd., ☎ 02/537–6595), a minute's walk north of the King George–Jaffa Road intersection, occupies a 19th-century stone house with a small art gallery and a shaded courtyard. Its specialty is a delightful selection of teas and coffees served in tastefully selected china and sweet treats from both "Olde England" and "New England" (whence hails the owner). Light meals—not especially cheap—provide additional gastronomic nostalgia for expat Anglos and ex-colonials. There is live music some evenings.

Some neighborhoods, like the **German Colony,** can be good hunting grounds for restaurants and cafés. On summer evenings in particular, these places teem with the young set, and it is worth arriving in mid-evening to beat the after-the-show crowd. For something different, try Nili's sensational Belgian waffles, washed down with hot or cold chocolate, in the hole-in-the-wall **Hachagiga Shel Babette** (⌧ 17 Emek Refaim St., at the bus stop, no sign and no phone).

Jan's (⌧ 20 Marcus St., ☎ 02/561–2054), literally under the plaza of the Sherover (Jerusalem) Theater, is a one-of-a-kind café. You sit or lounge on soft pillows and rugs, with low lights adding to the mysterious atmosphere. The menu isn't very big—ambience is all—but what is served is very good—and not cheap. It's better for romantic assignations than clubby conversation.

LODGING

There are travelers for whom a central location is a priority; others prefer a hotel that's a haven at the end of the day, with ambience more important than accessibility. Jerusalem has more of the first than the second, and even hotels once considered remote are in fact no more than 10 minutes by cab or hotel minibus from the city center. In truth, with only a few exceptions, most hotels are modern establishments with little claim to Old World charm.

Many hotels in Jerusalem are grouped in the following locations: on or near the downtown triangle formed by King George Street, Jaffa Road, and Ben Yehuda Street (Sheraton Jerusalem Plaza, Lev Yerushalayim, Jerusalem Tower, Kikar Zion, Eyal, Zion); close to the city center (and most convenient to Jaffa Gate and the Old City), near the intersection of King David and Keren Hayesod streets (King David, Laromme, King Solomon, Radisson Moriah Plaza, Mt. Zion, Windmill, Ariel, YMCA [West], Scottish Hospice); in West Jerusalem between the Central Bus Station and Givat Ram, on major city bus routes (Holiday Inn Crowne Plaza, Renaissance Jerusalem, Caesar, Jerusalem Gate, Park Plaza, Four Points Jerusalem); a few city locations not part of the above (Hyatt Regency, Ramat Rachel, Waterman-Wise). An interesting alternative is the rural ambience of kibbutz guest houses in the forested hill country, a 20-minute drive from the city center (Neve Ilan, Ma'aleh Hahamisha, Kiryat Anavim, and Shoresh guest houses); to get to these, it's best to have a car (☞ West of Jerusalem *in* Chapter 3).

Hotels in Arab East Jerusalem, predominantly in the less-expensive categories, were seriously affected by Palestinian street violence in the late 1980s and early '90s, and the resultant shrinking of hotel occupancy there has, with only a few exceptions, led to a decline in standards as well. Still recommended, however, is the American Colony Hotel.

Rates quoted by hotels are maximum regular-season rates; it is quite common to find a room at a price below the published rate, especially off-season. High season typically includes 10 days to a month around the Jewish holiday of Passover (March/April), a similar period over the Jewish holidays in September and October (High Holy Days and Sukkoth), part of the summer, and for some hotels, the Christmas season. Because there is considerable variation in what different hotels consider high season, and because the dates of Jewish holidays shift annually in accordance with the Jewish calendar, the difference in room rates can be significant, and it is worth confirming the room rate before making a firm reservation.

All hotels have heating. Hotels in the $$$$ and $$$ categories have air-conditioning and telephones in the rooms; many moderately priced properties have them, too.

CATEGORY	COST*
$$$$	over $200
$$$	$100–$200
$$	$60–$100
$	under $60

All prices are for two people in a standard double room, including breakfast and 15% service charge.

$$$$ 　🏨 **American Colony Hotel.** This onetime pasha's palace, a hotel for over
★ 　a century, is a 10-minute walk from the Damascus Gate in East Jerusalem, but worlds away from the hubbub of the Old City. This cool limestone oasis, with its flower-bedecked outdoor courtyard, is a favorite haunt of American and British expats, international journalists, and Palestinian officials. You're paying for the ambience and the excellent service, rather than a luxurious property. The whitewashed guest rooms tend toward the spartan, with simple turned-wood pieces, the occasional Turkish or Syrian antique, and small area rugs covering stone floors; the better rooms are spacious (and the marble bathrooms huge). Decorative touches, such as turquoise-and-blue tile work, rattan chairs, and plenty of potted palms, lend a Mediterranean atmosphere to the public areas. The restaurant serves good (nonkosher) cuisine, mainly Continental, with several Middle Eastern offerings as well. ⊠ *Nablus Rd., Box 19215, 97200,* ☎ *02/627–9777,* 🄵🄰🄷 *02/627–9888. 96 rooms with bath. 3 restaurants, bar, 2 pools. AE, DC, MC, V.*

$$$$ 　🏨 **Holiday Inn Crowne Plaza.** A quintessential business and convention hotel, the Crowne Plaza is in Givat Ram. The Lounge, the lobby-level dairy restaurant–bar–coffee shop, serves superb cakes and pastries. The in-house Kohinoor Indian restaurant is a real treat. The hotel's lofty location gives almost all rooms—particularly those on the top five floors—fine views of some part of Jerusalem. Rooms are not especially large, but redecoration in tasteful pastels and light earth colors has given them a much lighter and airier feel. The small, informal health club is privately owned and not included in the room rate. A complimentary shuttle bus takes guests to downtown Jerusalem and the Old City. ⊠ *Givat Ram (West Jerusalem), 91130,* ☎ *02/565–8888,* 🄵🄰🄷 *02/651–4555. 397 rooms with bath. 3 restaurants, bar, pool, sauna, whirlpool bath, miniature golf, tennis courts, health club, shops, playground, business services. AE, DC, MC, V.*

$$$$ 　🏨 **Hyatt Regency.** Cascading down Mt. Scopus, the Hyatt Regency has the most dramatic setting of any hotel in Jerusalem—and the boldest design (it's built around seven courtyards). The lobby is a stylish combination of stone, leather seating, and greenery. Guest rooms, about one-third of which have views of the Old City, are spacious, decorated with stone-top tables, Castel prints, and light colors. The hotel's pool

area, with an adjacent playground, is a cool enclave of palms and plants. The independently owned, sophisticated Jerusalem Spa offers cosmetic and therapeutic treatments in addition to the expected facilities; hotel guests receive a discounted day rate. Valentino's, the in-house Italian restaurant, is recommended (☞ Dining, *above*). ⊠ *32 Lehi St., 97856,* ☎ *02/533–1234,* FAX *02/581–5947. 503 rooms with bath. 3 restaurants, bar, 3 pools, beauty salon, sauna, steam room, whirlpool bath, tennis courts, health club, shops, nightclub, business services. AE, DC, MC, V.*

$$$$ ⊞ **King David Hotel.** The grande dame of Israeli luxury hotels opened
★ in 1931 and has successfully defended its premier status ever since. Management efforts have had some success in inducing the veteran staff to shake off its old snootiness. The lobby, with its ceilings, columns, and walls covered with "ancient" geometric decoration, is comfortable but very much part of the bustle of the nearby reception area. For more privacy try the bar (☞ Nightlife and the Arts, *below*). Renovations have transformed most of the already spacious and elegant rooms into a cream-and-brown symphony of good taste, with old-fashioned writing tables a gracious addition. The pricier rooms have a view of the Old City. The large pool, in a beautifully landscaped garden behind the hotel, may tempt you away from your touring in hot weather. ⊠ *23 King David St., 94101,* ☎ *02/620–8888,* FAX *02/624–6847. 249 rooms with bath. 3 restaurants, bar, 2 pools, tennis court, exercise room, shops, business services. AE, DC, MC, V.*

$$$$ ⊞ **Laromme.** A low-rise building of Jerusalem stone (limestone) wrapped around a central courtyard and atrium, the Laromme is more appealing for its architecture and friendly, energetic staff than for its decor. The furnishings of the public areas are rather ordinary, though helped by a profusion of plants. Recent refurbishing has improved the guest rooms, some of which have balconies and fine views. Despite its unexceptional features, there is something about the hotel—the lively atmosphere and amiable staff, perhaps—that has made the Laromme one of the most popular in its category. Its location next to Liberty Bell Garden is a plus for families. ⊠ *3 Jabotinsky St., 92145,* ☎ *02/675–6666,* FAX *02/675–6777. 302 rooms with bath. 2 restaurants, bar, pool, beauty salon, sauna, whirlpool bath, shops. AE, DC, MC, V.*

$$$$ ⊞ **Radisson Moriah Plaza.** Although the Moriah is outclassed by its luxury peers, it nevertheless offers an excellent location, convenient to downtown and the Old City, and an efficient staff. The guest rooms, although comfortable, are unexceptionally decorated and not overly large. There is a small health club attached to (but not affiliated with) the hotel, discounted to NIS 20 ($6.70) for guests (for the gym alone). ⊠ *39 Keren Hayesod St., 94188,* ☎ *02/569–5695,* FAX *02/623–2411. 292 rooms with bath. 3 restaurants, bar, pool, beauty salon, shops. AE, DC, MC, V.*

$$$$ ⊞ **Renaissance Jerusalem.** Polished stone walls and copper fixtures in the reception and lounge areas add class to this large, modern hotel, whose rates are modest for this price category. Rooms are quite spacious, with a pleasing pastel decor; bathrooms are small. The hotel's best features are its large outdoor pool and its equally large heated indoor pool and health club, all free to hotel guests. It's on the west side of town, adjacent to Hebrew University's Givat Ram campus. A complimentary shuttle bus transports guests to downtown and Jaffa Gate. ⊠ *6 Wolfson St., 91033,* ☎ *02/652–8111,* FAX *02/651–1824. 650 rooms with bath. 3 restaurants, 2 bar/lounges, indoor and outdoor pools, beauty salon, saunas, whirlpool bath, tennis court, health club, shops. AE, DC, MC, V.*

$$$$ ⊞ **Sheraton Jerusalem Plaza.** Close by the lively shopping area of Ben Yehuda Street, the 22-story Sheraton looks like any big business hotel anywhere, complete with look-alike guest rooms (modern built-in cherry-wood furniture, large beds, big closets), but it does have more to recommend it. The balcony views of the Old City are spectacular (those of the New City are almost as impressive), and in general the staff is welcoming. Its nonmeat Italian restaurant, the Primavera, has won kudos locally, and the in-house French restaurant, Cow on the Roof, is expensive but justly celebrated. ⊠ *47 King George St., Box 7686, 91076,* ☎ *02/629–8666,* FAX *02/623–1667. 300 rooms with bath. 4 restaurants, bar, pool, beauty salon, massage, sauna, shops. AE, DC, MC, V.*

$$$ 🏨 **Four Points Jerusalem.** Although there is little that is extraordinary about the look of this hotel on the west side of town, its recreational facilities make it a standout in its price category. The health club, complete with indoor pool, exercise room, sauna, and whirlpool bath, and the grassy pool area provide a delightful, relaxing environment at the end of a day of touring. ⊠ *4 Wolfson St., 91036,* ☎ *02/655–8888,* FAX *02/651–2266. 198 rooms with bath. Restaurant, bar, 3 pools, health club. AE, DC, MC, V.*

$$$ 🏨 **Jerusalem Gate.** Adjacent to the Central Bus Station and on many convenient bus routes, though not a close walk to anywhere, the Jerusalem Gate caters to business travelers and tour groups. Guest rooms are reasonably spacious; the pastel colors contribute to the effect. Ask for a north-facing room, which will have a view across the hills and beyond the city. The attractive bar on the mezzanine terrace overlooking the lobby has a copper ceiling. The rooftop sundeck is a welcome haven from the bus station bustle. ⊠ *43 Yirmiyahu St., 94467,* ☎ *02/538–3101,* FAX *02/538–9040. 298 rooms with bath. Restaurant, bar, shops, business services. AE, DC, MC, V.*

$$$ 🏨 **Jerusalem Tower.** This hotel, with renovated guest rooms and partly renovated public areas, is in a choice location: bang in the center of downtown. The café/bar is an inviting asymmetrical room with arched windows, cane furniture, and quiet corners. Guest rooms are small but tastefully decorated with upholstered headboards and stone tabletops. Ask for a room above the sixth floor to guarantee a view. ⊠ *23 Hillel St., Box 2656, 94581,* ☎ *02/625–2161,* FAX *02/625–2167. 120 rooms with bath. Restaurant, bar, café. AE, DC, MC, V.*

$$$ 🏨 **Kikar Zion.** Although this seven-story building dominates downtown Zion Square (Kikar Zion in Hebrew), the entrance is a very modest doorway off Shamai Street a half block away, where the elevator takes you up to the huge lobby. High above street level, rooms are quiet and spacious, with light gray felt wall coverings that lend a feeling of warmth and intimacy. The rooms wrap around the building, affording good views of the city, but insist on high floors facing either the Old City or Independence Park. Hotel guests pay a nominal fee for the privately owned health club. ⊠ *25 Shamai St., 94631,* ☎ *02/624–4644,* FAX *02/624–4136. 120 rooms with bath. 2 restaurants, bar, health club. AE, DC, MC, V.*

$$$ 🏨 **Kings.** Less than 10 minutes' walk from the city center, though on a noisy intersection, the Kings has been transformed by ongoing renovations (make sure to ask for one of the new rooms). Cane furniture and deep sofas create comfortable, if not particularly intimate, public areas. Most guest rooms are fairly spacious, the renovated accommodations enhanced by light colors. ⊠ *60 King George St. (entrance on Ramban St.), 94262,* ☎ *02/620–1201,* FAX *02/620–1211. 187 rooms with bath. 2 restaurants, bar. AE, DC, MC, V.*

$$$ 🏨 **King Solomon.** After a slump in the late 1980s, the King Solomon has bounced back, as it deserves to. The lobby has as a centerpiece a huge globe-shape sculpture of Jerusalem by Frank Meisler. Alcoves in the coffee shop offer some degree of privacy from the lobby crowds. A split-level atrium reveals shops one floor down and restaurants below that. Standard rooms are a bit cramped, but the more deluxe ones are quite large. The rooms are attractive; brown and beige predominate, with sepia prints above the beds. The well-equipped bathrooms are more spacious than most. Rates are low for this category. ⊠ *32 King David St., 94101,* ☎ *02/569–5555,* 🗚 *02/624–1774. 142 rooms with bath, 6 suites. 2 restaurants, bar, pool, beauty salon, shops. AE, DC, MC, V.*

$$$ 🏨 **Lev Yerushalayim.** One of the best bargains in its price category, this
★ all-suite hotel is in the heart of the city center. The heat and noise are left behind as you enter the stone-walled, plant-filled lobby. Suites are decorated in tasteful pastel pinks and grays. Prices are per suite for two guests; additional guests using the sofa beds pay only an extra $25 per night for an adult and $17 per night for a child. Deluxe suites are defined by an additional room having sofa beds—for a family, easily worth the small extra charge—not by a higher grade of furnishings. Breakfast is included, but you can make other meals in the suite's kitchenette. Samson's Gym, on the premises (gym, whirlpool bath, sauna), is free to hotel guests. ⊠ *18 King George St., 91079,* ☎ *02/530–0333,* 🗚 *02/623–2432. 58 suites, 28 deluxe (double) suites. Restaurant, exercise room, coin laundry. AE, DC, MC, V.*

$$$ 🏨 **Mount Zion.** The core of the hotel is a renovated 19th-century building that was a British eye hospital, to which a new, similar wing was added in the 1970s. Columns, arched doorways, and windows in Jerusalem stone all frame ethereal views of Mt. Zion and create atmospheric nooks filled with wall hangings, Armenian tiles, and plants. Only the tacky carpeting detracts from the otherwise excellent taste. At press time the new management was promising to improve the once mediocre service and realize the hotel's phenomenal potential. Guest rooms in the new wing have been recently renovated; the superior rooms of the old wing offer more character and better views. An octagonal swimming pool and adjacent children's pool overlook the Hinnom Valley. ⊠ *17 Hebron Rd., 93546,* ☎ *02/672–4222,* 🗚 *02/673–1425. 130 rooms with bath. Restaurant, bar, pool, health club. AE, DC, MC, V.*

$$$ 🏨 **Ramat Rachel.** As a rustic kibbutz hotel at the southern end of the
★ Bus 7 route, less than 15 minutes by car from downtown, Ramat Rachel enjoys the best of both worlds. Most of its rooms have stunning views of Bethlehem and the Judean Desert. They have all been recently renovated in order to bring them up to the standard of the new wing, due to open at the end of 1997. The pleasant if unexceptional decor is offset by the brilliant colors of Calman Shemi quilted-fabric "soft-art" originals above each headboard. With its fine pool and other sports and health facilities, all free to guests, Ramat Rachel feels like a resort far removed from a major city. ⊠ *Kibbutz Ramat Rachel, M.P. North Judea 90900,* ☎ *02/670–2555,* 🗚 *02/673–3155. 91 rooms with bath (85 more to open by Dec. 1997). Restaurant, bar, pool, beauty salon, saunas, whirlpool bath, 3 tennis courts, basketball, exercise room, playground. AE, DC, MC, V.*

$$$ 🏨 **Windmill.** The unobtrusive decor of this comfortable but fairly nondescript hotel includes many plants in public areas. Its rates are high for what it offers, but the good location (on a side street opposite the Radisson Moriah Plaza, near the city center and on good bus routes) counts for something. ⊠ *3 Mendele St., off Keren Hayesod, 92147,* ☎ *02/766–3111,* 🗚 *02/761–0964. 133 rooms with bath. Restaurant, bar. AE, DC, MC, V.*

$$–$$$ 🏨 **Ariel.** An early conversion from a planned apartment hotel left the Ariel with a good number of spacious guest rooms, some large enough to accommodate families. About a third of the rooms have excellent views of Mt. Zion. Extensive bathroom renovations and some new bedroom furniture have added to guest comfort. The public areas—lobby, bar, dining room—have been completely redone as well, with many plants balancing the new marble. The hotel is close to the railway station. ✉ *31 Hebron Rd., 93546,* ☎ *02/671–9222,* 𝖥𝖠𝖷 *02/673–4066. 125 rooms with bath. Restaurant, bar. AE, DC, MC, V.*

$$–$$$ 🏨 **Caesar.** Functional rather than fun, the Caesar is an unexceptional hotel. Rooms leave few memorable impressions and have no views at all. It is a base from which to venture out, rather than a home to which to return. ✉ *208 Jaffa Rd., 94383,* ☎ *02/538–2801,* 𝖥𝖠𝖷 *02/538–2802. 84 rooms with bath. Bar, coffee shop. AE, DC, MC, V.*

$$–$$$ 🏨 **Park Plaza.** This West Jerusalem hotel—the old Sonesta—has a good local reputation. Its rooms are small and its facilities limited, but recent renovations have made a difference. Attractive cane furniture adds brightness and a touch of style to guest rooms and public areas. ✉ *2 Wolfson St., Box 3835, 95435,* ☎ *02/652–8221,* 𝖥𝖠𝖷 *02/652–8423. 217 rooms with bath. Restaurant, bar. AE, DC, MC, V.*

$$–$$$ 🏨 **YMCA (West).** Built in 1933, this limestone building with its famous domed bell tower is a Jerusalem landmark. Stone arches, exotic murals, wooden cupboards, and Armenian tiles give it charm and character. Guest rooms are not large, but renovations have lifted them from their once-spartan character to attractive air-conditioned comfort. That and an excellent location make the Y an attractive deal at the upper end of the price category. On the premises are excellent sports facilities, an auditorium where concerts and folklore performances are held, and the privately run Le Tsriff restaurant (☞ *Dining, above*). ✉ *26 King David St., Box 294, 91002,* ☎ *02/625–7111,* 𝖥𝖠𝖷 *02/625–3438. 66 rooms with bath. Restaurant, café, pool, sauna, 4 tennis courts, basketball, exercise room, indoor track, squash. AE, DC, MC, V.*

$$ 🏨 **Bet Shmuel.** This relatively new stone building with cool inner
★ courtyards and a fabulous view of the Old City from the roof (and from almost half the rooms) was not built exclusively as a guest house but as a cultural/educational center of the World Union For Progressive Judaism. Its spacious rooms, which can sleep six, are bright, with blond-wood furniture—pleasant, if a little spare. The location is excellent: five minutes' walk to the Old City, 10 to the center of town. One drawback: In good weather the central courtyard is used for Friday night concerts and occasional receptions, thus making the guests in many rooms involuntary participants. ✉ *13 King David St. (entrance on Shamma St.), 94101,* ☎ *02/620–3491 or 02/620–3473,* 𝖥𝖠𝖷 *02/620–3467. 41 rooms with shower. Restaurant, coffee shop. DC, V.*

$$ 🏨 **Eyal.** A central downtown location makes this well-kept hotel a good choice in its price range. Rooms are not too cramped, and although the decor is unexceptional (veneer paneling), the presence of TVs and refrigerators—unusual for this category—makes the hotel a good value. Ask for an "outer" room facing the street. ✉ *21 Shamai St., 94631,* ☎ *02/623–4161 through 02/623–4168,* 𝖥𝖠𝖷 *02/624–4136. 71 rooms with bath. Restaurant, bar. AE, DC, MC, V.*

$$ 🏨 **Jerusalem Inn.** All rooms have little balconies overlooking shaded side streets near Zion Square downtown. Recent renovations have added new wooden furniture, private (though tiny) shower and toilet facilities in most rooms, TVs, and extra bunk beds in some larger rooms. Breakfast is not included. ✉ *7 Horkonos St., Box 2729, 94230,* ☎ *02/625–2757,* 𝖥𝖠𝖷 *02/625–1297. 18 rooms, 15 with private showers and toilets. Restaurant, coffee shop. Cash preferred; 5% more for credit cards (AE, DC, MC, V).*

$$ 🏨 **Palatin.** At this personable family-run hotel just off the intersection of King George Street and Jaffa Road, the guest rooms are small, but the updated decor includes pine furniture, moldings and other details, brighter colors, and TVs in the rooms. Complimentary coffee and tea are always available. ✉ *4 Agrippas St., 94301,* ☎ *02/623–1141,* ℻ *02/625–9323. 28 rooms with bath. AE, DC, MC, V.*

$$ ⚜ **Scottish Hospice.** Part of the St. Andrew's Church complex, the Presbyterian-operated hospice is as much a retreat as a place to overnight. Opened in 1930, the building has the pleasing stone arches, alcoves, and atriums that characterize the architecture of the period. The rooms are small, a bit sparsely furnished, and not air-conditioned, but most compensate with views of the garden, and some have a view of Mt. Zion. Refreshments are always available, and meals can be requested. ✉ *Off corner of King David and Emek Refaim Sts., opposite railway station, Box 8619, 91086,* ☎ *02/673–2401,* ℻ *02/673–1711. 19 rooms with shower. Shops. MC, V.*

$$ ⚜ **Zion.** A Parisian-style hotel, Zion is right in the center of town and its little balconies overlook one of the pedestrian-only side streets of the Ben Yehuda mall. The downside is a lot of street noise till late hours. Renovations have preserved many of the stone walls and alcoves of this 140-year-old building, and traditional furniture and brass ornaments in some of the public areas add to the Old World ambience. Simply but pleasantly furnished guest rooms are two and three flights above street level and *can be reached only by stairs.* Rooms have TV and fans but no air-conditioning. The hotel is at the lower end of the price category. ✉ *10 Dorot Rishonim St., 94646,* ☎ *02/625–9511,* ℻ *02/625–7585. 26 rooms with bath. Bar. AE, MC, V.*

$–$$ ⚜ **Christ Church.** This is the guest house of the adjacent Anglican church, the oldest Protestant church (1849) in the Middle East. Rooms in the two old stone buildings are comfortably furnished, if not exactly luxurious, as you might expect from this former pilgrim hospice. The location, in the Old City just inside Jaffa Gate, is excellent for sightseeing, though many visitors are more at ease in modern West Jerusalem. Prices drop to $ November 1–December 19 and January 1–March 14. ✉ *Jaffa Gate, Old City, Box 14037, 91140,* ☎ *02/628–2082,* ℻ *02/628–9187. 23 rooms with bath. Dining room. No credit cards.*

$ ⚜ **Louise Waterman-Wise.** Jerusalem's largest youth hostel has added a guest-house wing, with simply but neatly furnished private rooms. The hostel's setting, opposite Mt. Herzl in the Bayit Vegan area of West Jerusalem, has sweeping views of the Judean Hills. Downtown is a 15-minute drive by taxi (the hostel is next to a taxi stand) and city bus (Nos. 13, 18, 20, 23, 27, and 39). Guests have access to a garden and other common rooms and to occasional evening activities, such as folk dancing and movies. Meals are substantial and very cheap. There are no age requirements. ✉ *8 Hapisga St., Bayit Vegan, Box 16350, 91162,* ☎ *02/542–3366 or 02/542–0990,* ℻ *02/542–3362. Hostel: 172 beds in 43 rooms, each room with bath. Guest-house wing: 128 beds in 24 rooms, each room with bath. No credit cards.*

NIGHTLIFE AND THE ARTS

Nightlife

Jerusalem's nightlife, almost provincial, is a great deal more limited than Tel Aviv's, but *some* lively spots are open until the wee hours.

Bars and Lounges

All the major hotels have bars, but the watering hole at the **King David Hotel** (✉ 23 King David St., ☎ 02/620–8888) is a standout. A quiet room with comfortable lounge chairs and subdued lighting provides an intimate atmosphere unusual for Jerusalem.

Dance Clubs

Primarily the preserve of the 17- to 21-year-old crowd (the drinking age is 18), Jerusalem dance clubs come alive on Thursday, Friday, and Saturday nights. Admission runs NIS 25–NIS 30 ($8.35–$10). Don't even *think* about going before midnight.

The veteran downtown **Underground** (⊠ 1 Yoel Salomon St., off Zion Sq., ☎ 02/625–1918) looks like something out of Dante's *Inferno,* with rough black walls, murals, and sculptures of prisoners. The bar at street level, which is above the disco, is only marginally saner. You can also have a drink at the upper level, where the dance floor is free. The Hyatt Regency Hotel's **Orient Express** nightclub (⊠ 32 Lehi St., ☎ 02/533–1234), on Mt. Scopus, has old-fashioned decor that recaptures the bygone era of that famous train, but the sound system is marvelously new-fangled. Tuesday is '60s nostalgia, Wednesday draws the students from the adjacent campus, and on Thursday and Saturday everything goes.

The **Talpiot Industrial Zone,** 4 km (2½ mi) out of the city center, is perhaps an unlikely place to find a clutch of discos but not illogical in a city where the Jewish Sabbath is sacrosanct to so many. Nothing much happens before midnight, but by then parking is tight, and the snack bars are crowded. Most places are geared to the 17-to-21 age group, a few to a slightly older crowd. Individual clubs appear and disappear with such bewildering rapidity that specific listings have little long-term significance. Ask your hotel staff for recommendations.

Folk-Music Clubs

There is a modest folk scene in Jerusalem, with performances by local artists and the occasional visit by international performers. Watch for listings, usually under Entertainment in the *Jerusalem Post* and elsewhere, or call folksinger Jill Rogoff (☎ 02/679–0410) for connections with the local folk community.

Jazz Clubs

The **Pargod Theater** (⊠ 94 Bezalel St., ☎ 02/623–1765 or 02/625–8819) hosts a regular jam session on Friday afternoon and often features jazz programs during the evening (especially in July and August).

Pubs

A half-dozen totally nondescript pubs populate a courtyard off **31 Jaffa Road,** where a drink is just a drink, and the ambience is secondary. In and around the **Russian Compound,** a cluster of pubs sells drinks, but the pubs themselves have little atmosphere.

The Arts

For schedules of performances and other cultural events, consult the Friday weekend section of the *Jerusalem Post* and its insert *In Jerusalem,* the free local booklets *Your Jerusalem* and *This Week in Jerusalem,* and the monthly *Hello Israel.* All these publications are in English. Particularly useful is the Ministry of Tourism's monthly bulletin, *Events in Jerusalem,* available at TIOs and most better hotels.

The main ticket agencies for performances in Jerusalem are **Ben-Naim** (⊠ 38 Jaffa Rd., ☎ 02/625–4008); **Bimot** (⊠ 8 Shamai St., ☎ 02/624–0896); and **Kla'im** (⊠ 12 Shamai St., ☎ 02/625–6869). If you are a student, present your card at the ticket office; sometimes discount tickets are available.

Top Israeli and international orchestras, choirs, singers, drama companies, and dance troupes participate in the **Israel Festival,** usually held in May or early June and covering all the performing arts from the classical to the avant-garde.

Dance

Although the **Israel National Ballet** and the modern **Bat-Dor** have a varied performance record, the better-known **Batsheva** modern dance troupe is the one to look out for.

Film

The usual Hollywood fare is available at the cinemas clustered in the center of town, in the Jerusalem Mall, and farther out in the Talpiot Industrial Zone. They close Friday night. Movies are subtitled in Hebrew and (when appropriate) English. The **Jerusalem Cinemateque** (⊠ Hebron Rd., ☎ 02/672–4131) specializes in old, rare, and art films, but its wide-ranging programs often include quite current offerings. The theater is open Friday night. Its monthly series focuses on specific directors, actors, or subjects. Its annual **Jerusalem Film Festival,** held in July, is a must for film buffs.

Music

Classical music abounds in Jerusalem, with Israeli orchestras and chamber ensembles performing year-round and a trickle of international artists passing through.

The International Convention Center, or ICC (☎ 02/655–8558), still known locally by its old name Binyanei Ha'ooma, is opposite the Central Bus Station and is the local venue for occasional concerts by the internationally renowned **Israel Philharmonic Orchestra.** For tickets, contact the orchestra's offices in Tel Aviv (⊠ Hechal Hatarbut, 1 Huberman St., ☎ 03/525–1502). The **Jerusalem Center for the Performing Arts** (⊠ 20 Marcus St., ☎ 02/561–7167), still best known as the Jerusalem Theater, houses the Jerusalem Sherover Theater, the Henry Crown Auditorium, and the more intimate Rebecca Crown Theater. All in all, this is the city's most active and interesting venue.

Bet Ticho, or Ticho House (⊠ Off Harav Kook St. near Zion Sq. ☎ 02/624–5068), holds intimate recitals on Friday mornings in a charming setting. The atmosphere is rustic at the **Targ Music Center,** in Ein Kerem (⊠ Hama'ayan St., ☎ 02/641–4250), 7 km (4 mi) from the city center, where noontime chamber-music performances are common on Friday and Saturday. The popular (and free!) **Etnacha** series of concerts, produced by Israel Radio's classics station, takes place Monday at 5 PM, October through June, at the Henry Crown Auditorium (⊠ 20 Marcus St., ☎ 02/561–7167). Always check listings to be sure.

Hearing music at one of Jerusalem's many **churches** can be a moving experience. The most common venues are the Church of the Redeemer (⊠ Muristan, in the Old City's Christian Quarter, ☎ 02/626–4608 or 02/626–4750) and Dormition Abbey (⊠ Mt. Zion, ☎ 02/671–9927).

A rousing concert of Israeli folklore—mostly singing and folk dancing—is presented at the **YMCA (West)** (⊠ King David St., ☎ 02/625–7111). The concerts usually take place on Monday, Thursday, and Saturday evenings, but call ahead to confirm. As the 500-seat hall is generally inundated by tour groups and seats are unreserved, it is advisable to arrive early. Concerts with folk dancing and singing, similar but less elaborately produced than the YMCA's, take place at **Binyanei Ha'ooma,** in the International Convention Center complex (opposite the Central Bus Station) on Sunday, Tuesday and Thursday evenings, except in July. Performances are subject to demand; verify with the producers (☎ 02/563–6663).

The **Bible Lands Museum** (✉ Givat Ram, adjacent to the Israel Museum, ☎ 02/561–1066) has Saturday evening concerts, preceded by cheese and wine in the foyer. Their delightfully eclectic programs range from chamber music to jazz and gospel to folk music and country-and-western. An added attraction: The museum's galleries are open to patrons for a half hour before and after the concert.

To rub shoulders with the locals, look into the Friday night Oneg Shabbat series at **Bet Shemuel** (✉ Eliyahu Shama'a St., off King David St., ☎ 02/620–3456), which typically hosts some of the top performers on the Israeli pop scene. The evening will be in Hebrew, of course, but the music and the atmosphere may speak to you in an international language of good feelings.

Theater
Most plays are performed in Hebrew, but there is the odd offering in English. Some performances have simultaneous translation. Your best bet for plays in English is the **Khan Theater** (✉ 2 David Remez Sq., near the railway station, ☎ 02/671–8281), but check newspaper listings for other venues as well.

OUTDOOR ACTIVITIES AND SPORTS

For a change of pace from sightseeing, you can keep in shape or pursue a favorite sport at facilities around Jerusalem.

Bicycling
The informal **Jerusalem Bicycling Club** (✉ 16 Ha'arazim St., call Gershon at ☎ 02/643–8386 or Benny at 02/561–9416) leads rides on Saturday morning at 7 starting from the International Convention Center, Binyanei Ha'ooma (opposite the Central Bus Station). The club is a good source for information on bike rentals and can recommend routes to take in the city.

Bowling
The **Jerusalem Bowling Center** (✉ Achim Yisrael Mall "Kenyon Talpiot," 18 Yad Harutzim St., Talpiot Industrial Zone, ☎ 02/673–2195) has 10 lanes and a small cafeteria and billiard tables. The center is open daily 9 AM–2 AM. The cost per game (including shoe rental) is NIS 14 ($4.70) 10 AM–6 PM, and NIS 18 ($6) 6 PM–2 AM.

Health Clubs
The best health clubs in Jerusalem are in hotels; some are privately run concessions. All welcome visitors who are not hotel guests. The most comprehensive facilities are at the **Holiday Inn Crowne Plaza** (✉ Givat Ram, ☎ 02/653–5821), **Hyatt Regency** (✉ 32 Lehi St., Mt. Scopus, ☎ 02/532–2906), **Four Points Jerusalem** (✉ 4 Wolfson St., ☎ 02/655–8888), and **Renaissance Jerusalem** (✉ 6 Wolfson St., ☎ 02/652–8111). The following have good facilities but no pools: **Kikar Zion** (✉ 25 Shamai St., Zion Sq., ☎ 02/624–4644) and **Lev Yerushalayim** (Samson's Gym; ✉ 18 King George St., ☎ 02/530–0333).

Horseback Riding

A number of stables offer lessons and trail riding, including those suitable for children, as well as longer (and more interesting) trails. **King David's Riding Stables** (⊠ Neve Ilan, north of Rte. 1, ☎ 02/534–0535), in the wooded Judean Hills, 16 km (10 mi) west of Jerusalem, charges NIS 70 ($23.40) for a full hour. Longer guided trails in the area are offered at a lower hourly rate. **Meir Mizrachi Stables** (⊠ Kfar Adumim, north of Rte. 1, ☎ 02/535–5419 [stables], 02/535–4769 [home]), in the Judean Desert, 17 km (11 mi) east of Jerusalem, charges NIS 50 ($16.70) for an hour. **The Riding Club** (⊠ Kiryat Moshe, behind Angel's Bakery, ☎ 02/651–3585; do not call between 1 and 3 PM), run by Yehuda Alafi, breeds Arabians. The charge is NIS 70 ($23.40) for an hour.

Squash

The **YMCA (West)** (⊠ 26 King David St., ☎ 02/625–7111) has three squash courts for hourly rental. They are available for NIS 30 ($10) an hour 7:15 AM–8:45 PM, Monday–Saturday.

Swimming

The enthusiast can swim year-round at the pools listed below. Indoor: **Djanogly** (⊠ Bet Avraham Community Center, Ramot Allon, ☎ 02/586–8055), **Renaissance Jerusalem Hotel** (⊠ 6 Wolfson St., ☎ 02/652–8111), and **Bet Hano'ar Ha'ivri** (or **YMWHA;** ⊠ 105 Herzog Blvd., ☎ 02/678–9441). Outdoor (covered and heated in winter): **Laromme Hotel** (⊠ 3 Jabotinsky St., ☎ 02/675–6666).

Recommended outdoor pools (except in winter) include the **Jerusalem Pool** (⊠ 43 Emek Refa'im St., ☎ 02/563–2092), a public facility that gets very crowded in July and August, and the beautifully landscaped facilities of the following hotels: **Hyatt Regency** (⊠ 32 Lehi St., Mt. Scopus, ☎ 02/533–1234); **Holiday Inn Crowne Plaza** (⊠ Givat Ram, ☎ 02/565–8888); **King David Hotel** (⊠ 23 King David St., ☎ 02/620–8888); and **Renaissance Jerusalem** (⊠ 6 Wolfson St., ☎ 02/652–8111). A little less expensive are the facilities at the **Four Points Jerusalem** (⊠ 4 Wolfson St., ☎ 02/655–8888) and **Mt. Zion Hotel** (⊠ 17 Hebron Rd., ☎ 02/672–4222), also in attractive locations.

Tennis

Tennis has really taken off in Israel during the past decade. Advance reservations are always required. **Hebrew University at Mt. Scopus** (☎ 02/581–7579 or 02/588–2796) has 10 lighted courts; equipment can be rented. Courts go for NIS 20 ($6.70) an hour weekdays, and NIS 24 ($8) an hour evenings and Friday–Saturday. The courts are open Sunday–Thursday 7 AM–10 PM, Friday and Saturday 7–5. The **Israel Tennis Center** (⊠ 5 Almaliach St., Katamon Tet, ☎ 02/679–1866 or 02/679–2726) has 18 lighted courts that can be rented at NIS 17 ($5.70) per hour Sunday–Thursday 7 AM–3 PM; and NIS 25 ($8.40) per hour Sunday–Thursday 7 PM–10 PM, Friday 7–5, Saturday 8–3. The **YMCA (West)** (⊠ 26 King David St., ☎ 02/625–7111) has four courts that rent at NIS 20 ($6.70) per hour. They are open Monday–Saturday 8 AM–sunset. Several major **hotels** have their own courts but often restrict usage to guests or club members. Ask your concierge to make inquiries if you are determined to play at a particular hotel.

SHOPPING

There is good shopping in Jerusalem, from jewelry and art to crafts and souvenirs. The several distinct shopping areas make it easier to plan expeditions. Generally there are fixed prices on merchandise in the city center and the Jewish Quarter of the Old City, although you can sometimes negotiate for significant discounts on high-priced art and jewelry. Shopping in the Old City's colorful Arab bazaar, or souk (pronounced shook in Israel), is fascinating but can be a trap for the unwary. Never buy gold, silver, or gem-studded jewelry here.

New store hours in the city on weekdays are generally 8:30 or 9–1 and 4–7, but many stores now stay open through the day with no break. Some close on Tuesday afternoon, a traditional but not mandatory half day. Jewish-owned stores (West Jerusalem and the Old City's Jewish Quarter) close on Friday afternoon at 1 or 2, depending on the kind of store and the season (food and souvenir stores tend to stay open later), and reopen on Sunday morning. Some stores geared to the tourist trade, particularly in the center of town (bounded by Jaffa Road, King George Street, and Ben Yehuda Street), are open on Saturday night after the Jewish Sabbath ends, especially in summer. Arab-owned stores in the Old City and East Jerusalem are busiest on Saturday and quietest on Sunday, when many (but not all) Christian storekeepers close for the day.

Shopping Streets and Malls

Arts and Crafts Lane (known in Hebrew as Hutzot Hayotzer), opposite and downhill from the Jaffa Gate, has goldsmiths and silversmiths specializing in Judaica, generally done in an ultramodern, minimalist style. The work is exquisite and is priced accordingly. You can also find excellent jewelry, weaving, fine art, and musical instruments.

The **Cardo,** in the Old City's Jewish Quarter, began life as the main thoroughfare of Byzantine Jerusalem, was a street during the Crusader era, and today has been converted into a major shopping area. Apart from souvenirs and Judaica, some good-quality jewelry, art, and objets d'art can be found in stores here.

King David Street is lined with a sizable number of prestigious stores, with the emphasis on art, Judaica, and antiquities, and a lot of interesting jewelry as well.

The **Midrachov** is simply downtown Ben Yehuda Street, the pulse of downtown Jerusalem. The selection of clothing, shoes, jewelry, souvenirs, T-shirts, and street food is prodigious on this pedestrians-only street. You'll be serenaded by street musicians at every turn. It's a real scene, best appreciated from one of the many outdoor cafés. Summer evenings are lively, as the mall fills with peddlers of cheap jewelry and crafts, especially attracting the younger crowd.

Salomon Street, in the old neighborhood of Nahalat Shiva, just off Zion Square, has been developed as a pedestrian mall. Here and in adjacent alleys and courtyards, eateries abound, but you can also find some attractive crafts galleries and arty jewelry and clothing stores.

Hatachana (the Mill) is a small arcade on Ramban Street near the intersection with King George Street. Built around an old windmill, the complex houses expensive fashion stores, a children's clothing store, a jewelry store, and an excellent beauty salon.

The new **Jerusalem Mall,** known locally as Kenyon Malcha, is—at 500,000 square feet not counting parking—the largest in the Middle

East. It includes a department store, supermarket, eight cinemas, and almost 200 shops and eateries (Pizza Hut and Burger King among them). The interior is an attractive mix of arched skylights and wrought-iron banisters in a quasi–art deco style. There are clearly signposted turnoffs to the mall from Eliyahu Golomb Street (on the way up to Kiryat Hayovel) and from the Pat Junction–Gilo Road.

Street Markets

The first and foremost market, of course, is the **souk** in the Old City. Spreading over a warren of intersecting streets, the souk is primarily the market for the Old City's Arab residents. It is awash with color and redolent with the clashing scents of exotic spices. Village women's baskets of produce vie for attention with hanging shanks of lamb, fresh fish on ice, and fresh-baked delicacies, and food stalls are interspersed with those selling fabrics and shoes. The baubles and trinkets of the tourist trade often seem secondary, except along the well-trodden paths of the Via Dolorosa, David Street, and Christian Quarter Road.

The atmosphere in the Arab Quarter has relaxed a great deal since the tense years of the late 1980s. On the other hand, haggling with merchants—a time-honored tradition—is not the good-natured experience it once was. Unless you know what you want, know how much it's *really* worth, and enjoy the sometimes aggressive give-and-take of bargaining, you are better off just enjoying the local color (stick to the main streets and watch your wallet or purse) and doing your shopping in the more modern and familiar New City.

Off Jaffa Road, near the Clal Center office buildings, is the **Machaneh Yehuda** produce market. The block-long alleyway is a blur of brilliant primary colors as the city's best-quality fruit and vegetables, pickles and cheeses, fresh fish and poultry, confections, and falafel await inspection. Thursday and Friday, when Jews shop for the Sabbath, are the busiest days. The market, like the rest of Jewish West Jerusalem, is closed on Saturday.

On Thursday and Friday, **Hamartef** (the Cellar) arcade, beneath City Tower (⊠ Corner of King George and Ben Yehuda Sts.), hosts jewelers and vendors of bric-a-brac and secondhand books. It's fun just to browse, but sometimes there is something really worth buying.

Specialty Stores

Art Galleries

Several galleries representing a range of Israeli artists are close to the city's premier hotels, on **King David Street.** For large wall decorations (with similar-size prices!), check out the unique appliqué-like soft art of **Calman Shemi** (⊠ 22 King David St., ☎ 02/249557). The marvelous effects must be seen to be appreciated. **Frank Meisler** (⊠ 21 King David St., ☎ 02/242759) has an original and whimsical sense of humor. His caricaturish silver-plated pewter sculptures cover subjects from Noah's ark and Jerusalem cityscapes to Freud and animal figures that seem to be sharing Meisler's secret joke.

Clothing

Clothing tends to be expensive in Israel, and in Jerusalem you have to search for really stylish clothes. One homegrown women's clothing store with definite class is **A.B.C.** (⊠ 33 King George St., ☎ 02/234934). The very pricey **Miss Lagotte,** in the Hatachana arcade (⊠ 8 Ramban St., ☎ 02/665059), stocks well-designed women's wear.

High-quality leather and suede jackets, pants, a[...]
styles and colors are very good buys in Israel; try **Be[...]**
Yehuda St., ☎ 02/256902), on the Midrachov.

Israeli swimsuits and beach accessories have revolutionize[...]
ket overseas. They are rightfully known for their dazzling desi[...]
colors. **Gottex** swimwear is available at the downtown department [...]
Hamashbir (⌧ 28 King George St.). Names (⌧ 23 Ben Yehuda St.,
02/625–8430) sells **Gideon Oberson** suits. Well worth a look is **Gluck[...]**
a Haifa-based company that now has a Jerusalem store (⌧ 16 Hillel
St., ☎ 02/624–7399). They will alter a suit to fit you perfectly and—
given enough time—will even make one to measure especially for you.
Their motto is "a bathing suit for everyone."

Crafts

For ceramics, glass, jewelry, wooden objects, and embroidery, try the
Jerusalem House of Quality (⌧ 12 Hebron Rd., ☎ 02/671–7430), which
presents the work of some excellent Israeli craftspeople. The building's
second floor is home to their studios, where you can often find the artists
themselves at work.

For Armenian hand-painted pottery—predominantly blue and brown,
with geometric or stylized natural motifs—one of the best artisans is
Stefan Karakashian of **Jerusalem Pottery,** at the VI Station of the
Cross, on the Via Dolorosa in the Old City. His work is of a particularly high standard and includes plates, plaques, and bowls. Drop in
at **Cadim** (⌧ 4 Salomon St., ☎ 02/623–4869), in Nahalat Shiva, for
a selection of interesting contemporary ceramics by Israelis. **Shemonah
Beyachad** (⌧ 11 Salomon St., ☎ 02/624–7250) displays the work of
a number of artists. At **7 Artists** (⌧ 6 Salomon St., ☎ 02/623–4210),
pottery shares the showcases with embroidered and woven fabrics. **Danny
Azoulay**'s store (⌧ 5 Salomon St., ☎ 02/623–3918) has fine porcelain items. Although many are traditional Jewish ritual objects—some
of which are expensive—you can also find less pricey items such as nap-
kin rings and bottle stoppers—all beautifully painted by hand in rich
blues, reds and golds.

If ethnic embroidery is your interest, take a look at the items in **Kuzari**
(⌧ 17 Salomon St., ☎ 02/623–3905), where traditional stitchery is
applied in bright colors to a variety of traditional and modern items.
Rain-Beau Gallery (⌧ 16 Salomon St., ☎ 02/624–1918) carries a wide
variety of delightful handcrafted items.

Opaque smoky-color Israeli **glass** is available in both decorative and
practical items in many of the tourist shops. The miniature vases,
sometimes decorated with silver, are particularly attractive.

Klein (⌧ 3 Ziv St., off Bar Ilan St., ☎ 02/538–9992 and 02/538–8784),
in the north part of Jerusalem, offers some of the best-made olive-wood
objects in the country. This is actually the factory, which has a showroom that stocks everything they make, from bowls and yo-yos to attractive trays of Armenian pottery tiles framed in olive wood, picture
frames, boxes, and desktop paraphernalia.

Paper-cutting was a well-established Jewish art form until about a
century ago. **Yehudit Shadur,** who has been primarily responsible for
the Israeli revival of this tradition craft, does pieces ranging from simple contrasts to richly colored and varied textures (⌧ 12 Hovevei
Zion St., ☎ 02/566–3217); call for an appointment. **Archie Granot,**
working with traditional motifs, has evolved his own complex multi-

paper-cut Judaica (⊠ 22 Yosef Rivlin St., ☎ 02/624–

Druze weavings in the form of cloths, pillow cov-
ings can be found at **Ben Shalom** (⊠ 19 Ben Yehuda
8), which has a wide variety of beautiful items at
G.R.A.S. (⊠ 20 King George St., adjacent to the
t store, ☎ 02/625–6599) offers its own special
ats, vests, pillow covers, and curtains in their dis-
Israeli-made "Eastern" (read: exotic) fabrics. The pillow covers are an especially good value and make great, easy-to-pack gifts.

Harps

The **House of Harrari,** in Nahalat Shiva (⊠ Ma'alot Nahalat Shiva 7,
☎ 02/625–5191), sells a selection of beautiful harps, ranging from decorative door harps to 22- and 34-string folk instruments. You can choose
from a variety of ornamentation, and the little door harps can be decorated with an appropriate inscription. The gallery will ship your purchase home. The store also stocks (since no mention of human beings
named Harrari) recorded klezmer music by local artists.

Jewelry

Jewelry in Israel is of a high international standard. The ubiquitous **H.
Stern** (⊠ Just inside Jaffa Gate and at many major hotels) has high-
quality, conventional pieces. **Meshulash** (⊠ 17 Salomon St., ☎ 02/624–
1762) makes and sells exquisite ultramodern pieces, characterized by
their clean, almost minimalist lines. The very affordable **G.R.A.S.** (☞
Crafts, *above*) does a lot of modern adaptations of traditional Yemenite
silver jewelry. **Idit** (⊠ 16 Ben Yehuda St., ☎ 02/625–5836) has fine
merchandise of a more formal style. One particularly outstanding
craftsman is **Danny Alsberg** (☎ 02/628–9275), in the Arts and Crafts
Lane (Hutzot Hayotzer), near the Jaffa Gate.

The **National Diamond Center (NDC),** one of the country's largest diamond manufacturers, has a factory and showroom for jewelry and loose-
cut gems (⊠ 143 Bethlehem Rd., ☎ 02/733770). Guided tours of the
facility are also available on request.

Perfumes

Judith Muller produces scents that come in pretty, smoky-glass flacons
shaped to look like ancient bottles. The bottles are available in the usual
measures, but you can also find gift sets of two, four, six, and eight
miniature bottles. Try the Hamashbir department store, on King George
Street, or any perfumery or pharmacy.

T-Shirts

Light and inexpensive, T-shirts are a fun gift to bring home. The stores
all stock the same range of machine-stamped shirts (some crude, some
very attractive); most will also decorate shirts from a selection of designs. There are several on Ben Yehuda Street: Army/Navy Surplus (also
on Ben Hillel St., adjacent to Ben Yehuda), Best Line, Happy T-Shirt,
Sweet, and Happening. Mr. T. and Lord Kitsch, on Zion Square, also
stock a good selection.

JERUSALEM A TO Z

Arriving and Departing

By Bus

The **Egged** National Bus Cooperative (☎ 02/530–4555) serves Jerusalem
with comfortable air-conditioned buses from all major cities in Israel
to the **Central Bus Station** (⊠ 224 Jaffa Rd.). Egged buses in and out

of Jerusalem stop service about a half hour before sunset on Friday and religious holiday eves and resume after dark on Saturday or religious holidays. The **East Jerusalem Bus Station** (⊠ Sultan Suleiman St., opposite Damascus Gate) is the terminus for private Arab-run lines serving West Bank towns such as Bethlehem and Hebron.

By Car

Route 1 is the chief route to the center of Jerusalem from both the west (Tel Aviv, Ben-Gurion Airport, Mediterranean Coast) and the east (Galilee via Jordan Valley, Dead Sea area, Eilat). From Tel Aviv, Route 1 becomes Jaffa Road, which runs into the city center. The road from Tel Aviv is a divided highway that presents no problems except at morning rush hour (7:30–9), when traffic backs up at the entrance to the city.

By Plane

INTERNATIONAL FLIGHTS

Most visitors entering Israel fly into **Ben-Gurion International Airport** (☎ 03/971–0000 for information), outside Tel Aviv and 50 km (31 mi) from Jerusalem.

Egged Buses 423, 945, and 947 run from the airport to Jerusalem's Central Bus Station on a reasonably frequent schedule (it's seldom more than 30 minutes' wait), except in the evenings, and cost NIS 15.50 ($5). There is no bus service from Friday afternoon to Saturday night, or on religious holidays. For bus schedules, call 02/530–4555.

The **drive** from the airport, on Route 1 east, takes about 35 minutes. A "special" taxi (as opposed to a shared one, a *sherut*) should cost NIS 110 ($36); NIS 140 ($46) after 9 PM and on Saturday and holidays.

Seven-seat **sherut** taxis (limo-vans) depart when they fill up and drop passengers off at whatever address they request for NIS 29 ($9.70). To get from Ben-Gurion Airport to Jerusalem by **limousine,** call Nesher (☎ 02/625–3233 or 02/623–1231) to book a place, preferably the day before. They will pick you up at any Jerusalem address. Nesher also makes the reverse trip; look for their stand outside the terminal.

DOMESTIC FLIGHTS

Atarot Airport (☎ 02/583–3440), 8 km (5 mi) north of Jerusalem off Ramallah Road, provides domestic flights only—specifically, daily flights to and from Eilat, Haifa, and Rosh Pina on Arkia, Israel's domestic carrier. Arkia runs a shuttle service geared to its flight schedule and costing NIS 10 ($3.40), between the airport and Arkia's downtown office at the Clal Building (⊠ 97 Jaffa Rd., ☎ 02/625–5888, or toll-free 177/022–4888).

By Sherut

Seven-seat sheruts (stretch cabs or minivans) available to share ply the same routes as the Egged buses to and from Tel Aviv, Haifa, and Beersheba and charge about the same fares (25% more on Saturday and holidays, when the buses do not run). In Jerusalem, **Ha'ooma/Habira** (⊠ 1 Harav Kook St., near Zion Sq., and at the old Ram Hotel, behind Central Bus Station, ☎ 02/538–9999) goes to Tel Aviv. **Aviv/Kesher** (⊠ 12 Shammai St., ☎ 02/625–4034 or 02/625–7366) goes to Haifa. **Yael Daroma** (⊠ 12 Shammai St., ☎ 02/625–6985) has routes to Beersheba and Eilat. Sheruts from Tel Aviv to Jerusalem congregate at the Tel Aviv New Central Bus Station. Sheruts to Jerusalem from Haifa leave from the Hadar district.

By Train

One rides the train between Tel Aviv and Jerusalem for the scenery and novelty of the experience (it's great for kids), not for the convenience.

There is only one train a day in each direction: from Jerusalem, Sunday–Thursday at 2:55 PM and Friday at 12 noon; and from Tel Aviv Sunday–Friday at 10 AM. There is no service on Saturday and religious holidays. The schedule is subject to change, so call ahead before setting out for the station. The trip takes twice as long as the bus, about 1¾ hours, and costs NIS 13.50 ($4.50) for adults, with discounts for children, students, and senior citizens. The railway station in Jerusalem (⊠ David Remez St., ☎ 02/673–3764) is on several city bus routes (Nos. 4, 7, and 8), and you can normally hail a passing cab. The route ends at Tel Aviv Central on Arlozorov Street, well served by taxis and numerous bus routes.

Getting Around

By Bus

The **Egged** National Bus Cooperative (☎ 02/530–4555 for local information) enjoys a monopoly on bus lines within Jerusalem. Routes within the city are extensive. Service begins at 5:30 AM and ends around midnight (depending on the route). There is no service from half an hour before sunset on Friday (or on the eve of a religious holiday) until half an hour after sundown on Saturday. The fare on all routes is NIS 3.75 ($1.25); you need to use Israeli money, but you do not need exact change. There are no transfers. Buses do not automatically stop at every bus stop; you need to signal the driver. Bus maps are sometimes available at the Central Bus Station, on Jaffa Road in West Jerusalem. Your best bet is to get advice from your hotel or the locals.

The two small Arab-run bus stations in **East Jerusalem** primarily serve routes to towns in the West Bank (☞ Around Jerusalem A to Z *in* Chapter 3).

Egged's **Bus 99** runs a loop that sets out from the small terminal on Ha'emek Street (near Jaffa Gate) and takes about 1½ hours to complete. The 35 stops include the downtown area (the New City), the Jerusalem Theater, the Jerusalem Mall, the Holyland Hotel (with its scale model of ancient Jerusalem), Mt. Herzl, Yad Vashem, the Israel Museum, the Knesset, the Central Bus Station, Mt. Scopus, and a circuit of the Old City walls (with stops at Damascus Gate, the Rockefeller Museum, Gethsemane, the Western Wall and Mt. Zion). Almost all the hotel districts are serviced by this bus. The route stops at sites that are otherwise difficult to reach except by taxi. Buses leave the Jaffa Gate station Sunday–Thursday at 10, 11, noon, 1, 2, and 4, and on Friday and holiday eves at 10, 11, and noon only. There is no service on Saturday or religious holidays. The cost is NIS 15 ($5) for a one-day ticket or NIS 24 ($8) for a two-day ticket, with unlimited transfers on this route.

By Car

Navigating a rental car through unfamiliar territory and looking for legal parking make driving in the big cities a dubious pleasure. A combination of walking and cabs or a guide-driven tourist limo-van is often more time-effective—and even more cost-effective. In Jerusalem the only sights that might be easier to get to by car are West Jerusalem and the panoramic overlooks, which are a bit out of the way.

Note that curbs painted with alternate bands of blue and white indicate legal parking, but only with the use of inexpensive parking cards, available for purchase at post offices and at many refreshment stands or curb vendors in or near the downtown area.

Gas stations are easily found, and some never close, but gasoline is expensive in Israel—about $4 a gallon at press time. Drive defensively: Many local drivers take hair-raising risks on the road.

By Taxi

Taxis can be flagged on the street, ordered by phone, or picked up at a taxi stand or at major hotels. There are usually taxis waiting outside the Israel Museum and Yad Vashem. The law requires taxi drivers to turn on their meters; passengers can insist on it. Negotiating the fare puts you at a disadvantage unless you are familiar with the distance involved. A 10- to 15-minute ride (day rates until 9 PM) should cost between NIS 12 and NIS 18 (between $4 and $6). The fare is 25% higher after 9 PM and on Saturday and holidays. Any serious problem with the cabby can be reported to the Ministry of Tourism: Be sure to note the number on the illuminated yellow sign on the roof of the cab.

Contacts and Resources

Car Rental

Avis (✉ 22 King David St., ☎ 02/624–9001). **Budget** (✉ 8 King David St., ☎ 02/624–8991 or 02/624–8992). **Eldan** (✉ 24 King David St., ☎ 02/625–2151). **Europcar (National)** (✉ 8 King David St., ☎ 02/624–8464). **Hertz** (✉ 18 King David St., ☎ 02/623–1351; ✉ Hyatt Regency Hotel, 32 Lehi St., ☎ 02/581–5069). **Reliable** (✉ 14 King David St., ☎ 02/624–8993).

Consulates

United States Consulate-General: 18 Agron Street, in West Jerusalem, and 27 Nablus Road, in East Jerusalem (for consular services); ☎ 02/625–3288 for both. **British Consulate-General:** Tower House, next to St. Andrew's Church, Remez Street, in West Jerusalem, ☎ 02/671–7724; and for consular services, Sheikh Jarrah, East Jerusalem, ☎ 02/582–8281. This consulate also serves citizens of Australia and New Zealand.

Doctors and Dentists

Magen David Adom (✉ 7 Hamag St., Romema, ☎ 02/652–3133) is an emergency ambulance service. The privately run, 24-hour **Terem Emergency Care Center** (✉ 7 Hamag St., Romema, ☎ 02/652–1748) offers first aid and other medical attention. **Yad Sarah** (✉ 43 Hanevi'im St., ☎ 02/624–4242) is a voluntary organization that lends medical equipment such as wheelchairs, crutches, and canes. There is no charge, but a contribution is expected. It is open Sunday–Thursday 9–7 and Friday 9–noon.

Dr. Barzilai runs an emergency dental clinic (✉ 16 King George St., Entrance B, 8th floor, ☎ 02/625–4779) Sunday through Thursday, with alternating morning and afternoon hours.

Emergencies

Ambulance (☎ 101 or 02/652–3133). The Magen David Adom is the Israeli version of the Red Cross. **Police** (☎ 100 or 02/539–1111).

HOSPITAL EMERGENCY ROOMS

Emergency rooms in major hospitals are on duty 24 hours a day in rotation. The duty list is published in the daily press. In an emergency, call Magen David Adom (☎ 101) to find out which hospital is on duty that day for your specific need (orthopedic or gastric, for example). Be sure to take your passport with you. A fee will be charged. The major hospitals in Jerusalem are **Bikur Holim** (✉ Strauss St., ☎ 02/670–1111); **Hadassah** (✉ Ein Kerem, ☎ 02/677–7111, emergency room 02/677–6555, children's emergency room 02/677–7204); **Hadassah** (✉ Mt. Scopus, ☎ 02/584–4111); **Sha'arei Tzedek** (✉ Bayit Vegan, ☎ 02/655–5111, emergency room 02/655–5508).

Guided Tours

ORIENTATION

Two tour operators offer half- and full-day tours of Old and New Jerusalem, with different itineraries covered on different days of the week: **Egged Tours** (⌧ 224 Jaffa Rd., ☎ 02/530–4422) and **United Tours** (⌧ King David Hotel Annex, 23 King David St., ☎ 02/625–2187, 02/625–2188, or 02/625–2189). A tour costs about $23 for a half day and $44–$55 for a full day, depending on itinerary. The price includes pickup and drop-off at your hotel, and bookings can be made directly or through your hotel concierge.

PERSONAL GUIDES

At press time the daily rate for a private guide with an air-conditioned car or limousine was $280–$360, depending on the size of the vehicle. Many guides will offer their services without a car for about $130–$160. The customary rate for a half day is 60% of the full-day rate. For listings of private guides, contact Eshcolot Tours (⌧ 36 Keren Hayesod St., ☎ 02/563–5555) or Fodor's writer and guide Mike Rogoff (☎ FAX 02/679–0410).

SPECIAL-INTEREST TOURS

The **Society for the Protection of Nature in Israel** (⌧ 13 Helene Hamalka St., ☎ 02/625–2357 or 02/624–4605, FAX 02/625–4953), or SPNI, emphasizes nature in its tours, often in off-the-beaten-path locations. Tours in English cater to visitors, but sometimes the experience matters more than the explanations, so the richer menu of Hebrew-language tours might be considered. Tours change throughout the year, so call for details.

WALKING TOURS

Archaeological Seminars (☎ 02/627–3515) specializes in visiting sites of archaeological importance. A slide lecture precedes the tour, and the guides are generally excellent. Three two- to three-hour itineraries ($12–$15) are offered Sunday through Thursday several times a week, with expanded summer offerings. No reservations are required. Discounts are available for students, and are also offered when you take more than one tour. All tours depart from 34 Habad Street, in the Jewish Quarter of the Old City.

Walking Tours (☎ 02/652–2568 or 02/581–8758) operates tours with two comprehensive half-day itineraries. Some are offered several times a week. Prices range from $10 to $14. Discounts are available for students and senior citizens, and there are package deals. Tours depart from the office of the associated Zion Walking Tours (☞ *below*), inside Jaffa Gate opposite the police station. **Zion Walking Tours** (☎ 02/628–7866) has a number of itineraries, among them the Mount of Olives area. Tours last about 3½ hours and cost $10 to $16, with student discounts available. Some tours are repeated during the week.

Late-Night Pharmacies

The daily press publishes the addresses of pharmacies on duty at night, on Saturday, and on holidays. This information is also available from Magen David Adom (☎ 02/652–3133). **SuperPharm** (⌧ 5 Burla St., Nayot, ☎ 02/678–4139) is open Sunday–Thursday 8:30 AM–midnight, Friday 8:30 AM–3 PM, and Saturday 9 PM–midnight. Its downtown location (⌧ 3 Hahistadrut St., ☎ 02/624–6249) closes at 11 PM.

Taxis

Twenty-four-hour service: **Hapalmach** (☎ 02/679–2333); **Rehavia,** (☎ 02/625–4444, 02/625–4445, or 02/625–4446); **Hapisgah** (☎ 02/542–1111 or 02/542–2222; not on the Sabbath).

Travel Agencies

American Express (✉ 40 Jaffa Rd., ☎ 02/623–1710 or 02/623–1908). **ISSTA** (✉ 31 Hanevi'im St., ☎ 02/625–7257); for students and academics. **Vaintours** (✉ 33 King George St., ☎ 02/625–2984). **Ziontours** (✉ 19 Hillel St., ☎ 02/625–4326 or 02/625–4327).

Visitor Information

There is a **Tourist Information Office** at the Jaffa Gate in the Old City (☎ 02/628–0457 or 02/628–0382) and another at 17 Jaffa Road (☎ 02/625–8844). Both offices are open Sunday–Thursday 8:30–5 and Friday 8:30–1 (until 2 at the Jaffa Gate office).

The **Christian Information Center** at Jaffa Gate in the Old City (☎ 02/627–2692) is open Monday–Saturday 8:30–1 (closed Sunday and Christian holidays).

3 Around Jerusalem

Including Bethlehem, Masada, and the Dead Sea

West of Jerusalem, rugged pine-forested hills fold down to a green region of soft landscapes, biblical echoes, and chalk caves. To the east, in stark contrast, you plunge at once through the Judean Desert to Masada and the Dead Sea, the lowest spot on earth, with bleak but dramatic vistas counterpointed by brilliant green oases. And just south of the holy city is Bethlehem, birthplace of Jesus. For Tel Aviv–based travelers, these areas are easily accessible with an investment of not more than an hour in each direction.

By Mike Rogoff

JERUSALEM'S LOCATION IN THE HEART of Israel's central mountain range makes it an excellent base for day tours in the area. Furthermore, many visitors feel visiting Jerusalem is so intense that they need excursions like these for a change of pace and scenery.

By far the most interesting, dramatic, and unmissable sites are those of the Judean Desert–Dead Sea region. This is a rocky desert of extraordinary barrenness, throwing into brilliant relief the waterfalls and greenery of Ein Gedi, the springs and reed thickets of Ain Fashcha, and the sprawling oasis of the town of Jericho.

The road that skirts the Dead Sea (Route 90) is hemmed in by awesome fractured brown cliffs that soar in many places to heights of more than 1,600 feet. Slicing through these immense desert precipices are Ein Gedi's two canyons of Nahal David and Nahal Arugot, both refreshing surprises of rivulets, pools, waterfalls, and subtropical vegetation. Wildlife abounds here, particularly the ibex (wild goat) and the hyrax (coney), though you cannot rely on always seeing them.

The Dead Sea itself—actually a lake—is a unique phenomenon: It is the saltiest body of water in the world at the lowest point on earth. Feel the tension seep away as you float in the balmy brine or smooth mineral-rich black mud all over your body. Bathing options range from free-access public beaches with minimal facilities to well-equipped spas. Some of the best are in the Ein Bokek hotel district at the southern end of the Dead Sea (☞ Chapter 8).

Masada, the great mountaintop palace-fortress built 2,000 years ago by King Herod, overlooks the Dead Sea. Its palaces, mosaics and frescoes, ingenious water system, and baths are a tribute to Herod's grand style; the remote location and almost unassailable position are evidence of his paranoia. Add the human drama of Masada's defense and fall during the Jewish revolt against Rome a century later, and it is easy to understand why this is one of the most visited sites in Israel.

For Christian visitors, Bethlehem is a major place of pilgrimage, a stone's throw from Jerusalem. The cavernous and colonnaded Church of the Nativity, the oldest church in the country, is built over the grotto where Jesus is believed to have been born. Bethlehem is a West Bank Arab town of some 35,000 souls, one-third Christian, two-thirds Muslim, straddling the ancient high road through the rocky, olive-groved Judean Hills.

Still on the trail of the Bible, you will find echoes of Joshua, though not his walls, at the palm-studded oasis of Jericho to the east; and persuasive topographical detail of the dueling ground of David and Goliath in the Elah Valley to the west.

In the planted pine and cypress forests west of Jerusalem, there are an abundance of delightful views, picnic spots, and a few nature reserves. Do not miss the Sorek Cave, an almost fantastical cavern of stalagmites and stalactites; or the extraordinary network of ancient man-made chalk caves—the huge "bell caves" of Bet Guvrin and the adjacent underground storage, burial, and industrial complexes of Maresha.

Pleasures and Pastimes

Bird-Watching

Israel's varied climate and position on major migratory routes make it a fascinating place for bird-watchers. Especially interesting in this region are the raptors seen in the skies of the Judean Desert.

Dead Sea Beaches, Spas, and Mineral Pools

You bathe in the briny Dead Sea; you cannot actually swim in it. The incredible density of its water—about 10 times that of the ocean—makes it impossible to sink. The Dead Sea area has gained recognition as one of the world's primary health retreats for sufferers of psoriasis and various rheumatic and arthritic ailments. But the hale, too, will enjoy the benefits of the incredible mineral concentration in the Dead Sea water and mud, the natural warm mineral springs, and the oxygen-rich atmosphere at the lowest point on earth. There are several swimming spots along the Dead Sea and the good Ein Gedi Spa. (For the sophisticated spas and therapeutic facilities of the Ein Bokek/Neve Zohar area, *see* Chapter 8.)

Doctors recommend not remaining in the water for more than 15 minutes at a time because of the enervating effect of the salt, and a heart condition or high blood pressure is a reason not to bathe here at all. Avoid the discomfort of getting the brine in your eyes and mouth, though you can rinse off at the outdoor showers and faucets found at recognized beaches. It is imperative to drink a lot of water, especially in the hot season: April to October. Many beaches are rocky (and hot in summer), and it's a good idea to wear protective rubber sandals, shoes, or sneakers. Do not leave your possessions unguarded on the beach.

Dining

Other than passably good lunch cafeterias, there are no restaurants at all that might tempt you out in the evening in the areas covered by this chapter. In most cases, the tours have you back by nightfall in your Jerusalem or Tel Aviv hotel, where there is no shortage of good places to dine (☞ Dining *in* Chapters 2 and 4).

Hiking and Rappelling

The Judean Desert offers some excellent hiking trails. Ein Gedi's two nature reserves of Nahal David and Nahal Arugot are the best for beginners. For the serious hiker, several other spectacular canyons have more challenging walks but should not be attempted without expert local guidance. A hat and copious amounts of water are essential when hiking in this region. Some of the awesome limestone cliffs near the Dead Sea are favorites with local rappelling clubs.

Lodging

The lodgings of the Dead Sea region are much patronized by visitors, both local and international, who come to "take the waters." Many enjoy the quiet ambience between cliffs and coastline. For others, it's just a convenient overnight from which to strike out over the Judean Desert. Facilities range from youth hostels to luxury hotels. Excellent hotels are also available in the nearby Ein Bokek area (☞ Chapter 8).

West of Jerusalem is typically explored as a day trip from Jerusalem or Tel Aviv. The area's only decent lodgings are some fine guest houses 15 to 20 minutes outside the capital. Bethlehem, now governed by the Palestinian Authority, has a few unprepossessing hotels; Jerusalem, only 10 minutes away, is a far more convenient and congenial base. For price-category definitions, *see* Lodging *in* Chapter 2.

Exploring Around Jerusalem

This area offers day-trip options in three different directions. The Dead Sea region provides the richest fare and requires the most time, but some of its sights can be picked up en route to the Galilee via the Jordan Valley. The other two areas—west of Jerusalem and Bethlehem and the West Bank—are closer to Jerusalem and can be combined with Jerusalem sightseeing or in a pinch, with each other.

Great Itineraries

To explore the **Dead Sea Region,** you journey east through the arid Judean Desert to Qumran, where the Dead Sea Scrolls were found; the salty Dead Sea, the lowest point on earth; the canyons and waterfalls of Ein Gedi; and the ancient palace-fortress of Masada. An interesting side trip (political climate permitting) includes the oasis town of Jericho, the oldest city known.

With an early start, most of the sights can be done in one day. A good combination is Masada (with its dramatic story and interesting archaeological remains), the Dead Sea (total relaxation), and one of the Ein Gedi nature reserves (a refreshing antidote to the heat and the brine of the Dead Sea). From April to October, later closing times allow a visit to Qumran as well. Jericho (again, if accessible) can be seen together as a day tour from Jerusalem, on the way to an overnight trip along the Dead Sea, or en route to the Jordan Valley and Galilee.

The area **west of Jerusalem** encompasses part of the Judean Hills and to its southwest, the lowland area known as the Shefelah. Highlights include the exquisite Sorek stalactite cave, the Elah Valley where David and Goliath clashed, and the intriguing man-made caves of Bet Guvrin and Maresha. It's a full but comfortable day's touring.

Bethlehem, with its famous Church of the Nativity, is no more than a 10-minute drive south of Jerusalem, and you can see this church and be back in Jerusalem within two hours. There is the option (recommended if you are with a licensed guide) of continuing deeper into the West Bank as far as the Etzion Bloc. The Arab villages on the way are not friendly, and though there are fewer instances of stone throwing than there were once, the visitor is advised to use Egged buses or a guide-driven limo to get around. From the Etzion Bloc, Route 367 descends west to the Elah Valley (☞ West of Jerusalem, *below*), if you want to link two areas on your trip.

When to Tour Around Jerusalem

The Dead Sea region is pleasant in the cool season (October through April) but often very hot at other times. A very early start, and beginning the day with Masada, can help beat the heat and the crowds. *Ending* the day with Masada often achieves the same result. Bethlehem is best first thing in the morning or late afternoon if you want to avoid the crowds, especially the seasonal cruise-boat traffic, but note the Grotto of the Nativity hours. West of Jerusalem is good anytime, although the Sorek Cave has more limited hours and no tour on Friday.

Throughout this chapter, numbers in the margin correspond to points of interest on the Around Jerusalem map.

DEAD SEA REGION

From the ridges of Jerusalem's Mt. Scopus and Mount of Olives, the view to the east is of barren hills that cascade down to the Dead Sea, almost 4,000 feet below. Clouds off the Mediterranean warm and disperse as they cross the high ridge and descend toward the chasm of the Dead Sea, creating what is called a "rain shadow." Within a map distance of about 24 km (15 mi), the average annual rainfall drops from 22 inches in Jerusalem to 2 inches at the Dead Sea. This "shadow" region is the Judean Desert, and its proximity to Jerusalem has always made it part of that city's consciousness. Refugees fled to it; hermits sought its solitude; and in ancient times, before the Jewish Day of Atonement, the scapegoat symbolically bearing the sins of the people was driven into oblivion among its stark precipices.

Around Jerusalem

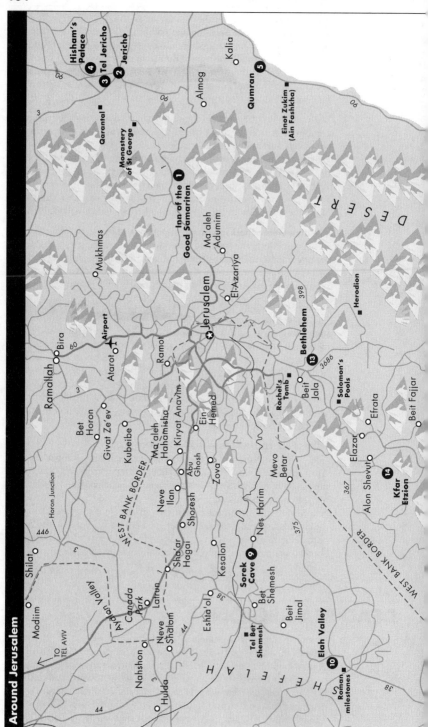

Modiin

Shilat

446

3

Canada Park

Ayalon Valley

TO
TEL AVIV

Nahshon

Hulda

3

44

Neve
Shalom

Latrun

Sha'ar
HaGai

Eshta'ol

38

Kesalon

Bet
Shemesh

Tel Bet
Shemesh

Beit
Jimal

Elah Valley 10

Roman
milestones

38

Nes Harim

Sorek
Cave 9

Zova

Shoresh

Neve
Ilan

Abu
Ghosh

Kiryat Anavim

Ma'aleh
HaHamisha

Kubeibe

Givat Ze'ev

Bet
Horon

Ramallah

Bira

60

3

Horon Junction

WEST BANK BORDER

Mukhmas

Atarot

Airport

Ramot

Jerusalem ★

Ein
Hemed

Mevo
Betar

375

Rachel's
Tomb

Beit
Jala

Bethlehem 13

3686

Solomon's
Pools

Efrata

Elazar

Alon Shevut

367

Kfar
Etzion 14

Beit Fajjar

WEST BANK BORDER

Herodion

398

El-Azariya

Ma'aleh
Adumim

Good Samaritan

Inn of the 1

Monastery
of St George

Qarantal

3

90

Hisham's
Palace 4

3 Tel Jericho

2 Jericho

90

Almog

Kalia

Qumran 5

Einot Zukim
(Ain Fashkha)

90

D E S E R T

S H E F E L A H

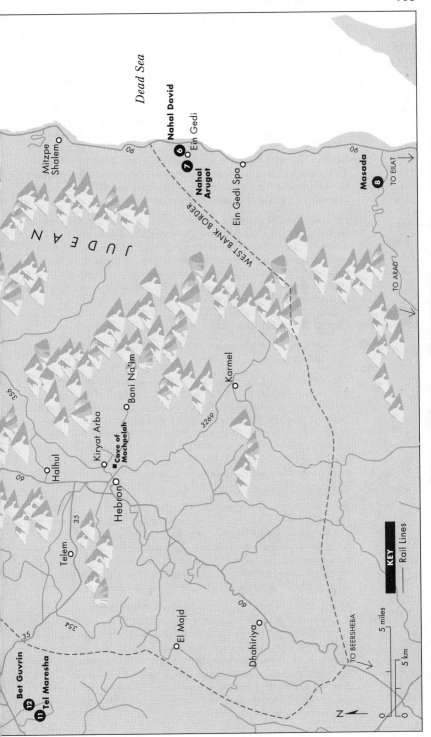

Dead Sea

Nahal David

Nahal David

6 Ein Gedi

7 **Nahal Arugot**

Ein Gedi Spa

Mitzpe Shalem

06

WEST BANK BORDER

J U D E A N

8 **Masada**

TO EILAT

TO ARAD

Karmel

3269

Bani Na'im

Kiryat Arba

Halhul

Cave of Machpelah

356

06

Hebron

35

Telem

354

El Majd

80

Dhahiriya

TO BEERSHEBA

35

Bet Guvrin

12 **Tel Maresha**

11

KEY

Rail Lines

N

5 miles

5 km

0

0

Important words of caution: It is vital to wear a hat and drink water copiously in this area in hot weather. The desert is an area to be approached with respect—do not attempt unfamiliar trails without expert guidance.

Route 1 leaves Jerusalem just north of the French Hill neighborhood, runs east, swings back below the eastern slopes of Mt. Scopus and the Mount of Olives (look for their distinctive towers on your right), and begins its steep descent to the Dead Sea. Some 8 km (5 mi) on, ahead and above you, is the edge of the town of Ma'aleh Adumim, built in the 1970s and '80s as a bedroom community of Jerusalem. This and the handful of small Jewish villages in the Judean Desert are some of the so-called West Bank settlements so often in the news. Because of their isolation, however, they have been spared the constant friction with Palestinian Arab neighbors typical of such settlements in the mountain region.

On both sides of the road, you will frequently see encampments of Bedouin, tent-dwelling Bedouins (Arab nomads) still clinging to the traditional way of life of their ancestors and eking out a livelihood by herding sheep and goats. Yet concessions have been made to modernity: water tanks and tractors, synthetic fabrics flapping on clotheslines, and even an occasional TV antenna sprouting out of a tent are witnesses to a culture in change.

Inn of the Good Samaritan

❶ *20 km (13 mi) east of Jerusalem on Rte. 1, 500 yards east of the junction with Rte. 458.*

The lone one-story building, its courtyard surrounded by a low stone wall, was a Turkish police fort a century ago, the half-way point on what was then a two-day journey between Jerusalem and Jericho. Known in the Hebrew Bible as Ma'aleh Adumim (the Red Ascent) because of its distinctive patch of red limestone, this spot was once the border marker between the biblical Israelite tribes of Benjamin to the north and Judah to the south (Joshua 15). (Don't confuse it with the town of the same name closer to Jerusalem.)

The popular name of the site, the Inn of the Good Samaritan, is spurious. The New Testament (Luke 10) relates the parable of a man ambushed on the Jericho road and helped only by a Samaritan (a member of a people hostile to the Jews), who lodged him at the nearby inn. Because Jesus' parables used images familiar to his listeners, it is not unreasonable that he had a specific inn in mind and that it was at this perennially strategic spot. The original Jericho road, now tarred but not much used, is off to the right of the highway as you continue east.

No remains of a 1st-century inn have been found, but other ages have left their mark. If you're energetic, turn your back on the commercialized "Inn," carefully cross the road, and climb the dirt track to the top of the hill opposite. Amid the scanty ruins of the small 12th-century Crusader fort of **Maldoim**—with the outskirts of Jerusalem and Jericho visible—the gospel passage comes alive. The medieval Burchard of Mt. Sion wrote that the Red Ascent (called the "Blood Ascent" by Arabs) got its name "from the frequent blood shed there. Of a truth it is horrible to behold and exceedingly dangerous! . . ."

Jericho

★ **❷** *45 km (28 mi) northeast of Jerusalem.*

The oasis town of Jericho, immortalized as the place where "the walls came tumblin' down" at the sound of Joshua's trumpets, is the oldest city in the world; at 850 feet below sea level, it is (currently) the lowest as well. Just to be able to say, "I was there" is arguably worth a trip through the town, but there is enough to hold you a little longer. The wide, tree-lined main artery is more country lane than city street. The riot of greenery—date palms, orange groves, banana plantations, bougainvillea, and papaya trees—takes the edge off the neglect and dilapidation that is everywhere apparent. The Arab population of about 12,000 is mostly Muslim, with a small Christian minority.

Jericho has been under Palestinian autonomous control since May 1994, and though the atmosphere at press time (fall 1996) was generally relaxed, the situation is not always predictable and should be checked before planning your tour. There have been times recently when tourists in private cars were discouraged from visiting the town.

Entering the town from the south, take the left fork at the traffic island. A few hundred yards farther, the road swings sharply to the left. To the right of the bend and one block away (no entry for vehicles) is a huge sycamore tree, which tradition (and the fellow across the way who sells postcards of it) identifies as the very one Zacchaeus climbed to watch Jesus pass by (Luke 19). The fruit stands and garden restaurants that dot this route closed under the pressure of local Palestinian activists after the eruption of the *intifada,* the Arab unrest, in December 1987, but some have reopened in the changed climate—and administration—of the town.

❸ Tel Jericho is the mound of accumulated earth that entombs the famous ancient city. Archaeologists have extensively excavated it, looking for its most famous ruins: the walls that, in the words of the spiritual, "came tumblin' down" at the blast of Joshua's ram's horns (Joshua 6). Jericho was the first Canaanite objective of the Israelite army in the mid-13th century BC. The Israelites marched around the city once a day for six days, relates the Bible. On the seventh day, they marched around seven times, and on the seventh time they blew their ram's horns and shouted, "and the wall fell down flat, so that the people went up into the city, every man straight before him, and they took the city" (Joshua 6:20).

Those walls have not been found, but remains of the world's oldest walled city have. An excavation pit at the top of the *tel* (hill) reveals a massive, round stone tower 30 feet in diameter, preserved to a height of 25 feet and attached to an 8-foot-thick wall. The structures predate the invention of pottery, and carbon-14 tests have placed human skulls and bones found at the site in the Neolithic period (Late Stone Age), between 7800 and 6500 BC. Little is known about who these early urbanites were, or why they needed such stout fortifications thousands of years before they became common in the rest of the region, but a wealth of artifacts, most displayed in the Israel and Rockefeller museums in Jerusalem (☞ Exploring Jerusalem *in* Chapter 2), give insights into their domestic life and rituals. One such ritual was decapitating the bodies of deceased relatives and burying the head beneath the floor of the house, apparently to keep the ancestor's spirit—and thus his strength and wisdom—within the home.

From the sun shelter at the top of the tel, there is a fine sweeping view of Jericho, the biblical "City of Palms." The generous spring that was always the secret of its fecundity is across the road, capped today by a pump house. It is known as **Ain es-Sultan,** the Sultan's Spring, or Elisha's Spring, in recognition of the Old Testament prophet's miracle of sweetening the water with a bowl of salt (I Kings 2). In the distance to the east is the high range of the mountains of Ammon and Moab in Jordan, among them the peak of Mt. Nebo, from which Moses viewed the Promised Land.

To the south, among the banana trees some 3 km (2 mi) away, is a small but distinctive earth mound. This is **Tel Abu Alaik,** where archaeologists' spades have uncovered the remains of the royal palace of the Jewish Hasmonean dynasty (2nd–1st centuries BC), described by the Jewish historian Josephus Flavius (AD 37–circa 100). In the last decades of the 1st century BC, Mark Antony gave the valuable oasis of Jericho to his beloved Cleopatra. The humiliated King Herod, Antony's local vassal, was forced to lease the property back from the Egyptian queen. Herod expanded and improved the palace, turning it into his winter retreat. It was here that he died in 4 BC.

To the west is the **Mount of Temptation,** identified by tradition as the "exceedingly high mountain" from which Satan tempted Jesus with dominion over "all the kingdoms of the world" (Matthew 4). The peak is surrounded by a modern wall. Halfway down the mountain and a bit to the left is a remarkable Greek Orthodox monastery, built right into the cliff face on Byzantine remains (note also the many caves, which once served hermits). Both mountain and monastery (the Monastery of Temptation) are known locally as Qarantal, a corruption of *quarantena* (a period of 40 days; the source for the English word *quarantine*), the period of Jesus' temptation. ⊠ *Turn left at sharp bend in the road, entrance is from the west,* ☎ *02/992–1909.* ◪ *NIS 4 ($1.40).* ☉ *Apr.–Sept. 7:30–6, Oct.–Mar. 7:30–5; subject to change.*

NEED A
BREAK?

The **Temptation Restaurant,** which abuts the parking lot of Tel Jericho, has excellent *bourma,* a honey-rolled pastry filled with whole pistachio nuts. The lunches offer good value, with tasty *mezes* (Middle Eastern salads) and meats. The nearby fruit stands tend to overcharge, but try the pomelo (related to the grapefruit), in season from December to March.

---

❹ A spacious site in pastoral surroundings, the remains of **Hisham's Palace** have some interesting stonework and a spectacular mosaic floor. Hisham was a scion of the Ummayad dynasty, which built the Dome of the Rock and El-Aqsa Mosque, in Jerusalem. Like Herod eight centuries earlier, he was attracted by the balmy winter climate of the Jericho oasis and decided to build what is known as Hisham's Palace (Hirbet el-Mafjar in Arabic). While still under construction, the structure was badly damaged by the great earthquake of AD 749 and never completed, but the high quality of the mosaics and stone and plaster reliefs that survive are evidence of its splendor.

To get here from Tel Jericho, go north for 2 km (1 mi), where a turnoff to the right leads to the site. The left turnoff to the site itself is another km (½ mi) down the road but marked only by a low stone pillar on the right side of the road. The entrance to the ruins is through a small gatehouse and into a wide plaza dominated by a large star-shape stone window that once graced an upper-floor chamber. A basement bathhouse and one of the palace's two mosques (open to the sky) are an interesting juxtaposition of both the worldly and the spiritual characters of the Arab empire of the time. North of the plaza is a series of columns—some artless reconstructions in concrete—that supported the roof of a large bath and recreation area. Several sections of the fine geometric mosaics have been left exposed; others are covered by sand.

Undoubtedly the most impressive part of the complex is the adjacent reception room. Its intricate **mosaic floor** depicting a lion hunting a stag is one of the most beautiful in Israel, the tiny colored tesserae producing a realism astonishing for this medium. Still visible on some of the walls are fragments of ornate stucco reliefs, but the best examples found here are now displayed in Jerusalem's Rockefeller Museum (☞ Exploring Jerusalem *in* Chapter 2). The balustrade of an ornamental pool reflects the artistic influences of both East and West. ⊠ *Jericho,* ☎ 02/992–2522. 🎫 *NIS 4 ($1.40).* ☉ *Apr.–Sept. 7:30–6, Oct.–Mar. 7:30–5; subject to change.*

En Route Route 90 south brings you back toward the **Dead Sea.** A milestone by the side of the road just before the gas station (at the Kalia Junction) announces you have now reached the bottom of the world, and a Bedouin is often here with his camel to help you immortalize the moment. The Dead Sea has shrunk in recent years, and the shore at this point is almost a kilometer (½ mile) away. Heaps of white potash, the primary product of the Dead Sea, can be seen off to the left, though today all extraction of potash, bromine, and magnesium takes place at the huge plant at Sodom, at the southern end of the lake.

Qumran

❺ *6 km (4 mi) south of the Kalia Junction on Rte. 90, 20 km (13 mi) south of Jericho, 50 km (31 mi) east of Jerusalem.*

The ancient remains of Qumran are not especially impressive to the layperson, but caves in the cliffs west of the small site yielded the most significant archaeological find ever made in Israel: the **Dead Sea Scrolls,** found under extraordinary circumstances. In 1947, a young Bedouin goatherd stumbled on a cave containing a cache of the now-famous scrolls, hidden in earthen jars. Because the scrolls were written on parchment, which is treated animal hide, one of the nomads sought out a Bethlehem shoemaker to turn them into sandals! The shoemaker alerted a local antiquities dealer, who brought them to the attention of Professor Eliezer Sukenik of the Hebrew University of Jerusalem. Five other major scrolls and several thousand fragments subsequently came to light in later years, some from pirate digs conducted by the Bedouin themselves in other caves in the area, others from methodical excavations by Israeli, French, and British archaeologists.

The scrolls were written by an ultradevout Jewish sect generally identified as the Essenes, who had set up a monastic community at Qumran in the late 2nd century BC. During the Great Revolt against Rome (AD 66–73), they apparently spirited away their precious scrolls to the caves visible in the cliffs and canyons behind the town. Their fears were well founded, and Qumran was destroyed in AD 68, giving scholars an end point for the scrolls.

The Dead Sea Scrolls include books of the Old Testament and sectarian literature of the Qumran community. Among the biblical scrolls is one containing the full 66 chapters of the Book of Isaiah. Except for minor variations, the text of the scroll is almost identical to that used in Jewish communities to this day, conclusively putting to rest any doubts about the authenticity of the modern edition. Sectarian texts include their constitution, known as the "Rule of the Community" (or as the "Manual of Discipline"); a description of an end-of-the-world final battle ("War of the Sons of Light Against the Sons of Darkness"); and the "Thanksgiving Scroll," containing hymns reminiscent of biblical psalms.

Apart from the bonanza the scrolls represented for Bible scholars and students of ancient Hebrew, they afforded researchers rare insights into this previously shadowy Jewish sect. Christian scholars have long been intrigued by the suggestion that John the Baptist, whose lifestyle seems to have paralleled that of the Essenes, may have been a member of the

Qumran community. Several of the scrolls are on display in the Israel Museum in Jerusalem (☞ Exploring Jerusalem *in* Chapter 2).

Qumran sits on a narrow plateau between the craggy limestone cliffs to the west and the narrow shores of the Dead Sea to the east. The site was excavated in the 1950s. Climb the tower for a good view and note the unusual number of water channels and cisterns that gathered run-off winter floodwater from the cliffs to the west. Just below the tower (in front of you as you look toward the Dead Sea) is a long room identified as the **scriptorium.** A plaster writing table and bronze and ceramic inkwells found here confirm that this was where the scrolls were written. A good air-conditioned cafeteria and gift store serve the site. ⊠ *Rte. 90,* ☎ *02/994–2235.* ⊠ *NIS 10 ($3.40).* ☉ *Apr.–Sept., Sat.–Thurs. 8–5, Fri. and holiday eves 8–4; Oct.–Mar., Sat.–Thurs. 8–4, Fri. and holiday eves 8–3.*

Beaches and Pools

Attraktzia offers a Dead Sea beach, freshwater pools with water slides, two go-cart tracks, and full facilities. ⊠ *3 km (2 mi) north of Qumran off Rte. 90,* ☎ *02/994–2393.* ⊠ *NIS 45 ($15); after 2 PM NIS 35 ($11.70).* ☉ *Aug., daily 9–6; Sept.–July, daily 9–5.*

Hof Benyamin has a Dead Sea beach with showers and changing rooms. ⊠ *3 km (2 mi) north of Qumran off Rte. 90,* ☎ *02/994–2781.* ⊠ *NIS 15 ($5).* ☉ *Apr.–Oct., Sun.–Fri. 9–4.*

Hiking and Rappelling

Metzukei Dragot, the Center for Desert Tourism (⊠ M.P. Jericho Valley, ☎ 02/996–4501, FAX 02/996–4505), is on a cliff top overlooking the Dead Sea. The turnoff from Route 90 is 17 km (10½ mi) south of Qumran, 16 km (10 mi) north of Ein Gedi; it's about 5 km off the main road. Run by Kibbutz Mitzpe Shalem, it specializes in desert safaris in go-anywhere vehicles and in rappelling (even for novices) on the impressive cliff faces nearby.

Shopping

Kibbutz Mitzpe Shalem (⊠ 20 km, or 12½ mi, south of Qumran, ☎ 02/994–5100) manufactures the excellent—but not inexpensive—Ahava line of skin and hair-care products based on (but not smelling like!) the Dead Sea minerals. The factory outlet here is open Sunday–Thursday 8–5, Friday and holiday eves 8–3:30, and Saturday 8:30–5:30, but the products are sold elsewhere (at Masada and the Ein Gedi Spa, for example) and at pharmacies in major cities.

Einot Zukim (Ain Fashka)

3 km (2 mi) south of Qumran on Rte. 90.

A Dead Sea beach, fresh (though brackish) springs, a variety of trees and reeds rare in the arid Judean Desert, and picnic and changing facilities make the nature reserve Einot Zukim (Ain Fashkha) a popular spot; its name translates as Cliff Springs. It is especially crowded on Friday and Saturday. The most beautiful part of the reserve, with bubbling brooks and thickets of giant reeds, is closed to the general public to preserve its fragile ecosystem. The Nature Reserves Authority does occasionally conduct tours of the section, however; call for information. ☎ *02/994–2355.* ⊠ *NIS 20 ($6.70).* ☉ *Mar.–Oct., daily 8–5; call ahead for Nov.–Feb.*

En Route   Four kilometers (2½ miles) south of Qumran, Route 90 enters a wider area, the delta of the dry **Kidron stream.** One of the very few canyons in the area with a gentle enough slope to allow its use as an ancient caravan route, the Kidron comes down from the heart of Jerusalem itself. Look for the remains of a 21-centuries-old Hasmonean fort on your left, built to protect royal caravans carrying valuable tropical produce from Ein Gedi to the Mediterranean world.

Ein Gedi

★ *33 km (21 mi) south of Qumran, 20 km (12½ mi) north of Masada, 83 km (52 mi) east and south of Jerusalem.*

The wondrous oasis of Ein Gedi—two nature reserves and a verdant kibbutz-type village—bursts upon you with a splash of vivid green against ❻ the burnt browns and beiges of the desert rock. **Nahal David** (David's Stream) is a delightful natural reserve; it was here 3,000 years ago that David hid from the wrath of King Saul (I Samuel 24). The cliffs soar to more than 1,600 feet above the streams, waterfalls, and tropical reeds of the nature reserve. These features plus the wildlife would make this a delightful spot anywhere; in the midst of a harsh desert, it is nothing short of spectacular. The first turnoff to the right takes you to the parking lot at the entrance to Nahal David.

It's a bit of a climb up the clearly marked trail, which takes you past several pools and small waterfalls to the beautiful top waterfall, but it's not too daunting a prospect. Allow at least 1¼ hours to include a refreshing dip under one of the lower waterfalls. Look out for ibex (wild goat), especially in the afternoon, and for the small furry hyrax, often seen on tree branches. Leopards were rediscovered in the area some years ago but are facing extinction again because of breeding problems. They are seldom seen nowadays and never in the reserve.

If you're a hiker, don't miss the trail that breaks off to the right some 50 yards down the return path from the top waterfall. It passes the remains of Byzantine irrigation systems and offers breathtaking views of the Dead Sea. The trail doubles back on itself toward the source of Nahal David. Near the top, a short side path climbs to the remains of a 4th-millennium BC (Chalcolithic) temple. The main path leads on to a streambed, again turns east, and reaches Dudim (Lovers') Cave, formed by boulders and filled with the crystal-clear spring water. You are exactly above the waterfall of Nahal David (don't throw stones—there are people below). Since this trail involves a considerable climb (and hikers invariably take time to bathe in the "cave"), access to the trail is permitted only up to 2½ hours before closing time. ✉ *Ein Gedi,* ☎ *07/658–4285.* ▣ *NIS 11 ($3.70); includes Nahal Arugot on same day only (☞ below).* ☉ *Sat.–Thurs. 8–4, Fri. and holiday eves 8–3; closes 1 hr later during daylight saving time (late spring and summer); last admission 1 hr before closing.*

A somewhat rocky **public beach** (☞ Beaches, *below*), 200 hundred yards south of Nahal David behind the gas station, has free access to the Dead Sea, freshwater showers (absolutely essential) by the water's edge, and basic changing facilities. A word of advice: Avoid getting the salt water in your eyes and mouth, and do not leave valuables unguarded.

❼ **Nahal Arugot,** like Nahal David to its north, is a fine nature reserve. Aside from its natural beauty, or perhaps because of it, Ein Gedi has attracted settlement for thousands of years. Near the mouth of the canyon is a small mound known as **Tel Goren.** Excavations here in the 1960s exposed five noncontinuous strata of settlements from the 7th century BC (Israelite period) to the 6th century AD (Byzantine period). An intriguing Hebrew and Aramaic inscription removed from a 6th-century AD mosaic synagogue floor nearby invokes the wrath of heaven on troublemakers of different stripes, including "whoever reveals the secret of the town to the Gentiles." The "secret" is believed to refer to the revived cultivation of the balsam tree, which produced the prized perfume for which the town was once famous.

Although not quite as green as Nahal David, the deep canyon of Nahal Arugot is, if anything, more spectacular. Enormous boulders and slabs of stone on the opposite cliff face seem poised in mid-cataclysm, and the whole effect is powerfully primordial. The hour-long hike to the **Hidden Waterfall** (quite a lot of steps, but not especially steep) takes you by delightful spots where a stream bubbles over rock shelves and shallow pools offer relief from the heat. The Hidden Waterfall is reached by a short marked trail down to the left. Do not continue on the trail beyond the waterfall without prior arrangement with the Nature Reserves Authority. From the waterfall, if you're adventurous, you can return through the greenery of the streambed, leaping the boulders and wading the pools (appropriate footwear obviously necessary). ⊠ *Ein Gedi,* ☎ *07/658–4285.* ▤ *NIS 11 ($3.70); includes Nahal David on same day only (*☞ *above).* ⊙ *Sat.–Thurs. 8–4, Fri. and holiday eves 8–3; closes 1 hr later during daylight saving time (late spring and summer); last admission 2 hrs before closing.*

Beaches and Pools

Ein Gedi Spa offers decent facilities (changing rooms with lockers, and indoor showers), access to the Dead Sea, a freshwater pool, free Dead Sea mud, and marvelously relaxing, warm indoor sulfur pools. Disposable towels can be purchased. A restaurant is downstairs from the changing rooms and snack bar. ⊠ *3 km (2 mi) south of Ein Gedi gas station,* ☎ *07/659–4813.* ▤ *NIS 41 ($13.70) including locker and restaurant discount; NIS 23 ($7.70) if accompanied by licensed guide.* ⊙ *Apr.–Sept., daily 7–6; Oct.–Mar., daily 7–5.*

The free **public beach** at Ein Gedi (behind the gas station) has open-air showers at the water's edge, and shower-and-changing rooms for NIS 3 ($1).

Lodging

🏨 **Kibbutz Ein Gedi.** A motel-style guest house on the kibbutz grounds is set between 1,600-foot-high cliffs and the Dead Sea and surrounded by subtropical landscaping. There is no maid service. Prices (per couple) range from $174 to $204 (according to season) and include breakfast and another full meal daily and unlimited entry to the nearby spa. ⊠ *Rte. 90, M.P. Dead Sea 86980,* ☎ *07/659–4222,* ℻ *07/658–4328. 120 rooms with shower. Kitchenette, pool, 2 tennis courts. AE, DC, MC, V.*

Camping facilities (⊠ Rte. 90, M.P. Dead Sea, ☎ 07/658–4342, ℻ 07/658–4455) are available at Ein Gedi, including tent sites (but not the tents themselves), air-conditioned bungalows, and aging "caravans" with cooking facilities and refrigerators. The site has beach access. There's also a **youth hostel** (⊠ Bet Sarah, Rte. 90, M.P. Dead Sea, ☎ 07/658–4165, ℻ 07/658–4445).

Outdoor Activities and Sports

Ein Gedi has well-marked trails through magnificent scenery for the newcomer to the area to do alone. For advice on other, and more serious, trails in the region and for information on organized hikes, contact **SPNI** (⊠ 13 Helene Hamalka St., Jerusalem, ☎ 02/624–4605; ⊠ 3 Hashefela St., Tel Aviv, ☎ 03/638–8677; or ⊠ Society's field school in Ein Gedi, ☎ 07/658–4288).

Masada

★ ❽ *19 km (12 mi) south of Ein Gedi on Rte. 90, 103 km (64 mi) east and south of Jerusalem, 20 km (12½ mi) north of Ein Bokek.*

The great isolated flattop rock of Masada commands its surroundings, its Herodian remains a witness to the chimera of ancient power and glory. But its very name has become a symbol and a rallying cry, entering history as the dramatic last stand of Jewish rebels against the legions of Rome. Herod the Great, King of the Jews by the grace of Rome, hated by his subjects and threatened by Cleopatra of Egypt, built a fortress here in the 1st century BC to which he could escape if necessary. Horrified at the thought of being an uncomfortable refugee, he had the mountaintop complex constructed in the best palatial style. Nowhere in the land are both his paranoia and sense of grandeur more in evidence: Long before you reach it, Masada is visible to the west of the highway.

With Herod's death in 4 BC and the exile of his oldest son, Archelaus, 10 years later, the central districts of Judea and Samaria (south and north of Jerusalem, respectively) came under direct Roman control. Decades of oppression and misrule precipitated the Great Revolt of the Jews against Rome in AD 66, spearheaded by an ultranationalist group called the Zealots. Masada fell to the rebels early on, but with the Roman reconquest of the country and the fall of Jerusalem in AD 70, the fortress became the last refuge for almost a thousand men, women, and children. The new governor, Silva, came down with a full legion of troops and thousands of slaves to crush the last vestige of resistance. The thoroughness of the siege can be seen by the long Roman siege wall at the foot of the mountain and by the eight square Roman camps in strategic locations on all sides.

The 1st-century Jewish historian Josephus Flavius sets the final scene. Despite the vigorous defense, the Romans succeeded in constructing a massive earth assault ramp from the high western plateau to the very summit of the mountain. Seeing the battle was lost, the rebel leader, Elazar Ben Yair, assembled his warriors and exhorted them to "at once choose death with honor, and do the kindest thing we can for ourselves, our wives and children" rather than face the brutal consequences of capture. The decision was not an easy one, relates Josephus, but once taken, it impelled each man to "carry out his terrible resolve" without delay. Having dispatched their own families, the men then drew lots to select 10 executioners for the rest; and the 10 similarly chose the last man, who would kill them all and afterward take his own life.

Josephus, who went over to the Romans in the course of the revolt, has long been suspect in the eyes of modern historians, and his melodramatic account was taken with more than a grain of salt. His description of Masada has been borne out by archaeologists, however, and the human skeletal remains and inscribed potsherds (the lots, perhaps?) seem to give weight to his version of events as well.

Most visitors ride the large cable car up to Masada (three minutes). The intrepid climb the **Snake Path** (45 minutes of steep walking), some even going before dawn to watch the sunrise. Others take the easier western Roman Ramp path, accessible only from Arad (☞ Exploring Eilat and the Negev *in* Chapter 8). The desert climate makes it imperative to drink lots of water and to wear a hat. Running water (but not refreshments or snacks) is available on Masada itself, so save your bottles for refilling. Allow at least 1½–2 hours to explore the site. Maps, brochures, and a very useful electronic guide are available at the top entrance to the site.

The 90 steps from the cable car to the top of Masada pass a large plastered cistern, one of a dozen (many are much larger) that gave Herod's fortress an incredible 10 million gallons "on tap." The secret was the winter floodwaters in streambeds west of the mountain, diverted to cisterns in the slope and then hauled to the top by hand.

The entire mountaintop—an area of more than 20 acres—is surrounded by a 4,250-foot-long **casemate,** a double wall that included living quarters and guardrooms. Most of the important buildings are concentrated on the high northern area of the site. A street passes between storerooms, where quantities of broken jars, seeds of grain, and dried fruit pits were unearthed, bearing out Josephus's assertion that the Jews did not burn their food supply (as they did their possessions) in order to show the Romans that they did not die out of want.

At the highest and most northerly point of Masada stands the **Northern Palace,** an extraordinary structure that seems to hang off the mountain. The wonderful view from its upper terrace takes in the Roman camps and "runner's path" (used for communication between the camps), as well as Ein Gedi 16 km (10 mi) to the north, from which Silva had to get his water. The effect is awesome: baked brown precipices and bleached valleys shimmering in the midday glare or awash in the gentler light of the early morning or late afternoon. The plastered wall protecting the palace—it could serve as an inner citadel—is original.

Facing you as you return from the upper terrace is the **bathhouse,** in Herod's time a state-of-the-art facility with its *apodyterium* (changing room), *frigidarium, tepidarium,* and *caldarium* (cold, lukewarm, and hot rooms, respectively). Frescoes and floor tiles are evidence of the Herodian opulence; intrusive benches and a pool represent alterations by the later occupants. The caldarium was once a closed room, heated sauna style from below and through wall pipes by hot air pumped in from an outside furnace. West of the bathhouse, steps descend to the middle and lower terraces—interesting (note Herod's hidden spiral staircase as well as the columns and frescoes of the lower terrace), but a long climb back up.

The **mikveh** is one of two Jewish ritual baths found on Masada and built during the revolt. Their discovery created a sensation in Jewish ultra-Orthodox circles in Israel, especially after a rabbinic inspection team confirmed that they were built in precise obedience to Jewish law, thus demonstrating both the length and tenacity of the religious tradition.

Continue down to the western casemate and the **synagogue** of Masada, one of only three ever found from this period. The building's orientation toward Jerusalem suggested its function, but the stone benches (synagogue means "place of assembly") and man-made pit for damaged scrolls (a *geniza*) confirmed it. It was likely here, in the community's spiritual center, that Elazar's men took their fateful decision.

At a break in the walls of the western edge, a modern winch marks the place where the Roman legionnaires broke into Masada; the original wedge-shape **ramp** (the upper part has since collapsed) is below. Here, too, is the Western Gate, from which a modern trail takes you down this side of the mountain (access via Arad only).

The small **Byzantine chapel,** complete with mosaic floor and wall designs, comes as something of a surprise on Masada. The monastic movement of the 5th century swirled and eddied into the most remote corners of the Byzantine Empire and found solitude here too. South of the chapel is the **Western Palace,** the largest structure on Masada and originally its residential and administrative center. Its most interesting features are two colorful Herodian mosaics, the larger with especially meticulous geometric and fruit motifs.

The message of the last stand of the Jews of Masada was not lost on Palestinian Jews fighting for independence in the 1930s and '40s or on the modern Israel they created. "Masada shall not fall again!" became not merely a rallying cry, but a state of mind. It reflected a determination (made more poignant by the Nazi Holocaust) to become masters of their own destiny in their own land.

If you have energy and time, explore the sparser southern part of Masada with its huge water cistern and spectacular view from the southern citadel. Test the echoes at this southern point.

✉ *Off Rte. 90,* ☎ *07/658–4207 or 07/658–4208. Site:* 💳 *NIS 14 ($4.70).* 🕐 *Apr.–Sept., Sat.–Thurs. 8–5, Fri. and holiday eves 8–4 (eve of Yom Kippur until noon). Cable car:* 💳 *NIS 15 ($5) one-way; NIS 26 ($8.70) round-trip.* 🕐 *Scheduled run every ½ hr from 8; intermediate runs depending on demand. Last car down: Apr.–Sept., Sat.–Thurs. 5* PM, *Fri. and holiday eves 3* PM, *eve of Yom Kippur noon; Oct.–Mar., Sat.–Thurs. 4* PM, *Fri. and holiday eves 2* PM. *Sound-and-light show (access only from Arad;* ☞ *Exploring Eilat and the Negev in* Chapter 8): 💳 *NIS 27 ($9).* 🕐 *Mar.–Oct., Tues. and Thurs. at 9* PM. *Translation headsets (from Hebrew):* 💳 *NIS 12 ($4). Shuttle bus by prior reservation: Yoel Tours,* ☎ *07/658–4432 or 07/695–4791; Arad Tourist Information Office,* ☎ *07/995–9333 or 07/995–8993.* 💳 *NIS 32 ($10.70) from Arad, NIS 37 ($12.40) from Ein Bokek (Dead Sea); call ahead to verify show times.*

Beaches and Pools

The **Ein Bokek** hotel district, about 15 minutes' drive south of Masada, has a free public beach with showers only (next to Kapulsky's Restaurant); there are better facilities at the adjacent **Hammei Zohar** (☎ 07/658–4161). Nonguests can pay to use the beaches and freshwater pools at the **Lot** (☎ 07/658–4321 or 07/658–4324) and **Tsell Harim** (☎ 07/658–4121 or 07/658–4122) hotels. Also available to nonguests are the beaches, pools, and full spa facilities at the more expensive **Hod** (☎ 07/658–4644), **Radisson Moriah Plaza** (☎ 07/659–1591), and **Nirvana** (☎ 07/658–4626) hotels. Nirvana is open to guests only on some holidays and weekends; call ahead. For more information about Ein Bokek, *see* Chapter 8.

Lodging

One option near Masada itself is the **Taylor Hostel** (✉ Rte. 90, M.P. Dead Sea, 86935, ☎ 07/658–4349, 🖷 07/658–4650). About 15 km (9 mi) south of Masada are the excellent hotels of **Ein Bokek** (☞ Beersheva to Ein Bokek *in* Chapter 8).

WEST OF JERUSALEM

The rugged and reforested Judean Hills let you down—with a stop at an exquisite stalactite cave—to the gentler landscapes of the Shefelah lowland. This is not a region of towns but of rural landscapes, biblical ghosts, and ancient fingerprints. To get here from Mt. Herzl in West Jerusalem, take the steep descent down to Ein Kerem and out the other side. One kilometer (about a half mile) beyond the neighborhood is the Kerem Junction. Continue straight (left fork) on Route 386. On the hills to your left is the Hadassah Hospital complex (☞ West Jerusalem *in* Chapter 2), one of the largest in the Middle East. Most hillsides are terraced, some simply following the natural strata of the sedimentary limestone, many having been created laboriously by farmers over the centuries. One of the landscape's dominant features is the result of reforestation undertaken by the Jewish National Fund to restore something of the area's ancient scenery. The mostly pine and cypress groves have begun restoring the topsoil lost through centuries of erosion, providing recreation areas and a new lease on life for animals such as the gazelle, now seen close to Jerusalem itself.

The road crosses the Jerusalem–Tel Aviv railway line, where the Refaim Valley merges with Nahal Sorek, and at once begins climbing, offering fine views of the deep gorge below. Most of the villages in these hills are *moshavim,* cooperative farming settlements of a kind pioneered in the 1920s by veteran settlers who found the communal life of the kibbutz too stifling. In a moshav, the family unit is completely autonomous but is contractually bound to other members in areas such as cooperative purchasing and marketing, social and educational services, and mutual assistance in time of need.

The socialism of the kibbutz also didn't hold any attraction for Jewish refugees from Arab lands in the 1950s. Most went to the towns, of course, but for those who settled the land, the moshav lifestyle, in which the patriarchal family structure of the old country could be preserved, was an ideal solution. There are more than 450 moshavim in Israel today, accounting for about 3% of the population. Moshavim in this area typically raise poultry and dairy cattle or sheep and cultivate fruit orchards in the lowland valleys.

Sorek Cave

★ ❾   *25 km (17 mi) southwest of Jerusalem on Rtes. 386 and 3866, 16 km (10 mi) east of Bet Shemesh on 3855.*

The Avshalom Reserve contains the justly renowned Sorek Cave, a stalactite cave that is small in comparison with similar caverns in other countries but is said to include every type of formation known. It was discovered in 1967 when a routine blast in the nearby quarry tore away the rock face, revealing a subterranean wonderland never before seen.

In developing the site, the Nature Reserves Authority faced the problem of how to allow the cave public access yet minimize impact on its unique environment. In general, the authority has won kudos for its sensitive solutions. Colored lights have been eschewed in favor of "regular" lighting to highlight the natural whites and honey browns of forms with names like "macaroni," "curtains," and "sombreros," the products of guides vying with each other to find imaginative familiarity in the shapes of the formations. In one "interfaith" series, some guides find rocky evocations of Moses, the Madonna and Child, Buddha, and the Ayatollah Khomeini. Photography is allowed only on Friday morning, when there are no guided tours. Despite the almost 100% humidity, the temperature and the general atmosphere in the cave are very comfortable year-round.

A stepped path winds down to the cave entrance: Visitors with medical problems should bear in mind the climb back to the parking lot. Local guides take groups into the cave every 15 minutes for a 30-minute tour (English tours on request). A video in an acclimatization room (English version available) explains how the cave was formed. ✉ *Avshalom Reserve. Rte. 3866,* ☎ *02/991–1117.* 🎫 *NIS 13 ($4.30).* ☉ *Sat.–Thurs. 8:30–4, Fri. and holiday eves 8:30–1.*

Lodging

There are four very good kibbutz guest houses in wooded Judean Hills locations 15–20 minutes' drive west of Jerusalem, about 10 km (6 mi)

north of the Sorek Cave. All have commanding hilltop views, quiet surroundings, rural ambience, comfortable if not luxurious accommodations, and good swimming pools. Bed-and-breakfast for two runs
$75–$150 depending on season.

🏨 **Kiryat Anavim.** Besides the better-appointed rooms in the main
building, there are garden rooms, more spartan but also more private,
with quiet little arbors nearby. ✉ *8 km (5 mi) west of Jerusalem, north
of Rte. 1, M.P. Judean Hills, 90833,* ☎ *02/534–8999,* 🖷 *02/534–8848.
85 rooms, 50 with bath. AE, DC, MC, V.*

🏨 **Ma'aleh Hahamisha.** In the largest, and thus least intimate, of the
guest houses, new building additions have added a health club, including
an indoor heated pool, gym, saunas, and whirlpool baths. Some rooms
lead to a garden patio. ✉ *12 km (7 mi) west of Jerusalem, north of
Rte. 1, M.P. Judean Hills, 90835,* ☎ *02/533–1331,* 🖷 *02/534–2144.
239 rooms, most with bath. AE, DC, MC, V.*

★ 🏨 **Neve Ilan.** A grade above its neighbors, this guest house has larger,
better-furnished rooms. Also available are superior-grade rooms and
mini-suites with their own whirlpool bath. Their pool is covered year-
round and heated in winter. The views are still somewhat scarred by
the great forest fire of the summer of 1995. ✉ *10 km (6 mi) west of
Jerusalem, north of Rte. 1, M.P. Judean Hills, 90850,* ☎ *02/533–9339,*
🖷 *02/534–8197. 160 rooms with bath. AE, DC, MC, V.*

🏨 **Shoresh.** An ambitious building program will convert this guest house
to the largest and, it is claimed, best appointed in the area. The new
pool will be covered and heated year-round. The worst hit by the
1995 forest fire, Shoresh is working hard to landscape the surroundings anew. ✉ *15 km (8½ mi) west of Jerusalem, south of Rte. 1, M.P.
Judean Hills, 90860,* ☎ *02/533–8338,* 🖷 *02/534–0262. 94 rooms
with bath (eventually 250), 120 2-bedroom apartments (eventually 150).
AE, DC, MC, V.*

Swimming

In the Judean Hills to the north of the Sorek Save, several villages and
kibbutzim have beautiful pools in wooded locations (☞ Lodging,
above).

Kiryat Anavim. ☎ *02/534–8999.* 🎫 *Sun.–Fri. NIS 27 ($9), Sat. and
holidays NIS 30 ($10).* ⊘ *May–mid-Oct., Sat.–Thurs. 9–6, Fri. and
holiday eves 9–5:30; closes 1 hr later during daylight saving time (late
spring and summer).*

Ma'aleh Hahamisha. ☎ *02/533–1331.* 🎫 *Sun.–Fri. NIS 33 ($11), Sat.
and holidays NIS 40 ($13.40).* ⊘ *May–June and Sept.–mid-Oct.,
Sun.–Thurs. 9–6, Fri.–Sat. 9–7; July–Aug., 9–7 daily.*

Neve Ilan. ☎ *02/534–1241.* 🎫 *Sun.–Fri. NIS 35 ($11.70), Sat. and
holidays NIS 45 ($15).* ⊘ *Year-round, Fri.–Sat. 8–6, Sun. 8–8, Mon.
and Wed. 6 AM–8 PM, Tues. and Thurs. 6 AM–9 PM; only for members
Sat. June–Aug.*

Shoresh. ☎ *02/534–1477.* 🎫 *Sun.–Fri. NIS 25 ($8.40), Sat. and hol-
idays NIS 30 ($10).* ⊘ *May–Sept., daily 8–6.*

Tel Bet Shemesh

*12 km (7½ mi) west of Sorek Cave on Rtes. 3855 and 38, 35 km (22
mi) from Jerusalem.*

The modern town of Bet Shemesh takes its name from its ancient predecessor, now entombed by the *tel*, or archaeological mound, on a rise
on Route 38, 2 km (just over 1 mi) south of the town's main entrance.
This is Samson country. Samson, one of the judges of Old Testament

Israel, is better known for his physical prowess and lust for Philistine women than for his shining spiritual qualities. But it was here "between Zorah and Eshta'ol" that "the Spirit of the Lord began to stir him" (Judges 13). Eshta'ol is today a moshav a few minutes' drive north, and Tzora (Zorah) is the kibbutz immediately to the west.

There is a clearing to pull off the road for the tel. From the top of the tel there is a fine view of the fields of Nahal Sorek, where Samson dallied with Delilah (Judges 16). The city of Bet Shemesh controlled access through the valley to the mountains of Judah to the east. When the Philistines captured the Israelite Ark of the Covenant in battle (11th century BC), they found that, according to the Bible, their prize brought divine retribution with it, destroying their idol of Dagon and afflicting them with tumors and their cities with rats (I Samuel 5). In consternation and awe, they rid themselves of the jinxed ark by sending it back to the Israelites at Bet Shemesh.

Elah Valley

⓿ *10 km (6 mi) south of Bet Shemesh, 42 km (26 mi) west of Jerusalem.*

The Elah Valley is one of those delightful places, not uncommon in Israel, where one can relate the scenery to a specific biblical text and confirm the maxim that once you've visited Israel, you'll never read the Bible the same way again!

Just beyond the junction of Route 38 with Route 383, and up to your right above the pine-wooded slopes is a distinctively bald flattop hill, **Tel Azekah,** the site of an ancient Israelite city. Dirt roads, especially delightful in spring when the wildflowers are out, crisscross these hills (access to Tel Azekah is by the first left from Route 383).

You have just entered the Elah Valley. A small bridge spans a usually dry streambed. Just after crossing, carefully park on the shoulder. If you have a Bible with you, open it to I Samuel 17 and read about the dramatic duel between David and the giant Philistine champion Goliath. The battle took place, one may claim with some confidence, within a half mile or so of where you're standing. Skeptical? Review the following biblical quotation.

Now the Philistines gathered their armies for battle; and they were gathered at Socoh, which belongs to Judah [identified by a mound 800 yards east of the junction ahead of you], and encamped between Socoh and Azekah [exactly your location]. . . And Saul and the men of Israel were gathered, and encamped in the valley of Elah, and drew up in line of battle against the Philistines. And the Philistines stood on the mountain on the one side, and Israel stood on the mountain on the other side, with a valley between them.

Try this: As you look east up the valley (across the road), you'll see the mountains of Judah in the distance and the road from Bethlehem—now, as then—by which David reached the battlefield. The white northern ridge, a spur of the mountains of Judah, may have been the emplacement of the Israelite army; the southern ridge (where the gas station is today)—including Tel Socoh, where, as the Bible says, the Philistines gathered—ascends from the Philistine territory to the west. And the stream you crossed is the only one in the valley: "And David. . . chose five smooth stones from the brook . . .; his sling was in his hand, and he drew near to the Philistine." The rest, as they say, is history.

En Route   About 1½ km (1 mi) south of the Elah Junction (Rtes. 38 and 383), a terrace on the right is planted with a few slim cypress trees. The five broken pillars here are **Roman milestones** that were found nearby. The second from the left bears a lengthy (though damaged) Latin inscription dedicated to the glory of the emperors Septimus Severus and Caracalla and to the latter's brother (later murdered by him), Septimus Geta. Dated to around AD 210, the milestones marked the road from Ashkelon through the Elah Valley to Bethlehem and Jerusalem, by then the renamed Aelia Capitolina. The Latin was for the benefit of the Roman legionnaires; but Greek was the language of the region, and the last three lines say, "COL[onia] AEL[ia] CAP[itolina], MIL[le], KΔ [24]," meaning 24 Roman miles to Aelia Capitolina, measured from Jerusalem's Damascus Gate.

About 2 km (1¼ mi) farther, a road to the right climbs to the forest watchtower of Mitzpeh Massua. A small restaurant (closed on Saturday) serves light meals and draft beer, and there are picnic facilities at the site. The fabulous view is free.

Tel Maresha and Bet Guvrin

21 km (13 mi) south of Bet Shemesh, 52 km (33 mi) from Jerusalem.

The National Park of Bet Guvrin-Maresha is a wonderland, below ground and above it. The flattop mound of ancient Maresha, known today as **Tel Maresha,** was already the site of an important city in the Israelite period (early 1st millennium BC); but it was in the Hellenistic period (4th–2nd centuries BC) that the endless complexes of chalk caves that riddle the site—and make it so delightful—were excavated. Maresha was finally destroyed by the Parthians in 40 BC, and its place was subsequently taken by the new nearby Roman city of Bet Guvrin.

Even before you enter the park, the antiquities greet you: Sprawled around the kibbutz of Bet Guvrin, on the junction of Routes 30 and 35, are bits and pieces of the 2nd- to 3rd-century AD "free city" of Bet Guvrin, renamed (around the year 200) Eleuthropolis, "the city of free men." A particularly great find was the amphitheater, an arena for blood sports, one of only a handful discovered in Israel. The main part of the Roman city was on the southeast side of the road, where a few old buildings, at least one of them Roman, peek tantalizingly out of a rubble-strewn hill that still awaits the archaeologists' attention. (The scanty ruins of a 12th-century church are virtually the only evidence of the Crusader town of Bethgibelin.)

The layout of the roads in the park encourages but does not compel you to begin with its older sites. Nothing remains of earlier excavations that unearthed the Hellenistic city on the tel's top, but more recent digs have exposed the masonry of ancient fortifications of the Old Testament period at the corner of the mound. The view from the tel is worth the short climb. What you have really come for, however, is a vast series of underground chambers carved out of the soft chalk by the Hellenistic citizens more than 2,000 years ago.

One impressive complex (to the right before you reach the tel) is the so-called **"Columbarium,"** dug underground in the shape of a double cross (no religious significance; this is older than Christianity) some 30 feet deep. The walls are lined with symmetrical niches. The Latin word *columba* means dove or pigeon in English, and a leading theory is that these birds were raised here for food and to provide fertilizer from the droppings, but most especially for ritual sacrifices. Other scholars question this because chemical analysis of the surrounding chalk has failed to support the pigeon theory; they suggest instead that the niches contained urns with cremated human remains. The term *columbarium* has nevertheless entered the archaeological lexicon to describe this style of niche-filled walls, whatever their purpose.

The most interesting and extensive of the mazes is just off the road on the opposite side of the tel. Here, under their houses, the ancient Mareshans did excavations to create their own personal water cisterns and storerooms. The excitement of exploration makes this a must for kids (with close parental supervision, though the safety features are good), but the many steps make it impractical for the infirm. The last chamber of the maze route displays a restored ancient olive press in situ where, it is estimated, 9 tons a year of that precious commodity were processed.

Warning: Other fascinating but undeveloped complexes of caves near the tel have dangerous pits and are off-limits to visitors. Keep to the marked sites only. The leaflet you're given with your ticket has a good diagram of the site.

On a ridge to the north of Tel Maresha, look for a large **apse** standing in splendid isolation on the ridge to the north. Known as Santahanna in Arabic, it has been identified by scholars as a remnant of the Crusader Church of St. Anne.

★ ⑫ The great "bell caves" of **Bet Guvrin** date to the Late Roman, Byzantine and even Early Arab periods (2nd century–7th century AD), when the locals created an ecologically sound quarry to extract lime for cement. These caves are very different from the functional underground chambers of Maresha. At the top of each "bell" is a hole through the 4-foot-thick hard stone crust. The moment they reached the soft chalk below, the diggers began reaming out their quarry in the structurally secure bell shape, each bell eventually cutting into the adjacent one. The effect of the soaring domed ceilings and the interplay of shadow with shafts of sunlight is awesome.

The open areas outside the bell caves were once such caves themselves, but their roofs have since collapsed. They have a wild character, as fig trees, cacti, and small bushes struggle for dominance. Several natural rock bridges (climbing is not permitted) add to the amazingly photogenic nature of the site. (Photographers: The caves are not dark, yet the light is dim in places.) Claustrophobes need have no fear here: The cavernous bell caves reach up 50 feet in places and are open to the outdoors.

Although not built to be inhabited, the caves may have been used as refuges by early Christians. In the North Cave, a much later cross high on the wall, at the same level as an Arabic inscription, suggests a degree of coexistence even *after* the Arab conquest of the area in AD 636. Movie scenes in the rock musical *Jesus Christ Superstar* were filmed here. At press time, some parts of the bell caves were closed for restoration work. ⊠ *Rte. 35,* ☎ *07/681–1020.* 🎟 *NIS 14 ($4.50).* ☉ *Apr.–Sept., Sat.–Thurs. 8–5, Fri. and holiday eves 8–4; Oct.–Mar., Sat.–Thurs. 8–4, Fri. and holiday eves 8–3.*

An attractive alternative route back to **Jerusalem** is east from the Elah Valley on Route 375, past Israel's main satellite communications receiver, and up through fine wooded hill-country to Tzur Hadassah (look out for the rock-hewn Roman road on the right). Route 386 runs north to Jerusalem. The right turn (continuation of Route 375) takes you to Bethlehem and on to Jerusalem, but this road goes through some inhospitable West Bank villages and at press time is not recommended. Avoid as well Route 35 from Bet Guvrin to Hebron.

BETHLEHEM AND THE ETZION BLOC

Warning: The sites covered in this section are in the West Bank. Because of sporadic Arab unrest in the area, most visitors confine themselves to nearby Bethlehem. You are strongly urged to explore other sites in the region only in the company of a licensed guide and, in any event, to remain on the main arterial roads.

The West Bank is that part of the onetime British Mandate of Palestine, west of the Jordan River, that was occupied by the Hashemite Kingdom of Transjordan in its war with Israel in 1948 and unilaterally annexed shortly afterward. Consequently, that kingdom changed its name to Jordan in order to reflect its new territorial reality. The territory was lost to Israel in the Six-Day War of 1967 and, with the exception of recently autonomous urban areas, has remained under Israeli military administration ever since. In Israel itself, the ancient biblical names of the region are most commonly used: *Yehuda,* or Judea, for the area south of Jerusalem, and *Shomron,* or Samaria, for the much larger area north of it. The term *Green Line* is used to denote the pre-1967 border between the West Bank and Israel proper.

The West Bank is a kidney-shaped area, a bit larger than the U.S. state of Delaware and almost half the size of Northern Ireland. The Arab population of almost 1 million is more than 90% Muslim, the Christian minority living mostly in the Greater Bethlehem area (in Judea), and in Ramallah (in Samaria).

Palestinian nationalism in the West Bank and the Gaza Strip flared into street violence in the late 1980s (the intifada); however, in the last few years, the series of negotiated agreements between Israel and the Palestinians and related political developments have had a significant effect on the general atmosphere in the Territories, as they are sometimes called. On the one hand, the Autonomy Agreement, signed in Cairo in 1994, gave Palestinian Arabs control of their own internal affairs in the Gaza Strip, Jericho, and, more recently, seven other West Bank cities. On the other hand, Muslim fundamentalists who reject the entire peace process with Israel (like the Hamas and Islamic Jihad movements) have stepped up their attacks on Israeli citizens. In response, Israel has severely restricted the access of Palestinian Arab workers from these areas into Israel proper, a probably necessary security measure to contain the violence, but one that has caused economic hardship among the Palestinians. At press time, the impact on the Territories of the 1996 general elections in Israel, which brought in a more conservative government, was still hard to predict.

The nonviolent majority of Palestinians is caught between a rock and a hard place. Despite the frustration of living under military occupation, the economic development, educational standards, and medical services in the West Bank have improved dramatically since 1967; but these developments do not impress a new generation for whom political independence is the top priority. The prognosis is not entirely bleak, however: Since the beginning of the current peace process in Madrid in 1991, the street activists and clandestine terrorist cells have had to share local glory with a legitimate, recognized leadership representing its people's cause.

The Jewish population in Judea and Samaria numbers about 135,000 in a handful of small towns and more than 100 villages. Although some of the towns are really suburbs of Jerusalem and Tel Aviv, other settlements were set up by fiercely nationalist Israelis—the majority of them religious Jews—who see the region as an integral and inalienable part of their ancient homeland, and who see the almost miraculous "homecoming" in 1967 as nothing less than a first glimmer of the messianic age. With its mountain heights dominating Israel's main population centers and the area thrusting to within 14 km (9 mi) of the Mediterranean Sea, the West Bank has a strategic value that has convinced many more moderate Israelis of the folly of relinquishing it to potentially hostile Arab control. A person's attitude toward the questions of continuing settlement in the West Bank and the ultimate status of the region is an important touchstone of political affiliation in Israel, and the country is completely divided on these issues.

This section takes in Bethlehem, less than 16 km (10 mi) south of Jerusalem, and continues southwest to the Jewish settlements of the Etzion Bloc. The Hebron Road leaves Jerusalem heading south to become Route 60.

Bethlehem

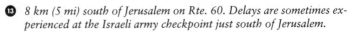 *8 km (5 mi) south of Jerusalem on Rte. 60. Delays are sometimes experienced at the Israeli army checkpoint just south of Jerusalem.*

Christian visitors are often surprised by how close Bethlehem is to Jerusalem (10 minutes' drive), as if the temporal separation of the two in the New Testament should somehow be reflected in distance. As you leave Jerusalem, a good view of the modern city opens up on your right. Kibbutz Ramat Rahel, on the hill to your left, was an important Israeli position in the War of Independence of 1948 and then a border outpost in the years that followed, when the Green Line ran through the valley immediately below it. The next ridge is capped by the Greek Orthodox monastery of Mar Elias (St. Elijah)—once a Jordanian stronghold—and immediately beyond is your first view of Bethlehem.

Way off on the eastern horizon is a prominent flattop hill. This is Herodion, one of Herod's great palace-fortresses, later used by the Zealots in the Great Revolt against Rome (AD 66–73) and by Bar Kochba's fighters in the 2nd century AD. On the ridge to the right as you pass Jerusalem's Gilo neighborhood is Tantur, an ecumenical institute set up in the afterglow of the Second Vatican Conference as a sabbatical retreat for Christian clergy of all denominations.

Rachel's Tomb, at the entrance to Bethlehem, is more readily identifiable by the Israeli security outside this important Jewish holy site than by its small white dome. The biblical patriarchal couples (Abraham and Sarah, Isaac and Rebecca, Jacob and Leah) are all buried in the Cave of Machpelah, in Hebron to the south—all but Rachel, Jacob's second and favorite wife. The Bible relates that Rachel died in childbirth on the outskirts of Bethlehem, "and Jacob set up a pillar upon her grave" (Genesis 35).

The present building is probably medieval, with additions in the 19th century made by the renowned British Jewish philanthropist Sir Moses Montefiore. The large velvet-draped, blocklike cenotaph inside is certainly not the original pillar set up by Jacob, and the thread of authenticity is lost in the distant past, but centuries of prayers have hallowed the spot for observant Jews. The interior of the tomb is decorated with Hebrew biblical quotations referring to Rachel. People come to pray here for good health and fecundity (Rachel was long barren), and the keening of a particularly afflicted soul is not an unknown sound. Another tradition is to wind a red thread seven times around the tomb marker and to give snippets of it as talismans to cure all ills.

Rachel is respected by Islam as well, and adjacent to the site is a Muslim cemetery, reflecting the Middle Eastern tradition that it is a special privilege to be buried near a great personage. ⊠ *Rte. 60.* 🎫 *Free.* ☉ *Sun.–Thurs. 8–5, Fri. 8–1.*

Even from a distance, **Bethlehem** is easily identified by the minarets and church steeples that struggle for control of its skyline. Immediately beyond Rachel's tomb, the road forks; the right fork goes toward the Etzion Bloc and Hebron, the left into Manger Street and onto Manger Square. Note that Bethlehem is now an autonomous Palestinian enclave, with all security and tourism matters in the hands of the Palestinian Authority.

The wide Manger Street winds into town past the large gift shops and high stone walls of religious institutions. To the east are occasional panoramas of what geographers call "marginal land," still more or less arable, but very close to the desert. Fields now part of the adjacent town of Beit Sahour are traditionally identified with the biblical story of Ruth the Moabite, daughter-in-law of Naomi, who "gleaned in the field" of Boaz, Naomi's kinsman. Boaz eventually "took Ruth and she became his wife" (Ruth 4); and it was in Bethlehem that their great-grandson, King David, was born.

Flocks are more common than fields on the edge of the desert. Christian tradition identifies Boaz's barley fields as those where the shepherds, "keeping watch over their flock by night," received word of the birth of Jesus in Bethlehem. Several denominations maintain sites in the valley purporting to be the authentic "Shepherds' Fields."

★ Manger Square is Bethlehem's central plaza and the entrance to its primary sight, the **Church of the Nativity,** built over the grotto thought to be the birthplace of Jesus. The square has a tourist information office, a couple of restaurants, and some shops. At press time the atmosphere in Bethlehem was fairly relaxed and the area of the Nativity well monitored by the Palestinian Tourist Police, but the town's political vicissitudes and occasional incidents in recent years make it inadvisable to wander away from Manger Square into the *souk* (market) and narrow alleys.

The unprepossessing stone exterior of the Church of the Nativity is crowned by the crosses of the denominations sharing it: Above the central gable is the Greek Orthodox cross; to the left, the square Jerusalem cross of the Franciscans; and to the right, the Armenian cross. The now-blocked but still impressive square entranceway dates from the time of the Byzantine emperor Justinian (6th century AD). Twelfth-century Crusader repairs created the arched entrance (also now blocked) within the Byzantine one. The current low entrance (watch your head) was designed in the 16th century to protect the worshipers from attack by their then-hostile Muslim neighbors.

The church interior is vast and gloomy. On the left side of the central nave, a wooden trapdoor reveals a remnant of a mosaic floor from the original church built in the 4th century by Helena, mother of Constantine the Great, the Roman emperor who first embraced Christianity. Emperor Justinian's rebuilding two centuries later enlarged the church, giving it its present-day structure and plan. The high columns, which run the length of the nave in two paired lines, are 6th century too, making this the oldest standing church in Israel. In AD 614, the country was invaded by the Persians, who destroyed every Christian church and monastery across the land, except the Nativity. The story goes that when they reached Bethlehem, they discovered the splendid Byzantine church with wall mosaics or frescoes depicting the events of the Nativity, including the tale of the Three Wise Men of the East. For the local artist, "east" meant Persia, and he thus dressed his wise men in Persian garb. The Persians understood nothing of the significance of the picture, but "recognizing" themselves in it, they spared the church.

The church was pillaged by the early Muslims in the 7th century (much of the marble used at the Temple Mount in Jerusalem came from here), but the patches of 12th-century mosaics high on the walls and the faded burned-wax figures of saints on the Corinthian pillars give some hint of its revived medieval splendor. The ceiling beams are medieval English oak and are said to have been covered by lead, which was later melted down for bullets by the Turks in their wars with the Venetians.

The elaborately ornamented front of the church serves as the parish church of Bethlehem's Greek Orthodox community. The right transept is theirs, too, but the left belongs to the Armenians. All three "shareholders" in the church have vied with each other for centuries for control of the holy sites of the Holy Land. A 19th-century status quo agreement that froze their respective rights and privileges in Jerusalem's Church of the Holy Sepulcher and the Tomb of the Virgin pertains here, too: Ownership, the timing of ceremonies, the number of oil lamps, and so on are all clearly defined. It has not, however, prevented undignified fisticuffs between rival monks in recent years over the privilege of cleaning this or that part of the birthplace of Jesus.

Below the altar is the **Grotto of the Nativity.** Once a cave—exactly the kind of place that might have been used as a barn—the grotto has been reamed, plastered, and decorated beyond recognition. Immediately on your right as you enter is a small altar, and on the floor below it is the focal point of the entire site: a 14-point **bronze star** with the Latin inscription HIC DE VIRGINE MARIA JESUS CHRISTUS NATUS EST (Here of the Virgin Mary, Jesus Christ was born). The original star was placed here in 1717 by the Roman Catholics, who lost control of the altar 40 years later to the more influential Greek Orthodox. In 1847 the star mysteriously disappeared, and pressure from the Turkish sultan compelled the Greeks to allow the present Latin replacement to be installed in 1853. The Franciscan guardians do have possession, however, of the little alcove a few steps down on your left as you enter the Grotto (behind the candles). This is said to be the manger where the infant Jesus was laid. There is clear evidence of the fire that gutted the grotto in the 19th century; the asbestos wall hangings were a French gift to prevent a recurrence. ⊠ *Manger Sq.,* ☎ *02/674–1020.* ☉ *Daily 6–6 (access to grotto restricted until 10 AM daily because of Armenian mass).*

The **Church of St. Catherine,** adjacent to the Church of the Nativity and accessible by a passage from its Armenian chapel, is Bethlehem's Roman Catholic parish church. Completed in 1882, the church incorporates remnants of its 12th-century Crusader predecessor and has fine acoustics but is otherwise unexceptional. It is from this church that the midnight Christmas mass is broadcast around the world. Steps descend from within the church to a series of dim grottoes, clearly once used as living quarters. Chapels here are variously dedicated to Joseph, to the Innocents killed by Herod, and to St. Jerome, bishop of Bethlehem in the late 4th century, who is said to have written here the Vulgate, the Latin translation of the Bible. At the end of a narrow passage, a small wooden door (kept locked) connects the complex with the Grotto of the Nativity.

The cloister outside the church, with its restored Crusader minicolumns, flower beds, and young lemon trees, is probably one of the most tranquil spots in Bethlehem. ⊠ *Manger Sq.,* ☎ *02/674–2425.* ☉ *Daily 5–noon and 2–6.*

Manger Square is brilliant with lights and bursting with life on Christmas Eve (December 24, that is; the Greek Orthodox celebrate Christmas Day on January 7, the Armenians on January 19). Traditionally, choirs from around the world perform carols and sacred music in the square between 8:30 PM and 11:30 PM, and at midnight the Roman

Catholic mass from the Franciscan Church of St. Catherine is simultaneously relayed on closed-circuit television onto a large outside screen and by satellite to all parts of the globe.

There have been changes, however. The celebration of Christmas 1995 came just days after Bethlehem had become an autonomous Palestinian zone and thus was far more a political rally than a religious event. The traditional framework of the Christmas Eve celebrations will most likely be preserved in seasons to come, but the logistics and other arrangements for tourists need to be clarified close to the date. For information, contact your regional Israel Government Tourist Office at home and (especially) the Office of Tourism of the Palestinian Authority in Bethlehem (☎ 02/674–1581 or 02/674–1582). Regarding the mass, contact the Christian Information Center at Jerusalem's Jaffa Gate (☎ 02/627–2692). In general, you will probably need to leave your car in Jerusalem and take public transportation to Bethlehem; there is no seating in Manger Square; very warm clothing is essential; you should have your passport with you; bringing in alcohol is forbidden; and large bags are discouraged (because of security checks). The Israel Ministry of Tourism will be involved with parallel Christmas celebrations in Nazareth in the future.

Shopping

Bethlehem craftspeople make carved olive-wood and mother-of-pearl objects, mostly of a religious nature, but the many stores along the tourist route in town sell jewelry and a range of baubles and notions as well. For quality and reliability, most of the half-dozen or so large establishments on Manger Street, where the tour buses stop, are worth investigating, but some of the merchants near the Church of the Nativity, on Manger Square, have good-quality items as well.

Etzion Bloc

24 km (15 mi) south of Jerusalem on the new bypass road, which begins near the Jerusalem Mall. From Bethlehem, return to Jerusalem and take the bypass, rather than continuing south on Rte. 60.

Midway between Jerusalem and Hebron, the Etzion Bloc—*Gush Etzion* in Hebrew—is today made up of two small Jewish towns (Efrat and Alon Shevut) and a handful of rural communities. In the 1940s there were four kibbutzim, built because of their strategic proximity to the important Jerusalem–Hebron highway. During Israel's War of Independence, their ability to disrupt troop movements of the Jordanian (then Transjordanian) Arab Legion led to the Legion's attack, conquest, and destruction of the Bloc in May 1948. Jewish settlers, some of them survivors of the 1948 disaster, returned there after the Six-Day War of 1967, when the area came under Israeli control. The Bloc had been an area of Jewish settlement long before Israel became a state, which makes it sacrosanct even among Israelis who would otherwise support a large-scale Israeli withdrawal from the West Bank.

At the entrance to the Etzion Bloc, facing the Jerusalem–Hebron road (Route 60), is a small fortresslike building: a turn-of-the-century Russian Orthodox monastery that was the Bloc's forward position in the War of Independence. Although the walls are intact, the monastery is nothing more than a shell today. The road west passes Alon Shevut on the right.

⑭ Kfar Etzion, the oldest settlement in the Etzion Bloc, was founded as far back as 1921, but the poor land, lack of water, and harsh winters deterred many. By the early 1940s, however, the situation had stabilized, with the addition of three more villages: Revadim, Ein Tzurim, and Massu'ot Yitzhak. When the Arab Legion overran the Bloc, the survivors of these three kibbutzim were taken prisoner. Those of Kfar Etzion were not so lucky: Almost all were gunned down after their surrender. Among the group that resettled the site in the late 1960s were those who had been evacuated as children before the battle. Take time for the story of Kfar Etzion, told through a dramatic audiovisual presentation in the auditorium, and at the small museum. To get to the settlement, ignore the first gate and continue along the periphery of the village to the second, southern gate. Park at the cafeteria/gift shop, and ask for directions to the museum and auditorium. ⊠ *Rte. 367, just west of Rte. 60,* ☎ *02/993–5160. Visits by prior arrangement only.* ☎ *NIS 5 ($1.70).* ☉ *Sun.–Thurs. 8:30–12:30 (July–Aug., occasional afternoon hrs according to demand), Fri. 8:30–11.*

From the Etzion Bloc, Route 367 descends west to the Elah Valley (☞ West of Jerusalem, *above*).

Shopping

Kibbutz Kfar Etzion (⊠ Off Rte. 367, near the junction with Rte. 60, ☎ 02/993–5148) sells its own attractive decorative candles in its little coffee shop/gift store.

AROUND JERUSALEM A TO Z

Arriving and Departing

The points of departure for the three areas explored in this chapter are Jerusalem and Tel Aviv. For information about arriving and departing, please *see* Jerusalem A to Z *and* Tel Aviv A to Z *in* Chapters 2 and 4, respectively.

Getting Around

By Bus

With few exceptions, the **Egged Bus Cooperative** enjoys a nationwide monopoly on intercity bus routes. Buses are modern, comfortable, air-conditioned, and reasonably priced. Service on main routes is good, but infrequent to outlying rural districts. For fares and schedules, call 02/530–4555 (Jerusalem) or 03/537–5555 (Tel Aviv).

The **Central Bus Station,** in Jerusalem, is in the city's northwestern corner, on Jaffa Road. Give yourself ample time to buy a ticket and get into line for the often crowded Dead Sea routes. Since Jericho became autonomous under the Palestinian Authority, Egged no longer services the town. For the Dead Sea area (Qumran, Ein Gedi, Masada, and Ein Bokek), take Bus 421 or 486 (or 487 only as far as Ein Gedi), and the busy 444 to Eilat (which does not drive into Masada). Service is approximately hourly. Only one bus departs daily from Tel Aviv to the Dead Sea area—Bus 421, currently at 8:30 AM.

Bus 160 (the Hebron route) runs every hour, with stops at Rachel's Tomb and the Etzion Bloc Junction. Bus 161, which runs less frequently, takes you into Kfar Etzion itself. Both originate at the Central Bus Station, but can be picked up as well near downtown Jerusalem, on **Keren Hayesod Street** opposite the Radisson Moriah Hotel, and at the **Jerusalem Train Station.** From the **East Jerusalem Bus Station,** on Sultan Suleiman Street near the Damascus Gate, an Arab company operates Bus 22 to Manger Square in the heart of Bethlehem. There is no direct bus service from Tel Aviv to Bethlehem.

The sights west of Jerusalem are difficult to reach by public transportation. The only bus going to Bet Guvrin (Bus 011) leaves at 8 AM from the town of Kiryat Gat. There are frequent buses to Kiryat Gat—Bus 446 from Jerusalem and Bus 369 from Tel Aviv.

By Car
This is a much better option than public transportation because many sights in this chapter are on secondary roads, where bus services are infrequent or in some cases nonexistent. Roads range in condition from fair to excellent, and most places are clearly marked. Drive defensively—many Israeli drivers are frustrated fighter pilots! Gas stations are plentiful, and some never close. Still, it's wise to play it safe and never let your gauge drop below half. Pay special attention to keeping the radiator topped in the hot Israeli summer.

Masada, the farthest of the Dead Sea sites in this chapter, is 100 km (62 mi) from Jerusalem, about 1½ hours' drive, on Routes 1 and 90; add one hour from Tel Aviv. Jericho, which is 40 km (25 mi) from Jerusalem, can be reached in 35 minutes via Routes 1 and 90 north. Since this is now a Palestinian Autonomous Zone, check the town's accessibility before you set out. Heading southwest from Jerusalem, it takes 40 minutes to get to the Sorek Cave via Route 386 (about 24 km, or 15 mi) and another 30 minutes' driving time (about 30 km, or 19 mi) to Bet Guvrin via Route 38. From Tel Aviv (east on Rte. 1, south on Route 38), Bet Shemesh can be reached in about 40 minutes. Bethlehem is a mere 8 km (5 mi) from downtown Jerusalem—a 15-minute drive—and the Etzion Bloc 16 km (10 mi) farther south on Route 60. A new bypass road from the Jerusalem Mall avoids Bethlehem en route to the Etzion Bloc. Driving your own car in other areas of the West Bank is definitely not recommended.

By Guide-Driven Limousine/Minivan
This is by far the best way to see the areas covered in this chapter. With a private licensed guide in a 4-, 7-, or 10-passenger, air-conditioned limousine/minivan, *you* determine the tour's character and pace (☞ Guided Tours *in* Contacts and Resources, *below*).

By Sherut and Taxi
A *sherut* is a shared taxi (seating up to seven passengers) that runs along a set route. Usually it follows a major bus route, and the fare is similar to that of a bus. From Jerusalem you can get an Arab sherut to West Bank towns such as Bethlehem and Jericho, which will give you some local flavor—and sometimes a hair-raising driving experience. An Arab taxi is likely to be delayed at military checkpoints, however. Depending on the destination, Egged buses (☞ By Bus, *above*) are a more comfortable and reliable alternative.

Using a regular **taxi** to tour is not cheap. Define your itinerary, get a quote from one of the main West Jerusalem taxi companies, and use that as a starting point for negotiating a better deal with an individual cabbie (outside your hotel, or the Arab cabbies at the Jaffa Gate). Hiring a taxi for seven hours to Ein Gedi, the Dead Sea, and Masada, for example, costs at least NIS 500–NIS 600 ($170–$200). Hiring a qualified tour guide with an air-conditioned limo for the same trip is far better value for money.

Contacts and Resources
Bird-Watching
For more information on birds in this area, contact the **Society for the Protection of Nature in Israel** (SPNI), which has a bird-watching center and a center for raptors; the group is based in Tel Aviv (☎ 03/682–6802 or 03/518–2644).

Car Rental

Jerusalem: Avis (✉ 22 King David St., ☎ 02/624–9001); Budget (✉ 8 King David St., ☎ 02/624–8991); Eldan (✉ 24 King David St., ☎ 02/625–2151); Europcar (National; ✉ 8 King David St., ☎ 02/624–8464); Hertz (✉ 18 King David St., ☎ 02/623–1351; ✉ Hyatt Hotel, ☎ 02/581–5069 [open on the Sabbath]); Reliable (✉ 14 King David St., ☎ 02/624–8993).

Tel Aviv: Avis (✉ 113 Hayarkon St., ☎ 03/527–1752); Budget (✉ 99 Hayarkon St., ☎ 03/523–1551); Eldan (✉ 112 Hayarkon St., ☎ 03/527–1166); Europcar (National; ✉ 126 Hayarkon St., ☎ 03/524–8181); Hertz (✉ 144 Hayarkon St., ☎ 03/522–3332); Reliable (✉ 112 Hayarkon St., ☎ 03/524–9794).

Emergencies

Ambulance and medical emergencies—Magen David Adom (☎ 101).

The major **hospitals** in Jerusalem are: **Bikur Holim** (✉ Strauss St., ☎ 02/670–1111); **Hadassah** (✉ Ein Kerem, ☎ 02/677–7111, emergency room ☎ 02/644–6555, children's emergency room ☎ 02/677–7215); **Hadassah** (✉ Mt. Scopus, ☎ 02/584–4111); **Sha'arei Tzedek** (✉ Bayit Vegan, ☎ 02/655–5111, emergency room ☎ 02/655–5508).

Police (☎ 100).

Guided Tours

Regular bus tours, as they're known locally, pick you up at your hotel and bring you back there at the end of the tour. Guided bus tours departing from Tel Aviv offer the same itineraries as those leaving Jerusalem. There are discounts for children. The two main operators are **Egged Tours** (✉ 224 Jaffa Rd., Jerusalem, ☎ 02/530–4422; ✉ 59 Ben Yehuda St., Tel Aviv, ☎ 03/527–1212, 1213, 1214, and 1215); and **United Tours** (✉ King David Hotel Annex, Jerusalem, ☎ 02/625–2187 or 625–2188; ✉ 113 Hayarkon St., Tel Aviv, ☎ 03/693–3412 or 03/522–2008). Most hotels carry the tour companies' brochures and can book them for you.

Both companies offer full-day tours of Masada, the Dead Sea, and sometimes Jericho. Tours cost between $64 and $67 per person (not including lunch), and there are daily departures. The Church of the Nativity, in Bethlehem, and sometimes Rachel's Tomb can be seen as part of a half-day tour that includes some Jerusalem sites (daily departures, $22 per person).

Touring in a private **guide-driven limo/van** can be comfortable and convenient (☞ Getting Around, *above*); for four or more people it becomes cost-effective as well. Current rates (always quoted in U.S. dollars) are $280–$310 per day for four- or seven-passenger vehicles. Rates include all guiding and car expenses (up to 200 km, or 120 mi, per day, averaged out over all the days of the tour). There is a charge for the guide's expenses for overnights away from home base.

Some guides have organized into cooperatives, but all are essentially freelancers. In Jerusalem, try **Eshcolot-Yehuda Tours** (✉ 36 Keren Hayesod, ☎ 02/563–5555, FAX 02/563–2101); and in Tel Aviv, **Twelve Tribes** (✉ 29 Hamered St., ☎ 03/510–1911, FAX 03/510–1943) or **TarHemed** (✉ 59 Hayarkon St., ☎ 03/517–6101, FAX 03/510–0165). You can get advice from two of Fodor's in-field writers, themselves qualified guides: Mike Rogoff (✉ 67/35 Shahal St., 93721 Jerusalem, ☎ FAX 02/679–0410) and Judy Goldman (✉ Gan Rehavia A, Apt. 6, 92461 Jerusalem, ☎ 02/624–5827). Hotel concierges can usually recommend guides.

Metzukei Dragot (⊠ Kibbutz Mitzpe Shalem, M.P. Jericho Valley, ☎ 02/996–4501, 4502, 4503, and 4504) provides one variety of desert adventure. It offers twice weekly one-day "safaris" from Jerusalem to the Judean Desert in a go-anywhere 31-seater safari truck; the cost is $55, including a picnic lunch. If you cannot live without air-conditioning and plush seats, don't consider it. But if you want unforgettable desert vistas that really are off the beaten track, this is for you.

The **Society for the Protection of Nature in Israel** (⊠ 13 Helene Hamalka St., Jerusalem, ☎ 02/624–4605, FAX 02/625–4953; ⊠ 3 Hashefela St., Tel Aviv, ☎ 03/638–8677, FAX 03/688–3940; U.S. office ⊠ 89 5th Ave., Suite 800, ☎ 212/645–8732 or 800/323–0035, FAX 212/645–8749), also known as SPNI, runs several off-the-beaten-track excursions, with an emphasis on nature and some hiking. Their English-speaking tours in this region include Masada, the Dead Sea, and the Ein Gedi Nature Reserve (easy hike); a trip into the Judean Desert in a go-anywhere vehicle (no hiking); a more energetic trip into Wadi Kelt, with its marvelous desert spring and St. George's Monastery; and a monthly moonlight hike into the same area, timed with a bright moon. A rare tour to the area west of Jerusalem includes the Neot Kedumim Biblical Landscape Reserve, the Sorek Cave, and Bet Guvrin. Day tours range from $48 to $59; and longer, more complex packages are available.

Visitor Information
There are Tourist Information Offices (TIOs) at the following locations:
Bethlehem (⊠ Manger Sq., opposite the Police Station, 3rd floor, ☎ 02/674–1581 or 02/674–1582).
Jerusalem (⊠ Jaffa Gate, ☎ 02/628–0382 or 02/628–0457; ⊠ 17 Jaffa Rd., ☎ 02/625–8844).
Tel Aviv (⊠ Shop No. 6018, 6th floor, New Central Bus Station, ☎ 03/639–5660).

4 Tel Aviv

Although it does not retain the official title of capital of Israel—a right reserved for age-old Jerusalem—Tel Aviv is the beating pulse of the country, the center for Israel's economy, business, culture, and cuisine. Brash and unlovely at first glance, this teeming, cosmopolitan city on the Mediterranean has fine sandy beaches, excellent restaurants and nightlife, and a performing arts scene that invite a serious look. It's hard to believe that less than a century ago, the area was only sand dunes.

PROUD RESIDENTS CALL IT the city that never stops, and if you don't believe them, just come around at 4 AM, when you may find yourself waiting in line

By Lisa Perlman

for a table at a café or stuck in a traffic jam on Hayarkon Street. True, there are no buses at that hour, but that doesn't stop the young and the restless of surrounding towns from finding their way to the country's throbbing heart.

Next to the magical holy city of Jerusalem, Tel Aviv seems more like the city of sin. Your first reaction to it may be negative—to the newcomer it appears muggy, congested, ill-planned, and scarred with boxy, concrete buildings. But what it lacks in grandeur, Tel Aviv makes up for in vitality. One-third of the country's population—a number approaching 2 million Israelis—lives in this 138-square-km (55-square-mi) metropolis. Half a million cars go in and out of the city every day. Residents of other towns swell the population further on the weekends, when they make Tel Aviv their playground. The city is Israel's center of commerce, culture, and people. It bustles with museums, art galleries, restaurants, and beaches.

Having risen from empty sand dunes less than a century ago, Tel Aviv can hardly boast the ancient beauty of Israel's capital. Still, the city's southern border, the port of Jaffa, is as old as they come: Jonah set sail from here before his journey in the belly of a whale. The cedars of Lebanon that were used in the construction of Solomon's Temple arrived in Jaffa before being transported to Jerusalem. According to archaeologists, Jaffa was founded in the Middle Canaanite period, around 1600 BC. For the next thousand years it was dominated by one ancient people after another: Egyptians, Philistines, Israelites, Phoenicians, and Greeks. After being taken by Crusaders twice, in the 11th and 12th centuries, Jaffa was recaptured by the Muslims and remained largely under Arab domination until the 20th century. During much of this time it was abandoned, and it did not regain its importance as a port until the 19th century.

In the second half of the 19th century, Jewish pioneers began emigrating here from other parts of the world. Their numbers strained the capacity of the small port, and by the late 1880s, Jaffa was overcrowded, rife with disease, and stricken with poverty. A group of Jewish families moved to the empty sands north of Jaffa and founded Neve Tzedek, the first Jewish neighborhood. This was followed by Ahuzat Bayit (literally, "housing estate"), an area to the north of Neve Tzedek that became the precursor of Tel Aviv. Arab riots in Jaffa in the 1920s spurred further growth, as more Jews moved to Ahuzat Bayit. They were joined by emigrants from Europe, mostly Poland, and a decade later by an influx of German Jews fleeing the Nazis. These new, urban immigrants—unlike the pioneers from earlier immigrant waves—brought an appreciation for the arts and a passion for the sidewalk cafés that sprouted like mushrooms throughout the city. It was they who made the strongest social and cultural impact on Tel Aviv.

The fact that Tel Aviv began as separate neighborhoods helps to explain its eclectic (some would say discordant) appearance, its Mediterranean-style buildings jostling each other in the shadow of towering skyscrapers. In the 1930s and '40s, the city became known as the "white city," because it was the only one in the world dominated by the International Style of Le Corbusier and Mies van der Rohe—a style of functional forms, flat roofs, and whitewashed exteriors. By the 1950s, however, shoddy imitations of the style led to its decline, and many of its buildings fell into disrepair. Happily, recent efforts by preservationists are helping to reclaim these architectural treasures.

The Tel Aviv of today is already vastly different from the Tel Aviv of half a century ago. Although northern Tel Aviv has traditionally been the glitzy, affluent part of the city, it's the oft-neglected south that wins attention now. Here city-backed gentrification projects in many neighborhoods are changing the area's face; each week the scaffolding rises on another building, and new restaurants and shops continue to appear. Tel Aviv has come a long way in its short history, and as you gaze around, you may find it hard to believe that 80 years ago this modern, teeming metropolis was nothing but sand.

Pleasures and Pastimes

Beaches

Tel Aviv's western border, an idyllic stretch of sand on the Mediterranean, has miles of beaches and a beachfront promenade. Sunsets here are spectacular. Still, the Med can be moody: For most of the year, the lapping of gentle waves offers respite and relaxation, but it doesn't always provide the refreshment you would expect. Because the Med is a closed sea, its water turns warm and decidedly unrefreshing in the dead of summer. If the jellyfish are out in force—which they are in July and August—you may decide that an air-conditioned café with a *view* of the sea is a much more civilized choice.

Cultural Activities

As Israel's undisputed cultural capital, Tel Aviv puts on a pretty good show—even at street level. There's a stimulating range of museums; dance and music of all kinds are popular; opera is budding; and theater, almost all in Hebrew, is prolific. As for popular culture—it's all around you.

Dining

Tel Aviv's culinary scene has radically improved in the last few years, and the city's cosmopolitan character is now happily represented in its food. That's not to say that you can't still enjoy the Middle Eastern fast foods that this part of the world is so famous for: The ubiquitous stands proffering falafel or *shwarma* (spit-grilled meat) in pita still occupy countless street corners, but beyond these are restaurants serving everything from American burgers to Chinese dim sum. Surprisingly perhaps, in contrast to Jerusalem, you have to really look to find a kosher restaurant outside the hotels, where all restaurants are required to be kosher.

Tel Aviv is also very much a café society. Everyone from idle shoppers to hard-driving businesspeople frequent the scores of coffee shops dotting the city. Don't miss an opportunity to join them at least once; the murmur of varied languages and the range of exotic coffees at these cafés will convince you as nothing else that you are truly in a cosmopolitan locale.

Many of Tel Aviv's restaurants are concentrated in an area known as Little Tel Aviv, at the northern end of Ben Yehuda and Hayarkon streets (the area of the old Tel Aviv port). In addition, numerous establishments are along the seafront south of Little Tel Aviv—all the way to Jaffa at the city's southern end—as well as east of there, in the inner city. In Herzliya Pituach, a suburb north of Tel Aviv, most restaurants are concentrated in one complex in the industrial area, about a 10-minute walk from the Herzliya hotels.

CATEGORY	COST*
$$$$	over $35
$$$	$22–$35
$$	$12–$22
$	under $12

per person for a three-course meal, excluding drinks and 10%–15% service charge

Lodging

Nothing stands between Tel Aviv's luxury hotels and the Mediterranean Sea except the golden beach and the Tayelet (promenade), outfitted with chairs and gazebos. Even the small hotels are just a short walk from the water. Tel Aviv's hotel row is along Hayarkon Street, which becomes Herbert Samuel Esplanade as you proceed south, between Little Tel Aviv (the old port area) and Jaffa. This means that wherever you stay, you're never far from the main thoroughfares of Ben Yehuda and Dizengoff streets, with their shops and outdoor cafés, or the city's major concert hall, museums, art galleries, and the open-air Carmel Market.

Tel Aviv is known for a dearth of middle-price hotels, but the few hotels listed in the $$ and $ categories are generally clean and comfortable, with friendly employees who create a warm atmosphere.

In the winter (mid-November to March or thereabouts), the outdoor pools at Tel Aviv hotels are closed, and the lifeguards at the public beaches take a break as well. Most hotels, except the Hilton, don't have room for tennis courts. The hotel health clubs are open to anyone over age 18.

CATEGORY	COST*
$$$$	over $120
$$$	$80–$120
$$	$60–$80
$	under $60

All prices are for a standard double room, including breakfast and excluding 15% service charge.

Water Sports

There is no shortage of water-sports opportunities in Tel Aviv—even some that come as a surprise: in addition to the more obvious swimming, sailing, and windsurfing, pleasure boats can be rented on Hayarkon River, and waterskiing is possible—not in the sea but on a cable in a man-made lake.

EXPLORING TEL AVIV

Tel Aviv's western border is the Mediterranean. The beachfront Tayelet runs from north Tel Aviv to Jaffa, some 3 km (2 mi) to the south, and provides a great walk, especially at sunset. The north–south thoroughfares of Hayarkon, Ben Yehuda (which becomes Allenby), Dizengoff, and Ibn Gvirol streets run more or less parallel to the shore. The hotels are almost all concentrated on the seafront, along Hayarkon Street, which is also bursting with cafés, restaurants, and pubs. Allenby Street, one of the oldest in the city, crosses Hayarkon and Ben Yehuda streets and becomes the latter at its southern terminus. The change in affluence is as immediate as the change in street name, with a different socioeconomic situation reflected in the shabbier buildings and more budget-oriented shops along Allenby. The "border" between south and north might be considered Carmel Market, a real junction of east-meets-west and old-meets-new. In the north, the business center dwindles north of Arlosoroff Street, which runs east–west near Kikar Hamedina

(Hamedina Square). The residential part of the city continues north and takes in the Yarkon River, once the city's northern boundary and now a popular recreational spot. South of downtown is Jaffa, once a separate city but now part of the municipality of Tel Aviv. An ancient port, Jaffa now includes an impressively restored section known as Old Jaffa.

Technically, there are boundaries between Tel Aviv and the numerous towns and cities that surround it, but the urban sprawl is so great that residents of these surrounding municipalities will often tell you they live in Tel Aviv.

Numbers in the text correspond to numbers in the margin and on the Exploring Tel Aviv map.

Great Itineraries

Spending three or four days in Tel Aviv is ideal. You'll have time to explore a variety of neighborhoods and museums—and still have enough time for cooling off on the beach as well. Fewer days than that will make your visit quite action-packed, though you'll be able to catch the highlights.

IF YOU HAVE 2 DAYS

Begin in Old Jaffa, wandering around the restored section and delving into the small galleries and shops. Take in a fresh fish meal on the waterfront at the port and walk along the coastal Tayelet (promenade) back to central Tel Aviv. In the afternoon, head for the Sheinkin Street area (Israel's wannabe Greenwich Village) to get a feel of contemporary Israeli culture and lifestyle. The area is a meeting point between the city's trendiest trendy and a local ultra-Orthodox (Hasidic) Jewish community. In a way, it's hard to tell the difference: wearing black is de rigueur for both groups. Nearby Rothschild Boulevard has good examples of the city's changing architecture over the years—from Middle East–influenced to Bauhaus to '90s styles.

On the second day, take in a museum on a subject that interests you: the Tel Aviv Museum of Art, the Eretz Israel Museum with its excellent archaeological exhibits, or Beth Hatefutsoth (Diaspora Museum), which depicts Jewish life around the world through the ages. You may want to get some shopping in after that and then spend a couple of hours doing what Tel Avivians do best: it's called *beten-gav* (tummy-back) in Hebrew—in other words, cooling off on the beach. There's no shortage of eating options in the evening.

IF YOU HAVE 4 DAYS

If your first day is a Tuesday or a Friday, head straight for the Nahalat Binyamin street fair and the Carmel produce market. From there, it's a hop, skip, and a jump to Sheinkin Street for a coffee break. Spend the afternoon at the Tel Aviv marina, either on the port or on the Mediterranean (rent a small boat with or without a captain). The next day walk through Old Jaffa and Neve Tzedek, and you'll get an excellent feel of Tel Aviv's beginnings. Rest up in the late afternoon and go for a late dinner on Ha'arba'a Street, which is lined with bars and eateries. Begin the third day on the beach and then take in a museum (☞ If You Have 2 Days, *above*). Spend the evening in Jaffa again; the atmosphere is very different at night. Leave the last day for wandering around the city center—browsing and shopping. Walk on the Tayelet again before you leave Tel Aviv.

From the Market to the Theater

It is only 2 km (1 mi) from the *souk,* or marketplace, to the national theater, and yet this space traverses a good part of the city's nine-decade history, its ethnic mix, and its various social strata.

A Good Walk

Begin at **Bialik Street** ① (off Allenby Street), one of the quaintest corners of the city, containing well-preserved architecture characteristic of Tel Aviv's early years. The change from bustling, polluted Allenby to Bialik is striking: quiet descends around you in an instant. Walk to the end of the street, and you'll find a mosaic and a fountain (it rarely flows). Strolling from the fountain back toward Allenby Street, stop in at No. 22, **Bet Bialik** ②, the residence of the "father of Hebrew poetry." Three doors down, at No. 14, is **Bet Rubin** ③, an art gallery that houses painter Reuven Rubin's works as well as changing shows.

Return to Allenby Street, cross at the traffic light, and head south (left). In less than a minute you will be at the entrance to the **Carmel Market** ④; soak up the bustling atmosphere and perhaps purchase some dry goods or examples of the country's fresh produce. On Tuesday and Friday, the city's artisans and would-be artisans set up shop, creating a street fair along **Nahalat Binyamin** ⑤, east of the market.

Nahalat Binyamin forms a V with the marketplace at Allenby Street at **Kikar Magen David** ⑥. Cross Allenby at this intersection by taking the underpass (otherwise you risk life and limb), and you will end up on the corner of Sheinkin and Allenby streets. Cross narrow Sheinkin Street to King George Street and make your way downhill. Midway down King George Street, on the right, the alley called **Simtat Plonit** ⑦ can be identified by the two obelisk-style plaster structures at its entrance; take a walk here to see some of the city's older architecture.

Gan Meir ⑧, a park that's a bit farther along on the other side of King George, provides a place to rest your feet. Proceed north from the park and turn right onto Ben Zion Boulevard. It's a few minutes' walk up a slight incline to **Kikar Habimah** ⑨, a culturally significant square, with buildings that house the **Habimah National Theater**; the **Helena Rubinstein Pavilion,** an annex of the Tel Aviv Museum (TAM); and the **Mann Auditorium.** A half-mile detour northeast to Shaul Hamelech Boulevard would bring you to another cultural highlight, the **Tel Aviv Museum of Art.**

Ben Zion Boulevard swings right (south) at Kikar Habimah to become **Rothschild Boulevard.** It's a 15-minute walk south to get to the **Independence Hall Museum** ⑩; you'll see it on your left after you cross Allenby. Here, Israel's statehood was announced in 1948. Nearby, in the middle of the boulevard, stands the stark, square **Founders' Monument and Fountain** ⑪.

TIMING
This walk can take the better part of the day—including time spent at the Nahalat Binyamin street fair and stops for coffee and a light meal along the way. Allow about three hours for simply strolling it.

Sights to See

★ ❷ **Bet Bialik.** Bialik House is the charmingly restored home and library of Chaim Nachman Bialik (1873–1934), the national poet who is considered the father of Hebrew poetry. Bialik was already a respected poet and publisher by the time he moved to Tel Aviv from Russia in 1924. In the remaining 10 years of his life, his house became the intellectual center of Tel Aviv, and Bialik himself became the city's inspiration. His two-story, cream-color house, with its pointed arches and turrets, is a

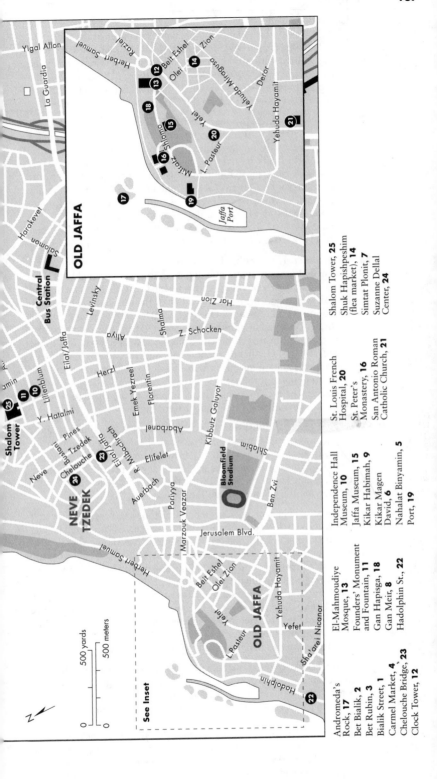

OLD JAFFA

Jaffa Port

Shalom Tower, **25**
Shuk Hapishpeshim
(flea market), **14**
Simtat Plonit, **7**
Suzanne Dellal
Center, **24**

St. Louis French
Hospital, **20**
St. Peter's
Monastery, **16**
San Antonio Roman
Catholic Church, **21**

Independence Hall
Museum, **10**
Jaffa Museum, **15**
Kikar Habimah, **9**
Kikar Magen
David, **6**
Nahalat Binyamin, **5**
Port, **19**

El-Mahmoudiye
Mosque, **13**
Founders' Monument
and Fountain, **11**
Gan Hapisga, **18**
Gan Meir, **8**
Hadolphin St., **22**

Andromeda's
Rock, **17**
Bet Bialik, **2**
Bet Rubin, **3**
Bialik Street, **1**
Carmel Market, **4**
Chelouche Bridge, **23**
Clock Tower, **12**

Central
Bus Station

Shalom
Tower

NEVE
TZEDEK

Bloomfield
Stadium

OLD JAFFA

See Inset

500 yards
500 meters

harmonious blend of Mediterranean and European styles. Built in 1927, it was almost palatial by the harsh standards of the time: mosaic-tile floors; Islamic-style arches and pillars; a small tower for meditating; sturdy, dark wood; and European-style furniture, including shelves to hold some 3,000 books. At press time, all labels were in Hebrew only, but the house is still a highly recommended stop. ⊠ *22 Bialik St.,* ☎ *03/525–4530.* ☞ *Free.* ☉ *Sun.–Thurs. 9–5, Sat. 10–2.*

❸ **Bet Rubin.** Recognized as one of Israel's major painters, Reuven Rubin (1893–1974) bequeathed his house to the city, together with 45 of his works, which make up the permanent collection here. Unlike the still-furnished Bet Bialik (☞ *above*), this house functions solely as an art gallery, with changing exhibitions by Israeli artists in addition to the great Rubin's work. There is also a small but well-stocked art library upstairs where you can pore over press clippings and browse through art books. Most days, though, the museum has limited hours. ⊠ *14 Bialik St.,* ☎ *03/525–4230.* ☞ *NIS 9 ($3).* ☉ *Sun.–Mon. and Wed.–Thurs. 10–2, Tues. 10–1 and 4–8, Sat. 11–2 (Sept.–June).*

❶ **Bialik Street.** This area has been more successful than many other Tel Aviv neighborhoods in maintaining its charming older buildings. Bialik has long been a popular address for many of the city's artists and literati, so it's not surprising that some of the houses have been converted into small museums. One end of the street has a fountain and a **mosaic.** Designed by painter-cum-writer Nahum Gutmann, the mosaic depicts the history of the city from the ancient days of Jaffa to the rise of Tel Aviv. Gutmann, a renowned children's author as well as a painter, was among the elite group of Tel Aviv's first artists and one of the first pupils at the city's first school, in Neve Tzedek. His writer father, Simcha Ben Zion, had a special place in the city's beginnings, too: A boulevard, Ben Zion, is named for him.

★ ❹ **Carmel Market.** Consisting of one long street and numerous short streets branching off it in both directions, this market, commonly referred to as the souk, is invariably crowded on weekdays from about 9 through the afternoon, especially on Friday, as people rush to finish the shopping before the Sabbath and the weekend. Take a deep breath before you plunge into the hubbub.

The first section is mainly devoted to dry goods and assorted items: If you're looking for a pair of slippers or a can opener, you'll find it here. A little farther down is the fruit and vegetable section—where everybody yells. Here, Israel's famous oranges, avocados, and mangoes are as fresh as they get, and if you think the vendor is insulting you for not taking a large enough quantity, he probably is—but it's all part of the show. With prices fixed, the days of market-style bargaining are over, but all the atmosphere and vigor of the past are retained. These days, in addition to veteran Tel Avivians, you'll find newly arrived Russian immigrants looking for bargains, even if they don't yet understand the Hebrew of the merchants who squawk the praises of the produce.

If you feel like trying something new, stop at one of the stalls that sells dried fruits and ask for *ledder* (a variation on the English *leather*). It's a Moroccan version of the dried apricot, beaten to a pulp and rolled out into a superthin, square sheet that resembles. . . leather.

NEED A
BREAK?
The Carmel Market borders the **Yemenite Quarter,** which contains a score of delicious and cheap little eateries (closed Friday night and Saturday) offering shwarma and barbecued skewered meats, all kosher. Dig into any that takes your fancy and wash your meal down with a cold beer.

⓫ Founders' Monument and Fountain. Dedicated in 1949, the Founders' Monument names those who founded Tel Aviv. This large slab of stone also encapsulates the city's past in three bas-relief panels representing the earliest pioneer days of planting and building as well as modern structures and houses. ⊠ *Rothschild Blvd. on the island at Nahlat Binyamin St.*

❽ Gan Meir. In this park you can rest on one of the benches and take in a free performance by city birds. It's something of a green haven in muggy Tel Aviv, and although also favored by local derelicts, it is perfectly safe. On summer nights, musicians sometimes gather for jam sessions.

You are now close to the Dizengoff Center, Israel's first shopping mall (☞ Shopping, *below*). Before the center opened in the early 1980s, this area was known as the **Nordiya** Quarter, a neighborhood set up in the 1920s by Jewish refugees seeking a home in the wake of Arab attacks against them in Jaffa. If you proceed north from Meir Park, you will reach Bograshov Street, named for the man who founded the Nordiya Quarter and who was one of the headmasters of the first school in Tel Aviv.

Habimah National Theater. The origins of the national theater are rooted in the Russian Revolution, when a group of young Jewish actors and artists in Russia established a theater that gave performances in Hebrew—this at a time when Hebrew was barely considered a living language. Subsequent tours through Europe and the United States in the 1920s won wide acclaim. In the late 1920s and '30s, many of the group's members moved to Israel and helped to establish the theater here. The cornerstone was laid in 1935; the current large, rounded glass-front building dates from 1970. ⊠ *Kikar Habimah.*

NEED A BREAK? | Stop in for a coffee and a strudel topped with whipped cream at **Cafe Habimah** (⊠ 2 Tarsat St., ☎ 03/620–4113), in the Habimah National Theater complex's section with the wide, round window. If you do attend one of the Habimah plays, you may even recognize some of the actors at the next table. In any case, this café is something of a theater in itself, with many of the who's who of Tel Aviv vying for a moment in the spotlight.

Helena Rubinstein Pavilion. This annex of the Tel Aviv Museum of Art (☞ *below*) has regularly changing contemporary art exhibitions. The gallery is next to the Habimah National Theater (☞ *above*), on Tarsat Street: Tarsat is the Hebrew-calendar acronym of 1948, the year in which Israel became independent. ⊠ *6 Tarsat St.,* ☎ *03/528–7196.* ⌖ *Combination ticket with Tel Aviv Museum of Art: NIS 20 ($6.70).* ☉ *Sun.–Mon. and Wed.–Thurs. 10–6, Tues. 10–10, Fri.–Sat. 10–2.*

❿ Independence Hall Museum. This impressive structure, with its wide ground-floor entrance and narrow horizontal windows, was originally the home of longtime mayor Dizengoff. He donated it to the city in 1930 for use as the first Tel Aviv Museum. More significantly, the settlement's leaders assembled here in May 14, 1948, to announce to the world the establishment of the State of Israel. Today the museum's **Hall of Declaration** stands as it did on that dramatic day, with the original microphones on the huge table where the dignitaries sat; behind it is a portrait of the Zionist leader Herzl. ⊠ *16 Rothschild Blvd.,* ☎ *03/517–3942.* ⌖ *NIS 6 ($2).* ☉ *Sun.–Thurs. 9–2.*

❾ Kikar Habimah. Habimah Square is a center of culture in Tel Aviv. The buildings here house the ☞ **Habimah National Theater,** the ☞ **Mann Auditorium,** and the ☞ **Helena Rubinstein Pavilion,** an annex of the

Tel Aviv Museum (TAM). Nestled between the theater and the museum is a charming little junglelike garden, **Gan Ya'akov,** whose centerpiece is a sycamore that's been here almost longer than the city itself. The story goes that camels were brought here to relax in the shade of the sycamore and drink from the nearby well.

❻ Kikar Magen David. This meeting point of six streets is named for the six-point Magen David, or Star of David. The intersection gives you an all-too-close look at the hair-raising style of Israeli driving: If you need to cross the street, use the underpass here.

OFF THE   **SHEINKIN STREET –** This street off Kikar Magen David recalls New York's
BEATEN PATH Greenwich Village, with its artists and would-be artists, trendies and
             wannabes, and café after café. Shopping here is fun, too–if you're not
             looking for anything in particular. Half the street is closed off to vehicu-
             lar traffic on Friday afternoons, allowing for street performances (in
             good weather).

Mann Auditorium. One of the cultural facilities on Kikar Habimah (☞ *above*), this is the country's principal concert hall and the permanent home of the Israel Philharmonic Orchestra, headed by maestro Zubin Mehta. The low-slung gray building, among the most distinguished and sophisticated halls in Israel, has excellent acoustics and a seating capacity of 3,000. It's also a venue for pop and rock concerts (☞ Nightlife and the Arts, *below*).

★ ❺ Nahalat Binyamin. The selection at this street market (open Tuesday and Friday) is large: from tacky plastic trinkets to sophisticated crafts items such as hand-carved wooden boxes and attractive glassware, but the real drawing card is the handmade silver jewelry. Nahalat Binyamin is further enlivened with the relatively new (for Israel) profusion of street performers and buskers. As a final spot of local color, cafés serving cakes and light meals line the street. Throughout the summer, the street is packed on market days, and you have to slalom between other pleasure seekers and bargain hunters to see anything. The area is more enjoyable in spring and autumn, when you actually have time to appreciate the wares as you wander among stalls.

When the city first began to spread out from Jaffa, Nahalat Binyamin served as the eastern border of Tel Aviv's premier neighborhood, **Ahuzat Bayit.** In those days, this area was so far removed from the center of things that only the poorest Jews ended up here. In recent years, much of Nahalat Binyamin has undergone gentrification, although the contrast between the "befores" and "afters" is all too clear. Look up while strolling here, for some of the architectural detail is particularly interesting. For example, at **No. 8,** built in the early 1920s, a number of Jewish symbols were incorporated into the original eclectic design. Note particularly the way the bricks at the top form steps: This kind of deliberate incompleteness is a common motif to remind viewers of the destruction of the Temple in Jerusalem.

Rothschild Boulevard. Half a century ago, this was *the* most exclusive street in the city, and it still commands sky-high real-estate prices. Dating from the 1940s, many buildings have been allowed to deteriorate; others have been restored. Still others are examples of the International Style, a style that is charming on this tree-lined street, but poorly imitated elsewhere in Tel Aviv.

❼ Simtat Plonit. It's worth taking a minute to wander down this alley to see old Tel Aviv decorative (and now derelict) architecture at its best. Note the stucco lion in front of **No. 7,** which used to boast glowing eyes fitted with lightbulbs. The tract of land that incorporates this alley was bought in the '20s by an outspoken builder from Detroit named Meir Getzel Shapira. (He established what is still known as the Shapira Quarter, just south of the Central Bus Station, now one of the city's seedier neighborhoods.) After purchasing this land, Shapira insisted that this pint-size street be named after him, and the story goes that he fought furiously with Tel Aviv's first mayor, Meir Dizengoff, to get his way. (Dizengoff had already planned to name another street Shapira, after a *different* Shapira.) The mayor emerged victorious and named the alley Plonit, meaning "what's-his-name."

Tel Aviv Museum of Art. The TAM houses a fine collection of Israeli and international art, including works by Israeli artist Reuven Rubin and a Roy Lichtenstein mural commissioned for the museum in 1989. There's also an impressive French impressionist collection here as well as an extensive collection of sculptures by Aleksandr Archipenko. ⊠ *27 Shaul Hamelech Blvd.,* ☎ *03/696–1297.* ⌦ *NIS 20 ($6.70), includes entry to the Helena Rubinstein Pavilion (☞ above).* ☉ *Sun.–Thurs. 10–6 (Tues. until 10), Fri.–Sat. 10–2.*

Jaffa

The origin of Jaffa's name is unclear: Some say it is derived from the Hebrew *yafeh* (beautiful); others claim the town was named after its founder, Japhet, son of Noah. Nor is it certain when Jaffa was established. What is sure is its status as one of the oldest ports in the world—perhaps *the* oldest. Excavations have turned up artifacts as much as 4,000 years old. The Bible names Jaffa as the site of a number of significant events: The cedars used in the construction of the Temple passed through Jaffa on their way to Jerusalem; the prophet Jonah set off from Jaffa before being swallowed by the whale; and here St. Peter raised Tabitha from the dead. In the ancient world, Jaffa was an important stop on the Via Maris, the trade route that extended from Egypt to Mesopotamia.

Jaffa's history has been one of fits and starts. The city has been razed and rebuilt scores of times as various powers fought to control it. Napoléon was but one of a succession of invaders who brought the city walls down. These walls were rebuilt for the last time in the early 19th century by the Turks and torn down yet again as recently as 1888.

By that time, Jaffa was a thriving cosmopolitan center, host to international businesspeople, bankers, and diplomats. Christian and Jewish pilgrims on their way to Jerusalem were a familiar sight here. Jewish immigrants lived peacefully with Arabs here until the riots of 1921, when discord sent most of Jaffa's Jews fleeing to the sandy north that would become Tel Aviv. Today a part of the municipality of Tel Aviv, Jaffa has a Jewish majority (most hailing from North Africa and from other Middle Eastern countries) and is also home to many Arab Christians and Muslims.

The restored section, Old Jaffa, is only a small part of this fascinating port; today it caters primarily to tourists and fishermen. Besides the restored section, a visit to the area can take in a shabbier side of Jaffa, where trading, bargaining, and arguing are as much a part of life today as they were in days of old.

A Good Walk

To get to Jaffa, you can take Buses 8, 10, 25, 46, or 90 from downtown Tel Aviv. If you're driving, you can park for free during the day on weekdays and Sunday; there's a charge on weekday evenings and Saturday.

A good starting point is on the northwestern corner of Jaffa's main square, known familiarly as the "clock square," in front of the **police station** on Yefet Street. On the empty patch of land across the road, you can see the remains of what used to be Jaffa's northern wall. This patch was the *saraya* (administrative center) of the Turkish government in the early part of the century and was one of the corners of what was later called Government Square (its official though rarely used name is Jewish Agency Square). The square was eventually destroyed by a Jewish underground group seeking to root out Arab terrorist gangs.

Head south on Yefet for about 100 feet, passing the **clock tower** ⑫, on an island in the middle of the street—a renowned meeting place for anyone with a rendezvous in Jaffa. On the southwestern corner of the square is the beautifully preserved **El-Mahmoudiye Mosque** ⑬.

Turn onto Bet Eshel Street, opposite the mosque, and wander through what was a bustling business district some 300 years ago: the old Jerusalem Road, with handy access to the harbor. Number 11, which you'll recognize by the numerous arches forming the building's facade, was the local *khan*, equivalent to a motel today. Built in the early 18th century by an Armenian family named Manouli, the ground floor was used as stables, with rooms upstairs for travelers. Today the building is a furniture store. Any of the small streets leading south from Bet Eshel Street will take you into the **shuk hapishpeshim** ⑭, a flea market where you can find anything from silver earrings and Indian-style clothes to a kilo of shrimp. The ambience seems a world away from modern Tel Aviv.

Return to Yefet Street, south of the clock tower, crossing it and entering the passage between Nos. 10 and 12. This used to be the local fish market. The aroma lingers—there are still a couple of very good fish stores and restaurants in the vicinity—but you'll find more shoe stores than seafood here now.

You are now very close to the ancient port. Walk south (you'll be going uphill) on Mifratz Shlomo Street until you come to a square on the left. Note the fountain here: When built by Turkish governor Mohammed Abu Najat Aja in the early 19th century, the fountain boasted six pillars and an arched roof, providing shade as well as water. The archway just beyond this formed the entrance to the *hamam*, or old Turkish baths. Today archaeologists are digging beneath the floor of what is now an events hall here in search of ancient artifacts. Their finds—most of which were parts of Jaffa's ancient fortifications dating from the town's beginnings around 2000–1500 BC—have been preserved beneath the hamam's center stage as well as in the **Jaffa Museum** ⑮, also on Mifratz Shlomo Street.

Before you continue up the hill to the main square of Old Jaffa, cast your gaze north to see the dramatic contrast between the ancient and the modern, linked by the softly lapping waves of the Mediterranean. As you make your way toward **Kikar Kedumim,** Old Jaffa's central plaza, you cannot help but notice the beautiful ocher-and-russet-color **St. Peter's Monastery** ⑯, on the right.

Before leaving the square, go through the Yamit restaurant (it's on an outdoor terrace, with a narrow walkway beside the tables), on the western side, for the best view of an unassuming piece of rock that rises from the sea here and is known as **Andromeda's Rock** ⑰. Now climb the hill from Kikar Kedumim, passing wide shade-giving yucca and fig trees, and cross the wooden bridge to a park called **Gan Hapisga** ⑱, literally Summit Garden.

Return to Kikar Kedumim and follow one of the alleyways with steps leading down to the **port** ⑲, which makes for pleasant exploring. If you have the energy to continue walking, some very interesting sights and sounds remain. You can either follow the coast north for about five minutes to return to the clock tower or take the official port exit, walk a few steps up the hill, and turn left onto Louis Pasteur Street. About 300 feet ahead, you'll notice a bronze sculpture of a roly-poly little whale by sculptor and jewelry maker Ilana Goor, a resident of Old Jaffa. The whale keeps watch over a small parking area, beyond which stands a remnant of the city's ancient wall.

Continue on Louis Pasteur Street and return to **Yefet Street** a few strides ahead, which links Jaffa sights, both old and new. Most face you at the T-junction of Pasteur and Yefet streets, including the **St. Louis French Hospital** ⑳. A little farther south, on the left at no. 51, is the **San Antonio Roman Catholic Church** ㉑.

A few steps farther south, turn right into Sha'arei Nicanor Street and wander down to the charming little **Hadolphin Street** ㉒. The walk ends here, but to the south is the **Ajami** Quarter of Jaffa, one of many neighborhoods around the country benefiting from a rejuvenation program known as Project Renewal, financed by Jewish communities around the world.

TIMING
Allow about three hours for walking around Jaffa. Jaffa Port and the restored area of Old Jaffa are good for a stroll at any time; you can come at night for a romantic dinner.

Sights to See
Ajami. Though still suffering from poverty, lack of infrastructure, and a crime and drug problem, Ajami boasts some of the most luxurious, gracious houses in the country; some ambassadors and other diplomats call this area home while in Israel. Tel Aviv has numerous projects in store for Ajami, and property prices are rising rapidly. Within a few years this part of Tel Aviv may be radically different—just as Old Jaffa, though still retaining the flavor of the past, is unrecognizable to anyone who was there 30 years ago. ✉ *South of Old Jaffa.*

⑰ **Andromeda's Rock.** To look at this rock from Kikar Kedumin (☞ *below*) is to see the stuff of myth and legend: Nireus, father of mermaids, was incensed that Andromeda, daughter of King Copeus of Ethiopia and his queen, Xaiopa, was more beautiful than the mermaids. He implored Poseidon, the god of the sea, to intervene. Poseidon obligingly set the sea astorm and sent a monster to eat whatever approached. In an attempt to restore calm, the people tied Andromeda to this rock. Only Perseus, riding the winged horse Pegasus, dared to save her. Soaring down from the sky, he beheaded the monster, rescued the lovely Andromeda, and promptly married her.

⑫ **Clock tower.** The tower is the focus of Jaffa's central square and stands at the town's center, with restored Old Jaffa lying to the west and the flea market to the east. The clock tower was completed in 1906, in time to mark the 30th anniversary of the reign of Sultan Abdul Hamid II; similar clock towers were built for the same occasion in Akko and in Jerusalem. The four clocks employed at this tower stood still for many years until 1965 when the city renovated the tower and set the clocks in motion again; the renovation also added stained-glass windows depicting events in Jaffa's history. ✉ *Yefet St.*

NEED A BREAK? There is always a line outside **Abulafia Bakery** (✉ 7 Yefet St.), south of the clock tower. The Middle East's answer to pizza goes like hot cakes here—literally. For a simple snack with an exquisite flavor, order a pita topped with the indigenous herb *za'atar* (hyssop, a relative of marjoram). Other pitas are topped with egg or mushroom, or stuffed with salty cheese and baked till crisp.

⑬ El-Mahmoudiye Mosque. Built in 1809, the mosque was renovated for the first time in 1812 by Turkish governor Mohammed Abu Najat Aja. The governor rebuilt much of the city during his rule (1807–22), including the city walls that Napoléon's army tore down in 1799.

The mosque, with its minaret and two colorful domes, managed to escape the fate of other sites in Jaffa that were destroyed during the War of Independence. In the late 19th century a separate entrance was built into the east wall to save the governor and other dignitaries the bother of having to push through the market-square crowds at the main entrance on the south. Not usually open to tourists, this is one of the local Muslim community's most important mosques.

The original mosque included a huge, splendid **drinking fountain** built into its southern wall, where travelers refreshed themselves after long journeys. In recent times, however, the Suleiman Fountain has lost its glory, and it sits sadly between two soft-drink stores that offer today's travelers a less romantic but more practical means of quenching their thirst. ⊠ *Yefet St.*

⑱ Gan Hapisga. You might have to vie for space in this Summit Garden with a long line of newlyweds who come here to be photographed in their wedding garb at sunset. Seven archaeological layers have been unearthed in a section of the park called Ramses II Garden. The oldest wall sections (20 feet thick) have been identified as part of a 17th-century BC Hyksos city. Other remains include part of a 13th-century BC city gate inscribed with the name of Ramses II, a Canaanite city, a Jewish city from the time of Ezra and Nechemiah, Hasmonean ruins from the 2nd century BC, and traces of Roman occupation. At the summit and disturbing the ancient aura is a kitschy stone sculpture— *Statue of Faith*—from the 1970s and in the shape of a gateway.

㉒ Hadolphin St. This enclave is a hive of activity, with an art gallery, a superb French restaurant, a Greek Orthodox church dating from 1924, one of the best hummus joints in the city (open in the mornings only), and a ceramics store run by local potter Eytan, all within a stone's throw of one another.

⑮ Jaffa Museum. The museum building has a lengthy history: It was first constructed during the Crusades; in the 18th century, the Turks added to what was left of the original building and used it as their Government House until 1897. In the first half of this century it was a soap factory. Since 1961 the upper level has been operating as the Jaffa Museum, displaying many of the finds unearthed during archaeological digs here and in other parts of Tel Aviv. ⊠ *10 Mifratz Shlomo St.,* ☎ *03/682–5375.* ☞ *NIS 6 ($2).* ☉ *Sun.–Mon. 9–2, Tues.–Wed. 9–7, Thurs. 9–2.*

Kikar Kedumin. This is Old Jaffa's central plaza. Old Jaffa used to be Tel Aviv's red-light district; it also had a high crime rate and raw sewage in the streets. Today, however, thanks to efforts begun by the Tel Aviv municipality in the late 1950s, it is chockablock with excavation sites, restaurants, expensive gift and souvenir shops, and galleries. The artists who live here complain of too much noise on summer nights; some visitors say it is *too* touristy. But Old Jaffa is charming and should not be missed. The labyrinthine network of tiny alleyways snakes in all directions from Kikar Kedumim down to the modern port.

Serving as the focus of Kikar Kedumim is an archaeological site that exposes 3rd-century BC catacombs.

Police station. Overall an uninteresting structure, the station contains an Ottoman-designed arch above its entrance. The design over the door is the seal of Turkish sultan Abdul Hamid II. During the British Mandate, the British used the building to intern both Arabs and members of the Zionist group Irgun. ⊠ *Yefet St.*

★ ⑲ **Port.** Here you will find many fishing boats stuffed into the small marina, as well as a handful of houseboats. Along the waterfront are a plethora of restaurants, all expensive but most pretty good.

⑳ **St. Louis French Hospital.** This building was named for Louis IX, leader of the Seventh Crusade, who landed in Jaffa in 1251. Established by Roman Catholic nuns in the late 19th century, it was Jaffa's first modern hospital. Its neo-Renaissance style, popular in Europe at the time, includes high ceilings and tall arched windows. The building also had strategic importance, occupying the southwestern corner and highest point of Jaffa's encircling wall. It is now a community health center. ⊠ *Yefet St.*

⑯ **St. Peter's Monastery.** Dedicated to the apostle Peter, the monastery was established by Franciscans in the 1890s. It was built over the ruins of a citadel that dates from the Seventh Crusade, which was led by King Louis IX of France. St. Peter's remained Jaffa's principal Roman Catholic church until the church of San Antonio was built in 1932. A monument to King Louis stands today at the entrance to the friary. Napoléon is rumored to have stayed here during his Jaffa campaign of 1799. To enter, ring the bell by pulling the string on the right side of the door. You will probably be greeted by one of the custodians, who speak Spanish and some English. ☎ *03/682–2871; call ahead if you want to visit.*

㉑ **San Antonio Roman Catholic Church.** Although it looks quite new, with its clean white-stone bricks, the church actually dates to 1932, when it was built to accommodate the growing needs of the Roman Catholic Church in Jaffa. (St. Peter's, *above,* was in a heavily populated Muslim area and was unable to expand due to lack of land.) The church is named for St. Antonius of Padua, friend and disciple of St. Francis of Assisi. ⊠ *51 Yefet St.*

★ ⑭ **Shuk hapishpeshim.** The flea market actually began as one of many small bazaars that surrounded the clock tower in the mid-19th century, but it is now the only survivor of that era. The market's main street is **Olei Zion,** but there are a number of smaller streets and arcades to explore at your leisure, so take your time. There's more junk than treasures now, and bargaining is not as vigorous as it once was; but it's still important to play the game, so don't agree to the first price the seller demands.

Yefet Street. Think of Yefet as a sort of thread between eras: Below it is the old market area, while all around you stand the Christian and Western schools and churches of the 19th and 20th centuries. Nos. 21, 23, and 25 deserve mention. The first is the **Tabitha School,** established by the Presbyterian Church of Scotland in 1863. Behind the school is a small cemetery where some fairly prominent figures are buried, including Dr. Thomas Hodgkin, the personal physician to Sir Moses Montefiore and the first to define Hodgkin's disease, who died in Jaffa in 1866. **No. 23** was a French Catholic school (it still carries the sign COLLÈGE DES FRÈRES) from 1882, but has long since been used by the French Embassy for administrative purposes. And next door, the neo-Tudor, fortresslike **Urim School,** with its round tower, was set up as a girls' school in 1882 by nuns of the same order that built the hospital. Today it is a local school.

Neve Tzedek

In 1887, a small group of Jewish families concentrated their efforts to get out of crowded, poverty-stricken Jaffa and began creating an infrastructure on the sand to the north of the mainly Arab port town. Building at a rate of 10 houses a year, they laid the cornerstone for Neve Tzedek (Dwellings of Justice) in 1890. This was the forebear of Tel Aviv. The area is off the beaten path for most tourists, although as time and money are being invested in restoration, it is attracting renewed interest. Today Neve Tzedek is the home of some of Tel Aviv's artists, rich and poor; it also has a splendid dance and arts complex (the Suzanne Dellal Center) and a growing number of small trendy galleries and gift stores. Though bordered on three sides by heavily trafficked streets (Eilat Road to the south, Herzl Street to the west, and Kaufman Street along the sea), this little quarter is very tranquil. Made up of only about a dozen very small streets stuffed with one- and two-story dwellings in various stages of depressing disrepair or enthusiastic renovation, Neve Tzedek is rich with tales of a century ago.

A Good Walk

Begin your visit at **Chelouche Bridge** ㉓, on Chelouche Street just in from Eilat Road. Get used to the name: The Chelouches, one of the quarter's founding families, are remembered all over Neve Tzedek. The shell of Aaron Chelouche's house, the first in the quarter, still stands at what later became **32 Chelouche Street.**

Continue on Chelouche Street to Yehieli Street to see the main attraction of Neve Tzedek, the **Suzanne Dellal Center for Dance and Theater** ㉔. The two buildings from early in the century are now venues for a wide range of performances. Backtrack on Chelouche Street; the restored house at **No. 35,** at the corner of Rokach Street, was home to Nobel Prize–winning writer S. Y. Agnon from 1909 to 1912.

Turn right into Rokach Street. As you approach the intersection of Rokach and Neve Tzedek streets, consider what life was like before there was electricity or running water. In fact, on the northwestern corner, where the cream-color bomb shelters stand today, lay Neve Tzedek's wells. There residents waited eagerly for their "water man," a Yemenite by the name of Yosef Minz, who pumped the water and would even home deliver. Toward the end of the century people began digging their own wells; running water did not start to flow until after World War I.

At **36 Rokach Street** stands the house of another of the quarter's founders, Shimon Rokach; family members still live here. A few steps on and you will come to Pines Street. To the left and across the road, on the corner of Pines and Lilienblum streets, the pink-and-yellow shell of a building was the Eden Cinema, the first movie house in the country and a curious phenomenon altogether in 1914, set up as it was in the middle of the sand. The Eden became a cultural center, and the city's earliest opera and theater performances were also held here.

Continue up Lilienblum to Herzl Street and turn left. End your walk at the huge, ungainly **Shalom Tower** ㉕, where the view from the rooftop observatory takes in both the sprawling city and the Mediterranean.

TIMING
Allow around two hours for this walk, including time for coffee or a light meal. There are few sites to enter, but these are closed on Friday afternoon and Saturday, so it's better to visit on a weekday.

Sights to See

㉓ Chelouche Bridge. The bridge was na[...]
began his career as a money changer[...]
property north of Jaffa with his profit[...]
railroad track to be constructed in [...]
Jerusalem, the railroad was laid in 18[...]
erated by a French company. Aaron C[...]
for the French firm, and he added th[...]
line as a convenient means of getting [...]

32 Chelouche St. Prior to Neve Tzedek's inception, Aaron Chelouche was prominent in Jaffa's Jewish community, but he was intent on setting up a Jewish town. He thus built the first house here, in 1887. The shell of the huge house still stands, with hints of its grandeur in the arched terrace that spans the facade on the second floor. It held more than the Chelouche clan (including Aaron's two daughters, three sons, and their families): By the time Aaron "persuaded" other Jews to come here to live—by selling them cheap plots—the house was doubling as a community center. There was even a synagogue out back. The dynasty would continue, and one of Aaron's grandsons—Moshe—even became mayor of Tel Aviv—albeit for a day. Following the 1936 death of Meir Dizengoff, the city's first mayor, Moshe was elected to replace him. But he was quickly deposed by the city's rightist bloc, backed by the ruling British, who preferred another son of Neve Tzedek, Yisrael Rokach.

35 Chelouche St. Drawn to the quarter like so many others of the country's literati and artists, writer S. Y. Agnon lived here from 1909 to 1912. At the time, the young Agnon was working as a literary assistant to the more senior writer Simcha Ben Zion, the namesake of the city-center boulevard leading from King George Street to Habimah Square. Agnon's first story was published in the literary editions Ben Zion produced. Indeed, much of Agnon's writings reflects these very surroundings.

36 Rokach St. Shimon Rokach moved to the area from Jerusalem in 1884, and his son was born here three years later. The grandiose house, which changed the face of the street, was designed by an Austrian architect whose touch included a bronze dome at the rear. In fact, Rokach became known as the Parisian Street because of its obvious grand European influence.

Rokach the younger was already ensconced in politics by the time he was 28. After Mayor Dizengoff died in 1936, Rokach bumped out Moshe Chelouche as the preferred choice to succeed him. He served as mayor until 1952. In 1953, he became Israel's interior minister. The house is still occupied by the family: Shimon's sculptor granddaughter renovated it and sometimes opens it up to the public.

㉕ Shalom Tower. This building stands on the site of the first high school ever to hold its classes all in Hebrew: the Herzliya Gymnasium (named, like the street for the founder of the Zionist movement, Theodor Herzl). Israel's first skyscraper is today just another office block, but it has a rooftop observatory well worth a visit for its magnificent city and sea views. ✉ *Herzl St.,* ☎ *03/517–0991.* 📷 *NIS 9 ($3).*

㉔ Suzanne Dellal Center for Dance and Theater. The two large whitewashed buildings that make up this attractive complex started as schools, one in 1892 and the other in 1908. Both were used for educational purposes until the 1970s, although they also served as headquarters for the forces of Etzel and the underground Haganah that marched on Arab Jaffa in the 1940s, when Arab residents terrorized Jewish neighbor-

s. The complex was always something of a meeting place for the
r folk, and it opened as a dance center after extensive renovations
in 1990 (☞ Nightlife and the Arts, *below*). You can enter the attractive grounds, but the halls are open only for performances. ⊠ *6 Yehieli St.,* ☏ *03/510–5656.*

rthern Tel Aviv

Among the sights north of the Yarkon River are two important museums. The Eretz Israel Museum of Israeli Life is close to Tel Aviv University; Bet Hatefutsoth (Diaspora Museum) is farther north, on the campus of the university. The museums are about 8 km (5 mi) from the downtown hotels; Buses 24, 25, 27, 45, or 49 will take you to both. Allow at least two hours for each.

Sights to See

★ **Beth Hatefutsoth (Diaspora Museum).** Presented here are 2,500 years of Jewish life in the Diaspora (the settling of Jews outside Israel), beginning with the destruction of the First Temple in Jerusalem and chronicling such major events as the exile to Babylon and the expulsion from Spain in 1492. Also covered is the world of Eastern Europe before the Holocaust. Films and music enhance the experience. One highlight is a replica collection of miniature synagogues throughout the world, both those destroyed and still existent. ⊠ *Tel Aviv University Campus (Gate 2), Klausner St., Ramat Aviv,* ☏ *03/646–2020.* ✉ *NIS 22 ($7.30).* ☉ *Sun.–Tues. and Thurs. 10–4, Wed. 10–6, Fri. 9–1.*

★ **Eretz Israel Museum.** This national museum comprises eight pavilions that present such facets of Israeli life as ethnography and folklore, ceramics and other handicrafts, and numismatics (coins); the displays span 3,000 years of history. In the center of the complex is the ancient site of Tel Kassile, where archaeological digs have so far uncovered 12 layers of settlements. ⊠ *2 Levanon (University) St.,* ☏ *03/641–5244.* ✉ *Museum NIS 18 ($6); planetarium NIS 10 ($3.30).* ☉ *Sun.–Tues. and Thurs. 9–2, Wed. 9–7, Sat. 10–2.*

DINING

Most Tel Aviv restaurants are open throughout the day and well into the night year-round, except Yom Kippur. Keep in mind that many serve lunch at reasonable prices, making them less expensive options than the price categories suggest (eating well in Tel Aviv can be very expensive). Israelis, like many of their counterparts around the Mediterranean, dine late. Chances are you'll have no trouble getting a table at 7 PM, whereas at 10 you may be waiting on a long line. Casual attire is always acceptable, even in the fanciest Tel Aviv restaurants.

Although the quality of the cuisine has improved a lot, be warned that the same cannot be said about service. Even in good restaurants, staff members may make you feel as though they're doing you a favor by waiting on you. It's customary to leave a 10%–15% tip, but don't feel obliged to leave it if you've received poor service. Occasionally, the service charge is added to the bill; however, this is so rare that it generally goes unnoticed and diners end up paying twice for service.

$$$$ ✕ **Keren.** Ranked among the top restaurants in Israel, Keren is housed in the only fully restored building in the run-down American Colony area of Jaffa. The bar downstairs proves a restful spot after the inevitable daytime traffic jam on Eilat Street. The state of neighboring buildings is forgotten when you enter the upstairs dining room, with its fine white-lace tablecloths and smooth wood floors. The trademark stuffed zuc-

chini flowers are filled with something different on a regular basis. And that's just the beginning. . . . ⊠ *12 Eilat St., at Auerbach St., Jaffa,* ☎ *03/681–6565. Reservations essential. AE, DC, MC, V. No lunch Fri.*

$$$$ ✕ **King Solomon Grill.** Dim lights and partial curtains between tables create an intimate atmosphere here, despite the restaurant's large size. The eclectic menu ranges from Continental (pâté de foie gras, baked sweetbreads) to Middle Eastern (hummus and tahini) to North American (New York–style pastrami on rye)—there's even sushi. And all of it is kosher. ⊠ *Hilton Hotel, Independence Park,* ☎ *03/520–2222. Reservations essential. AE, DC, MC, V. No lunch.*

$$$$ ✕ **Le Relais Jaffa.** Here the traditional French cuisine is *très* fine, and
★ so is the ambience of this 150-year-old stone building. Built in Ottoman times, the structure retains not only the original marble floors, but also some engravings made to ward off the evil eye. On a balmy summer evening, ask for a table on the terrace. Whether you opt for the fixed menu or à la carte, top it off with a chocolate charlotte. ⊠ *13½ Hadolphin St., Jaffa,* ☎ *03/681–0637. Reservations essential. AE, DC, MC, V. No lunch Sun.*

$$$$ ✕ **Mul-Yam.** This is Israel's first true-to-life oyster and seafood bar. Every-
★ thing is flown in fresh from abroad—including Nova Scotia lobsters— which makes this an expensive option. Still, it's truly pleasurable: The dishes are tasty and well presented, and the great location, in the old port by the Mediterranean, adds to the flavor. ⊠ *Tel Aviv Port,* ☎ *03/546–9920. Reservations essential. AE, DC, MC, V. No dinner Sat.*

$$$$ ✕ **PastaLina.** One of the most innovative restaurants in Tel Aviv, PastaLina is worth the trek to a less-well-known corner of Jaffa, near the American Colony. Antipasti cover a large table by the entrance, and you are served generous samples upon being seated. The fixed menu, which changes daily, includes antipasti and a pasta, meat, or fish dish. Glass bricks in the front wall allow natural light to highlight the russet walls and wood furniture. ⊠ *16 Elifelet St., Jaffa,* ☎ *03/683–6401. Reservations essential. AE, DC, MC, V. No dinner Fri.*

$$$$ ✕ **Prego.** The easygoing atmosphere here makes lingering over your fine Italian meal a very good idea. Most of the restaurant occupies a terrace overlooking Rothschild Boulevard, in an older quarter of Tel Aviv. For something delicate and tasty, go for the spinach-and-ricotta ravioli with tomato sauce, accompanied by a glass of cold white wine from the Golan. ⊠ *9 Rothschild Blvd.,* ☎ *03/510–7319. AE, DC, MC, V.*

$$$$ ✕ **Taboon.** The restaurant's stone oven imparts a rich and faintly barbecued flavor to the fresh fish and seafood here. For starters, the carpaccio of salmon and grouper is delectable. Whitewashed walls and turquoise-color trimmings lend sophistication to the Mediterranean ambience. ⊠ *Main Gate, Jaffa Port (turn left at pier),* ☎ *03/681–1176. Reservations essential. AE, DC, MC, V.*

$$$$ ✕ **Twelve Tribes.** Regulars claim it's the best hotel restaurant in Tel Aviv.
★ They don't come here for the '70s decor, which is out of synch with the menu's New Israeli cuisine (reflecting the many nationalities of this melting pot). Favorite dishes include deep-fried goose liver wrapped in pastry on caramelized fruits and a sliced rack of lamb with red-wine sauce. ⊠ *Sheraton Hotel, 115 Hayarkon St.,* ☎ *03/521–1111. Reservations essential. AE, DC, MC, V. Closed Fri. (also Sat. in summer). No lunch.*

$$$$ ✕ **Yin Yang.** You won't find a better Chinese restaurant in the coun-
★ try, with food served up by owner–wonder chef Yisrael Aharoni. The atmosphere is enhanced with "Chinese red" walls and Asian prints. Yin Yang now serves dim sum between 4 PM and 6 PM. ⊠ *64 Rothschild Blvd.,* ☎ *03/560–6833. Reservations essential. AE, DC, MC, V.*

$$$ ✕ **Dixie.** This bar and grill is away from the main tourist areas and serves mostly the surrounding offices and commercial centers. But

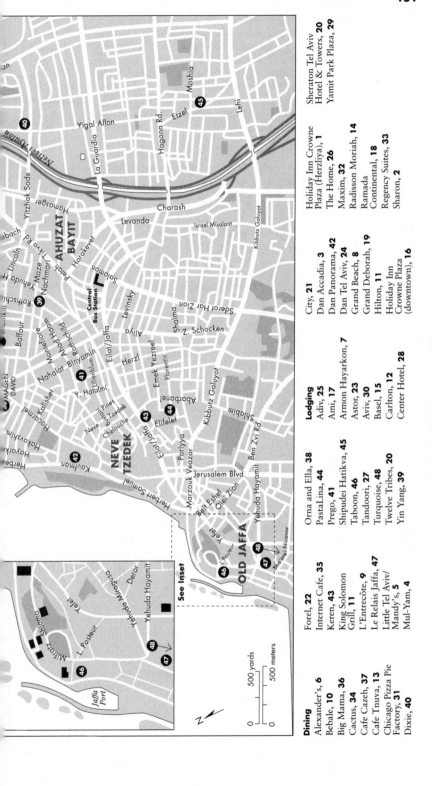

Dining
Alexander's, **6**
Bebale, **10**
Big Mama, **36**
Cactus, **34**
Cafe Cazeh, **37**
Cafe Tnuva, **13**
Chicago Pizza Pie Factory, **31**
Dixie, **40**

Forel, **22**
Internet Cafe, **35**
Keren, **43**
King Solomon Grill, **11**
L'Entrecôte, **9**
Le Relais Jaffa, **47**
Little Tel Aviv/ Mandy's, **5**
Mul-Yam, **4**

Orna and Ella, **38**
PastaLina, **44**
Prego, **41**
Shipudei Hatikva, **45**
Taboon, **46**
Tandoori, **27**
Turquoise, **48**
Twelve Tribes, **20**
Yin Yang, **39**

Lodging
Adiv, **25**
Ami, **17**
Armon Hayarkon, **7**
Astor, **23**
Aviv, **30**
Basel, **15**
Carlton, **12**
Center Hotel, **28**

City, **21**
Dan Accadia, **3**
Dan Panorama, **42**
Dan Tel Aviv, **24**
Grand Beach, **8**
Grand Deborah, **19**
Hilton, **11**
Holiday Inn Crowne Plaza (downtown), **16**

Holiday Inn Crowne Plaza (Herzliya), **1**
The Home, **26**
Maxim, **32**
Radisson Moriah, **14**
Ramada Continental, **18**
Regency Suites, **33**
Sharon, **2**

Sheraton Tel Aviv Hotel & Towers, **20**
Yamit Park Plaza, **29**

grab a taxi and go (anytime—it's open 24 hours a day) if you're in the mood for the Nebraska-style porterhouse steak or hints of Cajun food. The bar is well stocked. ✉ *120 Yigal Allon St.,* ☎ *03/696–6123. AE, DC, MC, V.*

$$$ ✕ **Forel.** Pleasant, unassuming, and always friendly, Forel (which means "trout") has a consistently good menu of—you guessed it—trout of all kinds, forms, and flavors: blue trout, stuffed trout, smoked trout, and more. An antipasti table near the entrance whets the appetite. The decor is simple and attractive, too. ✉ *10 Frishman St.,* ☎ *03/522–3167. AE, DC, MC, V.*

$$$ ✕ **Tandoori.** This is the original restaurant of the popular Tandoori chain,
★   which introduced Israelis to fine Indian cuisine. Sari-draped owner Reena Pushkarna greets customers and makes each feel like a special guest. Curries come in three strengths, but tandoori chicken is the specialty here. It comes to the table sizzling hot, and finger bowls of rosewater mean you can tuck in with abandon. ✉ *2 Zamenhoff St. (Kikar Dizengoff),* ☎ *03/629–6185. AE, DC, MC, V.*

$$$ ✕ **Turquoise.** The location—perched above a (relatively) quiet beach in Jaffa on a no-name street—and the food somehow compensate for what has to be among the worst service in town. Still, it's a good spot for seafood served in a romantic setting. Grouper fillet with crab sauce is great, as are the dessert parfaits. The circular outdoor bar is particularly delightful. ✉ *153/1 St. (turn down unnamed street toward sea), Jaffa,* ☎ *03/658–8320. Reservations essential. AE, DC, MC, V.*

$$ ✕ **Alexander's.** Dress trendy if you want to fit in: The crowd here is Tel Aviv yuppie to the hilt, in keeping with the atmosphere along this street. The menu runs the gamut from roast beef sandwiches to lasagna. You may have to wait for a table if you haven't made reservations, but service is generally quite good. ✉ *81 Yehuda Hamaccabi St.,* ☎ *03/546–3591. AE, DC, MC, V.*

$$ ✕ **Cactus.** "Across-the-border"–inspired graphics in bold yellows, reds, blues, and greens complement the terra-cotta tones of this small, happy Tex-Mex restaurant. The menu includes close-to-traditional fare of nachos and salsa, burritos, chili con carne, and fajitas. The margaritas are not quite the real thing but still do the trick. ✉ *66 Hayarkon St.,* ☎ *03/510–5969. MC, V.*

$$ ✕ **Cafe Cazeh.** It's one of the city's "in" hangouts and deservedly so: The food is good, the service is warm, and a little courtyard/garden in back provides a very relaxing atmosphere. No meat is served, but the vegetable pies and quiches are hearty and come with fresh salad. Desserts are the real specialty, though, and you may have trouble deciding between lemon meringue or pecan pie, apple cake or brownies. ✉ *19 Sheinkin St.,* ☎ *03/629–3756. No credit cards. No dinner Fri. Closed Sat.*

$$ ✕ **Cafe Tnuva.** Big, hearty salads and fresh juices can help perk you up on a day of touring Tel Aviv on foot—or you can end a relatively healthy meal with one of the many tasty cakes. ✉ *34 Ben-Gurion Blvd.,* ☎ *03/527–2972. AE, DC, MC, V.*

$$ ✕ **Chicago Pizza Pie Factory.** Order either the specialty deep-dish pizza or the thinner-crust variety here; both use only fresh ingredients and are very good. Leave room for the house cake, a sinful concoction of thick chocolate, nuts, whipped cream, and a meringue topping. The half-price happy hour runs weekdays from 5 to 7. ✉ *65 Hayarkon St.,* ☎ *03/517–7505. MC, V.*

$$ ✕ **L'Entrecôte.** The mood is distinctly Parisian in this intimate restaurant with wood beams and a cozy upper-level garret. As the name implies, mostly steaks are served here. There are only a few tables, so the noise level is low. ✉ *195 Ben Yehuda St.,* ☎ *03/546–6726. AE, DC, MC, V.*

$$ ✕ **Little Tel Aviv/Mandy's Candy Store.** The "Mandy" here refers to a principle figure in Britain's Profumo scandal of the '60s; she later married the original owner, a prominent local restaurateur with a string of his own scandals. The restaurant is a popular veteran on the Tel Aviv scene, with an extensive menu, including particularly memorable hamburgers. ✉ *300 Hayarkon St.,* ☎ *03/605–5539. AE, DC, MC, V.*

$$ ✕ **Orna and Ella.** Consistently good for light meals and excellent for cakes and desserts, Orna and Ella is worth going back to again and again. Start with the sweet potato latkes but don't leave here without trying something from the dessert corner, such as a *tarte tatin* (apple tart) or pear pie. ✉ *33 Sheinkin St.,* ☎ *03/620–4753. MC, V.*

$ ✕ **Bebale.** Serving old-style Jewish food amid photographs and mementos from the past, Bebale is enjoying something of a revival among young, hip Israelis newly appreciative of their Eastern European roots. Specialties include gefilte fish, chopped liver, and *cholent* (slow-cooked meat-and-bean stew)—all traditional Sabbath lunch fare in the old shtetls of Europe. ✉ *177 Ben Yehuda St.,* ☎ *03/546–7486. MC, V. No dinner Fri.*

$ ✕ **Big Mama.** The thin-crust pizza here is the best in town, and the
★ owners take pride in using only the freshest ingredients. Toppings range from the traditional basil to more unusual ones, such as zucchini or prosciutto and egg. In the heart of the Carmel Market, Big Mama avoids the market crowds by opening only for dinner. It's an ideal spot for a quick, light meal. ✉ *22 Rabbi Akiva St.,* ☎ *03/517–5096. No credit cards. Closed Sun. No lunch.*

$ ✕ **Internet Cafe.** If you *must* check out the latest sites on the World Wide Web, you might as well do it with an espresso alongside. Don't be surprised, though, if your neighbors don't acknowledge you when you ask the time—the Net can do that. ✉ *18 Ha'arba'a St.,* ☎ *03/562–6288.*

$ ✕ **Shipudei Hatikva.** This family-style restaurant is one of many along
★ Etzel Street in the Hatikva Quarter. The Las Vegas–style lights along the street contrast with the plain Formica tables and fluorescent lighting inside, where a range of sumptuous skewered meats grilled over hot coals is offered. The specialty is barbecued goose liver. ✉ *37 Etzel St., Hatikva Quarter,* ☎ *03/687–8014. MC, V. No dinner Fri., no lunch Sat.*

LODGING

Hotel reservations are essential during all Jewish holiday periods and are advised throughout the year. Keep in mind that most hotels (except as noted) include breakfast in the price: fresh vegetables, salads, and fruit; cereals and pastries; and eggs and cheeses are some options.

Tel Aviv

$$$$ 🏨 **Carlton.** The warm European ambience is evident as soon as you enter the lobby, with its muted colors, pale wood paneling, and soft music. The Carlton caters to its clientele, a mix of tourists and businesspeople, with efficient yet personal service. Most rooms have sea views, as does the swimming pool, which is on the roof. ✉ *10 Eliezer Peri St., 61064,* ☎ *03/520–1818,* ℻ *03/527–1043. 278 rooms with bath. 2 restaurants, bar, 2 coffee shops, pool, beauty parlor, chapel, parking (fee). AE, DC, MC, V.*

$$$$ 🏨 **Dan Panorama.** Its location south of the main stretch of hotels and near Jaffa is less convenient to town, but rates are lower than at comparable luxury establishments. Rooms at this high-rise hotel are compact and attractive, with decorative wall hangings adding spots of color. Each room has a tiny balcony overlooking the sea, either south toward Jaffa or north facing the hub of the city. Poolside barbecues in summer are a plus. ✉ *10 Y. Kaufman St., 68012,* ☎ *03/519–0190,*

FAX *03/658599. 504 rooms with bath. Restaurant, bar, coffee shop, pool, massage, sauna, exercise room, health club, nightclub, parking (fee). AE, DC, MC, V.*

$$$$ 🏨 **Dan Tel Aviv.** Despite its exclusive reputation, this landmark hotel
★   has a warm, congenial atmosphere. Patterned coverlets decorate olive green furniture in the rooms; bathrooms have hair dryers, phones, and radios. Rooms are larger in the luxurious King David wing and have panoramic sea views, as well as double-glazed windows to muffle city noise; however, none of these have balconies. Guests have access to free golf at the Dan Accadia Hotel, about 25 km (15½ mi) north of Tel Aviv. Tel Avivians come to La Regence, the hotel's restaurant, for elegant dining. There is direct access to the beach from the hotel. ⊠ *99 Hayarkon St., 63903,* ☎ *03/520–2525,* FAX *03/524–9755. 238 rooms with bath, 50 suites. 3 restaurants, bar, café, minibars, pool, sauna, steam room, health club, parking (fee). AE, DC, MC, V.*

$$$$ 🏨 **Grand Beach.** All rooms have turquoise-and-yellow decor, and the furniture is gray accented with yellow. The reading lamps are particularly good. There is a rooftop pool, and the hotel is a five-minute walk from the beach. The main dining room has a view of city streets, and light food is served in the large lobby lounge. ⊠ *250 Hayarkon St., 63113,* ☎ *03/543–3333,* FAX *03/546–6589. Bar, lobby lounge, pool, shops, chapel. AE, DC, MC, V.*

$$$$ 🏨 **Hilton.** The country's most expensive hotel and the one most clearly catering to business travelers, the Hilton fairly bristles with the high energy of negotiations and deal making. A full range of executive services is offered, including Japanese-language services and two business lounges. The Hilton's large seawater pool is the best in town; this is also the only Tel Aviv hotel with its own beach, so you don't need to get dressed to get undressed again. In addition to enjoying classic French cuisine in the first-class King Solomon Grill, you can get a pastrami on rye in the Deli Room or kosher sushi in the lobby. Unlike other hotels listed here, breakfast is not included in the price. ⊠ *Hayarkon St., Independence Park, 63405,* ☎ *03/520–2222,* FAX *03/527–2711. 600 rooms with bath. 2 restaurants, 2 bars, deli, sushi bar, pool, tennis court, health club, beach, shops, parking (fee). AE, DC, MC, V.*

$$$$ 🏨 **Holiday Inn Crowne Plaza.** The light and attractive Holiday Inn Crowne Plaza is decorated in soothing pastels, both in the guest rooms and public spaces. Each room is equipped with a voice-mail box for messages. Executive floors are available. The main restaurant, Bellissima, serves meat at lunchtime and becomes an Italian dairy restaurant at night. In addition, there is the Pacific China Grill, which serves Western food cooked with an Eastern influence; and the English-style Pub Inn, a nice spot for a seaside beer. ⊠ *145 Hayarkon St., 63453,* ☎ *03/520–1111,* FAX *03/520–1122. 220 rooms with bath. 2 restaurants, pub, 2 snack bars, sushi bar, in-room safes, no-smoking floors, beauty parlor, massage, sauna, health club, parking (fee). AE, DC, MC, V.*

$$$$ 🏨 **Radisson Moriah Plaza.** In this 17-floor hotel, all rooms (except singles) have sea views from their balconies. Public areas have been freshly redecorated in earth tones; the lobby has photos of old Tel Aviv. Rooms have Mediterranean color schemes and good reading lights. The outdoor pool (children's activities are held here daily in the summer) overlooks the beach, to which there is direct access. The restaurant presents a wide range of Israel dishes, including *taboon* (clay oven) baked fish. ⊠ *155 Hayarkon St., 63453,* ☎ *03/521–6666,* FAX *03/527–1065. 372 rooms with bath. Restaurant, bar, patisserie, in-room safes, minibars, room service, saltwater pool, parking (fee). AE, DC, MC, V.*

$$$$ 🏨 **Ramada Continental.** Guest rooms, decorated in a variety of soft hues, all have double-glazed windows and balconies with sea views; some even have queen-size beds, unusual in Israel. Bathrooms include hair dryers and scales. The lobby, with windows that overlook the sea, has a bar with a pianist and a coffee shop, and the main dining room has doors that open onto a patio, where barbecues are held. An outdoor terrace restaurant overlooking the sea serves light meals. ⊠ *121 Hayarkon St., 61032,* ☎ *03/521–5555,* FAX *03/521–5588. 330 rooms with bath, 10 suites. Restaurant, 2 bars, coffee shop, 2 pools, sauna, exercise room, parking (fee). AE, DC, MC, V.*

$$$$ 🏨 **Regency Suites.** This Best Western hotel is made up entirely of fully equipped, modern one-bedroom suites, each of which also has a small living area. A tad cheaper than the big hotels, its other advantages include being able to cook for yourself and entertain a few people. The decor is tasteful and the atmosphere is homey, especially in the tiny coffee shop, where breakfast is served (for an extra charge). ⊠ *80 Hayarkon St., 63432,* ☎ *03/516–3266,* FAX *03/516–3276. 20 suites. Coffee shop. AE, DC, MC, V.*

$$$$ 🏨 **Sheraton Tel Aviv Hotel and Towers.** Combining a personal touch
★ with the efficiency and experience of the international Sheraton chain, this is one of the most attractive lodging options in Tel Aviv. An excellent lobby design allows for private areas within the public space; there's a lounge bar, often with live entertainment. The rooms, most of which have soft hues and color-coordinated fabrics, all have double-glazed windows. The well-run executive Sheraton Towers floors have their own check-in and a 24-hour business center. The Twelve Tribes restaurant (☞ Dining, *above*) is widely considered the best hotel restaurant in Tel Aviv. ⊠ *115 Hayarkon St., 61032,* ☎ *03/521–1111,* FAX *03/523–3322. 346 rooms with bath. 2 restaurants, bar, minibars, 2 pools, health club, nightclub, business services, parking (fee). AE, DC, MC, V.*

$$$$ 🏨 **Yamit Park Plaza.** Roughly half the accommodations in this beach-front hotel are in suites with kitchenettes, unusual for Tel Aviv. One building contains the one- and two-bedroom suites, which include living areas as well as fully equipped kitchenettes. Standard rooms, housed in an adjacent building that opened in 1991, are less expensive. ⊠ *79 Hayarkon St., 63903,* ☎ *03/519–7111,* FAX *03/517–4689. 42 rooms with bath, 43 suites. 2 restaurants, bar, pool, nightclub, parking (fee). AE, DC, MC, V.*

$$$ 🏨 **Armon Hayarkon.** Though hardly the palace of its English translation, this small, family-run hotel is pleasant enough to garner a high percentage of repeat customers. It's in Little Tel Aviv, at the northern end of Hayarkon Street; a number of good restaurants are there, and the beach is just a minute's walk. The small rooms are decorated in basic brown, and some have balconies facing the sea. The small lobby has coffee-making facilities and a cold-drink machine. ⊠ *268 Hayarkon St., 63504,* ☎ *03/605–5271,* FAX *03/605–8485. 24 rooms with bath. Parking (fee). AE, DC, MC, V.*

$$$ 🏨 **Astor.** Built on a rise on the corner of Frishman and Hayarkon streets, the Astor has an excellent view of the sea. Rooms in this 30-year-old hotel are not large, but those facing the sea have enclosed balconies with picture windows. The small, homey lobby has prints of Israeli scenes and a shop selling handmade jewelry. The Shangri-La restaurant serves authentic Thai cuisine and has a beautiful canopied terrace that faces seaward. ⊠ *105 Hayarkon St., 63903,* ☎ *03/522–3141,* FAX *03/523–7247. 70 rooms with bath. Restaurant, bar, free parking. AE, DC, MC, V.*

$$$ 🏨 **Basel.** It is not on the beach side of Hayarkon Street, but this seven-story hotel lives up to its reputation as a good deal. All but five rooms on each floor have sea views; decor includes well-designed wooden furniture and patchwork-style fabrics. Expect personalized service (perhaps a legacy of the original Swiss owners). The lobby with its corner bar overlooks the small swimming pool. ⊠ *156 Hayarkon St., 63451,*

☎ *03/524–4161,* ⅋ *03/527–0005. 120 rooms with bath. Bar, coffee shop, room service, pool, parking (fee). AE, DC, MC, V.*

$$$ ⊡ **City.** On a quiet street near the beach, this six-story hotel is at the
★ bottom of the $$$ price range. The light, airy lobby has a small seating area on one side, a cozy dining room on the other. The outdoor café, which faces the neighbor's hedge across the street, consists of a dozen plastic chairs and tables under a sidewalk canopy. The rooms have blond-wood furniture and TVs. The City is known for its fine food, including an acclaimed Israeli breakfast and a Friday night Shabbat (Sabbath) dinner with gefilte fish. ⊠ *9 Mapu St., 63577,* ☎ *03/ 524–6253,* ⅋ *03/524–6250. 96 rooms with bath. Restaurant, café, room service, free parking. AE, DC, MC, V.*

$$$ ⊡ **Grand Deborah.** The bar and the reception area are one and the same at this newly renovated hotel, so you can have a drink as you check in. There's also a spacious lobby. The pleasant guest rooms are decorated with warm colors and wood trim. The Grand Deborah provides equally easy access to the city center and the beach. ⊠ *87 Ben Yehuda St.,* ☎ *03/527–8282,* ⅋ *03/527–8304. 60 rooms with bath. Dining room, lobby lounge, free parking. AE, DC, MC, V.*

$$ ⊡ **Ami.** Its name means "my people," and there are lots sitting at tables in the pleasant sidewalk café in front of this hotel. This small establishment is half a block from the sea, on a side street off Hayarkon Street. Most rooms are not large, though each has a small desk and chair. On each floor, four rooms have balconies with views of rooftops and cityscapes. ⊠ *4 Am Yisrael Hai St., 63455,* ☎ *03/524–9141,* ⅋ *03/523– 1151. 60 rooms with bath. Café, room service. AE, DC, MC, V.*

$$ ⊡ **Center Hotel.** This is one of the new breed of tourist-class hotels in Tel Aviv—simple rooms and warm but basic service, and much less expensive than the luxury spots on the beach, just a 15-minute walk away. The Center Hotel is well situated in town, on Dizengoff Square, adjacent to the Tandoori Indian restaurant (☞ Dining, *above*). Rooms are small and tasteful, though there is no Mediterranean view. ⊠ *2 Zamenhoff St.,* ☎ *03/629–6181,* ⅋ *03/629–6751. 56 rooms with bath. AE, DC, MC, V.*

$$ ⊡ **Maxim.** Moderately priced and amid more expensive accommodations, Maxim is a good value. Although the rooms are basic, most have views of the sea. Many Europeans like to stay here, and there is indeed a kind of Continental atmosphere about the place, due in part to the many European languages heard in the lobby. Guests can often be found relaxing in the café in the lobby. ⊠ *86 Hayarkon St.,* ☎ *03/ 517–3721,* ⅋ *03/517–3726. 60 rooms with bath. Bar, café. AE, DC, MC, V.*

$ ⊡ **Adiv.** This amiable hotel is on a side street off Hayarkon Street. Rooms have pleasing modern furnishings and pastel-print bedspreads and curtains; there are no sea views, however. The staff is polite. ⊠ *5 Mendele St., 63907,* ☎ *03/522–9141,* ⅋ *03/522–9144. 68 rooms with bath. Bar, café, room service. AE, DC, MC, V.*

$ ⊡ **Aviv.** More a hostel than a hotel, this three-story 1950s hotel was renovated when the trendy Picasso restaurant opened on its ground floor. Guests enter through the restaurant and register at a desk behind the kitchen. There's no elevator, and decor is spare; don't expect telephones or TVs. The rooms in the back are said to be quiet, but their location on Hayarkon Street and over the restaurant (which is open until 5 AM) is not the place for those who seek serenity. A real plus here is the breakfast (omelet, salad, juice, and bread) at Picasso, which is included in the price. ⊠ *88 Hayarkon St., 63432,* ☎ *03/510–2784,* ⅋ *03/522–3060. 20 rooms with bath. DC, MC, V.*

$ ⊡ **The Home.** Someone converted a regular residential block into furnished "studio apartments"—basic, but clean and well kept, at budget prices—right in the midst of the big, expensive hotels. A small kitchenette in each room can contribute to a budget stay in an otherwise expensive city. Don't expect much in the way of luxuries or facilities. ⊠ *106 Hayarkon St.,* ☎ *03/522–2695,* ᚎ *03/524–0815. Kitchenettes. AE, DC, MC, V.*

Herzliya Pituach

Herzliya Pituach, or Herzliya-on-the-Sea, is a resort area 12 km (7½ mi) up the coast from Tel Aviv. It has three beachfront resort hotels and several high-quality restaurants, as well as some fish eateries on the beach, two squares with outdoor cafés and shops, and a new marina. Affluent suburbanites live here, as do diplomats and foreign journalists. There's a cosmopolitan, holiday air to the place. An express tourist bus (Bus 90) plies the route between the Herzliya hotels, city center, and ancient Jaffa.

$$$$ 🏨 **Holiday Inn Crowne Plaza.** Almost anywhere you stand (or recline) in the Holiday Inn, you can see the sea—from the rooms, restaurant, and lobby. One of the pluses of this hotel is the state-of-the-art spa, where facilities include an indoor pool and single and double treatment rooms. All rooms have a view of the Mediterranean; deluxe rooms have balconies. Rooms are very tastefully decked out in sea blue and mustard hues. ⊠ *60 Ramot Yam, Herzliya-on-the-Sea, 46769,* ☎ *09/954–4444,* ᚎ *09/954–4675. 200 rooms with bath. 4 restaurants, bar, sushi bar, room service, outdoor and indoor pools, spa, tennis courts, shops, business services, parking (fee). AE, DC, MC, V.*

$$$$ 🏨 **Sharon.** The Sharon opened its doors as a hotel in 1948. Today's rooms—renovated of late—have light-color furniture, pink-and-gray color schemes, and bright reading lamps; most overlook the sea. Garden rooms are near the seawater pool. The Sharon's health club (popular with Tel Avivians) has a heated indoor pool, a workout room, dry and wet saunas, massage, and Dead Sea mineral baths. ⊠ *5 Ramot Yam, Herzliya-on-the-Sea, 46748,* ☎ *09/957–5777,* ᚎ *09/957–2448. 150 rooms with bath. Restaurant, bar, room service, 2 pools, beauty salon, tennis court, health club, shops, free parking. AE, DC, MC, V.*

$$$ 🏨 **Dan Accadia.** This well-known seaside hostelry (part of the Dan Hotel chain), open since 1956, is going strong. Its two buildings are surrounded by plant-filled lawns, with a pool at the center that overlooks the sea. Sixty rooms face the pool (with direct access to the beach), while others face the marina in front of the hotel. Rooms are not huge but have balconies with sea views; decor includes quilted bedspreads and matching blue-and-pink drapes. Organized activities for children and teenagers are held on Saturday and during the summer and holidays. Guests have access to the golf course at the Dan Caesarea farther north. The dining room has a glass wall that overlooks the sea, and a poolside restaurant is open for lunch. The Wednesday night barbecue poolside, with a band and dancing, has been a local fixture for years. ⊠ *Herzliya-on-the-Sea, 46851,* ☎ *09/955–6677,* ᚎ *09/956–2141. 185 rooms with bath. 2 restaurants, bar, coffee shop, pool, beauty parlor, massage, sauna, tennis courts, exercise room, shops, parking. AE, DC, MC, V.*

NIGHTLIFE AND THE ARTS

Nightlife

"The city that never stops" stays up later than many of the world's capitals. Peak hours on Hayarkon Street on a Friday or Saturday night continue until about 3 AM, when things finally begin to wind down.

Party goers are not daunted that nightspots come and go here about as quickly as the tides.

Bars and nightspots in Tel Aviv usually open in the day, long before the night owls descend; typically, these establishments offer either full dinners, beer and fries, or at the least, the coffee and cake they've been serving throughout the afternoon.

Bars, Pubs, and Nightclubs

Bar Ganza (⌧ 26 Sheinkin St., ☎ 03/528–1053) is really a bar only—there isn't a table in sight. Techno music is the norm.

Bar Mitzvah. (⌧ 16 Ha'arba'a St., ☎ 03/561–1869), one of numerous fun corners that line this street, makes an admirable play on words. Have some light smoked snacks with your beer.

Camelot (⌧ 16 Shalom Aleichem St., ☎ 03/528–5222), sometimes called a "neo-yuppie" place (by the Tel Aviv local paper), has quiet jazz as the main item on the menu, with some blues, too. The bar is upstairs, the music downstairs.

Echoes (⌧ 14 Twersky St., ☎ 03/562–8250) focuses on music from the '80s and particularly appeals to a younger set.

Fresco (⌧ 11 Rambam St., ☎ 03/516–3764) can make for an interesting experience; it specializes in Middle Eastern music and Israeli sing-alongs.

Hakossit (⌧ 6 Kikar Malchei Yisrael, ☎ 03/522–3244) appears to be nothing more than a simple pub, but some of Israel's most successful jazz musicians began their careers on a wooden bar stool here.

Hamisba'a (⌧ 344 Dizengoff St., ☎ 03/604–2360) is usually packed, and don't be surprised if you find a number of people dancing on the tables.

Hard Rock Cafe (⌧ Dizengoff Center, ☎ 03/525–1136), the Israeli version of the international pub/café, serves up music with your hamburger.

Hashoftim (⌧ 39 Ibn Gvirol St., at the corner of Hashoftim St., ☎ 03/695–1153), one of the first Israeli pubs, has really stood the test of time. Regulars still hang out here, and newcomers will also enjoy the atmosphere.

Lemon (⌧ 17 Hanagarim St., ☎ 03/681–3313) showcases a variety of music and often attracts an over-30 crowd (unlike many Tel Aviv nightspots). A small place with a nice bar, it also organizes parties.

Logus (⌧ 8 Hashomer St., on corner of Nahalat Binyamin, ☎ 03/516–1176) has live music inside, for which there's a cover charge, but it's usually loud enough to hear from the mall outside, where food and drinks are also served.

Omar Khayyam (⌧ Kikar Kedumim, Old Jaffa, ☎ 03/682–5865), one of the very oldest nightspots in Israel, still thrives by offering Israeli and Middle Eastern–style entertainment.

Rose (⌧ 147 Yehuda Halevy St., ☎ 03/685–0340) is one of the chicest bars in town; there's good music, too.

Soweto (⌧ 6 Frishman St., ☎ 03/524–0825) keeps going strong after all these years. Reggae and black music are de rigueur here.

Yuazar (⌧ 2 Yuazar Ish Habira, near clock tower in Jaffa, ☎ 03/683–9115), a swank wine bar, is owned and operated by one of the country's best-known gourmets.

Zanzibar (⌧ 13 Ibn Gvirol St., ☎ 03/561–9840), a very trendy, pine-furnished bar, attracts the twenty-something set.

Gay Bars

Believe it or not, in Tel Aviv a park serves the purpose of a gay bar: It is perfectly acceptable for gays to meet in Independence Park, next to the Hilton Hotel. Elsewhere, gay bars open and close even faster than other bars and restaurants, though a couple seem to be standing the test of time.

Names (⌧ 22 Ahad Ha'am, ☎ 03/510–7722) provides an interesting experience. Nothing has been done to renovate this shell of a building, but that hasn't stopped its popularity as a place for loud music and dancing.

Cafe Nordau (⌧ 145 Ben Yehuda St., ☎ 03/524–0134) is one of the oldest establishments around, with especially good cakes.

The Arts

Tel Aviv is Israel's cultural capital, and it fulfills this role with relish. Like New York, the city is full of people who devote their lives to the arts without necessarily getting paid for it. It's very likely that your waitress, taxi driver, or salesperson is also a struggling performer, painter, or musician.

You can purchase tickets to events at the box office or through one of Tel Aviv's three major ticket agencies: **Hadran** (⌧ 90 Ibn Gvirol St., ☎ 03/527–9955), **Castel** (⌧ 153 Ibn Gvirol St., ☎ 03/604–4725), and **Le'an** (⌧ 101 Dizengoff St., ☎ 03/524–7373). All accept major credit cards. You must pick up your ticket from the agency. Although there is never a shortage of events here, some areas of the arts—opera in particular—are still developing. The English-language *Jerusalem Post*'s Friday edition contains an extensive entertainment guide for the entire country.

Dance

The **Suzanne Dellal Center for Dance and Theater** (⌧ 6 Yehieli St., Neve Tzedek, ☎ 03/510–5656) is where you'll find most of the country's dance groups, and Neve Tzedek is home to artists and a growing number of trendy galleries and gift stores. A visit here is a cultural experience, as the complex itself is an example of new Israeli architectural styles used on some of the oldest buildings in Tel Aviv (for more about Neve Tzedek, *see* Exploring Tel Aviv, *above*).

Music

The **Mann Auditorium** (⌧ 1 Huberman St., ☎ 03/528–9163), Israel's largest concert hall, is home to the Israel Philharmonic Orchestra. It also serves as a venue for rock, pop, and jazz concerts.

Large outdoor concerts are held in **Hayarkon Park** (☎ 03/642–2828); there's a smaller venue called the Wohl Amphitheater inside the park.

Opera

The **Tel Aviv Performing Arts Center** (⌧ 28 Leonardo da Vinci St., ☎ 03/692–7788) is home to the budding New Israeli Opera.

Theater

Performances are rarely in any language other than Hebrew. Most of the plays at **Bet Liessin** (⌧ 34 Weizmann St., ☎ 03/695–6222) are by Israeli playwrights. The **Cameri Theater** (⌧ 101 Dizengoff St., ☎ 03/524–5211) sometimes offers simultaneous (taped) English translations of its productions. **Habimah** (⌧ Habimah Sq., ☎ 03/526–6666) is the national theater. Plays here are all in Hebrew, but some have simultaneous translation. **Hasimta Theater** (⌧ 8 Mazal Dagim St., ☎ 03/681–2126), in Old Jaffa, offers avant-garde and fringe performances.

OUTDOOR ACTIVITIES AND SPORTS

Beaches

In the heart of the city, beaches are free. On the northern edge of Tel Aviv, Hatzuk charges an entrance fee as do beaches in Herzliya (except Sidney Ali).

Beaches are generally named after something nearby—a street or a hotel, for example. So you have Hilton Beach in front of the hotel of that name, Gordon Beach at the end of Gordon Street, and likewise Bograshov Beach. Sometimes, however, this gets a bit confusing: Sheraton Beach is at the site of the first Sheraton Hotel in Tel Aviv, about 1 km (½ mi) north of today's Sheraton; and Jerusalem Beach, at the bottom of Allenby Road, is named after the city, not something in Tel Aviv.

When choosing a beach, look for one with timber lifeguard huts, where first aid is available. Lifeguards are on duty from roughly May to October, from 7 AM until between 4 PM and 7 PM, depending on the month (check with your hotel's concierge). Be prepared: Tel Aviv's lifeguards are fond of yelling commands through the loudspeakers if they think swimmers are breaking any rules. All beaches have public amenities, including bathrooms and changing rooms. Many have kiosks, too, as well as the omnipresent ice cream man, who paces up and down the sand proffering his treats throughout the summer. These days, he even hangs on to the wrappers when he hands over the goods—his part in the effort to prevent littering.

Participant Sports

Boating
Hayarkon Park (☎ 03/642–0541), in the northern part of the city, rents out pedal boats and rowboats (NIS 42, or $14, per hour) and motorboats (NIS 60, or $20, per half hour). Also here are pleasure boats that take up to 120 people for 15-minute rides (NIS 8, or $2.70, per person).

Health Clubs
Most of the city's luxury hotels have health clubs that are usually free for guests. The **Hilton** (⊠ Hayarkon St., ☎ 03/520–2291) has the largest gym and is open to nonguests. The fee for each visit is $17 plus VAT. The club is open Sunday–Thursday 6:30 AM–11 AM and 1 PM–9 PM (Friday until 5 PM).

The **Gordon Health Club** (⊠ 165 Hayarkon St., at the end of Gordon St., ☎ 03/527–1555), a Tel Aviv institution since the 1950s, includes an Olympic-size saltwater pool, a gym, and a sauna. Entrance to the health club alone costs NIS 60 ($20), and pool use is an additional NIS 38 ($13); you must present a passport. It's open daily from 6:30 AM–10 PM, except during July and August, when it's closed on Saturday.

Sailing
The **Sea Center** (⊠ Tel Aviv Marina, ☎ 03/522–4079, with another branch at the Hilton) rents out sailboats and windsurfing equipment by the hour. Windsurfers cost NIS 55 ($18) per hour; small boats, NIS 90 ($30) per hour; and catamarans, NIS 120 ($40) per hour. The unskilled can hire a boat with an instructor.

Swimming
The **Gordon Health Club** (☎ 03/527–1555) has an Olympic-size saltwater pool. This is a real Tel Aviv landmark. In addition to the pool, there is a health club and sauna (☞ Health Clubs, *above*). The pool is open daily from 5 AM–7 PM; admission (which does not include the health club) is NIS 38 ($13) and a tad extra on Saturday.

Waterskiing
Park Darom (☎ 03/739–1168), in the city's south, runs waterskiing without boats: Cables attached to a revolving crane pull you around an artificial lake, a system that holds no appeal for some but is particularly good for beginners.

Spectator Sports

Yad Eliahu Stadium (☎ 03/537–6376) is the place to go for basketball games. **Bloomfield Stadium** (✉ 1 Hatehiya St., Jaffa, ☎ 03/682–1276) is one of two venues for football (soccer). **Israel Football Stadium** (✉ Abba Hillel Rd., ☎ 03/579–9966), in east suburban Ramat Gan, is a venue for football (soccer).

SHOPPING

The shopping scene has made rapid advances in recent years, as prosperous Israelis have begun demanding higher-quality goods.

Shopping Districts

Kikar Hamedina, in the northern part of the city and arguably the most expensive real estate in the country, is where the wealthy shop. On the circular street, you can pick up a Sonia Rykiel or Chanel suit, perhaps a Kenzo creation, or indulge in a kilo of Godiva chocolates from Belgium. The middle of the square is an unkempt plaza that—although the perfect foil to the luxury surrounding it—does nothing to bring prices down.

The northern end of **Dizengoff Street** has a number of boutiques, including those of such popular Israeli designers as Yuval Kaspin (check out his wedding dresses), Tovale (very avant-garde), and Hagara (for all body types).

Dizengoff Center (✉ Dizengoff and King George Sts.), Israel's first shopping mall, thrives with shops selling everything from air-conditioners to camping equipment; you'll find many fashion stores and gift shops here. Avoid the center during school holidays if you don't like crowds of teenyboppers.

Opera Tower (✉ 1 Allenby St.), near the sea, has a small but eclectic range of stores. It's particularly good for jewelry.

Allenby Street, a less affluent option in the southern part of the city, offers some real bargains on clothes, jewelry (especially gold), and Judaica (religious and decorative objects).

Department Store

Hamashbir (✉ Dizengoff Center, Dizengoff and King George Sts., ☎ 03/528–5136) carries, for the most part, a rather banal selection of goods, often at prices a little higher than you'll find in smaller stores. On the second floor, however, its Designer Avenue features women's clothing by local designers. These designers also have boutiques at the northern end of Dizengoff Street or in the surrounding area, so ask for the address if you'd like to see even more of a particular designer's offerings. Hamashbir is also the Israeli outlet for the British St. Marks label (of Marks & Spencer).

Street Markets

At the **Nahalat Binyamin** street fair, held Tuesday and Friday, local crafts ranging from handmade puppets and pincushions to olive-wood sculptures and silver jewelry attract throngs of shoppers and browsers (☞ Exploring Tel Aviv, *above*). The **shuk hapishpeshim,** in Jaffa, is mostly full of junk these days, but you can still find a bargain—even if it's not an authentic antique. The flea market has a wide selection of reasonably priced Middle Eastern–style jewelry that uses chains of small silver coins and imitation stones and amber.

Specialty Stores

Jewelry, Judaica, and Ethnic Crafts

You can find good gold prices in the many hole-in-the-wall jewelry stores on **Allenby Street.** For silver, head for the **Nahalat Binyamin** street fair on Tuesday and Friday (☞ Street Markets, *above*). Sophisticated gems and jewels can be found at **H. Stern** (branches in the Dan, Sheraton, and Hilton hotels).

Leather

You can opt for traditional browns or blacks or go for the bolder reds, purples, and mustards. **Beged-Or** (✉ Dizengoff Center, Gate 3, ☎ 03/525–4294) has sophisticated fashions. **Ofnat Or** (✉ 134 Dizengoff St., ☎ 03/523–9021) can deck you out in the latest styles.

Swimwear

Although swimsuits and accessories sometimes cost less in the United States than they do in their country of origin, it's worth checking out the sales here. **Gideon Oberson** (✉ 6 Yirmiyahu St., ☎ 03/546–7436) is well known and is based in Tel Aviv. **Gottex** (✉ 148 Dizengoff St., ☎ 03/524–5383) is internationally known for its swimwear designer.

TEL AVIV A TO Z

Arriving and Departing

By Bus

Traveling around Israel by bus is extremely convenient. The main interurban bus company, **Egged** (☎ 03/537–5555), operates primarily from the **Central Bus Station** (✉ Levinsky St.), but also from the **Central Railway Station,** on Arlosoroff Street. The Central Bus Station may look like a big, confusing marketplace, but the bus service is actually very efficient. (For most of the day, buses between Jerusalem and Tel Aviv leave every 15 minutes.) You can purchase your ticket at the booth on each platform (signs at each platform state destinations) or, if your booth is closed, from the driver on the bus. Only the Eilat line requires advance reservations—particularly necessary in peak season.

By Plane

Israel's international airport is **Ben-Gurion** (☎ 03/971–0000 or 03/971–0011), 16 km (10 mi) southeast of Tel Aviv. All international flights to Israel land here, except for charters to Eilat. Most major American and European carriers fly into Ben-Gurion, offering frequent and convenient connections to major cities around the world. Having undergone extensive renovations in the last few years, Ben-Gurion has joined the ranks of efficient and modern airports.

At **Sde Dov Airport** (☎ 03/690–2222), 4 km (1½ mi) north of the city center, the domestic airline Arkia flies to Eilat (some 10 flights per day), Jerusalem (three flights), Haifa (three flights), and the Upper Galilee (two flights or more).

BETWEEN BEN-GURION AND CENTER CITY

United Bus 222 operates between the airport and the city about every hour from 4 AM to midnight on weekdays, and on Saturday at 45-minute intervals from noon to midnight. From the airport it stops at the Central Railway Station (✉ Arlosoroff St.), the youth hostel (✉ Weizmann St.), and at numerous points along the promenade, where Tel Aviv's main strip of hotels is located. The fare is NIS 15 ($5).

Bus 475, a local, runs to the Central Bus Station (✉ Platform 613) from 5:10 AM to 11 PM. The fare is NIS 8 ($2.90). Like all regular buses, it does not run on the Sabbath (Friday afternoon to Saturday evening) or on holidays.

Tal Limousine Service (✉ Ben-Gurion Airport, ☎ 03/972–1701, ℻ 03/972–1705) can supply a limousine and driver into Tel Aviv for NIS 102 ($34). (It's slightly cheaper from Tel Aviv to the airport because the driver has to pay taxes only to exit the airport.)

There is a fixed tariff for **taxis** from the airport into town (and vice versa); it's printed in a booklet that the driver carries. Verify the price before you get in and don't let the driver switch the meter on. The rate is NIS 65 ($22); it goes up to NIS 75 ($25) after 9 PM and on the Sabbath. The price includes one piece of baggage per person; for each additional piece there is a baggage charge of NIS 2 (70¢). There is a supervised taxi stand at the airport.

BETWEEN SDE DOV AND CENTER CITY

City **Bus 26** runs between Sde Dov and the Central Bus Station every 10–15 minutes, following Ibn Gvirol Street. The fare is NIS 3.70 ($1.20); there is no service on the Sabbath or on holidays. Taxi is the most convenient way to get from Sde Dov. Fare is determined by the meter (unlike from Ben-Gurion, where it's a fixed rate); the cost is NIS 20–NIS 25 ($7–$8) to the center (excluding baggage charge).

By Sherut

Sherut taxis are a fleet of stretch Mercedes-Benzes at the Central Bus Station that run the same routes as the buses, at comparable prices for one-way tickets (unlike buses, sheruts do not offer round-trip tickets). The "schedule" of arrivals and departures is determined by how long it takes to fill all seven seats of each car. You'll find sheruts at various points (depending on destination) in front of the bus platforms; you can usually hear someone yelling the destination long before you get close (if you don't, try yelling yourself; someone is sure to point you in the right direction). Sheruts, unlike buses, run on Saturday.

By Train

Train travel is not as common as bus travel in Israel, yet this is one of the most scenic and relaxing ways to travel between Tel Aviv and cities and towns to the north, such as Netanya, Hadera, Haifa, and Nahariya. The northbound train leaves the **Central Railway Station,** on Arlosoroff Street (☎ 03/693–7515; information office open Sun.–Thurs. 6 AM–9 PM and Fri. 6–2), about every hour on weekdays from 6 AM to 8 PM; there are fewer trains on Friday and holiday eves and no service on Saturday or holidays. There are two trains daily to Jerusalem. Timetables in English are available at all railway stations.

Getting Around

By Bus

The city bus system is well developed, with lines run primarily by the Dan bus cooperative, as well as by Egged. Fare is a fixed NIS 3.70 ($1.20) within the city center, and passengers buy tickets on the bus. If you think you might use the buses between 21 and 25 times during your stay, you can buy a *kartisia*, which offers 25 journeys for the price of 20. Remember, however, that Dan's kartisia is only good for Dan lines and Egged's for Egged (although you'll be able to use the Egged ticket in other cities as well).

Two of the major lines, Bus 4 (Ben Yehuda and Allenby streets) and Bus 5 (Dizengoff Street and Rothschild Boulevard), are also serviced by privately run red minibuses. You can flag these down and ask to get off at any point along their routes; fare is the same as on the reg-

ular buses. Minibuses also operate on Saturday, when regular buses
do not.

By Car

Driving in Tel Aviv is not recommended, especially if you get nervous
on the road. Aside from the aggressive tactics of other drivers, Tel Aviv's
layout more closely resembles the creation of an absent-minded philosopher than a city planner. Moreover, some street names may not be marked
in English—or, indeed, at all—which makes getting to your destination nothing short of a headache. Parking, too, is a problem, and the
last thing you want is to deal with the Israeli bureaucracy if your ille-
gally parked car has been booted.

Tel Aviv is more fun on foot, anyway. Most attractions and sites are
situated in the heart of the city within walking distance of one another,
and when you get tired, a bus or taxi is never far away.

By Taxi

Taxis here can be any car model or color and are identified by lighted
signs on top. Drivers will toot their horns to catch your attention, even
if you're not looking for a taxi; cabs are plentiful except in bad weather.
If you're traveling in the metropolitan area, make sure the driver turns
the meter on when you get into the car. Rates are NIS 6 ($2) for the
first 18 seconds, 30 agorot (10¢) for each 18 seconds thereafter. For
interurban trips, there is a fixed tariff; if you think you're being quoted
a price that's too high, ask to see the tariff in the booklet each driver
carries. Expect night rates to be about 25% higher than day rates. Tipping taxi drivers is not customary in Israel.

Contacts and Resources

Car Rental

Car rental companies include **Budget** (⊠ Dan Hotel, 99 Hayarkon St.,
☎ 03/523–1551), **Hertz** (⊠ Sheraton Hotel, 115 Hayarkon St., ☎ 03/
527–1881), and **Eldan** (⊠ 112 Hayarkon St., ☎ 03/527–1166), the
largest Israeli rental company.

Dentists

Ichilov Hospital (⊠ Weizmann St., ☎ 03/697–3696 or 03/697–3676)
has dental service Sunday, Monday, and Wednesday, 8–6; Tuesday,
Thursday, and Friday, 8–1. The **dental clinic** inside the Dizengoff Center (⊠ Gate 3, 50 Dizengoff St., ☎ 03/629–6716 or 050–502050) is
open from 8 AM to 10 PM.

Embassies

United States (⊠ 71 Hayarkon St., ☎ 03/517–4338). **United Kingdom**
(⊠ 192 Hayarkon St., ☎ 03/524–9171). **Canada** (⊠ 220 Hayarkon
St., ☎ 03/527–2929). **Australia** (⊠ Europe House, 37 Shaul Hamelech
St., ☎ 03/695–0451).

Emergencies

Ambulance (☎ 101). **Fire** (☎ 102). **Police** (☎ 100).

Magen David Adom (⊠ 2 Alkalai St., ☎ 03/546–0111) provides 24-
hour emergency first-aid service.

Tokens or telecards are not required at public phones for **emergency
calls.**

HOSPITAL

The casualty ward of **Ichilov Hospital** (⊠ Weizmann St., ☎ 03/697–
4444) has 24-hour emergency service. Bring your passport.

POLICE

The main **police stations** are at 14 Harakevet Street (☎ 03/564–4444), near the Central Bus Station, and at 221 Dizengoff Street (☎ 03/545–4444). Harakevet Street also has a lost-and-found.

English-Language Bookstores

The **Steimatzky** chain has two of its main stores at 107 Allenby Street (☎ 03/566–4277) and at 109 Dizengoff Street (☎ 03/522–1513).

Guided Tours

BOAT TOURS

Kef (✉ Jaffa Port, ☎ 03/682–9070) and **Sababa 5** (✉ Jaffa Port, ☎ 03/681–6739) run hourly boat tours (weekends only) from the Jaffa Port to the Tel Aviv Marina and back. Fare is around NIS 15 ($5).

ORIENTATION TOURS

Egged (✉ 15 Frishman St., ☎ 03/527–1222) and **United** (✉ 57 Ben Yehuda St., ☎ 03/523–6676 or 03/523–6677) bus companies offer half-day tours of the city for $25 per person. The tour takes in Neve Tzedek, Jaffa, Bet Hatefutsoth (Diaspora Museum), the Habimah Theater complex, and the Oppenheimer Diamond Museum.

PERSONAL GUIDES

Twelve Tribes (✉ 29 Hamered St., ☎ 03/517–2436, FAX 03/510–1943) and **Tar-Hemed Tours** (✉ 59 Hayarkon St., ☎ 03/517–6101, FAX 03/510–0165) provide personal guides (usually with a car), who are available for anywhere in the city and even around the country.

SPECIAL-INTEREST TOURS

Late Night Tel Aviv (✉ 14A Pinsker St., ☎ FAX 03/525–6484) organizes evening walking and dining tours of the city. You can join one of their regular tours or tailor one to your own interests.

WALKING TOURS

The Tel Aviv–Jaffa municipality has laid out four tours of the city called the **Tapuz (Orange) Routes.** The routes cover numerous points of interest in the city, covering historic and cultural sites of significance. Maps are available from the Tel Aviv Tourist Information Office in the Central Bus Station (☞ Visitor Information, *below*). Free city-sponsored walking tours of **Old Jaffa** begin at the clock tower on Wednesday at 9 AM; no prior registration is required.

Late-Night Pharmacies

Pharmacies take turns keeping late hours, and the duty roster changes daily. Check the *Jerusalem Post* for the day's details.

Travel Agencies

Ben Yehuda Street in central Tel Aviv is full of travel agencies, large and small. Among the biggest are **Diesenhaus** (✉ 21 Ben Yehuda St., ☎ 03/517–2140) and **Ophir Tours** (✉ 32 Ben Yehuda St., ☎ 03/526–9777). **Meditrad** (✉ 16 Ben Yehuda St., ☎ 03/629–4654) is an American Express representative.

Visitor Information

The **tourist bureau** at Ben-Gurion Airport is open 24 hours. You'll find the latest local information at the **Tel Aviv Tourist Information Office** (✉ Store No. 6108, Central Bus Station, Levinsky St., 6th floor, ☎ 03/639–5660, FAX 03/639–5659). It's open Sunday–Thursday 9–5, Friday 9–1. They can also provide a listing of *zimmerim* (bed-and-breakfast-type accommodations).

5 Northern Coast and Western Galilee

Including Haifa, Caesarea, and Akko

North of Tel Aviv and up to the border with Lebanon lies the only part of the country where you can drive for long stretches with unimpeded views of the Mediterranean. Coastal cities speak from the past: Caesarea, the 2,000-year-old port city built by King Herod; and Akko, whose vast underground ruins hark back to Crusader victories. The city of Haifa marks the meeting place of Mt. Carmel and the sea; steep streets climb upward to meet sharp white hotel towers at the crest of the Carmel, a backdrop for the sparkling golden dome of the Baha'i Shrine.

By Karen
Wolman

Updated by
Judy Stacey
Goldman

STRETCHED TAUT ON A NARROW COASTAL STRIP between urban Tel Aviv and the chalky cliffs of the Lebanese border, this region offers much more than the balmy Mediterranean beaches that line its shore. There are numerous historical sites as well as a diverse landscape of gently undulating sand dunes, flat fields, and citrus groves on the Sharon Plain, which is a fertile swath encompassing Netanya, Hadera, and Caesarea. Early in the century the plain was converted from a malarial swamp by toiling Jewish pioneers. Today, Caesarea is a delightful resort town with whitewashed villas and romantically crumbling Roman and Crusader ruins. Unforgettable here are the sights of ancient Roman aqueduct arches disappearing into the sand and of Israeli children splashing in the cove of the walled Crusader city, seemingly unaware of the engineering wonders of Herod's port.

At the base of Mt. Carmel, the softly contoured foothills and valleys, dotted with vineyards, are the site of Baron Edmond de Rothschild's generosity in helping Israel create a wine industry that has been one of the country's most successful businesses. The Carmel Range then rises dramatically to its pine-covered heights, which overhang the coast of Haifa, a modern port city with friendly and hardworking inhabitants. Haifa was the site of many heartrending scenes in the decade prior to Israel's independence: Scores of ragtag ships filled with Jewish refugees fleeing Nazi persecution were turned away by the British just offshore of Haifa, within view of relatives and residents. North of Haifa you can roam the Western Galilee, which runs along a fertile plain up to the Lebanese border. Just across the sweeping arc of Haifa Bay lies Akko, a jewel of a Crusader city that is a medley of Romanesque ruins, Muslim domes and minarets, and swaying palms. To the north are the resort of Nahariya, especially popular among Israelis; Montfort, arguably the country's most magnificent Crusader castle; more Crusader ruins at Kibbutz Hanita; and straddling the border, the caves at Rosh Hanikra, scooped out of rock by the relentless tides.

As the scenery changes, so does the ethnic mix of the inhabitants: Druze, Carmelite monks, Baha'is, Christian and Muslim Arabs, and Jews. You can also retrace the steps of the forebears of those with the most ancient claim to these lands: the prehistoric people of the caves of Nahal Me'arot, on Mt. Carmel, whose artifacts continue to be studied onsite by paleontologists. In Haifa and perhaps at absorption centers of kibbutzim, you will meet the region's latest arrivals, Jews from Ethiopia and the former Soviet Union. The Baha'is, whose universalist religion embraces the teachings of many others, dominate Haifa's mountainside setting with their gleaming golden temple and handsome gardens. The robed Carmelite monks quietly preside over their religious shrines at the monasteries in Haifa and in Mukhraka, on Mt. Carmel, just next door to the Druze villages. Although the Druze, who reside along the northern coast, consider themselves an integral part of Israeli society, they maintain a unique cultural and religious enclave on Mt. Carmel, with the secret rites and rituals of their faith and the distinctive handlebar mustaches and white head scarves favored by the older men. Arabs and Jews live side by side in Akko, where many dilapidated buildings and cramped and dusty streets in the Old Quarter would seem to belie the town's pristine, picture-postcard reputation. Yet its subterranean knights' halls, Ottoman skyline, and outdoor *shuk* (market) awhirl with fascinating colors and sounds can still enchant. You will meet the ghosts of the Crusaders at the castles and fortifications that were erected throughout the region to maintain the warriors' tenuous hold over Palestine, which ended in 1291, after two centuries, with the fall of Akko to the powerful Mamluk dynasty from Egypt.

Pleasures and Pastimes

Archaeology

It is said that wherever you put down a shovel in Israel, you'll find ancient ruins—even one-time visitors to Caesarea have been known to find old coins after a rainfall. The northern coast and Western Galilee are home to two stellar archaeological sites, Caesarea and Akko. In Caesarea, archaeologists continue to uncover history, restorers put together shattered pieces and patch up ancient buildings, and sites are lovingly restored. Herod's harbor, Sebastos, which was ruined in an earthquake beneath the Caesarea waters two millennia ago, beckons scuba divers. In Akko, more underground Crusader ruins have come to light. Haifa University's Nahsholim and Hecht museums exhibit archaeological finds in unusually engaging styles.

Beaches

From Tel Aviv to the northern border with Lebanon there are miles and miles of beautiful sandy beaches; most are public and have lifeguards from early May to mid-October (beware of swimming where there are no lifeguard stations as there may be dangerous currents or undertows). Many beaches are unattended off-season, and trash does collect. But not to worry: As soon as warmer weather sets in, they are generally kept clean and well maintained.

Dining

You won't have to hunt long in this region for a restaurant with an excellent view of the Mediterranean and good fresh fish. Most often menu will include grilled or baked fish with a variety of sauces: *locus* (grouper), *mulit* (red mullet), *churi* (red snapper), and *farida* (sea bream). Also fresh, but hailing from commercial fish ponds and the Sea of Galilee, are *buri* (gray mullet) and the ubiquitous *tilapia* (St. Peter's fish), as well as the hybrid *iltit* (salmon-trout).

Coastal restaurants are generally not as refined as those in Tel Aviv, with some notable exceptions in Haifa and Mt. Carmel. Not unlike Tel Aviv, Haifa has a growing number of cafés sprouting up in residential and commercial neighborhoods. Even at the most expensive restaurants in this region, dress is always informal (but tasteful), and ties are never required. In the Druze village of Daliyat el Carmel you will find renowned falafel and other authentic Mediterranean-style fare. Netanya has the region's highest concentration of kosher restaurants. Otherwise, you'll wine and dine on cuisines that run the gamut from pita and hummus to sophisticated French.

CATEGORY	COST*
$$$$	over $35
$$$	$22–$35
$$	$12–$22
$	under $12

*per person for a three-course meal, excluding drinks, service, and sales tax

Lodging

Along the coast you'll find everything from campgrounds to new luxury hotels. You won't, however, find that the selection and quality of deluxe accommodations compare with those in, say, Tel Aviv or the Red Sea resort of Eilat. In some places, such as Akko, the pickings are less than slim, but because distances here are never daunting, you can tour many towns along the coast from a single base.

The chart below lists peak-season prices, usually charged in July and August and during major Jewish holidays (Passover, which generally falls in April; Rosh Hashanah and Yom Kippur, in September or October; and Hanukkah, in December). There are variations, however, so be sure to inquire at each hotel. In addition, many hotels are considerably less expensive—sometimes by 40%—during low season, from November through February.

Camping facilities, including some bungalows and cabins only several notches above a spartan tent, dot the coastline north of Netanya to the Lebanese border. However inviting, the wooded slopes of Carmel National Park do not have facilities. Contact the Tourist Information offices in Tel Aviv and Haifa (☞ Contacts and Resources *in* Northern Coast and Western Galilee A to Z, *below,* and Tel Aviv A to Z *in* Chapter 4) for complete lists of campgrounds and maps as well as a brochure on Isra-chalets and bungalows.

CATEGORY	COST*
$$$$	over $120
$$$	$80–$120
$$	$55–$80
$	under $55

All prices are for a standard double room, including breakfast and excluding service charge.

Nightlife and the Arts

On many a balmy summer night in towns up and down the coast, chances are you'll find an outdoor concert or a dance or theater performance; particularly worth attending are any events held under the stars on the reconstructed stage of the Roman theater at Caesarea. In other seasons, chamber music concerts are held in Ein Hod and at Zichron Ya'akov.

Parks and Nature Reserves

Magnificent parks and nature reserves, large and small, grace the coastal area, both along the seashore and in the hilly areas to the east. The largest of these is the flourishing Carmel Park, which comprises 20,000 hilly acres and covers the top of Mt. Carmel. Several parks and reserves have information offices where helpful staff members will explain maps and trails; all have parking lots, toilets, and picnic areas. Though the parks and reserves are generally not signposted in English from the road, distinctive dark wooden boards marked in white or yellow letters indicate their entrances.

Wine

Wine lovers, take note: This is one of the country's prime wine-growing areas (its classification is Shomron). Though wine has been produced in Israel for thousands of years, and the Rothschilds updated viniculture around Zichron Ya'akov some 120 years ago, it is only in the last decade or so that truly high-quality wines have appeared on the market. The Zichron Ya'akov Carmel Winery's best (and most expensive) wines are those in the Rothschild series; their best vintage is the 1985 cabernet sauvignon. Also distinctive are the wines of the less exclusive Selected series, especially the chardonnay. In high demand among Israelis is the semidry Emerald Reisling, a fruity and aromatic choice.

Exploring the Northern Coast and Western Galilee

Running the length of the region up to Haifa are two main highways: Route 2, a multilane highway that takes you from Tel Aviv to Haifa in just over an hour, and the inland Route 4 (Old Haifa Road), which continues all the way to the border. Most sights are a short drive from one of these two roads, so it's tough to get lost even if you make a wrong turn.

Starting from Tel Aviv, Route 2 (the Coastal Road) hugs the coast, introducing travelers to the northern coast—Netanya, Caesarea, and Haifa, with the sites of Nahsholim and Atlit in between. Zigzagging along to the east and parallel to Route 2 (at the most about 10 km, or 6 mi, away) is Route 4, also known as the Old Road. Just off Route 4 is the Rothschild wine country and Mt. Carmel, the back-door route to Haifa. It meanders through the foothills and up the spine of the mountain, taking in Zichron Ya'akov, Shuni, the Carmel National Park, the Carmelite monastery of Mukhraka, and two Druze villages not far from Haifa. (A branch of Route 4, going north and then inland, winds through the huge Carmel National Park and later connects with Road 672 leading to the Druze villages.) The Western Galilee is the area north of Haifa, including Akko, Nahariya, and up to Rosh Hanikra, with several sites along the way, as well as a few just inland. In this relatively small part of the country, all the sites on the northern coast and in Western Galilee are within easy driving distance of Caesarea and Haifa, the former a quiet overnight location and the latter a thriving city.

Great Itineraries

Keep in mind that there's a golf course at Caesarea and plenty of Mediterranean beaches along the coast, as well as wonderful nature reserves to walk in and many sports to pursue. So be sure to factor in time for the beach, golf, or hiking.

Numbers in the text correspond to numbers in the margin and on the Northern Coast and Western Galilee map.

IF YOU HAVE 2 DAYS

You'll have time to see the highlights of the region: Start with King Herod's port city of **Caesarea** ②, where there are many Roman, Byzantine, and Crusader ruins. Then travel through Rothschild wine country in the rolling Carmel Hills to visit the pioneer village of **Zichron Ya'akov** ㉒, the picturesque Druze villages of **Daliyat el Carmel** ㉕ and **Isfiya** ㉖, and the modern port city of ⓣ **Haifa** ⑤–⑲. The next day, get an early start so you can see the Baha'ai Shrine and Gardens on your way down the hill and out of Haifa, heading north to the walled Crusader city of **Akko** ㉙–㊲. After a late lunch at the old port, head up to the border with Lebanon where you take a short cable-car ride down the cliff to see the waves crash through the sea grottoes at **Rosh Hanikra** ㊶.

IF YOU HAVE 3 DAYS

Start off with a visit to the **Carmel Wine Cellars** (reserve a tour in advance) and **Zichron Ya'akov** ㉒, then head through the hilly wine country to see the Carmelite Monastery at **Mukhraka** ㉔. Your next stop will be **Daliyat el Carmel** ㉕, as you head for ⓣ **Haifa** ⑤–⑲. The next morning, bright and early, visit the Baha'ai Shrine and Gardens in Haifa, head north to **Akko** ㉙–㊲, and zip up the coast to **Rosh Hanikra** ㊶ and back to Haifa for the night. Your destination the next morning is **Caesarea** ②, and then the artists' village of **Ein Hod** ㉗.

IF YOU HAVE 4–5 DAYS

This itinerary covers four days, but you can easily add another if part of the trip appeals to you. Start with a drive through Rothschild wine country to the restored Roman theater and Ottoman fortress at **Shuni** ㉑, continuing to the **Carmel Wine Cellars** (reserve a tour in advance) and the pioneer town of **Zichron Ya'akov** ㉒. Then travel through the rolling hills of the Carmel to the Carmelite Monastery at **Mukhraka** ㉔, after which the undulating road will take you to the Druze

villages of **Daliyat el Carmel** ㉕ and **Isfiya** ㉖ as you head for ⛯ **Haifa** ⑤–
⑲. Overnight in Haifa and explore the city the next day. Get an early
start on Day 3, when your first destination will be the walled Crusader
city of **Akko** ㉙–㉛. Just north of Akko is the Holocaust memorial museum at **Kibbutz Lochamei Hageta'ot** ㊴, and straight up the coastal road
is the seaside town of **Nahariya** ㊵. A short drive farther north brings
you to the exciting sea grottoes at **Rosh Hanikra** ㊶. If you don't have
the energy left for the walk up to **Montfort,** the medieval castle perched
high on a wooded mountain, you can admire it from Goren Park if
you remembered your binoculars. Overnight in ⛯ **Caesarea** ②, a good
base to take in the area's sights, which require a bit of zigzagging between Routes 2 and 4. Explore the town and then head south to
Nahsholim-Dor ③ to see the intriguing Underwater Museum; the reconstructed British detention camp of **Atlit** ④; the artists' village of **Ein
Hod** ㉗; and lastly, the prehistoric **Carmel Caves,** nearby the entrance
to the **Nahal Me'arot Nature Reserve** ㉘. You might earmark a few hours
for a hike on the wooded slopes of the Carmel.

When to Tour the Northern Coast and Western Galilee

Summer's strong sun heats the region (though there's no humidity),
and the soft sea and mountain breezes cool it down. Spring (April–May)
and fall (October–November) are balmy and crisp. Winter (late December–March) brings chilling winds and cold rain interspersed with
sun. If you're warmly dressed, you can tour comfortably—and the crash
of the waves and the roar of the sea provide just the right backdrop
for Roman and Crusader ruins.

As in the rest of Israel, hotels are heavily booked on weekends; make
reservations well ahead of time. On Saturday and national holidays
Israelis take trips, so it's best not to even consider traveling from north
to south (to Tel Aviv or Jerusalem). Beaches and national sites are also
very crowded during this time. If you're taking a two-day trip, consider doing it on Thursday and Friday (Shabbat calm reigns on the highway Friday night) or Saturday and Sunday.

Summer brings theater and dance performances in Caesarea's Roman
theater and the blues festival in Haifa (usually held in July).

In spring, you'll ride by fields ablaze with the colors of wild anemones,
tulips, and buttercups; cyclamen and narcissus grow a bit higher up.
And you don't have to be an ornithologist to appreciate the astonishing variety of birds you'll see—some simply perched on telephone
wires and flocks of migrating storks and pelicans overhead. In late fall,
herons, cormorants, and ducks come to pass the winter.

THE NORTHERN COAST

As you head north from the pleasant city of Netanya, the major sights
along the coast include Caesarea, Nahsholim-Dor, and Atlit, all of which
have reminders of the country's long history. Haifa, also on the Mediterranean, lies to the north of Atlit and could be another stop on your
itinerary.

Netanya

❶ *30 km (18 mi) north of Tel Aviv, off Rte. 2; take the second exit (Central Netanya).*

Netanya is a seaside resort city, the geographic capital of the verdant
Sharon Plain, and a diamond-polishing center. Once a sleepy town of
farmers and orange groves, Netanya, named after Jewish philanthropist

Northern Coast and Western Galilee

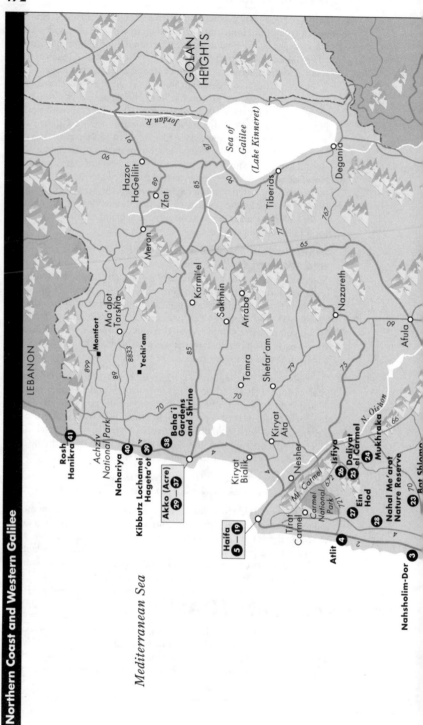

Mediterranean Sea

LEBANON

GOLAN HEIGHTS

Jordan R.

Sea of Galilee (Lake Kinneret)

Rosh Hanikra **41**

Achziv National Park

Nahariya **40**

Kibbutz Lochamei Hageta'ot **39**

Akko (Acre) **29 — 37**

Baha'i Gardens and Shrine **38**

Montfort

Ma'alot Tarshia

Yechi'am

Meron

Zfat

Hazor HaGelilit

Karmi'el

Sakhnin

Arraba

Tamra

Shefar'am

Tiberias

Degania

Nazareth

Afula

Kiryat Ata

Kiryat Bialik

Nesher

Haifa **5 — 19**

Tirat Carmel

Mt. Carmel

Carmel National Park

Isfiya **26**

Daliyat el Carmel **25**

Mukhraka **24**

N. Oishon

Ein Hod **27**

Nahal Me'arot Nature Reserve **28**

Bet Shlomo **23**

Atlit **4**

Nahsholim-Dor **3**

899

90

91

89

85

85

70

70

79

75

89

8833

87

90

77

767

65

09

672

721

70

66

60

4

2

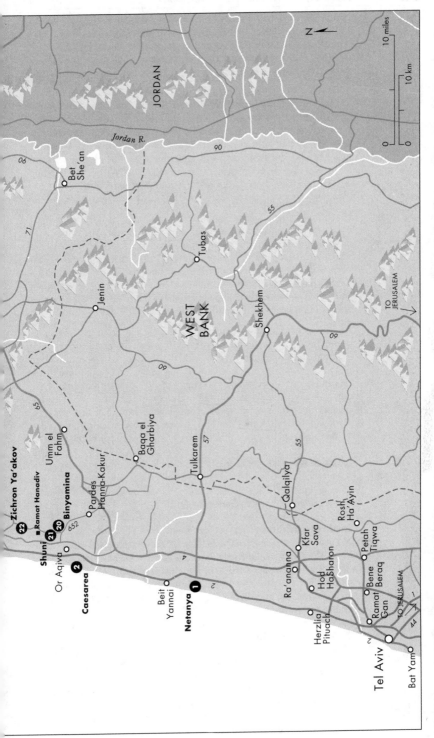

JORDAN

10 miles

10 km

Jordan R.

90

06

Bet She'an

71

55

Tubas

Jenin

WEST BANK

Shekhem

TO JERUSALEM

60

09

65

80

Umm el Fahm

Baqa el Gharbiya

Tulkarem

57

55

Zichron Ya'akov

■ Ramat Hanadiv

Pardes Hanna-Kakur

Binyamina

652

Shuni

22 **21** **20**

Or Aqiva

2

Caesarea

4

Qalqilya

Rosh Ha'Ayin

Kfar Sava

Beit Yannai

1

Netanya

2

Ra'anana

Hod HaSharon

Petah Tiqwa

Bene Beraq

Herzlia Pituach

Ramat Gan

TO JERUSALEM

1

Tel Aviv

44

Bat Yam

Nathan Strauss, has steadily burgeoned from a few settlers in 1929 to its present population of 160,000. Russian immigrants are now a permanent part of the local scene. Netanya attracts droves of French tourists, and in the summer their lilting tones float above the café au lait and croissants (now popular all over the country) served in the outdoor cafés.

Though citrus farming is still evident on Netanya's rural outskirts, there are few traces of small-town grace and few sights to see in the rambling concentration of apartment buildings, some built on the coast itself. Still, what visitors come here for are unspoiled, sandy public beaches, ideal for swimming and sunbathing, and the pleasurable café area. Netanya contains a self-contained resort within its bustling streets. It's also a base for guided bus tours in the region.

Lively **Ha'atzmaut Square** is the heart of the city; it's close to the beach and lends a special ambience, surrounded as it is by open-air cafés and restaurants that are filled until late at night. The square also has an outdoor amphitheater for free summer concerts. The hotels are near the square, and the beaches lie just below the cliffs, with windsurfers and paragliders slicing though sea and sky. To get to your hotel or the beach, drive down the town's main artery, Herzl Street, which ends at the **pedestrian mall** and Ha'atzmaut Square. Access to the beaches is south and north of the mall.

Israel's large diamond industry (its leading export is polished diamonds) was launched with the arrival of Jewish diamond cutters from Belgium and Holland during World War II, many of whom settled in Netanya. You can get a free tour of one of the larger **diamond factories** and showrooms, where raw stones of various hues and quality are cut, polished, and set into jewelry. Tours wind up in the showroom, where prices are generally good, though not better than those in New York City's wholesale diamond district. *See* Shopping, *below,* for phone numbers of shops that will pick you up at your hotel.

OFF THE BEATEN PATH | **FIELDS OF FLOWERS** – In February and March, detour a few kilometers south of the city to see the famous fields of rare, exotic, deep-indigo wild irises indigenous to the area. There are marked paths to the iris fields and a parking lot on Ben-Gurion Boulevard.

Dining and Lodging

$$$ ✕ **Lucullus.** Owner Bernard Gabay of Tunisia has run this reliable French restaurant on the southern edge of town for more than 20 years (there's also a kosher version at 5 Ha'atzmaut Square). Although the menu is French, the ambience is Israeli. Candles and fresh flowers add a touch of class, and there's a pianist in the bar several times a week. Gabay recommends his coquilles St. Jacques or the chateaubriand, and for dessert the chocolate mousse or profiteroles. ⊠ *2 Jabotinsky St.,* ☎ *09/861–9502. Reservations essential.*

$$ ✕ **Apropo.** This restaurant—a bit like a glorified coffee shop—is in King George Park and serves breakfast, lunch, and dinner, with a view of the scalloped curve of coastline below a jutting cliff. There's something for everyone on the eclectic menu: fresh fish, Italian pastas, soups and salads, and a variety of omelets. For the adventuresome there are even a few Thai specialties. All dishes are glatt kosher, meaning that meal preparation undergoes extra-strict supervision by the kashrut authorities. ⊠ *Gan Hamelech Park, at end of Ha'atzmaut Sq.,* ☎ *09/862–4482 or 09/862–4483. Reservations essential for Sat. dinner and Apr.–Sept. AE, DC, MC, V. No dinner Fri., no lunch Sat.*

$$ ✕ **Casa Mia.** Replete with pizza oven, this centrally located family-run restaurant is not unlike a traditional Italian trattoria, albeit a bit short on charm. The chef, who takes pride in being well versed in the language and cuisine of Italy, makes a mean *fegato alla veneziana* (liver prepared Venice style, with bacon and onion in a red-wine sauce), fried calamari, lasagna, and minestrone; or you can stick with a simple pizza. ⊠ *10 Herzl St.,* ☎ *09/834–7228. Reservations essential for Fri. and Sat. dinner. AE, DC, V.*

$ ✕ **Kfar Vitkin Pancake House.** This local equivalent of a truck stop does a brisk roadside business with its down-home cooking. Yes, you can actually get pancakes and eggs in addition to Middle Eastern mainstays such as hummus and pita bread. It's open daily 6 AM–1 AM. ⊠ *7 km (4¼) mi north of Netanya on Rte. 2,* ☎ *09/866–6112. No reservations. No credit cards.*

$ ✕ **Pundak Hayami.** Owned by three brothers who have run the restaurant for 28 years, this unprepossessing place just off Herzl Street is a favorite among locals. It's a no-frills diner with Middle Eastern cooking, counter seating, and wooden tables. You can find fresh fish, *shishlik*, kebabs, and roast goose as well as the usual salads. ⊠ *1 Harav Kuk St.,* ☎ *09/861–5780 or 09/834–1222. Reservations not accepted. MC, V. No dinner Fri. and holiday eves.*

$$$$ 🏨 **Blue Bay.** It's out of the bustle of the downtown area (3 km/2 mi away), but there's an hourly hotel shuttle or public bus to the center. Blue Bay has direct access to the beach below, and all rooms in the main wing have a sea view. Five of the seven floors, including the lobby, have been recently renovated. ⊠ *37 Hamelachim St., 42228,* ☎ *09/860–3603,* FAX *09/833–7475. 196 rooms with bath. Restaurant, bar, coffee shop, pool, beauty parlor, sauna, whirlpool bath, 2 tennis courts, health club, dance club. AE, DC, MC, V.*

$$$$ 🏨 **Carmel.** This sparkling new hotel, built on a cliff over the sea, has a lobby with floor-to-ceiling windows. Glass elevators ride up the 20 stories, and the decor of the rooms reflects the blue and green of the sea. Each room has its own air-conditioning unit, and most have kitchenettes for which equipment may be requested. The swimming pool (containing a whirlpool) is covered and heated in winter. It's fun to sit in the garden and watch the paragliders, who use the grass as their springboard into the blue. ⊠ *Jabotinsky St., near main square, 42228,* ☎ *09/860–1170,* FAX *09/860–1171. 200 rooms with bath. Restaurant, lobby lounge, pub, pool, wading pool, saunas, health club. AE, DC, MC, V.*

$$$$ 🏨 **La Promenade.** This five-year-old apartment hotel with its snappy modern design is on the south side of King George Park, near the city center and the beach. Each unit has a bedroom and a living room, furnished with marble tiles and sleek furniture, plus a kitchenette. A balcony with a sea view completes the picture. An unusual feature is the indoor pool, which includes a whirlpool bath. ⊠ *6 Gad Machnes St., 42279,* ☎ *09/862–6450,* FAX *09/862–6450. 20 apartments with bath. Restaurant, coffee shop, indoor pool, exercise room. AE, DC, MC, V.*

$$ 🏨 ★ **Seasons.** A good hotel, well maintained and dependable for fine service, Seasons is just outside the downtown area, with easy stairway access to the beach below. Though it was built 26 years ago, most rooms and all public rooms were redecorated recently. Bedrooms are spacious, with private terraces and sea views. The newer rooms are especially comfortable—decorated in pleasing pastels—and the baths are luxurious. ⊠ *Nice Blvd., 42269,* ☎ *09/860–1555,* FAX *09/862–3022. 85 rooms with bath. Restaurant, coffee shop, pool, massage, sauna, whirlpool bath, tennis court, exercise room. AE, DC, MC, V.*

Outdoor Activities and Sports

BEACHES

The standard facilities, including staffed lifeguard stations, a first-aid station, showers, toilets, and changing rooms, are free and available at all the Netanya beaches (☎ 09/860–3118 or 09/603155), which cover 12 km (7 mi) of soft, sandy coastline. Chairs and umbrellas are available for rent. The main beach, **Sironit,** is open year-round. Its parking lot is on the beach, just off Jabotinsky Street south of the main square, and costs NIS 9 ($3) per car. There are two eateries and volleyball nets here. South of town is the Orthodox beach **Kiryat Sanz,** where men and women have different bathing days and hours. Near the **Seasons Hotel** is another beach, with a restaurant and refreshment stand as well as standard facilities. In front of the main square is **Herzl Beach,** with a water slide, restaurant, and refreshment stand. **Goldmintz Beach** has a refreshment stand but no chair or umbrella rentals. At press time Netanya's southernmost beach, **Poleg** (Green Beach) was closed because of high pollution levels, which are monitored regularly by the Health Department; the other beaches have a clean bill of health.

Five km (3 mi) north of Netanya and next to Moshav Bet Yannai, you'll find a lovely **private beach** (☎ 09/866–6230) with grills, some picnic tables, and a lifeguard on duty in season. There are toilets near the parking lot and cold showers on the beach, where you can also rent chairs and umbrellas. There is no entrance fee, but parking costs NIS 20 ($6.70) per car Sunday–Friday and NIS 25 ($8.35) on Saturday and holidays. Because this stretch of beach is only 2,400 feet long and cannot comfortably accommodate crowds, it's wise to come on weekdays.

There's a very popular beach at **Mikhmoret,** 7½ km (4½ mi) north of Netanya. A huge dirt parking lot, which charges NIS 15 ($5) per car, is 1 km (½ mi) after the turnoff from Route 2. There are three lifeguard stations, a restaurant and café, and umbrellas and chairs for rent.

FITNESS

Much of the sophisticated equipment at the **Wingate Institute** (8 km [5 mi] south of Netanya, ☎ 09/863–9521, ℻ 09/865–3070) is now available to the public, albeit generally only in the afternoon. Facilities include a 25-meter pool with a retractable roof, squash courts, tennis courts, and a fitness center. A full medical checkup is available at the sports medicine division.

GOLF

Wingate Institute (☎ 09/863–9546 after 10 AM, ℻ 09/865–3070; ☞ Fitness, *above*) has the **Center for Golf Instruction and Practice,** which includes a driving range, putting and pitching greens, and video analysis. The center is open year-round, day and night.

HORSEBACK RIDING

The **Ranch** (☎ 09/866–3525) is in northern Netanya, 2 km (1¼ mi) up the road from the Blue Bay Hotel. It's wise to reserve for Saturday or for moonlight rides on the beach—or consider a pastoral ride though orange groves. The stables are open daily 9–6; the cost is NIS 50 ($16.70) per hour.

PARAGLIDING

If you're between the ages of 6 and 60 and want to fly without an engine and a cockpit—albeit with the instructor beside you—call **Dvir Paragliding** (☎ 09/834–9679, portable 052/546077) for a thrilling experience. It's like hang gliding, but two can participate.

Shopping

Netanya is known for quality diamond shopping; clients will be dazzled by the profusion of stone-studded earrings, necklaces, bracelets, and loose stones with international diamond certificates. A reliable establishment is **Inbar Jewelry** (✉ 1 Ussishkin St., ☎ 09/882–2233). Also try the **National Diamond Center** (✉ 90 Herzl St., ☎ 09/862–0436). Prices are competitive. You can check with the Tourist Information Office for the names of other firms recommended for their fairness and authenticity.

Caesarea

❷ *16 km (10 mi) north of Netanya, 49 km (29½ mi) south of Haifa.*

By turns port city of Herod the Great, Byzantine capital, and Crusader stronghold, Caesarea is at the northern tip of the Sharon Plain. Covered with Roman, Byzantine, and Crusader ruins, it is a delightful place to stop for a half day of sightseeing and a leisurely lunch or swim at the beach. You will see, stretched out over 3 km (2 mi), the Roman theater, the Crusader city, and the newly discovered Roman-Byzantine remains, which include a bathhouse complex, an amphitheater and parts of the port from Herod's time, and the ancient aqueduct in the sand dunes, just farther north.

Herod the Great gave Caesarea its name, dedicating the magnificent Roman city he built to his patron Augustus Caesar; the port he called Sebastos, which is Greek for Augustus. It was the Roman emperor who elevated Herod—born to an Idumean family that had converted to Judaism—to his position as King of the Jews around 30 BC. Construction began in 22 BC at the site of an ancient Phoenician and Greek port called Strato's Tower. Herod spared nothing in his elaborate designs for the port facilities—a major engineering feat at the time—as well as for the city, which included palaces, temples, a theater, a marketplace, a hippodrome, and water and sewage systems. When it was completed 12 years later, only Jerusalem outshone the splendor of Caesarea. Its population under Herod grew to around 100,000, larger than that of Jerusalem; the city was spread over some 164 acres.

In AD 6, a decade after Herod died, Caesarea became the seat of the Roman procurators. Herod's kingdom had originally been divided among his surviving sons, with his eldest, Archelaus, getting Judea and Samaria. But the Romans were unhappy with Archelaus's rule and banished him to Gaul. With Jerusalem a predominantly Jewish city, the Romans preferred the Hellenistic Caesarea with its Jewish minority as the seat of their administration.

Religious harmony did not prevail here. The Jews and the Greek-speaking population repeatedly clashed, with hostilities exploding in the Jewish revolt of AD 66. The first Jewish rebellion was squelched by Vespasian, who was proclaimed emperor here by his legions in AD 69. A year later his son and coruler, Titus, captured and razed Jerusalem and celebrated his brutal suppression of the Jewish revolt. Henceforth Caesarea became a Roman colony and the local Roman capital of Palestine for nearly 600 years. It was here that Peter converted the Roman centurion Cornelius, a milestone in the spread of the new faith, and this was where Paul preached and was imprisoned for two years. In the 2nd century, Rabbi Akiva, the spiritual mentor of the Bar Kochba Revolt, was tortured to death here.

Caesarea is distinguished by well-marked signs in English. The **Roman theater,** along with the port area, is under the aegis of the National Parks Authority. One ticket admits visitors to both the theater and the

Crusader City, so save your stub. At the entrance you can get a free brochure with a basic map and layout of the sites. (Be sure to lock your car and keep valuables out of sight.)

Entry to the theater is through one of the vomitories, the arched tunnels that led the public into Roman theaters. Herod's theaters—here and elsewhere in Israel—were the first of their kind in the ancient Near East and Middle East. Although smaller than the better-preserved Roman theater of Bet She'an (☞ Chapter 6), Caesarea's has become famous in its own right. The theater today seats 3,600 and is a spectacular venue for summer concerts and other performances (☞ Nightlife and the Arts, *below*). The view of the sea as a backdrop steals any show, especially when the sky is ablaze with the setting sun.

What you see today is predominantly a reconstruction; only a few seats of the *cavea* (where the audience sat)—those near the orchestra—are original, in addition to some of the stairs and the decorative wall at the front of the stage. Just inside the site's main gate is proof that one of the Roman rulers who resided here was Pontius Pilate, governor of Judea when Jesus was crucified. It is the only archaeological evidence of the governor's presence in Palestine. On a mounted plaque, a replica of the original (now housed in the Israel Museum in Jerusalem) is a fragmented Latin inscription believed to read, "Pontius Pilate, the prefect of Judaea, built and dedicated the Tiberieum [probably a temple or shrine dedicated to the emperor Tiberius] to the Divine Augustus." ☎ 06/636–1358. ☛ *Theater and Crusader City NIS 15 ($5).* ☉ *Daily 8–4, Fri. and holiday eves 8–3.*

In the large area of **ongoing excavations** along the seashore, you will see the streets of a Roman-Byzantine administrative area, built over vaults that served as storehouses—of special note are the beautiful and imaginative mosaic floors of the bathhouse complex. The huge horseshoe-shape "entertainment area," its sloping sides filled with rows of stone seats, is the amphitheater built by Herod (most likely the one mentioned by 1st-century historian Josephus), where 2,000 years ago some 10,000 spectators saw horse races, chariot races, and various sports shows.

★ The walls that surround the **Crusader City** were built by Louis IX of France. They enclose both the remains of the Herodian port and the Crusader City itself, which was actually only one-third the size of Herod's original city. The bulk of what you see today—the moat, escarpment, citadel, and walls that once contained 16 towers—dates from 1251, when the French king actually pitched in and spent a year restoring the existing fortifications. The Crusaders first laid siege to and conquered Caesarea in 1101 after nearly five centuries of rule by Arabs, who allowed the port to silt up.

Access to the Crusader City is over a dry moat. However impressive, the 42-foot-deep moat scored scant success in repelling an attack under Sultan Baybars in the late 13th century. The Mamluks then destroyed the city to prevent its resettlement by the Christians. Still, the fortifications and the gatehouse (at the entrance) are fine examples of medieval architecture. Note the sloping glacis against the outer wall, the shooting niches, and the groined vaults of the gatehouse.

Arrows and signs direct visitors on a designated walking tour. Especially after heavy rains, keep a vigilant eye out for old bronze coins, some smaller than a dime. As you walk under a series of four graceful arches that cover a Crusader street, you can see just to your right the remains of a Frankish house. At the southeastern corner of the fortress, there is a postern gate designed for counterattack against an invading enemy. Here the surefooted can climb up onto the walls for a view of the sea and ruins, walking for about 60 feet toward the beach and then down the stairs. To the right are the remains of the unfinished **Crusader cathedral,** built on the site of a Byzantine church; the three graceful curves of its apses stand out. Both churches stood on the ruins of the Temple Herod, dedicated to Augustus, on this promontory dominating the port. The collapse of the underlying vaulted chambers halted construction of the Crusader church.

At the railing in front of the church ruins is a lookout over the ancient port, now underwater, as well as a view northward to Zichron Ya'akov and Haifa, all the way up the coast. On a clear day, the shadowy outlines of the submerged harbor construction can be best observed, however, from the top terrace of the tower, now the Citadel restaurant. Underwater tours with marked maps of the port area are offered by the port's scuba-diving center (☞ Outdoor Activities and Sports, *below*).

NEED A BREAK?	You can relax in the shadow of the vaulted remains of Herod's inner harbor, on the raftered patio in the middle of the Crusader City (near the rest rooms). The kiosk here sells hot and cold drinks, snacks, and ice cream. Over by the water's edge are souvenir shops and restaurants overlooking the sea.

Even today, **Herod's port** may be regarded as an awesome achievement. The 1st-century Jewish historian Flavius Josephus glowingly described the wonders of the port and compared it to Athens's port of Piraeus. Once the underwater ruins were explored, it became clear that what had been long dismissed by many historians as hyperbole was as Josephus described it.

Its construction was an unprecedented challenge; never before had such a large artificial harbor been built. There was a total absence of islands or bays as natural protection; furthermore, work was hindered by bad weather. During preliminary underwater digs in 1978, archaeologists were stunned to discover concrete blocks near the breakwater offshore, an indication of the highly sophisticated use of hydraulic concrete, which hardens underwater. Although historians knew the Romans had developed such techniques, before the discoveries at Caesarea, it was never known hydraulic concrete was used on such a massive scale. The main ingredient in the concrete, volcanic ash, was probably imported from Mt. Vesuvius, in Italy; it is likely that the wooden forms were, too. Teams of professional divers actually did much of the trickiest work, laying the foundations hundreds of meters offshore. To inhibit the natural process of silting, engineers designed sluice channels to cut through the breakwaters and flush out the harbor. Herod's engineers had also devised underwater structures to break the impact of waves.

When finished, two massive breakwaters—one stretching west and then north some 1,800 feet from the Citadel restaurant, the other extending 600 feet, both now submerged—sheltered a 3½-acre area from the waves and tides. The port also featured two towers, each mounted by three colossal statues at the entrance on the breakwaters; although neither the tower nor the statues has been found, a tiny medal that bears their images was discovered in the first underwater excavations here in 1960. The finished harbor also contained the dominating temple to Augustus as well as cavernous storage facilities along the shoreline. The port was devastated by an earthquake in AD 130. The Crusaders only reutilized a small section of the harbor when they conquered Caesarea in 1101. ☎ 06/636–1358. *☐ Theater and Crusader City NIS 15 ($5).* ⊙ *Daily 8–4, Fri. and holiday eves 8–3.*

A small, sunken fenced-in area encloses the **Byzantine street.** It was during this period and in late Roman times that Caesarea thrived as a center of Christian scholarship and as an episcopal see; in the 7th century, Caesarea had a famous library with some 30,000 volumes that originated with the collection of illustrious Christian philosopher Origen (185–254), who lived in Caesarea for two decades. Eusebius, who was an ecclesiastical adviser to Emperor Constantine and is known as the Church's first historian, became Caesarea's first bishop in the 4th century. Once lined with workshops and stores, the street is paved with marble slabs, and a mosaic has been uncovered. Towering over the street are two monumental marble statues that face each other, both probably carted here from nearby Roman temples. The provenance of the milky white one is unknown; the purple porphyry figure could have been commissioned by Emperor Hadrian when he visited Caesarea. In Byzantine times the city grew an estimated eight times as large in area as the fortified Crusader City. The Byzantine street is outside the Crusader City, just across the street from the entrance.

The **Caesarea Museum** houses many of the artifacts that were found by kibbutzim as they plowed their fields in the 1940s. The museum possesses arguably the best collection of late-Roman sculpture in Israel, impressive holdings of rare Roman and Byzantine gemstones, and a large variety of coins minted in Caesarea over the ages, as well as oil lamps, urns excavated from the sea bottom, and fragments of jewelry. ⊠ *On the grounds of Kibbutz Sdot Yam, about 600 feet south of the theater entrance,* ☎ *06/636–4367.* ☞ *NIS 4 ($1.35).* ☉ *Sat.–Thurs. 10–4, Fri. 8–2.*

★ A wonderful finale to your visit at Caesarea (especially at sunset) is the **Roman aqueduct** on the beach. The chain of arches, tumbling north toward the horizon where they disappear beneath the sand, is a captivating sight, and they form a unique backdrop for a swim at the pretty beach (☞ Outdoor Activities and Sports, *below*). During Roman rule, the demand for a steady supply of water for the city's drinking needs, household use, public baths, and city fountains was considerable. The source of water, however, was a spring about 13 km (8 mi) away, in the foothills of Mt. Carmel. Workers labored to cut a channel approximately 6½ km (4 mi) long through solid rock before the water was piped into the aqueduct, whose arches also spanned a length of 6 km (4 mi). In the 2nd century, Hadrian doubled its capacity by adding a new channel. Today, you can walk along the sea side of the aqueduct and find marble plaques dedicated to the support troops of various legions that toiled here. On your way back to the road, you might like to drive around the villa area and admire some of Israel's tonier and brand new residences, many covered with swaths of brilliant bougainvillea. ⊠ *Villa area, north of the Crusader City.*

Dining and Lodging

$$$ ✕ **Charley's.** On a clear day, it's a delight to eat on one of several patios here, right above the sandy cove beach in the Crusader City. In the center of the port under the stone watchtower, Charley's is especially known for its way with fresh seafood, grilled or baked. Depending on the catch of the day, supplied by fishermen from a neighboring Arab village, there's red snapper, mullet, or grouper. Or you can order a simple, inexpensive snack of Middle Eastern salad or coffee and crème caramel or cheesecake. ⊠ *Old City,* ☎ *06/636–3050. Reservations essential in high season. MC, V.*

$$$ ✕ **Harbor Citadel.** By Israeli standards this is a venerable institution: It's been open for 26 years. You'll spot it under the Israeli flag at the far end of the port, at the top of a spiral stone staircase. Its elevated

location affords a spectacular view of the coast. The versatile menu showcases seafood and salads as well as schnitzel and chicken livers. In warmer weather you can sit on the outdoor patio, shaded by a yellow awning, and savor the view of the ruins of the ancient port. ✉ *Old City,* ☎ *06/636–1988 or 06/836–1989. Reservations essential. AE, DC, MC, V.*

$$$ 🎦 **Dan Caesarea.** You will find quiet comfort here as well as accessi-
★ bility to a range of sport facilities and the archaeological sites of Caesarea. The four-story hotel is unobtrusively set in landscaped grounds. All the rooms have balconies, some facing the open countryside and others with sea views. Especially recommended are the renovated deluxe doubles, with marble bathrooms and modern decor in cheerful hues. Stretching adjacent to the hotel's 15-acre gardens are the 18 holes of Israel's only golf course, which offers Dan guests a discount. ✉ *Opposite entrance to villa area, north of the Crusader City, Caesarea 30600,* ☎ *06/636–2266,* 📠 *06/636–2392. 114 rooms with bath. Restaurant, bar, café, pool, sauna, golf privileges, 2 tennis courts. AE, DC, MC.*

$$ 🎦 **Illana Berner's.** Tucked away at the end of a cul-de-sac in the town's residential quarter, Illana rents out holiday units on the grounds of her home, a leisurely 10-minute walk from the beach. Each has an air-conditioned bedroom and fully equipped kitchen. Your hostess is a licensed guide and for an extra fee offers tours of Caesarea and beyond to guests, as well as free tips on planning itineraries. ✉ *23 Harimon St., Caesarea 30600,* ☎ *06/636–3936,* 📠 *06/836–0212. 3 units with bath. Pool. No credit cards.*

Outdoor Activities and Sports

BEACHES

Bathers have three choices here. In the **Old City,** in a sandy cove in Herod's ancient harbor, is the small **Caesarea Beach Club** (☎ 06/636–1441). The adult admission of NIS 15 ($5) includes chairs, umbrellas, and hot showers. The beach offers a diving platform and rented kayaks; the Gal-Mor scuba-diving center is next door. In the residential area at the **Roman aqueduct,** just north of the Crusader City, is a considerably more spacious beach, with the dramatic backdrop of Roman arches disappearing into the sand. The amenities, however, are few: toilets and a lifeguard in season. There is no entrance fee, but parking runs about NIS 5 ($1.70) per car. The beach and swimming areas have been cleared of rocks and debris, but it is forbidden to swim outside the demarcated area supervised by a lifeguard (never swim unless one is on duty). The largest and most popular sandy beach in the area is **Hof Shonit** (☎ 06/636–2927), just south of Caesarea. When approaching from Route 2, turn left (instead of right toward the main site). The parking lot here accommodates 400 vehicles and costs NIS 10 ($3.35). There are lifeguards (in season), a refreshment stand, and a restaurant, as well as cold showers and toilets.

GOLF

Israeli and foreign visitors flock to the **Caesarea Golf Club** (☎ 06/636–1172). Adjacent to the Dan Caesarea Hotel, the club is open from sunrise to sunset, and the course is built on sandy soil so it's playable even after heavy rainfall. Reservations are advisable on Friday, Saturday, and holidays. The greens fee is NIS 250 ($83.35) Tuesday–Friday; NIS 300 ($100) weekends; the weekly rate is NIS 960 ($320). Golf club rentals run NIS 60 ($20), and an electric caddie car can be hired for NIS 91.20 ($30.40).

SCUBA DIVING

The Gal-Mor Diving Center (☎ 06/636–1787), in the Old City, provides courses in scuba diving, windsurfing, underwater photography, and swimming. A unique diving tour offers the opportunity to explore Herod's largely submerged port; a detailed map shows four different routes through the underwater ruins.

Nightlife and the Arts

At **Caesarea's Roman theater** evening performances by local and international troupes of the highest caliber are generally held from May to mid-October. For advance information on the program, contact the National Parks Authority (⊠ 35 Jabotinsky St., Ramat Gan, ☎ 03/576–6888). Tickets can be purchased in advance at the Le'an (⊠ 101 Dizengoff St., Tel Aviv, ☎ 03/523–6193) ticket agency; the box office in Caesarea is open on performance days.

Shopping

The **Glass Center** (☎ 06/636–1890) is a small store on the southern side of the port selling handblown colored glass. The pale-color vases and vessels, lightly veined and streaked, are reminiscent of ancient glass. The factory warehouse, open Sunday–Friday 9–5, is next to a Paz gas station on the road to the highway toward Tel Aviv.

Nahsholim-Dor

❸ *20 km (12 mi) north of Caesarea.*

Founded 35 centuries ago, biblical Dor was once the maritime capital of the Carmel coast. Its small bay made it the best harbor between Jaffa and Akko, and thus a target for many imperial ambitions, from the ancient Egyptians and the "Sea Peoples" through King Solomon and on down. It was renowned in antiquity for its precious purple dye called Tyrian purple. This color, reserved for royalty, was extracted from a mollusk that was abundant along the coast. During the Arab period, it was renamed Tantura, which is also the name of its popular beach today. **Tel Dor,** an ongoing archaeological excavation, is not formally open to tourists, but if you call the Nahsholim Museum (☞ *below*), someone will take you around and explain what's been uncovered. Among the finds are remains of a Crusader fortress, a temple to Zeus, and the industrial area for production of the purple dye.

★ The **Nahsholim Museum** (or Mizgaga Museum) and the Center for Nautical and Regional Archaeology, a five-minute walk from Tel Dor, are housed in the partly restored former glass factory opened by Baron Rothschild in 1893 to serve the wineries of nearby Zichron Ya'akov. The enterprise, run by the first mayor of Tel Aviv, Meir Dizengoff, failed two years later because the poor quality of the sand used made the bottles black. The museum contains a rich trove of the finds of local nautical digs and of excavations at nearby Tel Dor. The various peoples who settled, conquered, or passed through Dor—from the Phoenicians to Napoléon and his army—can be traced through the artifacts on display here. Of particular interest is the bronze cannon that Napoléon's vanquished troops dumped into the sea during their retreat from Akko to Egypt in May 1799. Treacherous currents and winds made this shoreline a graveyard for ships, which have yielded many of the finds. In 1982, a storm revealed a shipwreck about 300 feet offshore, bringing to light a treasure: over a ton of coins, bronze figurines, silver plates, and bracelets that date from the Byzantine and Mamluk periods. An interesting film in English gives background to the seminal work of Kurt Raveh, a Dutch-born member of Kibbutz Nahsholim, who spearheaded many of the underwater digs in the area. ⊠ *Kibbutz Nahsholim,*

☏ 06/639–0950. ✉ NIS 8 ($2.70). ⏱ Sun.–Fri. 8:30–1, Sat. and holidays 10:30–3.

Beach

Dor Beach (✉ 06/839–0922), also known as Tantura Beach, is one of the most frequented in the country because of the fine sand that lines its 1½ km (1 mi) of coastline. The fee is NIS 7.50 ($2.50) per person, and there is parking for 2,000 cars. Facilities here are ample: lifeguards in season, a snack bar and restaurant, a first-aid station, a trampoline (an additional fee), and chair and umbrella rentals, as well as changing rooms and showers. Motorized dinghies can be rented for NIS 20 ($6.70) for a 20-minute ride.

Lodging

$ 🏠 **Nahsholim Guest House.** Next to the museum and at the water's edge on the white sand of Tantura Beach (one of the nicest along the coast), this unadorned, well-maintained place is ideal for a family beach holiday and as a base for sightseeing. Set among the lawns is the guest house's series of one-story buildings, each housing several units. These are furnished in the quintessential austere style of the kibbutz, although many have kitchenettes. The dining room serves three meals a day; guests must take half board during half board. ✉ M.P. Hof Carmel, 30815, ☏ 06/639–9533, ✆ 06/397614. 80 rooms with bath (40 sleep 6). Dining room, coffee shop. AE, DC, MC, V.

Atlit

❹ 9 km (5½ mi) north of Nahsholim-Dor, 15 km (9¼ mi) south of Haifa.

Atlit is a peninsula jutting into the Mediterranean where the jagged remains of an important Crusader castle still stand; there are also reminders of the more recent past. A **detention camp,** on your right about 1,500 feet from the highway, was used by the British during the decade prior to Israeli independence. The reconstructed barracks, fences, and watchtowers stand as reminders that Jewish immigration was practically outlawed under the British Mandate after the publication in 1939 of the infamous White Paper. More than a third of the 120,000 illegal immigrants passed through this camp from 1934 to 1948. The 45-minute tour includes the living quarters, complete with laundry hanging from the rafters. The authenticity of the exhibit is striking, re-created from accounts of actual detainees and their contemporaries. Visitors are advised to call ahead. ✉ Rte. 2, ☏ 04/984–1980. ✉ NIS 5 ($1.70). ⏱ Sun.–Thurs. 9–3:30, Fri. 9–12:30, Sat. 9–3.

Since 1948, the **Crusader castle** has been off limits, property of the Israeli navy. However, there is a good view of it from the windswept beach just north of the walls. To view the castle, continue straight from the detention camp 1 km (½ mi) along the road toward the beach, passing the left turnoff to the new town of Atlit (or take Bus 122 from Haifa) and then cross the railroad tracks.

Built in 1217 by the Crusader order known as the Templars, this fortified castle with its natural port was known as Château des Pelerins, or the Pilgrims' Castle. After the fall of the Crusader capital in Akko in 1291, the Château des Pelerins became the last surviving Crusader fortress in the Holy Land. It was never taken by siege. But in August of that year, the last Crusaders set sail, and after their departure the Mamluks dismantled the fortifications just in case the Crusaders had second thoughts.

Its strategic location made the castle a natural stronghold that only needed fortification on the side facing toward land, along which several towers were erected. The ruins of two of them are visible today. There was once a moat along the eastern side that could be flooded with seawater. During the Seventh Crusade, Louis IX of France extended the fortifications, and his wife gave birth to a son here. In the 18th century, stones from the castle were used to fortify Akko; an 1837 earthquake wreaked heavy damage, leaving it in its present ruined state.

HAIFA

Spilling down from the pine-covered heights of Mt. Carmel to the blue Mediterranean is Haifa, whose vertiginous setting has led to perhaps hyperbolic comparisons with San Francisco. Israel's largest port and third-largest city, Haifa was ruled for four centuries by the Ottomans and gradually grew up the mountainside into a cosmopolitan city whose port once served the entire Middle East. In 1902, Theodor Herzl enthusiastically dubbed it "the city of the future."

With the 1924 opening of the Technion Institute, Haifa was becoming a center for science and technology. The turn-of-the-century construction by the Turks of the Hijaz Railway, which stretched from Constantinople via Damascus to the Muslim holy cities of Mecca and Medina, proved a boon to Haifa (which had its own branch of the new line to Damascus). Under the British Mandate, a deep-water port was dug and opened to world traffic in 1933; the following year Haifa was hooked up by an oil pipeline to Iraq. After Israel's independence, Haifa's links with neighboring Arab states were broken, but today cruise ships from abroad ply its waters, and the Technion is still the nation's citadel of scientific research.

First mentioned in the Talmud, the area of Haifa was the site of two settlements in ancient times: To the east, in what is today a congested industrial zone in the port, lay Zalmona; 4¾ km (3 mi) west around the cape was Shiqmona. The Crusaders conquered Haifa, then an important Arab town, and maintained it as a fortress along the coastal road to Akko for two centuries. Like much of the Crusader kingdom, Haifa was lost and regained repeatedly by the Christians. During this period, in 1154, the Order of Our Lady of Mount Carmel (the Carmelite order) was founded on the slopes of Mt. Carmel by a group of hermits following the principles of the prophet Elijah and the rules of poverty, vegetarianism, and solitude. After Akko and Haifa succumbed to Mamluk sultan Baybars in 1265, Haifa was destroyed and left derelict, just as it had been at the end of Byzantine rule. For centuries, Haifa remained a sleepy fishing village.

It reawakened under the rule of Bedouin sheikh Dahr el-Omar, who had rebelled against direct Ottoman rule in the mid-18th century and independently governed Akko and the Galilee. Dahr recognized that Haifa's location made it vulnerable to attack; in 1761 he ordered the city to be demolished and moved a couple of miles to the south. The new town was fortified by walls and protected by a castle. The new port began to compete with that of Akko across the bay, for although its harbor was not as good as Akko's, Mt. Carmel offered a natural barrier against the strong southwesterly winds and, therefore, a comfortable anchorage.

Napoléon, too, came to Haifa, though only briefly and on his way to ignominious defeat at Akko during his eastern campaign. Napoléon left his wounded at the Carmelite Monastery (☞ *below*) in Haifa when he beat a retreat in 1799, but the French soldiers there were killed and the monks driven out by Ahmed el-Jazzar, the victorious pasha of Akko.

Exploring Haifa

Haifa is divided into three main levels, which run parallel to the harbor, crisscrossed with parks and gardens. The downtown port encompasses the largely uninhabited Old City; the midtown area, called Hadar HaCarmel, or Hadar for short, was an early Jewish neighborhoods and is today a bustling shopping area; and central Carmel, or Mercaz HaCarmel, is on top, home to upscale residential developments and the posher hotels. The most striking landmark on the mountainside is the gleaming golden dome of the Baha'i Shrine. The Carmelit subway (☞ Getting Around *in* Northern Coast and Western Galilee A to Z, *below*), which reopened in July 1992 after six years of repair, rises from the port to the upper city with numerous stops along the way. It is Israel's only subway.

Numbers in the text correspond to numbers in the margin and on the Haifa map.

A Good Walk and Tour

A good way to orient yourself is to gaze down at Haifa as you stroll along **Yefe Nof** ⑤, which descends the mountain and has great views of the port and beyond. At No. 89 Yefe Nof is the **Mané Katz Museum** ⑥, the lattice-windowed home of the Ukrainian-born expressionist painter Emmanuel Katz. Hanassi Avenue runs parallel and west of Yefe Nof; No 88 is the **Tikotin Museum of Japanese Art** ⑦, with its attractive displays. Leaving the museum, return to Yefe Nof and head north, accompanied by great vistas in the direction of the bay. Continue on Yefe Nof to Shomron Street; turn right and then right again, into Sderot Hatziyonut (Zionism Boulevard).

On your left is the entrance to a **sculpture garden** ⑧ that overlooks Haifa Bay. A bit farther along you'll come upon the ornately carved gates of the **Baha'i Shrine and Gardens** ⑨; it is the dazzling gold dome of the Shrine of the Bab that's the landmark of Haifa postcards. Haifa is the Baha'i faith's world center.

Keep heading down the hill to the intersection of Zionism Boulevard and Shabbetei Levy Street. The **Haifa Museum** ⑩, with its modern art collections, and **Bet Hagefen** ⑪, the Arab-Jewish Center, are on either side of the junction. Turn left onto Hagefen Boulevard and walk three blocks to Ben-Gurion Boulevard, where you'll turn right, into what's known as the **German Colony** ⑫. This late-19th-century colony established by the German Templar religious reform movement is the most important Templar area in the Holy Land.

If you don't have time for this entire tour, you can start a short walk by taking a taxi, bus, or the Carmelit subway down to the **Carmelite Monastery** ⑬. Across the street is a fine observation point and the Stella Maris Lighthouse. A 20-minute walk takes you down to **Elijah's Cave** ⑭, sacred to Jews, Christians, and Muslims. Next, walk down the stairs that lead to Allenby Road, turn left, and cross the road to the **Clandestine Immigration and Naval Museum** ⑮, which tells of the often heroic efforts by Jews to bring Jewish refugees from war-torn Europe to Palestine. Up the road is the **National Maritime Museum** ⑯, which brings to life thousands of years of maritime history.

Three additional sights are a bit farther afield. The closest of these, still downtown, is the **National Museum of Science and Technology** ⑰, with its hands-on exhibits. Bus 30 take you to Haifa University and the **Hecht Museum** ⑱, well-known for its archaeological collections. To visit the **Technion** ⑲, take Bus 31.

186

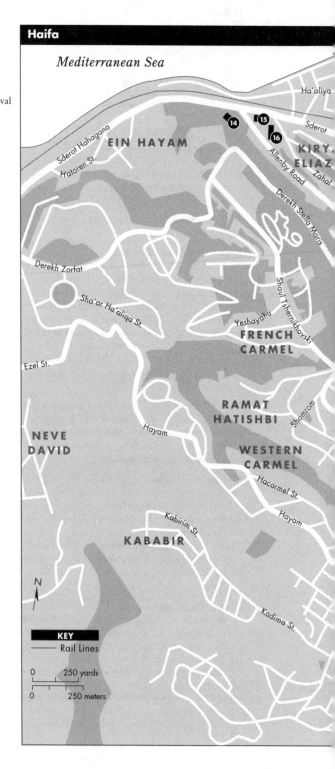

BAT GALIM

asharon

Hashnia

hagana

R

Mediterranean Sea

Hey Hayam St.

Tel Aviv St.

KIRYAT
ELIAHU

Harbor

Deror

de Rothchild

Yitzhaq Sade St.

Sderot Hameginim

Haganin St.

Ben Gurion Blvd.

Allenby Rd.

Hagefen Blvd.

Sderot Ha'atzma'ut

Jaffa

13

12

Blvd. I. Khouri St.

11

Wadi
Nisnas

Zionism

10

Y. L. Perez St.

Sderot Hatziyonut

8

9

Yefe Nof

Shabbetai Levy St.

Hassan

Gid'on St.

Baerwald St.

Bialik

Shukri

Hanassi Avenue

5

6

Eliyahu Golumb St.

Hahashmona'im St.

Arlosoroff St.

Spinoza

Balfour St.

Pevsner St.

Herzl St.

Nardau St.

Kibbutz Galuyot St.

7

17

HADAR
HA'CARMEL

Bilu

Hakishon

19

Sderot Wedgewood

Sderot Wingate

Sderot Krish

Hapoel St.

Geula St.

CENTRAL
CARMEL

TEL AMAL

18

Ha'asif St.

Sights to See

★ ❾ **Baha'i Shrine and Gardens.** The most striking feature of the gardens is the **Shrine of the Bab,** whose gilded dome dominates as well as illuminates Haifa's skyline. Haifa is the world center for the Baha'i faith, founded in Iran in the 19th century and whose central belief is the unity of humankind. For Baha'is, religious truth is not dogmatic; rather, it consists of progressive revelations of a universal faith. Thus the Baha'is teach that great prophets have appeared throughout history to reveal divine truths. Among these have been Moses, Zoroaster, Buddha, Jesus, Muhammad, and most recently, the founder of the Baha'i faith, Mirza Husayn Ali, known as Bahaullah—the Glory of God. Bahaullah was exiled from his native Persia by the shah and then by the Ottomans to Akko, where he lived as a prisoner for almost 25 years. (The holiest shrine for Baha'is is on the grounds of Bahaullah's home, where he lived after his release from prison and the site of his final resting place, just north of Akko; *see* Western Galilee, *below.*)

At the center of the shrine's magnificently manicured gardens is the mausoleum built for the Bab—which literally means "the Gate"—who heralded the coming of a new faith revealed by Bahaullah. The Bab was martyred by the Persian authorities in 1850. The gardens and shrine were built by Bahaullah's son and successor, who had the Bab's remains reburied here in 1909. The 128-foot-high building, made of Italian-cut stone, gracefully combines the canons of classical European architecture with elements of the East and also houses the remains of Bahaullah's son. The dome glistens with some 12,000 gilded tiles imported from Holland. Inside, the floor is covered with rich Oriental carpets and a filigree veil divides visitors from the inner shrine.

The hush of the largely geometric gardens is now periodically disturbed by construction work that will create terraces down the slope all the way to the ☞ **German Colony** as well as up the mountain to Yefe Nof Street. The Shrine of the Bab, along with the Shrine of Bahaullah, north of Akko, are sites of pilgrimage for the worldwide Baha'i community. Visitors to the shrine are asked to dress modestly. ⊠ *65 Hatziyonut Blvd.,* ☎ *04/835–8358.* ⊠ *Free.* ☉ *Shrine daily 9–noon; gardens daily 9–5.*

⓫ **Bet Hagefen.** The Arab-Jewish Center is a striking but simple two-story stone building. Founded 33 years ago, it is the first and only such Arab-Jewish institution in Israel. Bet Hagefen's location is not accidental: It stands at the meeting place between Wadi Nisnas (☞ Off the Beaten Path, *below*), with its large Arab population, the ☞ **German Colony,** with its mixed population, and central Carmel, which is predominantly Jewish. Throughout troubled times, the center has continued to promote the principles of coexistence and understanding between Arabs and Jews through cultural projects and exhibitions.

Open regularly is the visitor center and a small art gallery, with works on display by Arab and Jewish painters and sculptors. The center's involvement in the community extends far beyond holding art shows. Activities include meetings between Arab and Jewish schoolchildren and performances by an Arab-Jewish dance group and an Arab theater company. Call ahead to see what's on the calendar. ⊠ *2 Hagefen,* ☎ *04/852–5252.* ⊠ *Free.* ☉ *Sun.–Thurs. 8–1 and 4–8, Fri. 8–1, Sat. 10–1.*

....

OFF THE   **WADI NISNAS –** A colorful quarter laced with narrow streets and shops
BEATEN PATH   selling housewares and groceries, this neighborhood east of Bet Hage-
                fen, around Khouri Street, is a slice of modern Arab life in Israel. Yet you
                will still see men crouched on stools in front of stoops and women in tra-
                ditional dress peering out from behind curtains or ducking in doorways.

St. John's pedestrian mall is a humming marketplace of stalls heaped with fruit and vegetables. Open on Saturday, when many other stores in the city are closed, this market draws many Jewish customers from far-away neighborhoods. You'll find some great falafel here, too.

⑬ Carmelite Monastery. During the Crusader period, on the steep mountain slope, groups of hermits emulating the life of the prophet Elijah lived in caves near the present monastery. In the early 13th century they united under the leadership of the Italian pilgrim (later a saint) Berthold, who petitioned the patriarch of Jerusalem for a charter for the group. Thus was born the Carmelite order, which spread across Europe. The Carmelite monks were forced to leave their settlements on Mt. Carmel at the end of the 13th century, when Akko fell to the Mamluks, and did not return until nearly four centuries later. When they found Elijah's Cave inhabited by Muslim dervishes, they set up a rudimentary monastery nearby. Dahr el-Omar drove them out again in 1767.

The church of the present monastery dates from 1836 and was built with the munificence of the French monarchy; hence the surrounding neighborhood is known as French Carmel. The French connection is explained by a small pyramid topped with an iron cross that stands before the entrance of the basilica-style church. The monument commemorates the French who were slaughtered here by the Turks in 1799 after the retreating Napoléon left his ailing troops behind to be treated in what was then a military hospital at the monastery. Inside, the academic paintings in the dome depict Elijah in the chariot of fire in which he ascended to heaven, as well as Old Testament prophets. The small cave a few steps down, at the end of the nave, is traditionally associated with Elijah and his pupil, Elisha. A small museum near the entrance contains some fossils and Byzantine artifacts discovered in the area. Across the street from the church, at the tip of the promontory, is the **Stella Maris Lighthouse** (Star of the Sea), built for the Turkish fleet in the early 19th century and still in use. Collectively the lighthouse and the monastery are known as Stella Maris. The lighthouse is not open to the public. ⊠ *Stella Maris Rd.,* ☎ *04/833–7758.* 🎫 *Free.* ☯ *Daily 6:30–1:30 and 3–6.*

⑮ Clandestine Immigration and Naval Museum. The rather dull name of this museum belies the dramatic nature of its contents. The Clandestine Immigration and Naval Museum chronicles the story of the often heroic efforts to surreptitiously bring Jewish immigrants to Palestine, many refugees aboard ships fleeing war-torn Europe. The exhibits are labeled in English. In addition to a clearly marked map that pinpoints the immigration routes, there are video presentations, photographs, and documents that record both deportations and successful missions.

Emigration to Palestine was well nigh impossible after the British imposed a naval blockade, bowing to pressure by Arabs opposed to Jewish immigration. In 1939, on the eve of World War II, the British issued the White Paper, which effectively strangled Jewish immigration to Palestine and prohibited Jews from buying land there. Little boats sometimes managed to elude the vigilant British warships and put ashore their human cargoes at secret landing beaches. But for bigger ships the odds were daunting. Out of 63 clandestine ships that tried to run the blockade after the war's end, all but five were intercepted and their passengers deported to Cyprus.

The museum is full of moving stories of courage, tenacity, and disaster. A photomural of the celebrated ship, the *Exodus,* recalls the story of the 4,530 refugees aboard who were forcibly transferred back to Germany in 1947, but not before the British forces opened fire on the rebellious ship, convincing the passengers and crew to surrender. Another tragic episode took place aboard the *Struma,* a leaky vessel that was forced to anchor in Istanbul for repairs in 1941. The Turks refused to assist the ship after warnings from the British. So, unable to continue and its passengers unwilling to return, the boat wallowed in Istanbul's harbor for two months and finally sank a few miles offshore. There was one survivor among the 767 aboard.

One of the blockade-runners was an old American tank-landing craft, renamed *Af-al-pi* (Nevertheless), which serves as the centerpiece of the museum, accessible from the roof. This ship left Italy in 1947 for Palestine and was intercepted by the British. Its 434 passengers, all survivors of the Holocaust, were sent to internment camps in Cyprus. ⊠ *204 Allenby Rd.,* ☎ *04/853–6249.* ⊠ *NIS 5 ($1.70).* ☉ *Sun.–Thurs. 9–4, Fri. and holiday eves 9–1.*

⑭ Elijah's Cave. This site is considered sacred by Jews, Christians, and Moslems. An early Byzantine tradition identified it as the cave in which Elijah found refuge from the wrath of Ahab, king of Israel, from 871 BC to 851 BC. Graffiti made by pilgrims of various faiths and from different centuries are scrawled on the right wall. Written prayers are often stuffed into crevices; some supplicants come to ask for fertility, others for better fortune or to be cured of an illness. Modest dress is requested. It's a 20-minute walk to the cave down the fairly steep path across from the entrance to the Carmelite Monastery and its church. The cave can also be reached from Allenby Road, from which you'd walk up about 100 feet. ⊠ *230 Allenby Rd.,* ☎ *04/852–7430.* ⊠ *Free.* ☉ *Sun.–Thurs. 8–5, Fri. and holiday eves 8–1.*

⑫ German Colony. Ruler-straight Ben-Gurion Boulevard is the heart of what was, in the late 19th century, a colony established by the German Templar religious reform movement. Note the robust two- and three-story stone houses with red-tile roofs, which are typical of the neighborhood. There are a few good restaurants along the walk uphill. Some houses still bear German names on the lintels above the doors. The Templars' colony in Haifa was the most important one in the Holy Land. The early settlers formed a self-sufficient community that enjoyed quite a comfortable standard of living. By 1883 there were nearly 100 houses built and as many families.

The Germans introduced several improvements in transportation to Haifa. Until their arrival, the horse-drawn wagon was unknown. The Germans in Palestine (Israel) started to make wagons locally and then built with their own funds a road from Haifa to Nazareth as a pilgrimage route. Their labors gave rise to modern workshops and warehouses; under their influence, Haifa began to take on the semblance of a modern Western city, with well-laid-out streets, gardens, and attractive homes.

Haifa's importance to Germany was highlighted in 1898 when Kaiser Wilhelm II sailed into the bay as the first stop on the first official visit to the Holy Land by a German emperor in more than 600 years. For the occasion, the ruling Turkish sultan ordered a new jetty built. During World War II the Germans living in the colony were expelled, suspected of being Nazis.

The German Templars and the French Carmelite monks on the hill were on no better terms than their compatriots back home. A battle took shape in 1885 along nationalistic lines when the Germans bought some acreage on the mountain, and the French monks refused to let them cross monastery land to get there. The case ended up in a Haifa court, and the monks were ordered to allow the Germans access to their land.

⓪ Haifa Museum. Until recently, the museum was three museums in one building: Now this building holds the Museum of Modern Art. The ancient art collection is housed at the ☞ **National Maritime Museum,** while the music and ethnology section has yet to find a home. One admission ticket is good for the Haifa and Maritime museums, as well as the ☞ **Tikotin Museum of Japanese Art,** also under the auspices of the Haifa Museum.

The Museum of Modern Art exhibits work from all over the world, dating from the mid-18th century to the present. This is a good venue to learn about Israeli modern art: The many pieces include 20th-century graphics and contemporary paintings, sculpture, and photography. The print collection is of special note, and international photography shows are mounted several times a year. ⊠ *26 Shabbetai Levy St.,* ☎ *04/852–3255.* 🎫 *NIS 12 ($4), includes all 3 museums.* ☉ *Sun.–Mon. and Wed.–Thurs. 10–5, Tues. 4–8, Fri. 10–1, Sat. 10–2.*

⓲ Hecht Museum. It's worth the trip to Haifa University for the fine archaeological holdings of this museum. At the summit of Mt. Carmel, in the main tower on campus—designed by Brazilian architect Oscar Niemeyer—the collection spans the millennia from the Chalcolithic era to the Roman and Byzantine periods. The artifacts, all Jewish, range from religious altars and lamps to two coffins and figurines from the Early Bronze Age. Featured prominently are finds from the excavations of the Temple Mount in Jerusalem. In a separate wing, there is a small collection of paintings, mostly impressionist and from the Jewish School of Paris. Bus 30, which departs from the Nof Hotel, will take you to the museum. ⊠ *Abu Hushi St.,* ☎ *04/824–0577.* 🎫 *Free.* ☉ *Sun.–Thurs. 10–4, Fri. and holiday eves 10–1, Sat. 10–2.*

❻ Mané Katz Museum. This is actually the studio and house where the expressionist painter Emmanuel Katz (1894–1962) lived and worked from 1958 until his death. The whitewashed building with ornamental grillwork on the windows houses a collection of Katz's paintings, drawings, and sculptures—the Ukrainian-born artist's legacy to the city. Katz spent the 1920s in Paris, where he exhibited with a group of Jewish artists from the École de Paris. As on the canvases of fellow members Marc Chagall and Chaim Soutine, a recurring theme in his work is the village life of Jews in Eastern Europe. The artist was an avid collector of rugs and 17th-century antiques from Spain and Germany, which are also on display along with objects from his Judaica collection. ⊠ *89 Yefe Nof St.,* ☎ *04/838–3482.* 🎫 *Free.* ☉ *Sun., Mon., Wed., Thurs. 10–4, Tues. 2–6, Fri. and holiday eves 10–1, Sat. and holidays 10–2.*

⓰ National Maritime Museum. Here, 5,000 years of maritime history is told (and made more interesting than it sounds) with models of ships, archaeological finds, coins minted with nautical symbols, navigational instruments, and other artifacts. There are also a number of intriguing underwater finds from nearby excavations and shipwrecks. A new addition to the museum is the ancient art collection, formerly housed in the Haifa Museum. One of the most notable in the country, this collection is mostly Greek and Roman stone and marble sculptures, Egyptian textiles, Greek pottery, and encaustic grave portraits from El Faiyûm in Egypt. Particularly rare are the figures of fishermen from the Hellenistic period. Among numerous terra-cotta figurines from Syria and Egypt are several curious animal-shape vessels, once used as playthings, incense burners, or funerary gifts, found in Haifa's nearby Shiqmona excavation. Also from Egypt is a group of finely carved alabaster vessels and funerary masks. ⊠ *198 Allenby Rd.,* ☎ *04/853–6622.* 🎫 *NIS 12 ($4); includes admission to Museum of Modern Art* *and Tikotin Japanese Art Museum.* ۩ *Sun.–Mon. and Wed.–Thurs. 10–5, Tues. 4–8, Fri. 10–1, Sat. 10–2.*

⑰ National Museum of Science and Technology (Technoda). Children and adults alike will be captivated by the hands-on chemistry and physics exhibits displayed in the beautifully designed building that was the original home of the ☞ **Technion.** ⊠ *Balfour St.,* ☎ *04/862–8111.* ☜ *NIS 6 ($2).* ۩ *Sun.–Mon. and Wed.–Thurs. 9–5, Tues. 9–7, Fri. 9–1, Sat. 10–3.*

⑧ Sculpture garden. From one of the benches on a winding path through the garden, you can contemplate the life-size bronzes of humans and animals by sculptor Ursula Malbin. Malbin, a refugee from Nazi Germany, divides her time between the artists' village of Ein Hod (☞ The Rothschild Wine Country and Mt. Carmel, *below*), south of Haifa, and a village near Geneva, Switzerland. ⊠ *Just to the west of the Baha'i Shrine.*

⑲ Technion. Israel's foremost center for applied research, the 300-acre Technion City was relocated to this area in 1953. Founded in 1912, the doors to the original institute (known as the Technoda) in midtown opened 12 years later, due in part to the hardships of World War I. Today, the Technion is highly fertile ground for the nation's scientific innovations: Two-thirds of Israel's university research in such fields as science, technology, engineering, medicine, architecture, and town planning takes place here. Visitors can get an idea of the vast scope of studies and research conducted here at Technion's **Coler-California Center,** in an architecturally striking cubical concrete building. You can see descriptions of the various Technion departments on laser disc videos. Call ahead to find out when the introductory 30-minute film in English will be screened. You can catch Bus 31, across from the Nof Hotel, to reach the Technion. ⊠ *In Kiryat Ha-Technion,* ☎ *04/832–0664.* ☜ *Free.* ۩ *Sun.–Thurs. 8–2.*

⑦ Tikotin Museum of Japanese Art. Established in 1957 by Felix Tikotin, this graceful venue adheres to the Japanese tradition of displaying beautiful objects in harmony with the season; therefore exhibits change frequently. The Japanese atmosphere, emphasized by sliding doors and partitions made of wood and paper, accompanies viewers through a display of scrolls, screens, pottery and porcelain, lacquer and metalwork, paintings from several schools, and fresh flower arrangements. ⊠ *88 Hanassi St.,* ☎ *04/837–4497.* ☜ *NIS 12 ($4); includes admission to Museum of Modern Art and Maritime Museum.* ۩ *Sun.–Mon. and Wed.–Thurs. 10–5, Tues. 4–8, Fri. 10–1, Sat. 10–2.*

⑤ Yefe Nof. This street, also known as Panorama Road, descends the mountain past the Baha'i Shrine. On a clear day from any of several observation points, the naked eye can take in the smokestacks of the port below, Akko across the bay, and the cliffs of Rosh Hanikra, with Lebanon in the distance. It's a superlative view.

Dining

$$$$ ✕ **La Chaumière.** Occupying a two-story stone building in the German Colony, this restaurant is graced with authentic French charm, both in its ambience and the virtuosity of its cuisine. Owner Michel Kaminski and his wife, Danielle, who take turns in the kitchen, see to it that everything from the goose-liver pâté to the chocolate mousse and bread is fresh and homemade. Particularly outstanding is the fillet *Chaumière* with a cream sauce of tomatoes, cognac, and port. ⊠ *40A Ben-Gurion Blvd.,* ☎ *04/853–8563 or 04/855–3154. Reservations essential. AE, DC, MC, V. No lunch Fri.*

$$$$ ✕ **La Trattoria.** It's not your typical Italian restaurant, because along with pizza, pasta, and minestrone, there are the likes of couscous and chicken livers on the menu. Yet the homey hodgepodge of Italian, French, and Tunisian atmosphere and cuisine is precisely what makes La Trattoria so popular among locals. Owner Edy Barby presides with a jovial manner over this family-style establishment. ✉ *119 Hanassi Blvd.,* ☎ *04/837–9029 or 04/838–9618. Reservations essential Fri., Sat. AE, DC, MC, V.*

$$ ✕ **Palermo Pizza.** If you're searching for genuine thin-crusted pizza,
★ you've come to the right place. Looking more like a fashionable salad bar than a pizzeria, this parlor in the Panorama Center displays jars of spicy peppers and fresh flowers that add a dash of color. The range of toppings is prodigious—from tuna and salami to pineapple and peppers—and the crust is crisp. There are also plenty of other Italian specialties, like a *caprese* salad (sliced mozzarella topped with tomatoes and basil leaves and drizzled with olive oil), gnocchi, and ravioli. Palermo also serves meat, fish, and salads. ✉ *In Panorama Center, Hanassi Ave.,* ☎ *04/838–9129. AE, MC, V.*

$$ ✕ **Recital.** The ambience at this small restaurant is decidedly artistic,
★ with classical music playing softly in the background and black-and-white photos adorning the otherwise plain walls. Watch for the white awning out front—the sign is in Hebrew only. The pastries and desserts here are divine: a finger-licking hot apple pie served with ice cream or whipped cream and unbeatable cheesecakes. For something more substantial, try the chicken medallions, served with sauces such as avocado or pesto, or choose a quiche or a salad with fresh fruit and nuts. ✉ *131 Moriyya Blvd.,* ☎ *04/834–1269. AE, DC, MC, V. No dinner Fri.*

$$ ✕ **Taiwan.** This is considered one of the better Chinese restaurants in the city. The chef is from Taiwan, and the restaurant is a family-owned establishment in the German Colony that has been operating for 23 years. House specialties are meat and seafood with satay sauce, and lemon chicken. ✉ *59 Ben-Gurion Blvd.,* ☎ *04/853–2082. Reservations essential Fri. and Sat. AE, DC, MC, V.*

$$ ✕ **Voilà.** This whitewashed hideaway tucked downstairs off the Nor-
★ dau pedestrian mall is an exclusive haunt. The mood is cozy and offbeat—tilted doorways, odd wooden trestle tables, a Bedouin woman's headdress hung with British soldiers' dog tags, flowering pots, dolls, decorative pieces from churches, and Oriental rugs. Inside are only eight tables, but the garden enclosure is heated during winter. Famous for its fondues (beef, cheese, and chocolate varieties), the restaurant also prides itself on its beef fillet with port sauce and goose-liver pâté. A welcome accompaniment is another house specialty, the traditional Swiss potato dish called *roesti.* For dessert, don't miss the ice cream–filled crepes draped with wild blackberry or raspberry sauce. Less expensive three-course business lunches—for NIS 48 ($16) and NIS 67 ($22.50)—are available noon–4. ✉ *21A Nordau St.,* ☎ *04/866–4529. Reservations essential. AE, DC, MC, V.*

$ ✕ **Shishkebab.** You'll find lots of locals slipping in for down-home kosher Middle Eastern food here in the German Colony. There is a no-nonsense approach to the quick service and decor (Formica tables and chairs). Shishkebab is famous for its high-quality grilled meats, arrayed on skewers in a small glass counter by the entrance. Don't balk at sharing a table; it's customary here. Also available are Middle Eastern salads and *kube* soup (ground beef dumplings, often with pine nuts or raisins, rolled in cracked wheat and floating in a consommé). Aromatic coffee is served in tiny cups with cardamom. ✉ *59 Ben-Gurion Ave.,* ☎ *04/852–7576. Reservations not accepted. No credit cards. Closed Fri.–Sat. and holiday eves.*

Lodging

$$$$ 🏨 **Dan Carmel.** The deluxe rooms on the upper floors of this central Carmel hotel on the slopes of Mt. Carmel really stand out for their sumptuous furnishings, including satin bedspreads and richly stained wooden bureaus. Other doubles aren't as luxurious, but they're cheerfully decorated in pastels and well maintained; all have balconies with views of the city or sea. Also pleasant is the large outdoor garden beside the pool, landscaped with potted plants. The gourmet restaurant, Le Rondo, is a study in fine dining. ⊠ *85–87 Hanassi Ave., 31060,* ☎ *04/830–6211,* FAX *04/838–7504. 219 rooms with bath. Restaurant, café, pool, beauty salon, sauna, exercise room, travel services. AE, DC, MC, V.*

$$$ 🏨 **Dan Panorama.** A member of the Dan hotel chain, this one is glitzier
★   than its sister hotel down the road. The rooms, like the gleaming marble lobby, are spacious and sparkling; the pale blue-and-yellow color scheme, like the furnishings, is low-key. Some rooms look out onto the Baha'i Shrine and the bay. The hotel is connected to the Panorama Center shopping mall, filled with small eateries and boutiques. ⊠ *107 Hanassi Ave., 31060,* ☎ *04/835–2222,* FAX *04/835–2235. 266 rooms with bath. Restaurant, 3 cafés, piano bar, 2 pools, sauna, exercise room, shops, baby-sitting. AE, DC, MC, V.*

$$$ 🏨 **Haifa Tower.** This hotel is in a brand-new 17-floor office tower in the downtown area, a busy shopping district on the old Technion campus. Room sizes are ample and the decor subdued, tasteful, and fresh. All rooms have either a sea or a city view. The breakfast area, which looks out over Haifa Bay, is bright and cheerful. ⊠ *63 Herzl St.,* ☎ *04/867–7111,* FAX *04/862–1863. 96 rooms with bath, 4 with shower. Restaurant, bar. AE, MC, V.*

$$$ 🏨 **Nof.** The rooms in this small pleasant hotel are done in shades of turquoise. Unbeatable here is the location atop Mt. Carmel, with its view of the city spreading down to the sea. The front desk and room service are quick and efficient. The Chinese restaurant and coffee shop also offer superb views. ⊠ *101 Hanassi Ave., 31063,* ☎ *04/835–4311,* FAX *04/838–8810. 93 rooms with bath. Restaurant, bar, café, coffee shop, dance club. AE, DC, MC, V.*

$$$ 🏨 **Shulamit.** A bit off the beaten track, on Mt. Carmel near the Ahuza district, this medium-size hotel is nonetheless surrounded by restaurants and a lively nightlife. It is set in a wooded residential area on a quiet street, with parking spaces right out front. The furnishings are monochromatic, but the service is spirited. ⊠ *15 Kiryat Sefer St., 34676,* ☎ *04/834–2811,* FAX *04/825–5206. 84 rooms with bath. Restaurant, bar. AE, DC, MC, V.*

$$ 🏨 **Beth Shalomi.** Across the street from the city's luxury hotels in cen-
★   tral Carmel, this guest house operated by an evangelical Christian organization gets high points for its prime location. The management runs a tight ship while preserving a family atmosphere, true to the reputation of Swiss-owned hotels around the world. The rooms and lobby are spotless and well maintained, even if the furnishings aren't the most up-to-date. Only reservations for a minimum of three nights are accepted. ⊠ *110 Hanassi Ave., Box 6208, 31061,* ☎ *04/837–7481 or 04/838–3019,* FAX *04/837–2443. 30 rooms with bath. Cafeteria. AE, DC.*

Nightlife and the Arts

For the latest information on performances, festivals, exhibitions, and other special events taking place in and around Haifa, check the 24-hour **What's On** recording (☎ 04/837–4253). For current cultural listings along the coast, pick up the Friday issue of the *Jerusalem Post* or the monthly brochure "Events in Haifa and the Northern Region," available at hotels and Tourist Offices. The following nightspots come and go, so call first; some operate only on certain evenings.

Bars

Some popular gathering spots are **Migdalor** (⊠ At Stella Maris, ☎ 04/833–6292), **Mizpor** (⊠ 115 Yefe Nof St., ☎ 04/837–7577), and **Back Door** (⊠ 120 Yefe Nof St., ☎ 04/837–6183).

Dance Clubs

Among the city's hot spots are **Butterfly** (⊠ 137 Hanassi Ave., ☎ 04/838–8052) and **Shmura** (⊠ 38 Pica Rd., ☎ 04/834–7727).

Downstairs in the basement of Haifa's Dan Panorama Hotel is the **Chaplin Club,** a disco that caters to the thirty-something crowd, especially those nostalgic for 1960s dance music. There's never a cover charge and no minimum on weekdays; on Friday the minimum per person per table is NIS 45 ($15) plus 10% service. The club is open from 10:30 PM to 2 AM daily. On Friday, make a reservation (☎ 04/838–4186).

Film

In October, near the holiday of Sukkoth, Haifa hosts an international **film festival.** Contact the Haifa Cinemateque (☎ 04/838–3424) for the schedule and venues.

Music

A **blues festival** takes place in July in the unusual venue of Haifa's port. For information call 04/837–4010 or check with the TIO (☎ 04/866–6521).

The **Israel Philharmonic Orchestra** gives approximately 30 concerts at the Haifa Auditorium (⊠ 138 Hanassi Ave., ☎ 04/838–0013) from October through July. Although most seats are sold through subscription, some tickets are usually available. Ticket prices range from NIS 75 to NIS 175 ($25–$58.35) and generally are sold only at IPO theater box offices in Haifa (⊠ 16 Herzl St., ☎ 04/866–4167), Jerusalem, and Tel Aviv. Concerts start at 8:30 PM or 9 PM. The box office opens one hour before performances. The **Haifa Symphony Orchestra** also plays at the Haifa Auditorium about four times a week. It's best to buy tickets about 30 minutes before the performance, which generally begins around 8:30 PM. For information check with the box office (⊠ 50 Tezner St., ☎ 04/862–1973). Ticket prices range from NIS 25 to NIS 60 ($8.35–$20).

Outdoor Activities and Sports

Beaches

The coastline south of Haifa is lined with one fine, sandy public beach after another. From north to south, **Carmel, Zamir,** and **Dado beaches** (☎ 04/852–4231) cover 2½ km (1½ mi) of coast and have six lifeguard stations among them. There is no entrance fee and parking is free. These beaches have showers, toilets, and a promenade that connects them. There are also several refreshment stands and seven restaurants. At press time additional Haifa beach developments, including the construction of nearby hotels, are in the planning stages.

Ice Skating

One of the country's few ice-skating rinks (☎ 04/841–5388) can be found in the **Lev Hamifratz shopping center,** in northern Haifa on the road to Akko. The rink is open daily from 10 AM to midnight, but call ahead as practice sessions may take place in the afternoons. Admission, including skate rental, is NIS 22 ($7.35).

Tennis

The public tennis court at **Kfar Samir** (⌧ Kfar Samir St., ☎ 04/852–2721) is close to Hof Dado and Carmel beaches and is open all year, barring bad weather. There are 20 floodlighted courts open Sunday–Thursday 7 AM–10 PM, Friday 7–7, and Saturday 8–6, with more court availability in the morning. Call ahead to book. Rates are NIS 20 ($6.70) during the day and NIS 25 ($8.35) on Friday, Saturday, and after 7.

Shopping

Haifa is studded with modern indoor shopping malls replete with boutiques, small eateries, and movie theaters. **Horev Center,** in the Ahuza district on Horev Street at the intersection of Pica Street, is one of the three main malls. The **Panorama Center** in Central Carmel is adjacent to the Dan Panorama hotel. **Migdal Haneve'im,** in the Hadar district on Khouri Street, is one of the main indoor malls.

The **Nordau Street pedestrian mall** makes for a pleasant stroll amid shops, cafés, and restaurants; it draws a local crowd as well.

Gourmet visitors will appreciate a new shop called **Special Reserve** (⌧ 87 Hanassi St., near the Dan Carmel Hotel, ☎ 04/836–1187), claimed by the owner to be Israel's smallest wine shop, yet with the largest stock. You can try a sample at the counter, and wine-tastings conducted in English are held once a month.

THE ROTHSCHILD WINE COUNTRY AND MT. CARMEL

This is the back-door route to Haifa, one that meanders through the foothills and up the spine of Mt. Carmel through Druze villages. The Druze are an Arabic-speaking people who practice a secret religion. This close-knit and respected minority (just 2% of Israel's population) is one of the most colorful and intriguing parts of the Israeli mosaic. So exclusive is this sect that only around 6% of the community is initiated into its religious doctrine, one tenet of which is a belief in reincarnation. The Druze broke away from Islam about 1,000 years ago, believing in the divinity of their founder, al Hakim bi Amir Allah, the caliph of the Egyptian Fatimid dynasty from AD 996 to 1021.

Route 4 goes smoothly along, with the Carmel looming to the east, through cultivated fields and huge banana plantations (you may not actually see bananas since they're usually bagged in blue or gray plastic). Traveling inland, the road leads through an undulating countryside dotted with cypresses, palms, and vineyards.

Binyamina

⓴ *55 km (34 mi) north of Tel Aviv on Rte. 652.*

Coming from the south, you'll drive through Binyamina, the youngest of the settlements in the area, founded in 1922 and named after Baron Edmond de Rothschild (1845–1934; his Hebrew name was Benyamin), the head of the French branch of the famous family, who took a keen interest in the welfare of his fellow Jews in Palestine. With his contributions, prestige, and vision, Rothschild laid the foundations starting in the late 19th century for three towns along this itinerary as well as others along the coastal plain and in parts of the Upper Galilee.

At least in this region, the advice of viniculture experts Rothschild hired in the 1880s paid off handsomely, and after years of initial adversity and setbacks, the fruits of the vine flourished in the 1890s. The paternalistic system he set up, however, was not without its pitfalls. Some of his administrators ruled his colonies like petty despots: for instance, trying to impose use of the French language despite the desire of the local settlers to speak Hebrew. As in many Rothschild towns, note the unmistakable and respectfully preserved signs of early settlement in Binyamina: the rows of lofty, willowy Washingtonian palms introduced to the area by the local hero and agronomist Aaron Aaronson of neighboring Zichron Ya'akov; and the modest one-story stucco homes capped with red terra-cotta roofs evocative of the charming towns of Provence, which were models for these settlements.

Shuni

㉑ *At railroad tracks in Binyamina, turn left onto Rte. 652, then 1 km (½ mi) north.*

This stone fortress was built by effendis in the 18th and 19th centuries on the site of existing ruins because of their sweeping command over surrounding lands, some planted with grain; *shuni* is Arabic for granary. The surrounding land, the landscaped **Jabotinsky Park,** was part of a parcel purchased by Rothschild in 1914, but its chief attractions today are Shuni (the Ottoman fortress) and the Roman theater; you can also dine in the fortress (☞ *below*). The spring at present-day Shuni was also the source of the spring water that was tapped for the aqueducts of ancient Caesarea. In the 1930s and '40s, because of its remote location, the site was chosen as a training ground for members of self-organized units inspired by Ze'ev Jabotinsky (1880–1940), the right-wing Zionist leader who was the spiritual leader of the Jewish underground organization Irgun Zvai Leumi; armed Irgun units later launched attacks from here.

Excavations of the **Roman theater** have brought to light the remains of bathing pools lined with 2nd-century Roman mosaics and a marble statue of the Greek god of medicine, Aesculapius, both now in storage at the Rockefeller Museum in Jerusalem. These finds support the theory that this was once a sacred spa whose waters had healing powers. Indeed, an early 4th century pilgrim mentioned in his writings that women who bathed here always became pregnant, like it or not. On the right, before entering the fortress, you can still see part of a mosaic floor. An ancient olive press, carved lintels, and fragments of columns lie in the well-preserved 2nd-century Roman theater, entered through the fortress. Call ahead to arrange for a guided tour of the site. ⊠ *Rte. 652,* ☎ *06/638–9730.* ⊡ *Fortress and theater: NIS 4 ($1.35).* ☉ *Sun.–Thurs. 9–4, Fri. and holiday eves 9–12:30.*

OFF THE BEATEN PATH

RAMAT HANADIV – Literally "the Benefactor's Heights" and also known as Rothschild Memorial Gardens, Ramat Hanadiv is the splendid setting for the tomb of the baron and his wife, the baroness Adelaide. Set on 1,112 acres of parkland, the stunning gardens that surround the family crypt lie 2 km (1¼ mi) up an unpaved road with memorable views of the Sharon Plain you just left behind. Over the wrought-iron gateway to the garden is the family coat of arms, a bronze shield supported by a gilded lion and unicorn, capped by a coronet. Inside, the well-tended gardens are filled with a mixture of indigenous and foreign flora. Cedars of Lebanon and cypresses grow on lawns interspersed with rose and palm gardens. On the western edge is a panoramic view of Caesarea and Hadera to the south and Dor and the fish ponds of Kibbutz Ma'agan Michael to the north; a stone map marks the regional settlements founded or sponsored by the baron. The Rothschilds' wish to be buried here was carried out only after the Jewish state was established;

in 1954, an Israeli warship brought their remains from France. Opposite
the exit is a refreshment kiosk and picnic tables. A map is available and
marks several hikes that begin here, some with great views of the coast.
⊠ *3½ km (2¼ mi) east of Shuni,* ☎ *06/639-7821.* ☑ *Free.* ☉
Sun.–Thurs. 8–4, Fri. and holiday eves 8–2, Sat. 8–4.

Dining

$$$ ✕ **Shuni Castle.** The setting alone—a few upper rooms in the stone fortress
★   with views of Israel's wine country—is memorable. Add to that the coun-
try charm of artfully arranged baskets of red peppers and dried sausage
laid out beside chubby loaves of homemade bread under hanging pots
of trailing vines, and you've got a winner. The view's divine from the
three tables on the patio, so you'd do well to call ahead and request
one. In keeping with the informal style (chef Antoine likes to banter with
regular customers), there's no written menu, but you can expect to find
some of the following: leg of duck with honey and fruit, *boeuf bour-
guignon* with mushrooms, veal with white wine and artichokes, and
braised entrecôte with peppers and tomatoes. Local red and white
wines are served, or you can ask for the Riesling from Antoine's vine-
yard. ⊠ *In Jabotinsky Park just off Rte. 652, 1 km (½ mi) north of
Binyamina,* ☎ *06/638–0227. Reservations essential. DC, V. Closed Sun.*

Zichron Ya'akov

★ ㉒   *5 km (3 mi) north of Shuni, 61 km (36½ mi) north of Tel Aviv.*

At the planted roundabout is the entrance to Zichron Ya'akov, named
by the original settlers in honor of Rothschild's father, James. Just op-
posite is a Tourist Information Office, next to the Founders' Monu-
ment and the Central Bus Station. Here you can obtain a map of the
town; most of the main sites are signposted in English.

Founded in 1882 by Romanian pioneers, this settlement nearly foundered
until rescued by Edmond de Rothschild. A decade later, the town's win-
ery took off, the same **Carmel Wine Cellars** that can be reached by veer-
ing to the right from the traffic circle and driving up Jabotinsky Street.
Where the street ends, turn right on Hanadiv Street. Today, the win-
ery is the nation's second largest, producing more than 80 kinds of wines
and spirits. A three-day wine festival takes place here after the harvest,
around the time of the Jewish holiday of Sukkoth. The original stor-
age vats and oak barrels are still on view, but storage is now mostly
in stainless-steel vats and concrete tanks. A guided tour follows the stages
of local wine production—the winery uses a computerized fermenta-
tion system and automated bottling lines—from the weighing in of trac-
tors laden with grapes to grape pressing and the aging of wine in
caves. The 75-minute tour includes a wine tasting of some five vari-
eties and an audiovisual presentation that is frankly so rudimentary it
might have you yawning *before* you taste the wine. The first tour—
tours leave whenever there's a large enough group—starts at 9 AM and
the last at 3 PM. You'll find a much better selection of wine sold here
than in wine stores elsewhere, and you get a 15% discount. The finest
wines are the Rothschild vintages of cabernet sauvignon, sauvignon
blanc, and *fume blanc.* Locally made gin, vodka, and brandy are also
available. ⊠ *Hanadiv St.,* ☎ *06/639–1241; call for reservations.* ☑
NIS 12 ($4). ☉ *Sun.–Thurs. 9–3, Fri. 9–12:30.*

Hameyasdim Street, the town's main street, starts at the Founders' Mon-
ument. To get here from the wine cellar, retrace your steps back up
Jabotinsky Street to the traffic circle at the entrance to town. Zichron
Ya'akov townspeople have made every effort to keep the short thor-

oughfare looking as it did originally—you'll see many small, red-roofed homes built in 100-year-old style on the cobblestone street. In those days, people needed courtyards behind their homes to house animals, carts, and farm equipment. Several of these have been fixed up and look exactly as they did long ago, except now they house small eateries, crafts shops, and offbeat clothing stores.

The late-19th-century architecture of **Bet Aaronson** (Aaronson's House), about midway down Hameyasdim Street, is a successful combination of art nouveau and Middle Eastern traditions. This museum was once the home of the accomplished agronomist Aaron Aaronson (1876–1919), who gained international fame for his discovery of an ancestor of modern wheat, a wild and hardy strain that grew in the surrounding mountains. The house is preserved as it was after World War I, with family photographs and French and Turkish furniture. The museum also houses the library, diaries, and letters of Aaronson, who in his youth was sent to France by Rothschild to study agriculture.

Aaronson and his sisters became local heroes as leaders of the spy ring called the NILI (an acronym for a quote from the Book of Samuel: "The Eternal One of Israel will not prove false"), a militant group dedicated to ousting the hated Turks from Palestine by collaborating with the British during World War I. They were spurred on by the harshness of such Turkish policies as the expulsion of Russian Jews from Palestine (the Russians were enemies of the Turks during World War I) and the confiscation of Jewish property.

Both sisters, Sarah and Rebecca, were in love with Aaron's assistant, Absalom Feinberg. A double agent was disrupting NILI's communications with the British, so Feinberg set off to cross the Sinai Desert to make contact. He was killed in an ambush in the Gaza Strip. His remains were recovered some 50 years later from a grave marked only by a palm tree that had sprouted from some dates in Feinberg's pockets (after the Six-Day War, Feinberg's body was reburied in Jerusalem). Sarah Aaronson was captured by the Turks and subsequently committed suicide in her brother's house after being tortured. Other NILI leaders were executed by the Turks when they discovered the secret organization. Aaron returned to Zichron Ya'akov with the victorious British in 1918, but the following year his plane mysteriously vanished while en route from London to the Paris peace conference. ⊠ *40 Hameyasdim St.,* ☎ *06/639–0120.* 🎟 *NIS 6 ($2).* 🕐 *Sun.–Thurs. 8:30–1, Tues. 3:30–5:30, Fri. 9–noon.*

Binyamin Pool, a few doors up from Bet Aaronson on Hameyasdim Street, is actually the town's water tower, built in 1891. Zichron was the first village to have water piped to its houses. Meir Dizengoff, first mayor of Tel Aviv, came to town to see how it was done. Its facade resembles that of an ancient synagogue. At the corner of Hanadiv and Meyasdim Streets stands the actual town synagogue, **Bet Ya'akov,** built in 1885 to fulfill the settlers' first request to Rothschild. Hanadiv Street has a children's park and the **former town hall.** Commissioned by Rothschild, this is a fine example of late-19th-century Ottoman-style architecture in white stone, with a central pediment capped by a tile roof. The building is being restored as a museum dedicated to the town's first pioneers.

NEED A BREAK? An inviting venue in which to relax and watch the action in a rural town is **Tnuva b'Moshava** (⊠ Hameyasdim and Hanadiv Sts.). At the main crossroads in town, this vegetarian streetside café offers in-season fresh fruit drinks (try mango or peach), ice cream, high-rise cakes, and a wide choice of light meals.

Bet Daniel (Daniel's House)—a small cluster of one- and two-story buildings—is a tranquil oasis for writers, musicians, and artists, set in the woods on the western edge of town, with a wonderful view of the Carmel coast. Lillian Friedlander built the retreat in 1938, after the death of her son Daniel, a highly gifted pianist. The child prodigy was sent to study at the Juilliard School in New York, where he committed suicide at the age of 18.

Today, Bet Daniel remains a setting for concerts, music classes, and workshops, in addition to being a public guest house (☞ Dining and Lodging, *below*). Daniel's 1905 Steinway from New York still stands in the dining room, and the closely guarded guest roster bears such illustrious names as Isaac Stern, Leonard Bernstein, Aaron Copland, and Arturo Toscanini. A chamber music festival is held twice a year in a small concert hall on the grounds (☞ Nightlife and the Arts, *below*). To get here, turn right off Hanadiv Street into Herzl Street, then left into Habroshim Street. ⊠ *Habroshim St.,* ☎ *06/639–9001.*

Dining and Lodging

$$$ ✕ **Aroma.** Up the hill from the winery and right in the heart of town, this charming restaurant has a sophisticated menu and an old-fashioned setting. There's a small wood-paneled bar, and peach-color walls are hung with paintings of the surrounding countryside. The floor is terracotta, and 18th-century implements used by the pioneers who settled Zikron are used as decoration. On the menu are French-style meat dishes, fish, and seafood. Start with marinated calamari heads, then move on to selections such as beef fillet, smoked trout, or shrimp with capers and lemon. For dessert, try marzipan parfait or homemade apple pie. ⊠ *66 Hameyasdim St.,* ☎ *06/639–0728. Reservations essential. AE, DC, V. Closed Sun.*

$$$ ▦ **The Baron's Heights and Terraces.** Spread over the hillside on 14 terraced levels, this hotel is designed with modern, clean, geometric lines. The rooms are furnished in pastel color schemes, with a combination of terra-cotta tiles and carpeting, a separate living area and a kitchenette; each has a terrace with a view. A specially designed mountain elevator was installed to reach all levels. The pool, alongside the large coffee shop, is on the 15th floor, overlooking the blue sea. ⊠ *Box 332, Zichron Ya'akov, 30900,* ☎ *06/639–3900,* ☒ *06/639–3930. 154 rooms with bath. Restaurant, bar, café, pools, hot tub, sauna, steam room, exercise room, children's programs. AE, DC, MC, V.*

$$$ ▦ **Bet Maimon.** On the western slopes of Zichron Ya'akov, this family-run hotel offers a spectacular view of the coastal valley and the sea. The terrace restaurant serves both Middle Eastern and Eastern European cuisine. Inquire about the special health-vacation packages. Guests who are less than fit will feel the climb to the sundeck on the roof—there's no elevator in this three-story lodging. ⊠ *4 Zahal St., 30900,* ☎ *06/639–0212,* ☒ *06/639–6547. 22 rooms with bath. Restaurant, hot tub, sauna. DC, MC, V.*

$$$ ▦ **Radisson Moriah Gardens.** From an existing building, which now houses the guest rooms, a new hotel was fashioned. A large and very contemporary wing houses the public rooms, and it's surrounded by trees and gardens, on a mountainside 1 km from Zichron Ya'akov. The site provides stunning views of the Mediterranean coast. The public rooms are decorated beautifully, using off-white heavy wooden furniture, plumped with seat covers and lots of pillows covered in white with designs of blue, brown, or beige. Polished stone floors set off the ultramodern decor, and there's an outdoor terrace with a waterfall splashing down the slope of the hill to a pool below. The hotel is designed for conventions, but the public areas are so large and spread out that

a crowd of people would probably not disturb guests. The rooms (reached by 10 steps) are functional though not fancy, and each has a smashing view. ⊠ *Western entrance to Zichron Ya'akov, 1 Etzion St., 30900,* ☎ *06/630-0111,* ℻ *06/639-7030. 112 rooms with bath. Lobby lounge, pool, massage. AE, DC, MC, V.*

$$ 🏠 **Bet Daniel.** Set in a verdant park on Mt. Carmel, this guest house was founded in 1938 as a retreat for musicians. Gradually, its guests also included artists and writers; today it is open to the public. Those who place a premium on quiet and charm will love it. In the living room stands a 1905 Steinway and other antiques brought from England. Old photographs hang on the walls, and the library is well stocked, with books in German, Yiddish, French, and Hebrew. Rooms in two stone buildings have been newly redecorated in the style of the 1930s. The Summer House has several apartments, each accommodating four guests. If you want to stay here during the biannual chamber music festival (☞ Nightlife and the Arts, *below*), reserve well in advance. Good home cooking is available under various meal-plan options. ⊠ *Box 13, Habroshim St., 30900,* ☎ *06/639-9001,* ℻ *06/639-7007. 14 rooms, most with bath. V.*

Nightlife and the Arts

The pastoral retreat for musicians and artists at **Bet Daniel** (☎ 06/639-9001) is a perfect setting for the two **chamber music festivals** held here during the Jewish holidays of Sukkoth and Passover, which generally fall in October and April, respectively. The programs feature open rehearsals and discussions by musicians and teachers as well as alternating afternoon and evening concerts. In between concerts, guests can walk around the lovely landscaped grounds set in the woods, with a fine view of Mt. Carmel. Book well in advance.

Bat Shlomo

㉓ *5 km (3 mi) northeast of Zichron Ya'akov on Rte. 70.*

Bat Shlomo was established in 1889 and named after Baron Edmond de Rothschild's mother, Betty, the daughter of Solomon ("bat Shlomo," in Hebrew). This tiny hamlet established for the children of Zichron Ya'akov farmers failed to grow, and the town remains virtually unchanged. There is only one street in the old part of the village; it's a charming stroll past small, square houses with red-tile roofs, the space between them enough room for a farmer's horse and wagon. The old synagogue is in the middle of the street. A few of the owners still cultivate the land and sell locally made cheese, olive oil, and honey (some for sale), much like their forebears. The short walk ends with a dramatic view of vineyards below and, opposite, the lushly forested hill, established as a nature reserve in 1941 by the British.

Mukhraka

㉔ *18 km (11 mi) from Bat Shlomo, off Rte. 672.*

Past open, uncultivated fields and a goatherd's rickety shack is the **Carmelite Monastery** at Mukhraha. This monastery stands on the spur of the Carmel Range, at an altitude of almost 1900 feet, on or near the site where tradition has it that the struggle between Elijah and the priests of Ba'al took place. *Mukhraka* is the Arabic word for a place of burning, referring to the fire that consumed the offering on Elijah's altar. The conflict developed because the people of Israel had been seduced by pagan cults introduced by King Ahab's wife, Jezebel. Elijah demanded a contest with the priests of Ba'al in which each would erect an altar with a butchered ox as an offering and see which divinity sent down fire. Elijah drenched his altar with water, yet it burst into flames. On his orders, the priests were taken down to the Brook of Kishon and executed.

The stark stone monastery was built in 1883 over earlier Byzantine ruins. Records show the site was revered as early as the 6th century, when hermits dwelled here. The Carmelites, a Roman Catholic monastic order established in the 13th century, view Elijah as a role model for their monks (Muslims and Jews also honor Elijah as a prophet). Today, the monks who live here have no telephones and only a generator for power. In the courtyard is a statue of a fearless Elijah brandishing a knife. Climb to the roof of the monastery for an unforgettable panorama: To the east stretches the Jezreel Valley and the hills of Nazareth, Moreh, and Gilboa. On a clear day you can even see the Gilead Mountains beyond the Jordan River and Mt. Hermon. To get here from Bat Shlomo, go 7 km (4¼ mi) north on Route 70 to Elyakim Junction; turn left onto Route 672. Drive north 8 km (5 mi); bumpy road continues 3 km (2 mi) to east. ⊠ *Off Rte. 672. No phone.* ☏ *NIS 1 (35¢).* ☽ *Mon.–Sat. 8–1:30 and 2:30–5. Closed Sun. after noon mass.*

Daliyat el Carmel

㉕ *2 km (1¼ mi) west of Mukhraka (at junction with Rte. 672).*

The largest Druze village in Israel is Daliyat el Carmel. The Druze who live in the two existing villages on Mt. Carmel (the second is Isfiya; ☞ *below*) serve in the Israeli army, a sign of their loyalty to Israel. Though many of the younger generation wear jeans and T-shirts, some older men and women are easily recognizable in their traditional garb. Head coverings indicate the degree of religious belief, from high white turban (resembling a fez) to white kerchief covering the head and shoulders. Many men sport a bushy, walruslike mustache, a hallmark of the Druze, and some older men wear flowing dark robes and black pantaloons. Although many women wear Western garments, they retain the diaphanous white headdress, often worn with an embroidered dress.

About 1 km (½ mi) inside town, take a right turn into the marketplace, a colorful jumble of shops lining the street. You can be assured to eat excellent falafel at any of the roadside stands or restaurants.

Shopping

Along a brief stretch of the main road that winds through Daliyat el Carmel are shops that sell light throw rugs, handwoven baskets, brightly colored pottery, brass dishes, characteristic woven wall hangings, and embroidered skullcaps (worn by men). Bargaining is expected. Some shops close on Friday, and the area is crowded on Saturday.

Isfiya

㉖ *1 km (½ mi) north of Daliyat el Carmel on Rte. 672.*

Isfiya (also spelled Ussifiya) is very similar to its neighbor, Daliyat el Carmel. Both have flat-roofed homes built closely together into the hillside, many of them raised on pillars, with arched windows. Hospitality is second nature to the Druze. You may visit a village home and watch as the woman of the house bakes crispy-thin pita in the courtyard, then eat her work with yogurt cheese and spices and hear about Druze life while seated on an ornate sofa in the living room (☞ Guided Tours *in* Northern Coast and Western Galilee A to Z, *below*). As you leave the village at the top of the hill, note the vista of the Jezreel Valley suddenly opening on your right. The final approach to Haifa also affords a magnificent view of the coast that stretches from Akko across the bay to south of the city.

Dining

$$$$ ✕ **Pine Club Restaurant.** This restaurant, nestled in the woods at the
★ crest of Mt. Carmel, is one of the region's finest. You'll dine in a glass-enclosed pavilion, where the fireplace is always stoked in winter. Fresh flowers and crisp white linen match the French-inspired cuisine in elegance. Try the local venison with sour-cherry sauce or rabbit cooked in stock and served with artichoke hearts. Dessert lovers will swoon over the dark-chocolate and white-chocolate mousses. ⊠ *On road to Bet Oren near Damon Jail,* ☎ *04/832–3568. Reservations essential. AE, DC, MC. Closed Sun. No lunch Mon.–Fri.*

$–$$ ✕ **Nof Carmel.** Don't bother to look for an English-language sign to
★ identify this Druze establishment. Instead, watch for the unfailingly familiar red Coca-Cola symbol overhead after driving to the northern edge of the village; it will be on your left encircled by a picket fence. Diners come for the fine Middle Eastern fare, especially the thick homemade hummus with pine nuts or *foule* (a baked broad-bean concoction seasoned with oil, garlic, and lemon juice) and well-seasoned kebabs. Those with a sweet tooth will want to sample the scale-bending baklava or the *sahlab* (a warm winter drink—like a liquid custard of crushed orchid bulb, thickened with milk, sweetened with sugar, and topped with raisins, almonds, or cinnamon). ⊠ *Rte. 672,* ☎ *04/839–1718. No reservations. AE, MC, V.*

Ein Hod

❷❼ *5 km (3 mi) west of Isfiya.*

Today the artists' village of Ein Hod is home to around 135 families of sculptors, painters, and other artists. The setting is an idyllic one, with rough-hewn stone houses built on the hillside with sweeping views. As the Dadaist painter Marcel Janco (1895–1984) wrote of the deserted Arab village slated for demolition after his first trip there, in 1950: "The beauty of the place was staggering." Though the place was ruled by scorpions and snakes and was without water or electricity, Janco and a group of 20 artists set up a colony here two years later. To get here from Isfiya, take Route 672; turn left (west) on Route 721. At Route 4, turn left (south). The exit for Ein Hod will be on your left. You can also take Bus 921 or Bus 202 from Haifa.

The town square is bordered by a restaurant and a large **gallery** where works by present and past Ein Hod artists are exhibited (☞ Shopping, *below*). The **Janco-Dada Museum,** near the town square, recognizes the contributions of one of the founders of the dadaist movement. The Romanian-born Janco had a well-established professional reputation when he immigrated to Israel in 1941. The museum, which opened in 1983, houses a permanent collection of works in various media by the artist, reflecting Janco's output in both Europe and Israel. A 20-minute slide show chronicles the life of the artist and the dadaist movement. Also exhibited are works by other Israeli modern artists. Don't miss the view from the rooftop. ⊠ *Town square,* ☎ *04/984–2350.* 🎟 *NIS 5 ($1.70).* ⊙ *Sun.–Thurs. and Sat 9:30–5, Fri. and holiday eves 9:30–4.*

From the town square, walk up the stone staircase that skirts the restaurant to a ruined building with an old olive press. It leads to the Ein Hod's open-air **theater,** where summer concerts are held (☞ Nightlife and the Arts, *below*). Paths branch off to artists' studios and homes on a lovely walk along the road that encircles the village.

Dining

$$ ✕ **Ein Hod Restaurant.** This rustic place is in the heart of the quaint village. At wooden tables beside arched windows or outside on a stone patio, choose from the restaurant's specialties: stuffed vegetables, soups, Greek kebab with pine nuts, or steak with mustard or pepper sauce. Salads are also available, as are desserts such as fresh fruit and homemade cakes. ✉ *Town square,* ☎ *04/984–2016. Reservations not accepted. No credit cards.*

Nightlife and the Arts

For chamber music Saturday evenings at 6:30, try **Ein Hod's Gertrud Kraus House** (☎ 04/984–1058), just off the central square of this artists' community. There are no performances in July, August, and September. Admission is NIS 27 ($9), and coffee and cake are on the house.

Also in Ein Hod, the outdoor stone **theater** (☎ 04/984–2029) at the top of the hill resonates with music every Friday night from June to September. This theater features mostly quality pop, classical, and jazz performances by local performers. Tickets can be bought in advance on the second floor of the Gallery (☞ *below*) in town.

Shopping

The best place in the region to find a wide range of quality handicrafts is at the **Gallery** (☎ 04/984–2548), on Ein Hod's main square. You can also buy directly from the artisans at various workshops in the village. Arrayed in the front room of the village's official gallery are silver, enamel, and gold jewelry; handblown glass; and ceramic jugs, mugs, and teapots. Three rooms are devoted to paintings, watercolors, sculptures, and graphic works by the town's resident artists, some of them internationally known. Tourists can ask for a small discount. The Gallery is open Sunday–Thursday and Saturday 9:30–5, Friday and holidays 9:30–4.

An Israeli fine art photography gallery, **Silver Print** (✉ 4-minute walk from town square, ☎ 04/984–1067), is run by Vivienne and Roy Silver. A sideline here is greeting cards, some of which are old photos of the Holy Land. They also sell (NIS 15, or $5) a map with a walking tour of the village and stickers with photos of the 18 sights along the way.

Nahal Me'arot Nature Reserve

28 *3 km (2 mi) south of Ein Hod, 1 km (½ mi) east of Rte. 4.*

You can allot time to hike in this verdant, hilly reserve. Major attractions at Nahal Me'arot are the prehistoric **Carmel Caves.** Three excavated caves are beyond a steep flight of stairs, on a fossil reef that was under the sea 100 million years ago. The first discoveries of prehistoric remains were made when this area was being scoured for stones to build the Haifa port. In the late 1920s, the first archaeological expedition was headed by Dorothy Garrod of England, who received assistance from a British feminist group on the condition the dig be carried out exclusively by women. It was. In Tannur Cave, the first on the tour, Garrod's team excavated spanning about 150,000 years in the life of early humans. The most exciting discovery in the area were the remains of Homo sapien and Neanderthal skeletons; such evidence that both lived here has raised fascinating questions about the relationship between the two and whether they lived side by side. The daily life of early humans as hunters and food gatherers is displayed in Gamal Cave.

The last cave you will visit, Nahal, is the largest—cutting deep into the hillside—and was actually the first discovered. A burial place with

84 skeletons was found outside the mouth of the cave, where you can see a hunched-up skeleton. The bone artifacts and stone tools discovered in Nahal Cave suggest that people who settled here, about 12,000 years ago, were the forebears of early farmers, with a modified social structure more developed than that of hunters and gatherers. There is also evidence that the Crusaders once used the cave to guard the coastal road. Inside, an audiovisual show sheds light on how early humans in the area lived. There's a snack bar and parking lot at this site. ⊠ *Off Rte. 4,* ☎ *04/984–1750 or 04/984–1752.* ☎ *NIS 12 ($4).* ☺ *Sat.–Thurs. and holidays 8–4, Fri. and holiday eves 8–1.*

At the entrance to the Carmel Caves is the stone-built office of the **Nature Reserves Authority** (☎ 04/984–1750), where trained staff members provide maps and information about two well-marked nature walks that depart from this point. The Botanical Path walk takes 2 hours, while the Geological Path takes 40 minutes; both include specially built lookout points.

WESTERN GALILEE

The sights in this region encompass many eras in the country's history and much natural beauty. To the south, on the coast, is the historic city of Akko; to the north are Nahariya, the area's earliest Jewish settlement, and the spectacular cliffs and grottoes of Rosh Hanikra, near the border with Lebanon. Inland are the fortresses of Montfort and Castle Judin, reminders of the many nations who have battled here.

Akko (Acre)

22 km (13½ mi) north of Haifa.

Akko, with its enchanting mixture of mosques, markets, khans, and vaulted Crusader ruins, is at the northern tip of Haifa Bay. You approach the Old City on Weizman Street, proceeding through a breach in the surrounding walls. Once inside, park at the Knights' parking lot, where you'll start a walking tour (the circular route brings you back to your car). Plan on at least two hours here or half a day if you want to include everything.

You can approach Akko from Haifa on Route 4. A much slower but far prettier route to Akko takes you north on Route 70. This scenic drive runs roughly parallel to Route 4, about 7 km (4¼ mi) to the east through rolling hills and Arab villages, avoiding the unattractive industrial pockets and drab satellite towns of Haifa. Continue north past a small jog in the road, about 10 km (6¼ mi) ahead. Take Route 85 west some 14 km (8¾ mi) to Akko's Old City.

Numbers in the margin correspond to points of interest on the Akko Old City map.

You enter the **Old City** at its walls. History clings to the stones of old Akko; each twist and turn along its warren of streets tells another tale. The city's history begins 4,000 years ago, when Akko was first mentioned in Egyptian writings that refer to the mound, or tel, northeast of the walls on which you stand. Judges 1 of the Old Testament explains that, after the death of Joshua, the tribe of Asher was unable to drive the Canaanite inhabitants from Akko and so lived among them. Akko was a prize worth fighting for throughout the course of history. It had a well-protected harbor, a well-watered and fertile hinterland, and a strategic position on the coastal road that links Egypt and Phoenicia (present-day Lebanon). In the 4th century BC, Akko eclipsed

Tyre and Sidon as the principal port of the eastern Mediterranean. Alexander the Great's high regard for Akko is apparent in the mint he established there in the 3rd century BC; it remained in operation for six centuries. For long periods Akko was a Phoenician city, but when the Hellenistic king Ptolemy II of Egypt gained control of the country in the 2nd century BC, he renamed it Ptolemaïs, the name it retained through the Roman and Byzantine periods.

㉙ Climb the signposted blue-railing stairway at the entrance to the Old City for a stroll on the **ramparts.** Walking right you can see the stunted remains of the 12th-century walls built by the Crusaders, under whose brief rule—just under two centuries—Akko flourished as never before or since. The indelible signs of the Crusaders, who made Akko the main port of their Christian empire, are much more evident inside the Old City itself.

The wide wall on which you are walking girds the northern part of the town and was built by Ahmed el-Jazzar, the pasha of Akko, who added these fortifications following his victory over Napoléon's army in 1799. With the help of the British fleet, which sunk the French heavy artillery sent by sea, el-Jazzar turned Napoléon's attempted conquest into a humiliating rout. Napoléon had dreamed of founding a new empire in the East, thrusting northward from Akko to Turkey and then seizing India from Great Britain. His defeat at Akko hastened his retreat to France, thus changing the course of history.

Walk around to the guard towers and up an incline just opposite; there's a commanding view of the moat below and Haifa across the bay. Turn around and let your gaze settle on the exotic skyline of Old Akko, the sea green dome of the great mosque its dominating feature. Walk down the ramp, crossing the **Moat Garden** at the base of the walls, and continue alongside the round arches on the backside of **Shuk el Abiad** (White Market). This market was built by Dahr el-Omar, the Bedouin sheikh who defied Turkish rule and set up his own fiefdom in the Galilee in the 18th century. In 1749 he moved his capital from Tiberias to Akko and rebuilt the walls of the city. Dahr el-Omar's rule here ended more than four centuries of desolation and isolation that had beset Akko after the Mamluks drove the Crusaders out in 1291. He rebuilt the port and also built access roads to the city. Continue along a pedestrian walkway, with a bank on your right. Turn right after the bank into a large square with stalls and outdoor eateries. On your left at the top of a short flight of stairs you will see a mosque.

★ **㉚** The **El-Jazzar Mosque** is one of the most beautiful in Israel. Ahmed el-Jazzar, who succeeded Dahr el-Omar simply by having him assassinated, ruled Akko from 1775 to 1804. During his reign he built this mosque along with other public structures. The Albanian adventurer's cruelty was so legendary he earned the epithet "the Butcher." (He is buried next to his adopted son in a small white building to the right of the mosque.)

Just beyond the entrance, in the middle of the courtyard, is a pedestal mounted with a marble reproduction of a seal. Engraved with graceful calligraphy, it re-creates the seal of a 19th-century Ottoman sultan. Some of the marble and granite columns that adorn the mosque and courtyard were plundered from the ruins of Caesarea. On your left is the entrance to the underground **reservoir;** the ornate fountain with eight slender columns opposite the entrance to the mosque is used by the faithful for ritual washings of hands and feet. Bordering the courtyard are outbuildings once used as a religious school. Inside the mosque, enshrined in the gallery reserved for women, is a reliquary containing

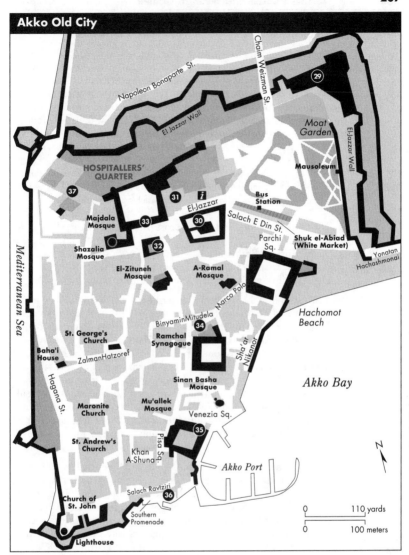

Akko Old City

Chaim Weizman St.

Napoleon Bonaparte St.

El Jazzar Wall

Moat Garden

El Jazzar Wall

Mausoleum

HOSPITALLERS' QUARTER

37

31

i

Bus Station

El-Jazzar

Majdala Mosque

33

30

Salach E Din St.

Shuk el-Abiad (White Market)

Shazalia Mosque

32

Parchi Sq.

Yonatan Hachashmonai

Mediterranean Sea

El-Zituneh Mosque

A-Ramal Mosque

Marco Polo

Hachomot Beach

St. George's Church

BinyaminMitudela

34

Ramchal Synagogue

Baha'i House

ZalmanHatzoref

Sha'ar Nikanor

Akko Bay

Sinan Basha Mosque

Hagana St.

Maronite Church

Mu'allek Mosque

Venezia Sq.

St. Andrew's Church

Pisa Sq.

35

Khan A-Shuna

Akko Port

Church of St. John

Salach Ravtziri

36

Southern Promenade

Lighthouse

N

0   110 yards
0   100 meters

Crusader Vaults and Halls, **31**
El-Jazzar Mosque, **30**
Khan el-Umdan, **35**
Museum of the Underground Prisoners, **37**
Pisan Harbor, **36**

Ramparts, **29**
Refectory, **33**
Souk, **34**
Turkish bath, **32**

a hair believed to be from the beard of the prophet Muhammad; it is removed only once a year, on the 27th day of Ramadan.

The reservoir dates from the Crusader period and was actually a cathedral until converted into cisterns by Ahmed el-Jazzar. You can traverse the cavernous depths on a wooden walkway (keep an eye on children, who like this path). The cisterns still fill with rainwater. Since the mosque is a functioning mosque, it closes five times a day for prayers, necessitating a short wait for visitors, who should dress modestly. ⊠ *Off El-Jazzar St., in square opposite entrance to Crusader Vaults and Halls.* ☎ *NIS 1.50 (50¢).* ⊘ *Sat.–Thurs. 8–5, Fri. 8–11 and 1–5.*

NEED A BREAK?
In the central plaza outside the mosque are several outdoor restaurants where you can enjoy falafel or just a pita with coffee or freshly squeezed orange juice while sunning yourself or watching the world go by.

③ The **Crusader Vaults and Halls,** across from the El-Jazzar Mosque, are one of the Old City's highlights. Your ticket provides admittance to the ☞ **Turkish Bath** and ☞ **Refectory** as well, so hang on to it. You can obtain brochures and maps here as well, and the Tourist Information Office staff is helpful (there's also a post office along one wall).

You will tour a 12th-century subterranean city, above which are the buildings of today, constructed in the 18th and 19th centuries. Deep inside, after following the arrows that take you past fragments of marble capitals, you arrive in the **Knights' Halls,** a series of barrel-vaulted rooms, one of which is sometimes used for chamber concerts. Six such halls have been discovered so far. Above this part of the Crusader city stands an Ottoman **citadel,** which you can glimpse from the courtyard. Raised by Dahr el-Omar on the rubble-filled Crusader ruins, the citadel was the highest structure in Akko. It was later converted by the British into a prison (☞ the Museum of the Underground Prisoners, *below*). Archaeologists are always busy delving deep into the mysteries of Akko, but signs are posted to direct you to current excavation sites.

The Crusaders who conquered Akko in 1104 were led by King Baldwin I and assisted by the Genoese fleet. The principal link to their homeland was the port city, renamed by the victorious French Hospitallers, the Knights of St. John, for their patron saint, Jean d'Acre. Commerce thrived, and the European maritime powers of Genoa, Pisa, Venice, and Marseilles developed separate quarters here. After the disastrous defeat of the Crusader armies at the Horns of Hattin in 1187, Akko surrendered to the victorious Saladin without a fight. But four years later, Richard the Lionhearted of England recaptured the Crusader stronghold. In the 13th century, Akko became the effective capital of a shrunken Latin kingdom after the fall of Jerusalem to the Moslems. During its Crusader heyday, Akko boasted about 40 churches and monasteries, and its population swelled to 50,000. Today, its residents number 45,000, with an ethnic mix of Jews and Arabs.

The seeds of the Crusaders' downfall in Akko were probably sown by the divisive factions that held sway within its walls. The Hospitallers and Templars, the so-called fighting monks, each had their own quarters (the Templars, also French, lived near the lighthouse by the western Crusader seawall). By the mid-13th century, open fighting broke out between the Venetians and the Genoese. When the Mamluks attacked with a vengeance in 1291, the Crusaders' resistance quickly crumbled. The city's devastation was complete, and it remained so for centuries. Yet even today, Akko retains a medieval cast. ⊠ *Opposite the El-Jazaar Mosque,* ☎ *04/991–1764.* ☎ *Knights' Halls, Turkish Bath, and Refectory: NIS 8 ($2.70).* ⊘ *Oct.–Mar., Sun.–Thurs. 8:30–*

5, Fri. 8:30–2, Sat. 8–3; Apr.–Sept., Sun.–Thurs. 8:30–7, Fri. 8:30–2, Sat. 8–5.

★ ㉜ The remarkable **Turkish Bath,** built for Pasha el-Jazzar in 1781, was in use until 1947, when it was damaged by the explosion at the nearby British prison. The bathhouse has recently been restored to pristine condition, after serving for years as a municipal museum (at press time the building was slated to be a museum, with copper objects, jewelry, coins, and other artifacts from the city collection as well as new archaeological finds from Akko on display). You'll notice the colored glass bubbles that protrude from the roof domes send a green, filtered light to the steam rooms below. These skylights were actually ordered from the same Hebron workshop that made the original ones a century ago. The dressing room is decorated with colorful handmade Turkish tiles and capped with a cupola; note the inlaid marble floors. For admission and hours, *see* Crusader Vaults and Halls, *above.*

㉝ The **Refectory** was once known as the Crypt of St. John; before excavation it was erroneously thought to have been an underground chamber. The dimensions of the colossal pillars that support the roof (note they're girdled with metal bands for extra support) make this one of the more monumental examples of Crusader architecture in Israel. Moreover, it is one of the oldest Gothic structures in the world. In the right-hand corner opposite the entrance is a fleur-de-lis carved in stone—the crest of the French House of Bourbon—leading some scholars to postulate that this was the chamber in which Louis VII convened the Knights of the Realm.

At the wooden stairs that descend next to the base of one of the columns is an opening to an extremely narrow **subterranean passageway.** This was a secret tunnel cut in stone that the Crusaders probably used to reach the harbor when besieged by Muslim forces. When you emerge, you will find yourself in the cavernous vaulted halls of the **Posta,** the fortress guardpost, with a 13th-century marble Crusader tombstone and a map of the Crusader city displayed at the exit. Climb the stairs to the left and turn right, into the covered market. Here, artisans beat copper pieces into bas-relief plates and bowls, and other handcrafted items are sold. Exit to the left.

㉞ The local **souk** (market), south of the whitewashed **El-Zituneh Mosque,** has stalls where heaps of fresh produce are artfully arranged. It also has specialty stores: a pastry shop with an astonishing variety of exotic Middle Eastern delicacies; a spice shop filled with the aromas of the Far East; a bakery with steaming fresh pita. You will often see fishermen sitting on doorsteps, intently repairing their lines and nets to the sounds of Arabic music blaring from the open windows above.

NEED A BREAK? In the souk, you can duck into the **Oudah Brothers Cafe** (☎ 04/991–2013) and sit in the courtyard of the 16th-century Khan el-Faranj (Franks' Inn). While sipping coffee or eating hummus or kebabs, note the 18th-century Franciscan monastery and tower to your left.

㉟ The **Khan el-Umdan** (Inn of the Pillars), off Venezia Square in the southern part of the Old City, is the largest of four Ottoman khans in the city. Before you explore it and the Pisan Quarter beyond, take a stroll around the **port,** with its small flotilla of fishing boats, yachts, and sailboats. Then walk through the khan's gate beneath a square clock tower built at the turn of the century. During Akko's golden age of commerce in the 18th century, the khan served vast numbers of merchants and travelers. The 32 pink-and-gray granite pillars that give the khan its name are compliments of Ahmed el-Jazzar's raids on Roman Caesarea. At the center of the colonnaded courtyard there was once a market.

36 At the **Pisan Harbor,** you can take a walk along the seawalls. If you're coming from the Khan el-Umdan, make a sharp left when you exit to enter the Pisan Quarter. Start at the café perched on high—a great lookout (in the summer, boys dive off the rocks into the sea). Then head west in the direction of the 18th-century **Church of St. John.** You will end up at the southwestern extremity of Akko, next to the **lighthouse.** The Templars once occupied this area. Head north along Haganah Street, which runs parallel to the crenelated western seawall. After five minutes you will reach the whitewashed, blue-trimmed **Baha'i House** (not open to the public), where the religion's founder and prophet, Bahaullah, spent 12 years of his exile. His burial site is just north of Akko (☞ Baha'i Gardens and Shrine, *below*).

37 The **Museum of the Underground Prisoners** is housed in several wings of the citadel built by Dahr el-Omar. The citadel was added onto by Ahmed el-Jazzar in 1785, and it became a British prison under the Mandate. On the way in, you pass the outside wall of the citadel; the difference between the large Crusader building stones and the smaller Turkish ones above them is easy to spot. The original cells and their meager contents tell of day-to-day life in the prison, supplemented by displays of photographs and documents that reconstruct the history of the Jewish resistance to British rule in the 1930s and '40s. During the Mandate, the citadel became a high-security prison whose inmates included top members of Jewish resistance organizations, including Ze'ev Jabotinsky. In 1947, a dramatic prison breakout by leaders of the Irgun captured headlines around the world and provided Leon Uris's *Exodus* with one of its most dramatic moments.

As you leave the museum, turn right after 60 feet, and follow the massive walls around the northern part of town to the breach at Weizmann Street and the parking lot where you entered the Old City. ⊠ *Haganah St. (a few minutes north of the lighthouse),* ☎ *04/991–8264.* ☞ *NIS 6 ($2).* ☉ *Sun.–Thurs. 9–5, Fri. 9–12:30.*

Dining and Lodging

$$ ✕ **Abu Christo.** This popular waterfront fish restaurant at the north-
★ ern edge of the Crusader Port actually stands at one of the original 18th-century gates built by Pasha Ahmed el-Jazzar when he fortified the city after his victory over Napoléon. A family business dating from 1948 and passed from father to son, Abu Christo serves up the daily catch—often grouper, red snapper, or sea bass—simply prepared, either grilled or deep fried. Shellfish and a selection of grilled meats are also on the menu. The covered outdoor patio right on the water is idyllic in summer. ⊠ *Crusader Port,* ☎ *04/991–0065. Reservations essential July–Sept. AE, DC, MC, V.*

$$ ✕ **Galileo.** Sit on the terrace alongside the old city's ancient walls for a meal of fresh fish, grilled meats, or Middle Eastern salads. You'll be right on the water in the Pisan Harbor, with nothing but a few ruins and an expanse of blue before you. ⊠ *Crusader Port,* ☎ *04/991–4610. Reservations essential Fri.–Sat. DC, MC, V.*

$$$ 🏨 **Beit Hava.** Eight km (5 mi) north of Akko and close to the resort town of Nahariya, this country hotel was founded in 1938 by German Jews. With the beach and a 4th-century Byzantine church a few minutes from your front door, the surrounding countryside is inviting for strolls. The guest rooms are adequate but nothing fancy. Above all, you get peace and quiet here. The real bonus is the sports facilities. If you're traveling by public transportation, take Egged Bus 271 or the train from Akko or Haifa. Both bus and train leave you within a five-minute walk of the hotel. ⊠ *Box 82, Shavei Zion 25227,* ☎ *04/982–0391,* FAX *04/982–0519. 90 rooms with bath. Dining room, pool, 2 tennis courts, baby-sitting. AE, MC, V.*

$ 🏨 **Akko Youth Hostel.** In the Crusader quarter near the lighthouse and
★ Pisan Harbor, this no-frills hostel is in a historic stone building that has been beautifully restored with wood-beamed high ceilings. The dormitory-style rooms, which sleep four to eight people, are mostly on the second floor. Meals (kosher, if desired) are served upon request. ⊠ *Box 1090, 24110,* ☎ *04/991–1982. 80 beds share 4 baths. No credit cards.*

$ 🏨 **Palm Beach.** On a beach off the highway just south of Akko, this hotel has a fine view of Haifa Bay and the rooftops of the Old City. Guests can use the facilities of the adjoining country club, which include a swimming pool and whirlpool bath. ⊠ *Rte. 4, 24101,* ☎ *04/981–5815,* FAX *04/991–0434. 120 rooms with bath. Restaurant, dance club. AE, MC, V.*

Nightlife and the Arts

Nights of Akko, a free concert series that features mostly Israeli music and folk dancing, is held Saturday night at about 7:30 from July to mid-September. The concerts take place on an outdoor stage on Ben Ami Street, the main street in the new area of the city. There are also occasional chamber music concerts in the Crusader city and in Khan el-Umdan in the summer and winter. For more information call the Tourist Information Office (☎ 04/991–1764).

Outdoor Activities and Sports

BEACHES

Just south of the Old City on the Haifa–Akko road is a sandy stretch of **municipal beach** in Akko Bay, with parking, showers, toilets, and chair rentals. Admission is NIS 5 ($1.70).

SCUBA DIVING

In the marina in Akko is the **Ramy Diving Center** (☎ 04/991–8990). Ramy, a navy diver, runs the diving school and offers tourists guided dives. The three local dives explore the reef (NIS 120, or $40), the submerged wall of the city (NIS 90, or $30), and the wreck of an Italian World War II submarine (NIS 180, or $60). Prices include an instructor and equipment rental.

Shopping

A fascinating place to browse is **I. E. Dany's Archaeological Galleries** (⊠ 13/3 Salah Adin, ☎ 04/981–3770), in the Old City. You'll find the shop on your left before you get to the plaza of El-Jazzar Mosque. It is lined with glass cases whose contents, some more than 4,000 years old, range from ancient coins to small statuary, delicate Roman glass, and urns and pottery. The pieces carry government-issued certificates, and items for sale are officially approved for export. Prices range from $50 into the thousands.

Baha'i Gardens and Shrine

38 *1 km (½ mi) north of gas station at northern edge of Akko.*

For the Baha'is this is the holiest spot on earth, the site of the tomb of the faith's prophet and founder, Bahaullah (☞ Exploring Haifa, *above*). First, you'll pass the west gate (open only to Baha'is). Make the first right (no sign) and turn again, 500 yards up, through the north gate. He lived in the red-tile mansion here after his release from jail in Akko and was buried in the small building next to the mansion, now the Shrine of Bahaullah. Visitors to the Shrine are asked to dress modestly. The gardens and terrace are exquisitely landscaped. ⊠ *Rte. 4,* ☎ *04/981–2763.* 🗪 *Free.* ☉ *Gardens daily 9–4; tomb Fri.–Mon. 9–noon.*

En Route Less than 1 km (½ mi) north of the gardens, to the west of the highway, stands a segment of the graceful **aqueduct** built by Ahmed el-Jazzar in the late 18th century to carry the sweet waters of the Kabri Springs to Akko.

Kibbutz Lochamei Hageta'ot

39 *2 km (1¼ mi) north of Akko, 6 km (3¾ mi) south of Nahariya.*

Kibbutz Lochamei Hageta'ot (Ghetto Fighters) was founded in 1949 by survivors of the German, Polish, and Lithuanian Jewish ghettos and veterans of the ghetto uprisings against the Nazis. To commemorate their compatriots who perished in the Holocaust and to perpetuate the memory of those tragic events, the kibbutz members set up a **museum,** whose entrance is to the right of the main gate of the kibbutz. There is a vast collection of photographs that document the Warsaw Ghetto and the famous uprising, and halls devoted to different themes, among them Jewish communities before their destruction in the Holocaust, the death camps, and deportations at the hands of the Nazis. You can see the actual booth in which Adolf Eichmann, architect of the "Final Solution," sat during his Jerusalem trial.

Opened in 1996, **Yad Layeled** (the Children's Memorial) a white, cone-shaped building near the museum, is dedicated to the memory of the 1½ million children who perished in the Holocaust. Children see a series of scenes, tableaux, and images accompanied by recorded voices, which enable them to identify with the feelings of individual victims without seeing any shocking details. There is a small restaurant on the premises. ⊠ *Rte. 4,* ☎ *04/982–0412.* 🗪 *Donation appreciated.* ☉ *Museum and memorial: Sun.–Thurs. 9–4, Fri. 9–1, Sat. 10–5.*

Nahariya

40 *8 km (5 mi) north of Akko.*

Nahariya was the first Jewish settlement in the Western Galilee. The town (now a city) was founded in 1934 by German Jews who had fled the Nazis and had come to eke out a living from farming. Eventually these pioneers turned from the soil to what they realized was their greatest natural resource—some of the country's best beaches—for a more lucrative livelihood. Thus a popular seaside resort was born. The main thoroughfare, Haga'aton Boulevard, was built along the banks of a river, now dried up, lined with shady eucalyptus trees. The town's name, in fact, comes from *nahar,* the Hebrew word for river.

Once upon a time, Nahariya had a staid reputation and horse-drawn buggies took visitors slowly up and down the main street. And though once the German language was the hallmark of the town, today you're as likely to hear Russian or the Ethiopian tongue, Amharic. Blue-bereted U.N. soldiers from bases to the north are frequent visitors.

In July and August, there's dancing in the amphitheater at the mouth of the river, and Israeli stars come out at night to perform on the beach and in the town square.

The **Byzantine church** has an elaborate 17-color mosaic floor that depicts peacocks and other birds, hunting scenes, and plants. It was part of what experts consider one of the largest and most beautiful Byzantine churches in Western Galilee, where Christianity rapidly spread—as in the rest of Israel—from the 4th to the 7th centuries. Call the Tourist

Information Office (☎ 04/879800) to arrange a visit (it's not always open). To get to the church, which is next to the Katzenelson School, head east on Haga'aton to Route 4, make a left at the stoplight, then take the first right into Yechi'am Street. From here, you make the third left and then an immediate right onto Bielefeld Street. ⊠ *Bielefeld St.* ☎ *NIS 2 (70¢).*

Dining and Lodging

$$ ✕ **Maxims.** Locals consider a meal at this Chinese restaurant a special event. The Asian decor may be standard for Israel, but the authenticity of the cuisine is a pleasant surprise. Stir-fried shrimp with green peppers, onions, and mushrooms in a chili sauce is one of the more unexpected dishes, but there are also favorite standbys, such as lemon chicken, batter-fried and covered with a sweet-and-sour lemon sauce, and sautéed chicken on a skewer, smothered in peanut sauce. ⊠ *43 Weizmann St.,* ☎ *04/992–1088. Reservations essential Fri.–Sat. V.*

$$ ✕ **Uri Buri.** Buri is the Hebrew name for gray mullet, just one of the wide selection of freshly caught fish served with pride by proprietor Uri. This restaurant serves only fish and seafood; the day's catch is baked, grilled, fried, or steamed. Fittingly, it's right on the beach. On the menu are local fish, such as trout and salmon trout from the Dan River, St. Peter's fish, red snapper, and sea bass. Your choice is served with salad and potato or rice. As an entrée, try the Tunisian-style stuffed sardines, fragrant with coriander, garlic, basil, and hot chili. ⊠ *Last building on southern end of promenade (look for big glass windows with a yellow sign),* ☎ *04/992–4824. DC, MC, V.*

$$ ✕ **Yehiam Castle.** You too can eat in a medieval castle, or ruins thereof, 12 km (7½ mi) east of Nahariya. The 12th-century dining room was fixed up by an 18th-century Bedouin sheikh, and the finishing touches in 1996 were completed by the kibbutzim who run it. You sit in a high-ceilinged room with soaring arches and thick walls; the windows provide a view of blue sky (it's a lofty elevation) and Western Galilee countryside. The food? At press time, the place was new, but the emphasis is Hungarian. ⊠ *12 km east of Nahariya; take Rte. 89 and Rte. 8833 until you see sign for Castle Judin; restaurant is at this site.* ☎ *04/987–9122.*

$ ✕ **Pinguin.** Fresh spinach blintzes with melted cheese, pasta, and hamburger plates are some of the offerings at this casual eatery on Nahariya's main street. Management swears that its schnitzel gets accolades from Viennese visitors. All main dishes come with a green salad, rice, french fries, and cooked vegetables. There's Chinese food, too. You can get lighter salads and desserts next door at the soda fountain and frozen yogurt at the adjacent stand; both are owned by the same outfit that runs Pinguin. ⊠ *31 Haga'aton Blvd.,* ☎ *04/992–8855. V.*

$$$ ☷ **Carlton.** The best in town, this centrally located, six-story hotel has a staff that will go the extra mile. Rooms are spacious, and many have sea views or a view of the mountain range rearing up in the northeast. Furnishings are comfortable but not exceptional. The La Scala disco-nightclub, with its live music in the summer, attracts local fun lovers from all over the north. ⊠ *23 Haga'aton Blvd., 22381,* ☎ *04/992–2211,* 𝔽𝔸𝕏 *04/982–3771. 196 rooms with bath. Restaurant, bar, pool, sauna, nightclub, baby-sitting. AE, MC, V.*

$$$ ☷ **Frank.** At the lower end of its price category, this old, established hostelry is still managed by the family of the original owners. Very near the beach, the sedate two-story hotel has an intimate air, with a pink-and-purple color scheme in the dining room and appealing patio off the lobby. The modest but pleasant rooms obviously work for its regular patrons—mostly Europeans and locals who wouldn't dream of going anywhere else. ⊠ *4 Ha'aliya St., 22381,* ☎ *04/992–0278,* ℻ *04/992–5535. 50 rooms with bath. Pool, hot tub. AE, MC, V.*

$$ 🏨 **Erna.** A bit off the beaten track from the downtown area, this family-owned hotel is nonetheless only a five-minute walk to the main beach. The three-story building is unobtrusive from the outside but is spick-and-span and cheerful, and the service is solicitous. ⊠ *29 Jabotinsky St., 22383,* ☎ *04/992–0170,* ℻ *04/992–8917. 26 rooms with bath. Restaurant, bar, baby-sitting. MC, V.*

Nightlife and the Arts

Nahariya's flashiest disco is **La Scala** (☎ 04/992–2211; ☞ Carlton Hotel, *above*), which spins standard dance tunes with a throbbing beat and attracts an older crowd. This nightspot is in the passageway just west of the Carlton on Haga'aton Boulevard. The cover charge on Friday and Saturday is NIS 30 ($10); the doors open at 10 PM.

"Renaissance Nights" refers to music from the Middle Ages: church music and baroque- and Renaissance-period melodies, played on authentic instruments. Concerts take place at Judin Castle at Yehiam (☎ 04/985–6085), 12 km (7½ mi) east of Nahariya.

Shopping

The acclaimed glassware of **Nahariya Glass** (⊠ 100A Herzl St., ☎ 04/992–0066) has a distinctive style, often with a brightly colored naturalistic or abstract pattern embedded between two layers of glass. The trays, sets of dishes, small sculptures, and other items sold here can be shipped abroad. Visitors are also welcome to tour the factory; call ahead because hours are not regular.

Outdoor Activities and Sports

BEACHES

The public bathing facilities in Nahariya, at the **Galei Galil Beach,** just north of Haga'aton Boulevard, are ideal for families and not far from most hotels. There is an Olympic-size pool, a wading pool, playground, changing rooms, showers, and snack bar. In peak season, exercise classes are offered early in the morning. The entrance fee is NIS 9 ($3).

Beautifully maintained because it's in the Achziv National Park just north of Nahariya, **Achziv Beach** is great for kids, with a protected artificial lagoon, lifeguards, and playground facilities. You can picnic on the grassy slopes or make use of the restaurant. Admission, which is NIS 9 ($3), covers the use of showers and toilets. **Betzet Beach,** north of Achziv Beach, is part of a nature reserve and offers abundant vegetation, trees, and the ruins of an ancient olive press. There's a lifeguard on duty in season.

SCUBA DIVING

Trek Yam Ltd., or Sea Treks (☎ 04/982–3671 or 04/982–5089), takes scuba divers to explore the Achziv Canyon and the caves at Rosh Hanikra, along the northern coast.

OFF THE BEATEN PATH

YEHIAM – This kibbutz, set in a wooded area, has an unusual attraction, the ruins of the medieval Castle Judin. The memorial you pass on the way commemorates the convoy that set out to bring fresh supplies and reinforcements to the besieged kibbutz in Israel's War of Independence in 1948. Castle Judin was apparently built by the Templars in the late 12th century. It, too, was destroyed by Baybars, but its ruins so impressed the 18th-century Bedouin sheikh Dahr el-Omar that he transformed it into a palatial citadel 500 years later. You can see the remains of a large reception hall and mosque, as well as a tower and bathhouse. There are also picnic facilities, and the kibbutz has opened a restaurant in part of the ruins, called Yehiam Castle (☞ Dining and Lodging, *above*).

The kibbutz and castle are 12 km (7½ mi) east of Nahariya. Head east on Route 89 until you see sign to castle, off to the right. ⊠ *Off Rte. 8833,* ☎ *04/985–6004.* ⊠ *NIS 6 ($2).* ⊙ *Daily 8–4.*

Rosh Hanikra

🜚 *7 km (4¼ mi) north of Nahariya.*

The dramatic white cliffs at the coast signal the border with Lebanon and the sea grottoes of Rosh Hanikra. Even before you get in line for the two-minute cable-car ride to the grottoes, take a moment to look at the stunning view down the coast. Still clearly visible is the route of the railway line, now mostly a dirt road, built by the British through the hillside in 1943 to extend the Cairo–Tel Aviv–Haifa line to Beirut. The caves underneath the cliff were sculpted by relentless waves pounding at the chalky white rock. Footpaths lead from one section to another, and bursts of seawater plunge in and swirl around below you. ⊠ *Rte. 4,* ☎ *04/985–7109.* ⊠ *NIS 25 ($8.35).* ⊙ *Daily 8:30–4 (July–Aug. until 10 PM); in winter call ahead.*

NEED A BREAK?	The **cafeteria** perched on top of the Rosh Hanikra cliff might not be a gourmet's dream, but you'd be hard pressed to find a more gorgeous view. It's filled with light and breezy, with a wide range of snacks, drinks, and ice cream. Take a fun photo outside at the sign on the cafeteria wall: It points out the distance from Beirut.
OFF THE BEATEN PATH	**MONTFORT –** This formidable medieval mountaintop fortress is arguably the most majestic of its kind in Israel. There's a marked path up the long path to get there, but if you just want to look, there's an observation point at Goren Park (there are marked walking trails and picnic areas here as well). The walk takes anywhere from 30 minutes to an hour, depending on your fitness level. The slopes are steep and densely wooded, and the stark ruins of the fortress reach skyward from a narrow spur of hill above the bed of a bubbling stream. Built and named in the 12th century by French Crusaders, Montfort was part of the domain of the nearby Courtenay fiefdom at Mi'ilya. In the 13th century it was sold to the German Knights of the Teutonic Order, who greatly expanded it. They renamed the castle Starkenberg and used it to house their archives and treasury. Montfort was first conquered by the Muslims in 1187, but was regained five years later. It was lost for good by the Crusaders in 1271 to the Mamluk sultan Baybars, who allowed the knights to retreat to Akko. The layout of the castle was thoroughly explored in 1926 by a team from the Metropolitan Museum of Art, in New York.
	To get here from Route 4, turn east at exit for Shlomi to Hanita Junction. Turn east onto Route 899. Pass Kibbutz Eilon before reaching the sign for Goren Park, at the end of a 1½-km (1-mi) gravel road.

NORTHERN COAST AND WESTERN GALILEE A TO Z

Arriving and Departing

By Bus

The **Egged** bus cooperative (☞ Getting Around, *below*) serves the coastal area from Ben-Gurion Airport and from the Jerusalem and Tel Aviv central bus stations. Service to Netanya, Hadera, Zichron Ya'akov, and Haifa from both cities starts before 8 AM and usually ends around

8 PM. From Tel Aviv to Haifa, there is a bus that leaves every 20 minutes from 5:20 AM to 11 PM. Travel to Caesarea requires a change at Hadera; service from Hadera to Caesarea runs only until 12:30 PM. You must change buses at Haifa to get to Akko and Nahariya.

By Car

You can take either Route 2 or 4 north along the coast from Tel Aviv to Haifa, continuing on Route 4 all the way up to the Lebanese border. From Jerusalem follow Route 1 to Tel Aviv and then connect through the Ayalon Highway to Herzliya, where you can pick up Route 2.

By Plane

Most travelers from abroad arrive at **Ben-Gurion International Airport,** at Lod on the outskirts of Tel Aviv. The airport is 105 km (65 mi) from Haifa, about a 90-minute drive. Buses, sherut vans, and taxis to the northern coast are readily available at the airport. **Haifa Airport** (☎ 04/872–2220), a small airport in the port area, is served by Arkia Airlines (Jerusalem, ☎ 02/583–3440; Tel Aviv, ☎ 03/523–3285), which flies into the city from Jerusalem, Tel Aviv, Eilat, and the Dead Sea. There is bus service between the airport and Haifa.

By Ship

Many cruise liners that tour the Mediterranean stop at Haifa. To visit the city, you will exit the docks area through either Gate 5 or the Passenger and Customs Terminal, depending on whether you are required to go through customs. Taxis are usually waiting at the exits. Nearby, you can catch buses to the Central Bus Station, the Hadar district, and Mt. Carmel.

By Train

There is a line linking Tel Aviv to Netanya, Haifa, and Nahariya, with stops along the way. The portion of the trip from Tel Aviv to Haifa takes 90 minutes and costs NIS 15 ($5). There is also a direct train to Tel Aviv from Haifa, which is fast (one hour) and comfortable and runs hourly Sunday–Thursday 6 AM–10 PM (last train from Haifa 7 PM). It is advisable to buy tickets a day ahead, at the Tel Aviv train station (✉ Rakevet Zafon) or at the Northern Train Station (✉ 1 Arlozorov, ☎ 03/693–7515). Haifa has two train stations; the main one is Haifa Bat Gallim, at the Central Bus Station, ☎ 04/856–4564. The train station in Netanya is on Ha'Rakevet Road, just east of Route 2 (☎ 09/823470).

Getting Around

By Bus

The **Egged** network will get you just about anywhere in the region. Most connections are hourly during the weekday. For countrywide information on routes and schedules, call 02/530–4555; 03/537–5555; 04/854–9555, or contact the local bus stations directly: Haifa, 04/854–9131; Netanya, 09/833–7052.

By Car

Driving is probably the most comfortable and convenient way to tour the region and allows you to explore some of the more scenic back roads. The distances are short: for example, 29 km (18 mi) from Tel Aviv to Netanya, 22 km (13¾ mi) from Haifa to Akko, 37 km (23 mi) from Haifa to Zichron Ya'akov.

Traffic gets particularly snarled at rush hour along the coast, especially entering and exiting major cities. The worst times are after 5 PM weekdays and Saturday evenings. Expect gridlock during morning and evening rush hours in Haifa in the port area. Even in the best of con-

In case you want to see the world.

At American Express, we're here to make your journey a smooth one. So we have over 1,700 travel service locations in over 120 countries ready to help. What else would you expect from the world's largest travel agency?

do more ®

http://www.americanexpress.com/travel

Travel

In case you want to be welcomed there.

We're here to see that you're always welcomed at establishments everywhere. That's why millions of people carry the American Express® Card – for peace of mind, confidence, and security, around the world or just around the corner.

do more

Cards

In case you're running low.

We're here to help with more than 118,000 Express Cash locations around the world. In order to enroll, just call American Express before you start your vacation.

do more

Express Cash

And just in case.

We're here with American Express® Travelers Cheques and Cheques *for Two*.® They're the safest way to carry money on your vacation and the surest way to get a refund, practically anywhere, anytime.

Another way we help you...

do more

Travelers Cheques

ditions, Haifa traffic is sluggish, and because of the city's steep layout, streets zigzag up the slope and are difficult to negotiate. Remember to pay attention to street signs in Haifa indicating which streets close on Saturday.

By Train

This is a novel way to travel within the area, because this is the only part of the country serviced by rail except for the Tel Aviv–Jerusalem route. Many of the main cities and towns can be reached by train, including Netanya, Hadera, Binyamina, Zichron Ya'akov, Haifa, Atlit, Akko, and Nahariya.

Haifa possesses the only subway in Israel. The six-station Carmelit subway takes just six minutes for the run from Hanassi Avenue in central Carmel to Kikar Paris in the port area; the fare is NIS 3.50 ($1.20). The train operates Sunday–Thursday 6 AM–10 PM, Friday 6–3, and Saturday 7 PM–midnight.

Contacts and Resources

Car Rentals

Haifa: Avis (⊠ 7 Ben-Gurion St., ☎ 04/851–3050); Budget (⊠ 186 Yaffo St., ☎ 04/852–0666); Eldan (⊠ 95 Hanassi Ave., ☎ 04/837–5303); Hertz (⊠ 90 Ha'atzmaut St., ☎ 04/853–9786); Reliable (⊠ 33 Histadrut St., ☎ 04/842–2832). **Nahariya:** Budget (⊠ 62 Weizmann St., ☎ 04/992–9252). **Netanya:** Avis (⊠ 1 Ussishkin St., ☎ 09/833–1619); Budget (⊠ 2 Gad Machness, ☎ 09/861–4711); Eldan (⊠ 12 Ha'atzmaut Sq., ☎ 09/861–6982); Hertz (⊠ 8 Ha'atzmaut Sq., ☎ 09/882–8890); Reliable (⊠ 2 Gad Machness, ☎ 09/862–9042).

Consulate

Haifa: Jonathan Freidland, U.S. Consular Agent, ⊠ 12 Jerusalem St., ☎ 04/867–0616; ☉ Sunday–Thursday 9–1.

Emergencies

POLICE

Akko: ☎ 100. **Haifa:** ☎ 100. **Nahariya:** ☎ 100 or 04/992–0344. **Netanya:** ☎ 100.

AMBULANCE

Akko: ☎ 101 (Magen David Adom) or 04/991–2333. **Haifa:** ☎ 101. Nahariya: ☎ 101 or 04/982–3332. **Netanya:** ☎ 101.

HOSPITALS

Haifa: Rambam, ☎ 04/854–3111; Carmel, ☎ 04/825–0211. **Nahariya:** Western Galilee Regional Hospital, ☎ 04/985–0766. **Netanya:** Laniado Hospital, ☎ 09/860–4666.

Guided Tours

GENERAL INTEREST

In most cases, pickup at your hotel for the following tours can be made by prior arrangement.

Egged Tours offers a one-day bus trip from Tel Aviv or Netanya that takes in Caesarea and Akko and goes north to Rosh Hanikra at the Lebanese border. The tour, costing NIS 177 ($59), departs Sunday, Wednesday, and Friday at 8 AM. Bookings may be made in Tel Aviv (☎ 03/527–1212) or in Netanya (☎ 09/860–6206). For departures from Haifa call 04/854–9486.

For those in a hurry, **Egged** gives a half-day tour that follows the western coast to Nahariya and north to Rosh Hanikra and Crusader Akko on the way back. Sunday, Wednesday, and Friday are your choices, and the price is NIS 96 ($32).

A **United Tours** excursion from either Tel Aviv or Netanya takes you to Caesarea, the Baha'i Gardens in Haifa, and Rosh Hanikra; on the return trip there's a stop at Akko to see the Crusader city, the Arab market, and the mosque. A visit to the Diamond Center wraps up the trip. This one-day tour costs NIS 177 ($59) and leaves at 8 AM on Wednesday, Friday, and Sunday from the Tel Aviv train station. Contact United Tours in Tel Aviv (☎ 03/693–34123 or 03/522–2008).

Another United Tours offer is a free half-day tour to Netanya from Tel Aviv, driving through the coastal Sharon Valley and visiting a kibbutz. In Netanya there is a tour of the National Diamond Center. Departures are daily (except Saturday) from 9:15 to 10, returning at about 2 PM.

From April through November the **Society for the Protection of Nature in Israel (SPNI)** tours the Mediterranean coast and the Carmel Mountains on a two-day excursion. The tour, which costs NIS 294 ($98), leaves at 11:30 from Tel Aviv at the SPNI office (⊠ 3 Ha'shfela St., ☎ 03/638–8673 or 03/638–8677). Participants can swim at Dor Beach, explore the ancient tel (a man-made mound of layers of civilization) nearby, bird-watch at Kibbutz Ma'agan Michael, hike on Mt. Carmel, and visit the Carmel Caves. Accommodations are in a field-study center, which is a bit like a youth hostel; breakfast and dinner are included.

In Haifa the **Tourist Board** (☎ 04/983–7010) conducts a free 2½-hour walking tour on Saturday, which leaves at 10 AM from the corner of Yefe Nof (Panorama Road) and Sha'ar Ha'levanon Street. The itinerary includes the Mané Katz Museum and the Baha'i Shrine and ends at Haifa Museum. You can catch Bus 23 back to central Carmel.

SPECIAL INTEREST

Israel is a crossroads for European migratory birds heading for Africa and back, and thus is a paradise for bird-watchers. The best season to observe them is from November through February. Some of the birds you are likely to see along the northern coast include egrets, pelicans, storks, terns, spoonbills, mallard ducks, kingfishers, cormorants, and even some flamingos. You can hire a private guide for a day at the coastal **Ma'agan Michael Field School** (☎ 06/639–9655, FAX 06/639–1618), one of Israel's major centers for bird-watching, at the kibbutz of the same name, just north of Caesarea. The cost of the guided tour is NIS 390 ($130). Dormitory facilities are available for longer stays. Visitors are also welcome to roam without a guide; brochures in English are usually available at the school.

Carmelit (☎ 04/841–8765) offers boat tours of Haifa Bay from Kishon Port. The ride lasts one hour and costs NIS 15 ($5). Call ahead for departure times. From Akko's Crusader port the **Princess of Akko** ferry makes a 25-minute jaunt around the bay (☎ 04/991–0606). The boat sets out February through December whenever it fills up and costs NIS 12 ($4). From Nahariya, **Trek Yam** (☎ 04/982–3671 or 04/982–5089) takes you on a 45-minute ride up the coast in its high-speed motorboat, the *Tornado,* for a cost of NIS 50 ($16.70).

For an ethnic adventure in a Druze village in the Carmel, call **El Carmel** (☎ 04/839–0125) and ask Amit to make the arrangements. You'll be invited into a private home, usually one with a courtyard where pita is baked over a traditional stove, and the head of the house will discuss the distinctive life of the Druze. With lunch the cost is $21.50; without lunch it's $16.

PERSONAL GUIDES

Caesarea resident and authorized tour guide **Illana Berner** (☎ 06/636–3936) provides an upbeat 2½-hour walking tour through Caesarea for

$50. Haifa-based **Mitzpe Tours** (☎ 04/867–4341) offers guided tours in a private car or limousine tailored to individuals or small groups. **Carmel Touring Co. Ltd.** (☎ 04/838–8882) in Haifa uses cars or limousines for its tours for individuals and small groups.

Taxis
Akko: Akko Zafon, ☎ 04/981–6666. **Haifa:** Carmel-Ahuza, ☎ 04/838–8882; Mercaz Mitzpe, ☎ 04/866–2525. **Nahariya:** Kefarim, ☎ 04/992–6333. **Netanya:** Hashahar, ☎ 09/834–7777; Hasharon, ☎ 09/833–3338.

Travel Agencies
Akko: Shefi Tours (✉ 37 Ha'Arba'a St., ☎ 04/991–2730). **Haifa:** Histour (✉ 14 Nordau St., ☎ 04/867–1313). **Nahariya:** Ler Tours (✉ 19 Haga'aton Blvd., ☎ 04/982–5636). **Netanya:** Atlas Tours (✉ 29 Herzl St., ☎ 09/834–5183).

Villa Rentals
Modern whitewashed houses near the beach in Caesarea are available through **Chana Kristal Real Estate** (✉ 23 Hamigdal St., Cluster 8, Caesarea 36060, ☎ 06/636–3896 or 06/636–2691, FAX 06/636–0212), a real-estate broker. **Real Estate Caesarea** (✉ 32 Hadar St., Cluster 5, Caesarea 43660, ☎ FAX 06/636–0969) is a source for a variety of rentals.

Visitor Information
Akko: Tourist Information Office (✉ El Jazzar St., ☎ 04/991–1764), just inside the Knights Halls, is opposite the mosque and is open Sunday–Thursday 8–4, Friday 9–2.

Caesarea: Caesarea Development Corporation (✉ Old City, Box 1044, 30660, ☎ 06/636–0833) is open Sunday–Thursday 8–5, Friday 8–1.

Haifa: Haifa Tourist Board office (✉ 18/20 Herzl St., Bet Hakranot, ☎ 04/866–6521) is open Sunday–Thursday 9–5, Friday 9–1. Another office (✉ 106 Hannassi Ave., ☎ 04/837–4010) is open Sunday–Thursday 8–7, Friday 8–1. A third office (✉ Ground level, Central Bus Station, Haganah Blvd., ☎ 04/851–2208) is open Sunday–Thursday 9:30–5, Friday 9:30–1. Call the What's On in Haifa Hotline at 04/374253.

Nahariya: Tourist Information Office (✉ Nahariya Municipality, 19 Ga'aton Blvd., Box 78, 22100, ☎ 04/987–9800) is open Sunday–Thursday 9–1 and 4–7, Friday 9–1.

Netanya: Tourist Information Office (✉ Next to amphitheater on Ha'aztmaut Sq., ☎ 09/882–7286 or 09/884–1348) is open Sunday–Thursday 8:30–7, Friday 9–noon. The Association for Tourism Promotion (✉ 15 Herzl St., Box 2165, 42400, ☎ 09/833–0583 or 09/603–1150) is open Sunday–Thursday 7:30–3.

Zichron Ya'akov: Tourist Information Office (✉ Next to Central Bus Station, Gidonim, Box 10, ☎ 06/639–8811 or 06/639–2442) is open Sunday–Thursday 9–1, Friday 9–12.

6 Lower Galilee

Including Nazareth, Tiberias, and the Sea of Galilee

Nowhere does the Bible resonate more than in this land of soft cultivated valleys, harsh hills, and the freshwater Sea of Galilee. The Jezreel Valley is the land of Deborah, Gideon, King Saul, and Elijah. Nazareth and the Sea of Galilee are rich with significance for the Christian pilgrim. Yet this is also a region of parks and one of Israel's favorite vacation playgrounds.

By Mike Rogoff

THE GALILEE, TO MOST ISRAELIS, is synonymous with "the North," a land of mountains and fertile valleys, nature reserves and national parks. In short, they would claim, it's a provincial region too rustic and remote to live in, but great for vacations. Although much of the wild scenery associated with the North—the rugged highlands, waterfalls, and panoramas that seem to go on forever—is found in the Upper Galilee, the Lower Galilee has its own quiet beauty, varied landscape, and more than anything, rich history.

On a map, the Lower Galilee fits into a frame about 50 km (31 mi) square, divided into valleys, hill country, and the Sea of Galilee. To the south is the fertile Jezreel Valley, known in Hebrew simply as *Ha'e-mek*—the Valley—and sentimentally, if not scientifically, thought of by many Israelis as distinct from the rest of the Lower Galilee. To the east, the boundaries are easily defined by the Jordan Valley and the eastern shore of the Sea of Galilee (the *Kinneret* in Hebrew). To the north, the steep hillsides above the lake merge into the Upper Galilee, while farther west, Route 85 follows the Bet Hakerem Valley, the natural division between the two regions. Toward the Mediterranean Sea, the hills flatten out as you reach the coastal plain; Route 70 follows the region's western edge. Farming forms the economic base: fruit orchards; fish ponds; field crops such as wheat and cotton in the valleys, olive groves in the hills; livestock everywhere. The valley towns of Afula and Bet She'an are little more than small, nondescript rural centers, while the larger hill town of Nazareth, the region's automotive service center, has more character—a noisy clash of pistons and politics. Tiberias, on the Sea of Galilee, depends on tourism for its livelihood, but its location is more impressive than the town itself.

Historical traditions abound. In the Jezreel Valley, filled with Old Testament lore, you come face to face with the land of Deborah, Gideon, King Saul and Jonathan, King Solomon, the prophet Elijah, Ahab, and Jezebel. After the Assyrian devastation of the northern kingdom of Israel in the 8th century BC, the region declined as the stream of history was diverted elsewhere, but in the late Roman and Byzantine periods (1st century BC–6th century AD), the vibrancy and wealth returned. The magnificent city of Scythopolis/Bet She'an, the opulent spa of Hammat Gader, the exquisite mosaics of Hammat Tiberias and Zippori, and the synagogues of Bet Alfa and Capernaum all highlight the period.

For Christian pilgrims, of course, there is nothing more compelling than exploring the landscape where Jesus of Nazareth lived, walked, and forged his ministry. Although Nazareth and Cana play crucial roles in the story, it is the Sea of Galilee and the many sites around its shores that have the most powerful resonance. Here Jesus called his disciples, wrought miracles, cured the sick, and taught the multitudes.

But the Galilee is not all ancient history. It was here that early 20th-century Jewish pioneers tamed a hostile land, draining malarial swamps and clearing boulders, transforming it into some of Israel's richest farmland. Here, too, they invented a new way of living together in perfect equality—the kibbutz. Travelers in the Galilee should take the opportunity to visit a kibbutz settlement and one of the handful of small museums exploring this unique Israeli social experiment.

The kibbutzim in the region and a smaller number of moshavim (Jewish cooperative settlements) are concentrated in the Jezreel and Jordan valleys and in the Sea of Galilee region; the rockier hill country is predominantly Arab (*Israeli* Arab, of course; this is not disputed territory).

The enmities of the 1940s have yielded to a pragmatic and often even amicable modus vivendi between Jews and Arabs in the region. Arabs are only 17% of Israel's general population, but they have long been the majority in the Galilee. The demographics have shifted, however, and a half-dozen small Jewish towns and several dozen rural villages have brought the two communities to numeric parity.

Whatever your agenda is in the Lower Galilee, take time to savor the region's natural beauty. Follow a hiking trail above the Sea of Galilee or drive up to Belvoir, a mountaintop Crusader fortress; wade through fields of rare irises in the spring; bathe in warm mineral spas and spring-fed swimming pools; water-ski on the lake, canoe on the Jordan River, or slip down a water slide.

Culture and entertainment are not the region's strong suits; a number of annual festivals and other events are the highlights. Tiberias's pubs and restaurants probably come closest to providing lively nightlife; but there are worse fates than sitting by a moonlit lake washing down a good St. Peter's fish, lamb *shishlik* (grilled skewered meat), or some Chinese delicacies with one of the excellent Israeli wines.

Pleasures and Pastimes

Biblical History

Biblical echoes are what characterize this region most. The would-be scholar with Bible in hand will find the Jazreel Valley saturated with Old Testament sites. The hill country, and especially the Sea of Galilee, witnessed the beginnings of the ministry of Jesus and is second only to Jerusalem in its centrality in the Christian story.

Dining

Tiberias is the center of gravity for tourism in the Lower Galilee, and it is there that the better restaurants are to be found. St. Peter's fish is a regional specialty. With a few rare exceptions, the restaurants you are likely to encounter en route are cafeterias or native eateries, some very good, but places to grab a meal rather than dine out. Restaurant attire in the Lower Galilee, even at dinner, is strictly casual.

CATEGORY	COST*
$$$$	over $35
$$$	$22–$35
$$	$12–$22
$	under $22

*per person for a three-course meal, excluding drinks and 10% service charge

Festivals

Ein Gev, on the eastern shore of the Sea of Galilee, has a music festival in the spring—classics, jazz, folklore, and what you will. The Misgav area, at the region's western edge, is even more eclectic: Small and larger events alike take place during the week of Passover in a widespread series of venues, the better to encourage the public to mix some sightseeing in with their music. Bet She'an has revived its ancient Roman theater for a short series of events in May. And in early July, Jacob's Ladder, the annual national folk-music festival, fills the air above Gan Hashelosha (Sachne) with the traditional folk and country sounds of the British Isles and North America.

Lodging

Tiberias, the region's tourist center, has a large number of hotels for every pocket, from deluxe (though not top drawer) to tourist class—and even cheaper hostelries for those on a really tight budget. Within

Thank you for eating at McDonald's
San Felipe Store #24239
Store Manager STEPHANIE HAYNES
(408)528-9160, mcdonalds24239@yahoo.com

YERBA BUENA & SAN FELIPE
SAN JOSE, CA 95135

THANK YOU

MCDONALDS   TEL# (408)528-9160

03 KS#14 **S#1**   Aug.31'10(Tue)17:04
STORE# 24239

1 MCCHICKEN   1.00
1 MED WLDBRY SMOOTHIE   2.79

SUB TOTAL   3.79
TAKE OUT TAX   0.35

                                     4.14

CASH TENDERED   10.14

CHANGE   6.00

a radius of 20 to 30 minutes' drive from Tiberias are a number of excellent motel-type guest houses, some run by kibbutzim and some on the shore of the Sea of Galilee itself. A few of these also rent out cheaper huts or small mobile homes called caravans, with access to the same facilities as the better accommodations.

Nazareth has a few inexpensive hotels (not all recommended) that cater primarily to organized Christian pilgrim groups and attract few individual tourists. Tiberias, just 45 minutes away, has far more to offer after hours. In Nazareth, and to a lesser extent around Tiberias, are a number of hospices run by one or another of the Christian denominations or orders (in the Holy Land, a hospice is a hotel for pilgrims, not a facility for the ill; some are good or interesting enough to attract general traffic as well).

Bed-and-breakfasts have sprung up in such profusion in recent years that it's hard to keep track of them. Many are in or adjacent to private homes in rural farming communities; others are within kibbutzim, where the collective has renovated older buildings, creating units with a kitchenette and a bath. These are usually a good value for the money, especially for families.

The Sea of Galilee area is a magnet for Israeli vacationers, especially during the two major Jewish-holiday seasons: Passover (March–April) and the High Holidays and Sukkoth (September–October). Because they are based on the Hebrew lunar calendar, the dates of these holidays shift from year to year; be sure to verify the current dates before you decide when *not* to stay in the area. The weather is normally great during these periods, but everything is crowded, and rates soar. Some hotels charge high-season rates for part of the summer and during the week of Christmas. Some hotels raise weekend rates substantially.

Youth hostels are not what they used to be. Gone is the image of 10 to a room with iron beds and communal showers. The Youth Hostel Association has seriously upgraded its facilities (including five in this region alone), with many hostels offering suite-type arrangements suitable for families. These are generally the cheapest deals around.

CATEGORY	COST*
$$$$	over $180
$$$	$100–$150
$$	$60–$100
$	under $60

All prices are for a standard double room, including breakfast and 15% service charge.

Swimming and Water Sports

The Jezreel Valley has two fine pools—one actually a river—in national parks with delightful natural surroundings. The Sea of Galilee—in fact, a freshwater lake—is a refreshing but rocky place for a swim. There are both pleasant commercial beaches with shaded lawns, facilities, cafeterias, and the occasional water park; and free beaches with minimal facilities, particularly south of Tiberias. For the serious swimmer, there is the internationally recognized Kinneret Swim in September.

There are several locations around the Sea of Galilee at which to hire pedal boats, rowboats, kayaks, and motorboats. For very serious kayakers, there's an international competition held annually in March. Waterskiing is available, too. Water slides have suddenly appeared in the area like multicolored extraterrestrial life-forms, especially at some of the facilities just south of Tiberias and at the beaches on the northeastern shore, north of Ein Gev.

Walking, Jogging, and Running

Two annual 11-km (7-mi) Tza'adah (Big Walks) take place in March or April, one along the shore of the Sea of Galilee, the other along the trails of Mt. Gilboa. The events attract participants from all over the country. A promenade in Tiberias suitable for jogging follows the lakeshore for about 5 km (3 mi) to the south. Dedicated runners might want to participate in the Sea of Galilee Marathon and Half-Marathon, which take place in December or January. A triathlon takes place at the beginning of May.

Exploring Lower Galilee

The Lower Galilee embraces three distinct subregions: the Jezreel and Jordan valleys, which traverse the southern part of the region from Mt. Carmel in the west to the border with Jordan in the east; Nazareth and the rugged hill country north of the Jezreel Valley and west of the Sea of Galilee; and the Sea of Galilee itself.

The Jezreel Valley is most easily entered from the Mediterranean coast by Route 65 (the Wadi Ara Pass), which runs northeast from Caesarea. Coming from Jerusalem, you would more likely come up the Jordan Valley and begin exploring the area from the east. You'll find echoes of Old Testament stories throughout the area, but attractions include fine natural sites in addition to the archaeological ones.

One of the dominant themes of the hill country is the New Testament, but the area defies a simple label. Olive groves dominate the landscape like scriptural illustrations. The whole area can be comfortably covered in a day if you time it right. If your itinerary includes the drive between Nazareth or Zippori and Akko (Acre), on the Mediterranean coast, and you are not pressed for time or limited by impending nightfall, consider a scenic return route from the Nazareth end of Route 79 west, 784 north (just west of the Hamovil Junction), and then west again from Karmiel on 85.

The third part of the chapter takes the traveler clockwise along the shores of the entire Sea of Galilee beginning at Tiberias, the main town in the area. The shores are covered with sites hallowed by Christian tradition, but there are also important ancient synagogues at Capernaum and Hammat Tiberias, and Tiberias itself is one of Judaism's four holy cities. Those whose priorities lie elsewhere may want to concentrate on the recreational attractions of the Sea of Galilee.

Numbers in the text correspond to numbers in the margin and on the Lower Galilee map.

Great Itineraries

It is possible to get a feeling for the region in a couple of days; you may want to explore some highlights of the Upper Galilee and the Golan (☞ Chapter 7), too.

IF YOU HAVE 2 DAYS

Use Tiberias or the Sea of Galilee area as a base. Explore the archaeological excavations of **Megiddo** ① and/or **Bet She'an** ⑥ on the way into or out of the region. In hot weather, take a dip at Gan Hashelosha. Visit the Church of the Annunciation in **Nazareth** ⑨ and the fine mosaics of **Zippori** ⑪ nearby. A Christian itinerary might include **Mt. Tabor** ⑫ and **Yardenit** ㉑, on the Jordan River. For a more general approach, visit the ancient synagogue mosaics of **Bet Alfa** ⑤ or **Hammat Tiberias** ㉓, the Crusader fortress of **Belvoir** ⑦, and the cemetery of **Kibbutz Kinneret** ㉒. (The sequence will be determined by the direction from which you enter the region: from Jerusalem via the Jordan Valley or from the Mediterranean coast.)

If your orientation is toward Christian sights, spend the second day around the Sea of Galilee. Join a boat ride with a pilgrimage group, admire the ancient boat at **Ginosar** ⑭, read scripture by the lakeshore at **Tabgha** ⑯, eat a St. Peter's fish lunch near the water, explore the ruins of **Capernaum** ⑰, and end the day in the panoramic tranquillity of the **Mount of Beatitudes** ⑮. For a more general experience, ascend the Golan Heights via **Hammat Gader** ⑲ for the spectacular view and in the Upper Galilee explore the nature reserves of Banias and Tel Dan (with a trout lunch on the bank of one of the rivers) or the synagogues and cobblestone lanes of Zfat (☞ Chapter 7).

IF YOU HAVE 3 OR MORE DAYS
Spend the first day in the Jezreel Valley, including **Megiddo** ①, visiting the scenic attractions of **Mt. Gilboa** ②–⑤, **Bet She'an** ⑥, and—time permitting—either the catacombs of **Bet She'arim** ⑧ in the west, the Crusader castle of **Belvoir** ⑦ in the east, or the church and fine views atop **Mt. Tabor** ⑫. Overnight in 🕇 **Tiberias** or one of the kibbutz guest houses in the Galilee. (The sequence of the following days will be determined to some extent by where you overnight.)

The Christian pilgrim should spend the second day in the Sea of Galilee area (☞ If You Have 2 Days, *above*). On the morning of the third day, drive up to Banias and Caesarea Philippi of the Gospels in the Upper Galilee (☞ Chapter 7), and then head south via Nazareth's **Church of the Annunciation** ⑨ and the mosaics of ancient **Zippori** ⑪. A more general approach might include a more leisurely exploration of the Golan Heights and the Upper Galilee beauty spots on the second day (eat some trout, boat or tube the Jordan River in season—☞ Chapter 7). On the third day, explore the old synagogues and artists' quarter of the mystical mountaintop city of Zfat, in the Upper Galilee, and **Nazareth** ⑨ and **Zippori** ⑪ on the way south.

When to Tour the Lower Galilee
By far the best time to tour the Galilee (and Israel in general) is the spring—March, April, and early May—when the weather is usually great (though March is a bit less reliable) and the countryside is blanketed with wildflowers. At 700 feet below sea level, the Sea of Galilee area is very hot in summer. Avoid the week of Passover, when half the country is vacationing exactly where you are; also weekends in general (Thursday night through Saturday night) are more crowded. The fall—late September, October, early November—is fine, though avoid the Jewish holidays because of crowds and high-season prices. Most panoramas are better in the afternoon, when the sunlight is gentler.

JEZREEL AND JORDAN VALLEYS

"Highways of the world cross Galilee in all directions," wrote the eminent Victorian scholar George Adam Smith in 1898. The great international highway of antiquity, the Via Maris (Way of the Sea) swept up the coast from Egypt and broke inland along three separate mountain passes to emerge in the Jezreel Valley before continuing northeast to Damascus and Mesopotamia. The west–east through road that began at the Mediterranean coast just north of Mt. Carmel and led to the Jordan Valley at Bet She'an, ran through the Jezreel Valley as well. And then, as now, roads connected the valley with the hill country of the Galilee to the north and Samaria to the south. Its destiny as a kind of universal thoroughfare and its flat terrain made the Jezreel Valley a frequent and easy battleground, so much so that the New Testament

Lower Galilee

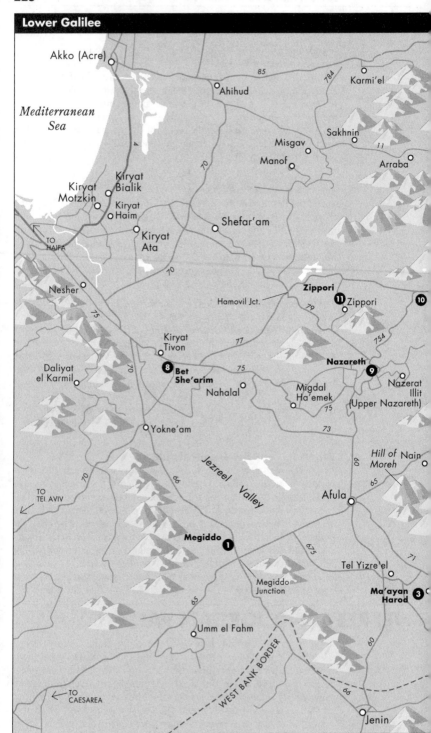

Mediterranean
Sea

Akko (Acre)

Ahihud

85

784

Karmi'el

Sakhnin

11

Misgav

Manof

Arraba

Kiryat
Bialik

Kiryat
Motzkin

Kiryat
Haim

70

Shefar'am

Kiryat
Ata

TO
HAIFA

70

Nesher

75

Zippori

Hamovil Jct.

79

11 Zippori

10

754

Kiryat
Tivon

77

Daliyat
el Karmil

70

8 **Bet
She'arim**

75

Nazareth

9

Nazerat
Illit
(Upper Nazareth)

Nahalal

Migdal
Ha'emek

75

Yokne'am

73

Jezreel

Hill of Nain
Moreh

80

Valley

65

Afula

TO
TEL AVIV

70

66

Megiddo **1**

675

Tel Yizre'el

71

Megiddo
Junction

65

**Ma'ayan
Harod** **3**

60

Umm el Fahm

WEST BANK BORDER

TO
CAESAREA

66

Jenin

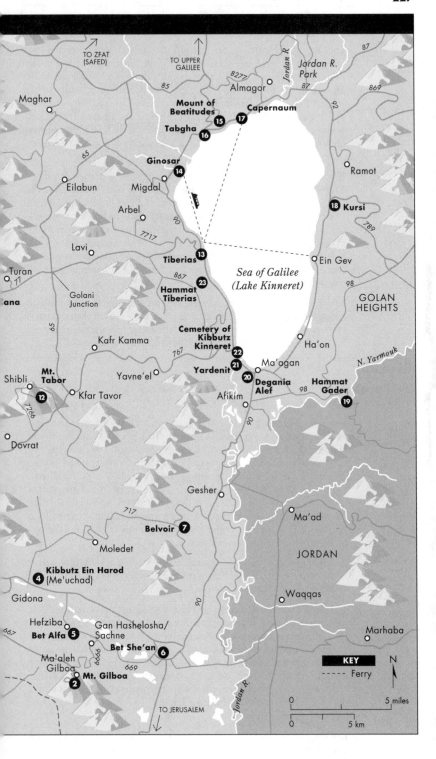

Book of Revelation identified it—by the name Armageddon—as the stage for humanity's apocalyptic finale.

On a topographical map, the Jezreel Valley appears as an inverted equilateral triangle, each side about 40 km (25 mi) long, edged by low mountains. The narrow Harod Valley extends the Jezreel southeast to Bet She'an, in the Jordan Rift. Your most immediate impression will be Jordan Rift—lush farmland as far as the eye can see, but as recently as 50 years ago, malarial swamps still blighted the area, and some early pioneering settlements had cemeteries before their first buildings were completed. Today the valley is one of the country's most fertile regions.

The sites here are described from west to east (though they can easily be explored in the reverse order): Begin with the ancient city of Megiddo, by way of Tel Jezreel and a clutch of diverse attractions on or near Mt. Gilboa, go through the famous dig at Bet She'an, and end (if time permits!) at the glorious Crusader castle of Belvoir, overlooking the Jordan River. There are no fewer than six national parks here, making the National Park Green Card (☞ Nature Reserves and Parks *in* Important Contacts A to Z) a worthwhile investment. Most people spend less than a day in these valleys, but a more leisurely pace will pay dividends.

Eating establishments in this rustic area are confined to roadside cafeterias, lunch-only restaurants adjacent to archaeological sites and parks such as Megiddo and Sachne/Gan Hashelosha, and eateries and snack bars in the towns of Afula (especially) and Bet She'an.

Megiddo

★ ❶ *2 km (1¼ mi) north of the Megiddo Junction, where Rtes. 65 and 66 meet; 12 km (7½ mi) west of Afula.*

Since the beginning of the century, several archaeological expeditions have exposed no fewer than 25 strata of civilization—from the 4th millennium BC to the 4th century BC—in the historical layer-cake mound of Megiddo that archaeologists call a *tel*. The ancient city owed its great importance to its strategic position at the mouth of a pass, the main branch of the international highway between Egypt and Mesopotamia. Pharaohs and Assyrian satraps rushed their armies up and down these passes on their way to attack the other, and Megiddo's coveted location made it as much a target for foreign conquest as it was the center of power of its own small region.

A tiny museum at the site's entrance offers some good visual aids to help you on your way, including three-dimensional maps and a model of the tel itself. The spot is served by an indifferent cafeteria.

The ramp up to the flattop mound brings you into the partially restored remains of a Late Canaanite (Late Bronze Age) **gate,** quite possibly the very one that unsuccessfully defended Megiddo against the Egyptian pharaoh Thutmose III in 1468 BC, as described in his victory stele. Above it is a larger and later gate, almost identical to those found at Hazor, in the north, and Gezer to the south. Long identified with King Solomon (10th century BC)—all three cities were his regional military centers— the gate has been redated by some scholars to the time of Ahab, king of Israel a century later.

Evidence of prehistoric habitation on the site has been found as well, but among the earliest remains of the *city* of Megiddo are a round **altar** dating from the Early Bronze Age and the outlines of several Early Bronze Age **temples,** almost 5,000 years old, visible in the trench between the two fine lookout points.

The connection to King Ahab (9th century) is strong at Megiddo. Ruins of **stables,** also once thought to be Solomon's, are now definitively dated to the reign of Ahab, who is known to have had a large chariot army. But nothing at Megiddo is as impressive as its **water system.** Before its construction, again apparently by Ahab, the citizens of the town had to leave the safety of their walls to draw water from the subterranean spring. In a masterful stroke, the Israelite engineers sunk a deep shaft and a horizontal tunnel through solid rock to reach the spring from within the city. With this access, the spring could be permanently blocked outside the defensive walls, securing the city's vital water supply. The spring, at the end of the tunnel, is nothing more than a trickle today, perhaps blocked by earthquakes of later centuries. Look for chisel marks and ancient steps hewed from rock as you descend 180 steps through the shaft, traverse the 65-yard-long tunnel under the ancient city wall, and climb up 83 steps at the other end. A 10-minute walk takes you back to the parking lot.

The Jezreel Valley has so often heard the clash of arms that the very name of the site that commands it—Har Megiddo, Mt. Megiddo, or Armageddon (Revelation 16)—has become synonymous with the final cataclysmic battle of all time. In 1918, General Allenby swept up the pass by way of Megiddo to outflank the Ottoman Turks and seal the British victory. He was subsequently knighted, taking as his title viscount of Megiddo! ⊠ *National Park, Rte. 66,* ☎ *06/652–2105 or 06/652–6815.* ⌨ *NIS 14 ($4.70).* ☉ *Apr.–Sept., Sat.–Thurs. 8–5, Fri. and holiday eves 8–4; Oct.–Mar., Sat.–Thurs. 8–4, Fri. and holiday eves 8–3; water tunnel closes 30 min before site as a whole.*

Shopping
A small **jewelry shop** at the Megiddo site (☎ 06/642–0314) specializes in handsome and reasonably priced silver and gold items, many made in nearby Kibbutz Megiddo. Particularly attractive is the jewelry incorporating pieces of ancient Roman glass.

En Route   From the Afula road (Route 65), Route 675 breaks southeast through a small farming region called the Ta'anach. On the left, 500 yards beyond the intersection with Route 60 and just after the entrance to Kibbutz Yizre'el, is the low-rise **Tel Yizre'el,** site of the Old Testament city of Jezreel. A short dirt road leads to a rise with a small thicket of trees. Here Ahab coveted Naboth's vineyard (I Kings 21), and his Phoenician wife, Jezebel, met the gruesome death predicted by the prophet Elijah (II Kings 9). From among the indecipherable ancient ruins recently unearthed by a Tel Aviv University expedition, you have a magnificent view of the valley below and a great place to sit and read those biblical passages.

Five hundred yards farther, the scenic Route 667 strikes up through the pine forests of Mt. Gilboa, eventually descending to Route 669 just east of Bet Alfa.

Mt. Gilboa

★ ❷   *17 km (10½ mi) from Megiddo (on Rte. 675) to Rte. 667, descending via Rte. 6666 to Rte. 69, just east of Bet Alfa.*

Mt. Gilboa, actually a small, steep mountain range rather than a single peak, is geographically a spur of the far greater Samaria Range (the biblical Mt. Ephraim) to the southwest. Literally half the mountain is freshly reforested with evergreens, with the other half left in its pristine rockiness. The environmentalists prefer the latter, to protect the profusion of wildflowers that splatter the slopes with color every March and April. From the gravel parking area off Route 667 on the summit of the ridge, well-marked and easy panoramic trails wind through the natural habitat of the rare black (actually purple) iris, which draws hordes of Israelis every spring to pay homage to Mother Nature. Years of tireless efforts by environmental groups such as the Society for the Protection of Nature in Israel (SPNI) have paid off, and every preschooler will tell you imperiously that you are not allowed to pick the wildflowers! The views of the valley below and the hills of Galilee beyond are great year-round, but on a good winter or spring day they are amazing, and the snowcapped Mt. Hermon is easily seen far to the north. Afternoon is the best time to come. The immediate area holds a number of attractions besides the view, too.

Three thousand years ago, the Israelites were routed by the Philistines on Mt. Gilboa, and Saul, their mortally wounded king, ended his own life on the battlefield. "On the morrow, when the Philistines came to strip the slain, they found Saul and his three sons fallen on Mt. Gilboa. And they cut off his head, and stripped off his armor, and sent messengers throughout the land of the Philistines to carry the good news to their idols and the people. . . and they fastened his body to the wall of Beth-shan." Thus the Bible (I Samuel 31) describes the aftermath of the debacle. The battle was presumably fought on the lower slopes of the mountain, for the upper reaches are too craggy and steep; but from a vantage point on the crest, it is easy to conjure up the din of battle below you. The death of Saul sowed panic in the ranks, and the Israelites "forsook their cities and fled; and the Philistines came and dwelt in them." In his lyrical eulogy, king-to-be David curses the battlefield—"Let there be no dew or rain upon you"—where "thy glory, O Israel" was slain (II Samuel 1).

❸ **Ma'ayan Harod** (the Spring of Harod), at the foot of Mt. Gilboa, is a small national park with an attractive area of lawns, huge eucalyptus trees, and a big swimming pool fed by a spring. Today it's a bucolic picnic spot, but almost 32 centuries ago, Gideon, the reluctant hero of the biblical Book of Judges, organized his troops to fight the Midianite desert invaders: "And the camp of Midian was north of them, by the Hill of Moreh, in the valley" (Judges 7). At God's command, in order to emphasize the miraculous nature of the coming victory, Gideon dismissed more than two-thirds of the warriors, and by selecting only those who lapped up water from the spring "as a dog laps," further reduced the army to a tiny force of 300 men. Equipped with swords, ram's horns, and flaming torches concealed in clay jars, the force divided into three companies and surrounded the Midianite camp across the valley in the middle of the night. At a prearranged signal, the Israelite warriors shouted, blew the ram's horns, and smashed the jars. Waking to the din and the appearance of flaming torches, the Midianites were panicked into flight, and the victory was won.

The spring has seen other armies in other ages. It was here in 1260 that the Mamluks stopped the invasion of the hitherto invincible Mongols. And in the 1930s, the woods above the spring hid clandestine Jewish self-defense squads training under British army officer Orde Wingate. Wingate died in the Burmese jungle in 1944; his trainees, among them Moshe Dayan and Yigal Allon, became top military commanders of the fledgling State of Israel in 1948, when Wingate's principles of unconventional warfare stood them in good stead. ⊠ *National Park off Rte. 71, next to Gidona,* ☎ *06/653-2211.* ⌚ *NIS 19 ($6.40).* ☉ *Apr.–Sept., Sat.–Thurs. 8–5, Fri. and holiday eves 8–4; Oct.–Mar., Sat.–Thurs. 8–4, Fri. and holiday eves 8–3.*

❹ **Kibbutz Ein Harod (Me'uchad),** across the highway from Mt. Gilboa, has an **art museum** with a permanent collection that showcases Jewish artists past and present, but its changing exhibits are far more general, spanning different cultures and genres. Don't confuse the place with its immediate neighbor to the west, Ein Harod (Ichud).

🕭 Also on the kibbutz is **Bet Sturman,** a museum of the natural history of the region (stuffed and preserved specimens) and of its human settlement. ⊠ *Rte. 71 opposite gas station. Art museum:* ☎ *06/653–1670.* 🎟 *NIS 10 ($3.40).* ☼ *Sun.–Thurs. 9–4:30, Fri. and holiday eves 9–1:30, Sat. 10–4:30. Bet Sturman:* ☎ *06/653–3284.* 🎟 *NIS 12 ($4).* ☼ *Sun.–Thurs. 8–3, Sat. and holidays 10–2. An English-speaking guide can sometimes be arranged; call ahead. Combined ticket to both museums (without guide): NIS 14 ($4.80).*

NEED A BREAK?

The National Park of **Gan Hashelosha (Sachne)** (⊠ Off Rte. 669, ☎ 06/658–6219) was recently cited internationally for its natural beauty. The official name, Gan Hashelosha, or the Garden of the Three, remembers three Jewish pioneers killed here by a land mine in 1938. This attractive park is developed around a warm spring (28°C, or 82°F, most of the year) and a deep stream (actually a small river deep enough to dive into at spots, with artificial cascades in others). The cost is NIS 19 ($6.40). There are changing facilities for bathers, a decent snack bar at the west end, and a good cafeteria at the east end. In good weather the park is especially crowded on Friday and Saturday. Don't leave your possessions unattended on the lawns.

❺ The ancient synagogue of **Bet Alfa** was accidentally discovered in 1928 by members of Kibbutz Hefziba who were digging an irrigation trench (serendipity is the most successful archaeologist, some claim). Their tools hit a hard surface, and careful excavation uncovered a lovely multicolored **mosaic floor,** almost entirely preserved. The art is somewhat childlike, but that, too, is part of its charm. An Aramaic inscription dates the building to the reign of Byzantine emperor Justinian in the second quarter of the 6th century AD; a Greek inscription credits the workmanship to Marianos and his son, Aninas. Following Jewish tradition, the synagogue faces Jerusalem, with an apse at the far end to hold the holy ark. The building faithfully copies the architecture of the Byzantine basilicas of the day, with a nave and two side aisles, and the doors lead to a small narthex and, at one time, an outside atrium. Stairs indicate there was once an upper story.

The large mosaic in the nave is divided into three panels. The top one leaves no doubt that this was a synagogue. All the classic Jewish symbols are here: the holy ark flanked by lions; the menorah, a seven- or nine-branch candelabra; the ram's horn, called a shofar; the incense shovel once used in the Temple; and the *lulav* and *etrog,* the palm frond and citron used in the celebration of Sukkoth, the Feast of Tabernacles. It is the middle panel, however, that is at once the most interesting and the most unexpected: It is filled with human figures depicting the seasons, the zodiac, and even more incredibly for a Jewish house of worship, the Greek sun god, Helios. Clearly these were more liberal times; perhaps the prohibition on making graven images didn't apply to two-dimensional art then. Most scholars agree the mosaic's motifs do not suggest some divergent Jewish sect or regional apostasy, but a convenient artistic convention to symbolize the orderly cycles of God's universe, since he could not be represented graphically. The last panel tells the story of Abraham's near sacrifice of his son Isaac (Genesis 22), again captioned in Hebrew. ⊠ *National Park on Kibbutz Hefziba, Rte. 669,* ☎ *06/653–2004.* 🎟 *NIS 7 ($2.40).* ☼ *Apr.–Sept., Sat.–Thurs. 8–5, Fri. and holiday eves 8–4; Oct.–Mar., Sat.–Thurs. 8–4, Fri. and holiday eves 8–3.*

Dining and Lodging

$$–$$$ ✕ **Herb Farm on Mt. Gilboa.** Just the view of the Jezreel Valley from
★ the wooden deck or the picture windows would be enough, but here
is a place that glories in the myriad tastes of fresh herbs (25 in use at
any one time) and good produce. The homemade bread and salads are
delicious starters, but an intriguing variety of original dishes—some
meat, some vegetarian—will tempt you as well. There are also several
fish and pasta dishes from which to choose. Try the excellent *tarte,* a
pie of shallots, forest mushrooms, and goat cheese; or the wonderful
stuffed quail (when available). ⊠ *Rte. 667,* ☎ *06/653–1093. Reservations essential for Sat. lunch. AE, DC, MC, V. Closed Sun.*

$–$$ ▥ **Hankin Youth Hostel.** "Youth" is a misnomer at this establishment
in Ma'ayan Harod National Park, next to the hamlet of Gidona, at
the foot of Mt. Gilboa—all are welcome. Mini-apartments sleep six;
20 "caravans" (cheaply built mobile homes) sleep four, with 2 more
sleeping nine. All units are air-conditioned, but conditions are functional and furnishings spartan. The surroundings—the pines and eucalypti of Mt. Gilboa and the park—are a compensation. July and August
rates are slightly higher and include both breakfast and dinner. ⊠
Ma'ayan Harod National Park off Rte. 71, M.P. Gilboa 19120, ☎ FAX
*06/653–1660. 146 beds (including 8 mini-apartments and 22 caravans,
all with private shower). Dining room. AE, DC, MC, V.*

Nightlife and the Arts

Folk music, mostly of the British and American varieties, is alive and
well in Israel and has its big bash once a year (usually first weekend
in July) at the **Jacob's Ladder Folk Festival,** at Gan Hashelosha National Park. "Folk" here is generously defined, and goes beyond the
traditional music to include country and bluegrass, contemporary
music in the folk mode, and even blues. Although the event draws many
young people—especially for the late-night acts—the atmosphere is a
very comfortable one for families, with kids' events as part of the program. In addition to some excellent local talent, foreign household names
like Tom Paxton sometimes appear. Accommodations are in your own
tent or under the stars; showers are available. Since the venue and the
date have occasionally changed, contact the organizer, Menachem
Vinegrad (☎ FAX 06/692–6631), for details.

Outdoor Activities and Sports

KITE FLYING

The **Janusz Korczak Kite-Flying Competition** is an annual event at
Ma'ayan Harod, drawing contestants from throughout Israel and
abroad. For the less professional kite flier, kites can be purchased on
the spot, and kite-building workshops are part of the fun. The event
is named after the great Polish Jewish educator, who visited the nearby
kibbutz in the 1920s and subsequently perished in the Holocaust. The
event takes place during the week of Sukkoth, usually in October. For
details, contact Hagilboa Community Centers (⊠ M.P. Gilboa 18120,
☎ 06/653–3242, FAX 06/653–3362).

WALKING

The annual **Gilboa Big Walk** (Tza'adat Hagilboa in Hebrew) takes place
in March and follows an 11-km (7-mi) route along Mt. Gilboa. Transportation to the jump-off point is provided from Ma'ayan Harod. The
views are delightful, and the weather, though still unstable in this season, can be superb. For details, contact Hagilboa Community Centers
(⊠ M.P. Gilboa 18120, ☎ 06/653–3242, FAX 06/653–3362).

Bet She'an

★ ❻ *23 km (14 mi) east of Afula, 39 km (24 mi) south of Tiberias.*

"The hottest archaeological dig in Israel" is what many have dubbed Bet She'an over the last decade or so. At the intersection of the Jordan and Jezreel valleys and surrounded by farming settlements and fish ponds, the town has one spectacular site but no other attractions. Once in Bet She'an, follow signs to the National Park or the Roman Theater. The theater was exposed over 30 years ago, but the rest of the great Roman-Byzantine city of Scythopolis, as the city was known in antiquity, came to light only in the current excavations and partial restoration.

The high tel dominating the site to the north was the location of **Canaanite/Israelite Bet She'an** three to four millennia ago. Few visible remains are left of the work done by a University of Pennsylvania expedition that partially excavated the site in the 1920s, but a current team of Israeli archaeologists has also turned its attention to this most ancient area. The climb to the top, though a bit strenuous, is short and worth every gasp. There is a fine panoramic view of the surrounding valleys and a superb bird's-eye view of the entire excavated area.

The impressive semicircular **Roman Theater** was built of contrasting black basalt and white limestone blocks around AD 200, when Scythopolis was at its height. Although the upper *cavea,* or tiers, have not survived, the theater is the best preserved and largest in Israel, with an estimated original capacity of some 10,000 people. The large stage and part of the *scaena* (backdrop) behind it have been restored, and Bet She'an again hosts late spring performances as in days of yore (☞ Nightlife and the Arts, *below*).

Until 1985, when the current excavations of the nearly 30-acre site began, the theater was ignored by most tourists in favor of the more famous one at Caesarea (☞ Chapter 5). Now it is the jewel in the crown of one of Israel's most extensive and fascinating digs in recent years. The expedition has systematically exposed the downtown area of one of the region's greatest and most cosmopolitan cities in the Late Roman and Byzantine periods (2nd–6th centuries AD). Masterfully engineered colonnaded main streets, complete with storm drains and lined with shops, converge on a central plaza that once boasted a fine temple, a decorative fountain, and a public monument. An elaborate Byzantine bathhouse, 1¼ acres in area and complete with *caldaria* (steam rooms) and mosaic-floored porticoes, once pampered the worthies of the town. And the enormous haul of marble statuary and friezes says much about the opulence of Scythopolis in its heyday. One of the most interesting finds was a multicolored mosaic floor in a small room near the ancient *odeon* (a small auditorium for chamber music), showing Tyche (Fortuna), Greek goddess of good fortune, holding a cornucopia. An ambitious restoration program is marching hard on the heels of the archaeological dig.

On the main thoroughfare of Sha'ul Hamelech (King Saul) Street, a few hundred yards east of Bank Leumi, are the impressive remains of Scythopolis's **amphitheater,** where blood sports and gladiatorial combats were once the order of the day. ⊠ *National Park off Sha'ul Hamelech St., at Bank Leumi,* ☎ *06/658–7189.* 🎟 *NIS 14 ($3.70).* ☉ *Apr.–Sept., Sat.–Thurs. 8–5, Fri. and holiday eves 8–4; Oct.–Mar., Sat.–Thurs. 8–4, Fri. and holiday eves 8–3.*

Nightlife and the Arts

Gesher Leshalom (Bridge to Peace; ☎ 06/658–5349, 🖷 06/658–4761) is the name of the newish festival in Bet She'an every May. The emphasis is on large-scale mainstream productions—opera, modern dance, ballet, classical and choral ensembles—largely with international artists. The main venue is the marvelous Roman Theater, but secondary locations throughout the town provide stages for local talent performing street theater, folk dancing, children's programs, and so on.

Belvoir

❼ *Rte. 717; turnoff 12 km (7½ mi) north of Bet She'an; continue 5 km (3 mi) to site. The road from Ein Harod via Moledet is passable but in very bad condition in places.*

The Crusaders chose their site well: *Belvoir,* they called it—"beautiful view"—and it was the most invincible fortress in the land. The Hebrew name Kochav Hayarden (the star of the Jordan) and the Arabic Kaukab el Hauwa (the star of the wind) merely emphasize its splendid isolation. The breathtaking view of the Jordan Valley and southern Sea of Galilee some 1,800 feet below you is itself worth the drive (best in afternoon hours).

The mighty castle was completed by the Hospitallers (the Knights of St. John) in 1173. In the summer of 1187 the Crusader armies were crushed by the Arabs under Saladin at the Horns of Hattin, west of Tiberias, bringing to an end the Latin Kingdom of Jerusalem. Its remnants struggled on to Tyre (in modern Lebanon) and into the Holy Land itself, but Belvoir alone refused to yield. Eighteen months of siege brought the Muslims no farther than undermining the outer eastern rampart. The Crusaders, for their part, even sallied out from time to time to do battle with the enemy; but their lone resistance had become pointless. They struck a deal with Saladin: They surrendered the stronghold in exchange for free passage, flags flying, to Tyre.

Do not follow the arrows from the parking lot; instead, take the wide gravel path to the right of the fortress. It brings you right to the panoramic view. It is also the best spot from which to appreciate the strength of the stronghold, with its deep, dry moat, massive rock and cut-stone ramparts, and series of gates. Once inside the main courtyard, you are unexpectedly faced with a fortress within a fortress, a scaled-down replica of the outer defenses. Little wonder the Muslims could not force its submission. Not much of the upper stories remains: In 1220, the Muslims systematically dismantled Belvoir, fearing another Crusade and the renewal of the fortress as a Frankish base. Once you have explored the modest buildings, exit over the western bridge (once a drawbridge), which allows you to spy on the postern gates, the protected and sometimes secret back doors of medieval castles. ⊠ *National Park, Rte. 717, 5 km (3 mi) west of Rte. 90,* ☎ *06/658–1766.* 🎟 *NIS 10 ($3.40).* ☉ *Apr.–Sept., Sat.–Thurs. 8–5, Fri. and holiday eves 8–4; Oct.–Mar., Sat.–Thurs. 8–4, Fri. and holiday eves 8–3.*

NAZARETH AND THE GALILEE HILLS

Remove the modern roads and power lines, and the landscape of this region would be an illustration from the Bible. Unplanned villages are splashed on the hillsides, seemingly haphazardly, freeing the valleys for small-scale agriculture. Acres of olive groves are still harvested by whacking the trees as in days of old, to bring in the source of the region's ancient wealth. New Testament reminders are numerous here: Nazareth, where Jesus grew up; Cana, with its miraculous wedding feast; Mt. Tabor, identified with the Transfiguration; and others. Jewish history resonates strongly, too: Tabor and Yodefat were fortifications in the Great Revolt against the Romans (1st century AD); between the 2nd and 4th centuries AD, Shefar'am, Bet She'arim, and Zippori were in turn the head-quarters of the Sanhedrin, the Jewish high court; and latter-day Jewish pioneers have been attracted to the region's wild scenery as well. The suggested route reflects the area's diversity, from the catacombs of Bet She'arim to Nazareth, then to Cana and Zippori, followed by a detour to Mt. Tabor before the descent to Tiberias and the Sea of Galilee.

Bet She'arim

❽ *20 km (12½ mi) southeast of Haifa, 25 km (15½ mi) west of Nazareth.*

The chalk slopes are honeycombed with catacombs around the attractively landscaped site of ancient Bet She'arim. A Jewish town flourished here after, and to some extent because of, the eclipse of Jerusalem. The little that was left of Jerusalem after Titus's legions sacked it and razed the Second Temple in AD 70 was plowed under by Hadrian in AD 135, following the Second (Bar Kochba) Revolt of the Jews against Rome. Hadrian built in its stead the pagan town of Aelia Capitolina, and access to their holy city and the venerated burial ground of the Mount of Olives was denied to Jews for generations. The center of Jewish life and religious authority retreated, first to Yavne, in the southern coastal plain, and then for several centuries to the Lower Galilee.

By around AD 200 the unofficial Jewish capital had shifted to Bet She'arim, a city that owed its brief preeminence to the enormous stature of one man who chose to make it his home: Rabbi Yehuda Hanassi, the Patriarch, or Prince, as he is sometimes called. The title was conferred on the nominal leader of the Jewish community, who was responsible both for its inner workings and for its relations with its Roman masters. Alone among his contemporaries, Yehuda Hanassi brought to his dual office both a worldly understanding of the ways of diplomacy (he was a personal friend of one of the emperors, possibly Marcus Aurelius) and an awesome reputation as the foremost Jewish religious scholar and spiritual leader of his day.

The rabbi eventually moved east to Zippori (☞ *below*) because of its more salubrious climate, and there he gathered the great Jewish sages of his day and compiled the Mishnah, which remains the definitive interpretation of biblical precepts for religious Jews. Nevertheless, it was in his hometown of Bet She'arim that Yehuda Hanassi was finally laid to rest.

If Bet She'arim was a magnet for scholars and petitioners in Yehuda Hannah's lifetime, it became a virtual shrine after his death. With Jerusalem still off-limits, Bet She'arim became the prestigious burial site of the Jewish world. It was considered a privilege and good afterlife insurance to be buried in the company of *rabenu hakadosh* (our holy teacher), for when the Messiah came, surely the rabbi would be one of the first resurrected to accompany the Messiah to Jerusalem! Bet She'arim's prominence lasted until AD 352, when Gallus destroyed the town during the suppression of (another) Jewish revolt.

In two major expeditions in the 1930s and '50s, a huge series of 20 **catacombs** was uncovered. Of these, the largest is open to the public; its 24 chambers contain more than 200 stone sarcophagi and *arcosolia* (arched burial niches). A wide range of both Jewish and Roman symbols are carved into the sarcophagi, and more than 250 funerary inscriptions in Greek, Hebrew, Aramaic, and Palmyrene throughout the site testify to the great distances traveled by some denizens of this necropolis—from Yemen and Mesopotamia, for instance—to be buried here. Without exception, the sarcophagi were plundered by grave robbers seeking the possessions with which the dead were interred.

The tiny but interesting **museum** adjacent to the catacombs includes a relic of Bet She'arim's industrial activity, a 9-ton slab of raw, unfinished glass, the largest such artifact from the ancient world. Remains of an olive press and a fine ancient synagogue are visible to the left of the road that descends to the park. ⊠ *Follow the signs in Kiryat Tivon, off Rte. 75 or 722;* ☎ *04/983–1643.* ☖ *NIS 10 ($3.40).* ☉ *Apr.–Sept., Sat.–Thurs. 8–5, Fri. and holiday eves 8–4; Oct.–Mar., Sat.–Thurs. 8–4, Fri. and holiday eves 8–3.*

Nazareth

★ ❾ *30 km (19 mi) east of Bet She'arim; about 56 km (35 mi) east of Haifa; 15 km (9½ mi) north of Afula.*

The Nazareth where Jesus grew up was an insignificant village nestling in a hollow in the Galilean hills. Today's city of 70,000 has burst out of the hollow with almost frenetic energy. It is a slightly bemusing and dissonant experience for the Christian pilgrim who seeks the spiritual Nazareth among the horn-blowing cars, vendors, and donkeys (at least *they* add some scriptural authenticity!) plying Paulus VI Street. The scene is hardly quieter even on Friday, the holy day of the Muslim half of the Arab population, but calms down somewhat on Wednesday afternoon, when many businesses are closed for a midweek sabbatical; on Sunday, the day of rest for the Christians who make up the other half of the town, it's positively placid. If you're out for local color (and traffic jams), come on Saturday, when Arab peasants come to town to sell produce and buy goods, and Jewish families from the surrounding area come looking for bargains in the *souk* (market).

If you're coming from Bet She'arim, Route 77 breaks off to the north—to Zippori, the Golani Junction, and Tiberias. Route 75 skirts the north side of the picturesque Jezreel Valley as it climbs into the hills toward Nazareth. At the crest of the hill, it is joined by Route 60 from Afula. A turn to the left takes you down to Paulus VI, the main street of Nazareth.

The Franciscan **Church of the Annunciation,** the largest in the Middle East, dominates the lower part of the town. Consecrated in 1969, it enshrines the Roman Catholic tradition that here the angel Gabriel appeared to Mary to announce the coming birth of Jesus. (Casa Nova Street climbs steeply to the entrance of the church. Parking is hard to find here: Try Paulus VI Street, in the direction of the Galilee Hotel.)

The artwork in and around the church is eclectic in the extreme, but the more interesting for that. The portico around the courtyard just inside the main gate is decorated with contemporary mosaic panels, mostly depicting the Madonna and Child theme, donated by Catholic communities around the world. Many carry the names of their countries of origin; for others you must rely on the script (like Korean or Gaelic) or the artistic style (like Thai) to decipher the piece.

The main entrance of the church is graced by tastefully designed doors made in Germany that relate in bronze relief the central events of Jesus' life. Enter the dimly lighted **lower church,** with its brilliant abstract stained-glass windows. The focal point of the entire church is the **grotto,** a small, hewed cave dwelling below floor level. The New Testament (Luke 1) relates, "The angel Gabriel was sent from God to a city of Galilee named Nazareth, to a virgin. . . and the virgin's name was Mary. And he came to her and said, 'Hail, O favored one, the Lord is with you! . . . And behold, you will conceive in your womb and bear a son, and you shall call his name Jesus.' " This is the event known to Christianity as the Annunciation, and Roman Catholic tradition identifies the grotto as the home of Mary and the place where the angel appeared to her. A seating area before the cave is surrounded by a fence with a gate only opened for groups of pilgrims holding prearranged masses. If you are on your own, you can sometimes dart in and out as groups arrive and depart. Crusader-era walls still stand beneath the modern windows, and some restored Byzantine mosaics are below the railings from which you view the grotto.

Just inside the main entrance, a spiral staircase leads to the vast **upper church,** some 70 yards long and 30 yards wide, the parish church of Nazareth's Roman Catholic community. Note that the beautiful Italian ceramic reliefs on the huge concrete pillars representing the Stations of the Cross are captioned in the Arabic vernacular. The cupola, which soars 195 feet above the cave of the lower church (seen through a well), is formed by ribs representing the petals of an upside-down lily chalice rooted in heaven. The lily, a symbol of purity, represents Mary's unblemished nature, and therefore the petals are repeatedly inscribed with the letter *M*. The huge Italian-designed mosaic behind the altar shows Jesus and Peter at the center and an enthroned Mary behind them, flanked by figures of the hierarchical church (to your right), and the charismatic church (to your left). The modern concrete trusses over the nave evoke the wooden roofs of the early Christian basilicas.

On the walls of the upper church are the so-called banners, large panels of mosaics and ceramic reliefs contributed by Roman Catholic communities abroad. Among those represented are the United States (a piece inspired by Revelation 12:1–2), Canada (a fine terra-cotta), and Australia. Noteworthy are the Madonna and Child–themed gifts from Japan (made with gold leaf and real pearls), Venezuela (a carved-wood statue), and Cameroon (a stylized painting in black, white, and brick red). In the courtyard, a glass-enclosed baptistery is built over what is thought to have been an ancient *mikveh,* a Jewish ritual immersion bath.

In the same complex as the Church of the Annunciation is the small **Church of St. Joseph,** just past Terra Sancta College, built over a complex of rock-hewn chambers traditionally identified as the workshop of Joseph the Carpenter. ✉ *Casa Nova St.,* ☎ *06/657–2501.* 💲 *Free.* ☉ *Apr.–Sept., Mon.–Sat. 8:30–11:45 and 2–5:45, Sun. 2–5:30; Oct.–Mar., Mon.–Sat. 8:30–11:45 and 2–4:30, Sun. 2–4:30.*

The **souk,** entered a few yards down Casa Nova Street from the exit of the Church of the Annunciation, is full of kitchenware, live chickens, and cassette tapes of Egyptian pop singer Oum Kultom (not religious souvenirs and ethnic trinkets, which you'll find around the lower part of Casa Nova Street and on Paulus VI Street, where the tour buses park). It's still fun to poke around, though: One person's kitchenware is another's curio. At press time, however, the souk was nearing the end of some serious municipal renovation, with the promise (if that is the right word!) of creating a true bazaar-type tourist attraction. This is all part of Nazareth's girding its loins for the year 2000—Christianity's bimillennium—and its expected rush of pilgrims.

The so-called **Synagogue Church,** on the right side of the main thoroughfare of the souk and clearly marked, is occasionally sought by pilgrims. The site belongs to the Melkites (Greek Catholics), who, the Franciscans complain, took it by force in the 18th century. The building, though old, was never a synagogue, but rather a church built on the traditional site of the synagogue to which Jesus came "on the Sabbath day. And he stood up to read; and here was given to him the book of the prophet Isaiah" (Luke 4). Jesus selected a prophetic passage that, according to Christian tradition, he himself was destined to fulfill. His rendition pleased his listeners, apparently, but his interpretation did not, and they drove him out of town. If the building is locked, ask for the key at the apartment upstairs (you will be expected to leave something in the collection box).

NEED A
BREAK?

Try the Arab pastries at the **Mahroum** confectionery, at the corner of Casa Nova and Paulus VI streets in Nazareth. The place is clean, has bathrooms, and makes wonderful *bourma*, a honey-soaked cylindrical pastry filled with whole pistachio nuts. Don't confuse the place with one nearby: Look for the Arab pastries, not the gooey Western imitations.

The Greek Orthodox **Church of St. Gabriel,** about 1 km (½ mi) north of the junction of Paulus VI and Casa Nova streets, contains a spring that, citing the non-canonical Gospel of St. James, the Greek Orthodox believe to be the site of the Annunciation. (As you approach the church, you will pass a round white stone structure on the left marked MARY'S WELL. This, however, is merely a modern fountain.) One may question the authenticity of that tradition—evidence of an earlier structure, perhaps a medieval church, suggests the tradition is not new— but one thing is certain: This is the only natural water source in Nazareth, and Mary must have come here almost daily to draw water.

The ornate church was built in 1750 and contains a fine carved-wood pulpit and iconostasis (chancel screen) with painted New Testament scenes and silver-haloed saints in the niches. The walls are adorned with frescoes of figures from the Bible and the Greek Orthodox hagiography. A tiny "well" stands over the running spring, and a modern aluminum cup on a cord gives a satisfying plop as it drops into the sacred water. (The water is pure spring water; the cup's sanitary condition is more suspicious.) The hours of the church are flexible; sometimes you can enter during the midday break, sometimes in late afternoon. ⊠ *Off Paulus VI St.* ⛨ *Small donation expected.* ☉ *Apr.–Sept., daily 8–11:45 and 3–6; Oct.–Mar., daily 8–11:45 and 3–5.*

Christianity speaks with many voices in Nazareth: The newly rebuilt **Baptist Church,** a few hundred yards north of the Church of St. Gabriel, along Paulus VI Street, is affiliated with the Southern Baptist Convention in the United States.

For unobstructed **panoramas** of the town, drive up to Upper Nazareth, on the eastern ridge, a Jewish town of about 35,000 founded as a separate municipal entity in the 1950s; or to the Salesian church on the opposite western ridge (accessible from the police station at the town's northern exit, where the road heads for Tiberias).

Dining and Lodging
Visitors tend to sightsee in this area and move along, and the result is a dearth of good restaurants. There is, however, a clutch of fairly decent little **Arab restaurants on Casa Nova and Paulus VI Streets,** in Nazareth, frequented mostly by locals. Dining here means supping on hummus, shishlik, baklava, Turkish coffee, and the like. Decor is incidental, atmosphere a function of the moment's patrons, and dinnertime early. Of course, there are no reservations taken, and dress is casual.

Roman Catholic **hospices** in Nazareth cater primarily to pilgrim groups and not all encourage individual travelers. Contact the Government Tourist Office (⊠ Casa Nova St., ☎ 06/657–3003) for listings of both hospices and other hotels.

Cana

 8 km (5 mi) north of Nazareth on Rte. 754, 1 km (½ mi) south of the junction of Rtes. 77 and 754; 50 km (31 mi) east of Haifa.

According to the New Testament (John 2), it was here—the Arab village of Kafr Kanna, the ancient Jewish village of Cana—that Jesus reluctantly performed his first miracle, turning water into wine at a wedding feast, and thus emerged from his "hidden years" to begin a three-year ministry in the Galilee. Approaching the town from Nazareth, the road winds through typical Galilean countryside. The profusion of olive groves, pomegranates, grape vines, fig trees, and even the occasional date palm (unusual at this altitude) is a reminder of how much local scenery is reflected in the Bible. Even the clutter of modern buildings, power lines and industrial debris cannot completely ruin the impression.

Within the village, red signs on the right lead to two rival churches—one Roman Catholic (Franciscan), the other Greek Orthodox—that enshrine the scriptural tradition. The alleyway to these churches is passable for cars, and you can park in the courtyard of the souvenir store opposite the Franciscan **Cana Wedding Church** (☎ 06/651–7011). The present church, built in the 1880s, is worth a short visit. Admission is free, and you'll generally find it open weekdays 8–noon and 2–5 (until 6 April–September), Saturday 8–noon. From the vestibule, a few steps take you up into the main chapel, while another staircase descends into a grotto, said by the Franciscans to be the very spot where the wedding took place. In the vestibule look for an ancient mosaic with an Aramaic inscription (indicating the presence of a pre-Byzantine synagogue) and for the water trough in the grotto. The stone jar on display here is not old, but rather just an illustration of the kind mentioned in the gospel passage. The Greek Orthodox priests of St. Nathaniel across the way show two older jars, which their tradition suggests are original. Fine *authentic* examples of such water jars are on view in the Herodian mansions of Jerusalem's Jewish Quarter.

Zippori

★ *9 km (6 mi) from Cana—via Hoshaya, 4 km (2½ mi) off Rte. 77; also accessible through village of Zippori, 4 km (2½ mi) off Rte. 79; 47 km (29 mi) from Haifa.*

For years the main attraction of Zippori was its charming hilltop location, surrounded by planted pine and cypress woods, cultivated fields, and a fine view of the valley below. The site has been transformed into a national park: Archaeologists have unearthed much of the large and prosperous city of the Roman period, including a most impressive water system and a dozen mosaic floors of considerable interest and sometimes of extraordinary fineness (at press time, only one was open to the public, though preparation of the others continues apace).

A Jewish town stood here from at least the 1st century BC through the early Middle Ages. Known as well by its Greek name, Sepphoris, it is identified in some Christian traditions as the birthplace of the Virgin Mary. In the Great Revolt of the Jews against the Romans (AD 66–73), the citizens of Zippori opted out of the struggle and sued for peace with Vespasian, thus creating a serious gap in the rebel defenses in the Galilee and earning the ire of their compatriots, but sparing their town the destruction that was the fate of so many Jewish towns.

In the late 2nd or early 3rd century AD, the legendary sage Rabbi Yehuda Hanassi (the Patriarch) moved here from Bet She'arim (☞ *above*) for health reasons. His enormous prestige and official status as the head of the Jewish community made the relocation to Zippori of the Jewish high court, the Sanhedrin, an obvious move. It was apparently here (the sources are equivocal on this) that Rabbi Yehuda convened the greatest Jewish sages of the time and compiled the Mishnah, the codification of Oral Law. For centuries, rabbis had given learned responses to real-life questions of civil and religious law, basing their judgments on the do's and don'ts and between-the-lines principles of the Torah, the biblical Five Books of Moses, which is the foundation of Judaism. These rabbinic opinions had been transmitted orally from generation to generation and, like court decisions, had become legal precedents and the heart of Jewish jurisprudence. Further commentary was added to the Mishnah in later centuries to produce the Talmud, the primary guide to Orthodox Jewish practice to this day.

Zippori was a town with a clearly cosmopolitan soul, however. There is evidence that Jewish, Christian, and pagan communities coexisted for a while around the 3rd century AD. A relatively small Roman theater—capacity about 4,000, its stone seats long since stolen by local villagers for their own building projects—tells mutely of the town's cultural life; the mosaic floors bespeak the opulence that could support it. One mosaic is made up of Egyptian motifs, including the famous lighthouse at Alexandria and a mythological depiction of the source of the Nile River. Another mosaic, once a synagogue floor, rather surprisingly depicts the signs of the zodiac, just like those found in Bet Alfa (☞ Jezreel and Jordan Valleys, *above*) and Hammat Tiberias (☞ Tiberias and the Sea of Galilee, *below*). The finest mosaic floor of all (and the only one open to the public at press time) reveals a series of Dionysian drinking scenes, as well as the exquisite face of a woman, at once dubbed "the Mona Lisa of the Galilee" by the popular press. On the crest of the ridge, that floor apparently adorned the living/dining room of the town's most prominent villa, perhaps the governor's residence. A reconstruction of the structure has tastefully highlighted the mosaics and has detailed explanations of the various parts.

Alongside the villa is a watchtower, Zippori's landmark. The lower Crusader part of the structure reuses Roman sarcophagi as the cornerstones. The upper Turkish levels have been renovated, and the roof offers superb views of the area. A good video and a small museum that includes interactive CD-ROMs along with archaeological artifacts add an extra dimension to your visit. East of the villa is an impressive Roman colonnaded street, maybe the *cardo maximus,* the main thoroughfare of the 3rd-century town.

One kilometer (½ mile) east of the main site—but still within the park—is a huge section of the water supply system of ancient Zippori, fed by springs just north of Nazareth. The ancient aqueduct is in fact a deep man-made plastered canyon, and the effect is extraordinary. ✉ *Between Rtes. 77 and 79,* ☎ *06/656–8272.* ☛ *NIS 14 ($4.70).*

Donkey-Back Riding
You can rent a donkey or be guided on one in the Nazareth hills (☞ Guided Tours *in* Lower Galilee A to Z, *below*) from **Donkey Tracks,** in nearby Hoshaya (✉ Kfar Kedem, M.P. Hamovil 17915, ☎ 06/656–5511, ℻ 06/657–0378).

Golani Junction

6 km (3½ mi) east of Cana at intersection of Rtes. 77 and 65, 50 km (31 mi) from Haifa.

One of the most important crossroads in the Lower Galilee, the junction was captured by the Golani Brigade of the Israel Defense Forces in the War of Independence in 1948. A monument and museum (and a McDonald's!) are on the east side of the junction.

All around the Golani Junction are new groves of evergreens planted by visitors as part of the **Jewish National Fund**'s (JNF) Plant a Tree with Your Own Hands. Over the last 90 years or so, the JNF has worked to redeem a land neglected for centuries. In an attempt to restore the forests that once covered the hills of Israel, more than 200 million trees have been planted countrywide. Jewish tradition elevates the act of planting a tree to the level of a mitzvah, a good deed given authority by the Bible. If you want to leave something living behind you, the JNF offices (open Sunday–Thursday) are to the left of Afula Road (Route 65), a few hundred yards from the junction. For NIS 35 ($10) you can pick out a sapling—dedicating it to someone if you wish—and plant it yourself.

At the **Horns of Hattin,** a small double hill that is an extinct volcano, Saladin crushed the Crusader army in 1187, bringing to an end the Latin Kingdom of Jerusalem. Richard the Lionhearted's Third Crusade a few years later restored some parts of the country to Christian control, but the power and the glory of the Latin Kingdom was gone forever. The hill is just beyond Kibbutz Lavi (☞ Dining and Lodging, *below*), about 2½ km (1½ mi) east of the Golani Junction on Route 77.

Dining and Lodging

$–$$ ✕ **Younes.** Don't look for elegant decor and ambience: Younes is a place for eating, not dining. This popular watering hole for locals and Israelis on the road serves up excellent Arab fare, including tasty Middle Eastern salads, shishlik, and grilled lamb chops. Big windows provide some fair views and an airy feeling, and you can sit outside when the weather is right. ✉ *Rte. 77 at gas station, 1 km (½ mi) west of Golani Junction,* ☎ *06/676–7343. Reservations not accepted. No credit cards.*

$$–$$$ ⊞ **Lavi Kibbutz Hotel.** The guest house at Kibbutz Lavi is designed like a hotel, with all the units in one building. The community is Jewish Orthodox, so there is no vehicular traffic into or out of the village (and thus no check-ins or checkouts) on the Sabbath, from sunset on Friday until Saturday after dark. Those inconveniences aside, the atmosphere at the kibbutz is warm and welcoming, and many Christian pilgrim groups make it their Galilee base. Rooms are comfortable and the food decent, but nothing is out of the ordinary. Still, the experience of waking to rural surroundings has much to commend it, and you're only 15 minutes from Tiberias. ✉ *On Rte. 77, 11 km (7 mi) west of Tiberias, Lower Galilee 15267,* ☎ *06/679–9450,* ℻ *06/679–9399. 112 rooms with bath, 12 with shower. Restaurant, pool, 2 tennis courts. AE, DC, MC, V.*

En Route   South of the Golani Junction, Route 65 passes through beautiful, green undulating countryside. Ilaniya is the first village on the right, still known by its old Arabic name of **Sejera.** At the beginning of the century, it was a training farm for young Jewish pioneers, among them a certain David Ben-Gurion, later to become Israel's first prime minister.

Mt. Tabor

★ ⓬   *16 km (10 mi) south of the Golani Junction off Rte. 7266, 17 km (10½ mi) northeast of Afula.*

Mt. Tabor and the nearby areas are rich with biblical associations and history. The large village of **Kfar Tavor,** a veteran pioneering community of the late 19th century, is dominated to the west by the domed mountain that gave it its name.

The modern kibbutz of **Ein Dor**—2 km, or 1½ mi, past Kfar Tavor, east on the turnoff for Route 7276—is the biblical Endor of I Samuel 28. Three thousand years ago King Saul communed here with the spirit of the prophet Samuel before his fateful battle against the Philistines. Saul got little consolation. "The Lord has torn the kingdom out of your hand, and given it to your neighbor, David," cried Samuel, "and tomorrow, you and your sons shall be with me. . . ." At the subsequent battle on Mt. Gilboa (☞ Jezreel and Jordan Valleys, *above*), Saul and his three sons were killed and the Israelite army was routed. "How are the mighty fallen . . . ," lamented David when the news reached him.

Shibli, on Route 7266, is a village of Bedouin who abandoned their nomadic life a few generations ago and became farmers. The narrow switchback road up Mt. Tabor begins from a clearing beyond Shibli and between Shibli and the next village of Dabouriya. A Nazareth-based taxi is usually waiting at the bottom of the mountain to provide a shuttle service to the top.

Christian tradition, as far back as the Byzantine period, has identified Mt. Tabor as the "high mountain apart" that Jesus ascended with his disciples Peter, James, and John. "And he was transfigured before them, and his garments became white as light. And behold there appeared to them Moses and Elijah, talking with him" (Matthew 17). Early churches on the mountain were designed to represent the three tabernacles Peter had suggested be built, one for Moses, one for Elijah, and one for Jesus himself. The altar of the present **Church of the Transfiguration** (☎ 06/676–7489), which was consecrated in 1924, represents the tabernacle of Jesus; those of Moses and Elijah are represented as chapels at the back of the church. The church is open Sunday–Friday, 8–noon and 2–5; admission is free.

Thirty-two centuries ago, somewhere near the foot of the mountain, the Israelite conscripts of the prophetess/judge Deborah and her general, Barak, routed the Canaanite chariot army. From the terrace of the Franciscan hospice adjacent to the church, you see the Jezreel Valley to the west and south; and from a platform on the Byzantine and Crusader ruins to the left of the modern church (watch your step), there is a panorama east and north over the Galilean hills. No wonder the Jewish general Yosef Ben Matityahu (Josephus Flavius) fortified the hill in the 1st century AD, during the Great Revolt against the Romans.

NEED A BREAK? The **Dovrat Inn** (✉ Rte. 65, ☎ 06/659-9520) is a rather good cafeteria. For a meal, try the piquant goulash soup; for a snack, get the apple strudel with your coffee. It's about 5 km (3 mi) south of the Shibli (Route 7266) turnoff.

Dining

$$$ ✕ **Tzela Hatavor.** The restaurant lies "in the shadow of Mt. Tabor" (a
★ fair translation of the name). Split-pane arched windows and solid wood tables create a fashionably rustic ambience. The menu is wide-ranging—soups and salads, pastas, fish, steaks, and a kid's meal—and the effort to provide a dining experience lifts it above the usual roadside eatery. This is especially felt in the subtle but well-flavored sauces: the tomato-and-basil sauce of the eggplant appetizer, the orange sauce that accompanies the mallard, the Dijon-mustard steak sauce, and the caramel sauce in which the white-chocolate parfait swims. ✉ *Rte. 65,*

Kfar Tavor, next to gas station, ☎ *06/676–9966. Reservations essential on weekends and holidays. AE, DC, MC, V.*

En Route   If you're heading to Lake Kinneret (Sea of Galilee), take Route 767, which breaks off Route 65 at Kfar Tavor. It is a beautiful drive of about 25 minutes. The first village, **Kafr Kamma,** is one of two in Israel of the Circassian (*Cherkessi*) community, Muslims from the Russian steppes who were settled here by the Ottoman Turks in the 19th century. The decorative mosque is just one element of the tradition they continue to preserve.

On the descent to the lake, there is a parking area precisely at sea level. The Sea of Galilee is still more than 700 feet below you, and the view is superb, especially in the afternoon. You meet Route 90 at the bottom of the road.

TIBERIAS AND THE SEA OF GALILEE

The great American writer and humorist Mark Twain was unimpressed by the area of the Sea of Galilee. He passed through in 1867 in the company of a group of pilgrims and Arab dragomans (interpreters) on horseback and found "an unobtrusive basin of water, some mountainous desolation, and one tree." He would scarcely recognize it now. Modern agriculture and afforestation projects have made the plains and hills green, the handful of "squalid" and "reeking" villages of his day have been supplanted by a string of thriving and well-landscaped kibbutzim, and the "unobtrusive basin of water" has become a lively resort area.

The Sea of Galilee is in fact a freshwater lake, 22 km (14 mi) long from north to south and 12 km (7½ mi) wide from east to west. The Jordan River feeds the lake from the north and leaves it from the south to meander to the Dead Sea. Almost completely ringed by cliffs and steep hills, the lake lies in a hollow about 700 feet below sea level, which accounts for its warm climate and subtropical vegetation.

The city of Tiberias provides a sort of anchor for the area and the logical starting point for a tour. Thereafter, the sites are described in sequence as you circumvent the Sea of Galilee in a clockwise direction (via Routes 90, 87, 92, and 98), ending at Hammat Tiberias, at the city's southern edge. It is worthwhile crossing the lake by boat if bringing your car around is easily done. Note that several of the Christian sites demand that visitors be modestly dressed.

Tiberias

★ ⓭   *38 km (23½ mi) north of Bet She'an, 36 km (23 mi) east of Nazareth, 70 km (43 mi) from Haifa.*

The splendid location of Tiberias as the only town on the Sea of Galilee has made it the natural center of the region. It is not a town with class, however: Almost 2,000 years old, Tiberias still has the atmosphere of a community yet to come of age. It is simultaneously brash and sleepy, a provincial town where falafel is far more popular than foie gras, where a few pubs with loud recorded music are what's happening most nights, and where its reputation as a resort has more to do with its great location and some decent hotels than with the town's own attractions.

Today's Tiberias, with a population of 35,000, spreads all the way up the slope behind it, from about 700 feet below sea level at the lake to an elevation of 800 feet above sea level at its highest hilltop neighborhoods—a difference big enough to create a serious temperature differential in midsummer. Tiberias itself is not lovely; it deserves better than the sort of development it has experienced. Most visitors, however, see little of the town proper and confine themselves to the lakeshore district, where most of the hotels and all the pubs and restaurants are crowded together. Indeed, tourism, as much Israeli as foreign, is one of the mainstays of the town's economy. You can eat well here, boogie a bit, and drink late along an incomparable subtropical lake.

Tiberias has an almost invisible history: Much has happened here, but you will find few footprints of the past. Part of the black-basalt medieval city wall crosses Habanim Street just south of the Radisson Moriah Plaza Hotel; the Tourist Information Office, on Habanim Street opposite the hotel, is framed by restored Crusader arches; and massive Crusader towers and ramparts behind the Scottish Centre dominate Dona Gracia and Gedud Barak streets. In the area of the Promenade, between the Radisson Moriah and Caesar hotels, is a cluster of old basalt synagogues and mosques and a 19th-century church. Some synagogues date from the Aboulafia period of the 18th century. The Franciscan Church of St. Peter commemorates the events described in John 21, in which Jesus entrusts Peter with the care of "my sheep."

In AD 18, the town was completed by Herod Antipas, son of the notorious Herod the Great, and dedicated to Tiberius, emperor of Rome at the time. Although Antipas, with the title of tetrarch, was able to surround himself with ambitious courtiers and functionaries, many common folk shunned the new town because it had been built on an old cemetery and was therefore considered unclean.

Rich men make poor rebels, and the Tiberians seem to have had little stomach for the Jewish war against Rome that broke out in AD 66. They surrendered to the Romans in 67, saving themselves from the vengeful destruction visited on so many other Galilean towns. In the 2nd century, the revered Rabbi Shimon Bar Yochai ceremonially purified Tiberias, opening the way for a wave of settlement and development that transformed the city. Jerusalem, devastated by Titus's legions in AD 70, lay in ruins, the Jews banished from the city. The center of Jewish life in Israel gradually gravitated to the Galilee. By the 4th century, the Sanhedrin had established itself in Tiberias. It was here around AD 400 that the final compilation of Jewish Oral Law into what became known as the Jerusalem Talmud took place.

This was something of a golden era in Tiberias, assuring it a place among Judaism's holy cities in the Land of Israel (together with Jerusalem, Hebron, and Safed). The community knew hard times under the Byzantines, stabilized under more tolerant Muslim dynasties (the Arabs conquered the region in the 7th century), and declined again under the hostile Crusaders, who made Tiberias the capital of their Principality of Galilee. The Arab Saladin besieged the city in 1187 and routed the Crusader army, en route with relief to Tiberias, at the nearby Horns of Hattin. Crusader fortifications of the town are still a prominent feature of the cityscape today.

Tiberias's decline was almost total after the debacle at Hattin. It wasn't until 1562, when the Ottoman sultan Suleiman the Magnificent gave the town to the Jewish nobleman Don Joseph Nasi, that an attempt was made to revive the community. Don Joseph resettled the town and planted mulberry trees in the hope—the vain hope, as it turned out—of developing a silkworm industry.

In the 18th century, Tiberias was rebuilt by renegade Bedouin governor Dahr el-Omar, who invited a group of Jews from Izmir, in Turkey, to settle the town. In conflict with the Ottomans and unable to trust his own subjects, this cunning ruler decided to populate his capital city with a citizenry loyal to him personally. The leader of the new settlers was Isaac Aboulafia, perhaps still the best-known family name in Tiberias today. The Jewish community swelled further with the arrival in 1777 of a group of Hassidim, members of a devout, charismatic sect from Eastern Europe.

In 1833, the Egyptian nationalist leader Ibrahim Pasha, enjoying his short-lived independence from Turkey, again rebuilt the town, but a cataclysmic earthquake just four years later left Tiberias in ruins and (it is told) 1,000 dead.

Relations between the Jewish and Arab citizens of Tiberias were generally cordial until the Arab riots of 1936, in which some 30 Jews were massacred. Confrontation during the 1948 War of Independence had a different consequence. An attack by local Arabs in anticipation of an imminent Syrian invasion brought a counterattack from Haganah forces (the Jewish underground army before Israeli statehood), and the Arab population abandoned the town.

Among the wealth of tombs in Tiberias is that of its most famous denizen, the great 12th-century sage **Moses Maimonides** (1135–1204). To get to the tomb from the tourist center of Tiberias, walk north up Habanim Street, taking a left at Hayarden Street. Walk two blocks and turn right onto Ben Zakkai Street. Continue for two blocks; you'll see the tomb on your right.

Born in Córdoba, Spain, Maimonides became renowned as a philosopher, the physician to the royal court of Saladin in Egypt, and, in the Jewish world, as the greatest religious scholar and spiritual authority since the Talmudic period of the 4th and 5th centuries AD. To his profound knowledge of the Talmud, Maimonides brought an incisive intellect honed by his study of Aristotelian philosophy and the physical sciences. The result was a rationalism unusual in Jewish scholarship and a lucidity of analysis and style admired by Jewish and non-Jewish scholars alike.

After his death, in Egypt, Maimonides's remains were interred in Tiberias (although he never resided here). His whitewashed tomb has become a shrine, dripping with candle wax and tears. Marble plaques on either side of the path approaching the tomb recall the many disciplines in which Maimonides distinguished himself. Less tasteful is the stall at the entrance displaying cheap religious trinkets for the faithful. ✉ *Ben Zakkai St.* 🎫 *Free.* ☉ *Sun.–Thurs. daylight hrs, Fri. and holiday eves until 2.*

On Derech Hagevura, in the uptown area, is the traditional tomb of **Rabbi Akiva,** the spiritual leader of the Bar Kochba Revolt against Rome (AD 132–135), who was captured and then tortured to death in Caesarea.

Dining and Lodging
Tiberias and the Sea of Galilee are a much livelier proposition than other parts of Lower Galilee. Because most visitors to the region actually stay in this area, some very good restaurants have appeared. Most are in Tiberias proper, but a few of the daytime watering holes around the lake stay open into the evening. The local specialty is St. Peter's fish (*tilapia*), which is native to the Sea of Galilee, but demand has far outstripped the capacity of the lake, and most restaurants serve the pond-bred variety. Meat options tend to be more of the Middle Eastern variety: shishlik and kebabs accompanied by hummus, pickles, and the ubiq-

uitous french fries. Along the Promenade in Tiberias is a string of virtually indistinguishable restaurants that specialize in this menu.

At a right angle to the Promenade is the newer *midrachov* (pedestrian mall), between the Radisson Moriah Plaza and Caesar hotels, with a wide range of eating options: hamburger joints, pizzerias, ice cream parlors, and restaurants offering light meals. Among the latter is a member of the nationwide Kapulsky chain, known for its sinfully rich cakes. Perhaps because of the competition, the "regular" restaurants, with their fish, grills, schnitzel, and *shwarma* (slices of spit-grilled meat served in a pita with salads and condiments), have kept their prices down; if you're not looking for a gourmet experience, you can eat quite well for $10 or less. Another category that has gained popularity is the pub, with wood-paneled rooms and smoky atmosphere, and meals to mitigate the effect of the excellent local Goldstar draft. Try Big Ben, on the mall, and Le Pirate Pub, below the Caesar Hotel.

If you're in Tiberias and have a hankering for falafel, the Middle Eastern fast food of deep-fried chickpea balls and salad in pita bread, rub shoulders with the locals on Hagalil Street. In fact, if you're into local color, look for the modest, tiny restaurants (where English really *is* a foreign language) on Hagalil Street and in the little streets that connect it to Habanim Street. The menus predictably emphasize fish and Middle Eastern salads and meat dishes. Even tourists have been known to strike gold here—and often at lower prices than those found in the high-rent locations. Beyond the standard fare, there are a small number of very good specialty restaurants: Chinese, Indian, Italian, French, and vegetarian.

The city has a range of hotels, but if camping interests you, Kfar Hittim (⊠ M.P. Lower Galilee 15280, ☎ 06/679–5921), in the hills to the west of Tiberias, has facilities. In addition, local authorities have developed a series of free or minimum-charge lakeside sites south of Tiberias; the facilities, however, are spartan.

$$–$$$ ✕ **Ha'Italkia.** The menu at The Italian is more eclectic than the name suggests. Salmon fettuccine wins approval from Israeli vacationers and locals, and there's a variety of pizzas. The steaks and fish (especially trout) have earned something of a reputation in the area. The listed salads are entrée-size, but an unlisted smaller chopped green salad makes a good side dish. Red-and-white-check tablecloths add an Italian air; the old-style wooden windowpanes and outside greenery allow you to forget how close you are to the main street. ⊠ *Corner of Hagalil and Habanim Sts.,* ☎ *06/672–3150. AE, DC, MC, V.*

$$–$$$ ✕ **Karamba.** The fare is not Latin American, as the name suggests, but fish and vegetarian dishes, some quite original, served in a courtyard a few steps from the shore. Try the excellent Galilee salad of lettuce, mushrooms, grapefruit, pecan nuts, and Roquefort cheese with garlic dressing. The onion quiche is very good, the others of that genre somewhat less successful. The best fish dishes are a trout with a coconut crust and a tangy pineapple and almond sauce, and the *bouri* (gray mullet) done in butter and garlic. The house parfait is delicious. The menu includes special items for children. Good background music, reasonably priced drinks and spiked coffees, and late hours make Karamba a popular watering hole. ⊠ *On Promenade,* ☎ *06/672–4505 or 06/679–1546. AE, DC, MC, V.*

$$–$$$ ✕ **Pagoda** and **The House.** These Chinese/Thai restaurants under one
★ management are part of the Lido Beach complex, which includes other eateries and boat anchorage. Pagoda, in a faux Chinese temple with wraparound windows, is spacious, with a generous patio for outdoor dining overlooking the lake. The House, across the road, has a maze

of smaller, more intimate rooms entered through a delightful garden. The restaurants have identical menus, with one difference: The Pagoda is kosher and is closed on the Sabbath and on Jewish religious holidays. The House is open only when the Pagoda is not. Neither serves pork and shrimp. The food is in general exceptionally good. Try the spicy Thai soup, the (veal) spare ribs, and strips of beef sautéed in satay (peanut) sauce. ⊠ *Gedud Barak St. (Rte. 90),* ☎ *06/672–4488 or 06/679–2564. AE, DC, MC, V. The House: closed Sun.–Thurs. and no lunch Fri. Pagoda: no dinner Fri. or lunch Sat.*

$$ ✕ **Kohinoor.** Elegance, superb service and tantalizing flavors are the
★ hallmarks of this member of a national chain of Indian restaurants. The cuisine is typical of northern India: more subtle and less fiery than the curries of the south. Just after you're seated in the peach-and-cream-color dining room, Indian breads are brought to your table, addictive when dipped in a mango or date chutney or piquant mint sauce. For the main course, try the house specialty: tandoori chicken, marinated and baked in a clay oven to a startling red. You won't go wrong with *rogan ghosh* (lamb curry) or chicken *tikka masala* (tandoor-baked and sautéed with onions, tomatoes, and spices). A traditional Indian dancer makes short appearances on a small stage from time to time throughout the evening. ⊠ *Radisson Moriah Plaza (entrance also from Promenade) off Habanim St.,* ☎ *06/672–4939. AE, DC, MC, V.*

$–$$$ ✕☑ **YMCA Peniel-by-Galilee.** One of the area's more unusual hostel-
★ ries, Peniel-by-Galilee was built as a retreat in the late 1930s by Archibald Harte, founder of the famous Jerusalem YMCA. It occupies a low cliff just north of Tiberias, where you can enjoy unobstructed lake views and a pebbly but clean beach. The common room is lined with 180-year-old Damascene wood and inlaid panels. The guest rooms and family-size apartments are less inspiring, though spacious and comfortable enough; apartments have kitchen facilities. Most units have views of the lake. Dinner is served only when demand justifies it (at least eight people; call ahead to verify)—it's worth trying to round up the quota of guests. The excellence of the lake-caught St. Peter's fish is matched by the other entrées, which might consist of grilled steak or lamb chops, roast chicken, and hamburgers. ⊠ *Off Rte. 90, 3 km (2 mi) north of Tiberias, Box 192, Tiberias 14101,* ☎ *06/672–0685. 9 rooms and 2 apartments with bath. Dining room, beach, playground. No credit cards.*

$$$$ ☑ **Caesar.** Part of a small national chain, the Caesar is one of Tiberias's newer hotels. The public rooms are all white marble and polished brass. All guest rooms have lake views and tasteful, if unexceptional, furnishings; every suite has a whirlpool bath. The hotel has a large outdoor swimming pool and adjacent children's pool, but the area would have been enhanced by more grass and less concrete. The dining room does a very creditable job. ⊠ *The Promenade, Box 275, 14102,* ☎ *06/672–3333,* ℻ *06/679–1013. 227 rooms with bath. Bar, coffee shop, dining room, 2 pools, sauna, exercise room, windsurfing, boating, waterskiing. AE, DC, MC, V.*

$$$$ ☑ **Gai Beach.** On Route 90 at the southern edge of town, this newcomer offers guest rooms that are well designed and comfortable, but smallish; not all face the lake. The marble lobby area is too vast for intimacy. The hotel's rare lakeshore location is a big plus, as is the adjacent water park with its beach, water slides, and wave pool (all free to guests). Despite the undeniable attractions of Gai Beach, the rates are high for a hotel of this class. ⊠ *Rte. 90, Box 274, 14102,* ☎ *06/679–0790,* ℻ *06/679–2776. 120 rooms with bath. Restaurant, water park. AE, DC, MC, V.*

$$$$ ⊞ **Galei Kinneret.** Built in 1943—note its Bauhaus-style exterior—the
★ grande dame of Tiberias hotels was a favorite retreat of David Ben-Gurion's. The Galei Kinneret's most attractive feature is its lakeside location (most of its rivals only overlook the lake), slightly removed from the raucous hotel-and-pub strip, with lawns and eucalyptus-shaded patios right on the water. Renovations have improved the standard of the rooms and have given the lounge area a face-lift (though in dubious, brassy taste). ⊠ *1 Kaplan St., 14100,* ☎ *06/679–2331,* ℻ *06/679–0260. 120 rooms with bath. 3 restaurants, bar, pool, hot tub, sauna, tennis court, health club, boating, waterskiing, shops. AE, DC, MC, V.*

$$$$ ⊞ **Radisson Moriah Plaza.** The lobby and bar of this ultramodern high-rise are bright, comfortable places in which to relax. Rooms are fairly ordinary, with darkish furnishings that only emphasize the relative lack of space. The service is generally quite professional and accommodating, but hotel maintenance is not all it should be. The hotel overlooks the lake but does not have lake frontage. The Kohinoor Indian restaurant (☞ *above*) is highly recommended. The new Texas restaurant and bar, often with live music, is a fun place to spend a few evening hours. ⊠ *Just off Habanim St., 14103,* ☎ *06/679–2233,* ℻ *06/679–2320. 272 rooms with bath. 3 restaurants, bar, pool, beauty salon, sauna, whirlpool bath, exercise room. AE, DC, MC, V.*

$$$ ⊞ **Four Points Tiberias.** Lording it high above the city, this hotel compensates for its distance from the center with a quiet location and superb lake views from every room. There's an attractive garden area (though a new wing has gobbled up some space), and the fairly spacious rooms have wooden furniture with blue upholstery; balconies are a plus. The Lodge Bar, with its wide picture windows, is a cozy evening hangout despite some bizarre touches of decor. ⊠ *18 Hashomer St., 14102,* ☎ *06/679–1484. 220 rooms with bath. 2 restaurants, bar, pool, hot tub, 2 saunas, exercise room. AE, DC, MC, V.*

$$ ⊞ **Astoria.** One of Tiberias's better moderately priced hotels, the Astoria is set halfway uptown—neither as picturesque nor as convenient as other hotels near the lake. Still, it is a comfortable and clean family-run establishment, with many of the new furnishings in attractive pastels. The prices jump to the low end of the $$$ category in July and August and during the Jewish holidays. ⊠ *13 Ohel Ya'akov St., 14223,* ☎ *06/672–2351,* ℻ *06/672–5108. 65 rooms with bath. Restaurant, bar, coffee shop, pool. AE, DC, MC, V.*

$$ ⊞ **Church of Scotland Centre.** Built in 1893 as a hospital of the Free
★ Church of Scotland, the building was ultimately converted into a pilgrim hospice. Today it welcomes all visitors, proclaiming its commitment "to build bridges of trust and respect among our neighbors, whoever they are and wherever they come from." The double-story stone buildings with their deep porches and high-ceilinged rooms are a pleasant change from the tackiness of many modern hotels. The rambling, slightly wild gardens make a challenging adventure land for kids and a pastoral refuge for their elders. The outer gate is closed at 6 PM, but your key gets you in at your convenience, as well as providing access to the private beach across the road. The location could not be more central. ⊠ *Gedud Barak and Hayarden Sts., Box 104, 14100,* ☎ *06/672–3769 or 06/672–1165,* ℻ *06/679–0145. 48 rooms with bath. Beach. AE, DC, MC, V.*

$$ ⊞ **Ron Beach.** The last hotel in Tiberias on Route 90 north, it's one
★ of the few with its own lake frontage. The amenities—box-spring mattresses, TVs, and blow-dryers—are impressive at this price category in this area. In addition to the main building, a row of 29 rooms with patios opens onto the lawn and the beach. The restaurant has good St. Peter's fish. It's an altogether excellent value. ⊠ *Gedud Barak St.*

It helps to be pushy in airports.

Introducing the revolutionary new TransPorter™ from American Tourister® It's the first suitcase you can push around without a fight. TransPorter's™ exclusive four-wheel design lets you push it in front of you with almost no effort—the wheels take the weight. Or pull it on two wheels if you choose. You can even stack on other bags and use it like a luggage cart.

TransPorter™ is designed like a dresser, with built-in shelves to organize your belongings. Or collapse the shelves and pack it like a traditional suitcase. Inside, there's a suiter feature to help keep suits and dresses from wrinkling. When push comes to shove, you can't beat a TransPorter™. For more information on how you can be this pushy, call 1-800-542-1300.

Stable 4-wheel design.

Shelves collapse on command.

Your passport around the world.

- Worldwide access
- Operators who speak your language
- Monthly itemized billing

MCI Calling Card

415 555 1234 2244
J. D. SMITH

Use your MCI Card® and these access numbers for an easy way to call when traveling worldwide.

Bahrain†	800-002
Brunei	800-011
China (CC)†	108-12
(Available from most major cities)	
For a Mandarin-speaking operator	108-17
Cyprus ♦†	080-90000
Egypt (CC) ♦†	355-5770
Federated States of Micronesia	624
Fiji	004-890-1002
Guam (CC)†	950-1022
Hong Kong (CC)†	800-1121
India (CC)†	000-127
(Available from most major cities)	
Indonesia (CC) ♦†	001-801-11
Iran ÷	(Special Phones Only)
Israel (CC)†	177-150-2727
Japan (CC) ♦†	
To call U.S. using KDD ■	0039-121
To call U.S. using IDC ■	0066-55-121
Jordan	18-800-001
Korea (CC)†	
To call using KT ■	009-14
To call using DACOM ■	0039-12

Phone Booths ÷	Press Red Button 03, then *
Military Bases	550-2255
Kuwait†	800-MCI (800-624)
Lebanon (CC) ÷	600-624
Macao†	0800-131
Malaysia (CC) ♦†	800-0012
Philippines (CC) ♦†	
To call using PLDT ■	105-14
To call using PHILCOM ■	1026-12
For a Tagalog-speaking operator	105-15
Qatar ★	0800-012-77
Saipan (CC) ÷†	950-1022
Saudi Arabia (CC)†	1-800-11
Singapore†	8000-112-112
Sri Lanka	(within Colombo) 440100
	(outside of Colombo) 01-440100
Syria	0800
Taiwan (CC) ♦†	0080-13-4567
Thailand ★†	001-999-1-2001
United Arab Emirates ♦	800-111
Vietnam ●	1201-1022

To sign up for the MCI Card, dial the access number of the country you are in and ask to speak with a customer service representative.

http://www.mci.com

(Rte. 90 N), 14101, ☎ 06/679–1350, FAX *06/679–1351. 74 rooms with bath. Restaurant, pool, beach. AE, DC, MC, V.*

$
★ ⓣ **Berger Hotel.** Run by the family of that name, this two-wing hotel has spacious, well-furnished rooms, each with a balcony. It's uptown, and more convenient if you have a car, but buses to the downtown area are frequent (except on weekends). No meals are available, but a supermarket across the road makes it easy to stock your kitchenette. Recent renovations have upgraded parts of the hotel, which offers more frills than it used to. ⊠ *27 Neiberg St., Box 535, 14105, ☎ 06/672– 0850,* FAX *06/679–1514. 45 rooms with bath. Kitchenettes. MC, V.*

$ ⓣ **Meyouhas Youth Hostel.** This large basalt building fronted by a lawn and trees is in the heart of downtown Tiberias, a minute's walk from the lake, the Promenade, and the mall. The term "youth" is inaccurate: The hostel is open to all. A few double rooms are available, and many larger ones, which can sleep six, have bunk beds. Pine furniture has lifted the place out of its old iron-bedstead image, but conditions are still somewhat spartan. Meals are cheap. If you don't mind lodgings that are strictly functional, you could do worse. ⊠ *Corner of Gedud Barak and Hayarden Sts., Box 81, 14100, ☎ 06/672–1775 or 06/679– 0350,* FAX *06/672–0372. 60 rooms (240 beds), ½ with private showers and toilets. Restaurant. DC, MC, V.*

Nightlife and the Arts

As you might expect in a resort area, entertainment is more common than culture. Much of it, especially in the larger hotels in Tiberias, is of the live-music-in-the-lounge variety: piano-bar players, dance-music musicians, and "sing along, folks!" crooners. Thursday and Friday are "nightclub" nights at some hotels, with dance music to please the weekend crowds. The clientele tends to be a bit older. The younger set in general wouldn't be caught dead here and prefer to hang out at the pubs along the midrachov and the Promenade, where the recorded rock music is good and loud and the beer is on tap. The **Lido** (⊠ Gedud Barak St., ☎ 06/672–4488 or 06/679–2564) has a dance club that operates most nights between May and October, in a balmy, palm-dotted lakeside location.

Some boat operators use their bigger boats as **floating dance clubs** in the summer, usually departing from the piers at the Promenade for a 45-minute cruise offshore from Tiberias. The cost is NIS 15–NIS 20 ($5–$6.70). These companies also occasionally offer a two-hour dinner-and-disco deal for about NIS 120–NIS 150 ($40–$50). For details call Lido Kinneret (☎ 06/672–4488, 06/672–1538, or 06/679–2564), or Kinneret Sailing (☎ 06/675–8007 or 06/675–8009).

The Ministry of Tourism sometimes sponsors **Israeli Folklore Evenings,** entrance free, at one of the big hotels; call the TIO information number (☎ 06/672–5666) for schedules. Sometimes a classier act comes through, often performing on one of the kibbutzim in the area. If it's not too language-specific (a Hebrew comedian might be a problem), the performances could be a delightful slice of Israel.

The Galilee Experience, a 27-projector, 36-minute audiovisual presentation, provides a good historical overview of the Galilee from a distinctly Christian viewpoint. ⊠ *At the Marina, southern end of Promenade, ☎ 06/672–3620.* ☞ *NIS 18 ($6). Screenings in English throughout the day and the evening, some only when there are group bookings; call ahead for details.*

Outdoor Activities and Sports

SWIMMING

There's good swimming at a number of beaches near Tiberias. **Lido** and **Blue Beach** (both: ⊠ Rte. 90 at northern exit from Tiberias), **Sironit** (⊠ Rte. 90 at southern exit from Tiberias), and **Gai Beach** (⊠ Next to Sironit) are all options.

WALKING AND JOGGING

A promenade in Tiberias follows the lakeshore for about 5 km (3 mi) to the south.

WATER SPORTS

Kayaks, pedal boats, and rowboats can be rented from: **Nof Ginosar,** north of Tiberias (☎ 06/679–2161); **Carmel Jordan River Hotel Marina** (☎ 06/679–2950) and **Ganei Hammat Hotel** (☎ 06/679–2890), in Tiberias. Water slides are available at the **Sironit** and **Gai beaches,** south of Tiberias.

For waterskiing, inquire at the private beaches around Tiberias: **Blue Beach** (☎ 06/672–0105 or 06/672–4137), **Lido** (☎ 06/672–1538), **Sironit** (☎ 06/672–1449), and **Gai Beach** (☎ 06/679–0790).

Shopping

Tiberias relies heavily on tourism, but despite its developing infrastructure, it has little good shopping. The exception is jewelry. Souvenirs, of course, are found everywhere.

The large **Caprice diamond factory** (⊠ Tabor St., ☎ 06/679–2616) offers a video about the industry and a tour of its workshops before releasing you into its showroom. A few smaller **jewelry stores** are near the intersection of Habanim and Yarden streets and in some of the better hotels.

En Route   Metulla Road (Route 90) north out of Tiberias hugs the steep hillside, leaving only a few rocky beaches between it and the Sea of Galilee. About 5 km (3 mi) from the town, the shore widens. Among the trees and holiday bungalows is an enclosure with a small, unimposing cluster of black basalt ruins. This is all that remains of ancient **Magdala,** a Jewish town of the Second Temple period and the probable home of Mary Magdalene. When the Great Revolt of the Jews against Rome erupted in AD 66, the Galileans spearheaded the struggle, but courage alone could not defeat the disciplined Roman legions. Magdala— called Tarichaeae by the Romans—saw one of the bloodiest battles of the campaign (AD 67). In a chilling passage, contemporary Jewish historian Flavius Josephus describes "the entire lake stained with blood and crammed with corpses; for there was not a single survivor."

Ginosar

🕙 *10 km (6 mi) north of Tiberias.*

Perhaps the site of the New Testament's Gennesaret, Ginosar is today a veteran kibbutz in a glorious lakeside location. For many Israelis, it is known as the home of the late Yigal Allon (1918–80), commander of the crack Palmach battalions in the War of Independence and deputy prime minister in the 1970s under Golda Meir and Yitzhak Rabin. The settlement's favorite son is immortalized in **Bet Allon** (Allon House), a basalt-and-concrete eyesore of a building that houses a museum of the region's natural and human history; it's a good rainy-day option.

For the tourist, however, the site is intriguing because of the brilliant archaeological find made on its shore: a 2,000-year-old wooden boat, the most complete of this age ever found in any inland lake. In January 1986, after three years of poor rainfall had lowered the level of the lake, fishermen from the adjacent kibbutz spotted the prow of the boat exposed in the mud. The 28-foot-long boat, excavated in a frenetic 11 days, became an instant media sensation. Considering the age of the boat (1st century AD) and the frequency of nautical references in the New Testament stories that took place in this area, the popular press immediately dubbed it "the Jesus Boat." Certainly, for a reader of the Gospels, it is a startlingly vivid image from the past.

The ancient boat was amazingly intact but extremely fragile, its timbers sodden like wet cardboard. To move it, the vessel was sprayed inside and out with a styrofoam mixture, giving it a buoyant "straitjacket." It was then towed a few hundred yards by rowboat and lifted by crane to its current temporary home on the lakeside of Bet Allon, where it sits in a specially constructed bath filled with a wax-based preservative solution. This experiment—with the aim of displacing the water molecules in the wood in order to exhibit the boat dry—seems to have succeeded, and the boat can be seen in all its modest but remarkably evocative glory. Bet Allon screens an excellent video, filmed during the excavation, that explains the boat's unique features. The plan is to eventually build a special permanent pavilion to display the boat with the pride it deserves. ⊠ *Rte. 90,* ☎ *06/672–2905.* 🎫 *Museum and boat NIS 13 ($4.40); boat only (including video) NIS 9 ($3).* ⊗ *Sat.–Thurs. 8–5, Fri. and holiday eves 8–1 (boat only, 8–4). Last entry to museum 1 hr before closing; last entry to boat 30 min before closing.*

Lodging

$$$ 🏨 **Nof Ginosar Guest House.** This is one of the largest and best established of the Galilee kibbutz guest houses. Its location right on the Sea of Galilee, with a private beach, makes Nof Ginosar especially popular. There are evening lectures on kibbutz life and a morning tour. Also on the grounds are a 2,000-year-old fishing boat, a small natural history and anthropological museum, and kayak, pedal boat, and rowboat rentals. Nof Ginosar has a rustic-resort style, with motel-like accommodations easily equivalent to hotels in the same price range. Rooms are comfortable and airy, if not overly spacious; all have TVs. Although one side of its large dining room serves good but unexceptional full-course meals, the other has a nonmeat (read: vegetarian) buffet, with tasty salads, hot fish, and outstanding blintzes with sweetened cheese. ⊠ *Rte. 90, M.P. Jordan Valley 14980,* ☎ *06/679–2161,* 📠 *06/679–2170. 170 rooms with bath. Restaurant, bar, coffee shop, pool, beach. AE, DC, MC, V.*

Outdoor Activities and Sports

There's a pleasant beach at **Nof Ginosar** (☞ Lodging, *above*), and you can also rent kayaks, pedal boats, and rowboats.

En Route   Just north of Ginosar, on your right on Route 90, is an electric installation that powers huge water pumps buried in the hill behind it. The Sea of Galilee is Israel's primary freshwater reservoir and the beginning of the National Water Carrier, a network of canals and pipelines that integrates the country's water sources and distribution lines. On the hill above it is the small tel of the Old Testament city of **Kinneret,** dominating the main highway of the ancient Near East, the so-called Via Maris (Way of the Sea). The scholarly assumption is that the Hebrew name of the lake—Kinneret—comes from that of the most important city on its shores in antiquity. The romantics contend the name is derived from the lake's shape, reminiscent of the biblical *kinnor,* or lyre.

Mount of Beatitudes

⑮ *8 km (5 mi) north of Ginosar, 3 km (2 mi) north of Capernaum Junction, where Rtes. 90 and 87 meet.*

Well-tended gardens and spreading ficus trees provide a tranquil setting to contemplate the Sermon on the Mount, with which this hill is identified. "And seeing the multitudes, he went up into a mountain; and when he was set, his disciples came unto him. And he opened his mouth, and taught them, saying: 'Blessed are the poor in spirit, for theirs is the kingdom of Heaven . . .' " Thus the Gospel of Matthew (5:1–7:29) begins the record of Jesus' most extensive teaching.

The domed **Roman Catholic church** (of the Italian Franciscan Sisters), built by the famous architect Barluzzi, was completed in 1930. On the marble walls are quotations from the Beatitudes, the initial "Blessed are they . . ." verses of the Sermon on the Mount. The church is surrounded by a terrace and well-tended gardens, offering a superb view of the Sea of Galilee (best in the afternoon, when the diffused western sun softens the light and heightens color). It is appropriate to the spirit of the place that this is one of the few Christian holy sites in the country where Catholics and Protestants seem to feel equally at ease. ⊠ *Rte. 8177 off Rte. 90.* ☉ *Daily 8–noon, 2:30–5.*

Tabgha

⑯ *14 km (8 mi) north of Tiberias, at Capernaum Junction (Rtes. 90 and 87).*

Greenery drapes the antiquities and frames the Roman Catholic churches at two neighboring sites. Tabgha is a corruption through the Arabic of the earlier Greek name Heptapegon (Seven Springs). The German Benedictine **Church of the Multiplication,** a large building on the west of Tabgha, is identified by Christian tradition with the "desert[ed] place" of Matthew 14. Toward evening, the gospel relates, Jesus miraculously "multiplied" two fish and five loaves of bread to feed the crowds that followed him. "And they did all eat, and were filled. . . . And they that had eaten were about 5,000 men, beside women and children." This is the event known as the miracle of the Multiplication of the Loaves and Fishes.

The church, built in Byzantine basilica style and dedicated in 1981, incorporates some remains of its 5th-century predecessor. Most impressive in this airy limestone building with a wooden truss ceiling is the beautifully wrought Byzantine mosaic floor depicting flora and birds and curiously including Egyptian motifs such as the Nilometer, a graded column once used to measure the water level of the Nile. In front of the altar is the small and simple *Loaves and Fishes,* perhaps the most famous mosaic in Israel. From the outer courtyard of the church, a path leads down to a quiet spot on the lake. ⊠ *Rte. 87.* ☉ *Mon.–Sat. 8:30–5, Sun. 9:30–5.*

The austere basalt **Church of the Primacy of St. Peter,** 200 yards east of the Church of the Multiplication, is built on the water's edge, over a flat rock known as Mensa Domini (the Lord's Table) or Mensa Christi (the Table of Christ). After his resurrection, relates the New Testament (John 21), Jesus appeared to his disciples by the Sea of Galilee and breakfasted on a miraculous catch of fish. Three times Jesus asked the disciple Peter if he loved him, and after Peter's reply of "you know that I love you," Jesus commanded him to "feed my sheep." Some scholars see this affirmation as Peter's atonement for having thrice denied Jesus in Jerusalem after Jesus' arrest. This event is seen as establishing

Peter's "primacy" and, in the Roman Catholic tradition, that of his spiritual descendants, the bishops of Rome. Part of the Franciscan "Custody of the Holy Land," the site was included in the itinerary of Pope Paul VI in 1964. ⊠ *Rte. 87.* ⊗ *Daily 8:30–1 and 2–5.*

Capernaum

🔞 *3 km (2 mi) east of Tabgha and the Capernaum Junction, 17 km (10½ mi) northeast of Tiberias.*

Once Capernaum was a thriving town of merchants, farmers, and fishermen; today it contains an archaeological site and two monasteries. The easterly one, distinguished by its red-domed whitewashed church, is Greek Orthodox and is seldom visited, since its own antiquities have not been developed for tourism. The westerly Franciscan (Roman Catholic) one, at the first and clearly-marked turnoff after Tabgha, is what you have come to see, along with the nearby excavations.

The prosperity of this ancient Jewish community is immediately apparent from the remains of its synagogue. Excavations by the Franciscan friars in the early years of the century exposed a large town on the lakeshore that had thrived from the Second Temple/Early Roman period (about the 1st century BC) to the Byzantine period (5th–6th centuries AD). It was here at Capernaum—Kfar Nahum in Hebrew—that Jesus established his base during the three years of his ministry in the Galilee. Here, the New Testament relates, he called many of his disciples ("Follow me, and I will make you fishers of men"), healed the afflicted, taught in the synagogue. . . and ultimately cursed the city for not heeding his message.

To the right of the cashier as you enter the site is a display of finely carved stones showing the typical range of Jewish artistic motifs of the time, including the native fruits of the land, grapes, pomegranates, figs, dates, and olives. A dedication to a donor of the synagogue's building fund, one Alpheus the son of Zebedah the son of John, is in Aramaic, the language spoken by Jews in the region at the time (compare the Gospel of Mark 15:34) and strong proof that this was a Jewish community. A horizontal stone—a lintel—shows an artist's depiction of the biblical Ark of the Covenant, typically carried in Old Testament times, but here seen on wheels, perhaps a reference to the two such instances recorded (I Samuel 6 and II Samuel 6).

Immediately before you is a modern church, literally suspended from its outer support pillars over the scanty remains of Capernaum's central Christian shrine, the **House of St. Peter.** The church follows the octagonal outline of the Byzantine basilica that once encompassed the house where Jesus is supposed to have visited.

The partly restored **synagogue** dominates the complex. The ancient community went to the expense of transporting white limestone blocks from afar to set off the synagogue from the crudely built black basalt houses of the town. Stone benches line the inside walls of the building, recalling its original primary function as a place of assembly where the Torah was read and explained on Sabbaths and holidays; formal prayer in Judaism came later.

Controversy still surrounds the dating of the Capernaum synagogue—sometime between the 2nd and 5th centuries AD—but one thing is certain: This is not the actual synagogue of Mark 1 where Jesus taught. Nevertheless, consecrated ground was often reused, and the small structure seen in the excavation pit in the southeastern corner of the present building may have been that of the 1st-century synagogue in which he spoke.

Near the deep shade of the ficus trees, look for the remains of a fine olive-oil press and some small hand mills made from hard and durable volcanic basalt. Its advantages over the limestone found in the rest of Israel gave the Sea of Galilee region the raw material for an important export commodity in ancient times: agricultural equipment. Such mills have been found as far afield as Masada, Jerusalem, and the Mediterranean coast. To the right of the olive-oil press is the capital of a column with Jewish symbols in relief—a seven-branched menorah, a shofar (ram's horn), and an incense shovel—to preserve the memory of the Temple, with which they were associated. A small 1st-century mosaic from Magdala shows a contemporary boat, complete with oars and sails—a dramatic illustration of the many New Testament and Jewish references to the traffic and fishing on the lake. ⊠ *Rte. 87.,* ☎ *06/672–1059.* ☜ *NIS 2 (70¢).* ⊙ *Daily 8:30–4.*

En Route   Route 87 continues east past Capernaum and crosses the **Jordan River**—somewhat muddy at this point—at the Arik Bridge. Those raised on spirituals extolling the Jordan's depth and width are often surprised to find how small a stream it really is. Seldom more than 30 feet wide, it is often shallow enough to wade in. However, record-breaking rains in the winter of 1991–92 swelled the river, which flooded fields and threatened homes farther south. The Jordan enters the Sea of Galilee only a few hundred yards to your right. In this wetlands area of the Jordan Delta, archaeologists in recent years have finally identified and begun exploring the elusive site of the ancient Jewish town of Bethsaida, Peter's birthplace according to the New Testament.

Kursi and the Eastern Shore

⑱   *Kursi is 17 km (10½ mi) from Capernaum.*

Route 92 skirts the lake's eastern edge under the imposing cliffs of the southern Golan Heights, stringing together a series of beaches, water parks, picnic spots and campgrounds, lodgings, a restaurant, and a few historical sites. If you stayed on Route 87, you would continue east to Katzrin and the central Golan Heights.

Kursi, at the junction with Route 789, is linked with the New Testament, which relates the story of a man of Gedara who was possessed by demons (Matthew 8; Mark 5, and Luke 8 have him from Gerasa). Jesus miraculously exorcised the evil spirits, causing them to enter a herd of swine grazing nearby, which then "ran violently down a steep place into the lake, and were choked." A 5th-century Byzantine tradition identified that event with this spot at the foot of the steep Golan Heights, so they built a monastery there. Those were days of intensive pilgrimages to holy places, and the monastery prospered. The partly restored ruins of a fine Byzantine church on the site is a classic example of the basilica style common at the time, and remains of the monastery can be seen perched higher up the hillside behind it. ⊠ *Rte. 92,* ☎ *06/673–1983.* ☜ *NIS 7 ($2.40).* ⊙ *Apr.–Sept., Sat.–Thurs. 8–5, Fri. and holiday eves 8–4; Oct.–Mar., Sat.–Thurs. 8–4, Fri. and holiday eves 8–3.*

Dining and Lodging

If you're interested in **camping,** this area has several campgrounds with full cooking and washing facilities, beach access, and stores. Try those at Ein Gev (⊠ Ein Gev 14940, ☎ 06/675–8027 or 06/675–8028), Ha'on (⊠ M.P. Jordan Valley 15170, ☎ 06/675–7555 or 06/675–7556), and Ma'agan (⊠ M.P. Jordan Valley 15160, ☎ 06/675–3753).

$$ ✕ **Ein Gev Fish Restaurant.** This lunch institution on the eastern shore of the lake is known for its St. Peter's fish (pay the extra cost for a large fish to ensure moist meatiness) but does offer alternatives: light entrées such as pizza and omelets. On the grounds of the Ein Gev Holiday Village (☞ *below*) at the water's edge, the restaurant is open for dinner only in July, August, and sometimes September. Its outdoor dining area has a view of Tiberias, the lights of which twinkle across the lake. ⊠ *Kibbutz Ein Gev,* ☎ *06/675–8035 or 06/675–8036. MC, V.*

$$$ 🏨 **Ramot Resort Hotel.** High up in the foothills of the Golan Heights, the hotel is still just a 10-minute drive from the excellent Golan and Lunagal beaches (the latter with a water park) and has fabulous views of the Sea of Galilee region. Its main building has well-designed, comfortable, and air-conditioned guest rooms, each with a very private balcony affording a lake view. Less expensive (and older), the cottages are not as well furnished and are a bit run-down, but have some charm, with their wooden paneling and shutters and green surroundings. Guided tours of the area are available in the summer. ⊠ *E. of Rte. 92, 12490,* ☎ *06/673–2636,* 🖷 *06/679–3590. 123 rooms with bath; 19 cottages. Bar, coffee shop, pool. AE, DC, MC, V.*

$$ 🏨 **Ein Gev Holiday Village.** The kibbutz at Ein Gev has been in the tourism business for many years and is best known for its fish restaurant (☞ *above*), cruise boats, campground, and air-conditioned caravans. Better-class guest rooms with patios have been added to the motel-style building, on a palm-shaded lakeside location of lawns and beach. Rates go up 25% on weekends and holidays. ⊠ *Rte. 92, 12 km (7½ mi) from Tzemach Junction, Post Office Ein Gev 14940,* ☎ *06/ 675–8027 or 06/675–8028. 144 rooms with bath. Restaurant, miniature golf, boating, shops. MC, V.*

$$ 🏨 **Ma'agan.** This kibbutz on the southern tip of the Sea of Galilee, 12
★ km (7½ mi) from Tiberias, has abandoned its old campsite-and-bungalow image for a more upmarket one: regular guest rooms, plus spacious and well-furnished suites that have a living room (with a lake-view picture window), two small bedrooms, a bathroom, a kitchenette, a patio, and barbecue facilities. A sandy beach, swimming pool, and extensive lawns among the palms and eucalypti make this the best deal in the area. Kids have two smaller pools, a play area, and a menagerie. ⊠ *Rte. 92, 1 km (½ mi) east of Tzemach Junction, M.P. Jordan Valley 15160,* ☎ *06/675–3753,* 🖷 *06/675–3707. 24 rooms with bath, 100 1-bedroom suites. Restaurant, coffee shop, 3 pools, windsurfing, boating, shops. AE, DC, MC, V.*

Nightlife and the Arts

The **Ein Gev Spring Festival** (☎ 06/675–8032 or 06/675–8039), which takes places within Kibbutz Ein Gev, celebrated its 50th anniversary in 1993. Chiefly a music festival, whose participants have ranged from Bernstein and Rampal to Dietrich and Sinatra, it has always been held during Passover week. Call ahead for the date.

Outdoor Activities and Sports

SWIMMING

Ma'agan (☞ Dining and Lodging, *above*) has a shaded lawn and eating facilities as well as a beach. **Ein Gev, Golan Beach** (parking fee), and **Lunagal** (parking fee) are good swimming spots on the eastern shore; all are along Route 92.

WATER SPORTS

Kayaks, pedal boats, and rowboats can be rented from **Kibbutz Ha'on** (☎ 06/675–7555) and **Kibbutz Ma'agan** (☎ 06/675–1360), on the southeastern shore; and **Kibbutz Ein Gev** (☎ 06/675–8027), **Golan Beach**

(☎ 06/676–3750), and **Ramot Resort Hotel** (☎ 06/676–3730), on the eastern and northeastern shores. Water slides are especially profuse at **Lunagal,** on the northeastern shore.

Hammat Gader

⓳ *10 km (6¼ mi) east of Zemach Junction, 22 km (14 mi) southeast of Tiberias, 36 km (22½ mi) northeast of Bet She'an.*

Named for its patron city of Gadara high up the southern bank of the Yarmuk, Hammat Gader in its heyday was the second-largest spa in the Roman Empire, after Baiae, near Naples. The drive to the site is itself an absorbing experience. The road clings to the gorge of the Yarmuk River, crossed here and there by defunct railway bridges that once carried the narrow-gauge Valley Railroad cars from Haifa via Bet She'an to Damascus. On the opposite bank is biblical Gilead, now part of Jordan. Just before the descent to Hammat Gader, Route 98 climbs off to the southern Golan Heights in a series of heart-stopping switchbacks.

Built around three hot springs, the impressive complex of baths and pools at Hammat Gader attests to the opulence that once attracted voluptuaries and invalids alike. In its time the entrance corridor was kept dimly lighted to dramatize the effect of the fine ornamental pool—in contrast well lighted by high glass-paned windows—to which it led. Niches are believed to have contained statues of Asclepius, the god of healing, and of Eros, the god of love, representing the two distinct attractions of the site.

The large number of ancient clay oil-lamps found in one small pool are proof of nighttime bathing and a hint that this area could have been set aside for lepers, to keep them out of sight of regular patrons. The original "hot tub"—test the water!—is fed by a spring at a temperature of 54°C (129°F). A large cool pool, once adorned with water-spouting gargoyle fountains, has been partly restored.

The site is immensely popular among the locals, who tend to make a day of it, picnicking amid the lawns and large trees near the outdoor warm pool. Also on hand are a freshwater pool, changing facilities, trampolines and other children's attractions, an alligator farm, a cafeteria, and a specialty Thai restaurant. It's delightful for a leisurely visit, but pricey if seeing the antiquities is your only purpose. ⊠ *Rte. 98,* ☎ *06/675–1039.* ☞ *NIS 27 ($9) Sun.–Fri., NIS 29 ($9.70) Sat. and holidays; NIS 20 ($6.70) for entry after 5 PM.* ☉ *Sun. 8–4:30, Mon.–Thurs. 8 AM–9:30 PM, Fri. 8 AM–11:30 PM, Sat. 8–8. Children's attractions close at 5 PM, alligator farm and antiquities close at dusk. Entrance up to 1 hr before closing.*

Degania Alef

⓴ *10 km (6¼ mi) south of Tiberias.*

The collective village of Degania Alef (aleph is the *a* of the Hebrew language)—not to be confused with its younger neighbor Degania Bet (for Hebrew's letter *b*)—on the banks of the Jordan River, is distinguished as the world's first kibbutz, founded in 1909 by Jewish pioneers from Eastern Europe and established here on its permanent site the following year. The kibbutz idea—there are now some 280 kibbutzim in Israel—is based on the principle of "from each according to his ability, to each according to his need." The early pioneers needed a unified communal structure to cope with the forbidding terrain and a hostile neighborhood; but more than that, they were seeking the perfect society, based on absolute equality and the subservience of individual desires to the needs of the community.

The principles of the founders remained remarkably resilient for years, but the dream has begun to fade a bit, and the commitment to the old ideals has become more tenuous and less relevant for a new, more materialistic generation. Nevertheless, about 2.5% of the general population live on kibbutzim, the swampland and rocky soil have been turned into fields and plantations, and light industry and tourism have been added as a major part of their economic profile.

Near the entrance to Degania Alef is a small, World War II–vintage Syrian tank. On May 15, 1948, the day after Israel declared its independence, the fledgling state was invaded from all sides by Arab armies. Syrian forces came down the Yarmuk Valley from the east, overran two other kibbutzim en route, and were only stopped here, at the gates of Degania, by a teenager with a Molotov cocktail.

Within restored stone buildings of the early kibbutz is the museum of **Bet Gordon** (A. D. Gordon House), named for the white-bearded spiritual mentor of the early pioneers. It houses two fascinating collections: one devoted to the natural history of the region, with a renowned collection of stuffed birds, the other examining the history and archaeology of human settlement in the surrounding valleys. Among the prehistoric sites represented is Ubeidiya, just south of the kibbutz and Israel's oldest, now dated by scholars to 1.25 million years ago. Another museum (☎ 06/675–8111), also on Degania Alef, tells the story of the kibbutz; admission is free. There are no English labels here, but the curator is usually on hand to explain, and the visitor with a taste for modern history and a love for getting off the tourist trail might pass a pleasurable hour here. ⊠ *Near Rte. 90,* ☎ *06/675–0040.* ≊ *Bet Gordon NIS 6 ($2).* ☉ *Sun.–Thurs. 9:30–4, Fri. and holiday eves 8:30–noon, Sat. and holidays 9:30–noon.*

Nightlife and the Arts
A welcome new addition to the region is **Bet Gabriel** (☎ 06/675–1175, FAX 06/675–1187), on the southern shores of the Sea of Galilee near Degania Alef. Its fine architecture, beautiful garden setting, and state-of-the-art facilities have already established it as a magnetic cultural center, a 10-minute drive from Tiberias. The TIO in Tiberias (☎ 06/672–5666) and major hotels carry information on the month's performances and art exhibitions.

Kinneret

2 km (1 mi) from Degania Alef, 10 km (6¼ mi) south of Tiberias.

Kinneret, a kibbutz just across the Jordan to the north of Degania, was founded in 1911 and named for the lake (the Sea of Galilee) nearby. Two places in the immediate vicinity are of interest to visitors. On a picturesque stretch of the Jordan, where huge eucalyptus trees droop into the quiet water, is **Yardenit,** developed in recent years as a baptism site for Christian pilgrims. Although the baptism of Jesus by John the Baptist (Matthew 3) is traditionally identified with the southern reaches of the Jordan River, near Jericho, that area became a hostile frontier between Israel and Jordan in 1949, and pilgrims began to seek out accessible spots near the Sea of Galilee. At Yardenit, there is safe access to the river, where groups of white-robed pilgrims are often immersed in the Jordan, with prayers, hymns, and expressions of joy. Showers and changing facilities are available, and towels and robes can be rented from the souvenir shop. ⊠ *Off Rte. 90,* ☎ *06/675–9486.* ≊

Changing facilities: NIS 3 ($1), free with towel and robe rental. ☉
Sun.–Thurs. 8–6 (winter 8–5); Fri.–Sat. and holiday eves 8–5.

㉒   The serene and somewhat enchanted **cemetery of Kibbutz Kinneret,** barely
1 km (½ mi) north of the Jordan River bridge at a bend in Route 90,
holds the grave of Rachel Hameshoreret (the poetess Rachel), which
has virtually become a shrine for many Israelis. An opening in the low
stone wall on the right leads by shaded paths to the shore of the Sea
of Galilee, with a superb view of the Golan Heights, and, rarely, of majestic Mt. Hermon, to the north. Among the other distinguished
denizens of the cemetery are some early philosophers and pioneer
leaders of the Zionist movement—Borochov, Hess, Syrkin, Katznelson.
A few steps down from the clearing to the next path brings you to
Rachel's grave.

The large number of pebbles left on her grave by visitors (a token of
respect in the Jewish tradition) is a tribute to her renown and to the
romantic hold she has on the national imagination. Born in Russia,
Rachel immigrated to Eretz Yisrael (the Land of Israel) in 1909, lived
in Degania and Kinneret, and was in France studying agriculture when
World War I broke out. Unable to get back into Ottoman Turkish Palestine because of her Russian citizenship, she spent the war years working with refugee children in Russia, where she contracted the tuberculosis
that eventually ended her life. She returned to her beloved lake, but
never regained her health, and died in 1931.

Rachel became a poet of national stature in Hebrew, her third language.
The modern flavor and immediacy of her poems made them natural
lyrics for a whole genre of modern Israeli folk songs. Rachel wrote with
great sensitivity of the beauty of the region, and with passion—knowing her end was near—of her frustrated dream of raising a family. Her
tombstone is eloquently devoid of biographical information; it carries
the only name by which she is known, Rachel, and four lines from one
of her poems: "Spread out your hands, look yonder:/nothing comes./Each
man has his Nebo/in the great expanse." (It was from Mt. Nebo that
Moses looked into the promised land that *he* knew he would never enter.)
In a recess in the stone seat by the grave site is a weatherproof canister usually containing a complete volume (in Hebrew) of her poems,
just a few steps from the spot where many were written. ✉ *Off Rte.*
90, 600 yards south of the junction with Rte. 767.

Hammat Tiberias

★ ㉓   *7 km (4 mi) north of Kinneret, 2 km (1¼ mi) south of Tiberias.*

Here you will find Israel's hottest spring, gushing out of the earth at
60°C (140°F). The healing properties of its mineral-rich waters were
already recognized in antiquity, attested by the ruins of ancient towns—
including an exquisite 4th-century AD mosaic floor of a synagogue. Legend says that Solomon, the great king of Israel, wanted a hot bath and
used his awesome authority to force some young devils belowground
to heat the water. The fame of the salubrious springs spread far and
wide, bringing the afflicted to seek relief. Seeing such gladness among
his subjects, Solomon worried about what would happen when he died
and the devils then stopped their labor. In a flash of the wisdom for
which he was renowned, he made the hapless devils deaf. To this day,
they have not heard of the king's demise and so continue to heat the
water out of fear of his wrath.

The scientific explanation is almost tame by comparison. This and other
hot mineral springs in Israel (Hammat Gader, Ein Gedi) were created
by massive upheavals along the Great Syrian-African Rift, the world's

longest fault line. Cracks in the earth's crust allow mineral-rich water to boil to the surface.

By the end of the Second Temple period (1st century AD), when settlement in the Sea of Galilee region was at its height, a Jewish town called Hammat (Hot Springs) stood on this site. With time, Hammat was overshadowed by its newer neighbor Tiberias and became known as Hammat Tiberias (Tiberias Hot Springs). The benefits of its mineral hot springs were already legendary—a coin minted in Tiberias during the rule of Emperor Trajan, around AD 100, shows Hygeia, the goddess of health, sitting on a rock with a spring gushing out beneath it. The spa's international reputation was assured.

Parts of ancient Hammat have been uncovered by archaeologists on the mountain side of the road, bringing to light a number of ruined synagogues built one upon the other. The most dramatic is from the 4th century AD, with an elaborate mosaic floor using motifs almost identical to those at Bet Alfa: classical Jewish symbols, human figures representing the four seasons and the signs of the zodiac, and the Greek god Helios at the center (☞ Bet Alfa *in* Jezreel and Jordan Valleys, *above*). The childlike art of Bet Alfa has its charm, to be sure, but the mosaics of Hammat Tiberias are among the finest ever found in Israel.

Later cultures exploited the hot springs, too, as the small adjacent Turkish bath bears witness. Behind Hammat Tiberias, a turquoise dome marks the **tomb of Rabbi Meir Ba'al Ha-Nes,** the "Miracle Worker," a legendary personality who supposedly took a vow that he would not lie down until the Messiah came—and was therefore buried in an upright position. His name has become a sort of emblem for charitable organizations, and many a miracle has been attributed to the power of prayer at his tomb. ⊠ *Rte 90,* ☎ *06/672–5287.* 🎟 *NIS 7 ($2.40).* ☾ *Apr.–Sept., Sat.–Thurs. 8–5, Fri. and holiday eves 8–4; Oct.–Mar., Sat.–Thurs. 8–4, Fri. and holiday eves 8–3.*

NEED A BREAK? **Tiberias Hot Springs,** on the lake side of the road, is one of the two modern spa facilities fed by the mineral spring (the other, on the mountain side of the road, is exclusively for medical purposes). In addition to possessing sophisticated therapy-related services and facilities, it has a large, pampering warm indoor mineral pool (35°C or 95°F) and a small outdoor one right near the lake's edge. There's also a restaurant serving lunch. ⊠ *Rte. 90,* ☎ *06/679-1967.* 🎟 *Pools (including locker and facilities): NIS 40 ($13.40), extra for massages and therapies, 20% discount for weekday entry after 4 PM.* ☾ *Sun., Mon., Wed. 8–8; Tues., Thurs. 8 AM–10:30 PM; Fri. 8–4 (in summer till 6).*

LOWER GALILEE A TO Z

Arriving and Departing

By Bus

The **Egged** bus cooperative provides frequent service from Jerusalem, Tel Aviv, and Haifa to Bet She'an, Afula, Nazareth, and Tiberias. There is no direct service from Ben-Gurion International Airport; change in Tel Aviv. From Tel Aviv, Bus 824 leaves for Afula and Nazareth about every 1 to 1½ hours; the ride takes 1¼ hours to Afula, another 20 minutes to Nazareth. Bus 830 departs from Tel Aviv to Tiberias about every 45 minutes; the ride takes two hours. To get from Haifa to Tiberias, take Bus 430, which leaves hourly; the ride is less than one hour. From Haifa, take Bus 301 or 302 to Afula (about every 30 minutes); Bus 434 to Bet She'an (infrequent); and Bus 431 to Nazareth (every 1 to 1½ hours).

Buses from Jerusalem to Bet She'an (Buses 961 and 963) depart about once an hour. The ride to Bet She'an is almost two hours, another 25 minutes to Tiberias. Bus 953 services Afula and Nazareth from Jerusalem once daily on Sunday and Thursday; travel time is 2½ hours. Buses 355, 823, and 824 make the 20-minute run between Afula and Nazareth.

By Car

From Tel Aviv, the Lower Galilee can be reached by taking Route 2 north (the Tel Aviv–Haifa Highway) and then heading northeast along one of two regional roads: Route 65 (near Caesarea), emerging into the Jezreel Valley at Megiddo (80 km, or 50 mi; a 1¼-hour drive); or Route 70 (near Zichron Ya'akov), emerging at Yokne'am (90 km, or 57 mi; a 1½-hour drive). Avoid driving north out of Tel Aviv midday Friday and heading south to Tel Aviv Saturday afternoon and early evening. Access from Haifa is on Route 75 east to Bet She'arim and Nazareth (35 km, or 22 mi; a 45-minute drive to Nazareth); or from Route 75 onto Routes 70 and 66 south to Megiddo (34 km, or 22 mi; a 40-minute drive). The best route from Jerusalem is Route 1 east, then Route 90 north to Bet She'an (124 km, or 78 mi; a two-hour drive).

Getting Around

By Boat

The Ein Gev–based boat company **Kinneret Sailing** (✉ Rte. 92, Kibbutz Ein Gev, ☎ 06/675–8007 or 06/675–8009) has regularly scheduled runs on the Sea of Galilee between Ein Gev (eastern shore) and Tiberias (western shore). The boats are large (100–170 passengers), and the 45-minute crossings are comfortable in almost all weather. The round-trip costs NIS 25 ($8.70); a one-way trip, NIS 16 ($5.40). Currently there are daily departures from Tiberias to Ein Gev at 10:30 AM year-round, with additional sailings in July and August and on Jewish holidays. You can usually time it to eat a fish lunch at Ein Gev before sailing back to Tiberias. Call ahead for current schedules and for information about special group charters.

Lido Kinneret (✉ Gedud Barak St., ☎ 06/672–1538, 06/679–2564, or 06/672–4488) specializes in group charters, especially (but not exclusively) between Tiberias and Kibbutz Ginosar or Capernaum.

By Bus

Although the most important sites in the region are accessible by bus, the sometimes infrequent local service and transfers can make getting around the Lower Galilee by bus a time-consuming exercise. Bet She'an, Nazareth, Tiberias, and Tabgha are on the main routes; others, such as Megiddo, the Mount of Beatitudes, and Bet She'arim, are a bit of a walk from a nearby junction—or even a good, long hike, as in the case of Capernaum and Mt. Tabor. Mt. Gilboa and Belvoir are essentially inaccessible without a car.

By Car

Since not all sites are easily accessible by public bus (☞ *above*), driving is the best way to explore the region. Main roads are fairly good—some newer four-lane highways are excellent—but some smaller roads are narrow and in great need of repair. Signposting is generally good (and in English), with route numbers clearly marked. Ask directions by destination because most Israelis are not yet familiar with the relatively recent innovation of route numbers. Most attractions and accommodations are indicated by brown signs. You'll find gas stations and refreshment stands all over.

By Guide-Driven Limo-Van
Although not cheap for a couple, this can be very time-effective and, for a larger party, cost-effective as well. Most visitors traveling this way reach the region in the company of their Jerusalem- or Tel Aviv–based guide; there are very few guides actually based in Galilee.

By Taxi
This is generally an expensive and uninspiring way to travel. For sightseeing it is often a much better deal to hire a private guide with a car or limousine (☞ *above*). Following are some of the area's main towns and taxi companies in them: **Afula** (Yizre'el, ☎ 06/659–5625), **Nazareth** (Abu-Assal, ☎ 06/655–4745; Diana, ☎ 06/655–1483; Hashalom, ☎ 06/657–2888), and **Tiberias** (Hagalil, ☎ 06/672–0353; Ha'emek, ☎ 06/672–0131; Kinneret, ☎ 06/672–2262).

Contacts and Resources

Car Rentals
Agencies close early Friday afternoon and are closed on Saturday (except in Nazareth).

In **Tiberias,** companies include Avis (⊠ Central Bus Station, ☎ 06/672–2766); Budget (⊠ Opposite Carmel Jordan River Hotel, Habanim St., ☎ 06/672–0864); Eldan (⊠ In Carmel Jordan River Hotel, Habanim St., ☎ 06/ 672–2831); Europcar (National) (⊠ Sonol Garage, Alhadeff St., ☎ 06/672–2777 or 06/672–4191); Hertz (⊠ In Jordan River Hotel, Habanim St., ☎ 06/672–3939 or 672–1804); Reliable (⊠ 9 Alhadeff St., ☎ 06/672–4112).

Emergencies
Ambulance service (☎ 101). **First aid** (☎ 101). **Pharmacies** offering late-night service (☎ 101). **Police** in the Lower Galilee region (☎ 100).

Guided Tours
A free walking tour of Tiberias leaves from the Radisson Moriah Plaza Hotel (⊠ Habanim St., ☎ 06/679–2233) on Saturday at 10 AM. Organized jointly by the hotel and the Society for the Protection of Nature in Israel (SPNI), the tours are given in both Hebrew and English. Call ahead to verify.

Few coach tours actually originate in the Lower Galilee. They start instead from Jerusalem, Tel Aviv, Haifa, and Netanya. Most hotels can book a tour for you. All buses will pick you up and drop you off at your hotel.

Both **Egged Tours** and **United Tours** conduct one- and two-day tours from Jerusalem, Tel Aviv, Haifa, and Netanya several times a week. Itineraries include (in different combinations) the following Lower Galilee sites: Megiddo, Nazareth, Zippori, Bet She'an, Hammat Gader, Tiberias, Tabgha, Capernaum, and a boat ride on the Sea of Galilee. Many two-day tours include the Upper Galilee and Golan Heights. Prices range from $54–$60 for a day trip to $187 (including overnight and dinner) for two days. For reservations, contact Egged Tours, in Jerusalem (⊠ 224 Jaffa Rd., ☎ 02/530–4422); in Tel Aviv (⊠ 59 Ben Yehuda St., ☎ 03/527–1212 or 03/527–1215); in Haifa (⊠ 4 Nordau St., ☎ 04/862–3131 or 04/862–3132); and in Netanya (⊠ Central Bus Station, ☎ 09/860–6206 or 09/860–6207). For reservations with United Tours, call Jerusalem (⊠ King David Hotel annex, ☎ 02/625–2187 or 02/625–2188) or Tel Aviv (⊠ 113 Hayarkon St., ☎ 03/693–3412 or 03/522–2008).

For the more adventurous and/or active visitor, the nonprofit **Society for the Protection of Nature in Israel** does things differently. Lower Galilee sites, including some hikes, feature in their three-day Galilee tour. For information call the society in Jerusalem (✉ 13 Helene Hamalka St., ☏ 02/624–4605) or in Tel Aviv (✉ 3 Hashefela St., ☏ 03/638–8677).

Vered Hagalil, at Korazim Junction, is an Israeli version of a dude ranch that offers comfortable accommodations and a good restaurant, not to mention short and long horseback tours above and around the Sea of Galilee. For more information contact Vered Hagalil (✉ Rte. 90, M.P. Korazim, ☏ 06/693–5785, FAX 06/693–4964).

Donkey-back riding is singularly appropriate in the hills of Nazareth and the Lower Galilee, a revival of an ancient tradition. **Donkey Tracks** conducts fully guided group tours (call ahead to see what's available), and individuals can rent a donkey for NIS 40 ($13) an hour, complete with map, directions, and safety instructions. Discounts are available if booked through some hotels in the area. For more information, contact Kfar Kedem (✉ Hoshaya, M.P. Hamovil 17915, ☏ 06/656–5511, FAX 06/657–0378).

Nightlife and the Arts

By far the best source of information for performances in the Lower Galilee is the TIO on Habanim Street in Tiberias (☏ 06/672–5666), between the Radisson Moriah Plaza and Carmel Jordan River hotels. Also *see* the individual attractions in this chapter for specific festivals or events.

Kibbutzim in the area periodically host theatrical, dance, and musical performers on tour from the "big cities" in the south. Consult a TIO and your hotel front desk for information about these special events.

Outdoor Activities and Sports

BICYCLING

There is a bicycle **marathon** around the Sea of Galilee at the end of October or the beginning November, with both popular and competitive categories. There are three distances: 12 km (7½ mi), 25 km (15½ mi), and a complete 65-km (40½-mi) encirclement of the Sea of Galilee. All end at the Tzemach Junction. For details, contact the Sports Department of the Jordan Valley Regional Council (✉ Tzemach Junction, 15132, ☏ 06/675–7630 or 06/675–7631, FAX 06/675–7641).

HIKING

For information on trails and organized hikes in the Jezreel and Jordan valleys, contact the SPNI's **Alon-Tavor Field Study Center** (✉ M.P. Lower Galilee 14101, ☏ 06/676–7798). The center also offers hostel-type accommodations.

HORSEBACK RIDING

The **Vered Hagalil** ranch (✉ Rte. 90, M.P. Korazim, ☏ 06/693–5785, FAX 06/693–4964), on Route 90 north of the Sea of Galilee at Korazim Junction, conducts horseback tours of the area (☞ Guided Tours, *above*).

SWIMMING

Thousands of swimmers take part in the **Kinneret Swim** in September, a tradition since 1953. Traditionally a 4-km (2½-mi) race, the event has now gained recognition as an international swim meet, and the tough swimmers cover distances of up to 10 km (6¼ mi). Most, of course, are amateurs just out for fun. For details, contact the Jordan Valley Regional Council (✉ Tzemach Junction, 15132, ☏ 06/675–7630 or 06/675–7631, FAX 06/675–7641).

WALKING AND RUNNING

The annual **Big Walk** (Hatza'adah in Hebrew), which takes place in March or April over a 11-km (7-mi) route along the Sea of Galilee shore, attracts participants from all over the country. For details, contact the Jordan Valley Regional Council (✉ Tzemach Junction, 15132; ☎ 06/675–7630 or 06/675–7631, FAX 06/675–7641).

Dedicated runners might want to participate in the **Sea of Galilee Marathon and Half-Marathon,** which take place in December or January. A triathlon takes place at the beginning of May. For details, contact the Sports Department of the Jordan Valley Regional Council (✉ Tzemach Junction, 15132; ☎ 06/675–7630 or 06/675–7631, FAX 06/675–7641).

WATER SPORTS

The so-called kayaks of **Abukayak** (☎ 06/692–2245 or 06/692–1078) are really inflated rubber canoes. Rented inside the Jordan River Park (✉ On Rte. 888, just north of the Sea of Galilee), they offer a delightfully serene 1½-hour route (decidedly not white water!) down the lower Jordan River. Life jackets are provided, and the experience is appropriate for young children.

For serious kayaking, look into the international competition held annually in March. For details contact the Sports Department of the Jordan Valley Regional Council, ✉ Tzemach Junction, 15132; ☎ 06/675–7630 or 06/675–7631, FAX 06/675–7641.

Visitor Information

There are Tourist Information Offices (TIOs) in **Nazareth** (✉ GTIO, Casa Nova St., ☎ 06/657–3003 or 06/657–0555) and in **Tiberias** (✉ Habanim St., between the Carmel Jordan River and Radisson Moriah Plaza hotels, ☎ 06/672–5666).

7 Upper Galilee and the Golan

Including Zfat (Safed)

With something for everybody, this area draws pilgrims and vacationers, serious hikers and bon vivants. You can walk around Zfat, the mystical hillside city, or kayak near a kibbutz guest house. Despite the political heat that pervades the region—the Golan Heights in particular—this is the part of Israel that best represents cool, comforting relaxation. The area's history dates back a million years, but today it is geared to the modern traveler, with a range of traditional as well as trendy options.

ISRAELIS CALL IT THE SWITZERLAND OF ISRAEL: The undulating hills of Western Galilee roll into sharper, more rugged limestone and basalt formations, bordered on the north by Lebanon and on the east by the volcanic, mountainous terrain of the Golan Heights, on the other side of which lies Syria. The dominant feature of the Upper Galilee and the Golan, the latter claiming less than 50 square km (31 square mi) in all, is Mt. Hermon, the highest mountain in Israel, one of the highest in the Middle East, and home to Israel's sole ski resort.

By Lisa Perlman

Most Israelis come here to get away from it all, indulging in everything from hiking and bird-watching to kayaking and wine tasting. The nature trails, the rustic restaurants, and the kibbutz guest houses make it easy to steer clear of the four urban centers found here; in fact, two of these—Kiryat Shmona and Ma'alot, both of which began life as development towns designed to absorb Jewish refugees, mainly from Arab countries—offer little of interest to the visitor. The other two—Zfat (Safed) and Katzrin—have unique personalities, the first the result of a long history of Jewish religious mysticism and the second the consequence of a hard-headed determination to secure Israel's border with Syria.

Towering at a height of more than 9,000 feet, Mt. Hermon is Israel's "sponge" as well as its ski slope: Huge volumes of water from snow and rain are absorbed into the ancient limestone rock, emerging at the base of the mountain in a series of gorgeous springs and feeding the Jordan River and its tributaries. Indeed, these rivers, all flowing through the region's Hula Valley, provide half of Israel's water supply. The abundant water sustains gazelles, wildcats, hyraxes and hares, hundreds of species of birds, and lush, verdant foliage that thrives year-round.

More than anything else, it is the water here that has been the source of political contention since time immemorial. (In second place is the hilltop view, which underscores the value of the Golan Heights, officially annexed by Israel in 1981.) For a million years this region has been a center of human settlement. In earliest times, people hunted the rhinos, elephants, and fallow deer that have since roamed to other parts. Later they learned to farm—and to trade, for the Galilee was smack bang on the Western world's first major trade route, the Via Maris, stretching from Egypt to Mesopotamia.

Consequently, the rivals for this prime real estate were many: In ancient times, Egyptians, Canaanites, Israelites, Romans, Ottomans, and Crusaders locked horns in various configurations; in the 20th century, the borders have been played with by Russia, Britain, France, and, of course, Israel and Syria.

In addition to the Jewish and Arab population, there has always been a small Druze presence here, particularly in the Golan Heights (about 17,000 Arabic-speaking Druze). After the Six-Day War in 1967, five Druze villages found themselves no longer in Lebanese or Syrian territory, but in Israel.

Borders are not the only things that have shifted in the region. A geological fault line, the Syrian-African Rift, cuts straight through the 30-km-long (19-mi-long) Hula Valley. Many symmetrical volcanic cones, hundreds of thousands of years old, daub the Golan; as for earthquakes, in 1837 Zfat and Tiberias were razed when the earth shook here, but no rumbles of significance have been heard since.

With plenty of water and rich fertile soil, the Upper Galilee and the Golan have always been agricultural centers. Since Jewish development of the area resumed a century ago, orange and apple orchards, fish cultivation ponds, cotton fields, and vineyards have become common sights. These are closely intertwined with the region's other main industry: tourism. Travelers come to see and stay at the many successful communal settlements—the kibbutzim and moshavim—that dot the area. They also come to roam the area's nature reserves, most of which are around the rivers and springs, and to witness the seasonal vacationing of migratory birds that flit between Africa and Europe.

The region's proximity to Lebanon and Syria does not deter visitors to the Upper Galilee and the Golan. On the contrary, the so-called Good Fence, at the Israeli-Lebanese border crossing in Israel's northernmost town of Metulla, draws the curious from all over the world; enologists come to taste the local wine, and hikers don their boots for the fauna-and-flora-filled reserves.

Whether the status of the Golan Heights changes as a result of the ongoing peace negotiations will not be known for some time. Since their arrival at the turn of the century, the Jews have fought malaria and other diseases, defended themselves in the face of Arab armies and terror bands, and confronted a host of other hardships and hurdles. And still the tenacious Galilean will tell you there's no better place. Whether a kibbutznik or living in town, whether born here or opting for this corner of the world, the pride is palpable, and it transcends politics. It's amazing that despite the embattled past and unsure future, the average Galilean remains laid-back and friendly. Only four hours' drive from hectic, humid Tel Aviv and from the visceral capital, Jerusalem, this truly is another world.

Pleasures and Pastimes

Dining

Only a few years ago, one hand was too much on which to count the number of good restaurants in this region. Decent light food, such as falafel in pita bread, is never far away, but the concept of real meals in real restaurants with real atmosphere is relatively new to Israel. The Upper Galilee and the Golan have inherent attractions for diners: With verdant hills, old stone dwellings, and crisp, appetite-whetting air, the landscape serves as an exquisite backdrop for a meal that can be savored. Today there are many restaurants in the area that make the best of the natural environment in order to offer all-sensory gastronomic experience. You can find hearty steaks in the middle of the forest, fresh grilled Dan River trout served in shady groves on the river's banks, Middle Eastern fare prepared by Druze villagers, and simple home-style Jewish cooking in the heart of the holy city of Zfat. The excellent local wines from Katzrin enhance any meal; try the Mt. Hermon red, Gamla cabernet sauvignon, and Yarden cabernet blanc and merlot. Most restaurants are open every day except Yom Kippur; in a few places, however (Zfat, for example), it is difficult to find an eatery open on Shabbat (Friday afternoon until Saturday sundown). Attire is always informal, but it's wise to dress modestly in Zfat.

CATEGORY	COST*
$$$$	over $30
$$$	$22–$30
$$	$12–$22
$	under $12

*per person for a three-course meal, excluding drinks and service

Hiking

Superbly maintained nature reserves and national parks make this region an obvious destination for hikers. Most trails are not too challenging and are well marked; stick to the tracks to avoid any trouble. Always carry water, and wear a hat, especially in summer, and comfortable shoes. In fact, you may want to take an extra pair of shoes in case you get wet—there's an abundance of water in these parts.

Horseback Riding

Horseback riding—on both long and short trails—has really taken off in the Upper Galilee. It is an excellent way to see and appreciate Israel's beautiful northern landscape. A variety of options exist for wandering over hill and dale by this means of transport.

Jeep Tours

The popularity of Jeep tours has soared in this region. Needless to say, more distance can be covered in less time in a motorized vehicle, which make Jeeps an attractive option. This is especially good for an afternoon embellished with excitement.

Kayaking and Rafting

One of the more adventurous sports and enormously enjoyable with visitors of all ages is skimming the Jordan River in a kayak, raft, or inner tube. Novices needn't worry—this is not white-water territory.

Lodging

The region's lodging options have burgeoned in recent years. There are no grand hotels, but an ample choice of guest houses and inns range from ranch style to home style. As the tourism industry in the region has developed, many settlements, especially kibbutzim and moshavim, have added a hotel, or simply a wing attached to a home, and provide an extensive range of amenities, including activities for children. Although most guest houses remain independent of the community's other industries, they sometimes offer lectures and tours of the communal settlement. In addition to offering restaurant facilities, many also arrange kayaking and rafting, horseback riding, Jeep tours, and other sports and services for guests and the general public. The choice can be difficult, as all are in pretty settings and have well-maintained grounds.

CATEGORY	COST*
$$$$	over $120
$$$	$80–$120
$$	$55–$80
$	under $55

All prices are for two people in a standard double room, including breakfast and 15% service charge.

Exploring Upper Galilee and the Golan

The northern Jordan Valley serves as the geographical border between these two regions, with the hilly Upper Galilee lying to the west and the Golan, a basalt plateau, to the east. Together, however, they are still small enough to be covered in a weekend trip.

Great Itineraries

Tel Avivians do it. Jerusalemites do it. But cramming the Upper Galilee and the Golan into a day trip is far from ideal for the first-time visitor. Although brief visits are certainly possible (a day trip to the Golan Heights from Tiberias, for example), a several-day sojourn here can be as leisurely or as hectic as you wish. In three or four days, you can learn about the country's military history, do a bit of wine tasting, hike

Upper Galilee and the Golan

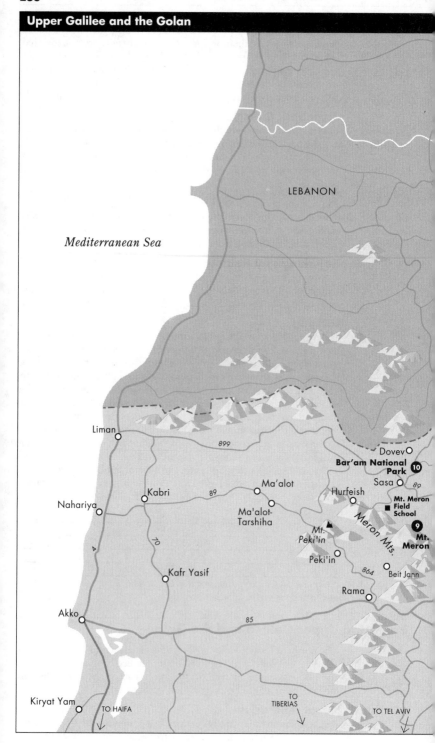

Mediterranean Sea

LEBANON

Liman

899

Dovev

Bar'am National
Park **10**

Sasa   89

Ma'alot

Hurfeish

**Mt. Meron
Field
School**

Kabri   89

Nahariya

Ma'alot-
Tarshiha

Meron Mts.

**9
Mt.
Meron**

70

Mt.
Peki'in

4

Peki'in

864

Beit Jann

Kafr Yasif

Rama

Akko

85

Kiryat Yam

TO HAIFA

TO
TIBERIAS

TO TEL AVIV

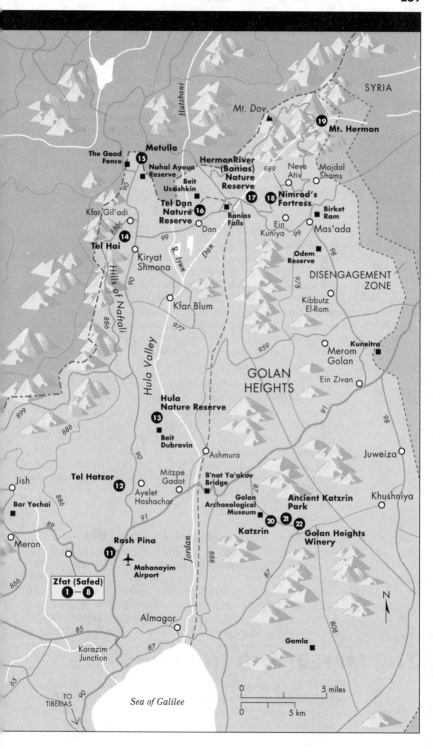

through a little piece of wilderness, relax over a hearty country meal, try your hand at kayaking, or sit quietly in a room with a view.

The distances in the Upper Galilee and the Golan are small (aren't they everywhere in Israel?). Still, the more time allowed here, the better; there is something about the soft gurgling of the brooks, the lush foliage of the forests, and the crisp mountain air of the Golan Heights that slow the pace. The ideal way to see the area is by car, but local buses will get you almost anywhere you want to go. In this chapter, towns and sites are arranged in the order you would most likely visit them when traveling by road, either from Tel Aviv or Tiberias.

Note: Touring in the Upper Galilee and the Golan is perfectly safe. If, however, security demands that caution be exercised, certain areas may be temporarily inaccessible to visitors.

Numbers in the text correspond to numbers in the margin and on the Upper Galilee and the Golan map and the Zfat (Safed) map.

IF YOU HAVE 1 DAY
If your base is Tiberias or elsewhere in the Lower Galilee (or the Western Galilee), spend it in the northernmost part of the country, starting with a walk through the **Tel Dan** ⑯ or **Hermon River (Banias)** ⑰ nature reserves, lunching over a Dan River trout. You can then either tackle **Nimrod's Fortress** ⑱ national park or, in spring and summer, take a chairlift to the top of **Mt. Hermon** ⑲; in winter, try wine tasting in **Katzrin** ⑳–㉒. Or, spend the morning strolling through the Old City in **Zfat** ①–⑧ and the afternoon kayaking on the Jordan River.

IF YOU HAVE 2-3 DAYS
A variety of options exists in the Upper Galilee and the Golan as well as the Lower Galilee if you have two to three days. Tiberias is a good starting point. Then, either spend a morning by the Sea of Galilee or head for **Zfat** ①–⑧ and take a walk in the Old City. Stop in **Rosh Pina** ⑪ for a cup of coffee and a break and then check out the swampy **Hula Nature Reserve** ⑬. Spend the night in one of the area's kibbutz guest houses; the following day, head for the Golan Heights, driving along Route 98, which overlooks the Disengagement Zone between Israel and Syria. The third day would be well spent on one of the region's adventure options—horseback riding, water sports on the Jordan River, or Jeep touring.

When to Tour the Upper Galilee and the Golan
The Upper Galilee and the Golan are best in spring and fall. If you're a flora fan, the range of full-bloom colors is wondrous in late winter and spring. In summer, days may be hot, but the region doesn't suffer from the humidity of other parts of Israel; in winter some rain can be expected. Note, however, that Zfat comes alive from July through September, when more galleries are open. There are many activities for visitors then—but also more crowds.

ZFAT (SAFED) AND ENVIRONS

Around the southern part of the Upper Galilee, attractions range from the narrow streets and historic synagogues of the Old City of Zfat to the wilderness of the Hula Nature Reserve. Other nature reserves such as Mt. Meron have both scenic appeal and spiritual importance. At Rosh Pina you can see where the first Zionist pioneers in the Galilee settled. And if you just want to relax at an inn or a kibbutz guest house and enjoy the wooded scenery, you can do that, too.

Zfat (Safed)

33 km (20 mi) north of Tiberias, 72 km (45 mi) northeast of Haifa.

At 3,000 feet above sea level, Zfat (Safed) is Israel's most elevated city. Perhaps this extra proximity to the heavens accounts for its reputation as the center of Jewish mysticism (Kabbala). For although like Jerusalem, Tiberias, and Hebron, it is one of the holy cities of Israel, Zfat possesses a spiritual dimension found nowhere else.

The Crusaders built a fortress here, and a thriving Jewish settlement grew up in the shadow of the castle walls. Although it declined with the eclipse of the Crusader presence in the Galilee, the town survived rule by the Ottomans, who retained Zfat as their capital through the 16th century. Soon after their expulsion in 1492, the Jews from Spain started streaming in, among them respected rabbis and other spiritual leaders, intellectuals, and poets who gravitated to Zfat as a center of the revival of Kabbala study.

The Kabbala—whose oral tradition dates to ancient times but which gained popularity starting in the 12th century, possibly as a reaction against formal rabbinical Judaism—is about reading between, behind, and all around the lines: Each and every letter and accent of every word in the holy books has a numerical value with specific significance, offering added meaning to the literal word. Zfat was the heart of the Kabbala, the great rabbis were its soul; under their tutelage religious and mystical schools and meeting places mushroomed here. Some of these leaders were to leave their mark on the age, on the generations to follow, and, of course, on Zfat itself.

For most of the year, Zfat can be something of an enigma to the tourist: It hibernates from October through June. The city's noted artists move to homes in warmer parts of the country, opening their galleries in Zfat infrequently, and other sites may (or may not) also be closed. This does not mean you should leave Zfat off your itinerary during those months. There is enough to occupy the curious wanderer for at least a couple of hours—and much is free. In summer, especially during school holidays (July and August), Zfat is abuzz with activity: Galleries and shops stay open late, the strains of klezmer music waft around corners, and the city extends a warm welcome to everyone. Moreover, everyone comes—so avoid Zfat at this time if you do not like crowds.

It doesn't take long to walk all around the labyrinthine Old City of Zfat and to get a feel for it. Take time to poke around the little cobbled passages that seem to lead nowhere or linger over some minute architectural detail on a structure from another era. And don't worry if you get lost—you're never far from the center. Yerushalayim (Jerusalem) Street runs through the heart of the Old City, encircling the Citadel in its center; from here there is easy access to the two main areas of interest, the Old Jewish Quarter and the Artists' Colony. There is no getting around the uphill–downhill of Zfat, so wear comfortable walking shoes. Also, modest dress is recommended in this Orthodox town.

A Good Walk

Begin by exploring the **Park of the Citadel** ①, site of what was the largest Christian fortress in the Middle East; you can leave your car here. As you return to the park entrance, on Hativat Yiftah Street, take in the sight of the old houses below and the undulating, pastoral panorama beyond. This image has been the inspiration for countless paintings and drawings that have emerged from Zfat since time immemorial, and you will no doubt see numerous modern interpretations at the General Exhibition (☞ *below*) and in the rooms of almost every Zfat hotel.

Turn right; after you walk about 300 feet, you'll come to the remains of the Citadel tower. It was destroyed over the years, mainly by earthquakes—the most recent and most devastating one occurred in 1837. A little farther along on the right is the **Israel Bible Museum,** with its impressive arched entrance.

Walk down the steps and cross Yerushalayim Street. Near No. 24, more steps lead to the parallel Bar Yochai Street. You are now entering the Ashkenazi (East European Jews) section of the Old Jewish Quarter, distinguished from the Sephardic (Middle Eastern Jews) section by its wider streets and more subtly colored buildings. Turn left and walk to **Kikar Hameginim** ②. Standing on the square, you will notice through the arch a stepped street leading down and to the right. This draws you into the 16th century and the Ashkenazi **Ha'Ari Synagogue** ③, with its impressive olive-wood holy ark.

After leaving the synagogue, go down the steps, turn left at cobbled Alkabetz Street and go down again at the first set of steps. Walk under the dome, and you'll shortly notice blue window frames and a door next to a little alley. You are now in the heart of Sephardic Zfat. If you haven't found the sign marking the spot, just ask for the **Abouhav Synagogue** ④, whose elements reflect Sephardic traditions. Head back under the arch and up the stairs to Caro Street, with its *souk*-style souvenir stores, and the compact **Caro Synagogue** ⑤, arguably the most charming in the quarter.

A little farther ahead you will find yourself in the middle of a stairway called **Ma'alot Olei Hagardom.** At this point, you have two options: You can take the stairs down, turn right at the bottom, and follow the road to the **cemetery** ⑥, with its intriguing gravestones old and new. En route you will pass Hameiri House, a museum devoted to Zfat's history, especially the last 100 years. The other choice is to continue straight ahead, crossing over the stairway to the **Artists' Colony.** You should make your first stop the **General Exhibition** ⑦, a selection of works by resident artists. A walk down Tet-vav Street brings you to one of the curiosities of the colony, the **Museum of Printing Art** ⑧.

Sights to See

❹ **Abouhav Synagogue.** This large Sephardic synagogue is named in honor of a 14th-century Spanish scribe, one of whose Torah scrolls found its way here with the Spanish Jewish exiles 200 years later. A look around reveals a number of differences between it and its Ashkenazi counterparts such as the Ha'Ari Synagogue (☞ *below*). The walls are painted a lively blue and are richly decorated with religious motifs, the benches run along the walls instead of in rows (so that no man turns his back on his neighbor), and the dome-shape roof is set atop four pillars.

Every detail is loaded with significance: There are three arks, for the three forefathers Abraham, Isaac, and Jacob (the one on the right is said to be the Abouhav original), and 10 windows in the dome, referring to the Commandments. The charmingly naive illustrations on the squinches include a depiction of the Dome of the Rock (referring to the destruction of the Second Temple) and pomegranate trees, whose 613 seeds are equal in number to the Torah's commandments. The original building was destroyed in the 1837 earthquake, but locals still swear the southern wall—in which the Torah scroll penned by Abouhav is set—was spared. This scroll is taken out only on the holy days of Rosh Hashanah, Yom Kippur, and Shavuot. ⌧ *Abouhav St.* ☉ *No set visiting hours.*

Artists' Colony. The colony was established in 1951 by six Israeli artists who saw the promise beyond Zfat's war-torn and dilapidated state;

Zfat (Safed)

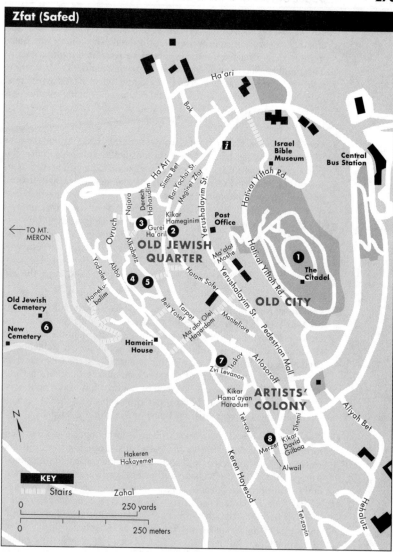

Abouhav
Synagogue, **4**
Caro Synagogue, **5**
Cemetery, **6**
General Exhibition, **7**
Ha'Ari Synagogue, **3**
Kikar Hameginim, **2**
Museum of
Printing Art, **8**
Park of the Citadel, **1**

for them, the old buildings, the fertile landscape, and the cool mountain air fused to form a veritable magic that they knew would help them create. Others soon followed until, at its peak, the colony was home to more than 50 artists, some of whom are exhibited internationally. The numbers have since dwindled somewhat, and gallery opening hours are unpredictable, especially in winter, when Zfat's artists tend to hibernate. In summer (July–September), however, things really come alive as the artists open their doors and display—or work on—their latest pots, paintings, and sculptures.

❺ Caro Synagogue. Rabbi Yosef Caro wrote the Shulchan Aruch, the code of law that has served as a foundation of Jewish religious interpretation to the present day. He arrived in Zfat in 1535 and served as its Jewish community leader for years. This synagogue was also destroyed in the great earthquake of 1837 and was rebuilt in the mid-19th century. It is said to have been Caro's study hall. If you ask, you can open the ark containing the Torah scrolls, one of which is at least 400 years old. A glass-faced cabinet at the back of the synagogue is the *geniza,* where damaged scrolls or prayer books are stored (but never destroyed because they carry the name of God). The turquoise paint here, considered the "color of heaven," is believed to help keep away the evil eye. ⊠ *Alkabetz St.* ☉ *No set visiting hours.*

❻ Cemetery. An old and a new cemetery are set into the hillside below the Old Jewish Quarter. The old plots resonate with the names and fame of the Kabbalists of yore, and their graves are identifiable by their sky blue markers. It is said that if the legs of the devout suddenly get tired here, it is from walking over hidden graves. In the new cemetery are the graves of members of the pre-State underground Stern Gang and Irgun forces, who were executed by the British in Akko prison (☞ Chapter 5). In a separate plot bordered by cypresses, the 24 teenage victims of the 1974 terrorist massacre at Ma'alot are buried.

❼ General Exhibition. The works inside this large space are a representative sampling of the works of Zfat's artists, ranging from oils and watercolors to silk screens and sculptures, avant-garde and traditional. The permission of the Muslim authorities was required for the General Exhibition, as it is housed in the old mosque, easily seen from afar thanks to its minaret. The Artists' Colony has recognized the growing presence of artists from the former Soviet Union, and the adjacent building holds the **Immigrant Artists' Exhibition.** In either facility, if any works take your fancy, just ask how to find your way to the artist's gallery for a more in-depth look. ⊠ *Isakov and Zvi Levanon Sts.,* ☎ *06/692–0087.* 🎫 *Free.* ☉ *Sun.–Fri. 9–6, Sat. and holidays 10–2.*

❽ Ha'Ari Synagogue. This Ashkenazi synagogue has associations going back to the 16th century. It is named for the renowned Ari, the great rabbi who left an indelible mark on Zfat and on Judaism. His real name was Isaac Luria, but he was known to all as the Ari, Hebrew for "lion" and an acronym for Adoneinu Rabbeinu Itzhak (our master and teacher Isaac). In the mere three years he was in Zfat, he evolved his own system of the Kabbala, which drew a huge following that was to influence Jewish teaching and interpretation the world over, right up to today. Even more astounding is that he died in his mid-thirties; it is said that one should not even consider study of the Kabbala before the age of 40, when one is thought to have reached the requisite level of intellectual and emotional maturity.

The synagogue itself is not outstanding but is typically Ashkenazi, with its pale colors and minimally decorated walls. The olive-wood holy ark, however, is a dazzling tour de force of carving, with two tiers of spiral columns and seemingly living plant reliefs. The synagogue was built after Luria's death, at the spot where the Ari is said to have come with his students on a Friday evening to welcome the Sabbath. The 1837 earthquake leveled it; it was rebuilt in 1857. (The Sephardic Ari Synagogue, where the rabbi prayed, is farther down the quarter, by the cemetery. The oldest of Zfat's synagogues, the 16th-century structure has especially fine carved wooden doors.) ⊠ *Ha'Ari St.* ☉ *No set visiting hours.*

Israel Bible Museum. This stone mansion was once home to the Ottoman governor; today it houses the somewhat dramatic paintings and sculptures of artist Phillip Ratner, all inspired by the Bible. ⊠ *Hativat Yiftah St.,* ☎ *06/699–9972.* ☜ *Free.* ☉ *Mar.–Sept., Sun.–Thurs. 10–6, Sat. 10–2; Oct.–Nov., Sat.–Thurs. 10–2; Dec., Sun.–Thurs. 10–2.*

❷ Kikar Hameginim. Defenders' Square is the Old Jewish Quarter's principal plaza and was once its social and economic heart. A sign points to a two-story house that served as the command post of the neighborhood's defense in 1948—hence the square's name.

Ma'alot Olei Hagardom. Part of Zfat's charm is its setting on the slope of a hill. This stairway, which extends all the way down from Yerushalayim Street, forms the boundary between the Old Jewish Quarter and the Artists' Colony (previously the Arab Quarter).

❽ Museum of Printing Art. The small but rich collection here spans the history of printing in Israel. On display are the first Hebrew press (operated in Zfat, in 1576), the first Hebrew book (which rolled off a year later), the first newspaper printed in Israel (1863), and a copy of the May 16, 1948, *Palestine Post* declaring the birth of the State of Israel. ⊠ *Merzer and Alwail Sts.,* ☎ *06/692–0947.* ☜ *Free.* ☉ *Sun.–Thurs. 10–noon and 4–6, Fri.–Sat. 10–noon.*

❶ Park of the Citadel. In Talmudic times, 1,600 years ago, hilltop bonfires here served as a massive beacon for surrounding communities to herald the lunar month, the basis for the Jewish calendar. The Crusaders, in the 12th century, immediately grasped the setting's strategic value and built the Citadel, only scattered sections of which remain. The Muslim ruler Saladin wrenched it from them in 1188, following his victory at the Horns of Hattin, but half a century later the Crusaders repossessed it, and the Order of the Templars turned it into the most massive Christian fortress in the East. For decades the Crusaders were able to keep the aggressive Mamluk sultan Baybars at bay, but his army eventually besieged the Citadel in 1266. Having already destroyed many of the cities along the coast, Baybars decided to move his capital from Akko to Zfat. This marked the beginning of the end of the Crusader empire.

The Jewish settlements outside the castle walls grew and prospered during and after the Crusader era, with the city becoming a center of Kabbala studies. Zfat remained predominantly Jewish until a devastating earthquake in 1837 razed the town and left few survivors. In 1929, Arab riots drove more of the town's inhabitants away. By 1948, only 1,500 Jewish residents remained. The departing British army left the town's key strategic positions to the Arab forces, which set about besieging the Old Jewish Quarter. A handful of Palmach fighters (part of the Jewish clandestine army during the British Mandate) penetrated the enemy lines and helped the mostly elderly devout Jews of the quarter successfully resist the offense in what became known as the Miracle of Zfat. Once again, with its sweeping views and slopes in the heart of Zfat, the Citadel was the focal point of battle. ⊠ *Old City.*

Dining and Lodging

$$$ ✕ **Bat Ya'ar.** It takes a little courage to find the place through the winding roads behind Zfat and into the Birya Forest, but this timbered, pub-style restaurant in the middle of nowhere serves tasty steaks and salads and excellent chicken with rosemary, all enhanced by the pine-wood mountaintop setting. You can work up an appetite on one of Bat Ya'ar's horseback-riding or Jeep tours. Outside the restaurant is a play area for children; they'll love the pony rides. ⊠ *Birya Forest (5 km, or 3 mi, from Zfat),* ☎ *06/692–1788. Reservations essential on weekends. MC, V.*

$$ ✕ **Ein Camonim.** The Galilee Hills make perfect pastureland for live-
★ stock—in this case, goats—and the output of Ein Camonim's dairy can be tasted fresh daily. The fixed menu consists of a platter of goat cheeses, home-baked bread, a wicker basket of raw garden vegetables, a small carafe of local wine, coffee, and dessert. There's a half-price menu for children up to age 12. A retail shop beside the restaurant sells the cheeses, and though very good, they are expensive. ⊠ *Rte. 85, 20 km (12½ mi) southwest of Zfat, 5 km (3 mi) west of Kadarim Junction (north of the highway),* ☎ *06/698–9894. AE, DC, MC, V.*

$$ ✕ **Hamifgash.** One of the veteran eateries on pedestrians-only Yerushalayim Street, Hamifgash lives up to its name, which means "meeting place": This is one of the most popular restaurants in town, possibly because it suits all tastes. There's self-service upstairs and table service downstairs, with anything from soups, salads, and snacks to substantial meat dishes. The most exclusive meals are served in the restaurant's renowned wine cellar—a rare find in Israel—which stocks a full range of Israeli wines. ⊠ *75 Yerushalayim St.,* ☎ *06/692–0510. AE, DC, MC, V. No dinner Fri. or lunch Sat.*

$$ ✕ **K'tse Hanof.** Living up to its name, the View's Edge café is perched high in the Birya Forest and commands a stunning vista of the surrounding hills. It's a wonderful place for a light fish or dairy meal. A gallery–gift shop displays and sells a range of works by local artists and craftspeople. ⊠ *Birya Forest before Amuka, 7 km (4 mi) from Zfat,* ☎ *06/697–3716. AE, DC, MC, V. Closed Sun.*

$$ ✕ **Pinati.** Question: What do goulash and Elvis Presley have in common? Answer: They are both drawing cards to Pinati. Images of Elvis cover the walls, and though nobody can explain his connection to the Polish–Italian–Middle Eastern menu, the heavy volume of customers indicates the success of the restaurant despite its many idiosyncrasies. Pinati serves up good wholesome food, and it has awards to show for it. It's also one of the few restaurants in town open Saturday. ⊠ *81 Yerushalayim St.,* ☎ *06/692–0855. AE, DC, MC, V.*

$$$$ ▣ **Rimon Inn.** Two hundred years ago, when the Turks were in charge,
★ this gracious old building was the local post office. Rooms were added later, and it became a khan, or inn. It opened as the Rimon Inn in 1961 and has enjoyed a reputation for charm and excellence ever since. With their stone walls, the rooms have a rustic feel, and they are tastefully decorated with local art; the former stables serve as the dining room. Half the rooms have a view over the mountain and gorges. At press time, the hotel was readying the adjacent building for guests. This wing will include a bar and gym. ⊠ *Artists' Quarter, Box 1011, Zfat 13110,* ☎ *06/692–0665,* FAX *06/692–0456. 86 rooms (including 50 in the new wing), most with bath. Restaurant, bar, pool, children's programs (in summer). AE, DC, MC, V.*

$$$$ ▣ **Ron.** This pleasant but unassuming hotel has a good restaurant with an eclectic menu of European and Middle Eastern dishes. Rooms are spacious, clean, and light-filled, and half have a mountain view. ⊠ *Near*

Metzuda Park, Hativat Yiftah, Box 22, Zfat 13214, ☎ *06/697–2590,* FAX *06/697–2363. 50 rooms with bath. Restaurant, bar, pool. V.*

$$$$ 🏨 **Sea View (Mitzpe Hayamim).** Midway between Zfat and Rosh Pina is this spot for all-around pampering, body and soul; there's a splendid view of the Sea of Galilee. The serene (but snobby) Sea View specializes in packages of up to a week that include a medical checkup and diet (vegetarian), massage, reflexology, shiatsu, a pedicure, a manicure, and hairdressing—as well as full board. Some rooms have been individually decorated (they all share a ban on smoking) to enhance the sense of luxury; a few have whirlpool baths. The lobby has a "tea corner," with a full range of herbal teas served round the clock. A gallery exhibits Israeli works at extremely high prices, and a gift shop sells homemade breads, cheeses, and other local products. ⊠ *Box 27, Rosh Pina 12000,* ☎ *06/693–7014,* FAX *06/693–7191. 81 rooms with bath. Restaurant, pool, beauty salon, hot tub, massage, sauna, exercise room. AE, DC, MC, V.*

$$$$ 🏨 **Vered Hagalil.** Stone and wood cottages, each with a front porch,
★ give guests a sense of privacy, yet the extremely popular restaurant and stables on this guest farm are only steps away. Owners Yehuda and Yona Avni haven't lost the almost-chauvinistic enthusiasm for the Galilee that drew them here (he's from the United States, she's from Jerusalem) decades ago, and it is reflected in the excellent running of their establishment. Accommodations range from cottage apartments with bedroom, living room, and kitchenette to studios and smaller cabins. All are ranchlike in decoration—earth tones, exposed wood, and stone walls, and big picture windows for Sea of Galilee–gazing. Trail riding packages of up to three days are a specialty. Overnight guests enjoy 10% off riding and meals in the hotel restaurant. ⊠ *Rte. 90, 15 km (9 mi) south of Zfat, next to Korazim, M.P. Korazim 12385,* ☎ *06/693–5785,* FAX *06/693–4964. 17 units with bath (2 for people with disabilities). Restaurant, bar, pool, horseback riding. AE, DC, MC, V.*

$$ 🏨 **Joseph's Well.** Rooms here are like cozy studio apartments, with pine furniture, coordinated tablecloths and sheets, and chintz curtains; each has a coffee corner, with an electric kettle, cups, and tea and coffee. They are all on the ground floor, in clusters of three with a shared patio. The kibbutz dining room—Joseph's Well is on Kibbutz Amiad, 10 km (6 mi) south of Zfat—doubles as the restaurant for guests. Unlike the bigger kibbutz hotels, Joseph's Well offers little to do—guests are here strictly to sleep. Amiad's main industry is wine, which it produces from unusual fruits such as kiwi and sells in a shop on the premises that also peddles a range of local and imported products. ⊠ *M.P. Upper Galilee 12335,* ☎ *06/693–3829,* FAX *06/693–3819. 24 rooms with bath. Dining room, pool, horseback riding. AE, DC, MC, V.*

Nightlife and the Arts

Zfat hosts a **klezmer festival** every summer. There could be no better setting than this mystical city, with its labyrinthine cobblestone lanes, for the three days of "Jewish soul music." The roots of klezmer are Hassidic, making it almost prayerlike in tone, especially with its emphasis on wind instruments. Many events are street performances and therefore free. Keep in mind, though, that Zfat is bursting at the seams with revelers, religious and secular alike, during this time. The festival is usually held in July. The Zfat Tourist Information Office (⊠ 50 Yerushalayim St., Box 227, Zfat 13010, ☎ 06/692–0961) can provide details.

Outdoor Activities and Sports

Bat Ya'ar (☎ 06/692–1788), in the Birya Forest 5 km (3 mi) from Zfat, has pony rides for kids and horseback riding in the area. It also has a steak house (☞ Dining and Lodging, *above*).

Vered Hagalil (☎ 06/693–5785), a guest ranch at the Korazim Junction at Route 90 (☞ Dining and Lodging, *above*) offers a variety of tours on horseback, with Western riding the specialty. These tours last up to three days. Pony rides for kids are also available. Prices for guided rides range from NIS 30 ($10) for a half hour to around NIS 400 ($130) for a day.

Mt. Meron

❾ *21 km (13 mi) west of Zfat on Rte. 89.*

The spiritual importance of Zfat extends beyond the city limits to Mt. Meron and its environs, a pilgrim site for both ultra-Orthodox Hassidic Jews and nature lovers.

Remote though it may seem, for centuries the village of Meron has drawn thousands upon thousands of Orthodox Jews paying homage to several of the great rabbis of the Roman era who are buried at the eastern foot of the mount. The most important site—and one of the holiest places in Israel—is the **tomb of Rabbi Shimon Bar Yochai**, a survivor of the Bar Kochba Revolt of almost two millennia ago and a leading exponent of the Talmud. Refusing to kowtow to the Romans after his succeeded in taking Jerusalem, he is said to have fled to a cave at Peki'in, not far from here, together with his son Elazar, where he remained for 13 years. It is believed by the faithful, beginning with the 16th-century mystics who settled in Zfat, that while holed up in the cave, Bar Yochai penned the Zohar (the Book of Splendor), the commentary to the Pentateuch, or the Five Books of Moses, the first five books of the Old Testament. Although firm opponents to this theory claim the Zohar dates to 13th-century Spain and not 2nd-century Meron, Hassidic pilgrims continue to make their annual visit to the great rabbi's tomb. Pieces of cloth and scraps of paper that hang from trees around the tomb are evidence of the pilgrims' devotion.

The pilgrimage is still celebrated en masse on Lag Ba'Omer, the festive 33rd day of the seven solemn weeks that begin with Passover and end with Shavuot (Pentecost). Mt. Meron comes alive as a grand procession of Hassidic Jews arrive on foot from Zfat, carrying Torah scrolls and singing fervently. Bonfires are lighted and barbecues follow. Many ultra-Orthodox still uphold the tradition of bringing their three-year-old sons here on Lag Ba'Omer for their first haircuts.

Mt. Meron itself, at 3,926 feet, is the highest mountain in the Galilee and the largest **nature reserve** in northern Israel, with 24,700 acres of preserved slopes. A good road past the Society for the Protection of Nature (SPNI) field study center takes you almost to the top (the actual summit is occupied by the Israeli army). There is a 1½-km (1-mi) nature trail that begins near the study center, and red markings guide the not-so-intrepid walker all the way.

The trail offers breathtaking views in all directions: the Druze villages of Western Galilee, Zfat, the Sea of Galilee, and on a clear day, the Golan Heights, Hula Valley, and mountains of Lebanon. You can also spot the ugly scars of bushfires. The blackened tree "skeletons" date to the summer of 1978, when fire destroyed a significant chunk of this reserve. Much of the rich and varied flora of Mt. Meron has since regenerated—if you're here in autumn, you'll be dazzled by the glowing yellow of the sunflowers—but reminders of the fire remain.

Nor has fire been the only misfortune. Not so long ago, bears, antelope, and even leopards here were hunted to extinction. Today, Israel's hunting laws protect the wild boar, marten, polecat, and other fauna that call the reserve home.

Lodging

$$$ 🏨 **Amirim Holiday Village.** The communal settlement of Amirim offers something a little different: Almost all 300 members of the moshav are vegetarians. This is a real get-away-from-it-all kind of place, atop a hill overlooking Mt. Meron and the Sea of Galilee. Guests have a choice of health and beauty treatments. The lodging units have one or several rooms and are run by different families. Although the units have kitchenettes, there is no shortage of eating options: Five families have minirestaurants with a range of vegetarian fare. ⊠ *Moshav Amirim, near Mt. Meron, M.P. Carmiel, 20115,* ☎ *06/698–9571. 90 units with bath. 6 restaurants, kitchenettes, pool, children's programs. No credit cards. No Sat. checkout in high season.*

En Route The Arab village of **Jish,** between Mt. Meron and Bar'am off Route 89, was called Gush Halav of the Second Temple period. In those days, it was renowned for its exceptional olive oil, and the milk from its cattle also received accolades. Gush Halav translates as "milk bloc," but it is unclear whether the name derived from the renown of its milk or from the whiteness of the chalky limestone that serves as the foundation of buildings in this area.

Bar'am National Park

❿ *15 km (9 mi) from Meron, 40 km (25 mi) northwest of Zfat.*

In an otherwise deserted spot lie the **ruins of Bar'am,** one of the best-preserved ancient synagogues anywhere. Although it is less grand than the synagogue at Capernaum on the Sea of Galilee (☞ Chapter 6), it is clear the community that built this synagogue devoted considerable funds and energy to their most important building. Like most synagogues uncovered in the area, it faces south toward Jerusalem. Unlike any other, however, this one has lavish architectural elements, such as an entrance with a segmental pediment and freestanding giant columns on its exterior.

The interior is in a worse state of repair than the facade. It resembles other Galilean synagogues of the period. Rows of pillars in the prayer hall apparently served as support for the ceiling, and there may have been another story to the building. A section of the facade's lintel, now in the Louvre in Paris, contains the Hebrew inscription, "May there be peace in this place, and in all the places of Israel. This lintel was made by Jose the Levite. Blessings upon his works. Shalom." ⊠ *Rte. 899,* ☎ *06/698–9301.* 🎟 *NIS 7 ($2.10).* ☉ *Apr.–Sept., daily 8–5; Oct.–Mar., daily 8–4.*

Rosh Pina

⓫ *10 km (6 mi) east of Zfat, 25 km (15½ mi) north of Tiberias.*

Rosh Pina, literally "headstone of the corner," derives its name from this biblical text: "The stone that the builder hath rejected hath become the headstone of the corner" (Psalm 118). This verse inspired the first Zionist pioneers settling the Galilee. The group came from Romania in 1882, determined to build a village. They bought this land, 1,500 feet above sea level at the foot of the mountain ridge east of Zfat, and arrived with all they needed for their new home, right down to the timber for construction. Ironically, the boat that brought them to the Holy Land was called the *Titus,* the name of the Roman general whose destruction of Jerusalem forced the exile of Jews from the city in AD 70.

The Romanians' main livelihood at Rosh Pina derived from the production of silk by silkworms; this industry was encouraged by the great philanthropist Baron Edmond de Rothschild, who gave them the fruit trees needed for the project. Despite grand efforts, however, the project did not yield the desired results: The residents were walking around in silk scarves and socks, but they had no bread to eat. Slowly, family by family, the immigrants moved away to other settlements, leaving only squatters for decades to follow.

Recent years have seen the little village restored, and although it has not been developed as a tourist attraction, it warrants a brief visit simply for its cobblestone charm. To get here, walk for 10 minutes up the path from the modern township of Rosh Pina. The two-story **Schwartz Hotel,** on Ha'elyon Street, built in 1890, was the first rest house to be built in the Galilee. Today it is quite literally a mere skeleton of the original, but try to imagine what it was like to check in here after a long, tiring journey and enjoy the tranquil view of the Sea of Galilee below and white-capped Mt. Hermon to the north.

The **synagogue** (⊠ Ha'elyon St.) is usually locked. However, someone in the office of Old Rosh Pina (☎ 06/693–6603), a development company, next door to the restaurant at the bottom of Ha'elyon Street, may open it. The interior of the no-longer-functioning synagogue is as it was when it was built in the mid-1880s; the dark pews and holy ark made of the timber brought from Romania have aged gracefully. Look at the ceiling: The depictions of palm trees and biblical motifs are painted in rich colors.

The **Old Rosh Pina office** occupies the house that belonged to Professor Gideon Mer, a leading expert on malaria in the 1930s. As the story goes, he used to inject his wife and children with his experimental remedies during his attempts to combat malaria in the region; all survived. The British were so impressed with Mer's work that they sent him to Burma to fight malaria epidemics there.

Old Rosh Pina is populated today by some 60 artists, although unlike their counterparts in the artists' village of Ein Hod (☞ The Rothschild Wine Country and Mt. Carmel *in* Chapter 5), they do not usually open their homes to visitors. There are, however, a couple of **galleries** that exhibit the creations of the locals.

Dining and Lodging

Rosh Pina is a budding center of tourism for this region. Many residents are now opening their homes as bed-and-breakfasts. There is no central reservation center, but the various visitor information centers in the area (☞ Visitor Information *in* Upper Galilee and the Golan A to Z, *below*) can help you find simple, pleasant accommodations. There are family rooms at the small (100-bed) youth hostel (☎ 06/693–7086).

$$$ ✕ **Hagome.** This red-roofed restaurant on Route 90 next to Rosh Pina offers fresh Middle Eastern dishes, from grape leaves to stuffed vegetables to chicken with dried fruit (check out the salad bar before ordering). Dining outdoors in Hagome's garden is especially pleasant. Its location makes it a natural stop for traveling Israelis; in fact, this is a good place to people-watch, as Hagome attracts all types. ⊠ *Opposite police station on west side of Rte. 90,* ☎ *06/693–6250. AE, DC, MC, V. No dinner Fri.*

$$ ✕ **Indigo.** This easygoing cafe offers another angle of the changing face of Rosh Pina: young. With wholesome salads and vegetarian pies on the menu, Indigo is a good spot to take a break in before or after walking around Old Rosh Pina, farther up the hill. ⊠ *30 Hechalutzim St.,* ☎ *06/693–5333. AE, DC, MC, V. Closed Mon.*

$$$$ ✕🏨 **Auberge Shulamit.** Opened in 1996 by veteran Galilee restaurateurs,
★ this charming inn takes its name from the original Hotel Shulamit, the
site of the signing of the 1948 Armistice Treaty. Among the delectables
on the menu—in addition to home-smoked meats—are salmon fillet in
crabmeat sauce and shrimp in gorgonzola sauce with wild rice. Besides
the restaurant, there are four guest rooms for those who really want to
indulge themselves for a day or two. ✉ *David Shub Rd., Box 259, Yesod
Hama'ala 12105,* ☎ *06/693–1494, 06/693–1495, or 06/693–1485,* 🆏
06/693–1495. Reservations essential. AE, DC, MC, V.

$ 🏨 **Village Inn.** These accommodations at Kfar Hanassi give a *real*
taste of kibbutz life. Each of the six units has two rooms that share a
kitchenette and bathroom facilities. All the units look out onto a garden, the site of many a barbecue. Although the units are rather old,
the decor is bright, with boldly colored sheets and cotton dhurrie rugs;
all the facilities are spotlessly clean. Meals are in the kibbutz's communal dining room. Amenities that will appeal to children include a
minizoo, picnic grounds, and a pagoda with a grand view of the Golan
and Mt. Hermon. Kfar Hanassi has several resident artists, and you
can visit their home studios. ✉ *Near Mahanayim Airport (10 km, or
6 mi, from Rosh Pina), M.P. Upper Galilee 12305,* ☎ *06/691–4870,*
🆏 *06/691–4017. 12 rooms share 6 baths. Dining room, kitchenettes,
pool, massage, miniature golf, tennis courts, basketball, boating, travel
services. AE, DC, MC, V.*

Kayaking and Rafting
Kibbutz Kfar Hanassi (☎ 06/691–4870; ☞ Dining and Lodging, *above*)
rents out lightweight paddleboats called catarafts.

Tel Hatzor

⑫ *8 km (5 mi) north of Rosh Pina.*

The large mound of Tel Hatzor, site of the ancient city of Hazor, is a
good stop for archaeology buffs. Over a period of thousands of years,
the city was built and rebuilt a total of 21 times, allowing latter-day
diggers to slice off layer after layer of differing lifestyles spanning the
ages. Situated on the Via Maris, which as the link between Egypt and
Mesopotamia was the most important trade route in antiquity, Hatzor is first referred to in Mesopotamian documents of the 2nd millennium
BC; an ambassador from Hammurabi's court resided here.

The Book of Joshua (Joshua 11:13) makes mention of ancient Hatzor
as "the head of all those kingdoms," although Joshua himself destroyed Canaanite Hatzor in the 13th century BC, and Israelites resettled it. Its next heyday came three centuries later when King Solomon
decided it would serve him well as one of his great regional military
and administrative centers, like Megiddo and Gezer. In 732 BC, Hatzor met its end when invading Assyrian king Tiglath Pileser III conquered the Galilee and forced its Israelite inhabitants off the land in
chains and into exile. The city was never to regain its former glory.

The site was first identified in 1928 as the ancient Hatzor, but the archaeologist who put it squarely on the modern map, from 1955 to 1959,
was the renowned Dr. Yigal Yadin, best known for his excavations at
Masada.

The huge site is divided into two areas: the *tel,* or **Upper City,** which
comprised the oldest settlements, and the **Lower City,** first settled in
the 18th century BC. Only the tel, covering less than a fifth of the total
area of the excavation site, is open to the public. The **Hatzor Museum**
(on the grounds of Kibbutz Ayelet Hashachar, on the other side of the

highway) houses many of the figurines, weapons, stone pots, and other artifacts unearthed in the two areas; still others are at the Israel Museum in Jerusalem. ✉ *Tel Hatzor National Park, off Rte. 90,* ☎ *06/693–4855.* 💷 *NIS 10 ($3.30).* ⊙ *Park and museum Apr.–Sept., daily 8–5; Oct.–Mar., daily 8–4.*

Lodging

$$$$ 🛏 **Ayelet Hashachar Kibbutz Guest House.** The first kibbutz to open a hotel, Ayelet Hashachar is run in a pastoral setting but with the efficiency and thoroughness of any city hotel. Guest quarters, next door to the Tel Hatzor Museum, resemble apartments, with rooms in two-story buildings surrounded by lawn and flower beds. Timber-framed windows add a soft touch. Jeep tours and guided tours of the kibbutz can be arranged. There are also facilities for persons with disabilities. This kibbutz is also one of Israel's biggest honey producers. ✉ *M.P. Korazim 12200,* ☎ *06/693–2611,* 📠 *06/693–4777. 144 rooms with bath. Cafeteria, dining room, pool, horseback riding, travel services. MC, V.*

Hula Nature Reserve

★ ⓭ *8 km (5 mi) north of Tel Hatzor.*

The last of Israel's swamplands and one of the last remaining vestiges of wilderness in Israel can be found at the Hula Nature Reserve. This is no accident: In the first half of the 20th century, British rulers under the Mandate, like the Ottomans before them, repeatedly refused Jewish settlers' requests to drain the swampland, a practice common in other parts of the tiny country as the need for arable land grew. Almost as soon as they could following independence, the Israeli authorities eagerly approved the project.

During much of the 1950s, the Hula Valley was drained and dredged again and again, until it was discovered that this was doing grave and irreversible harm to the ecosystem, particularly to the hundreds of thousands of migratory birds that stopped here as they flitted between Europe and Africa twice yearly. This crisis led the International Union for the Conservation of Nature (IUCN) to declare the Hula Valley a reserve of world importance, which it has remained since the early 1970s.

Pelicans, wild geese, storks, plovers, and a host of exotic birds once again have their sanctuary, but they would not be here were it not also for the swampy waters that abound with carp, catfish, and perch, and a reed habitat boasting rare thickets of papyrus through which a water buffalo or two might be seen roaming. Less recognized is the topminnow, an American fish that lives on mosquito eggs and has played a big part in helping rid the area of malaria. There is a visitor center with complete information about the 800-acre reserve, an observation tower, and a snack bar. Hunting and fishing are strictly forbidden. ✉ *East of Rte. 90,* ☎ *06/693–7069.* 💷 *NIS 13 ($4).* ⊙ *Daily 8–5 (1 hr later during summer holidays).*

NEED A BREAK?

For a rest stop with a bit of history, try **Bet Dubrovin** (✉ Yesod Hama'ala, ☎ 06/693–7371), near the entrance to the Hula Nature Reserve. The reconstructed farmhouse-cum-museum was once owned by immigrant converts from Russia, the Dubrovins. They were part of a movement of Christian Russians who converted to Judaism and moved to the Holy Land. In 1904, old man Dubrovin brought his family to the swamps of the Hula. Despite the hardships, these pioneers set up a model farm on their 173-acre estate, even winning first prize—for cattle in 1922 and for chick-peas in 1927—in the annual agricultural exhibitions in Rosh Pina. Eventually the property was donated to the Jewish National Fund, and it was opened to the public in 1986.

The estate consists of a series of stone buildings constructed on a square, surrounding a courtyard that holds some old farming equipment and even a few farm animals. An exhibit in the building where the family lived gives a history of both the area and the family. Also on the premises are a ceramics store selling locally made wares and the restaurant. The entrance fee to the museum (NIS 6.50, or $2.20) is deducted from the price of a main course, so hang on to your tickets.

Outdoor Activities and Sports
Baba Yona's Ranch (✉ Yesod Hama'ala Junction, ☎ 06/693–8773), near the Hula Nature Reserve, offers adventure packages that combine riding, canoeing, and Jeep rides; there's a steak restaurant here, too.

UPPER HULA VALLEY

The sights that hug the border with Lebanon show different sides of Israel. The towns of Kiryat Shmona and Metulla bear eloquent witness to the varying fortunes of Israel's relationships with its Arab neighbors. Tel Dan Nature Reserve, on the other hand, draws visitors with its huge trees, surging river, and wild beauty.

Kiryat Shmona

45 km (28 mi) north of Tiberias, 30 km (19 mi) north of Zfat.

The only urban center in the otherwise agrarian Upper Hula Valley, **Kiryat Shmona** in itself has little to offer travelers other than burger joints and similar fast-food stands in the shopping center on Route 90. Like Ma'alot, farther west, Kiryat Shmona made the headlines in 1974 when Arabs infiltrated into Israel from Lebanon one night, came down the mountain slope behind the town, and broke into an apartment at dawn, massacring an entire family. By 1982 the spate of terrorist attacks had reached such proportions that Israel responded by invading Lebanon, which was the first stage of the war with Lebanon. The city was in the news again in 1996 when, following a focused and continued attack on Kiryat Shmona and the environs by Hezbollah terrorists using katyusha rockets, the Israel Defense Forces responded by targeting their bases in southern Lebanon in a campaign that became known as the Grapes of Wrath.

❶❹ Perched on the northern edge of Kiryat Shmona is **Tel Hai,** meaning "hill of life" in Hebrew; the name was adapted from Arabic. In a sense the hill became a monument to life itself following a memorable battle in 1920. In the years immediately following World War I, while Britain and France bickered over who should have final control of the upper Hula Valley, bands of Arabs and Bedouins roamed the region, harassing and plundering the tiny Jewish farming settlements. They destroyed one such settlement completely, overran the communal settlement of Tel Hai, and caused the veteran village of Metulla to be temporarily abandoned; only Kibbutz Kfar Giladi was successful in defending itself, and it has since gone on to become one of the largest and most prosperous of kibbutzim (☞ Dining and Lodging, *below*).

In the wake of the Tel Hai terror, in which two settlement members were killed, Josef Trumpeldor and seven comrades were called on to defend the place. Trumpeldor had served in the czar's army in his native Russia, and though he had lost an arm fighting, he had already won a reputation as a leader. Fired by Zionist ideals, he moved to Palestine in 1912 at the age of 32 with a group of followers in tow. Soon after, he was fighting with the British against the Turks at the ill-fated battle of Gallipoli. Upon his return to Palestine, he moved to Kibbutz Tel Hai, became its commander, and like all the other Jewish settlers, was constantly on the alert against Arab terrorist bands.

In 1920 the final battle came. Trumpeldor and seven others were slaughtered on the kibbutz grounds (in fact, Kiryat Shmona—City of the Eight—is named for them). Trumpeldor's last words are believed to have been, "It is good to die for our country." Trumpeldor subsequently became not only a national hero but an inspiration, and he is still referred to with reverence. He is buried here, beneath the stone statue of a roaring lion on the hill behind the museum, once the stockade of Tel Hai. The heroic stand at Tel Hai was to have two important consequences for the area: It was the first modern example of Jewish armed self-defense, and it did much to change the local image of the Jew as timid and defenseless. Also, the survival of at least two of the Jewish settlements this far north determined that when the final borders were drawn by the League of Nations in 1922, those settlements would be included in the British-mandated territory of Palestine, and thus, after 1948, in the State of Israel.

The **museum** now displays agricultural equipment and tools used during Trumpeldor's time. Some of the implements are still put to use (especially during school holidays); you may be lucky enough to catch, for example, an old-style pita-making demonstration. ⊠ *Off Rte. 886,* ☎ *06/695–1333.* ⌑ *NIS 13 ($4.30).* ⊘ *Sun.–Thurs. 8–4, Fri. and holiday eves 8–1, Sat. 10–5.*

Dining and Lodging

In addition to the guest houses here, there's a large (200-bed) **youth hostel** in Tel Hai (☎ 06/694–0043). For camping, head for the **Hurshat National Park** (⊠ East of Hagoshrim on Rte. 99, 8 km [5 mi] east of Kiryat Shmona, ☎ 06/694–2360), opposite Kibbutz Dafna, but remember that it gets pretty cold here at night except in summer.

$$$ ✕ **Dag al Hadan.** Fresh trout and a cool glass of wine in a shady woodlet by the gurgling Dan River—it's as good as it sounds, except on crowded weekends. This was the first restaurant in the region to specialize in the fish the Dan yields in abundance; you can see the trout ponds in a small installation on the grounds. The restaurant is tucked away behind the main road but is well signposted. ⊠ *Off Rte. 99 near Kiryat Shmona, opposite Kibbutz Hagoshrim,* ☎ *06/695–0225. Reservations essential on weekends. No credit cards.*

$$$ ✕🏨 **Jordan Pagoda.** An unlikely place for a Chinese-Thai restaurant, perhaps, but somehow sitting in the timber pagoda (imported from Thailand, according to the owners) and eating South Asian delights on the banks of the Jordan River works! The restaurant is part of the Jordan's Source complex, which has 10 very reasonably priced wooden cabins. The complex is on the grounds of Kibbutz Sde Nechemia. ⊠ *Kibbutz Sde Nechemia (8 km, or 5 mi, from Kiryat Shmona), Rte. 918,* ☎ *06/ 694–7447. AE, DC, MC, V.*

$$$ 🏨 **Hagoshrim Kibbutz Hotel.** A delight of Hagoshrim is the waters of the Hermon River flowing through it, a setting the residents have wisely exploited in their "pub in nature" (open May to October). Tractor rides are one of Hagoshrim's more unusual activities. (Incidentally, Hagoshrim has had an impact on millions of women the

world over with its Epilady, a revolutionary depilatory appliance that has won the kibbutz kudos for technological initiative.) ⊠ *Rte. 99, east of Kiryat Shmona, Upper Galilee 12225*, ☎ *06/695–6231*, ⨳ *06/695– 6234. 121 rooms with bath. Restaurant, cafeteria, pub, pool, tennis court. AE, DC, MC, V.*

$$$ 🏨 **Kfar Blum Guest House.** Tucked in the northern Hula Valley, Kfar
★ Blum enjoys a reputation for attentive service that surpasses many of its rivals'. The home-style hospitality is enhanced by the garden setting, and photographs in the rooms depict kibbutz life as it is meant to be. Most members of Kfar Blum hail from English-speaking countries, so there are no language barriers here. One of the kibbutz's major attractions is its kayaks—what better way to experience the Jordan River? In the summer, the kibbutz hosts an annual chamber music festival (☞ The Arts, *below*). ⊠ *North of Rte. 977, near Kiryat Shmona, Upper Galilee 12150*, ☎ *06/694–3666*, ⨳ *06/694–8555. 113 rooms with bath. Restaurant, bar, pool, sauna, tennis courts, boating, shops, travel services. AE, DC, MC, V.*

$$$ 🏨 **Kibbutz Hotel Kfar Giladi.** Atop a hill behind Tel Hai overlooking the Hula Valley, this is one of the oldest and largest kibbutz hotels. It is run very efficiently but still manages to retain a homey atmosphere. Lovely woods just a stone's throw away make for great walks, and on the kibbutz grounds is the Bet Hashomer Museum, which explores the pre-State history of the kibbutz and the vicinity. Kfar Giladi produces sunglasses, which are for sale in the hotel. ⊠ *Rte. 886, Upper Galilee 12210*, ☎ *06/694–1414*, ⨳ *06/695–1248. 180 rooms with bath. Snack bar, pool, tennis court, health club. AE, DC, MC, V.*

The Arts

For the classically minded, Kibbutz Kfar Blum (⊠ Upper Galilee 12150, ☎ 06/694–3666) hosts **Chamber Music Days** each year late July–early August—a nationally renowned festival of chamber music in a pastoral setting.

Outdoor Activities and Sports

KAYAKING

Kibbutz Kfar Blum (☎ 06/694–8755; ☞ Dining and Lodging, *above*) rents two-person rubber kayaks for 1- or 1½-hour runs, transporting you back to the kibbutz at the end of the run. The cost is NIS 75 ($25) per couple, and the kayaks are available from March through October (call ahead at other times of the year).

TUBING

Ma'ayan Water Park (⊠ Kibbutz Ma'ayan Baruch, ☎ 06/695–1390) and **Sde Nechemia** (⊠ Kibbutz Huliot, ☎ 06/694–6010), both near Kiryat Shmona along Route 99, offer inner tubes at NIS 25 ($8.30) for an hour or so.

Metulla

⑮ *7 km (4 mi) north of Kiryat Shmona.*

Israel's northernmost town, Metulla, is so picturesque it is hard to believe this tranquil spot is just a stone's throw from a foe, Lebanon. And there is a happy story of cooperation between the Israelis and the Lebanese here that draws visitors from all over the world to see the so-called Good Fence.

Metulla was founded as a farming settlement in 1896 with the aid of Baron Edmond de Rothschild, and in the century since, its residents have shown such tenacity and determination that it has not only survived but thrived. Essentially, it has one thoroughfare, Harishonim Street (though this can hardly be called a main street), where hotels and eateries are located. Somehow the tensions of the Middle East dissipate here, at least briefly. One- and two-story limestone buildings with their European-style architecture line the street, and the Continental atmosphere is enhanced by the numerous signs that offer ZIMMER (German for "room") for rent. Even the weather is decidedly un-Mediterranean, with refreshingly cool mountain breezes in summer and snow in winter. And yet the cypresses and cedars recall a whiff of Lebanon.

The **Good Fence** is just a three-minute drive from the town center. Although you'll find little more than a thoroughly touristy kiosk and souvenir shop to greet you, there's a certain thrill to standing on the border of a country that has long been hostile to Israel. There's a twist, though: This segment of the Israel-Lebanon border has enjoyed its nickname since June 1976, when Israel first sent medical and other aid to residents of southern Lebanon. In one version of the story, Israeli soldiers noticed a Lebanese woman in labor at the border crossing. They rushed her to an Israeli hospital, where she delivered a healthy baby, and within days there were several very pregnant women waiting at the Good Fence. The peaceful interaction between the two sides has developed ever since: First Lebanese citizens with relatives in Israel were allowed to come over to visit, then summer camps were organized (and still are) for Lebanese schoolchildren and their Israeli counterparts, and today hundreds of Lebanese workers from the south of the country cross the border to go to their jobs in the Galilee.

NEED A BREAK?   Take a picnic down to the streams and waterfalls that flow year-round in the lush **Nahal Ayoun Nature Reserve** (⊠ Just south of Metulla next to Rte. 90).

Outdoor Activities and Sports

The multistory, multipurpose **Canada Centre** (⊠ At the top of the hill, ☎ 06/695–0370) has just about everything a sports complex could offer. For the price of admission—NIS 30 ($10)—you can spend the whole day here playing basketball, ice-skating, working out, swimming, using the water slide, or taking aim on the shooting range. And if that's all too much, go for the sauna or hot tub. There is a restaurant on the premises where you can put right back on all those calories you just burned up. The complex is open daily 10–10.

The ice-skating rink is one of only two in the Middle East—the other is in Saudi Arabia. But what the Saudis cannot boast are world-class former Soviet skaters. They now live in Metulla and teach the sport at the center. If you're lucky, you may catch a demonstration of their dazzling talent.

Tel Dan Nature Reserve

🔟 *25 km (15½ mi) from Metulla, 15 km (9 mi) from Kiryat Shmona.*

For sheer natural beauty, Tel Dan is hard to beat. A river surges through the reserve, and large, luxuriant trees, including majestic Mt. Tabor oaks, provide shade over wide paths. A host of small mammals inhabits the area, many partial to water, such as the otter and the mongoose. This is the home of Israel's largest rodent, the nocturnal Indian crested porcupine, and its smallest predator, the marbled polecat, recognizable by its bushy tail, which accounts for about half the creature's 1-foot length. There are wildcats in these parts, too, though they are rarely seen by day. The reserve has hiking trails and is also accessible to people using wheelchairs.

A rather majestic city occupied this land in biblical times. Dan was an urban center second only to Hatzor in importance in northern Palestine. According to Genesis, when Abraham "heard that his brother had been taken captive [by the four kings of the north] he armed his trained servants, born in his own house, three hundred and eighteen, and pursued them up to Dan." Five centuries later, when Canaan extended from Dan (then called Laish) in the north to Beersheva in the south, Joshua led the Israelites through the area to victory.

Fine ruins from several epochs can be found here. The Canaanite city of Laish existed here 5,000 years ago. Its name was changed when the Israelite tribe of Dan captured the tel, sometime in the period of Judges, and it became the northernmost point of the kingdom of Israel. When the kingdom was divvied up, the secessionist King Jeroboam I built a religious center here (and another at Bethel) and erected a cultic golden calf. Among the finds archaeologists have turned up are the city gate and a 9th-century BC paved plaza that was probably the town center. ⊠ *N. of Rte. 99,* ☎ *06/695–1579.* 🎟 *NIS 13 ($4.20).* ⊘ *Daily 8–5 (1 hr later during summer holidays).*

Kibbutz Dan

1 km (½ mi) from Tel Dan Nature Reserve.

This kibbutz adjacent to the Tel Dan Nature Reserve has an attraction that can enhance a visit to the area. The **Bet Ussishkin Museum** was founded in 1955 by the Jewish National Fund and is now operated jointly by Kibbutz Dan and the Society for the Protection of Nature in Israel. Children will appreciate the displays here, which document the wildlife and natural phenomena found around the Hula Valley, the Golan Heights, and the Jordan River. The audiovisual presentations give a concise and informative account of the area. ⊠ *Off Rte. 99,* ☎ *06/694–1704.* 🎟 *NIS 10 ($3.30).* ⊘ *Sun.–Thurs. 8:30–4:30, Fri. and holiday eves 8:30–3:30, Sat. 9:30–4:30.*

GOLAN HEIGHTS

Geologically distinct from the limestone massif of Mt. Hermon to its north, the basalt slopes of the Golan Heights extend about 60 km (37 mi) from north to south and between 15 km and 25 km (between 9 mi and 15½ mi) across. The whole region was volcanic in the not-so-distant past, and many symmetrical volcanic cones and pronounced reliefs still dominate the landscape, particularly in the upper Golan. Where the dark basalt rock has weathered or been cleared, the mineral-rich soil supports a wide variety of crops. The gentler terrain and climate of the Golan have attracted settlement far more than the less hospitable northern Upper Galilee. In spring the region, already greened by winter rains, comes alive with wildflowers; but when the summer heat has frizzled everything to a uniform yellow-brown, it seems a land of desolation. Sights here range from nature reserves in the north to a winery and archaeological sites near Katzrin in the south.

Hermon River (Banias) Nature Reserve

★ ⑰ *20 km (12½ mi) from Kiryat Shmona.*

One of the most stunning corners of Israel, this reserve contains gushing waterfalls, dense foliage along the riverbanks, and remains of a temple dedicated to the god Pan. There are two entrances, each with a parking lot: The first is indicated on a sign as Banias Waterfall; the other is 1 km (½ mi) farther along the same road and marked Banias. A circular walking trail connects the two and requires about two hours to complete. It is an easy trail, but if time is short, you may prefer to take a short walk to the falls, return to your car, then drive on to the second entrance to see the caves and the spring whence the Hermon River originates. The cost of admission covers entry at both sites.

At the lookout near the **Banias Waterfall,** maps point out the principal mountains and other features on the horizon. The approach to the waterfall, marked by a signpost, is enhanced by huge carob trees, maidenhair ferns, brier ivy, laurel (bay leaf) bushes, and other shrubs. Swimming at the waterfall is forbidden, but don't be surprised if there are groups of Israelis splashing and scrambling to photograph each other against the falls. There's a tremendous reverence for the 33 feet of cascading water, and people come from all over the country to see this unusual sight, especially in the rainless summer months.

Backtrack to the signpost and head in the other direction, passing walnut trees, willows, and lemon and fig trees as you proceed to the riverside walk to the spring and caves. Along the way, the trail passes two abandoned flour mills, and at times you will be walking on aqueducts that once brought water to these mills. About 1 km (½ mi) from the waterfall, a sign points to **hreichat haketzinim** (Officers' Pool), a pool built around the spring by Syrians for the use of their officers (swimming is forbidden, though).

NEED A BREAK? A few minutes' walk beyond the Officers' Pool is a little **stall** with a *nargila* (water pipe) standing sentry. Here you can buy Druze-style pita (bigger and flatter than the commercial version) not only baked on the premises but also milled here. The ancient flour mill is still powered by water from an aqueduct as it was in days of yore. In fact, until only a few years ago this was where local Druze villagers milled their flour. Now the mill and "bakery" service hungry hikers. Pull up a rock, and for a few shekels you'll be served a large rolled-up pita with *labane* (white goat's cheese) and Turkish coffee.

The remainder of the trail (about 600 feet) follows and crosses the river before reaching the spring. Note the pungent aroma of mint; blackberry bushes can be found here, too, and their fruit is particularly sweet at the end of summer.

Banias Spring emanates at the foot of mostly limestone Mt. Hermon, just where it meets the basalt layers of the Golan Heights. As the snow on the mountain melts, or when it rains, the water seeps through the Hermon's crannies and gushes forth at the foot of what is called Pan's Cave.

The name *Banias* is an Arabic corruption of the Greek *Panias,* the original name given to what was to become a cult center dedicated to the colorful Greek god Pan (Arabic has no *p* sound, hence the modification). Pan, the son of Hermes, god of herdsmen, music, and wild nature and patron of homosexuals and nymphs, was too hedonistic even for the ancient Greeks. In their attempts to keep him at some distance, they eventually built the half man–half goat a temple in this succulent corner of the world.

Take the path that crosses the spring and proceed toward **Banias Cave;** it is easily identified by the sturdy fig tree at the entrance. Note five niches hewed out of the rock to the right of the cave; these are what remain of the Hellenistic temple and probably once held statues. Three of the niches bear inscriptions in Greek mentioning Pan, the lover of tunes; Echo, the mountain nymph; and Galerius, one of Pan's priests. Archaeologists are only in the early stages of excavating, but they have already turned up what they believe are the remains of a second temple as well. All early references to the cave identify it as the source of the spring, but earthquakes over the years have changed its formations, forcing the water to emerge at the foot of the cave rather than from within it. (For those in a hiking mood, there is a long, very steep trail that leads from here through the oak and thorny broom forest up to Nimrod's Fortress [☞ *below*], a 40- to 60-minute climb.)

The path continues up to the whitewashed **tomb of Nebi Khader** (Arabic for "the prophet Elijah"), built on a ledge of the cliff. The tomb is closed, but from here there is a terrific view of the Hula Valley and the Hermon River. A little farther along the way are the remains of an ancient wall with a ceramic inlay that archaeologists believe was part of the white marble temple Herod built as a tribute to Caesar Augustus, who had given him the Hula Valley and Panias in 26 BC.

Herod's son Philip inherited this part of his father's kingdom, and when he made Panias his capital, he changed its name to Caesarea Philippi, to distinguish it from the Caesarea his father had founded on the Mediterranean coast. It was in Caesarea Philippi that Jesus changed Peter's name from Simon and gave him "the keys to the kingdom of heaven" after his disciple for the first time declared Jesus the Messiah: "Jesus came here and asked his disciples, 'Who do you say that I am?' and Peter replied, 'You are Christ, the son of the living god,' to which Jesus responded, 'Blessed are you, Simon, son of Jonah. And I tell you, you are Peter [*petros* means "rock" in Greek], and on this rock I will build my church and the powers of death shall not prevail against it'" (Matthew 16:13–20). Some scholars feel Christ may have deliberately selected the heartland of paganism for this great declaration of faith. A small Greek Orthodox church (now closed) nearby was built to commemorate the site.

Though Roman rule in this part of the kingdom would not last another generation past Philip, Panias continued to flourish for more than 1,000 years—and its original name, with only slight modification, has endured.

In the early 12th century, Banias was held by Crusaders, and just outside the second entrance (marked BANIAS) to the reserve are the ruins of what is thought to have been the marketplace of the day—a string of single "rooms" along a well-preserved section of wall might well have been shops. The archaeologist leading these excavations, Vassilos Tsaferis, believed that more of the city could be lying under the parking lot, and in mid-1994 a Roman-era health and leisure center for tired soldiers was unearthed within the reserve. The luxurious 1,613-square-foot facility dates to the 1st century and had marble floors, mosaics, and a series of subterranean (*under*-underground, if you will) passages. ⊠ *Off Rte. 99,* ☎ *06/695–0272.* 🎟 *NIS 13 ($4.35).* ☉ *Daily 8–5 (1 hr later during summer holidays).*

OFF THE BEATEN PATH	**TEL FAHER** – The large number of monuments to fallen soldiers in the Golan is a reminder of the strategic importance of the region—and the price paid to attain it. Among the easily accessible sites, where old Syrian bunkers give a gunner's-eye view of the valley below, is Tel Faher, in the northern Golan (⊠ Turnoff is to the right just above Banias, off Rte. 99). At Tel Faher—also known as Mitzpe Golani, for the elite Golani Brigade soldiers who died here in 1967—children can climb onto the tank that now sits passively. **Caution:** The sites are safe, but beyond the fences and clearly marked paths are old Syrian minefields that have not been completely detonated.

Nimrod's Fortress

★ ⑱ *5 km (3 mi) from Hermon River (Banias) Nature Reserve.*

The history of Nimrod's Fortress (Kal'at Namrud), the huge, burly fortress perched above Banias, is still vociferously debated. It was built around 1100, but was it, for example, Muslim or Crusader in origin? Academic controversy aside, a visit to the fortress is a real treat. The limestone fortress, overgrown with scruffy shrubbery and blending in with the surrounding stony mountain terrain, commands superb vistas, especially when framed by the arched windows or glimpsed through the narrow archers' slits in the walls.

What *is* known about the fortress is that it guarded the vital route from Damascus via the Golan and Banias to Lebanon and to the Mediterranean coast. Although Muslim legend says it was first built by Arabs, it is widely believed to have been a Crusader structure later modified by the Arabs. In any event, it changed hands between Muslims and Christians in the centuries to follow as both vied for control of the region. During one of the more curious periods of its history, from 1126 to 1129, Nimrod's Fortress was occupied by a fanatical sect of Muslims famous as murderers. Before heading out to track down their enemies, the cutthroats would indulge in huge quantities of hashish, thus earning the nickname *hashashin* (hashish users), from which the word *assassin* is derived. Nimrod functioned as a prison during the Mamluk period and was abandoned in the 16th century. In modern times, Syria observed Israeli troop movements from the fortress.

The entrance to the fortress, next to the parking lot, is through a breach in the western wall. There are several large vaulted cisterns on the site, which supplied the residents with water. These were particularly crucial during a siege: The cisterns could store enough water for 500 people for three years. Follow the path through the citadel ruins to the donjon, or keep, the central tower of the fortress. You may notice it faces east; the Crusaders expected attacks from this direction. It is possible to climb the donjon, 100 feet above the surrounding castle. This is where the feudal lord would have lived, and it is a kind of fortress within a fortress: The outer wall on the east and south sides is well protected by protruding towers, also equipped with slits. ⊠ *Nimrod's Fortress National Park, Rte. 989 (off Rte. 99),* ☎ *06/698–4316.* ▣ *NIS 10 ($3.30).* ☉ *Apr.–Sept., daily 8–5; Oct.–Mar., daily 8–4.*

Mt. Hermon

⑲ *12 km (7½ mi) from Nimrod's Fortress, 25 km (15½ mi) from Kiryat Shmona.*

The summit of Mt. Hermon, famous as Israel's highest mountain, at 9,232 feet above sea level, is actually in Syrian territory. Its lower slopes attract Israelis as the country's only ski resort, but the fun is significantly chilled by the high prices (☞ Skiing, *below*). In fact, summer is arguably the most interesting time on the Hermon: After the winter snows melt, hikers can discover chasms and hidden valleys on the mountain, the long-term result of extremes in temperature. Moreover, a powerful array of colors and scents emerge from the earth as cockscomb, chamomile, and scores of other flowers and wild herbs are drawn out by the summer sun. Getting here from Nimrod's Fortress, you will pass the new Jewish township of **Neve Ativ**, designed to look like a little piece of the Alps in the Middle East, replete with A-frame chalet-style houses. The residents of Neve Ativ operate the ski slopes 13 km (8 mi) above. You also go by the old Druze village of **Majdal Shams.**

Skiing

Don't compare the slopes of **Mt. Hermon** (☎ 06/698–1337) with those in Europe or the Americas. For Israelis, there is a certain thrill to having a ski resort in a hot Mediterranean country—and compared with flying to the Alps, it's a bargain (figure about NIS 250, or $83, per day for admission, lift tickets, and equipment rental). Frankly, though, Mt. Hermon has little to offer the serious, or even the novice, skier. The chairlifts and cafeterias run year-round; the site may be more attractive in summer, when it is bursting with wildflowers.

En Route **Ein Kuniya,** which appears across a valley on your left as you head east into the Golan on Route 99, is the most picturesque of several Druze villages in the area. The houses are built of the black basalt so prevalent in the Golan.

Merom Golan

20 km (12½ mi) from Mt. Hermon.

Kibbutz Merom Golan was the first settlement built in the Golan after the Six-Day War. Its fields and orchards are typical of the kibbutzim in the area. Apples are especially good in these parts, but man cannot live by apples alone, and Merom Golan runs Cowboys' Restaurant (☞ *below*), with good, reasonably priced steaks.

Dining

$$ ✕ **Cowboys' Restaurant.** Here's the best corral this side of the Israel-Syria Disengagement Zone. "Saddle" stools at the bar and cattle hides on the walls contribute to the frontier atmosphere. But, above all, it's the grub—specifically the excellent steaks—that people come for. The restaurant offers a 10% discount if you pay with a Visa card. ⊠ *Kibbutz Merom Golan, off Rte. 959,* ☎ *06/696–0206. DC, MC, V. No dinner Sun.*

Kuneitra/The Disengagement Zone

3 km (2 mi) from Merom Golan.

Syria is not far away. The ruined town of Kuneitra was captured by Israel in 1967, lost and regained in the 1973 Yom Kippur War, and returned to Syria in the Disengagement Agreement that followed. It is now a demilitarized zone, and Syria has made no effort to rebuild the town. The cluster of white buildings next to it houses the United Nations Disengagement Observer Force. ⊠ *Near Rte. 98.*

Katzrin

⓴ *20 km (12½ mi) from Merom Golan, 38 km (23½ mi) from Tiberias, 35 km (22 mi) from Zfat.*

The "capital" of the Golan Heights, Katzrin (Qazrin) was founded in 1977 on the site of a 2nd-century town of the same name. It is the administrative center of the Golan Heights and one of the most appealing residential areas in the north. To get here from the northern Golan, take Route 91 west and then go south on Route 87.

There is a very homey suburban feel about Katzrin, despite its strategic location and attendant sensitivity. It's not unusual to see bomb shelters decorated and converted into recreation centers or into Hebrew classrooms for Russian immigrants who have come to this corner of the country to begin life anew. The water here is very soft: Straight from the basalt bedrock, it is delicious to drink, and it also makes skin feel silky smooth.

Commercial Katzrin provides general services: There is a café (open during the day), a pizzeria (open at night), a gift store, a minimarket, and a library.

The **Golan Archaeological Museum,** though small, has a comprehensive collection of animal bones, stones, and artifacts that put the region into perspective. Among the exhibits is a Chalcolithic dwelling reconstructed from materials excavated close by. A room in the museum is devoted to the story of Gamla, the "Masada of the North" (☞ *below*), and includes an excellent audiovisual presentation of its history during the Great Revolt against the Romans and the discovery of the ancient site by archaeologists exactly 1,900 years later. The museum is run in conjunction with the Ancient Katzrin Park (☞ *below*). ⌂ *In Katzrin commercial center,* ☎ *06/696–1350.* 🎟 *NIS 11 ($3.60), includes Ancient Katzrin Park.* ⊙ *Sun.–Thurs. 8–5, Fri. and holiday eves 8–3, Sat. 10–4.*

㉑ **Ancient Katzrin Park,** 2 km (1¼ mi) east of the business center of Katzrin, is an excavation-in-progress of a Jewish village, possibly from the 3rd century, whose economy was based on the production of olive oil. In all such villages—it is believed there were once 27 in the vicinity—the synagogue was the focus of community activities. Its importance was reflected in the abundance and complexity of ornamentation. The Katzrin Temple, a contemporary of those at Bar'am and Capernaum, has decorative architectural details, such as a mosaic pavement and a wreath of pomegranates and amphorae in relief on the lintel above the entrance. Built of basalt, the synagogue was in use for 400 years until it was partly destroyed, possibly by an earthquake in 747.

Since 1967, when the excavations at Katzrin began, 10% of the ancient Jewish village has been uncovered. The two reconstructed buildings in the park, the so-called House of Uzi and House of Rabbi Abun (presumably a Talmudic sage), are attractively decorated with rope baskets, weavings, baking vessels, and pottery, based on remnants of the originals found at the site, and lighted with little clay oil lamps. ⌂ *Rte. 87,* ☎ *06/696–2412.* 🎟 *NIS 11 ($3.60), includes Golan Archaeological Museum.* ⊙ *Sun.–Thurs. 8–5, Fri. and holiday eves 8–3, Sat. 10–4.*

㉒ The **Golan Heights Winery,** in Katzrin's industrial zone, is one of Israel's top businesses. It launched the country into the international winemaking arena with its Yarden and Gamla labels (a third label is called, predictably, Golan). The area's unique volcanic soil, cold winters and cool summers, and state-of-the-art vinifying techniques have proven a recipe for success. Wine-tasting tours are generally available if booked in advance. A store here stocks the full line of wines, including the relatively new Yarden Gewurztraminer and the Gamla Muscat Canelli, as well as sophisticated accessories for the oenophile. If you don't feel like buying here (and you may find the wines a tad less expensive in city liquor stores), the winery can provide you with the business cards of their distributors around the world. ⌂ *Rte. 87 (east of town center),* ☎ *06/696–2001, 06/696–1646 for tours.* 🎟 *Tour and tasting NIS 10 ($3.30).* ⊙ *Sun.–Thurs. 9–5:30, Fri. 9–2.*

Nightlife

On the grounds of Katzrin Park, a **pub** (☎ 06/696–3033) is operated out of a century-old Syrian dwelling. The sheer experience of having a drink amid the ancient ruins is worth a detour if you are lodging in the area.

OFF THE   **MITZPE GADOT –** If you continued northwest on Route 87 from Katzrin
BEATEN PATH   and then west on Route 91, you would pass this tall, triangular concrete

monument to fallen Israeli soldiers. It's just above the B'not Ya'akov Bridge and is named after the kibbutz it overlooks. **Caution:** The site is safe, but don't explore beyond any marked paths because there may be undetonated Syrian minefields.

Gamla

20 km (12 mi) southeast of Katzrin; take Rte. 87 to Rte. 808 and watch for Gamla signpost.

Aside from offering a fascinating history of determination, struggle, and death, the "Masada of the North" is truly inspiring in its beauty. The rugged, hilly terrain of Gamla is softened in late winter and spring by the greenery and wildflowers that follow the rains. A collection of predatory birds returns here twice a year between migrations, and their nests are clearly visible from the Vultures' Lookout. Also, keep your eyes peeled for gazelles, porcupines, and foxes.

Digs have turned up a fortified town dating to the early Bronze Age, but the principal story of the camel-shape Gamla (the name *Gamla* is probably related to *gamal*, the Hebrew word for "camel") goes back 2,000 years. Those were the days when Herod was encouraging Jews to settle here in order to populate the frontiers of his kingdom. By AD 66, the Jews of Gamla had joined the Great Revolt against Rome. Herod's great-grandson Agrippa II, of Banias, sided with the Romans and challenged the zealous rebels. When he failed to overpower them, Rome dispatched Vespasian at the head of three legions. In 67, the Romans launched a bloody attack here that ended seven months later when the 9,000 surviving Jews flung themselves to their deaths in the abyss below the town.

Flavius Josephus related the story of Gamla in *The Jewish War*, and vivid descriptions from this tome are engraved in stones along the trails throughout the site. "Sloping down from a towering peak is a spur like a long shaggy neck, behind which rides a symmetrical hump, so that the outline resembles that of a camel. . . . On the face of both sides it is cut off by impassable ravines. Near the tail it is rather more accessible where it is detached from the hill. . . . Built against the almost vertical flank, the town seemed to be hung in the air . . . ." Indeed, this is precisely the first, dramatic image one has approaching Gamla from the hilltop entrance to the reserve.

It was that tough, steep terrain that almost caused Vespasian's three legions of Roman soldiers to fail in their siege. No sooner had the Romans succeeded in reaching the town than the defenders swung around and counterattacked; the Romans were "swept down the slope and trapped in the narrow alleys." Rallied by Vespasian, the Romans were able to drive the last defenders to the summit. Seeing no escape, the survivors opted for mass suicide.

The town subsequently fell into ruin and oblivion. This turned out to be a boon for visitors 1,900 years later. Because it was never rebuilt, Gamla is the only example of a Roman battlefield whose relics match the vivid stories from the past; among the finds are 2,000 "missile stones" and arrowheads. Moreover, there are about 200 **dolmens** scattered in the area—strange stone structures shaped like the Greek letter π. The effort required to erect these large basalt burial monuments, probably during the 2nd millennium BC, indicates the importance of death and burial rituals at that time.

Gamla offers a choice of three walking trails. There is an excellent short film on the story of Gamla at the Golan Archaeological Museum in Katzrin (☞ *above*). ⊠ *Off Rte. 808,* ☎ *050–509930.* 🖂 *NIS 11 ($3.70).* ☉ *Sun.–Thurs. and Sat. 8–5, Fri. and holidays 8–4.*

UPPER GALILEE AND THE GOLAN A TO Z

Arriving and Departing

By Bus

Egged buses (☎ 03/537–5555) run daily from Tel Aviv to Kiryat Shmona (Buses 842 and 845) and to Zfat (Bus 846); from Jerusalem to Kiryat Shmona (Bus 963) and to Zfat (Bus 964); from Haifa to Kiryat Shmona (Buses 501 and 502) and to Zfat (Buses 331 and 362); and to both cities from Tiberias (Bus 459).

By Car

Unquestionably, the best way to see the Upper Galilee and the Golan is by car. It takes three hours to make the 180-km (112-mi) drive from Tel Aviv; 1½ hours of driving from both Akko and Nahariya, about 60 km (37 mi) away; and four hours from Jerusalem, which is 200 km (124 mi) to the south. There are numerous approaches to the area. From Tiberias and the Sea of Galilee, Route 90 runs due north between the Hula Valley on the east and the hills of Naftali on the west. The more rugged Route 98 leads from the eastern side of the Sea of Galilee up through the Golan Heights to Mt. Hermon. Near the top of Route 98 you can pick up Route 91, which heads west into the Upper Galilee.

From the Mediterranean coast there are several options, but the main one is Route 85 from Akko. Route 89 runs parallel to Route 85 a little farther north, from Nahariya, and has some gorgeous scenery. From Haifa take Route 75 to Route 77, turning onto Route 90 at Tiberias, or Route 70 north onto Route 85 east. If you're starting from Tel Aviv, drive north on Route 4 or 2 to Hadera. From there you'll head northwest on Route 65, exiting onto Route 85 east.

By Plane

Arkia Israeli Airlines (⊠ In Tel Aviv, ☎ 03/690–2222; in Jerusalem, ☎ 02/625–5888), Israel's domestic airline, operates daily flights from Sde Dov Airport in Tel Aviv, and several flights per week from Jerusalem, to the small Galilee airport of Mahanayim (☎ 06/693–5301), part of the township of Rosh Pina. From the airport it is 10 km (6 mi) to Zfat and 30 km (19 mi) to Kiryat Shmona.

Getting Around

By Bus

Although local buses stop at all major sites in the region (partly because there is always a kibbutz, a town, or some other small residential settlement nearby), avoid buses if you are on a tight schedule; they can run infrequently. Call **Egged** (☎ 03/537–5555) for schedules. If you have trouble getting through to Egged, you can try the **local depots**: Kiryat Shmona (☎ 06/694–0740), Tiberias (☎ 06/679–1080), and Zfat (☎ 06/692–1122).

By Car

The state of Israel's **roads** is changing from bad-to-fair to fair-to-good. In the Upper Galilee in particular, the government is making an effort to improve the road infrastructure, but don't expect wide, even highways. The fact is, sometimes they're paved and sometimes, well, they just aren't. This is especially true in the Golan. Driving cautiously is tremendously important. Try to avoid driving during peak hours, which are usually late Saturday afternoon when city folk crowd the roads back to Jerusalem and Tel Aviv after a day out in the country.

The main north–south roads in the region are Route 90, which goes all the way up to Metulla at the Lebanese border; the 65-km-long (40-mi-long) Tiberias-Metulla Road; and the less-traveled Route 98, which runs from the eastern side of the Sea of Galilee through the Golan Heights (along the Disengagement Zone) to Mt. Hermon. The main west–east highways are Route 85, which runs for 60 km (37 mi) from Akko to Korazim, and Route 89, which connects Nahariya and Zfat, 50 km (31 mi) away.

Gas stations are easy to find along Route 90 and in the towns, such as Katzrin (Route 87) or Zfat (Route 89). It is best to fill up during the day, because it is difficult to find a gas station open after 9 PM. Gas stations are, however, generally open daily.

Contacts and Resources

Car Rental

It is much easier to rent a car in Tiberias (☞ Lower Galilee A to Z *in* Chapter 6), Tel Aviv, Jerusalem, or Haifa than to search for a dependable car-rental company in the tiny towns of the Upper Galilee. For travelers flying to the Galilee (☞ Arriving and Departing, *above*), **Arkia Israeli Airlines** (⊠ In Tel Aviv, ☏ 03/690–2222) can arrange for a rented car to be waiting at Mahanayim Airport, outside Rosh Pina.

Emergencies

Police (☏ 100). **Ambulance** (☏ 101). **Fire fighters** (☏ 102). Tokens or telecards are not required at public phones for emergency calls.

The main **police station** in the Upper Galilee is in Kiryat Shmona (⊠ 1 Salinger St., ☏ 06/694–3444 or 06/694–3445).

The **Magen David Adom** station in Kiryat Shmona (⊠ 3 Tchernichovsky St., ☏ 06/694–4334 or 06/694–9401) handles medical and dental emergencies 24 hours a day. It is near the central bus station.

Guided Tours

GENERAL INTEREST

Both of Israel's major bus companies, **Egged** (⊠ 15 Frishman St., Tel Aviv, ☏ 03/527–1222; ⊠ 224 Jaffa Rd., Jerusalem, ☏ 02/530–4422; ⊠ Zfat Bus Station, Zfat, ☏ 06/692–1122) and **United Tours** (⊠ 113 Hayarkon St., Tel Aviv, ☏ 03/522–2008 or 03/6933412; King David Hotel Annex, Jerusalem, ☏ 02/625–2187) offer one- and two-day guided tours of the region, departing from Tel Aviv and Jerusalem. Both give children under 12 a 10% discount.

SPECIAL INTEREST

The **Society for the Protection of Nature in Israel** (SPNI; ⊠ 4 Hashfela St., Tel Aviv 66183, ☏ 03/638–8666) sponsors excellent hikes and walking tours in the region. The tours are usually aimed at all ages, so Olympic-level fitness is not required; any hikes that require some physical exertion are clearly described as such.

Hospital

The largest hospital in the north outside Haifa is the **Rivka Sieff General Hospital,** in Zfat (⊠ Harambam Rd., ☏ 06/697–8822). Bus 6 from the Zfat bus station stops here.

Kayaking and Rafting

Whitewater Rafting (⊠ Rte. 91, not far from Mahanayim Junction, ☎ 06/693–6867 or 06/693–4622) operates professionally guided rafting trips through the rapids of the Jordan.

Lodging

Reservations for the area's kibbutz guest houses can be made directly or through a central reservation service, **Kibbutz Hotels Chain,** based in Tel Aviv (⊠ 90 Ben Yehuda St., ☎ 03/524–6161, FAX 03/527–8088), although not all the kibbutzim are represented by the agency. A central reservation service is also coordinated by **Moshav Beit Hillel** (⊠ M.P. Upper Galilee 12255, ☎ 06/695–1806 or 06/693–5016, FAX 06/695–9861).

Visitor Information

All hotels and kibbutz guest houses can provide tourist information, and many will arrange tours as well.

The Tourist Information Office (TIO) in **Tiberias** (⊠ Habanim St., ☎ 06/672–5666) can furnish information about the entire region. The Municipal Tourist Information Office in **Zfat** (⊠ 50 Yerushalayim St., Box 227, Zfat 13010, ☎ 06/692–0961) is useful for regional information and has a list of licensed guides in the city. **Tourist Information Center–Upper Galilee,** a small office, is at the Mahanayim Junction, adjacent to the gas station (⊠ Kibbutz Mahanayim, M.P. Hevel Korazim 12315, ☎ 06/693–5016), but they have little printed information in English. **Bet Ussishkin Museum** (⊠ Kibbutz Dan, M.P. Upper Galilee 12245, ☎ 06/694–1704) has information on the Upper Galilee's nature reserves, natural history, and bird-watching.

8 Eilat and the Negev

In the sun-drenched city of Eilat you can discover the wonders of the Red Sea while snorkeling through tropical reefs and relaxing on sandy beaches. To the north, in the desert landscape of the Negev, the biblical "southland," you can explore the quiet vastness of the desert landscape and the civilizations that have made it bloom. And to the east, on the Dead Sea at Ein Bokek, you can enjoy the beneficial properties of the famed waters at one of the area's many spas.

By Judy Stacey
Goldman

THE NEGEV IS THE SOUTHERNMOST PART OF ISRAEL, an upside-down triangle that constitutes about half the land mass of the country, though only about 6% of the population lives within its borders. The Negev's northern border, the base of the triangle, lies about 27 km (17 mi) north of Beersheva, known as the capital of the Negev and the only large city in the region. The Jordanian and Egyptian borders mark its eastern and western sides, respectively, and Eilat, on the Gulf of Eilat at the gateway to the Red Sea, is at its southernmost tip.

The Negev may well have changed more in the years since the foundation of the modern state of Israel than in the entire period since the end of the Roman Empire. The first kibbutzim in the Negev were established in the early 1940s, with new immigrants sent south after the War of Independence in 1948. Two years later, people started trickling into Eilat, where there was nothing but a few rickety huts. Arad put down its roots in 1961. The desert itself was pushed back, and the semiarid areas between Tel Aviv and Beersheva became fertile farming land. Today, agricultural settlements in the scorching Arava Valley make use of brackish water to raise flowers, vegetables, and dates that are sent to winter markets in Europe. (The greening of the desert is most evident when you fly over the Negev and see the patches of deep, rich green below you.) Tourism, aided and encouraged by the government, has taken off in earnest.

The army has been deployed over a large part of the Negev since the Sinai was handed over to Egypt. You'll feel a military presence at roadside diners, where soldiers stop off to eat; at bus stations, where they're in transit; and at tent-filled compounds here and there. Signs declaring FIRING ZONES indicate areas where the public may not enter, and checkpoints—where a smile and a wave-through are the order of the day—are scattered throughout.

The area has a long and varied human history. The ancient Israelites had fortifications in the Negev, as did the Nabateans and the Romans after them. These early settlers developed irrigation techniques that were remarkably sophisticated, even by modern standards. Throughout these periods of permanent settlement, the entire area was home to Bedouins, whose distinctive way of desert living, developed thousands of years ago, still can be observed.

Despite its rapid development, the Negev remains Israel's Wild West. It takes a certain kind of person to live and work here, someone who relishes the challenge of turning the hot, bone-dry desert into a hospitable place to live. The Negev draws people who have been seduced by the beauty of great canyons and cliffs spilling over with color at dawn and dusk; by the sight of thousands of migrating birds who fill the skies twice a year; by the endless areas of still, rocky terrain where the only movement might be a stone clattering down a hillside as an ibex makes a leap; by the sound of the wind coming up at the end of a dusty day; and by the pleasure of bright flowers carpeting the hills in winter.

The Negev contains some of Israel's most fascinating and dramatic scenery, from gigantic *makhteshim* (erosion craters) and the moonscape of the Dead Sea to carved-out wadis (ancient dry riverbeds), the red granite mountains around Eilat, and long cliff faces along the Arava Valley. You can visit the kibbutz home and grave site of Israel's first prime minister—David Ben-Gurion, the man whose dream it was to settle the desert—and the millennia-old ruins at Tel Beer Sheva, site of the biblical patriarch Abraham's visit. Farther south, the Hai Bar Nature Reserve is home to animals described in the Bible, and the Timna Valley Park is a wonderland of unusually colored rock formations. At the port city of Eilat you can see Technicolor tropical fish and coral formations, and in Ein Bokek you can get pampered at a spa.

Pleasures and Pastimes

Adventure Tours

A thrilling way to see the Negev is by Jeep or camel in the company of an expert guide who is not only knowledgeable about every facet of desert life but who also knows how to prepare open-air meals and to brew tea from desert plants (your guide might live in a desert settlement). If you have time, a trek of several days in the desert is not to be missed; tour companies provide all the camping equipment. Some desert expeditions combine camel riding, hiking, and rappelling. To find out more, *see* Hiking *under* Guided Tours *in* Eilat and the Negev A to Z, *below* (bookings can often be made through a travel agency or your hotel; it's wise to book ahead). Be aware that not all tours operate in summer, when it's very hot.

Dining

If the word dining conjures up starched and draped tablecloths, gliding waiters, and gleaming silver, and if that's what your heart is set on, head for the upscale restaurants and luxury hotels in Eilat and Ein Bokek. Although Eilat is at the southern tip of the Negev Desert, you won't miss out on any culinary treats—even Ben & Jerry's. If you like fish, you'll be especially happy in Eilat: Specialty fish restaurants abound, a rarity elsewhere in the country. Excellent sea fish, such as are raised in ponds around Eilat, and delicacies, such as *denise* (sea brim) and the Israeli specialty *furel,* salmon-trout bred in the Dan River up north, make wonderful meals. Flown-in fresh fruit and vegetables—Italian, Indian, French, Argentinean, Yemenite—can also be found in Eilat.

In the rest of the Negev, with the notable exception of the Mitzpe Ramon Inn, plan to dine in far humbler surroundings—typically a roadside diner—on meals that are apt to reflect the cook's ethnic background. You'll find, perhaps, Tunisian carrot salad, Moroccan *cigarim* (flaky pastry with a meat or potato filling), or standard Middle Eastern fare: hummus, pita, grilled meat, french fries (known as chips), chopped or shredded vegetable salads (*salatim*), strong coffee in small cups, and a dessert such as fruit or chocolate mousse. Keep in mind that outside Eilat restaurants close early on Friday and the main meal of the day is served at noon in all desert eateries, so lunch may be over if you arrive after 1:30.

As for what to wear: If people are dressed up anywhere, it will be at the fancy restaurants (and nightclubs and discos) in Eilat and Ein Bokek (though a tie is never required at any restaurant). The ritziest attire you'll see anywhere else is a clean T-shirt. Keep in mind, too, that it is always a good idea to make a reservation at Eilat and Ein Bokek restaurants, especially on Friday and Saturday night.

CATEGORY	COST*
$$$$	over $35
$$$	$22–$35
$$	$12–$22
$	under $12

per person for three-course meal, excluding drinks and service charge

Hiking

Hiking amid the splendid scenery, rugged heights, and steep cliff faces of the Negev requires skill and know-how. In summer the heat is extreme, and in winter the danger of floods is ever present. Hiking on your own is not recommended unless you are well versed in the art of reading topographical maps. The best way to hike the Negev is with one of several excellent organizations (☞ Hiking *under* Guided Tours *in* Eilat and the Negev A to Z, *below*). If you do venture out without a guide, be sure to give the details—where you're headed, your route, and when you expect to be back—to someone who is staying behind. Always follow the desert water-drinking guidelines (☞ Desert Precautions, *below*).

Lodging

Keep in mind that prices rise during peak season and holidays. High season is Hanukkah/Christmas, Passover/Easter, and July and August, when Israelis vacation. At Ein Bokek, high season is mid-March to mid-June and mid-September to the end of November. In Eilat, hotels are crowded with European tourists from October until April. Be sure to make reservations well in advance at any time of the year.

CATEGORY	EILAT AND EIN BOKEK*	OTHER AREAS*
$$$$	over $164	over $99
$$$	$125–$164	$70–$99
$$	$75–$125	$40–$70
$	under $75	under $40

All prices are for a standard double room, including breakfast for two and excluding 15% service charge.

Natural Wonders

The star of the Negev is the Makhtesh Ramon (Ramon Crater), a geological formation found only in Israel. But throughout the area other knock-out views abound: the changing colors of the Wilderness of Zin as the day passes; the sunsets that stain the Eilat waters a deep red; the snow-white salt blocks clumped on the surface of the Dead Sea; and the erosion sculptures surrounded by brooding mountains in Timna Park.

Scuba Diving

Eilat is at the gateway to the Red Sea, one of the best diving locations in the world. After the Six-Day War in 1967, Israeli divers opened diving facilities along the Sinai coast south of Eilat, and although the Sinai was returned to Egypt more than a decade ago, Eilat's dive centers still run regular dive safaris over the border. Amazing coral formations, underwater tropical plant life, and a dazzling array of fish live in waters that are warm year-round (22°C, or 72°F, in winter). The reefs are a mere 10 yards offshore, with an immediate deep drop, so a dive is just a walk away. Divers should bring their license, insurance certification, and appropriate footwear—the seafloor is rough and so are the sea urchins. Top-level dive courses are widely available.

Exploring Eilat and the Negev

Our peregrinations cover three basic areas in the inverted triangle of the Negev: The first is the heart of the Negev, with sites such as David Ben-Gurion's home and grave site, the ancient Nabatean-Roman-Byzantine ruins at Tel Avdat, and the amazing Ramon Crater. The second area includes the capital city of Beersheva, the spa-resort town of Ein Bokek at the Dead Sea, the ancient city of Tel Arad, and the modern city of Arad. The southern tip of the triangle encompasses the carefree resort town of Eilat, the Underwater Observatory at Coral Beach, and the Timna Valley Park. Eilat is also the setting-off point for one day or longer trips to both Jordan (ancient Petra), and Egypt (the Sinai Peninsula). Read Chapter 9 before making final travel plans.

As you travel from place to place in the Negev, you'll pass stretches of flat, uninhabited countryside under hot, blue skies, punctuated by the odd acacia tree, twisting wadi, or craggy mountain. In winter you'll see delicate desert flowers along the road. If you want to skip the desert driving experience, you might make Eilat or Ein Bokek your only destination in the area. In Eilat you can stay at a luxurious hotel, relax in the sunshine by the water, and scuba dive or snorkel. In Ein Bokek you can pamper yourself at the numerous spas that take advantage of the Dead Sea waters and medicinal mud.

Great Itineraries

The following itineraries cover the major (and some off-the-beaten-path) sites in the Negev for travelers who are driving and have a limited amount of time. All assume that you are coming from Tel Aviv or Jerusalem. A few places can be visited by bus, but it's definitely not the most comfortable way to get around. You might consider combining one of our suggested itineraries with a short guided tour (☞ Guided Tours *in* Eilat and the Negev A to Z, *below*).

Although Beersheva is considered the capital of the Negev, it is not included in the two-day or five-day itineraries because it is not of major importance nor does it have many good hotels (the new Hilton, however, may help rectify this situation). You might, however, want to stop there briefly for a snack or gas.

Numbers in the text correspond to numbers in the margin and on the Eilat and the Negev map.

IF YOU HAVE 1 OR 2 DAYS

In a day or two you can cram in a lot of varied Negev sites. Get an early start from Jerusalem or Tel Aviv: You can either stop at the **Bedouin Heritage Center** ① or drive to Beersheva (without stopping) on your way to **Mitzpe Revivim** ② to see the reconstruction of a 1943 fighting desert outpost. Next visit renowned prime minister **David Ben-Gurion's desert home** ③ and **grave site** ④, overlooking the Wilderness of Zin. Head down the twisting road near the grave site to get to **En Avdat** ⑤, a welcome respite of splashing waterfalls in the blazing summer and a green and picturesque sight in winter. It's a short drive from Ein Avdat to the 2,000-year-old Nabatean hilltop stronghold of **Avdat** ⑥, which you can explore on foot. If you have only one day, skip Ein Avdat and Avdat and drive straight to the visitor center at **Mitzpe Ramon** ⑦ to see the **Makhtesh Ramon** ⑦. If you have two days, spend the night in Mitzpe Ramon and the next morning explore the immense Ramon Crater or learn about it at the visitor center. (If you've brought children, they'll appreciate a visit to the **Alpaca Farm** just outside town.) Your return trip brings you back to **Beersheva** ⑨, where you can choose between visiting **Tel Beersheva** ⑪ and seeing the possible site of Abraham's Well or stopping at the **Israel Air Force Museum** ⑩, in Hatzerim, to see a field full of planes.

IF YOU HAVE 5 DAYS

Start at the **Museum of Bedouin Culture** ⑧ for an authentic look at the lifestyle of Israel's nomadic people. The sandy landscape along Route 31 takes you through ancient **Tel Arad** ⑫ and modern **Arad** ⑬. From Arad drive the dramatic 24-km (15-mi) descent on the sharply curving Route 31 to the Dead Sea, the lowest point on earth. Stay overnight in 🏨 **Ein Bokek** ⑭. Devote the next morning to enjoying your hotel's spa facilities and floating in the Dead Sea. By afternoon you'll feel well rested and can drive south to 🏨 **Eilat** ⑮ and spend two days taking advantage of all it has to offer. Back on the road on fourth day, going north, drive through the **Ramon Crater** ⑦ to reach 🏨 **Mitzpe Ramon** ⑦,

Eilat and the Negev

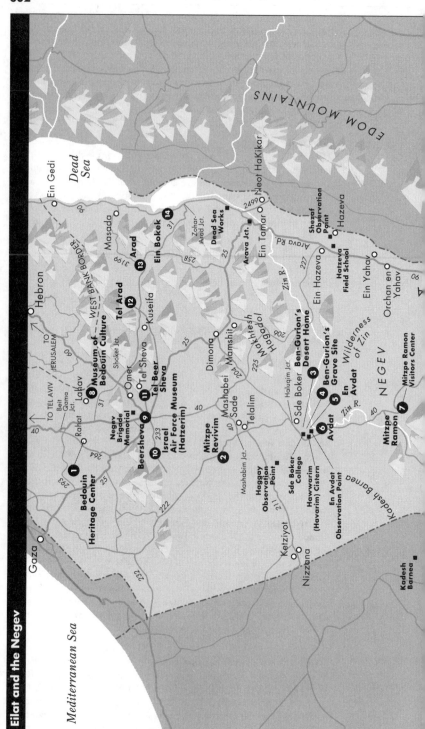

Mediterranean Sea

Dead Sea

EDOM MOUNTAINS

Ein Gedi

Gaza

Hebron

TO TEL AVIV

TO JERUSALEM

WEST BANK BORDER

Rahat

Lahav

Beit Qama Jct.

1 Bedouin Heritage Center

8 Museum of Bedouin Culture

Shoket Jct.

Omer

9 Beersheva

Negev Brigade Memorial

10 Israel Air Force Museum (Hatzerim)

11 Tel Beer Sheva

Tel Sheva

Masada

Arad **13**

Ein Bokek **14**

Tel Arad **12**

Kuseifa

Zohar-Arad Jct.

Dead Sea Works

Arava Jct.

Ein Tamar

Neot HaKikar

Shezaf Observation Point

Hazeva

Hatzeva Field School

Ein Hazeva

Ein Yahav

Orchan en Yahav

Dimona

Mamshit

Makhtesh Hagadol

Ben-Gurion's Desert Home

3 Ben-Gurion's Grave Site

Sde Boker

Wilderness of Zin

Zin R.

4 En Avdat

5

6 Avdat

Mitzpe Ramon Visitors Center

7

Mitzpe Ramon

NEGEV

Mashabei Sade

Telalim

Mitzpe Revivim **2**

Mashabim Jct.

Haggay Observation Point

Ketziyot

Nizzana

Sde Boker College

Hawwarim (Havarim) Cistern

En Avdat Observation Point

Kadesh Barnea

Kadesh Barnea

Halukim Jct.

Arava Rd

2499

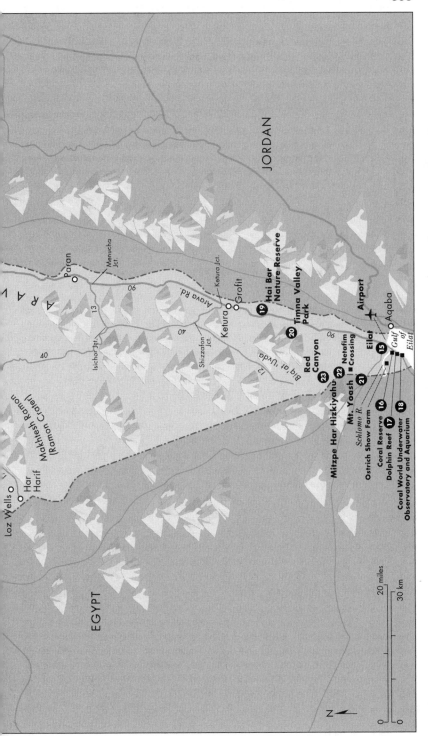

JORDAN

EGYPT

A R A V A H

Paran

Menucha Jct.

90

13

Isichor Jct.

40

40

Loz Wells

Har
Harif

Makhtesh Ramon
(Ramon Crater)

Mitzpe Har Hizkiyahu

Shizzafon Jct.

Ketura Jct.

Arava Rd.

Ketura

Grofit

Hai Bar
Nature Reserve

Timna Valley
Park

Airport

Aqaba

Gulf
of
Eilat

Eilat

Netafim
Crossing

Red
Canyon

Mt. Yaash

Schlomo R.

Ostrich Show Farm

Coral Reserve

Dolphin Reef

Coral World Underwater
Observatory and Aquarium

Big'at 'Uvda

12

90

19

20

23

22

21

15

16

17

18

N

20 miles

30 km

on the crater's edge; spend the night there. You might have time to get to the visitor center or at least enjoy the cliff-side Promenade before dark. On your last day head back to Tel Aviv or Jerusalem, stopping at either **Arad** ⑬, **Ben-Gurion's desert home** ③, **Ben-Gurion's grave site** ④, **Revivim** ②, or the **Israel Air Force Museum** ⑩ (you won't have time to see them all).

IF YOU HAVE 9 DAYS

Follow the first three days of the itinerary above, spending the third and fourth nights in **Eilat** ⑮. On the fourth and fifth days relax, learn to dive, swim with dolphins, bird-watch, hike, or take a guided tour of the Eilat area. On Day 6 drive north to the **Ramon Crater** ⑦. Stay overnight in 🏨 **Mitzpe Ramon** ⑦. Day 7 might be the day for a Jeep tour, plus the Alpaca Farm. Heading north on Route 40 on Day 8, visit ancient **Avdat** ⑥, **Ben-Gurion's home** ③, **Ben-Gurion's grave site** ④, or **En Avdat** ⑤ on your way to 🏨 **Beersheva** ⑨ for the night. If your last day (spent in Beersheva) is a Thursday, you can get an early start at the **Bedouin market** or visit **Tel Sheva** ⑪—or the **Israel Air Force Museum** ⑩, or **Revivim** ②—on your way to Tel Aviv or Jerusalem.

When to Tour the Negev

October through May is the best time to explore the Negev. In January and February it's dry and cold. Scorching-hot conditions prevail from June through late September (though there's no humidity), and you're best bet is to stay by the water in Eilat. Ein Bokek, with its unique Dead Sea properties, attracts visitors even in the wildly hot summer. In early March, you'll be treated to the sight of scarlet, bright yellow, white, and hot pink desert flowers bursting out against the brown desert earth. March is also when Eilat's International Bird-watchers' Festival takes place. In August don't miss the Jazz Festival.

Negev sites open at 8:30 AM and close by 4 PM in winter and 5 PM in summer. Restaurants (except for those in Ein Bokek and Eilat) serve their main meal of the day (hot food) at noon and often close by early evening; on Friday most places close early (roadside diners close at around 1:30 PM).

Try to get an early start, plan to be inside or resting at midday in summer, and make every effort to be at your destination by nightfall. If you are traveling long distances, stay alert and awake. Lock the car at all times, take your valuables when you leave the car, and keep your bags where they are not visible from the outside. Women should not hitchhike.

DESERT PRECAUTIONS

Certain rules of the desert must be observed so that you are comfortable, happy, and safe. You should drink 2 quarts of water a day in the winter, and if you are active, 1 quart per hour in the summer (dehydration sets in quickly in the desert). Keep a jerrican (which holds 19 liters/5 gallons) of water in your car, plus extra bottles of water. You'll find water fountains along the way, but they do not always function. Wear sunblock, sunglasses (on a string so you don't lose them), protective lip balm, and a hat (a must year-round). You'll soon forget personal vanity when you see *everyone* wearing hats you thought you wouldn't be caught dead in. Light hiking shoes and a small knapsack are indispensable for walks and hikes, as are bug spray and a flashlight.

Although it may seem incongruous in the desert, there is a very real danger of road flooding in the winter and early spring, especially the day after a rainfall farther north. Before setting out, if it is raining or has recently rained, call the police (☎ 100) or the SPNI (☎ 03/638–8696 in Tel Aviv, ☉ Sun.–Thurs. 9–2, Fri. 8–1) to ask if there is a problem on the road you intend to take. If you are already in the Negev, contact the local Tourist Information Offices (☞ Visitor Information *in* Eilat and the Negev A to Z, *below*) for an update on road conditions. If you are traveling and see water flowing across the road in front of you, stop and wait, even if it takes a while for the water to subside. Water on the road is a warning of possible imminent flooding. When hiking, do not enter canyons or dry riverbeds on rainy days or even if it has only rained farther north.

THE HEART OF THE NEGEV

Plunge right into the heart of the Negev—the area extending from the Negev Highlands to Eilat. You'll find a range of sights to explore: the Bedouin Heritage Center, in the village of Rahat; Mitzpe Revivim, a reconstructed desert outpost; David Ben-Gurion's kibbutz home and grave site; an icy desert pool at En Avdat; the 2,000-year-old Nabatean hilltop stronghold of Avdat; and the immense Ramon Crater.

Bedouin Heritage Center

🐚 ❶ *110 km (66 mi) south of Tel Aviv, 15 km (9 mi) north of Beersheva. After the sign for Rahat, drive 2 km (1¼ mi); the Bedouin Heritage Center is opposite the gas station.*

You can meet the Negev's indigenous inhabitants, the Bedouin, at the large black tent and fieldstone building that make up the Bedouin Heritage Center in the village of Rahat. (Notice the cemetery on your way in from the road; each grave has both a headstone and a footstone.) Rahat is a 22-year-old Bedouin village, with modern villas, schools, and a community center—and resident Salem Abu Siam's authentic tent. Seated inside are the Bedouin hosts who will welcome you by performing the traditional coffee ceremony: roasting the beans over a fire and rhythmically pounding them (to let neighbors know that guests have arrived) in a wooden container using a wooden pestle. You'll sit on rugs around the fire and drink coffee from small cups. Singing, playing the *rababa* (Bedouin violin), and storytelling (just as it has been done for centuries) are part of the visit. A nearby tent contains a rug-making loom. Demonstrations are given, and Bedouin crafts, such as embroidery and rugs, are for sale. Children will especially enjoy the short rides on camels and donkeys. ⊠ *Rte. 264, 27 km (16¼ mi) from Kiryat Gat,* ☎ *07/991–8263 or 07/991–8656.* 🎟 *NIS 12 ($4).* ۞ *Sun.–Fri. 8:30–8, Sat. 11:30–5.*

En Route   On your way south from the Bedouin Heritage Center, you'll drive through Beersheva (☞ *below*), where you might want to stop for gas or a snack. Look out for the rectangular tents and huts sprawling over the low hills on the outskirts of town. This is a settlement of the Azazme, a Bedouin tribe. Although Bedouin traditionally live in black goat-hair tents, the Azazme, like many other modern Bedouin, are leaving behind their nomadic way of life and settling down. What you see is a step in the modern-day transition from tents to hutlike structures to concrete homes in permanent villages (it's not unusual to see tents sitting beside these modern houses). But these traditionally desert nomads still depend on their flocks for sustenance—much as their ancestors did. As you drive, you will see Bedouin women, their faces covered and their embroidered black dresses flying in the wind, tending sheep and goats. Alongside the road (and all over the Negev), you will also see isolated, often oval-shaped, clusters of eucalyptus and tamarisk trees. Called a *liman* (Greek for a small port or haven), these are the results of Jewish National Fund desert afforestation efforts, in which trees are sown in depressions to catch even the smallest amount of runoff water. Keep an eye out for donkeys and sheep crossing the road!

Mitzpe Revivim

❷ *36 km (22¼ mi) southeast of Beersheva.*

Mitzpe Revivim is the site of an early desert outpost. In 1943, in a desolate and empty Negev, three outposts—one of them Mitzpe Revivim (*mitzpe* means "lookout," *revivim* means "showers")—were set up to gauge the feasibility of Jewish settlement in the southernmost part of the country. Revivim's very presence, along with a handful of other Negev settlements, influenced the United Nations decision to include the Negev as part of the State of Israel in the 1947 partition plan. During the War of Independence, isolated Mitzpe Revivim was besieged by Egyptian soldiers, and a hard-fought battle was won by a small band of pioneers and Palmach soldiers. The defenders' fort and living quarters have been preserved: The radio room, ammunition room, kitchen, and engineers' quarters contain their original equipment. Outside are a cave—actually a Byzantine-period cistern—where a medical clinic was set up, and two airplanes, which were used to bring supplies and evacuate the wounded. The kibbutz members who maintain the place act as guides. There is a small restaurant offering snacks and hot food during visiting hours. ⊠ *Rte. 222,* ☎ *07/656–2570.* 🎟 *NIS 6 ($2).* ☉ *Sun.–Thurs. 9–6, Fri.–Sat. and holiday/holiday eves 9–5.*

En Route Proceed south along Route 40, and you'll come to the **Mashabim Junction** gas station, which also serves as a roadside café (good for stocking up on bottled water) and a tourist information kiosk. Continue on Route 40 for 2 km (1¼ mi) past the station and make a left at the sign for Mitzpe Ramon, at Telalim Junction. Along this stretch of road heading southwest, you'll pass through areas where signs announce FIRING ZONES. The signs indicate closed military areas, which you may not enter without proper authorization. It is perfectly safe to travel on the main roads, but don't wander off them.

Continuing along Route 40, you'll see a sign on the right for the **Haggay Observation Point.** The parking lot is on the opposite side of the highway at a curve in the road. After parking the car, carefully cross the road to the observation point for a glorious first view of the **Wilderness of Zin**—stark, flat, beige-color terrain—and **Kibbutz Sde Boker.** Except for the greenery of the kibbutz, the area undoubtedly looks as it did to the wandering Children of Israel making their way from Egypt to the Land of Canaan more than 3,000 years ago, muttering complaints about the lack of figs or vines. . . and no water to drink.

Ben-Gurion's Desert Home

❸ *24 km (15 mi) south of Mitzpe Revivim. Don't turn in at Kibbutz Sde Boker; just afterward is the sign for Ben-Gurion's home.*

Amid the waving eucalyptus trees is David Ben-Gurion's simple dwelling. Ben-Gurion (1886–1973), Israel's first prime minister, was one of the great statesmen of the 20th century, yet his small Negev home is commonly known as "the hut" because of its humble ambience. It's not really a hut but a one-story wooden home with a small kitchen, an eating corner with table and two chairs, and simple furniture throughout. Visitors such as Dag Hammarskjöld, secretary-general of the United Nations, drank tea with Ben-Gurion in the living room, with its miniature version of Michelangelo's *Moses* on a side table and a picture of Lincoln on the wall. Ben-Gurion's library shelves contain 5,000 books (20,000 more are in his Tel Aviv home)—in fact, most of the space in the "hut" is taken up by the Old Man's (as he was locally known) books. On Ben-Gurion's desk are the papers on which he copied out sentences from the Old Testament: "I will even make a way in the wilderness, and rivers in the desert. . . . I give waters in the wilderness, and rivers in the desert, to give drink to my people, my chosen" (Isaiah 43). His bedroom, with its single picture of Mahatma Gandhi, holds the iron cot on which he slept (only three hours a night) and his slippers on the floor beside it. The house is as he left it, with only a porch added to exhibit various memorabilia, such as gifts from world leaders.

When Ben-Gurion resigned (later to return) from government in 1953, he and his wife, Paula, moved to the isolated, brand-new **Kibbutz Sde Boker** to provide an example for others. "Neither money nor propaganda builds a country," he announced. "Only the man who lives and creates in the country can build it." This said, the George Washington of Israel—whose interests were history, philosophy, and politics, as the artifacts in his home indicate—took up his new role in the kibbutz fold. In February 1955 he once again became prime minister, spending holidays and weekends at the kibbutz, and when he retired in 1970, he returned to Sde Boker to live. (He returned to his Tel Aviv residence some months before his death in 1973.) ☎ 07/655–8444. ⌦ *Free.* ☉ *Sun.–Thurs. 8:30–3:30, Fri. and holiday eves 8:30–1, Sat. and holidays 9–2:30.*

Dining

$ ✕ **Sde Boker Inn.** At this cozy, under-the-trees eatery, kibbutz members dish up hot homemade food, plus salads and sandwiches, for breakfast and lunch. Boxed lunches can be made up for the road. In season, delicious Sde Boker fruits are on the menu and for sale: apricots in June, plums in July, peaches in August. Bags of kibbutz-grown pistachio nuts may also be purchased. ⌂ *Next door to Ben-Gurion's home,* ☎ *07/656–0379. No credit cards. Closed after 4 PM Sun.–Thurs. and after 3 PM Fri. and holiday eves.*

Ben-Gurion's Grave Site

❹ *3 km (2 mi) southwest of Ben-Gurion's home, to the right of the main gate to Sde Boker College.*

After a visit to Ben-Gurion's home, you can visit his grave site, just a short distance away. Walk through the beautiful garden until you reach the quiet, windswept plaza, in the center of which are the simple raised stone slabs marking the graves of David and Paula Ben-Gurion (she died five years before her husband). The couple's final resting place—selected by Ben-Gurion himself—overlooks Zin Valley's geological finery: a vast, undulating drape of velvety-looking stone in shades of cream, ivory, coffee, and soft brown that slowly changes in hue as the day goes on. The cluster of greenery and palm trees to the right on the valley floor indicates En Avdat (☞ *below*), or the spring of Avdat. It is an awe-inspiring sight.

Sde Boker College

The entrance to Sde Boker College is through the gate with the traffic arm, next to Ben-Gurion's grave site.

Ben-Gurion envisioned a place of learning in the desert, and this campus became part of Ben-Gurion University of the Negev, whose main campus is in Beersheva. Although there isn't much to see here, the **National Solar Energy Center,** where a research program investigates new ideas for the harnessing of solar energy, is interesting. Primarily, the college is a good place to eat and spend the night. In the middle of the campus, under a peaked roof, the **Center** has a restaurant, a supermarket open till 8 PM, a post office, and the field school of the SPNI (☎ 07/656–5828).

Dining and Lodging

$ ✕ **Zin Inn.** As hot a spot as you'll find in the middle of the desert, this is where everyone hangs out—desert studies researchers from overseas, soldiers from the nearby base, visiting schoolchildren from all over the country, and field-school guides. The usual desert restaurant fare is served: soup, schnitzel (breaded and fried chicken cutlets), french fries, salad, ice cream, coffee, and soft drinks. ⌧ *On the grounds of Sde Boker College,* ☎ *07/656–5811. No credit cards. Closed after 2 PM Fri. and all day Sat.*

$$ ☷ **Desert Research Institute Guest House.** If you'd like the Wilderness of Zin as your backyard, consider this guest house. A university-run facility for visiting scientists, the guest house sometimes has rooms available for tourists seeking the simple life. On a winding path (with superb views) at the edge of a beautiful canyon, it is in a quiet, rather remote location. Each room has two beds (for a family, three cots may be added) and is equipped with a heater/air-conditioner and an alcove housing a small refrigerator, electric kettle, and a few dishes. Towels are supplied. There is a small TV lounge and a communal kitchen for light cooking (you can stock up at the nearby supermarket or eat at the restaurant). There are no phones in the rooms, but there is a pay phone in the Center. ⌧ *Ben-Gurion University of the Negev, Sde Boker campus, 84990,* ☎ *07/656–5079,* ℻ *07/655–5058. 14 rooms with bath. No credit cards.*

$ ☷ **SPNI Field School Hostel.** A short walk from the Commercial Center, this hostel is a cut above. Made up of a series of octagon-shaped units, each has a large room with a skylight, two bunk beds, two beds, a small desk, and a private bathroom (bring your own towel). You can use the large kitchen to prepare meals, and there's always hot water in the urn for making coffee. ⌧ *Sde Boker campus,* ☎ *07/656–5828 or 07/656–5016,* ℻ *07/656–5721. No credit cards.*

En Avdat

☽ ❺ *3 km (2 mi) south of Ben-Gurion's grave site and Sde Boker College.*

En Avdat (the spring of Avdat) lies at the foot of the canyon that divides the plateau between the ancient Nabatean city of Avdat and Kibbutz Sde Boker, in **En Avdat National Park.** To get to the spring from Ben-Gurion's grave site, head down the curving road to a clump of palm trees, the site of the admission booth. Ask for the explanatory leaflet when you pay. Lock the car, taking valuables with you. Walk toward the thickets of rushes, and about five minutes later you will see on the left, against the white-chalk cliff, a lone, ancient atlantica pistachio tree, the first of many reminders of a time when there was more water, and thus vegetation, in the area. Look for ibex tracks on the ground, made with hoofs that enable these agile creatures to climb sheer rock faces. Try to spot these animals, which are barely discernible against the cliff's rocks; the ibex even have striped markings on their coats that resemble the different strata formed over the millennia. Rock pigeons, Egyptian vultures (black and white feathers, bright yellow beak, and long pinkish legs), and sooty falcons use the natural holes in the soft rock and in the cliff ledges for nesting.

The big surprise at En Avdat is the pool of icy-cold spring-fed water, complete with a splashing waterfall. To reach this cool oasis shaded by the surrounding cliffs, walk carefully along the right side of the bank of the spring, which starts out as a trickle and eventually gets wider, and across the dam toward the waterfall. Swimming or drinking the water is not allowed (you'll not be *sorely* tempted, though—the water is swarming with tadpoles), but relaxing and enjoying the sight and sound of cold water in the arid Negev certainly is. ✉ *En Avdat National Park,* ☏ *07/655–5684.* 🅿 *Parking: NIS 12 ($4).* ⌚ *Apr.–Sept., Sun.–Thurs. 8–5, Fri. and holiday eves 8–4; Oct.–Mar., Sun.–Thurs. 8–4, Fri. and holiday eves 8–3.*

En Route For an eagle's-eye view of the waterfall and spring below, turn off of Route 40 at the orange sign for En Avdat to get to the **En Avdat Observation Point.** Below, in all its beauty is the white canyon carved out by the Zin River, with the waterfall (most of the year) tumbling into the pool, surrounded by greenery. From the lookout, a path leads around the top of the cliff (be very careful, especially with children), enabling you to see the rope marks in the rock made by Bedouin pulling up water buckets over the years from a now long-dry waterfall. (For information on the hike from here to ancient Avdat, consult the SPNI field school at Sde Boker College campus, *above*).

Avdat

★ ❻ *About 20 km (12 mi) south of Ben-Gurion's desert home and grave site.*

The Nabatean city of Avdat looms on a hilltop. Here you can see the stronghold and urban ruins of three peoples who have left their mark all over the Negev: the Nabateans, the Romans, and the Byzantines.

The Nabateans were seminomadic pagans who came from northern Arabia in the 3rd century BC. Establishing prosperous caravan routes connecting the desert hinterland with the port city of Gaza on the Mediterranean coast, they soon rose to glory with a vast kingdom whose capital was Petra, the great city cut out of rock (in today's Jordan). Strongholds to protect the caravans, which carried gold, precious stones, and spices, were established along these routes, usually at distances a day's journey apart.

The name *Avdat* is the Hebrew version of Oboda (30 BC–9 BC), a deified king who may have been buried here. Another king at Avdat, Aretas, is mentioned in the New Testament. The prominent local dynasty intermarried with the family of Herod the Great. The Nabatean kingdom was abolished by the Romans in AD 106, when it became a Roman province. Most of the remains on the acropolis date from the 3rd, 4th, and 5th centuries—the Byzantine period, when the Nabateans adopted Christianity. The city was sacked by the Persians in AD 620 and was only rediscovered in the 20th century.

To get to the 12-acre acropolis, drive to the admission booth just behind the parking lot. Be sure to ask for the National Parks Authority's explanatory leaflet and map. Drive up the road (save your energy for walking at the site), taking the right turn at the sign for the **Roman burial cave.** Park and walk the 300 feet for a quick viewing. The 20 burial niches cut into the rock date from the 3rd century BC.

Back in your car, drive up a little farther to the **lookout point** at the restored **Roman-period building.** The cultivated fields that lie below were re-created in 1959 by Professor M. Even-Ari of Hebrew University, who wanted to see if the ancient Nabatean and Byzantine methods of conserving the meager rainfall (measured in millimeters) for desert farming would still work. The proof is in the cultivated crops and orchards before you. Run-off water was collected and utilized owing to a clever system of catchment areas, conduit walls, dams, and cisterns. Barren slopes around Nabatean sites all over the Negev were put to use in this way. Groups (with a minimum of 10 people) may call ahead to arrange a tour of the farm (☎ 07/656–5741 or 07/655–8462); a small fee is charged.

After a stop at the **visitor center,** and with the help of the excellent National Parks map from the admission booth, trace the presence of the area's inhabitants at sites such as a reconstructed three-story Roman-period tower (there are good views from the tower corner of the 4th-century AD fortress walls); the unique Nabatean pottery workshop, where you might just find some eggshell-thin shards; a winepress (indicating that grapes were grown here, a testament to the Nabatean genius for conserving water); cisterns; two Byzantine-era churches; and a large baptismal font (to accommodate the newly converted). From the area of the baptismal font you can walk down the steps on the eastern slope to see the 6th-century AD Byzantine dwellings, each consisting of a cave, possibly used as a wine cellar, with a stone house in front of it. At the bottom of the hill, north of the gas station, is a well-preserved Byzantine bathhouse. ⊠ *Rte. 40,* ☎ *07/655–0954.* 🖅 *NIS 10.50 ($3.50) for all sights.* ⊙ *Apr.–Sept., Sat.–Thurs. 8–5, Fri. and holiday eves 8–4; Oct.–Mar., Sat.–Thurs. 8–4, Fri. and holiday eves 8–4.*

Makhtesh Ramon and Mitzpe Ramon

❼ *21 km (12½ mi) south of Avdat, 80 km (50 mi) south of Beersheva.*

The Ramon Crater is Israel's most spectacular natural sight. It's an immense depression 40 km (25 mi) long, 10 km (6¼ mi) wide, and 1,320 feet deep. Since it is a phenomenon known only in this country (there are three others in the Negev), the Hebrew term *makhtesh* (meaning mortar, as in mortar and pestle) is now accepted usage. By definition, a makhtesh is an erosion valley walled with steep cliffs on all sides and drained by a single watercourse.

Mitzpe Ramon is a tiny town on the edge of the crater. The populace numbers 5,500 people, including recently arrived Russian immigrants and Black Hebrews, who came to Israel from the United States. In Mitzpe Ramon there is one hotel, one swimming pool, one small shopping area, no movie house, and the biggest show in the whole Negev—the gigantic crater. The town's raison d'être is the crater; the promenade winds along the edge, the outdoor Sculpture Garden sits on the rim, outdoor activities take place within its cliff walls, and the main road runs through it.

Bear in mind that the four-year-old Ramon Inn is the only hotel in town. If accommodations are unavailable and you are continuing south to Eilat, you will still get to see the Ramon Crater because Route 40 goes right through it. If you aren't going to be staying in Mitzpe Ramon, remember to allocate your time so that you won't be driving to Eilat after dark. There are no gas stations between Mitzpe Roman and Yotvata, a distance of more than 100 km (62 mi).

The impressive **visitor center,** at the very edge of the makhtesh, is built in the shape of an ammonite fossil (spiral-shaped sea creatures that lived here when everything was under water millions of years ago). The helpful staff are rangers with the Israel Nature Reserve Authority. Guided tours of the center are available if booked ahead.

As you stand behind the glass at the visitor center, you'll be peering down at a world formed millions of years ago. The wall cliffs are made of layer upon layer of different-colored rock beds containing fossils of shells (there was a sea here once), plants, and trees. The makhtesh floor is covered with nature's creations: heaps of black basalt formed by volcanic activity, the peaks of ancient volcanoes themselves, jagged chunks of quartzite, huge blocks of overturned rock, and beds of multicolored clays used by potters today.

For a clear understanding of the makhtesh phenomenon (and a world-class view of it), the center offers an explanatory audiovisual presentation; a large, walk-around model of the makhtesh; and wall-to-wall, backlighted transparencies of geological points of interest. On the way to the top-floor lookout, be sure to peruse the panels describing the makhtesh's geological makeup, ecology, vegetation, and settlement. ⊠ *On the main road in Mitzpe Ramon,* ☎ *07/658–8691 or 07/658–8620.* 🖅 *NIS 12 ($4).* ☉ *Sun.–Thurs. 9–4:30, Fri. 9–2:30, Sat. 9–4:30.*

You might like to take a walk (about 1 km/½ mi) along the **Albert Promenade,** which winds east to west along the edge of the crater from the visitor center to the camel-shape Mt. Gamal. This is not the time to run out of film—the view is overwhelming. If it's late afternoon, you may see ibex along the cliffs and raptors wheeling overhead. The promenade is fashioned from local stone, as is the huge sculpture by Israel Hadani, the back of which faces town and represents the crater's geological layers.

With the crater as a magnificent backdrop, the **Desert Sculpture Park** exhibits a far-flung collection of huge stone sculptures. The park took shape in 1962 with the work of a group of Israeli and foreign sculptors under the direction of Negev artist Ezra Orion. Their idea was to add to the natural stone "sculptures" with geometrical rock formations of similar design. The sculptors, each allocated a space on the cliff's edge, brought their chosen rocks and formed their desert works of art with minimal hand shaping. ⊠ *Turn off near gas station on main road at sign marked* MA'ALE NOAH.

For a look at just one of the geological phenomena of the Ramon Crater, drive to the **Carpentry.** A path goes up to a wooden walkway, built to protect nature's artwork from visitors' feet. Long ago the sandstone was probably hardened and slightly warmed by volcanic steam. The rocks split into prisms, either due to cooling joints or another unknown process. The formations look like wooden chips piled up in a carpentry shop and have a lustrous patina caused by a chemical reaction brought on by climatic conditions. ⊠ *Along Rte. 40, going south.*

Another of nature's workings is the **Ammonite Wall,** which is on the right as you drive through the crater. A sign indicates a distance of 5 km (3 mi), which applies to the marked hike in the crater (take water—for fit walkers only). The rock face contains hundreds of ammonite fossils. They look like ram's horns and are indeed named for the Egyptian god Ammon, who had the head of a ram.

Just outside town is the **Alpaca Farm,** with its hundreds of sweet-faced alpacas and llamas. Young and old get a kick out of feeding the animals, receiving the occasional spit in the face from these long-eyelashed, gentle-looking animals. Children can take an alpaca ride. ⊠ *Turn off the main road opposite the gas station,* ☎ *07/658–8047.* 🖅 *NIS 9 ($3).* ☉ *Daily 9–6; call about shorter hrs in winter.*

En Route As you drive through the Ramon Crater, you enter the area known as "the ancient rivers." Here the wadis of the Negev increase in size from their source in the Sinai and cut through the Negev on their way to the Arava Valley to the east. The sight of the Mountains of Edom on the horizon to the east is beautiful, especially in the late-afternoon light.

After the Tsichor Junction with Route 13 (which connects with the nearby north–south highway Route 90) you will see strata of limestone that have "folded" over the millennia. After the Ketura Junction (where Route 40 ends) there are breathtaking views (to the left of the road) of the Arava Valley, which marks the Israel-Jordan border and is part of the Great Syrian-African Rift, a geological fault line formed millions of years ago. From here, Route 90 leads straight to Eilat (52 km/33 mi). It is not advisable to take Route 12 to Eilat because most travelers will wind up this tour after a long day's drive and/or toward dark, when Route 90 is the better and safer road.

Dining and Lodging

$$ ✕ Tsukit. If you're lucky enough to get a window table at Tsukit (Little Cliff), you'll be sitting on the edge of the Ramon Crater and the scenery will outshine whatever's on your plate. You can choose self- or waiter service for standard fare of beef, chicken, schnitzel, pasta, hummus, and stuffed vegetables. ✉ *Beside Mitzpe Ramon Visitors Center,* ☎ *07/658–6079. Reservations not accepted. DC, MC, V. No dinner.*

$ ✕ Dates. Run by Desert Shade, a center for desert tours, this roadhouse restaurant features self-service vegetarian cooking. It's conveniently open seven days a week (though only between 11 and 4). Except for Saturday night, you can also enjoy light meals, beer, and music from 9 PM onward. You'll run into other desert wayfarers at Dates, since Desert Shade runs a tent facility for groups here. ✉ *At the entrance to Mitzpe Ramon,* ☎ *07/658–6208. Reservations not accepted. No credit cards.*

$ ✕ Misedet Hanna. A cheerful roadside diner atmosphere—dark red
★ chairs and tables and fluorescent lighting that casts its dubious spell— prevails in this gas station–restaurant opposite the Makhtesh Ramon Visitors Center. The owner, who knows everyone here and talks warmly to all of them at the same time, says the food comes from "mother's kitchen." She does a very fine job with the food and the prices: A hearty breakfast of vegetable salad, *havita* (a crisp, plain omelet), cheese, bread, jam, and coffee costs only NIS 15 ($5). Breakfast starts at 5:30 AM. Lunch offerings include soups, salads (a round tray with six small, fresh vegetable dishes), oven-broiled ribs, schnitzel, chicken, fish, spaghetti, rice, and fries. Soup, salad, and an entrée cost NIS 27 ($9). ✉ *Paz gas station,* ☎ *07/658–8158. Reservations not accepted. AE, DC, MC, V. No dinner Fri.–Sat; no lunch Sat.*

$$ ⊞ The Ramon Inn. No hardship is involved in staying at this desert hotel.
★ On the contrary, the Ramon Inn offers modern, comfortable accommodations right in the middle of the Negev's natural wonder. The four-story building (no elevator) is on the cliff of the Ramon Crater. Stay in a pastel-and-white-hued studio apartment for two or a two- or three-room apartment (suitable for four to six people), the latter equipped with kitchenettes. The lobby has an open fireplace around which there is live entertainment on chilly winter nights. The homey atmosphere extends to the dining room, where local food is served, along with homemade condiments made by town residents. Ask at the desk about Jeep or camel trips. ✉ *Mitzpe Ramon, Box 318, 80600,* ☎ *07/ 658–8822,* 𝖥𝖠𝖷 *07/658–8151. 96 rooms with bath. Lobby lounge, kitchenettes, shops, coin laundry.*

$$ ⊞ Sukkah in the Desert. Deep in the Negev, Rachel Bat Adam, Ph.D., has created an out-of-the-ordinary encampment of sukkahs, the portable dwellings lived in by the Children of Israel when they wandered in this very same desert. You arrive in the middle of nowhere, and there on the rocky hillside are six small, isolated dwellings, each made of stone with a palm-frond roof. There is a central sukkah where you can prepare your own meals and congregate. The place offers an appealing combination: the starkness and purity of the desert with some modern amenities. Each sukkah has a carpet on the earthen floor and a bed that is a mattress with cozy blankets. There is a gas hot plate for cooking, a solar-powered heater, and a clay water jar and copper bowls for ablutions. You use the great outdoors for anything else. ⊠ *On road to Alpaca Farm, 7 km (4½ mi) west of Mitzpe Ramon, Box 272, 80600, ☎ 07/658–6280. 6 units that each sleep 2, none with bath. No credit cards.*

$$ 🏨 **The Youth Hostel.** Famed in Israel for its high standards, and fairly luxurious as hostels go, this one has to be booked way in advance (June and September are busiest). Fine for families, the place is done in bright colors, with a plant-filled lobby and a cheerfully decorated dining room. Most rooms have three to four beds, but there are also four double rooms. The mattresses are firm, and each room has a bathroom. Food is inexpensive and plentiful (box lunches can be ordered; nonguests must reserve for dinner). Check-in time is 5 PM–9 PM; knock if you arrive after hours. ⊠ *Opposite the visitor center, 80600, ☎ 07/658–8443, FAX 07/658–8074. 164 beds and 4 double rooms with bath. Dining room, snack bar, dance club. No credit cards.*

Nightlife and the Arts

There are three options in Mitzpe Ramon: Gaze at the stars, get a beer at **Dates,** or have a drink in the lobby of the **Ramon Inn** (☞ Dining and Lodging, *above*).

Outdoor Activities and Sports

ADVENTURE TRIPS

If you want to include a **camel or Jeep trip** in your Negev heartland experience, the well-established desert tour company **Desert Shade** (bookings are made from Tel Aviv, ☎ 03/575–6885, FAX 03/613–0160) offers a variety of trips (☞ Guided Tours *in* Eilat and the Negev A to Z, *below*). Desert Shade also supplies **personal guides** for a day or longer, rents **mountain bikes** for NIS 36 ($12) a day, and takes people **rappelling** down the spectacular cliffs of the Ramon Canyon.

HIKING

The staff at the visitor center (☎ 07/658–8691) in Mitzpe Ramon will help you plan a short local hike, though the explanatory maps are in Hebrew (☞ Desert Precautions, *above*, for planning information). The **Society for the Protection of Nature in Israel** (☎ 03/638–8673 or 03/638–8677) often includes this area in its trips.

SWIMMING

For swimming, the only body of water in town (and for miles around) is the **municipal pool** (⊠ Near the shopping center, opposite the gas station, at the entrance to town, ☎ 07/995–7702). Call for hours and admission costs.

Shopping

The **Amonit Gallery** (⊙ Daily 9–5) at the visitor center has a varied and rather unusual selection: jewelry and batiks made by the owner, as well as water pipes, Bedouin drums, Armenian pottery, hats, T-shirts, and small, framed sketches of the area. Alpaca wool is light as a feather, downy soft, and warm as toast; and comes in natural shades of white, gray, and brown. It's available in skeins at the **Alpaca Farm** (☎ 07/658–8047) and at the Amonit Gallery.

BEERSHEVA TO EIN BOKEK

This area stretches east from Beersheva, known as the capital of the Negev, to the resort town of Ein Bokek, on the Dead Sea. In between are ancient Tel Arad and modern Arad. Between Beersheva and Arad

you'll encounter scenes that seem like they're right out of the Bible—
black tents, Bedouin shepherds with robes flying, and sheep and goats
bumbling along. And after several twists of the road from Arad, you'll
come to the shores of the Dead Sea, the lowest point on earth.

Museum of Bedouin Culture

 ❽ *95 km (57 mi) south of Tel Aviv, 24 km (14 mi) north of Beersheva.*

At the Museum of Bedouin Culture (at the Joe Alon Regional and Folklore Center), you can learn all about the Bedouin who populate the Negev.
An orange sign directs you to the center, named for the late Colonel Joe
Alon, a pilot who took a great interest in the area and its people. The
one-of-a-kind museum, housed in a circular tentlike building, affords an
authentic look at the rapidly changing lifestyle of the Bedouin using various tableaux containing life-size mannequins. Each grouping is by subject: spinning wool and weaving carpets, baking bread, the coffee
ceremony, wedding finery (among them a camel elaborately decorated
for the event and bearing nuptial gifts), working with animals, and toys
made from found objects such as pieces of wire and wood. The tools
and artifacts, most handmade and many already out of use in modern
Bedouin life, form an outstanding collection. The film about Bedouin
life in the Negev adds a nice touch. Admission includes a cup of thick
coffee at a Bedouin tent, where the sheikh performs the coffee ceremony
over an open fire. ⊠ *Rte. 325, off Rte. 40.,* ☎ *07/991–8597 or 07/991–
3322.* 🎫 *NIS 9 ($3).* ⊗ *Sun.–Thurs. 9–4, Fri. 9–2, Sat. 9–4.*

Beersheva

❾ *24 km (14 mi) south of Museum of Bedouin Culture, 113 km (70 mi)
southeast of Tel Aviv.*

Beersheva's emblem consists of a tamarisk tree, representing the biblical past, and a pipe through which water flows, symbolizing the
city's modern revival. It was here that the patriarch Abraham constructed
his well (*be'er* in Hebrew) and swore an oath (*shevua* in Hebrew) over
seven (*sheva* in Hebrew) ewes with the king of Gerar, who vowed to
prevent his men from seizing the well. And here Abraham planted a
grove of tamarisk trees. The Book of Genesis describes how other patriarchal figures lived in this area, wandering the hills with their flocks.
It is easy to envision these scenes today owing to the cloaked figures
of Bedouin shepherds with their sheep and goats in the surrounding
hillsides.

Just outside the city, Tel Beer Sheva (☞ *below*) is the site of the biblical Beersheva, and could easily be the site of Abraham's well. An expression from the Book of Judges, "from Dan to Beersheva," once set
the northern and southern boundaries of the Land of Israel; in biblical times, living farther south of the city meant living a true desert (nomadic) life.

Romans and Byzantines built garrisons in Beersheva, but later the city
was abandoned. In 1900 the Ottoman Turks, who had ruled Palestine
since 1517, rebuilt Beersheva as their district center (the present Old
City) for the Negev. They set aside an area for a Bedouin market, which
still takes place every Thursday (☞ Shopping, *below*). During World
War I, the British took Beersheva from the Turks after a difficult battle. During the War of Independence the town became an Egyptian base,
and in 1948 it was conquered by the Israelis.

Beersheva, known as the capital of the Negev, is now the fourth-largest
city in Israel, with its own university—named after David Ben-Gurion,

who envisaged a flourishing Negev—and a regional hospital that serves Bedouin shepherds, kibbutzniks, and everyone else from the region. Once called "the wild east," this desert city now boasts a symphony orchestra, a light opera company, and an excellent repertory theater. A largely blue-collar city, Beersheva is struggling to provide housing for thousands of recent immigrants, many from the former Soviet Union and Ethiopia.

The city is a central starting point for Negev travel, although it is not a big tourist attraction. Main roads branch out from here, and it's a departure point for local buses to the south as well. But most sights lie outside Beersheva, and there are only two hotels. You might, however, want stop here for a meal or to spend the night on your way to somewhere else.

Dining and Lodging

$$ ✕ **Bulgarit.** On the pedestrian mall in the Old City, Bulgarit (Bulgarian) has been in business for 45 years; the third generation is now at the helm. The owner sits with his cronies at a corner table under a fancy silver sconce and reels off the selections from his "international" menu: roasted lamb and grilled meats, oven-baked meat, baked fish, moussaka, vegetables stuffed with meat and rice, *gvetch* (an assortment of vegetables cooked together), and chocolate mousse. If you speak Bulgarian, stories of pioneer days come with the meal. If you don't, you'll still get friendly, efficient service. ⊠ *K.K. le Israel St.,* ☎ *07/623–8504. Reservations not accepted. DC, MC, V. Closed Fri.*

$$ ✕ **Ilie's.** Although it's not much to look at from the outside, this eatery does offer the novelty of choosing your own piece of meat and then watching it cook over the charcoal grill. The emphasis at Ilie's, in the Old City, is definitely on meat, with various cuts of steak topping the menu. The tasty lamb chops and the fresh fish (Beersheva's daily outdoor market is the source) are also fine choices. Seasonal fruit salad complements the main course. If you'd rather have a nonhealthy dessert, the baklava fits the bill. ⊠ *21 Herzl St.,* ☎ *07/627–8685. Reservations not accepted. AE, DC, MC, V. No dinner Fri. or lunch Sat.*

$$ ✕ **Pitput.** An ivy-hung oasis in a desert city, this light-menu dairy restaurant has the look of a European *confisserie,* with its ironwork tables and chairs and pink-flowered tablecloths. Only homemade food is served—you can count on good cakes. To start with, though, choose from omelets, spaghetti, vegetable pies, lasagna, soups, salads, cheese sandwiches made on seeded rolls called *begeles,* and artichokes with fried mushrooms. The watermelon with salty cheese and the homemade ice cream are good dessert alternatives. ⊠ *122 Herzl St.,* ☎ *07/623–7708. Reservations not accepted. AE, DC, V.*

$$ ▦ **Beersheva Hilton.** This new hotel is changing travel in the Negev by providing up-to-date lodgings in the city that's the gateway to the desert. The pink-tinged brown stone of the 15-story building reflects its desert surroundings; arched windows soften the square look of the city. It's just a few minutes' walk to the Municipal Theatre and restaurants. ⊠ *Henrietta Szold St. near City Hall, 84100,* ☎ *07/640–5444,* FAX *07/628–7722. 264 rooms with bath. 2 restaurants, lobby lounge, pool, health club.*

$$ ▦ **Desert Inn.** Established 30 years ago and run in a down-to-earth manner, this friendly, small-town hotel is on the edge of Beersheva (when asking directions, use the Hebrew name for the hotel: Neot Midbar), in a huge garden. The staff is composed largely of Russian immigrants. Renovations (which should have extended to the vaguely '60s decor) include a new sauna and hot tub. Families will enjoy the well-equipped children's play area and the recreational facilities. ⊠ *Sderot Tuviyahu,*

84100, ☎ *07/642–4922 or 07/641–2772,* ℻ *07/641–2772. 110 rooms with bath. 3 restaurants, piano bar, 3 pools, hot tub, sauna, tennis court, basketball, Ping-Pong, playground. AE, DC, MC, V.*

Nightlife and the Arts

Both the **Beersheva Sinfionetta** (☎ 07/623–1616) and the **Beersheva Music Conservatory's Chamber Orchestra** (☎ 07/627–6019) are well regarded. Once a year, in March or April, the **Light Opera Group of the Negev** presents two performances of Gilbert and Sullivan in Beersheva; contact the Tourist Information Office in Beersheva for details.

Beersheva's yuppies congregate for postprandial drinks and coffee at the **Othello** (☎ 07/623–2230), in the Beersheva Theater Building.

Shopping

The Negev is home to the Bedouin, but today's Bedouin women may not be too thrilled about staying home all day to weave and embroider. That's why you should have the eye of an eagle and the patience of a saint to search through the bundles and stacks of rather ordinary stuff at the **Bedouin market** to find articles made by Bedouin grandmothers. The Thursday-only market, which starts at daybreak and goes until early afternoon, is on the eastern side of the huge outdoor market site near the bridge; follow the signs at the intersection of HaNesiim and Tuviyahu streets. The best time to be there is 6 AM, an hour or so later in winter. For sale (if you can find them) are wonderful embroidered dresses, yokes and side panels from dresses, woven camel bags, rugs, earrings, bracelets, amulets, nose rings, copper ware, *finjans* (Bedouin coffee utensils), coin headbands (used as dowry gifts), beaded bags, decorative beads, and tassels. An inexpensive necklace of simple beads and cloves, used to ward off evil spirits, also makes a rewarding purchase.

The older the better is the rule of thumb here; only the old work is handmade. Always examine the stitchery on pieces of material in good condition. Be warned that prices are high for articles of good quality. Bargaining over prices is part of the Arab culture, but you need your wits about you to succeed—and a local to act as a gladiator wouldn't hurt, either! You should end up paying 20%–30% less than the original asking price. If you are planning to take photographs at the market, bear in mind that Bedouin men usually don't mind being snapped, but the women do.

Convenient and cool in summertime, Beersheva's modern mall, **Kanionit** (✉ At the intersection of HaNesiim Blvd. and Eilat St.), has an underground parking garage that leads to an entire floor of fast-food places and another floor—reached by a glass elevator—on which there is a drugstore and shops that sell Israeli-made American-style clothes and accessories (heavy on jeans and sunglasses).

En Route   On one of the roads that runs northeast from Beersheva to Arad (Route 40), you can see the large and impressive **Negev Brigade Memorial.** Designed and built by Israeli artist Danny Karavan, the monument's 15 symbolic parts and Hebrew text tell the story of the battle by the Palmach's Negev Brigade against the Egyptians after the birth of the State of Israel. The tower, representing a Negev settlement water tower, offers a great view of Beersheva and the surrounding area.

Kafriat Shoket is a kibbutz-run way station at the intersection of Route 31 and Route 60. Its large cafeteria serves hot food, sandwiches, salads, cakes, and drinks; especially recommended are the apple turnovers and raisin Danish pastries. Snack inside at the long wooden tables or outside under the tamarisk trees. You can also purchase bottled water at a minimarket on the premises. ✉ *Intersection of Rtes. 31 and 60,* ☎ *07/646–9421.* ☉ *Sun.–Thurs. 6 AM–11 PM, Fri. 6–6, Sat. 8 AM–11 PM.*

Continuing along Route 31 east toward Arad, Bedouin encampments can be spotted along the way. The slow transition from a nomadic lifestyle to a more rooted one is demonstrated by Bedouin village of **Kuseifa,** already more than a decade old.

Israel Air Force Museum

🐣 ⑩ *7 km (4¼ mi) west of Beersheva.*

For plane lovers, this is a field of dreams. The open-air Israel Air Force Museum (also known as Hatzerim, for the nearby kibbutz) is a gigantic concrete field with 90 airplanes parked in rows. The fighter, transport, and training (plus a few enemy) aircraft tell the story of Israel's aeronautic history, from the Messerschmitt, obtained in 1948 from Czechoslovakia and one of four such planes that helped halt the Egyptian advance in the War of Independence, to the *Kfir,* Israel's first fighter plane. The young air force personnel who staff the museum give a guided tour that takes about 2½ hours and includes a movie about this branch of the military. (The movie house is an air-conditioned Boeing 707 that was used in the 1977 rescue of Israeli passengers held hostage in a hijacked Air France plane forced to fly to Entebbe, Uganda.) Another attention-getting display is a shiny black Supermarine Spitfire, with a red lightning bolt on its side. It was flown by Ezer Weizmann, the IAF's first pilot, who became defense minister and is now president of Israel. Be sure to wear a hat to protect against the sun. ✉ *Rte. 233,* ☎ *07/990–6428 or 07/990–6314.* 🎟 *NIS 15 ($5).* ☉ *Sun.–Thurs. 8–5, Fri. 8–noon.*

Tel Beer Sheva

⑪ *2 km (1¼ mi) east of Beersheva.*

Tel Beer Sheva, biblical Beersheva, is an artificial *tel* (mound) created by nine successive settlements that were here between 3,500 BC to 600 BC. The tel is a recent addition to the National Parks Authority roster; ask for the excellent explanatory leaflet.

Climb to the site traditionally associated with the patriarch Abraham. This is the only planned Israelite city uncovered in its entirety. Most of the visible remains date from the 10th–7th centuries BC. It is thought that the city, a fine example of a circular layout typical of the Iron Age, was destroyed around 706 BC by Sennacherib of Assyria. In the northeast, outside the 3,000-year-old city gate, is a huge well. More than 6 feet in diameter, it apparently once reached groundwater 90 feet below (the well has not been completely excavated). This ancient well served the city from earliest times, and scholars speculate that it could be the Old Testament Abraham's Well (Genesis 21:22–32). The observation tower is rather ugly, but it affords some beautiful views. ✉ *Rte. 60,* ☎ *07/646–7286.* 🎟 *NIS 6 ($2).* ☉ *Apr.–Sept., Sun.–Thurs. 8–5, Fri. and holiday eves 8–3; Oct.–Mar., Sun.–Thurs. 8–4, Fri. and holiday eves 8–2.*

Shopping

At **Mazkarot Keidar** (✉ Rte. 25, ☎ 07/646–0520), in the complex at Tel Beer Sheva, Dalia Schen has on hand a carefully selected and high-quality supply of old Bedouin weavings, rugs, embroideries, artifacts, and jewelry plus pillow covers, notepaper, and key rings that incorporate pieces of old embroidery and coins. Although normal business hours are 10–4, she will try to stay open later if you call ahead.

Tel Arad

12 *38 km (23 mi) east of Beersheva, 8 km (5 mi) west of Arad.*

Coming from the west to Tel Arad, site of the biblical city, takes you through flat fields of the low shrub called rotem (white broom). Ask for the National Parks Authority pamphlet that explains the excavations at the 25-acre site and be sure to purchase (for NIS 3, or $1) the plan of the early Canaanite city of Arad, with its map, recommended walking tour, and diagrams of the typical Arad house.

Arad was first settled during the Chalcolithic period (4,000–3,500 BC) by seminomadic pastoralists who lived and traveled together, herding and farming; it was they who first developed bronze. There was continuous occupation of Arad until the end of the Early Bronze Age (3,500–3,200 BC), but the city that you see most clearly here is the Early Bronze Age II city (2,950–2,650 BC). Here you can walk around a walled urban community and enter the carefully reconstructed one-room **Arad Houses.**

After the Early Bronze Age II, Arad was abandoned and hidden beneath the light loessial soil for nearly 2,000 years, until the 10th century BC, when a **fortress**—one of many in the Negev (the first may have been built by Solomon)—was constructed on the highest part of the site. It's worth the trek up the somewhat steep path to the fortress. First appreciate the view while taking your leave of the Early Bronze Age. At the top, which affords quite a view, you leave the Early Bronze Age and step into the Iron Age (10th–6th centuries BC). The small square fortress served the area intermittently until Roman times. Most of the visible remains are biblical and date from the end of the First Temple period (935–586 BC). Note the small Israelite temple sanctuary with its two standing stones (these are replicas—the originals are in the Israel Museum, in Jerusalem) and sacrificial altar of unhewn stone. In the 7th century BC, the southern part of the Israelite kingdom of Judah reached as far as today's Eilat. Artifacts found at the tel can be seen at the visitor center in Arad (☞ *below*). ⊠ *Off Rte. 31, no phone (call Arad Museum and Visitors Center,* ☎ *07/995–4409).* 🎫 *NIS 6 ($2).* ☉ *Sun.–Thurs. 8–5 (until 4 in winter), Fri. and holiday eves 8–4 (until 3 in winter).*

Arad

13 *46 km (28½ mi) east of Beersheva, 8 km (5 mi) east of Tel Arad.*

The modern town of Arad was established in 1961 by urban pioneers. Arad's population of nearly 25,000 now includes immigrants from Russia and Ethiopia; writer Amos Oz is its most famous resident. Breathe deeply: The town sits 2,000 feet above sea level and is famous for its clean, dry air and mild climate. Arad has made a name for itself as a healthy place for asthma sufferers. Industrial waste and the planting of trees and bushes are under government control so that pollution and pollen are not introduced into the air. Arad is a popular base for excursions to sites in the Dead Sea area (☞ Guided Tours *under* Around Jerusalem A to Z *in* Chapter 3) and is the *only* way to reach the sound-and-light presentation in nearby Masada.

In the middle of town is the **Arad Museum and Visitors Center.** The center's helpful staff dispenses maps, brochures, and information on hikes in the area. Its innovative "Meet the Israeli" program arranges for travelers to have coffee and a chat with locals. To get a sense of the desert, how floods occur and their results, how animals adapt to a wilderness diet, and other Negev issues, see the 20-minute audiovisual presentation. The small museum displays the work of local artists as well as presenting the archaeological discoveries from Tel Arad. You can see replicas of the Arad letters (the originals are in the Israel Museum), 2,500-year-old inscribed potsherds in ancient Hebrew script, some written by the fortress commander Eliashiv, concerning provisions of flour and wine for the soldiers. One has the name Arad inscribed on it seven times. ⊠ *28 Ben Yair St.,* ☎ *07/995–4409.* 🎟 *NIS 12 ($4).* ⊙ *Sun.–Thurs. 9–5, Fri. and holiday eves 9–2, Sat. 9–5.*

Dining and Lodging

$$ ✕ **Pundak Paz.** On Route 31 beside the Delek gas station, at the entrance to Arad, this roadside eatery recently changed hands and has been completely renovated. Mr. Steiner, the original owner, who had served local faithfuls and travelers since 1965, used to say that "people come to visit this restaurant as though it's a historical site." The cook is the same but there is a new bar, and the wood paneling lends a country air. You can order soups, 12 different meat dishes, and a variety of fish. House specialties are *cholent* (meat and bean stew simmered overnight), served on winter Saturdays, and apple strudel, known far and wide. ⊠ *Rte. 31,* ☎ *07/995–3328. Reservations not accepted. AE, MC, V.*

$$$ 🏨 **Margoa.** Well known for its asthma-treatment clinic and two-day packages, the seven-story Margoa carries on a 26-year tradition of pleasing its guests. Room furnishings are simple and subdued in color; those on the south side have a desert view across to the mountains of Moab. The 48 newer rooms, on ground level around the garden, have roomy, modern bathrooms and are connected to the pool area by an open walkway. The terrace is particularly pleasant. The brand-new spa center (skin treatments and reflexology available) is on the top floor, providing a wide-angle desert view. ⊠ *Moab St., Box 20, 80700,* ☎ *07/995–1222,* 🖷 *07/995–7778. 146 rooms with bath. Lobby lounge, pool, hot tub, sauna, spa, nightclub. AE, MC, V.*

The Road to the Dead Sea

The 24-km (15-mi) steep descent to the Dead Sea on Route 31 has one sharp curve after another. The drama of the drive is enhanced by the stunning canyons and clefts that unfold on every side. Keep an eye out for the sign on the right indicating that you've reached sea level.

Two observation points soon appear on the left side of the road; you cannot cross to the first—**Metsad Zohar**—from your side of the road. The second—**Nahal Zohar**—looks down (to the left) on the light marl of the ancient dry riverbed of Zohar, the last vestige of an eons-old body of water that once covered this area. The Dead Sea lies directly east, with the Edom Mountains of Jordan on the other side. To the right—which is south—is Mt. Sodom. You can walk back to the left to Metsad Zohar to see the Roman-built Zohar fort.

You'll soon see the southern end of the Dead Sea, sectioned off into the huge evaporation pools of the Dead Sea Works, where potash and salts such as bromine and magnesium are extracted. It's common to see row after row of plastic "tunnels," which act as hothouses for fruit (often tomatoes and melons) that is sold to Europe in winter there.

When you reach the T-shape junction with Route 90 (the Zohar-Arad Junction), you are at *the bottom of the world*: 1,292 feet below sea level. Although the Dead Sea (☞ Dead Sea Region *in* Chapter 3) can be as deep as 1,320 feet, it's much shallower at the southern end—only about 6½ feet deep. This area is now an artificial basin that serves the resort at Ein Bokek and provides an abundance of minerals for local use and for export.

Dining

$$ ✕ **Grill Michel.** A prime example of gas station eateries in the Negev, Grill Michel is a minimally decorated (just a few posters) *Baghdad Cafe*–style diner. It's run by a desert-hardened but friendly proprietor, usually surrounded by regular customers and friends. These truck drivers, Dead Sea Works employees, and other locals come as much for the conversation and laughter as for the grub, which features simple grilled meats, french fries, hummus, fresh chopped-vegetable salads, and good, strong coffee. ⊠ *At the gas station, north of Rte. 31, 10 km (6¼ mi) from the observation points. No credit cards.*

Ein Bokek

🔢 *8 km (5 mi) north of the Zohar-Arad Junction on Rte. 90.*

The rather startling sight of a tall hotel in this bare landscape signals your arrival at the Ein Bokek spa resort. According to the Bible, it was along these shores that the Lord rained fire and brimstone on the people of Sodom and Gomorrah (Genesis 19:24) and then turned Lot's wife into a pillar of salt (Genesis 26). The hot, sulfur-smelling air hangs heavy, the odd cry of the indigenous grackle bird is heard, and there is often a haze over the Dead Sea. The temperature of the oily water, where you can float but cannot sink, is 30°C (88°F) in July, August, and September; it's at its coldest in February, when the temperature gets as low as 19°C (66°F).

The resort area of Ein Bokek hugs the shore. It's a collection of hotels and spas, all linked by a palm-fringed promenade. This scene might seem like a mirage in such a desolate landscape, but it isn't. There's the added advantage of being a 30-minute drive from Masada and 45 minutes from Ein Gedi. Interesting local sites, such as the nearby white marl **Flour Cave** (from which you emerge dusted with white powder) may be explored with a guide, by arrangement through your hotel concierge.

The legendary Dead Sea, whose rare physical properties attracted glitterati such as King Herod and Cleopatra, retains its attractions for the modern-day visitor. Its salt content (six times denser than that of the Mediterranean), its high content of special minerals (bromine, for example, which has a calming effect on the nervous system), and its thick, black mud are sought after for their curative and beautifying properties.

Ein Bokek, at the southern tip of the Dead Sea, is the locale of sulfur-rich hot springs that have a temperature of 31°C (88°F). This water is used in combination with Dead Sea water and mud to treat rheumatic problems—even tennis elbow or a sore back. The sun's rays (it's sunny 320 days a year) seem to work wonders on psoriasis and other skin problems. (So positive are the results that German and Austrian health plans cover treatments at Ein Bokek.) Harmful rays are filtered out through the haze that floats over the Dead Sea; this means you can tan more safely, too.

At the lowest point on earth, the spas sit in an area that looks much as it did when Lot's wife looked over her shoulder. But don't compare them to the Baden-Badens of Europe. They have no grand, Old World elegance, so you won't find any string quartets performing amid potted palms. In fact, the sight of people's bodies smeared all over with thick black mud is quite the antithesis. However, the spa facilities are clean and modern, and the natural resources at your disposal are not to be found anywhere else in the world.

OFF THE
BEATEN PATH

A short jaunt south of the hotel district takes you to the **Arubotayim Cave** (Cave of the Two Chimneys). An orange sign on the right directs you to the cave, which is just off the road. Once inside the opening in the mountain, it's a five-minute walk to two chimney-shaped areas. Sit in the second of the two, a three-story-high chamber, and look at the amazing shapes hanging above and around you—you are actually inside Mt. Sodom, a mountain made of salt. Over thousands of years, the salt has been washed away by local rainfall, forming eerily shaped underground tunnels and deep caves dripping with long, knobbed salt "icicles." Although most caves in the area must be visited with a guide's assistance, this one is completely accessible alone. ⊠ *2 km (1¼ mi) south of the Zohar-Arad Junction.*

Dining and Lodging

$$$ ✕ **Hordus.** In 36 BC, Herod the Great built Masada—where the Hordus sits today—just up the road from Ein Bokek. Not quite as awesome as its namesake or his creations, this sprawling cafeteria-style restaurant offers sandwiches, hot dishes, fresh fruit (including local dates), baklava, and beer, until 8 in the evening. There's a falafel stand outside. ⊠ *Opposite Galei Zohar Hotel, Rte. 90, Masada,* ☎ *07/658–4636. Reservations not accepted. DC, MC, V.*

$$$ ✕ **Kapulsky.** In the center of the hotel area, this airy, cafeteria-style restaurant with big windows is attached to a Ben & Jerry's. Though best known for their luscious cakes and good coffee, the dairy dishes are also very good. You can choose from fresh salads, blintzes, pizza, St. Peter's fish, and sandwiches, plus beer and wine. A plus for customers is the free changing rooms for bathers. ⊠ *Beside the Kanionit shopping center,* ☎ *07/658–4382. Reservations not accepted. AE, DC, MC. Open 8 AM–4 AM.*

$$$$ 🏨 **Carlton Galei Zohar.** Established in 1971, when the vision of spas in the desert was considered a mirage, this two-building hotel has a seven-story wing housing a state-of-the-art spa (guests pay a small fee for its use) and 100 rooms, each one equipped with a kitchenette. The spa offers medical and beauty treatments. ⊠ *M.P. Dead Sea 86930,* ☎ *07/658–4311, 07/658–4422,* 📠 *07/658–4503. 250 rooms with bath. Restaurant, bar, pool, sauna, exercise room, shops, nightclub, baby-sitting, travel services. AE, DC, MC, V.*

$$$$ 🏨 **Hyatt Regency Dead Sea Resort and Spa.** Opened in September 1996,
★ this supermodern 17-story white building is said to contain the largest spa in the region—14 rooms devoted to beauty, fitness, and recreation. Features include use of Dead Sea properties such as therapeutic mud and two Dead Sea water pools, one indoors and one outside. Among the hotel facilities are a medical center offering such services as sport medicine, postsurgery recovery, and alternative medical treatments. The Italian restaurant serves Mediterranean specialties and the Bazaar restaurant has Caribbean, European, Far Eastern, and Middle Eastern fare. ⊠ *M.P. Dead Sea 86980,* ☎ *07–659-1234,* 📠 *07659–1102. 600 rooms with bath. 2 restaurants, bar, tennis court, squash court. AE, DC, MC, V.*

$$$$ 🏨 **Nirvana Resort and Spa.** You enter this hotel through a gleaming and inviting marble lobby, where WELCOME appears in many languages on the main wall, and the area is illuminated with table lamps and discreet ceiling lights. The huge outdoor pool is shaped like a dolphin, and the private beach is part of the Nirvana's own lagoon. You can savor your morning coffee on the terrace of the dining room. The in-house spa facilities, such as sulfur pools and a saltwater pool, are at your disposal for a small fee. The Nirvana also offers a complete health and fitness program that includes antistress strategies and beauty

treatments with Ahava Dead Sea products. ✉ *M.P. Dead Sea 84960,* ☎ *07/658–4614,* FAX *07/658–4620. 207 rooms with bath. 3 restaurants, bar, pools, beauty salon, mineral baths, sauna, whirlpool bath, beach, shops, dance club, car rental. AE, DC, MC, V.*

$$$ 🏨 **Hod.** There's a lot of traffic in the lobby (visitors from Germany consider this hotel a home away from home), but the feeling at the eight-year-old Hod is one of homey comfort in a friendly atmosphere. Room decor is modern, with multicolored check bedspreads and lots of pale wood. A walkway leads to the hotel's private beach, where the typical pebbled shore of the Dead Sea has been covered over with fine sand. Spa facilities (including Dead Sea hot mud treatments) as well as the Stauffer diet and relaxation system are available. The dining room looks out at the water. ✉ *M.P. Dead Sea 86930,* ☎ *07/658–4644,* FAX *07/658–4606. 205 rooms with bath. Restaurant, pool, massage, sauna, exercise room, Ping-Pong, beach, dance club. AE, DC, MC, V.*

$$$ 🏨 **Radisson Moriah Plaza Dead Sea.** A venerable beachside member
★ of the Moriah chain, this hotel keeps up with the times by constantly refurbishing and maintaining its modern and well-equipped spa. (Week-long beauty and relaxation packages are available, as are rheumatic treatment weeks.) The always busy but cozy lobby overlooks the outdoor pool. Rooms, decorated in pastel colors, have balconies that has been thoughtfully walled for privacy and lovely views of the pool or the Dead Sea. ✉ *M.P. Dead Sea 86910,* ☎ *07/659–1591,* FAX *07/658–4238. 225 rooms with bath. 2 restaurants, piano bar, snack bar, 2 pools, beauty salon, massage, mineral baths, sauna, spa, whirlpool bath, tennis court, basketball, exercise room, health club, beach, shops. AE, DC, MC, V.*

Nightlife and the Arts

Kapulsky (✉ Beside the Kanionit shopping center, ☎ 07/658–4382) is the place to go at night because there *is* nowhere else.

Outdoor Activities and Sports

BEACHES

Although pebbles line much of the shore of the Dead Sea at Ein Bokek, the Tamar Local Council has beautified two public beaches by bringing in desert sand and planting palm trees. The beaches lie between the Nirvana and Moriah Plaza Dead Sea hotels and the cluster of hotels about 2 km (1¼ mi) north. These well-maintained sandy stretches are free to the public and are usually fairly crowded. Facilities include changing rooms, rest rooms, and chairs to rent, and there is a lifeguard on duty from mid-March through November. There is ample parking alongside the promenade. Although there are no food stands on the beaches, the two shopping areas in Ein Bokek house eateries, and there are two restaurants on the promenade: Kapulsky and Hordus (which has changing rooms for its customers). Floating in the Dead Sea is the only water sport activity at Ein Bokek.

SPAS

If you are at Ein Bokek just for the day, head to the state-of-the-art public spa at **Hammei Zohar** (✉ Near the Moriah Plaza Dead Sea Hotel, ☎ 07/658–4161). It's open Sunday through Friday 7 to 3 and Saturday 7 to 1:30; the sulfur pool costs NIS 36 ($12), the sulfur bath NIS 63 ($21), the mud treatment NIS 90 ($30), and the dry massage, for which reservations should be made, NIS 75 ($25). Or you may reserve a treatment at one of the following spa-hotels: the **Moriah Plaza Dead Sea** (☎ 07/658–4221), the **Nirvana** (☎ 07/658–4626), and the **Galei Zohar** (☎ 07/658–4311). Each of these spas, which are under medical supervision, has an indoor Dead Sea–water pool, sauna, and hot tub and offers a range of beauty and health treatments. Individual treatments cost about NIS 85 ($28.35) for a half-hour massage, NIS 48 ($16) for a sulfur bath, NIS 66 ($22) for mud treatment. Hotel guests pay a lower fee. Other facilities and amenities often include fitness rooms, private solariums, and cosmeticians. Certain hotels offer one- or two-week spa-vacation packages. The **Ein Bokek Hotel** makes use of the facilities of the Hammei Zohar Spa, with regular shuttle bus service between the spa and the hotel.

Shopping

Several companies manufacture excellent bath and beauty **Dead Sea products** made from mud, salts, and minerals; the actual mud is sold in squishy, leak-proof packages. Ahava, DSD, and Jericho are three popular brands whose products are for sale at Kapulsky and most hotel shops.

Danny's (✉ In the Kanionit shopping center, ☎ 07/658–4435) has a wide selection of gold, silver, diamond, and Eilat stone jewelry. There's a workshop on the premises. Hours are Sunday–Thursday 10–10 and Friday 9–3. There are branches of Danny's in the Moriah Gardens Dead Sea Hotel and the Moriah Plaza Dead Sea Hotel.

Arava Road

North–south from Ein Bokek to Eilat.

Arava Road (Route 90) traverses Arava Valley from Ein Bokek and to Eilat and parallels the Jordanian border, almost touching it at some points. You'll see the spiky red-brown mountains of Moab, in Jordan, to the east. There is no obvious military presence, but you may be sure it's here.

Arava Road follows an ancient route mentioned in biblical descriptions of the journeys of the Children of Israel. The Arava (meaning "valley") is part of the Syrian-African Rift, that great crack in the earth stretching from Turkey to East Africa, the result of an ancient shift of land masses. Along the road are several agricultural settlements; the extremely hot climate is ideal for growing fruit, flowers, and vegetables in all seasons.

You'll pass signs for Neot HaKikar and Ein Tamar. The date palms in these settlements receive water from underground springs rather than from irrigation. Also in the area are commercial fishponds that breed gray mullet, St. Peter's, and other varieties plus fish to stock aquariums. Neot HaKikar's perimeter fence practically touches the border with Jordan.

With the Edom Mountains rising in the east (to your left), the road continues along the southern Dead Sea Valley. You'll cross one of the largest dry riverbeds in the Negev, Nahal Zin. It's hard to believe the large valley to the right can fill with water during the winter months (mid-December to early April), causing flash floods dangerous to hikers and drivers (☞ Desert Precautions, *above*). The landscape is dotted with acacia, the tree used by the wandering Children of Israel to build the Ark of the Covenant, which held the tablets given to Moses at Mt. Sinai. Today the acacia is a source of food for grazing goats and camels. On your left at one point, you'll see an experimental farming station's greenhouses, used for research and development by local flower and vegetable growers.

An orange sign on the way points to the **Shezaf Nature Reserve**, where the **Shezaf Observation Point** looks out over the reddish orange sandstone hills to the south and the Edom Mountains in Jordan and the Arava Valley, to the east, roughly the Israel–Jordan border.

NEED A
BREAK?
About halfway between Ein Bokek and Eilat is **Kushi Rimon** (Kilometer 101). Named for Shimon Rimon, whose nickname is Kushi, and the legendary army unit in which he served, this is the quintessential Negev road stop: One with every possible facility available in the desert. The place is huge and has lots of palm trees; small, wooden, red-roof bungalows behind it on the hill; and large metal-and-wire sculptures. There are also peacocks and ducks wandering about, a cage that contains monkey, and another cage that houses a tiger (a quotation from Jeremiah is affixed to its home). Inside is a cafeteria with all manner of hot food, a bar stocked with every liquor imaginable, and a minimarket. You'll also find a game room with a billiards table, other games, and a TV. ⊠ *Km 101 on Arava Rd.,* ☎ *07/658–1609.* ⊘ *Daily 24 hrs except Yom Kippur.*

EILAT AND ENVIRONS

The Arava Plain comes to an abrupt end where it meets the Bay of Eilat, site of the country's southernmost town: the sun-drenched resort town of Eilat. The Gulf of Eilat gives way to the gulf of the Red Sea, which lies between the Sinai Mountains, to the west, and the mountains of Edom, in Jordan, to the east. The Jordanian port of Aqaba is directly across the bay—Eilat residents will eagerly point out the Jordanian royals' vacation villa and yacht—and to the southeast is Saudi Arabia. The Sinai Desert is just over the Israeli border with Egypt.

Most visitors fly into or whiz down to Eilat to take advantage of its beaches and tropical reefs for snorkeling or scuba diving. But if you have time, give yourself a chance to see the vast desert landscape to the north of Eilat. You will find cliffs, canyons, formations at the Timna Valley Park, and indigenous animals at the Hai Bar Nature Reserve. Both of these make good side trips from Eilat; be sure to also include a sunset stop at Mt. Yoash or Mitzpe Har Hizkiyahu.

Eilat

🕔 *307 km (190 mi) from Jerusalem, 356 km (221 mi) from Tel Aviv.*

Eilat's strategic location as a crossroad between Asia and Africa dictated its place in history. The area was one of the stops of the Children of Israel as they fled from Egypt into the Promised Land. (Today, it's the sister city of Los Angeles!) It was long thought that King Solomon's fleet was in the area between Aqaba and Eilat: "And King Solomon made a navy of ships in Ezion-geber, which is beside Eloth, on the shore of the Red Sea. . . ." Later, because of its position on a main trade and travel route, every major power conquered Eilat: the Romans, Byzantines, Arabs, Crusaders, Mamluks, Ottoman Turks, and lastly, the British, whose isolated police station (headquarters of their camel corps) was taken by the Israelis in March 1949. Called Umm Rash Rash, this was the first building in modern-day Eilat, a town founded in 1951 and developed as a port in 1956 after the Egyptian blockade of the Tiran Straits was lifted.

A legend says that after the Creation the angels were painting the earth. They got tired and spilled their paints: The blue became the waters of Eilat, and the other colors became its fish and the corals. Add to this rainbow Eilat's year-round good weather, its superb natural surroundings of sculptural red-orange mountains, and its location on the sparkling Red Sea—with its exotic underwater life, including coral reefs just offshore that attract divers from all over the world—and you have the ingredients for a first-rate resort.

For many visitors, Eilat's natural assets more than make up for undistinguished architecture and overdevelopment. For wherever you are in Eilat, an eastward gaze will present you with the dramatic sight of the granite mountain range of Edom, whose predominant shades of red intensify and fade with the light of day, culminating in a red-gold blaze of sunset over the Red Sea. The incongruous name for a body of water that's brilliantly turquoise along the shore is the result of a 17th-century typographical error by an English printer. In setting the type for an English translation of a Latin version of the Bible, he left out an *e,* and thus "Reed Sea" became "Red Sea." The name was easily accepted because of the sea's red appearance at sunset.

With an average rainfall of about 7½ inches and an average winter temperature of 21°C (70°F), Eilat is a haven from the cold winter up north. Eilat's high season is mid-October to April, although the city is also crowded during Jewish and Christian holidays. It's the hottest here in July and August; many travel agencies close their doors, and Jeep trips and hikes are curtailed. The burning summer heat is a dry heat, however, without any mugginess. The wind picks up in the late afternoon, when the beaches, hotel terraces, and outdoor cafés become crowded with loungers sitting and sipping and watching the Edom Mountains turn red and the Saudi Arabian hills go purple. Walking in Eilat in summer is pleasant in the early morning and the latter part of the day; save the indoor attractions, shopping, and siestas for midday, when the heat can be still and stifling.

Arava Road (Route 90) runs north–south through the town, with the airport bordering it on the east side. The section of Eilat called the North Beach includes the Promenade south to the Marina and the Lagoon, surrounded by many of the luxury hotels, restaurants, boutiques, the Marina, and the local TIO (in the Khan Center). The foothills of the Eilat Mountains, which rise west of Route 90, are the location of Eilat's residential area, as well as the Central Bus Station and what is known as the New Tourist Center (in the area between Arava Road and Yotam, with its many restaurants).

South of Eilat, Route 90 (at this point called Eilat-Taba Road) continues past the port and navy base to Coral Beach; then to Coral Reserve, Dolphin Reef, and the Coral World Underwater Observatory and Aquarium; and finally on to the Taba border crossing to the Sinai in Egypt. To get to the sites south of Eilat, take Bus 15 (in the hotel area; at the Central Bus Station, on HaTmarim Boulevard, Eilat's main street; or on Arava Road) or grab a taxi. Although the sites are close enough together that you can walk from one to the next, the inexpensive taxis are a good alternative when the afternoon sun is searing.

Start exploring Eilat with a walk along the **Promenade,** beginning at King Solomon's Hotel (from Route 90 heading south, turn left into Durban Road and bear right; the hotel is the first large white building), at the northern curve of the Lagoon, where yachts are anchored, various small craft are for hire, and ice cream is for sale at a convenient Ben & Jerry's stand. Benches along the way face the Lagoon. The 2½-km-long (1½-mi-long) Promenade winds past shops and then the **Dutch Bridge,** which opens to allow passage to tall-masted vessels. On the other side of the bridge is the **Marina,** where cruise boats of all types wait to sally forth on the Red Sea (☞ Guided Tours *in* Eilat and the Negev A to Z, *below*). Now you are on the shore, a succession of glitzy hotels and beaches filled with people reddening in the sun. The scene includes sophisticated strollers, the backpack crowd, artists who do quick portraits, and vendors selling earrings, all accompanied by the strains of strolling street musicians. Across the bay in Jordan, the dark reddish gray shapes of the Edom Mountains form a jagged skyline.

At the southern end of the Promenade, just before the intersection of Durban and Arava, is **Pninat Eilat** (the Pearl of Eilat), a terrace full of eateries, one after the other, under blue-and-white wooden latticework domes. Choose from places such as McDavid's (the Israeli version of you-know-what), Dr. Lek Ice Cream, and Kapulsky café. Locals turn out in force here on Saturday to enjoy their day off: drinking coffee, chatting, and watching the tourists go by.

16 Less than 1 km (½ mi) south of Eilat, the **Coral Reserve** is one of the finest such protected areas in the world. Close to the shoreline, its coral reef is 1¼ km (¾ mi) long and is zealously protected by the Nature Reserves Authority. Divers (☞ Outdoor Activities and Sports, *below*) will enjoy the especially beautiful Japanese Gardens. Masks, fins, and snorkels may be rented. You can also try snuba, a form of diving in which you breathe through tubes connected to tanks carried in a boat on the surface. Landlubbers can traverse the beach and go into the shallow water to see part of the reef. Be sure to wear water-resistant shoes to protect your feet from the rough seabed and spiny sea urchins. If you do have a brush with one, don't pull out the stingers (doing so may cause infection); they dissolve in a day or two. Hot showers and a snack bar are on the premises. ⊠ *Rte. 90 (Eilat-Taba Rd.)*, ☎ *07/637–6829.* ⊠ *NIS 15 ($5).* ☼ *Nov.–Mar., daily 9–5; Apr.–Oct., daily 9–6.*

17 **Dolphin Reef,** 1 km (½ mi) south of Eilat, was developed for the study of marine mammals, specifically dolphins, in their natural habitat (only a flexible net separates them from the open sea). Dolphin Reef affords you the novel experience of meeting face to face with bottle-nosed dolphins: You can actually swim, snorkel, or scuba dive with them or join in on their training. The guide who takes you out and introduces you to the friendly creatures is there to protect the dolphins from people, not the reverse. Training of the dolphins can be seen daily at 10, noon, 2, and 4. Facilities (☞ Outdoor Activities and Sports, *below*) include a dive center, snorkel equipment rental, and a photo shop with on-the-spot film and video developing (you can watch yourself minutes after frolicking with the dolphins). You can really unwind under the palm-frond umbrellas on the pretty beach or at the Reef Bar, a thatch-roofed pub/restaurant serving tasty seafood. Eilatis patronize the place on Friday afternoons to "welcome" Shabbat (☞ Nightlife and the Arts, *below*). You must reserve a specific time to swim or dive with the dolphins. ⊠ *Rte. 90 (Eilat-Taba Rd.)*, ☎ *07/637–1846.* ⊠ *NIS 24 ($8).* ☼ *Daily 9–5.*

18 The **Coral World Underwater Observatory and Aquarium,** one of the area's star attractions, is recognizable by the tall space-needle structure that floats offshore. One of the highlights of the complex is the onshore **Red Sea Reef** (the building with stones piled around it), a circular aquarium surrounded by a coral reef. The aquarium's 12 windows provide views of rare fish so magnificent and some in such Day-Glo colors that it's hard to believe they are real. The **Aquarium** offers a look at fish from other parts of the world. There's an unlighted room where phosphorescent fish and other sea creatures glow in the dark. Nearby are the stingray and sea-turtle pool (one turtle is 250 years old) and the shark pools.

The **Underwater Observatory** is reached by a 110-yard-long wooden bridge. You might notice a yellow submarine docked to the right; it submerges several times a day to give passengers a view of the coral reefs (☞ Guided Tours *in* Eilat and the Negev A to Z, *below*). Once inside the observatory, you'll find yourself in an attractive bar and restaurant in the round, with big picture windows for enjoying the lovely view. Head right down the spiral staircase—and into the sea. You are 15 feet below water, in a round glass-windowed room, looking out at a coral reef. Swimming in and out of the reef are thousands of exotic tropical fish in often breathtaking colors and shapes you might have believed only Walt Disney could have invented. The **Observatory Tower**—reached by elevator or stairs—is 70 feet above sea level (there's a café here), from which you can see Israel's neighboring countries. ⊠ *Rte. 90 (Eilat-Taba Rd.),* ☎ *07/637–6666.* 🖃 *NIS 49 ($16.50).* ☉ *Sat.–Thurs. 8:30–4:30, Fri. and holiday eves 8:30–3.*

NEED A BREAK?	Head north on Route 90, past the Coral Reserve, taking a left at the sign directing you to the **Ostrich Show Farm**; stay on the gravel road for 20 minutes. There are no longer any ostriches here, but you can have a down-home meal, choosing from salad, cheeses, soup, sandwiches, *malawah* (a flaky Yemenite pastry, usually served with tomato purée), *labane* (a sour goat's-milk product), hot dogs, hamburgers, and ice cream in the railway car that houses the restaurant. Saturday is reserved for *hamin*, a Sephardic Shabbat stew of beans, meat, potato, wheat kernels, garlic, and onions. ☎ *07/637-2405.* ☉ *Mon.–Sat. 9–6.*

Dining and Lodging

Eilat has some of the finest restaurants in the Negev, but fast food can also be found, on HaTmarim Blvd. between the Central Bus Station and Hativat HaNegev St. (falafel stands) and at the Pninat Eilat center on the North Beach Promenade (cafés and various eateries). Café society is a way of life in Eilat: Business deals are made over café *hafuch* (strong coffee with a frothy hot-milk topping); friends have been meeting for years at the same café; and people come to see and be seen. Light food, such as cheese toast (grilled cheese sandwiches) and salads, is served, as are rich cakes, ice cream, iced drinks, and various types of coffee.

$$$ ✕ **Au Bistrot.** In this informal town it's fun to sit at a white-napped
★ table, with a small lamp gleaming on your gold-rimmed plate. This bistro only serves dinner, but it will not disappoint. The extensive menu (a separate one for dessert) includes Emperor fillet with goose liver and morel sauce (the house specialty); frogs' legs in butter and wine; fresh shrimp in Grand Marnier sauce; and lamb chops with tomato and basil sauce. The Moroccan chef studied in Belgium and returns yearly to collect recipes and know-how. Top-of-the-line Israeli and French wines are available. ⊠ *3 Elot St.,* ☎ *07/637–4333. Reservations essential. AE, DC, MC, V.*

$$$ ✕ **Blue Fish.** A fixture of the Eilat dining scene for the past 30 years, the Blue Fish has recently moved to a more central location. The new premises aren't pretentious: wood-paneling below peach walls with a starfish here and there provides a simple background for green tablecloths and dark turquoise chairs. Charcoal-grilled fish and seafood are house specialties, but if you prefer meat, carefully prepared grilled steak is available. The crème caramel is a tasty, light dessert. The wine list is lengthy. ⊠ *Across from entrance to Moriah Hotel (not on the sea side),* ☎ *07/633–7450. Reservations essential. AE, DC, MC, V. No dinner Fri.*

$$$ ✕ **Eddie's Hideaway.** As the name implies, this restaurant is slightly
★ hard to find. But the way affable Eddie prepares food makes it easy to understand why his place receives such rave reviews, especially for the delicious steaks. Eddie's devotees also appreciate his shrimp and fish

dishes. Starters such as Buffalo chicken wings and pâté *maison* may be followed by steak Eilat (with mushrooms, mustard, cream, brandy) or Shanghai fish with hot soybean paste. For a finale, try lime divine or pecan pie. ✉ *68 Almogim St. (enter from Elot St.),* ☎ *07/637–1137. Reservations essential. AE, DC, MC, V. Dinner only.*

$$$ ✕ **El Gaucho.** Just north of Eilat—a five-minute taxi ride gets you here—this restaurant has a larger-than-life figure of an Argentine cowboy outside. It's a good clue to what you'll be eating—beef. The owners proudly explain that the meat is cut on the premises and seasoned with special herbs and spices. The steaks, cooked on a charcoal grill that occupies one side of the restaurant, are served on thick wooden plates. Consistent with this two-fisted approach to eating, drinks are served in 14-inch-high glasses. The empanadas are homemade, and the chorizo sausage is excellent. ✉ *Arava Rd. (Rte. 90) at entrance to Eilat,* ☎ *07/633–1549. Reservations essential. AE, DC, MC, V.*

$$$ ✕ **The Last Refuge.** Right beside a marina in Coral Beach, this fine seafood ★ and fish restaurant is held in high esteem by many Eilatis, who take their guests from "up north" to eat out here. It is a large restaurant (the narrow terrace next to the water is especially romantic), with dark wooden paneling and predictable nautical motifs. Presented with a flourish are just-caught Red Sea fish, such as arichola and drumfish; shrimp on skewers; calamari; creamed seafood served in a seashell; and fish, crab, or lobster soup. The salads are enormous. The staff is harried but professional and eager to please. ✉ *Rte. 90 near overhead bridge, Coral Beach,* ☎ *07/637–3627. Reservations essential. AE, DC, MC, V.*

$$$ ✕ **La Trattoria.** *Bella*—and good food, too. Against a calm background of cream-color walls, beige-and-white furnishings, sheer white curtains, and softly-played Italian music, enjoy the Israeli-born, Italian-trained chef's cooking. His specialties are spaghetti with baby zucchini and dill in butter sauce and ravioli, but he also makes good fried mozzarella, sautéed forest mushrooms, 10 kinds of pizza, 10 types of fish, and four house pastas with 15 different sauces. Wines include some Italians and some Galilees. ✉ *At the Radisson Moriah Plaza Hotel, North Beach,* ☎ *07/636–1111. Reservations essential. No lunch. AE, DC, MC.*

$$$ ✕ **Tandoori.** Indian cuisine of the first order is graciously presented in ★ a setting of embroidered wall hangings, authentic Indian wooden carvings, and brass table appointments. The food is prepared to order; while you wait, you can enjoy an Indian drink of yogurt, fruit, and saffron or one of the many cocktails on the menu. Specialties of the house are various succulent meats cooked in a tandoor (a charcoal-fired clay oven), curries, and a selection of vegetarian dishes. If you can't afford dinner here, try the moderately priced business lunch (NIS 38, or $12). Indian musicians and dancers perform at night. ✉ *King's Wharf at the Lagoon (below Lagoona Hotel),* ☎ *07/633–3879. Reservations essential. AE, DC, MC, V.*

$$ ✕ **Mai Tai.** This small and serene restaurant serves Thai food that is authentic; it's not just another place serving up "Israelized" Asian cuisine. Thai cooking is popular in Eilat, and Mai Tai is often singled out by selective diners. The fixed menu of soup, egg roll, main course, rice, tea, and dessert comes to a moderate NIS 40 ($13.35); there is an à la carte menu as well. The lamp shades made of Thai food baskets and rice-paper umbrellas are a nice touch. ✉ *Yotam St.,* ☎ *07/637–2517. Reservations essential. DC, MC, V. Closed 3:30 PM–6 PM.*

$$ ✕ **Misedet HaKerem.** Family-run for 20 years, this Yemenite restaurant, not far from the Central Bus Station, has a low corrugated ceiling, fluorescent lights, and walls plastered with family snapshots, groups of smiling men, and huge portraits of two sisters in traditional Yemenite wedding headdress (one of these beauties could well be your waitress). The food is tasty: thick, spongy Yemenite pita with *za'atar* baked inside, vegetable soup, hummus, and the house specialty, meat cooked on the grill (try the chicken livers and hearts). End your meal with the coffee with *hawaj* (a spice mixture); no desserts are served. ⊠ *HaTmarim St.,* ☎ *07/637–4577. No credit cards. No dinner Fri. or lunch Sat.*

$$ ✕ **Spring Onion.** Vegetarians, front and center! Here's the place to get
★ garden-fresh salads nicely dressed with interesting toppings, as well as carefully cooked fresh fish, vegetable quiches, blintzes, and surprisingly authentic pizzas. Also served is a selection of what's known as cheese toast in Israel: A grilled cheese sandwich with tuna, tomato, or egg. Portions are large, but if you have room left try the layer cakes and the cream cakes. Beer and wine are available. The two floors at Onion are always crowded (in summer it's open 24 hours a day), but there's plenty of outdoor seating. ⊠ *At Bridge House, near the bridge over the Marina,* ☎ *07/637–7434. AE, DC, MC.*

$$$$ ⊞ **Ambassador.** This spiffy hotel shares its grounds and facilities with
★ the Red Sea Sports Club Hotel, which caters to divers, so you'll find wet-suit clad divers making their way through the splashily decorated lobby. (Ambassador guests get a discount at the Dive Club.) The hotel's entrance, facing the Eilat Mountains, is up a palm-lined lane. Inside, the decor is ultramodern. A balcony leads to the rooms, which face the pool and the sea and have light blue carpeting, wood furniture, and sea green bedspreads. The coffee corner in every room has a small refrigerator, a coffeemaker, and cups. ⊠ *Rte. 90 (Eilat-Taba Rd.), 88000,* ☎ *07/638–2222,* ⊠ *07/638–2200. 170 rooms with bath. Restaurant, pool, sauna, dive shop, children's program. AE, DC, MC, V.*

$$$$ ⊞ **Club-In Villa Resort.** This resort is a two-level arrangement of con-
★ necting, self-contained "villas" set into the mountainside opposite the Coral Beach Reserve. Each unit has two bedrooms, a kitchenette with microwave oven (there's a minimarket on the premises), a balcony, and a living room with TV. Picking up on desert colors, rooms are beige with sky blue ceilings and cacti painted on some walls. Front units face the pool; those in the rear provide a mountain view. There is a dining room if you don't want to prepare your own meals. ⊠ *Rte. 90, Coral Beach, Box 1505, 88000,* ☎ *07/633–4555,* ⊠ *07/633–4519. 168 villa units with bath. Restaurant, bar, 2 pools (1 for children), tennis court, exercise room, shops, dance club, children's program, coin laundry. AE, DC, MC, V.*

$$$$ ⊞ **Dan Eilat.** The 14-floor U-shaped Dan, on the North Beach near the
★ Jordan border, is the newest hotel in the city. Designed by Israeli architect Adam Tihani, the decor is nothing short of stunning. The lobby has a water cascade, a huge aviary, a fishpond, a rock pool with iguanas, and creative Italian furniture such as bright red chairs on green roller-skate wheels. The larger than usual terra-cotta and blue rooms have blond furnishings and lack for nothing in the luxuries department. One special feature is the dresser mirror that can be adjusted to reflect the sea. The large, lush pool and beach area features a 20-meter pool for serious swimmers; there is also a children's pool, a play pool with waterfalls and a slide, and a shaded hot tub. One of the three restaurants serves Lebanese and Mediterranean food, another French. ⊠ *North Beach,* ☎ *07/636–2222, 07/636–2333 (in Tel Aviv,* ☎ *03/572–1430). 374 rooms with bath. 3 restaurants, bar, sauna, spa, Turkish bath, health club, squash, shops, video games, children's programs. AE, DC, MC, V.*

$$$$ ⊞ **King Solomon's Palace.** The entire royal court of the eponymous Solomon could have been accommodated at this hotel, a senior member of the Isrotel chain and one of the five members of the chain grouped around the Lagoon. It's huge and utilitarian and has an expansive lobby furnished in pastel wicker. The staff pays attention to your every need, and everything runs like clockwork. Floor-by-floor renovations are in progress; the health club has already been completely refurbished. The large dining room is divided into three small restaurants (Continental, Chinese, and Italian); for breakfast, there is a vast buffet with fresh-cooked pancakes and croissants. The palm-fringed pool overlooks the Lagoon. The garden terrace suites have their own hot tubs. ⊠ *The Promenade, North Beach 88000,* ☎ *07/633–4301,* ℻ *07/633–4189. 420 rooms with bath. 3 restaurants, piano bar, pool, hot tub, massage, sauna, 2 tennis courts, health club, shops, dance club. AE, DC, MC, V.*

$$$$ 🏨 **Neptune.** On the Promenade near the Marina, this airy, modern hotel possesses a rare elegance. The lobby, with its potted plants and large wicker chairs, is especially appealing. Rooms, overlooking the pool with views of the Marina or the sea, are decorated in blue, green, and rose, complemented by strikingly designed furniture. The area around the pool has flower beds, palm trees, and potted plants. Adjoining the hotel and fronting the beach is a secluded grassy area with thatched umbrellas and a small restaurant. ⊠ *The Promenade, North Beach, Box 259, 88000,* ☎ *07/636–9369,* ℻ *07/633–4389. 279 rooms with bath. 3 restaurants, snack bar, pool, beauty salon, hot tub, massage, exercise room, bookstore, shops, dance club, nightclub, children's program. AE, DC, MC, V.*

$$$$ 🏨 **Orchid.** This replica of a Thai village is perched amid greenery and palm trees on the craggy mountainside. Everything—from the teak furniture and ceiling beams to the decorative statuary—was brought from Thailand. Individual cottages are connected by steep, winding pathways; you can be driven around in a special vehicle to get from place to place. Each has one bedroom downstairs, a sleeping loft for two under the pointed roof, and a balcony. The restaurant, overlooking the pool, serves delicious Thai food. ⊠ *Eilat-Taba Rd. Box 994, 88000,* ☎ *07/ 636–0360,* ℻ *07/637–5323. 135 units with bath. Restaurant, piano bar, pub, pool, beach. AE, DC, MC, V.*

$$$$ 🏨 **Princess.** Geographically the last hotel in Israel (it's five minutes from
★ the Egyptian border), the Princess is also the last word in sumptuous accommodations. The lobby faces a two-story-high sheer rock cliff, which can be seen through a glass wall. The public spaces are done in a dazzling white with gold trim; rooms include theme suites, such as the Chinese Suite. A variety of dining venues, decorated to reflect the style of food, serve Creole, Japanese, Cantonese, and French cuisine. The pool area is a country club in itself, with squiggly shape pools connected by bridges. The spa offers the ultimate in body care, with mineral baths, treatments using Dead Sea salts and mud, and Beizem body cleansing done with eucalyptus twigs. A self-contained world, amenities also include a shuttle into town and an El Al office on the premises. ⊠ *Eilat-Taba Rd., Box 2323, 88000,* ☎ *07/636–5555,* ℻ *07/637–6333. 418 rooms with bath. 4 restaurants, piano bar, pub, 2 pools, beauty salon, spa, health club, shops, dance club. AE, DC, MC, V.*

$$$$ 🏨 **Radisson Moriah Plaza.** Near the Marina, on the Promenade fac-
★ ing the beach, this sophisticated six-floor hotel is very convenient. The eye-catching lobby has a slanted glass roof, huge potted ferns, and statues in niches along the wall that separates it from the dining room. Rooms are nicely designed with color-stained pieces complementing the blond wood furniture. Three pool areas ensure your relaxation and enjoyment. ⊠ *Promenade, Box 135, Eilat 88000,* ☎ *07/636–1111,* ℻ *07/633–4158. 330 rooms with bath. 3 restaurants, pub, 3 pools, beauty salon, health club, shops. AE, DC, MC, V.*

$$$$ 🏨 **Riviera Apartment Hotel.** An apartment hotel can have an institutional air about it, but not the Riviera. It has a lively atmosphere with a fresh white-and-turquoise color scheme to match. Units sleep two–six people and have fully equipped kitchenettes; many have living rooms;

the premium ones have a small garden and patio and are set back from the pool. You can get food from the minimarket or the dining room, where breakfast and lunch are served. Young children can be cared for at the nursery or entertained in the kiddie pool. The beach is 165 yards away and the myriad facilities of the Country Club (at the nearby Sport Hotel) are offered to Riviera guests at a reduced rate. ⊠ *North Beach, Box 1738,* ☎ *07/633–3944,* ℻ *07/633–3939. 172 units with bath. Dining room, snack bar, 2 pools, baby-sitting. AE, DC, MC, V.*

$$$$ ⊞ **Royal Beach.** Isrotel's latest addition to their collection of hotels in Eilat, Royal Beach is the "jewel in their crown." It's not glitzy (though there is a glass elevator), but the Royal holds its own because of some offbeat attractions, including an interesting collection of works by Israeli artists. Another appealing touch is the three lobbies, which means that you can escape the nightly entertainment for a quieter evening. Rooms are done in warm blue and rose; all have comfortable sofas and chairs and a coffee corner; two are set up for people with hearing impairments. The hotel is on the beach and has four swimming pools (one for kids). You have access to the neighboring Sport Hotel's facilities. ⊠ *North Beach,* ☎ *07/636–8888,* ℻ *636–8811. 363 rooms with bath. 5 restaurants, bar, pub, 4 pools, massage, whirlpool bath, sauna, children's program. AE, DC, MC, V.*

$$$ ⊞ **Holiday Inn Crowne Plaza.** You can depend on competence at this beautifully designed nine-floor Holiday Inn. The public areas are decorated in cool white and beige; the entrance features a glass-domed ceiling. Rooms, all with air-conditioning, have tasteful light wood furniture and coral, pink, and blue bedspreads. The whole fifth floor is designated for nonsmokers. ⊠ *On the Lagoon, North Beach 88101,* ☎ *07/636–7777,* ℻ *07/633–0821. 226 rooms with bath. Air-conditioning, pool, hot tub, health club, children's program. AE, DC, MC, V.*

$$$ ⊞ **Moon Valley.** A laid-back, friendly place, Moon Valley is perfect for families. Each pastel-color unit, all on one floor, sleeps three and has air-conditioning and TV. They are next to the pool and close to each other. Europeans form a large part of the clientele. ⊠ *North Beach, Box 1135, 88100,* ☎ *07/633–3888,* ℻ *07/633–4110. 182 rooms with bath. Piano bar, air-conditioning, pool. AE, DC, MC, V.*

$$$ ⊞ **Red Sea Sports Club Hotel.** Attention, divers! Billed as the first hotel
★ in Israel for divers and adventurers, this white three-story hostelry houses the Manta Club, a fully equipped diving center with five-star PADI training center, qualified diving instructors, air-conditioned classrooms, personal lockers, diving equipment for sale, rinsing pools, and sauna. Diving trips to the Sinai can be arranged. Rooms, each with a balcony, have modern furnishings and are decorated in sea colors of green and bright blue. Red Sea Hotel guests share all facilities with the Ambassador Hotel (☞ *above*). A fun-loving atmosphere prevails, with dancing at night in the courtyard under the stars. Ed's Photo Shop (☞ Outdoor Activities and Sports, *below*) is on the same grounds. This hotel is a good value for its price category. ⊠ *Eilat-Taba Rd., Box 390, 88000,* ☎ *07/638–2222,* ℻ *07/637–4083. 86 rooms with bath. Restaurant, cafeteria, bar, sauna, pool, dive shop. AE, DC, MC, V.*

$$$ ⊞ **Sport Hotel.** The name says it all! This Isrotel hotel is designed with sports enthusiasts in mind. The Sport offers a full range of facilities for the active guest (a small fee is charged for equipment rental). Facilities include tennis, squash, racquetball, and basketball courts; a fitness center with the latest equipment and trainer; and a sauna and hot tub. There are two lobbies: One offers standard nightly entertainment; the other, peace and quiet. Nothing jars in this hotel; the peach-and-aqua color scheme is carried throughout the halls and into the rooms. Those in the newer wing look out on the Gulf of Eilat. ⊞ *North Beach 88000,* ☎ *07/637–9141,* ℻ *07/633–2766. 327 rooms with bath. 2* *restaurants, bar, 2 pools, massage, sauna, hot tub, tennis court, bas-ketball, exercise room, racquetball, squash, shops, dance club, children's program. AE, DC, MC, V.*

$$$ ⊡ **Taba Hilton.** If you want to get away from the hubbub of Eilat, you'll
★ appreciate the isolation of the Taba Hilton, which is just over the Egyptian border in the Sinai, 11 km (7 mi) south of Eilat. The quality of service and the excellent cuisine (Italian and Middle Eastern food are served at the two restaurants) put the Taba on a par with Israel's top hotels. There is also a three-floor gambling casino. Most rooms have balconies overlooking the pool or the sea. The large, free-form saltwater pool has one drawback: no lifeguard. The hotel beach (also unguarded) has sunshades, a snack bar, a children's playground, and a dive center. ⊠ *Taba Beach, Egypt (mailing address: Box 892, Eilat 88107),* ☎ *02/763677; in Israel, 07/632–6222; in Egypt,* F̄AX *02/747044; in Israel,* F̄AX *07/632–6660. 326 rooms with bath. 5 restaurants, 3 bars, pool, 2 tennis courts, health club, beach, dive shop, boating, water-skiing, shops, nightclub, travel services. AE, DC, MC, V.*

$$ ⊡ **Reef.** This modest, stucco beachfront hotel appeals to those who seek a quieter spot away from the main cluster of hotels. Appealing, too, is the direct access to the beach from the wooden sundeck and pool area. Water sports (including a dive center) are but a splash away. The modernized rooms in the four-floor hotel have balconies facing the sea; some are at pool level. ⊠ *Eilat-Taba Rd., Box 3367, 88100,* ☎ *07/636–4444,* F̄AX *07/636–4488. 80 rooms with bath. Piano bar. AE, DC, MC, V.*

$ ⊡ **Eilat Youth Hostel & Guest House.** The word *hostel* takes on new
★ meaning here, where each room is air-conditioned and has its own bath-room. The rooms are simply furnished and sleep 2–6. A 10-minute walk from the Central Bus Station—and right across the highway from the beach at the Red Rock Hotel—the hostel is a popular place, so make reservations well ahead of time. Three meals a day are pro-vided in the renovated dining room; snacks are also available. Bed linen and towels are provided. ⊠ *HaArava Rd., Box 152, 88101,* ☎ *07/637–0088,* F̄AX *07/637–5835. 80 rooms with bath. Dining room, air-con-ditioning, dance club, coin laundry. AE, DC, MC, V.*

Nightlife and the Arts

For an overview of events in the area, pick up a copy of the detail-filled leaflet called "Events and Places of Interest," available at the Tourist Information Office. For the coming week's arts and entertainment in-formation, check out Friday's *Jerusalem Post,* which carries listings for the entire country.

BARS AND CLUBS

Most hotels in Eilat have a piano bar (you can dance at some of them) and, in many cases, a disco; all are open to the public. Pubs also abound, although not quite in the same form as those in Great Britain or elsewhere. In Israel, a pub is almost any place where people come to hang out and drink (even a restaurant or café during the day); at many you can even expect a decent meal.

Dolphin Reef (⊠ Eilat-Taba Rd., ☎ 07/637–1846) is a good example of a bar/pub/restaurant. Eilatis have a soft spot for **Teddy's** (⊠ Ophira Park, ☎ 07/637–3949), with its long wooden bar and restaurant. For traditionalists, the nautically decorated **Yacht Pub** (⊠ King's Wharf, ☎ 07/633–4111) is the real McCoy: It was literally transported from England.

King's (⊠ Eilat-Taba Rd., ☎ 07/636–5555), at the Princess Hotel, tops the disco bill—with mirrored walls, fluted columns, and a checkered dance floor. **Sheba's Disco** (⊠ Promenade, ☎ 07/633–4111), at the

King Solomon Hotel, has laser light shows. **Yekev** (⊠ In the Industrial Area, ☎ 07/633–4343), where the noise goes unnoticed, is the scene of Israeli music and dancing on the tables; take a taxi there. Other options for dancing are **beach parties,** where bronzed bodies rock to recorded music all night long; keep an eye out around town for English-language posters listing times and places for these events; admission is free.

For a nautical nightlife in Eilat, consider dining and dancing under moonlit Red Sea skies while bobbing in a boat. **Eilat Cruises** (⊠ At the Marina, ☎ 07/633–3351) runs evening trips with live music for NIS 66 ($22). **Red Sea Sports Club** (⊠ King's Wharf, ☎ 07/637–9685) operates night cruises as well.

CONCERTS

One of the biggest events of the year is the **Red Sea Jazz Festival,** considered part of the international jazz circuit. It's held during the last four days of August in the unusual outdoor setting of Eilat's port. The festival spills into hotel lobbies in jam sessions that continue until dawn. Past participants have included Kurt Elling, Toots Thielmans and Wayne Shorter. Information is available at the **Tourist Information Office** in Eilat or from Multi Media, in Tel Aviv (⊠ 20 Amzaleg St., Tel Aviv 65148, ☎ 03/528–8989). **Music by the Red Sea,** which features chamber music concerts and workshops, takes place from December through January. Consult the Tourist Information Office for more information. **Philip Murray Cultural Center** (⊠ HaTamarim Blvd., ☎ 07/637–2257) is a year-round venue for classical music concerts as well as art exhibitions and other cultural events.

FOLK EVENINGS

From October to mid-April, you can enjoy evenings of Israeli folk dance and entertainment every Saturday night at **Kibbutz Elot,** 5 km (3 mi) north of Eilat. Tickets for the folk evening (including transportation and a buffet dinner) are NIS 108 ($36) and may be bought at your hotel or through the **Municipal Tourist Office** (☎ 07/637–4233).

Also on Saturday, you can be a Bedouin for a night: Enjoy traditional desert hospitality at a festive dinner in a sheikh's tent and listen to stories under the stars. With pickup at your hotel, the price of this **Desert Shade** (☎ 07/633–5377) outing is NIS 102 ($34).

LOCAL HOSPITALITY

Another way to spend an evening (or an afternoon) is with an Israeli family at their home. This is an unusual aspect of sightseeing that visitors to Israel appreciate. To organize it, call the Tourist Information Office or Mrs. Morris (☎ 07/637–2344).

Outdoor Activities and Sports

In the interest of convenience, many of the activities listed below can be arranged through your hotel or a travel agency. Several tour operators maintain desks in hotel lobbies where bookings can be made.

BEACHES

The beachfront of Eilat—the North Beach and the South Beach—is unusual in that none of it is private; rather, the municipality grants licenses to individuals to run certain sections. In turn, the beach managers must ensure the cleanliness of their section and provide open-air showers and deck chairs. The Tourist Patrol makes sure that standards are maintained and also can be called on for assistance. Most of the beaches are free and have a clublike atmosphere, with thatched-roof restaurant/pubs, beach chairs, contemporary music, and dancing, day and night. The beach at the Neptune Hotel is particularly pleasant. Although topless bathing is against the law, you'll often find European women going topless, mostly on the southern beaches.

Young people tend to hang out at the southernmost beaches, although families favor North Beach, which runs northeast from the intersection of Durban and Arava streets to the Royal Beach Hotel. North Beach is always full of action—you can go paragliding or rent paddle boats or a "banana" (a plastic boat towed by a motor boat); dancing goes on in the pubs until the wee hours. Sleeping on the beach is permitted (in sleeping bags, not tents). The southern beaches (south of the port, along the Eilat-Taba Road) share the coast with the Underwater Observatory, Dolphin Reef, and the Coral Reserve. The beach just south of the Red Rock Hotel (at Yotam and Arava Streets) has water-sports equipment for rent.

BIKING

Mountain bikes are available from **Red Sea Sports** (⊠ King's Wharf, ☎ 07/637–9685; Coral Beach ☎ 07/637–6569), where the staff will help you plan a route to places such as the bird-watching area or the Dolphin Reef.

BIRD-WATCHING

The **International Birdwatching Center** (⊠ Opposite the Central Bus Station, ☎ 07/637–4276; ⏲ Daily 9–1 and 5–7) conducts daily demonstrations during the migrating seasons at the Ringing Station, about a 20-minute walk from most hotels. It also organizes Jeep bird-watching tours (☞ Guided Tours *in* Eilat and the Negev A to Z, *below*).

BOATING

Boat rental and water-sports facilities are found either at the city's Marina or at Coral Beach, the area south of the port on the Eilat-Taba Road (Route 90). The **Red Sea Sports Club** (☎ 07/633–3771), in Eilat at King's Wharf on the Lagoon, rents paddleboats, canoes, and minispeedboats. You can also charter a 115-horsepower speedboat piloted by a water-ski instructor.

DEEP-SEA FISHING

The **Red Sea Sports Club** (⊠ King's Wharf, ☎ 07/637–9685) takes six people out for six hours aboard a chartered motor yacht. The price for catching, say, a tuna or the rare barracuda is NIS 1,140 ($380) for six people, including lunch and the use of fishing gear; each additional person pays NIS 36 ($12).

HEALTH CLUBS

The state-of-the-art fitness center at the **Sport Hotel's Country Club** (⊠ North Beach, ☎ 07/633–3333) is open to the public for NIS 21 ($7); use of both the sauna and hot tub costs an additional NIS 15 ($5).

HORSEBACK RIDING

Texas Ranch (⊠ Rte. 90, ☎ 07/637–6663 or 07/637–8638), in Coral Beach, takes riders on trails through Nahal Shlomo (Solomon's River) and into the desert; the sunset rides are particularly popular. The charge is about NIS 90 ($30); call ahead to reserve a horse. Children over 11 who know how to ride are welcome on the trails, and younger children may ride in the ring for NIS 30 ($10) a half hour.

PARASAILING

Red Sea Sports Club (⊠ King's Wharf, ☎ 07/637–9685) will give you a bird's-eye view of all those beach loafers for NIS 84 ($28) per 10 minutes.

RAPPELLING

Jeep See (⌑ Bridge House, near the Marina, ☎ 07/633–0133, FAX 07/ 633–0134) takes both novices and more experienced rappellers on trips. Call in advance to book; the trips are done only in groups.

SCOOTERS

See the sights on a Piaggio scooter, available from **Doobie** (⌑ North Beach, ☎ 07/633–6557), at the Dan Eilat hotel. Depending on the type of scooter, the price for half a day is NIS 42 ($14) to NIS 66 ($33). Double the sum for a whole day's scooting.

SCUBA DIVING AND SNORKELING

Excellent facilities can be found at the Marina in North Beach and at Coral Beach. Introductory dives for the whole family, diving courses, instruction, and night dives are offered. Equipment can be rented or purchased.

Aqua Sport International Red Sea Diving Center Ltd. (⌑ Coral Beach, ☎ 07/633–4404, FAX 07/633–3771) was the first diving center established in the Middle East. Aqua Sport offers one-day dive cruises with lunch (NIS 92, or $30.70 per person) plus weekly diving safaris that run from one to five days. You'll take a Jeep to explore the most exotic dive locations, such as the famous Blue Hole and Ras-Nasrani at Sharm-el-Sheikh in the Sinai. **Lucky Divers** (⌑ Promenade, ☎ 07/633–5990), at the Galei Eilat Hotel, operates a top-quality, full-service dive center. **Manta Diving Club** (⌑ Eilat-Taba Rd., Coral Beach, ☎ 07/637–6569), at the Red Sea Sports Club Hotel, is also an excellent dive center.

Coral Reserve (⌑ Eilat-Taba Rd., Coral Beach, ☎ 07/637–6829), open daily 8–5, is a great place to observe the fabulous fish and corals. Qualified divers, in limited numbers, can dive in a special area called the Japanese Gardens, so named for the way in which the closely packed, multicolored corals overlap each other. Call ahead to reserve a time slot. You can't rent diving equipment here, but wet suits and snorkeling equipment are available. Masks rent for NIS 6 ($2), snorkels for NIS 6 ($2), and fins for NIS 7 ($2.30). Admission to the Coral Reserve is NIS 12 ($4). Be sure to wear protective footgear. Hot showers, lockers, and a small restaurant are on the premises.

Families (children must be over 10) will have fun snuba diving at the **Caves Beach,** south of the Underwater Observatory. For information call 07/637–2722. In this cross between snorkeling and diving you breathe through tubes connected to tanks carried in a rubber boat on the surface. Instruction, a shallow-water practice session, and a guided underwater tour (a depth of up to 20 feet can be reached) may be arranged by calling ahead; the price is NIS 120 ($40) per person.

For certified divers who want to learn underwater photography, **Ed's Photo Shop** (⌑ Coral Beach, ☎ 07/637–6852), in the Ambassador Hotel, offers a two-day underwater familiarization program for the novice (NIS 750, or $250). Also offered are a three-day program (NIS 1,275, or $425) and a five-day advanced program, including two days along the Sinai coast at some of the world's best photography sites (NIS 2,550, or $850). Prices cover instruction only. Divers may rent cameras, and film is processed on-site, so you can see the results of one dive before you do another.

At **Dolphin Reef** (⌑ Eilat-Taba Rd., Coral Beach, ☎ 07/637–5935) you can dive with dolphins, using snorkel equipment (NIS 150, or $50 for a half hour) and preserve the experience on video for posterity (for an extra charge). It's a dive center as well. Be sure to call ahead for a reservation.

SPAS

The **Princess Hotel** (☎ 07/637–0195), the **Royal Beach Hotel** (☎ 07/636–8860), and the **Dan Eilat** (☎ 07/636–2222) all have state-of-the-art spas.

SWIMMING

Most hotels have outdoor pools, but you can also go to the **public pool** (⊠ Hativat HaNegev St., ☎ 07/633–2662). Call for hours and admission price.

TENNIS AND SQUASH

Floodlit tennis courts can be found at most hotels. At the **Sport Hotel's Country Club** (⊠ North Beach, ☎ 07/633–3333) tennis courts are available in the morning for the hourly rate of NIS 21 ($7) and in the evening for NIS 24 ($8); the price includes racquet and balls. Squash courts go for NIS 15 ($5) an hour; racquet rental is NIS 5. Book ahead to play at the **municipal courts** (⊠ Yotam St., ☎ 07/636–7235); a small fee is charged, and they're closed on Saturday.

WINDSURFING AND WATERSKIING

At the **Red Sea Sports Club** (⊠ King's Wharf, ☎ 07/637–9685) water-skiers can rent equipment and boats for a cost of NIS 45 ($15) for 10 minutes and NIS 5.10 ($1.70) for each extra minute. Windsurfing and equipment rentals, plus lessons, are also available at **Aqua Sport International Red Sea Diving Center Ltd.** (⊠ Coral Beach, ☎ 07/633–4404); one hour on the Windsurfer costs NIS 30 ($10). In addition, windsurfing requirements can be rented from **Mistral** (⊠ Coral Beach, ☎ 07/637–6416), at the Reef Hotel.

Shopping

Eilat is a tax-free zone, meaning all items are exempt from VAT and/or purchase tax. Articles such as bathing suits and jewelry sold in chain stores are less expensive in the Eilat branch. Items that are price controlled, such as gas, beer, cigarettes, and alcohol, are also cheaper.

The two shopping malls, **Kanion Adom** and **Shalom Plaza** (⊠ HaTamarim Blvd.), connected by a café-filled passage, sell similar merchandise. You'll find camera shops and music stores, but souvenir and gift shops are notably absent.

Le Drugstore (⊠ North Beach Promenade, ☎ 07/636–6667) and **Boutique Carnaval** (⊠ North Beach Promenade, ☎ 07/633–4111) are large stores housing mini-boutiques with everything from clothes to locally made gifts to baby clothes and newspapers. The WIZO counter in Boutique Carnaval sells modern and traditional handicrafts and religious articles.

Custom-made wet suits can be ordered from **Frog** (⊠ New Industrial Zone, ☎ 07/637–7465), where they do repairs and sell accessories as well.

Israel has a good international reputation for creative jewelry making, and though the Negev is not a center for this particular craft, certain shops in Eilat carry good examples of what Israel's jewelers are producing, most of it contemporary style. Diamonds—stones cut and polished in Israel are an important export item—are used imaginatively. Malachite, the indigenous "Eilat stone," in shades of turquoise blue streaked with various shades of green (and mined near Eilat in ancient times) is also a good choice. At the entrance to town and near each other are two good outlets for diamonds, gold, pearls, and Eilat stone jewelry: **Cadurit** (⊠ Eilat-Taba Rd., ☎ 07/637–8551) and **Eilat Stone Mines** (⊠ Eilat-Taba Rd., ☎ 07/633–6363). Both companies will pick you up from your hotel and are open daily.

Bijouterie Maccabi (⊠ At the end of the passage between Kanion Adom and Shalom Plaza, ☎ 07/637–2519) has a good selection of gold and costume jewelry. It's open Sunday–Thursday 9–9 and Friday 9–2. Also in Eilat, **Jerusalem of Gold** (⊠ King's Wharf) and **H. Stern** (☎ 07/637–1706 or 07/637–2898), in the King Solomon, Neptune, and Sport hotels, and the Khan Tourist Center, are tried-and-true firms where customers can count on top quality. **Malkit** (⊠ In the HaDekel neighborhood, ☎ 07/637–3372), which houses a workshop where indigenous Eilat stones are cut and polished and featured in a whole line of jewelry designed in-house, is another well-known store. It is open Sunday–Thursday 8–7, Friday 8–1.

Hai Bar Nature Reserve

⑲ *35 km (21½ mi) north of Eilat on Rte. 90. You will see the sign for Hai Bar and Predator Center, opposite the entrance to Kibbutz Samar. Drive in for 1½ km (1 mi) to the entrance. Excellent 1½-hour guided tours depart from here on the hr, every day.*

The Hai Bar Nature Reserve (wildlife preserve) can be seen on a day trip from Eilat and may be combined with a visit to the Timna Valley Park (☞ *below*) and a refreshing stop at the Ye'elim pool (☞ *below*). If you decide to do this, see Hai Bar in the morning, when the animals are most active. Timna Valley Park is especially beguiling at sunset. In very hot weather, plan on visiting one of the two sites early in the morning, spending the midday hours at the Ye'elim pool. If you are traveling north and not returning to Eilat, you may want to visit Timna Valley Park first and then Hai Bar, with a stop at Ye'elim pool.

The Nature Reserve consists of both a large natural habitat for biblical-era animals and birds and the Predator Center. The wildlife reserve was created not only as a refuge for animals that were almost extinct in the region but also as a breeding place; the animals are then set free to repopulate other parts of the Negev. Opened to the public in 1977, the 12-square-kilometer (4½-square-mile) area re-creates the ancient savanna landscape, with lots of acacia trees. Roaming around are the striped-legged wild ass, onagers (another species of wild ass), addaxes, gazelles and ibex, and white oryx. Ostriches come prancing over, ready to stick their heads into the van windows.

The 20-square-kilometer (7¾-square-mile) **Predator Center** is where local birds and beasts of prey are raised and displayed. An audiovisual presentation introduces both history and wildlife. You observe the animals without disturbing them because the glass you stand behind is one-way and soundproof. As you watch the hyena feed, notice that his front legs are stronger than his rear legs, enabling him to carry his heavy prey a long distance. (The meat fed to the center's animals comes from hit-and-run animal victims and sometimes animals that die of old age in local kibbutzim.) The birds of prey hang out in gigantic cages, where you'll see, among other species, the only lappet-faced vultures left in Israel, with average wingspans of about 10 feet. Hopes are high for some offspring from the resident couple. ⊠ *Rte. 90, 35 km (21½ mi) north of Eilat,* ☎ *07/637–3057.* 🎟 *Including tour: NIS 21 ($7); admission to Predator Center only: NIS 12 ($4).* ☉ *Daily, 8:30–3.*

NEED A
BREAK?
The **Ye'elim Restaurant, Swimming Pool, and Water Slide,** on Route 90, is a good place to stop for lunch and cool off. The large, spic-and-span cafeteria-style restaurant serves hot meals (a variety of meats, rice, and vegetables), plus soup and salad plates. The palm tree–lined pool area (with changing rooms and showers but no lockers) has children's play equipment and a water slide; poolside service for light meals may be ar-

ranged. (At press time, entrance to the pool was occasionally free if you ordered a full meal at the restaurant.) Also on the premises is a rooftop coffee shop with a terrace that offers a great view of the region. ⌧ *Rte. 90,* ☎ *07/637—3086.* ⌧ *Pool: NIS 12 ($4).* ☉ *Restaurant: daily 7 AM–9 AM, 11 AM–4 PM, 7 PM–8:30 PM; pool: daily 10–7.*

Timna Valley Park

★ ⑳   *From the Hai Bar Nature Reserve, get back on Rte. 90 traveling south in the direction of Eilat. Take a right 15 km (9 mi) down the road at a sign for Timna Park and Timna Lake. A 3-km (2-mi) access road (which passes Kibbutz Elifaz) brings you to the entrance booth of Timna Valley Park.*

At the entrance to Timna Valley Park, ask for a map and explanatory pamphlet. A small building just inside offers a video detailing humanity's 6,000-year-old relationship with the Timna area and with its precious copper ore, mined well before Solomon's time by the Egyptians; wall panels explain its fascinating geological makeup. There may be a map available to take with you or consult the posted wall map, which marks trails for experienced hikers (the hikes are from three to seven hours long and are best done in winter). Watch out for old mine shafts, take lots of water, and let the person at the gate know you are going and approximately when you'll be back. Because of the size of the park (60 square kilometers or 23 square miles), it is recommended that you drive from site to site, each of which you will be able to explore on foot (many of the sites are several kilometers apart).

You'll find a spectacular collection of cliffs, canyons, and rock formations surrounded by the Timna Mountains, whose highest peak is 2,550 feet. Millions of years of erosion have sculpted shapes of amazing beauty, such as the red-hued **Solomon's Pillars** (created by nature *not* by the biblical king). Another unusual geological feature is the 20-foot-high, freestanding **Mushroom.**

People also left their mark on Timna. You can see an ancient smelting camp, with living quarters for the copper miners. Near the Pillars are the remains of a small **temple** built by Egyptians who worked the mines 3,400 years ago during the Egyptian New Kingdom, which was also the time of Moses. The temple was dedicated to the cow-eared goddess Hathor. Archaeologists discovered in the temple a snake made of copper (*nehushtan* in Hebrew). According to Numbers 21:4–9, Moses made a serpent in the wilderness to heal people suffering from snake bite (the snake remains a symbol of healing to this day). The snake at Timna bears a resemblance to a votive copper snake—made by the people who followed the Egyptians in this area, the Midianites (Moses' father, Jethro, was a Midianite), which is now in the collection of the Eretz Israel Museum, in Tel Aviv (☞ Northern Tel Aviv *in* Chapter 4). Near the temple a path and stairway lead up to the observation platform overlooking the valley. Above the platform is a rock-cut inscription; with the aid of a sighting tube you can zero in on the hieroglyph, which shows Ramses III offering a sacrifice to Hathor. ⌧ *Rte. 90,* ☎ *07/635–6215.* ⌧ *NIS 15 ($5).* ☉ *Sat.–Thurs. 7:30–dusk, Fri. 7:30–3.*

NEED A   Here's a surprise in this desert landscape: a lake (man-made) and on its
BREAK?   shore the roomy, air-conditioned **Timna Oasis Restaurant,** built of local stone and using desert colors in its decor. This self-service eatery has on its menu hot dishes such as chicken schnitzel, dairy meals (cheeses and salads), sandwiches, hummus, and ice cream. Although swimming is not permitted, you can enjoy the lake from picnic tables in shaded areas on

the shore. From January through March, a 20-minute demonstration of ancient copper-mining and -smelting techniques is held on Sunday, Monday, and Thursday at 11 and 1; the staff will explain in English at your request. ⊠ *Timna Valley Park,* ☏ *07/637–4937.* ⊘ *Daily 11–5.*

Mt. Yoash

㉑ *Leave Eilat from the junction of Rte. 90 (the Arava Rd.) and Yotam Blvd., traveling west on Yotam (which will become Rte. 12), with the New Tourist Center on the left.*

This fine lookout along the border road with Egypt is easily reached from Eilat. Notice the huge tanks as you drive along Route 12; they belong to the Eilat-Ashkelon oil pipeline. After you pass the tanks, you enter the Eilat Mountains Nature Reserve, with Nahal Shlomo, a dry riverbed, to your left . Drive 12 km (7½ mi) and turn left at the orange sign for Mt. Yoash; then drive another 1 km (½ mi), bearing right up a rough, steep, and winding stone road. Park and gather yourself for knockout views of the alternating light and dark ridges of the Eilat Mountains; Eilat and Aqaba; the mountains of Edom behind Aqaba; to the south, the start of the Saudi Arabian coastline and the Nahal Geshron gorge, emptying into the Red Sea at Taba; and to the west, the plain of Moon Valley and the mountains of Sinai, in Egypt.

En Route   From Mt. Yoash, take Route 12 and drive north; look for a green sign labeled NATAFIM CROSSING. The Israeli flag flies over the **Natafim Crossing** checkpoint, where there are usually two soldiers. Nearby is a "base," with two prefab buildings—one on either side of the fence—the Egyptian flag flying from one, the Israeli flag from the other. The low fence is the border between the two countries. From this vantage point, looking toward Egypt, one often sees an Egyptian patrol, on foot or sometimes riding camels.

Mitzpe Har Hizkiyahu

㉒ *5 km (3 mi) from the Natafim Crossing on Rte. 12; you'll see a green sign for Mitzpe Har Hizkiyahu. Drive up a paved road for 3 min.*

As you drive along Route 12, you'll see an Israeli flag flying, and you'll be looking at Moon Valley, where the wadi Nahal Paran starts. There are two lookouts here, each with an excellent etched plan. From one you can see a base for the MFO (Multinational Force of Observers), a UN-sponsored international organization formed to supervise the Egypt-Israel peace accords of 1978; and an Egyptian military post that guards the adjacent border between the two countries. From the other observation point you can see Aqaba in Jordan, the salt ponds of Eilat, Aqaba's airport, and the Gulf of Eilat.

Red Canyon

㉓ *From the Mitzpe Har Hizkiyahu lookout, drive 4 km (2½ mi) down the road until you see the orange sign for the Red Canyon (Canyon Adom) to the right. Immediately turn left for another small sign. Drive 2 km (1¼ mi) on a packed gravel road, park, lock the car, and start your walk through the Red Canyon.*

At Red Canyon, you can absorb the dazzling panoramas you've just seen at Mitzpe Har Hizkiyahu (☞ *above*)on a nature walk that takes no longer than an hour. Although the hike isn't too difficult, it's not suitable for young children or older people. At the start, the ancient riverbed is made up of conglomerate (cemented silt and stones) that settled when the onetime river was much wider; you can see stones just sticking out, as though deliberately placed there. Walking along on the stony ground, you'll find yourself in a narrow part of the canyon—2 yards wide—where the colors have abruptly changed to the reddish hue of the sandstone walls of the Red Canyon, a startling sight. Follow the wadi of the canyon, a small part of Nahal Shani. When you meet the main course of Nahal Shani, follow the trail marked in green to a descent with metal handrails; descend in a sitting position. You'll then climb down a ladder, and shortly afterward you'll come to the end of the narrow gorge. Here, on the right, is a sign reading TO THE CARPARK still on the green trail. You will be retracing your route, except now you will be *above* the canyon rather than inside it. Once on top, walk on the edge of the canyon (watch your footing and keep an eye on your children) until you reach the parking lot. This makes a great side trip from Eilat.

EILAT AND THE NEGEV A TO Z

Arriving and Departing

By Bus

The national bus company, **Egged** (☎ 03/537–5555)—which is open Sunday–Thursday 6:30 AM–10 PM, Friday and holiday eves 6:30 AM–3 PM, and Saturday 4 PM–11 PM—provides frequent daily bus service (except on Saturday) from Tel Aviv's Central Bus Station and Arlozoroff Station (✉ Arlozoroff St. and Haifa Rd.) and from Jerusalem (✉ Jaffa Rd., ☎ 02/630–4555) to Beersheva; the trip takes 1½ hours. From the Beersheva Central Bus Station (✉ Ben Zvi St., ☎ 07/629–4311) buses depart four times a day to Arad, Avdat, Ein Bokek, Mitzpe Ramon, and Sde Boker. Most buses do not run on Saturday, although some routes do resume in the early evening.

Egged buses depart from Tel Aviv to Eilat at least four times a day and twice at night. A round-trip ticket costs NIS 84 ($28). Buses from Jerusalem to Eilat leave during daylight hours from the Central Bus Station; the trip takes about 5½ hours and çosts NIS 78 ($26) round-trip. Buy tickets in advance at the Central Bus Station to ensure a seat. Be sure to reserve a seat at Eilat's Central Bus Station for the return trip.

By Car

Beersheva is 113 km (70 mi) southeast of Tel Aviv. The drive from Tel Aviv, as well as from Jerusalem, takes about 1½ hours. To drive from Tel Aviv to Beersheva, take Route 2 (the Ayalon Highway) going south until the turnoff to Route 4, marked BEERSHEVA–ASHDOD. After the Ashdod turnoff you will be on Route 41, which runs into Route 40, 6 km (almost 4 mi) later. Continue on 40 to Beersheva; there are clearly marked signs all the way.

To reach Beersheva from Jerusalem, exit the city on Route 1 heading west to the Sha'ar Hagai Junction. Turn left (south) and follow Route 38, then Route 32, which turns into Route 35, to Kiryat Gat. Here you will pick up Route 40 south to Beersheva.

To drive to Ein Bokek from Tel Aviv, leave Tel Aviv via the Ayalon Highway (Route 2) south and join Route 1, following signs to Airport–Jerusalem. As you approach Jerusalem, stay left, on Route 1, which is marked JERICHO–DEAD SEA. Continue 30 km (18½ mi) to the unmarked Almog Junction (where Route 1 meets Route 90; there is a turnoff to the left, heading north, marked JERICHO). Stay on the same road, now called Route 90, for 10 km (6¼ mi) to the Dead Sea. Bear right, which will take you due south, and follow Route 90 along the coast, passing Qumran, Ein Gedi, and Masada (☞ Dead Sea Region *in* Chapter 3), to Ein Bokek. To reach Eilat, continue south along Route 90 (Arava Road) for another 177 km (111 mi). The trip to Eilat takes about five hours.

The most direct way from Tel Aviv to Eilat is Route 40 south to Beersheva. Leave Beersheva via Route 25 (marked DIMONA–EILAT), driving 69 km (43 mi) to the Arava Junction. Turn right (south) onto Route 90 (Arava Road) and travel straight to Eilat.

By Plane

Keep in mind that flights to the Negev are not always exactly on schedule, so call ahead for the status of your flight and arrive at the airport early (a shuttle operates from Jerusalem to the airport). Regularly scheduled flights use the **Eilat Airport,** in the middle of the city, a five-minute taxi ride to the hotels and a two-minute walk to the commercial center of town. Charter flights from Europe arrive at **Ovda Airport** (also known as Eilat West), 60 km (37 mi) north of Eilat; transportation to Eilat is arranged by the travel agencies who book the flight.

Arkia Israel Airlines (☎ 03/523–3285) serves Eilat from **Sde Dov Airport** (☎ 03/690–3333), in north Tel Aviv; from **Atarot Airport** (☎ 02/625–5888), 10 km (6¼ mi) north of Jerusalem; and from **Haifa Airport** (☎ 04/864–3371), with a stop in Tel Aviv or Jerusalem. The 55-minute flight to Eilat departs from Tel Aviv every 1½ hours Sunday–Thursday, 6:30 AM–10 PM, Friday 6:30 AM–4 PM, and Saturday 3 PM–10 PM. From Jerusalem, Arkia flies to Eilat three times daily, twice on Friday; there are no flights on Saturday. The flight lasts about 45 minutes. Flights from Haifa, which take about 1½ hours, depart three times a day; there are no flights on Saturday.

To reach Ein Bokek, you can take Arkia Airlines to the **Minhat HaShtayim Airfield** (☎ 07/658–4637) from Tel Aviv four times a week. The flight takes a half hour. An airline shuttle bus then travels the 5 km (3 mi) to the hotels at Ein Bokek. Be sure to book the shuttle ahead when reserving your flight. Arkia also flies twice on Wednesday from Tel Aviv to **Mitzpe Ramon Airfield** (☎ 07/658–8026); the flight takes a half hour.

By Sherut

Yael Daroma Aviv operates *sherut* (shared) taxis from Tel Aviv to Eilat. Seats—there are seven in each taxi—must be booked ahead in Tel Aviv (✉ 32 Rothschild Blvd., ☎ 03/566–0222) or Jerusalem (✉ 12 Shamai St., ☎ 02/625–7366). There are four departures from each city Sunday through Thursday, three on Friday, and none on Saturday; the trip takes five hours and costs NIS 45 ($15). The trip can be made from Eilat (☎ 07/633–6001) to the north as well. Yael Daroma also goes to Beersheva (✉ 195 K.K. le Israel St., ☎ 07/628–1144) from Tel Aviv, a trip of less than two hours; the trip costs NIS 15 ($5).

Getting Around

By Bus

Exploring the Negev on your own by bus *can* be done, but much time is wasted waiting for connections, and the heat can make standing at a bus stop in the middle of nowhere very uncomfortable. Besides, the buses don't go everywhere. However, from Beersheva (the transfer point for buses from Tel Aviv and Jerusalem), there is regular Egged bus service (☞ *above*) to all major towns in the Negev.

In Eilat, Buses 1 and 2 travel through the hotel area to town every 30 minutes. Bus 15 goes along Eilat-Taba Road, passing attractions such as the Underwater Observatory, Coral Beach, and the dive centers, to the Egyptian border crossing point at Taba.

In Ein Bokek, a shuttle bus takes guests from the hotels to the Solarium and to the spa at Neve Zohar (ask at your hotel for the timetable).

By Car
The only way to see the Negev Desert in a comfortable and efficient way is by car (air-conditioning in summer is a must). All roads are two lanes. The condition of secondary roads vary in quality; only those in good condition are mentioned here. Roads marked in Hebrew only are not for public travel. To avoid dangerous wintertime floods, proceed with caution when there is any indication of rain (☞ Desert Precautions *in* Exploring Eilat and the Negev, *above*). Driving at night in the Negev is not recommended; plan to reach your destination by 5 in winter and by 8 in summer.

Apart from locations in towns and cities, there are gas stations at Tel Avdat (near Sde Boker), Ketziyot (near Nizzana), Mashabei Sade Junction (40 km/25 mi south of Beersheva), Zohar-Arad Junction (near Ein Bokek), Ramat Hovev, and Shoket Junction (on the way to Arad). You'll find gas stations on Route 90 (Arava Road) at Ein Hazeva, Ein Yahav, Ketura (tires fixed here), and Yotvata. There's a tire repair shop in the industrial area just before the entrance to Mitzpe Ramon. Most gas stations share space with a roadside café; a majority are open 24 hours a day.

The following are the main roads in the Negev: Route 40 goes through the Negev highlands via Sde Boker, Mitzpe Ramon, and Makhtesh Ramon to Eilat; Route 90 (called Arava Road in the Negev), which starts in Metulla near the Lebanese border, runs through Ein Bokek and along the Jordanian border, and terminates in Eilat; Route 31 runs from Beersheva to the Shoket Junction, Arad, and Ein Bokek. Most of your driving will be along stretches of straight road; the exceptions are the winding (and in some parts rough and in disrepair) road through Makhtesh Ramon and the steep road between Arad and Ein Bokek (one hairpin turn after another). Beersheva is 45 km (28 mi) from Arad, 80 km (50 mi) from Mitzpe Ramon, and 241 km (151 mi) from Eilat. Mitzpe Ramon is 148 km (93 mi) from Eilat. Ein Bokek is 177 km (111 mi) from Eilat.

By Taxi
In Eilat, the preferred (and air-conditioned) way of hopping from one place to another is by taxi. Rides don't usually cost much more than NIS 15 ($5); taxis may be hailed on the street or ordered from **Arava** (☎ 07/637–3331) or **Taba** (☎ 07/633–3339). In Beersheva, **Netz Taxis** (07/627–0888) operates seven days a week. Taxis are not necessary in Ein Bokek or Mitzpe Ramon.

Contacts and Resources

Car Rental
Beersheva: Avis, ⊠ 11 Derech Hanessiim, ☎ 07/627–1777; Hertz, ⊠ 5 Ben Zvi St., ☎ 07/627–3878; Eldan, ⊠ 100 Tuviahu St., ☎ 07/643–0344; Reliable, ⊠ 1 HaAtzmaut St., ☎ 07/623–7123.

Eilat: Avis, ⊠ Eilat Airport, ☎ 07/637–3164; Budget, ⊠ Central Bus Station, ☎ 07/637–4124 or 07/637–4125; Eldan, ⊠ 143 Shalom Center, ☎ 07/637–4027; Hertz, ⊠ Red Kanion Shopping Center, ☎ 07/637–6682; Reliable, ⊠ Etzion Hotel, Hatmarim Blvd., ☎ 07/637–4126.

Ein Bokek: Hertz, ⊠ Galei Zohar Hotel, ☎ 07/658–4530.

Consulates

In Eilat, you can contact the honorary consul of the United Kingdom, Fay Morris (☎ 07/637–2344). English-speaking visitors whose countries are not represented may also apply to her for assistance.

Emergencies

Police: Dial 100.

Ambulance: Dial 101 (911, for English-speaking operator).

Hospitals: Beersheva: Soroka Hospital (⊠ Hanessi'im St., ☎ 07/640–0111); Eilat: Yoseftal Hospital (⊠ Yotam St., ☎ 07/635–8011).

Fire: Dial 102.

PHARMACIES

Call the **Magen David Adom Medical Service** (☎ 100), the Red Cross of Israel, for assistance with emergency prescriptions. In Eilat, the **Michlin Pharmacy** (⊠ Opposite the Central Bus Station, ☎ 07/637–2434) is open Sunday–Thursday 8–8:30, Friday 8–3:30. In the Negev, there are pharmacies in Arad, Beersheva, Eilat, and Mitzpe Ramon.

Guided Tours

AIRPLANE TOURS

From Sde Dov Airport in Tel Aviv, **Ayt Aviation & Tourism Ltd.** (☎ 03/699–0185) will take you for a two-hour flight over the *makhteshim* (canyonlike craters), the spring and waterfall of Ein Avdat, and along the Dead Sea; the cost is NIS 780 ($260) per person.

BEDOUIN EVENING

Spend Wednesday evening in a Bedouin tent enjoying a Middle Eastern dinner and listening to stories of the desert, for a cost of NIS 120 ($40). For reservations call 07/637–3565.

BIRD-WATCHING TOURS

In the spring and fall, millions of birds fly over **Eilat** on their long journey between winter grounds in Africa and summer breeding grounds in Eurasia. Migration activity takes place between mid-February and early June and between mid-September and the end of August, although the **International Birdwatching Center,** in Eilat (⊠ Opposite the Central Bus Station, Box 774, 88106, ☎ 07/637–4276), is aflutter year-round; it's open Sunday–Thursday 9–1 and 5–7 and Friday 9–1. The center conducts half- or full-day trips to bird-watching hot spots in the vicinity of Eilat. You'll see the ringing station, and you can plant a tree at the bird sanctuary, created on a landfill. The center provides binoculars for a better view of birds of prey, waterfowl, songbirds, and others. Based on a minimum of three people, prices range from $25 to $50 per person per trip.

BOAT TOURS

The spectacular underwater phenomena near Eilat—unusual coral, tropical plant life, and colorful fish of all sizes and shapes—may be seen from glass-bottom boats that depart from either the bridge at the Marina in Eilat or from the pier just north of Coral Beach on the Eilat-Taba Road. The **Jules Verne Explorer** (☎ 07/637–7702 or 07/633–4668; reservations are suggested), a mobile underwater observatory with two upper decks and a glass-sided underwater lower section, takes a two-hour trip past the Coral Reserve that costs NIS 55 ($18). There are three departures daily.

If you would like to see the fish and coral from down under, take a ride on **Yellow Submarine's** 72-foot-long *Jacqueline,* which leaves three to four times daily from Coral World Underwater Observatory (☎ 07/637–6666 or 07/637–6732), on the Eilat-Taba Road in Coral

Beach. The sub—which really *is* yellow—dives deep below the surface on a 40-minute guided journey to see the renowned reefs of the Coral Reserve. There's a camera mounted outside so you can see the water closing around you during the descent. Reservations are necessary; the sub does not operate on Sunday. The cruise costs NIS 195 ($65) and includes entrance to the observatory.

Choose a daylong cruise in the Gulf of Eilat (Aqaba) on one of the many boats anchored at the Marina, among them the **Orionia** (⊠ Red Sea Sports Club, ☎ 07/637–9685), a classic Spanish-built sailing yacht, whose skipper explains what's to see at sea; it's wise to book ahead. **Eilat Cruises Ltd.** (⊠ At the Marina, ☎ 07/633–1717, ℻ 07/633–3351) offers a barbecue-lunch cruise on an Old World–style sailboat to Coral Island, 17 km (10 mi) south of Eilat, with time to explore its Crusader fortress—all for NIS 135 ($45). In addition, there is a five-hour cruise on a Cutty Sark–style all-wood schooner that anchors at the Lighthouse, near Taba, and costs NIS 87 ($29). While you're out there, service boats come along and, for an additional fee, will take you parasailing, waterskiing, or for an introductory scuba dive.

For visitors who prefer more active sailing, the operators of the 47-foot ketch **Shooneet** (☎ 07/637–7925), out of the Marina, offer various trips, such as an overnight sail for NIS 120 ($40) and a 24-hour sail for NIS 270 ($90), in which guests can take the helm and hoist the sails. The skipper gives a short explanation of the surroundings while you are under sail.

CAMEL TOURS

When in Mitzpe Ramon, steel yourself and wake up early to get a breathtaking view of the awakening desert on **Desert Shade's** "Morning Tour" (book from Tel Aviv, ☎ 03/575–6885, ℻ 03/613–0160). It starts at 6:30, lasts for an hour and a half, costs NIS 66 ($22), and obligingly includes coffee (children must be over 5). Other camel trips offered are a one-hour ride along the ridge of the Makhtesh Ramon, and a two-day trip leaving every Monday that follows the ancient Spice Route, with a sleep-out under the stars.

Based in the heart of the mountains near Eilat, **Camel Riders** offers adventure-filled desert crossings. The two-day "Smugglers' Route" trek sets out from the Shacharut Desert Adventure Center (☎ 07/637–3218), 60 km (37 mi) north of Eilat. It crosses the Negev Highlands, through remote corners of the desert, on the route taken by smugglers in centuries past. The trip leaves on Friday, usually not in summer, and costs NIS 390 ($130). The **Camel Ranch** (☎ 07/637–6663 or at night 07/637–8638), at the Texas Ranch in Coral Beach, takes you into the mountains and canyons of the desert around Eilat. A half-day excursion (the sunset trip is smashing) costs NIS 120 ($40).

DIGS

Readers who would like to work all day in the dust under a blazing sun—with the hope of finding Abraham's tent peg (and also of contributing to Holy Land archaeology and meeting interesting people)—should contact the **Israel Antiquities Authority** (⊠ Box 586, Jerusalem 91004, ☎ 02/629–2607, ℻ 02/629–2628) for information about digs where volunteers are needed.

GENERAL INTEREST

Several Tel Aviv– and Jerusalem-based tour companies, including **Egged Tours** (⊠ 59 Ben Yehuda St., Tel Aviv, ☎ 03/527–1212; 224 Jaffa Rd., Jerusalem, ☎ 02/530–4422) and **United Tours** (⊠ 113 Hayarkon St., Tel Aviv, ☎ 03/522–2008 or 03/693–3412; King David Hotel Annex, 23 King David St., Jerusalem, ☎ 02/625–2187 or 02/625–2189), offer two-day air-conditioned bus tours to Eilat. Both companies will pick you up at your hotel. Among the highlights covered are David Ben-Gurion's home at Sde Boker, the Ramon Crater, and attractions in and around Eilat. At extra cost, participants can arrange to make the return trip by air. The trip costs NIS 600 ($200), with a small additional charge during peak season. Egged and United also organize half-day visits to Timna Park, Hai Bar Wildlife Reserve, and Kibbutz Yotvata from Eilat, which cost from NIS 108 ($36) to NIS 126 ($42).

Yoel Tours (✉ Carlton Hotel, ☏ 07/658–4311), in Ein Bokek, operates a half-day minibus tour to the Bedouin market in Beersheva, followed by a visit to a Bedouin family to drink coffee in their tent. The trip costs NIS 90 ($30) and runs every Thursday. Yoel also does a one-day trip to Eilat, which includes the Underwater Observatory and a swim in the Red Sea; there's also a yacht trip, which includes snorkeling.

Johnny Tours (☏ 07/631–6215 or 631–6216) organizes half-day tours of Eilat. The price of NIS 174 ($58) includes entrance to the Underwater Observatory, a visit to the Jordanian border, and the agricultural plantations of nearby Kibbutz Elot, as well as a hot lunch.

From Eilat, the **Timna Express** (☏ 07/637–4741) gives travelers a detailed exploration of Timna Park, with hotel pickups at 8 AM daily except Sunday. The price of NIS 108 ($36) includes a visit to a kibbutz and lunch at the Park Restaurant. You'll be back around 2 PM.

Amiel Tours (✉ Khan Center, ☏ 07/637–6308) takes sightseers north from Eilat to visit Hai Bar (with animals whose history dates from the biblical era), then to a dairy farm and Timna Park. The price of NIS 147 ($49) includes lunch.

Kibbutz Grofit (☏ 07/637–4362), 44 km (27 mi) north of Eilat, will take you to meet the kibbutzniks and hear about growing watermelons in the sand and how their dairy farm was developed. The tour, which leaves every Thursday at 8:30 AM and returns around 3 PM, costs NIS 108 ($36), and includes lunch with kibbutz members.

HIKING TOURS

A safer alternative to venturing out on your own—and more interesting—is an off-the-beaten-track hike led by professional guides of the **SPNI** (Society for the Protection of Nature in Israel; ✉ 4 Hashfela St., Tel Aviv 66183, ☏ 03/638–8673 or 03/638–8677; 13 Helene Hamalka St., Jerusalem 96101, ☏ 02/625–2357 or 02/624–4605). Although some one-day hikes are conducted in English, a hike led by a Hebrew-speaking guide should not be dismissed out of hand; English-speaking hikers in the group are often glad to translate, plus it's a good way to get to know nature-loving Israelis. SPNI day trips are planned only a short time ahead, so it's worthwhile calling to see what's going on.

For the ecology-minded, half-day tours around Eilat (especially pleasant is the Sunset Hike) are offered by **Nature's Way** (✉ Opposite the Central Bus Station, ☏ 07/637–0648). The company also gives free information about hiking on your own.

The expert nature guides of the **Nature Reserves Authority** (✉ Visitor Center, Box 340, Mitzpe Ramon 80600, ☏ 07/658–8691; 07/658–8698; 07/658–8620) may be hired to hike you (or accompany you in your vehicle) through the Makhtesh Ramon for the sum of NIS 369 ($123) from 8 to 5, starting from the Mitzpe Ramon Visitors Center. You must make a reservation at least two or three weeks in advance.

JEEP TOURS

Out of Eilat, the well-established **Red Sea Sports Club** (⊠ In the King Solomon Hotel, King's Wharf, ☎ 07/637–9685) takes Jeep trips through the Granite Mountains around Eilat to lookout points above Moon Valley; the jaunt may include a hike in the Red Canyon. The cost is NIS 84 ($28) per person for a half day and NIS 132 ($44) per person, including a picnic lunch, for a day trip.

If you're over 23 and would like to try your hand at driving a Jeep, contact **Johnny Tours** (☎ 07/631–6215), in Eilat, which also offers hard-top desert vehicles (not as romantic as Jeeps, which are open to the sky, but the air-conditioning has its appeal). Routes include Amram's Pillars, Timna Park, and the desert oasis of Ein Evrona. The half-day trip costs NIS 96 ($32); the one-day trips (with lunch) are $44–$55, entrance fees excluded.

Avi Desert Tours (⊠ In Jerusalem, Moshav Givat Yeshayahu 16, 99825, ☎ 02/991–8855; in Eilat ☎ 07/637–8871) leads carefully planned Jeep and four-wheel-drive expeditions out of Beersheva, Eilat, and Ein Bokek. From Eilat, **Jeep See** (⊠ Bridge House, near the Marina, Box 4188, 88100, ☎ 07/633–0133) offers a half-day trip to the red-sand Hidden Canyon costing NIS 90 ($30) and a 2½-hour trip to the Lost Valley and Black Canyon costing NIS 66 ($22). Jeep See also conducts full-day trips complete with picnic lunch, Bedouin tales, and a great sunset view that cost NIS 130 ($40).

Operating out of Mitzpe Ramon, **Desert Shade** (Tel Aviv office, ⊠ Box 238, 80600, ☎ 03/575–6885) provides a tour of the Ramon Crater, as well as a desert-style lunch, a camel ride and a visit to the Goes Alpaca Farm, on Sunday from February to April; the cost is NIS 264 ($88).

KIBBUTZ

Visit a desert kibbutz and see how watermelons are grown in the sand. The half-day tour at Kibbutz **Grofit** (☎ 07/637–4362) includes lunch, takes place on Thursday, and costs NIS 108 ($36).

SNORKELING

Know Before You Go (☎ 07/637–6666 or 07/637–6732) offers a cruise from the Marina to the Underwater Observatory, a tour of the Observatory, and then a snorkeling session at Coral Beach, where you will be among the fish you've just seen from the inside. The price for this 4½-hour jaunt is NIS 118 ($39.35).

Hiking

In Negev parklands and reserves, hiking trails have been marked by the SPNI, the National Parks Authority, and the Nature Reserves Authority. The SPNI publishes topographical maps (in Hebrew) on which the trails are color-coded to match the markings on the trails themselves. The trail marks are three short stripes: white/color/white, with the color either red, green, blue, or black. Yellow indicates military areas. The maps are available at SPNI headquarters in Tel Aviv and Jerusalem and at their field study centers in Sde Boker (☎ 07/656–5016), Eilat (⊠ Rte. 90, Coral Beach, ☎ 07/637–2021), Beersheva (⊠ Corner of Meshachrerim St. and Tuviyahu Blvd., ☎ 07/623–8527), and Har Hanegev (⊠ Mitzpe Ramon, ☎ 07/658–8616). Keep in mind that at least 60% of the Negev is occupied by the military; you are forbidden to enter these areas (firing zones and mines are marked in yellow on SPNI maps).

The **Nature Reserves Authority** (⊠ 78 Yirmiyahu St., Jerusalem 94467, ☎ 02/500–5444) is expertly represented at the visitor centers at Mitzpe Ramon (☎ 07/658–8691) and at the Coral Reserve in Eilat (⊠ Rte.

90, ☎ 07/637–3988). The rangers are knowledgeable and experienced and will help you with hiking information.

Travel Agencies

There are a host of travel offices in **Eilat** around the Central Bus Station, in the Khan Center, and at Bridge House, near the Marina. Well-established agencies in the Negev include **Galilee Tours** (⊠ North Promenade, ☎ 07/633–5147) in Eilat, **Amiel Tours** (⊠ Shopping center, ☎ 07/658–4433) in Ein Bokek, and **Lahish Tours** (⊠ 79 Herzl St., ☎ 07/727–6975) in Beersheva. Note that in July and August some travel agencies are closed.

Visitor Information

Tourist Information Offices are in **Arad** (at the visitor center, ⊠ 28 Ben Yair St., Box 824, 80700, ☎ 07/995–4409) and **Beersheva** (⊠ 6 Ben Zvi St., opposite the Central Bus Station, Box 591, 84104, ☎ 07/623–6001 or 07/623–6002). In **Eilat,** the **Municipal Information Center** (⊠ Arava Rd. at the corner of Yotam St., Box 14, 88100, ☎ 07/637–2111) offers comprehensive tourist information. Especially useful in Eilat is the detail-filled leaflet called "Events and Places of Interest," available at the center. Eilat also has a privately run **Information Center** (⊠ North Beach, Hapalmach, and Durban Sts., 88000, ☎ 07/637–4741) and the **Tourist Patrol** (⊠ Municipal Information Center, *above,* ☎ 07/636–7269 or 636–7209), open from 8:30–4 daily.

Visitor centers are in **Mitzpe Ramon** (⊠ At the top of the main street, Box 340, 80600, ☎ 07/658–8691, ☎ 07/658–8620) and **Arad** (⊠ In shopping center, ☎ 07/995–9333).

9 Side Trips to the Sinai and Petra

Egypt's Sinai Peninsula attracts adventurous travelers who want to trek in its granite mountains or dive in the magnificent coral reefs along its coast. The area also draws pilgrims seeking such sights as St. Catherine's Monastery and Mt. Sinai. Visitors to Jordan are flocking to Petra, the rose-red remains of an ancient Nabatean city carved into sandstone. Its gigantic monuments and royal tombs are treasures even in a region filled with impressive antiquities.

YOU CAN EASILY ADD SIDE TRIPS to Egypt or Jordan if you want to broaden your sense of the region or pursue a particular passion. The Sinai Peninsula's location along the ancient trading route linking Africa and Asia has made it a meeting place of cultures since time immemorial. Today people from all over the world are still drawn to this area of Egypt, with its pristine beauty. The Sinai coast is a world-class diving attraction; its year-round sunshine and dramatic granite mountains, which contrast with a teal-cobalt sea, are an allure to nature lovers.

Petra, in Jordan, combines awesome scenery with another element: artifacts of the mysterious and ancient culture of the Nabatean people. The Nabateans controlled the famed spice route stretching from Arabia to the Mediterranean, and Petra became both financial center and royal necropolis. Hidden from western eyes until the early 19th century, Petra's tombs, carved out of the rust-hued sandstone cliffs of the biblical region of Edom, have gigantic proportions and intricately carved facades. Its Roman remains provide a window on the culture that ruled the world 2,000 years ago. In a region studded with antiquities, Petra is without a doubt a crown jewel for students of ancient history.

THE SINAI

By Judy Stacey Goldman

Updated by Miriam Feinberg Vamosh

Today the Sinai is nothing less than a paradise for adventurers. Its interior seems untouched and even forbidding, yet Jeep and hiking trails beckon explorers. The Sinai coast is famous for the marvels of its coral reefs, but at the end of every day, the weary traveler is within a few hours of beautiful hotels and resorts.

The Sinai is a 61,000-square-km (37,820-square-mi) triangular peninsula, bounded on the east by the Gulf of Eilat/Aqaba and on the west by the Gulf of Suez. The apex of the triangle, pointing downward at the Red Sea, was the main route to the East for the traders of antiquity. Many legends of ancient Egypt are set in the Sinai: The goddess Isis came here to search for the body of her murdered husband, and the goddess Hathor, patroness of the Sinai's copper mines and known to the pharaohs as "Our Lady of Sinai," also sanctified the area. And, of course, biblical references to the Sinai are numerous. Pilgrims have long been drawn to the region that was the scene of the wanderings of the ancient Israelites.

The Sinai's vastness may mislead the uninitiated into regarding it as one geographical unit. In fact, the peninsula can be divided into three major subsections, each very different from the other. The plains of the northern Sinai are bounded on their southern edge by Darb el-Haj, the Muslim pilgrim's route connecting Egypt to Aqaba and, finally, to Mecca. The immense limestone massif of the Tih Desert, whose western reaches are rich in water sources and dramatic canyons, dominates the central Sinai. The word *Tih,* translated by some as "wanderers," has led some scholars to identify this wilderness with the wanderings of the Children of Israel. The southern Sinai is the most traveled part of the peninsula, as it is home to the traditional Mt. Sinai and, along the coast, to some of the best diving in the world.

Most travelers to the southern Sinai, the area covered in this side trip, follow a route leading from Eilat to St. Catherine's Monastery at the foot of Mt. Sinai. The simplest way to do this is by organized bus trip. This may not sound madly adventurous, but it does offer the security of knowing that everything from start to finish is taken care of, and the freedom to do nothing but gaze at the wonderful scenery. A whirlwind tour of the Sinai coast and a visit to St. Catherine's Monastery can be accomplished in a one-day tour. Longer tours, of two days or more, allow for swimming or snorkeling stops and visits to additional sites.

Individual travelers can see the region's highlights in a three-day trip. The road passes along the eastern coast, where the town of Nuweiba is both a crossroads to the interior and a vacation center. Nuweiba's beautiful beach has some of the best diving and snorkeling in the Sinai. It's also a stopover on the road west to Sinai's interior and St. Catherine's Monastery, or on the way south to the coral reefs of Dahab and Ras Muhammad, at the peninsula's southernmost tip.

Pleasures and Pastimes

Dining
While the Sinai's location on the coast ensures a number of fish restaurants, proprietors come and go, and so does the level of hygiene. Keep an ear to the ground, gleaning information from fellow travelers about the latest gems. Otherwise, trust that the most reliable dining opportunities are to be had in the resort hotels and leave your exploring for the scenery.

Diving
The Gulf of Eilat is an extension of the Indian Ocean, linked to it by the straits of Tiran and Bab el Mandeb. The water temperature is a constantly warm 21°C (70°F). This tropical sea is poor in plankton—accounting for the striking clarity of its waters—but rich in algae, which live in symbiosis with the coral among which they reside. The result of this symbiosis is nature's most magnificent regional work of art: the Sinai coast coral reefs, home to some 1,000 species of fish. Diving safaris are organized at several points along the eastern Sinai coast, and nondivers can rent snorkel equipment at many locations there. Some well-known diving sites are Ras-a-Sitan, 54 km (33 mi) south of Taba, and Ras-Abu Gulum, an unspoiled reef about 50 km (31 mi) south of Nuweiba and accessible by Jeep only. Dahab is another favorite, and the most famous of them all is the Ras Muhammad National Park.

Hiking and Trekking
The southern Sinai's landscape of gorges and valleys, over which tower multicolored granite mountains, provides virtually unlimited hiking opportunities. A few of the routes are well-traveled, and you can enjoy them even if you only have a short time. The area around St. Catherine's Monastery has several hiking trails besides the strenuous but not-to-be-missed hike up to the top of Mt. Sinai. Other widely available options for exploring are Jeep and camel tours.

For adventure-addicted, experienced hikers, there are treks to remote areas of the Sinai, like the Tih Desert or Mt. Sirbal. These trips should be undertaken only under the leadership of experienced guides. Caution: The trails in the Sinai are mostly unmarked, and attempting even the shortest ones without exact directions from touring experts can be risky.

Lodging
Travelers to the Sinai can pick luxury hotels and resorts at Nuweiba, Dahab, and Sharm el Sheikh. Medium- and low-price hotels are also available at these three locations. Campsites also abound and are well advertised, although some may not be very clean.

CATEGORY	COST*
$$$	over $130
$$	$45–$130
$	under $45

All prices are for a standard double room, including tax.

Gateway to Egypt

After leaving Eilat and border formalities behind, you will sense the freedom of the magnificent scenery that lies ahead. The turquoise waters of the Gulf of Eilat sparkle in the sunlight against the backdrop of the red and black mountains that nearly touch the water in many places. This is the landscape that will accompany you as you move down the eastern coast of the Sinai. The slopes are dotted with acacia trees, and wooden fishing boats bob offshore in the waters of the gulf.

Coral Island

17 km (11 mi) south of Eilat, 38 km (24 mi) north of Wadi Malkha.

With its ruined Crusader castle and Ottoman additions, Coral Island attracts roadside photographers and visitors. The recorded history of the island begins during the reign of Pharaoh Ramses III, who reigned from 1198–1166 BC. A document from this period relates that workers sent to mine copper from Timna, north of present-day Eilat, found shelter on the island. This is probably the source of the Arabic name for the island—Jezirat Phar'un, or Pharaoh's Island. The island next served as a port for the region's rulers during the Byzantine period, when busy shipping lanes connected India with the Land of Israel via the Gulf of Suez and the Gulf of Eilat.

The best-known period of the island's occupation is signaled by the dramatic remains visible from shore. These are the ruined walls of the **Crusader outpost** created here in 1115 by Baldwin I. For 55 years, the Crusaders controlled both the trade and pilgrimage routes that passed this way from the safety of the island. But in 1171, shortly after coming to power in Egypt, Saladin attacked the fortress by surprise, transporting his dismantled ships secretly through the Sinai on camelback. Despite repeated attempts, the Crusaders never again regained control of the island. Most of the remains seen today are from the Mamluk period (14th century).

If the mystery of the ruins attracts you enough to make this a full-blown stop, you can cross the 250 yards from the shore to the island in a boat that runs from the Saladin Motel from 9–5 every 15 minutes; a round-trip ticket costs $7.

Just a few miles south of Coral Island, take the time to stop at the Fjord, an impressively beautiful inlet, for another great photo opportunity.

En Route   At **Wadi Malkha-Sheikh Suleiman Junction** (38 km, or 24 mi, south of Coral Island; 10 km, or 6 mi, north of Nuweiba), there is a Bedouin-run kiosk with camels, guides, food, and water to rent for trips to some of the natural attractions inaccessible by car. Hour-long jaunts are also a possibility.

Nuweiba

48 km (30 mi) south of Coral Island, 125 km (78 mi) northeast of St. Catherine's Monastery.

Nuweiba is one of the eastern Sinai's fast-growing resort towns. Its name means "bubbling springs," and this oasis has long been an important

Sinai

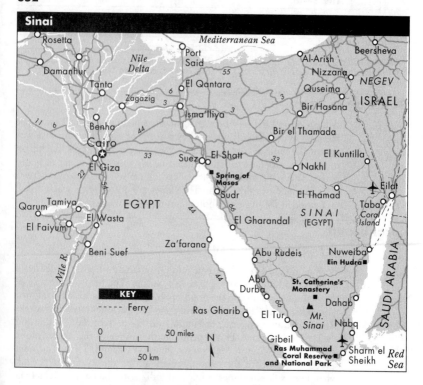

stopover for Muslim pilgrims en route to Mecca. Lovely, sandy beaches and colorful coral reefs accessible from the shore have also made its reputation as the perfect place for a resort-style vacation. It is also an excellent starting point for tours to the Sinai's interior.

Now a city of about 3,000, the oasis is the center for two tribes. Their members, once the outstanding fishermen of the Sinai coast, still inhabit the area in two villages: Nuweiba el Muzeina, south of Nuweiba city, and Nuweiba Tarabin, to the north. Nuweiba city also has a tourist center, with a Bedouin bazaar and a few shops and restaurants. But you will probably spend most of your time enjoying the beach and its coffeehouses, as well as the outstanding scenery.

An unusual attraction of Nuweiba el Mzeina is Holly, a solitary dolphin. Scientists are still studying solitary dolphins, loving and sociable creatures that sometimes break away from their pod and "move in" near human habitations. Holly has been a dockside resident of Nuweiba el Muzeina since 1994. She will often allow visiting swimmers to approach her and engage her in play.

From Nuweiba a car-and-passenger ferry runs daily to Aqaba in Jordan. It's the way the locals make the crossing but is slow going at 3½ hours' duration. A good alternative for tourists is the high-speed catamaran that makes the trip in 45 minutes, part of a package marketed by the Nuweiba Hilton Coral Resort (☞ Lodging, *below*), which makes a one-day round-trip to Petra, in Jordan, leaving Friday at 6 AM.

Lodging

$$$ 🏨 **Nuweiba Hilton Coral Resort.** Just beside the Nuweiba port, this quiet hotel is set on a beautiful sandy beach close to the oasis. The hotel offers numerous resort activities and the opportunity to join diving and hiking safaris. ✉ *Nuweiba port,* ☎ *520320 or 520321,* ☎ *800/445–*

8667 *in the U.S.,* FAX *520327 or 520423. 100 rooms with bath. 2 restaurants, 2 bars, 2 pools, tennis court, horseback riding, squash, beach.* AE, DC, MC, V.

$$ ☏ **El Salam Hotel.** This hotel has air-conditioned rooms with minibars, a swimming pool, and a private beach. ✉ *Nuweiba Tarabin,* ☏ *500441,* FAX *500440. 100 rooms with bath. No credit cards.*

$–$$ ☏ **Helnon Hotel.** The Helnon, in Nuweiba city near the bus station, has air-conditioned rooms and a private beach. Helnon Camping, on the hotel grounds, has bungalow accommodations in the $ category. ✉ *Nuweiba,* ☏ *500402 or 500403,* FAX *500407. 117 rooms with bath.* AE, MC, V.

En Route About 10 km (6 mi) past the junction of the Nuweiba–St. Catherine's road, you will see a Bedouin hut by the roadside. Stop here to walk (about 20 minutes to a half hour) to the point where you can get a view of an emerald green oasis, **Ein Hudra,** believed by some scholars to be the biblical site of Hatzeroth (Numbers 11:35). On the way, you can see a stone burial structure of the type known as *nawamis.* It is one of several in the vicinity and dates from the Chalcolithic period. There are also rock inscriptions along the path, carved by shepherds and pilgrims over the ages in Greek, Armenian, and Hebrew. Make sure you get walking directions from the Bedouin or better yet, rent a camel here for the trip. As well-known as these attractions are, they are not carefully signposted, and it's easy to get lost.

St. Catherine's Monastery

★ *125 km (78 mi) southwest of Nuweiba.*

The sight of St. Catherine's Monastery, utterly isolated and set in a valley surrounded by great, craggy mountains, is extraordinary. One of the most sacred monasteries in the world, it was constructed by the emperor Justinian in AD 530. But one look at the looming, fortresslike complex is enough to realize that religious fervor was not the emperor's only incentive. Right on the main caravan route carrying goods across the Sinai from Africa to Asia, the monastery no doubt served the emperor's soldiers as a base of operations against the bandits who plagued the route. Its surroundings are dotted with sites immortalizing various biblical stories, including what is said to be the exact location where the Israelites worshiped the Golden Calf.

The monastery comprises several buildings, each built or expanded at different times over the centuries. Among them are a church, several chapels, and a library (closed to the public). The library contains thousands of rare books, including a copy of the Codex Sinaiticus (the 3rd-century AD Greek translation by Jewish scholars of the Hebrew Bible), one of 50 copies commissioned by Constantine the Great in 331. Within the complex are also the monks' living quarters, an ancient refectory, and a white mosque with a minaret built in 1106 (not in use). All of this is encircled by high stone walls. Originally named after Mary, the monastery was later named for St. Catherine, martyred in Alexandria in the 4th century (the round firework called a Catherine wheel is named for the form of torture to which she was submitted); the faithful believe her bones were carried here by angels. About 12 Greek Orthodox monks currently live and work in the monastery. The archbishop, who resides in Cairo, visits at Easter and other important holidays. Outside and around the monastery live the Christian Bedouin of the Jabaliyeh tribe, who have long served the monks and work in the gardens and orchards.

Inside the **Church of the Transfiguration,** the apse is decorated with an ancient mosaic of the Transfiguration of Jesus, with Moses and Elijah. Oil lamps and decorated eggs hang from the ceiling of the church, while on its walls and those of the hallway and surrounding chapels, some of the monastery's unique collection of icons can be seen. All around are old and treasured works of art—inscriptions, wall coverings, inlaid metalwork, stone reliefs, and other carvings, and chandeliers (some of these are lighted on religious holidays). The doors to the church itself date from the 6th century, and the outer doors were built in the 11th century; the bell tower, a gift from the czar of Russia, was constructed in 1987.

The **chapel** behind the church is the most sacred part of the monastery. Unfortunately, it is not always open to the public. This chapel dates from the 4th century AD and is the oldest part of the church. Its walls are covered with icons. The monastery itself has 2,000 icons. You may see some more of them in the hall next to the library (the others are kept in secured rooms, closed to the public). One icon portrays the Sacrifice of Isaac and was painted in the 7th century. Outside the chapel, you can see the bush where tradition has it that God spoke to Moses.

Many visitors are intrigued by the **Room of the Skulls,** a chamber where the bones of deceased monks are kept, each transferred from the cemetery after five years of internment because their burial plot is very small. The skulls are lined up neatly in rows and number 1,500.

Above St. Catherine's Monastery looms the multipeaked summit of **Jabal Musa,** 6,855 feet above sea level. This, your local guide will tell you, is the place where Moses received the Ten Commandments as the Israelites waited impatiently below. But how reliable is this identification? Scholars have wrestled with this question for years with no solution. Most sites mentioned in the Bible are "internal"—they were named for events that happened to the Israelites but are not noted in external literary sources. Other locations have been suggested for the biblical Mt. Sinai, but Jabal Musa, probably because of its situation on the main trade route, has been the most enduring identification. Pilgrims' journals were the main guidebooks of earlier periods, and that is how Jabal Musa's sacred nature was passed on from one generation to the next.

Viewing Jabal Musa even from afar is an awe-inspiring experience. If you can climb to the summit in time for a sunrise, the sweeping view of the granite peaks from one end of the horizon to the other will very likely convince you no other place could serve better as the birthplace of Moses' vision. The climb to Jabal Musa takes 2½ to 3 hours, including 700 steps to the very top. There is a 3,000-step descent back down to St. Catherine's Monastery. ☎ 470346. 🎟 Free. ☉ Monastery Mon.–Thurs. and Sat. 9–noon; closed Greek Orthodox Christmas (Jan. 7) and Easter.

Lodging

$$$ 🏨 **El Raha Hotel.** The double-occupancy rate includes dinner and breakfast. ⊠ Village of St. Catherine, ☎ 470333, FAX 470323. 124 rooms with bath. No credit cards.

$$ 🏨 **Daniela Village.** This is a compound of double-bedded, air-conditioned bungalows. Its restaurant, the Hala, serves Middle Eastern as well as international specialties. ⊠ Near the Santa village town square, ☎ 202/470379 (Cairo), FAX 202/360–7750; or write ⊠ c/o 18 Shehab St., Monahdessin, Cairo. 54 rooms with bath. No credit cards.

$ 🏨 **Green Lodge.** Hostel and tent accommodations, each costing $15 per person per night, include breakfast. ⊠ 10 km (6 mi) east of St. Catherine's Monastery, ☎ 202/291–1491 (Cairo), FAX 202/470080. No credit cards.

$ 🏨 **Morganland Village.** Rooms are $45 per person, including dinner (high-season rates); hostel accommodations are $20 per person, including dinner. ⊠ *3 km (2 mi) from the monastery, just east of the main St. Catherine Rd. near the Zeituna area,* ☎ *202/356–2437 (Cairo),* 🖷 *202/356–4104. 70 rooms with bath. No credit cards.*

Side Trips from St. Catherine's

If you have an extra day to spare, you may want to go back to the coast and on to **Dahab,** another oasis and resort, 130 km (81 mi) east of St. Catherine's Monastery. **Sharm el Sheikh,** a three-hour drive from St. Catherine's at the southern tip of the peninsula, is a resort center with a number of hotels of various categories. The nearby Ras Muhammad National Park is considered one of the prime diving spots in the world.

The Sinai A to Z

Before You Go

BORDERS

The border crossing at Taba, in Egypt just over the border from Eilat, is open 24 hours a day, seven days a week, except for the Jewish holiday of Yom Kippur and the Muslim holiday of Id el Adkha. There is a NIS 45 ($15) tax on the Israeli side, and a $6 tax on the Egyptian side. The border crossing's phone number is 07/637–2104. Crossing the border on either side can take anywhere from five minutes to five hours, so arrive with plenty of patience!

CLOTHING

Although it's very hot during the day in the Sinai, temperatures dip at night. Even in summer it's wise to pack a jacket and socks. Winter days are generally warm and sunny, but the mountains around St. Catherine's are known for their freezing nights, including bouts of frost and snow. Modest dress is required to visit the monastery.

CURRENCY

Egyptian currency is calculated in pounds (L.E.) and piasters. The exchange rate at press time is approximately L.E. 3.38 to the U.S. dollar, L.E. 2.53 to the Canadian dollar, and L.E. 5.66 to the British pound.

Visitors to Egypt are obliged to convert currency at authorized exchange points, such as those found in all major hotels and banks. Convenient places to do this are the border exchange office and the bank in the Taba Hilton, which is usually open day and night, daily.

PASSPORTS AND VISAS

Valid passports are required for both children and adults entering Egypt. If a child shares a parent's passport, the parent cannot enter Egypt without the child, even for a one-day visit. Visas are obtainable on the spot at the border or through Egyptian consulates in Israel. Egyptian consulates are in northern Tel Aviv (⊠ 54 Basle St., ☎ 03/546–4151 or 03/546–4152) and in Eilat (⊠ 68 Avrony St., ☎ 07/637–6882). Holders of U.S. passports don't need visas to visit Nuweiba, Dahab, St. Catherine's, or Sharm el Sheikh, although they may be needed for other destinations in Egypt.

Arriving and Departing

BY BUS

From Eilat you can catch Egged Bus 15 from the Central Bus Station; at Taba you will switch to an Egyptian bus, which provides regularly scheduled daily service to Nuweiba, Dahab, St. Catherine's, and Sharm el Sheikh. Be patient; punctuality is optional here.

BY CAR

Only cars registered to their drivers may be driven over the border into Egypt. For further information on procedures for bringing your car into the Sinai from Israel, contact MEMSI, the Israeli branch of the AAA, with an office in Tel Aviv (☎ 03/564–1122).

BY FOOT

You may walk across the border from Eilat to reach the Taba Hilton Hotel in Egypt. A hotel representative has an office at the border crossing and will arrange transport to the hotel if you request it. However, if you're unencumbered by luggage, it's an easy walk.

BY PLANE

Arkia (⊠ Red Canyon shopping center, Eilat, ☎ 07/637–6102; ⊠ 11 Frishman St., Tel Aviv, ☎ 03/523–3285) and Air Sinai (⊠ Migdalor Bldg., 1 Ben Yehuda St., 13th floor, Tel Aviv, ☎ 03/510–2481) have biweekly flights to Sharm el Sheikh on Monday and Friday mornings. They operate jointly on this route, so you may make reservations by calling either company. A one-way ticket costs about $110.

Getting Around

BY CAR

For information on entering Egypt by car, *see* Arriving and Departing, *above*. No unleaded fuel is available in the Sinai. Drive with extreme caution on Sinai roads; there are an inordinate number of accidents, and emergency medical care is not always available.

BY TAXI

A popular means of transportation to Nuweiba, Dahab, and Sharm el Sheikh is by Bedouin taxis, which are found just across the Egyptian border or at the Taba Hilton. It is advisable to use the buddy system, at least two to a car, and negotiate the fare in advance, bargaining down if it sounds exorbitant (the taxis don't have meters). Typical fares from the Taba Hilton are Taba to Nuweiba, L.E. 130; Taba to Dahab, L.E. 250; Taba to Sharm el Sheikh, L.E. 350. Bedouin Jeep drivers are available for hire at the various tourist centers.

Contacts and Resources

CAR RENTALS

Rental cars are available from **Europcar** at the Taba Hilton Hotel (☎ 07/637–9222; ⊙ daily 8–1 and 5–8), with offices in Nuweiba, Dahab, and Sharm el Sheikh hotels as well. You can arrange to rent a car with a driver, too.

GUIDED TOURS

Reliable tour operators conducting day trips to St. Catherine's Monastery include **Geographical Tours Ltd.** (⊠ Neptune Hotel, North Beach, Eilat, ☎ 07/637–3410; ⊠ 37 Bograshov St., Tel Aviv, ☎ 03/528–4113); **Johnny Desert Tours** (⊠ Shalom Center, opposite the airport, Eilat, ☎ 07/637–2608); **Mazada Tours** (⊠ 141 Ibn Gvirol St., Tel Aviv, ☎ 03/544–4454; ⊠ 24 Ben Sira St., Jerusalem, ☎ 02/625–5453, FAX 02/625–5454; ⊠ Paul VI St., Nazareth, ☎ 06/656–5937); and **Neot Hakikar** (head office: ⊠ 67 Ben Yehuda St., Tel Aviv, ☎ 03/520–5858, FAX 03/522–1020; ⊠ Khan Center, Eilat, ☎ 07/632–6281).

Information on diving in Sinai, as well as diving safaris of varying durations and locations, are offered by several diving clubs in Eilat: **Aqua Sport** (⊠ Box 300, Coral Beach, ☎ 07/633–4404, FAX 07/633–3771), **Dolphin Reef Diving Center** (⊠ Box 104, Southern Beach, ☎ 07/637–5935, FAX 07/637–5921), and the **Red Sea Sports Club** (⊠ Kings Wharf, the Lagoon, ☎ 07/637–9685 or 07/637–6569, FAX 07/637–3702).

The Green Club (⊠ J.E.T. Travel and Tours, 3 Ben Sira St., Jerusalem, ☎ 02/623–5535, FAX 02/624–7270) offers a special five-day tour of the Sinai with specially equipped four-wheel-drive vehicles; the price is $445 per person. **Mazada Tours** (☞ *above*) has Sinai safaris from two to five days long at a cost of $160–$267 per person, depending on the length of the safari. **The Society for the Protection of Nature in Israel** (SPNI), Sinai Department (⊠ 3 Hashefela St., Tel Aviv ☎ 03/638–8675; ⊠ 13 Helene Hamalka St., Jerusalem, ☎ 02/625–2357) has a well-proven reputation for expert nature tours. It runs off-the-beaten path four- and seven-day tours, costing $380 and $525 per person, respectively. **The Red Sea Sports Club,** in Eilat (⊠ Marina Diving Center, ☎ 07/637–6569, FAX 07/637–4083), has hiking and combination camel/hiking and Jeep/water sports tours. Choices include a one-day minisafari leaving and returning to Eilat ($85 per person), a two-day tour to St. Catherine's Monastery ($125–$165 per person, depending on accommodations), and an eight-day Sinai dive safari ($749 per person, including accommodations).

In Egypt, **Abanoub Travel Agency** (☎ 500140, FAX 520206), at the new commercial center at Nuweiba, has camel, Jeep, and trekking tours of varying durations to all parts of the Sinai.

MEDICAL CARE
Medical care is available at Nuweiba, Sharm el Sheikh, Dahab, and El Tur. The hospitals are very basic, however; for serious medical conditions, a person would need to be evacuated by helicopter from the region. There is a decompression chamber for divers at the hospital in Sharm el Sheikh. There is a private pharmacy in Nuweiba and a hospital pharmacy at St. Catherine's. A doctor is in residence at the Nuweiba Hilton and is available 24 hours a day.

TELEPHONES
When calling Sinai listings from Israel, you add the prefix 002–062. The international country code for dialing Egypt is 20; the area code for the Sinai is 62.

VISITOR INFORMATION
In Israel, you can contact the **Sinai Department of the Society for the Protection of Nature in Israel** in Tel Aviv (☞ Guided Tours, *above*). In Egypt, the **Abanoub Travel Agency** (☞ Guided Tours, *above*) can be helpful.

PETRA

By Miriam
Feinberg
Vamosh

Poet Dean Burger described Petra as the "rose-red city, half as old as time." His words convey some of the mystery and grandeur of the place: its boulevards, temples, and theater, and its splendid royal and noble tombs, secreted among the high cliffs. Once inaccessible to all but an intrepid few, Petra's magnificent ruins were the epitome of romance. They remain romantic, but today they are far from inaccessible.

With open borders between Israel and Jordan, a trip to Petra to explore the ruins and stay overnight in an area hotel is an increasingly popular option. The jaunt is an unforgettable experience, as much because of the antiquities and breathtaking scenery as for the sense of being part of history. On your trip to Petra, you are crossing a peaceful border; what was a distant dream only a few short years ago is now a reality.

Petra lies in the biblical region of Edom, southeast of the Dead Sea in modern-day Jordan. According to the Book of Genesis, the Edomites were descendants of Esau, Jacob's brother and rival. When Moses led the Israelites into the promised land, he asked the Edomites permission to pass through their land and was refused. The water sources and agriculture of this highland region were probably considered too precious to share with the new arrivals from the wilderness (Numbers 20:14–21).

The fertile land was a magnet that desert dwellers could not ignore, however, and the Israelites were not the last to appear there. By the 4th century BC, a new group had arrived from the wilderness to take advantage of the riches of the highlands of Edom: the Nabateans. It is their spectacular tombs and city monuments that draw visitors to Petra today.

Little is certain about the origins of the Nabateans; historians assume they were nomads from Arabia. One rare source is an early 4th-century BC record kept by one of the officers of Alexander the Great. In it, he describes the Nabateans as inhabitants of the wilderness who wandered with their flocks. Later historical sources describe the Nabateans as traders in frankincense and myrrh, the most valuable of biblical spices. They were also mentioned as highway robbers and even as pirates. When Alexander the Great died, his empire was divided between the Seleucids in the north and the Ptolomies in the south. The Nabateans fought against their new rulers, the Seleucids, and gained independence. Historical and archaeological sources hint that they gradually abandoned their nomadic lifestyle and became the wealthy masters of the region's trade routes.

Aretas, who may have been the first Nabatean king, is mentioned briefly in the Book of Maccabees. According to the New Testament (I Corinthians 11:32), one of his descendants, also named Aretas, ruled in Damascus. In his book *The Jewish War*, the 1st-century AD Roman Jewish historian Josephus mentions "Petra, capital of Arabia." He speaks of a succession of Nabatean kings who ruled it and of a Nabatean bowman who served with the Roman army in quelling the Jewish revolt of AD 66–70.

Most of the famous tombs of Petra were carved during this period. Although the combination of a necropolis and a capital city may seem strange today, this custom was common among the ancients, who established cemeteries at the entrance to many of their capitals, including Rome itself. The existence of the tombs of Petra's rulers and wealthy class near the major monuments of the city was apparently part of a cult of the dead. When traders and travelers came to visit the marvels of the capital city, they would leave offerings at these tombs to ensure the success of their business venture or journey.

When the Nabateans emerged from the desert, they brought with them a faith in the deities who had protected them as nomads and traders. In the more well-watered northern regions into which they came, they met local people whose pantheon was composed of figures who protected their crops and their cities. The principal deity of the Nabateans had been Dusares, whose name means "Lord of Sarat." Near Petra, the Nabateans found an area called Shara, and Dusares easily changed his name to Dushara, "Lord of Shara." As Egyptian and Greek influences penetrated the area, Dushara became associated with the chief male gods of those pantheons. The chief Nabatean goddess was al-Uzza, who reigned together with her sisters Allat and Manat. She, too, took on Greek and Egyptian attributes. Her cult eventually became identified with Aphrodite, Greek goddess of love; Tyche, goddess of fortune and protector of cities; and the Egyptian Isis. Almost all the shrines at Petra were dedicated to Dushara and al-Uzza.

In AD 106, during the reign of Trajan, the Romans annexed the Nabatean Kingdom, making it a part of their new province of Arabia. In 130, Hadrian visited Petra, after which it acquired a name in his honor, Petra Hadriane. With the completion of the main north–south artery of the eastern Roman empire, the Via Nova Triana, Petra flourished as the region continued as a conduit for goods.

A unique combination of talents made the Nabateans the unchallenged masters of this route. Though they eventually abandoned their nomadic way of life, they did not forget its survival secrets. They carved cisterns in the rocky wilderness, into which they channeled every drop of precious water that condensed on the desert floor or fell in rare rainstorms. Control over water, the desert's most precious resource, enabled the cargo-laden Nabatean caravans to cross vast expanses efficiently. That cargo—frankincense, myrrh, and other spices—was worth its weight in gold.

The spices had their origin in what is now Yemen, and the caravan road stretched from Arabia to Petra. It then continued across the Arava Valley to the Negev highlands of what is now Israel, eventually reaching the Mediterranean port of Gaza. Another branch of the road continued north from Petra to Damascus and to the ports of Lebanon. Roman historian Pliny the Elder related that the journey from Arabia to Gaza took 65 days. Each night the caravan would put in at a trading post run by Nabateans. Caravan masters handsomely rewarded their hosts for the essential services they provided to the weary, thirsty, and hungry travelers.

After the arrival of Christianity in the early 4th century, churches were built in Petra, and the new faith gradually replaced the old one. Bishops from Petra appear in ecclesiastical records as participants in the ecumenical councils that decided the doctrinal issues of the early Church. By this time, Petra was far past its prime as a trade center. The ancient traders had learned they could use the prevailing winds to hasten ships across the sea. Armed with this knowledge, some Arabian goods began to make their way to Egypt and its Mediterranean ports via the Red Sea. The overland route that passed through Petra continued to be used, but to a lesser extent. A series of earthquakes left their ruinous mark on the city.

After Petra fell to the Muslims in 633, both strategic alliances and crossroads changed course, and the world lost interest in the area. Capitalizing on the ancient strategic value of the region, the Crusaders constructed fortifications among the old ruins in the 11th century, but in 1189 they surrendered to the Muslim warrior Saladin. For more than half a millennium after that, Petra sank into oblivion, all knowledge of it confined to a few references in history books. It was not until 1812 that Swiss explorer Johann Ludwig Burckhardt (who had converted to Islam to facilitate his travels through the unknown area) penetrated Petra on the pretext of offering a sacrifice at the traditional tomb of Aaron. It was Burckhardt who provided the Western world with its first contemporary description of the marvels of the ancient city.

A two-day trip to Petra from Eilat will provide the opportunity to see more than just the highlights of Petra. Crossing the border early in the morning should put you in Petra around noon. Drop your things off at your hotel, put on comfortable walking shoes, and take advantage of the rest of the day to tour the highlights of the city. The next day, you can go back for a second look; then choose one or two hikes off the main route to round out your experience. Petra is open daily from 7 AM to sunset; entrance fee is about $30.

Pleasures and Pastimes

Hiking

Of several short hikes within the immediate vicinity, one leads to the High Place of Sacrifice; another is to the monument on the mountaintop known as Jabal a-Deir. A third hike leads to Little Petra, to the north of the village of Wadi Musa. The first two involve strenuous climbs, but the views and the antiquities at the top are well worth the effort for people in good physical condition. The trip to Little Petra is usually made by car, with a short walk to the antiquities.

Dining

Hotel restaurants and food stands represent the limited range of dining choices. At the Taybet Zeman Hotel, a rich buffet offers dozens of salads in the Middle Eastern tradition and main courses leaning more toward European delicacies; it's worth the trip to the village of Taybeh. The Petra Forum Hotel also has a very good buffet. A cafeteria-style restaurant is run by the Petra Forum in the museum building. Not far from there, stands sell sandwiches and other snacks. Some fast-food chains are now operating in the village of Wadi Musa.

Lodging

New hotels are springing up in Petra. The ones closest to the site obviously provide the most convenient access, but except for the Movenpick you may find that they are not worth the price. Several hotels are in Wadi Musa, adjacent to the site. Even the less elaborate ones are worth considering; after all, you will not be spending much time in your room. Taybet Zeman, in the village of Taybeh 9 km (5½ mi) from Petra, is the farthest from the site. Still, its truly authentic flavor is well worth the small expense of the ride.

CATEGORY	COST*
$$$$	over $160
$$$	$100–$160
$$	$50–$100
$	under $50

*All prices are for two people in a standard double room, including taxes.

Shopping

You will find "sand artists" lined up in a row in the area known as the Open Siq. Artisans will fill a bottle with sand in a variety of designs. They will customize your purchase by including the name of your choice in sand. You give your order in the morning, and it's ready when you return in the afternoon. Part of the fun is watching the artist at work.

Exploring Petra

The walk that follows will take you through the main sites of Petra. There is also a hike to the High Place of Sacrifice and a side trip to Little Petra to enrich your visit.

Numbers in the text correspond to numbers in the margin and on the Petra map.

A Good Walk

After paying your entrance fee, you will see the **Horse Square** ①, with the lean-tos where horses are for hire. You soon come to the large **Djinn Blocks** ②, on the right of the path about 450 meters (1,485 feet) after the entrance. On the other side of the path is the **Snake Tomb** ③; step in and you'll see why. Back on the path, you will see a large two-story tomb on your left. The lower story is called the Triclinium Tomb; the upper story is the **Obelisk Tomb** ④ and Bas-a-Siq Triclinium. From **Bab**

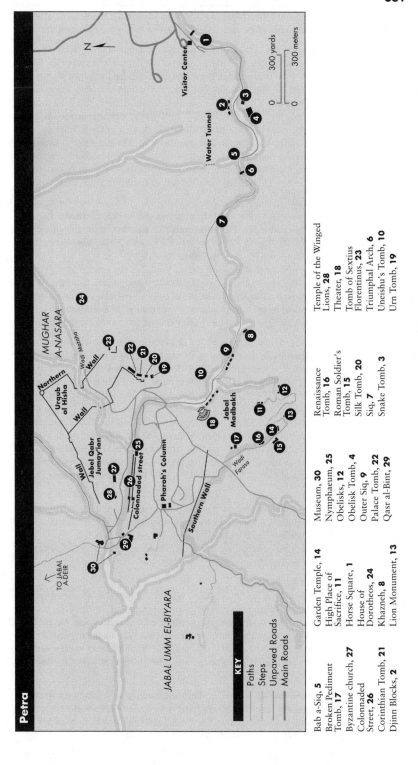

Petra

KEY

Paths
Steps
Unpaved Roads
Main Roads

Visitor Center, **1**
Water Tunnel

N

0   300 yards
0   300 meters

MUGHAR A-NASARA

Northern Wall

Urqub al Hisha

Wall

Jebel Qabr Jumay'ian

Wadi Mataha

JABAL UMM EL-BIYARA

TO JABAL A-DEIR

Colonnaded street

Pharoh's Column

Southern Wall

Jabal Madbakh

Wadi Farasa

Bab a-Siq, **5**
Broken Pediment Tomb, **17**
Byzantine church, **27**
Colonnaded Street, **26**
Corinthian Tomb, **21**
Djinn Blocks, **2**

Garden Temple, **14**
High Place of Sacrifice, **11**
Horse Square, **1**
House of Dorotheos, **24**
Khazneh, **8**
Lion Monument, **13**

Museum, **30**
Nymphaeum, **25**
Obelisks, **12**
Obelisk Tomb, **4**
Outer Siq, **9**
Palace Tomb, **22**
Qasr al-Bint, **29**

Renaissance Tomb, **16**
Roman Soldier's Tomb, **15**
Silk Tomb, **20**
Siq, **7**
Snake Tomb, **3**

Temple of the Winged Lions, **28**
Theater, **18**
Tomb of Sextius Florentinus, **23**
Triumphal Arch, **6**
Uneishu's Tomb, **10**
Urn Tomb, **19**

a-Siq ⑤, a 1¼-km (¾-mi) walk brings you to the main ruins of Petra; you can view the remains of a Nabatean water tunnel from this spot.

Travelers in the last century described a **triumphal arch** ⑥ that spanned the road at this point. As you traverse the narrow canyon of the **Siq** ⑦, nothing prepares you for the overwhelming first glimpse of the light at the end of the passage. The first burial monument is the magnificent **Khazneh** ⑧, or Treasury, adorned with figures from mythology. At this point the Siq widens and soon makes a sharp turn to the right. It is here, in the area called the **Outer Siq** ⑨, that you will meet the sand artists, ready to create a souvenir for you. On the right is **Uneishu's Tomb** ⑩. Across from the tomb, a flight of stairs leads to the path to the High Place of Sacrifice and the other tombs of Wadi Farasa ⑪–⑰, south and west of the main thoroughfare of antiquities (☞ Another Good Walk, *below*).

Continuing down the main street brings you to Petra's **theater** ⑱, a sign of Roman influence. The **Urn Tomb** ⑲ is the first in a series of some of the finest tombs in Petra, which also include the **Silk Tomb** ⑳, the **Corinthian Tomb** ㉑, and the **Palace Tomb** ㉒. No one really knows anything about those who were buried here, but the tombs' grandeur certainly suggests royal occupants. You can study these from the path or walk up and enter them. The main road now leads northeast toward the **Tomb of Sextius Florentinus** ㉓. The **House of Dorotheos** ㉔ is next, in an area where tombs were later reused for storage and habitation.

Returning to the main path in the city center, you will come to the **Nymphaeum** ㉕, one of the most important monuments in Petra. The ancient main street, known as the **Colonnaded Street** ㉖, was constructed by the Romans. The poorly preserved remains of a **Byzantine church** ㉗ stand on the slope to the north of the Colonnaded Street. Nearby is one of the city's most elaborate temples, the **Temple of the Winged Lions** ㉘. At the western end of the Colonnaded Street stood a monumental gateway to Petra's *temenos,* or sacred precinct. You can see the remains of statues of the deities worshiped here, including Hermes and Tyche. The temenos leads the visitor to a well-preserved temple, **Qasr al-Bint** ㉙. You can end your visit at Petra's **museum** ㉚.

TIMING

Plan on spending about six hours to see the highlights of Petra. It takes approximately 45 minutes to walk through the Siq to the main sites. If you want to hike to Jabal a-Deir, give yourself half a day. In summer the area is very hot, and you'll need to wear protection against the sun and to carry water.

Sights to See

❺ **Bab a-Siq.** The Gate of the Cleft is near the Siq, the canyon-lined passageway leading to the main sites. From here you can spot the remains of a Nabatean water tunnel, constructed to divert flood waters from coursing through the narrow cleft and flooding the necropolis. A dam, constructed for the same purpose in the second half of the 1st century AD, was restored by the Jordanians after particularly serious flooding some years ago.

㉗ **Byzantine church.** It appears that the church, richly decorated with mosaics in the style of the period, was destroyed by fire soon after its construction, perhaps in a severe earthquake that took place in AD 551. Unfortunately the remains are off-limits to visitors now.

㉖ **Colonnaded Street.** The Romans built the main street of Petra in the first part of the 1st century BC over earlier remains. In typical Roman style, it became the city's major thoroughfare, suitable for both commerce and grand ceremonial processions. After the Roman annexation of the Nabatean kingdom, restoration work was carried out on the street, as noted in an inscription dated AD 114 and dedicated to Emperor Trajan. In 363 an earthquake devastated Petra and the entire surrounding region. The city's inhabitants dug themselves out, but the street never again attained its former glory. Today visitors can see the remains of the columns that lined it in antiquity.

㉑ Corinthian Tomb. Set among some of Petra's finest tombs is one named for the large number of Corinthian capitals, now badly deteriorated, that once decorated its facade.

❷ Djinn Blocks. The function of these large structures is unclear: They may have been connected to Nabatean worship, perhaps symbolizing one of their deities. Their name in Arabic means "spirits," a common theme of Arab folklore.

❶ Horse Square. Horses used to be the conveyance of preference for the approximately 1-km (½-mi) trip to the main antiquities of Petra. This practice has been discontinued because of the growing numbers of visitors, but you can still hire horses to go the first 800 yards before the path narrows to become the Siq (☞ *below*), the 300-yard natural rock passageway to the site. Carriages ply the route for the benefit of those with difficulty walking. 🚪 *Horse or carriage hire, approximately $10, not including the expected minimum tip of $1.*

㉔ House of Dorotheos. The words THE HOUSE OF DOROTHEOS were found in this tomb in two Greek inscriptions. The area to the north of the tomb is called Mughar a-Nasara, meaning "caves of the Christians." Crosses carved on monuments here indicate their adaptation for use by the Christian inhabitants of the city.

★ ❽ Khazneh. Petra's most famous monument, this 130-foot-high structure has a splendid frontage graced by a number of mythological figures adopted by the Nabateans from Greek and Roman worship. Castor and Pollux (who after their death became the two brightest stars in the constellation Gemini), Amazons, Gorgons, eagles, and more march across the Khazneh's rosy facade. Between the columns of the tholos (the rounded section above the tympanum) are the remains of a female deity holding a cornucopia; she is believed to be the patroness of Petra, al-Uzza, the Nabatean version of the goddess of love, Aphrodite.

The Arabic name for this monument means "treasury"; its full name is Khaznet Fara'un, the Pharaoh's Treasury. Legends of treasures allegedly secreted within have led grave robbers here for centuries. The urn carved at the top of the tholos was thought to be the hiding place for the supposed hoard. The Bedouin have been taking potshots at it for generations in the hopes of dislodging its contents; the resulting damage can be clearly seen. The true function of the structure is unclear, but like most of the other large monuments at Petra, it is assumed to have been a tomb, constructed during the first century.

㉚ Museum. Petra's museum is in the building that also houses the Petra Forum restaurant, as well as rest rooms; another section is in a nearby tomb. A small number of Nabatean artifacts such as jewelry and pottery are on display.

OFF THE BEATEN PATH

JABAL A-DEIR – A strenuous 45-minute climb up a steep path that begins near the museum brings you to the summit of Jabal a-Deir, one of the most scenic places in Petra. The Mount of the Monastery received its name from the crosses carved into the rock of the giant monument at its summit by monks who inhabited the site in the 4th and 5th centuries.

The similarity between it and the Khazneh is remarkable, although this monument is much larger. Its relatively remote location might also suggest a greater degree of sanctity: The reason became clear when an inscription referring to the god Obodas was discovered. The Nabatean king Obodas I is remembered for his triumph over both the Hasmonean ruler Alexander Jannaeus and the Seleucid king of Syria Antiochus XII. Obodas died in 86 BC in the Negev and was deified shortly after. His burial place is somewhere in the ruins of the Nabatean city of Obodat (Avdat in Hebrew), in the Negev. This site was probably a shrine constructed in his honor, where supplicants gathered to perform rituals.

A clamber up the hill to the east of the monument affords a view of epic proportions: West of Petra, the highest peak in the region is the 4,455-foot-high sacred spot of Jabal Haroun, the traditional burial place of Aaron, brother of Moses. Beyond lies the wide expanse of the Arava Valley, and to the west, Israel's Negev Plateau.

㉕ Nymphaeum. Dedicated to the water nymphs, this fountain was both a place of refreshment and a place of worship. The fountains of this two-story structure were fed by a water channel that continued along the main street of Petra.

❹ Obelisk Tomb. The upper story of a two-story tomb is named for the four free-standing obelisks that decorate its facade. The lower story, the Triclinium Tomb, was so named because three walls of the empty room are lined with triclinia, a Latin word for this kind of bench. In other settings (not in a tomb), diners would partially recline on these.

❾ Outer Siq. As you traverse the area also known as Facade Street, you will see several tombs with variations on common Nabatean architectural themes. Among them are repeating triangular step patterns and pilasters topped with Nabatean or more classical capitals. Water pipes set into channels along the facades of the last tombs on the right-hand side were the continuation of the system that brought water from the Siq to the city beyond.

㉒ Palace Tomb. This partially constructed tomb is one of the few in Petra not carved entirely out of the rock. Many of the tomb's constructed segments have fallen away, so it is difficult to get an idea of its original dimensions. At the base of the Palace Tomb, remains of the northern city wall, constructed after the 1st century BC, can be seen.

㉙ Qasr al-Bint. The structure's full name, translated as the "Palace of the Daughter of Pharaoh," stems from a legend that the pharaoh's daughter promised she would marry the man who could channel water to the city where she lived. When she had to choose between two winners, she asked each how he had managed his appointed task. The one who answered in a manner most to her liking won her hand. In fact, the structure is a temple, constructed in the early 1st century AD. Its interior was approached through areas of gradually increasing sanctity. As in the Temple of the Winged Lions, the identity of the deity worshiped here is not known. A statue to him or her—perhaps Dushara, the greatest deity of the Nabatean pantheon—certainly stood in the temple's inner sanctum.

㉒ Silk Tomb. The striations of natural color in the rock of the Silk Tomb make it one of Petra's finest and also easy to identify. They seem to flow across the facade in a way that reminds the observer of a multicolor silk scarf blowing gently in the wind.

❼ Siq. The Siq (meaning "cleft"), a rocky passage between towering walls of stone, leads visitors to the main ruins. The colors of the rock are astounding, varying in hues of red and purple. Along the way, you may notice two locations where Nabatean paving is still visible. Niches, some of which contain inscriptions dating from the 2nd and 3rd centuries AD, show that this road was as much a ceremonial path as a passageway. One niche is carved into a small outcropping of rock near one of the paved patches of road. It is unusual because it faces away from the approach, and may have been designed to bestow a blessing on those leaving the city. Visitors may recall Harrison Ford riding through this area in some of the concluding scenes of *Indiana Jones and the Last Crusade*.

❸ Snake Tomb. No outward decoration marks this tomb, but within there are 12 burial niches carved into the floor. The name comes from a wall relief that shows two snakes attacking what may be a dog.

㉘ Temple of the Winged Lions. The sculptures that serve as capitals for the temple's columns gave this impressive building its name. The identity of the god or goddess worshiped within is unknown, but figurines of Isis, Egyptian goddess of the heavens and patroness of fertility, indicate she may have been the object of veneration. An inscription dates the construction of the temple to around AD 27.

⓲ Theater. This semicircular hallmark of Roman culture is a clear sign of the extent to which the Nabateans, like most peoples of the region, had adopted the Roman way of life. The Nabateans apparently had no qualms about constructing a theater in a cemetery; their stone masons even cut into some of the existing tombs (the remains of which can be seen at the back of the rock-cut theater) to do so. The capacity of the theater has been estimated at 10,000.

㉓ Tomb of Sextius Florentinus. The name of this Roman governor of Arabia appears in the tomb's inscription. Historical records note that he died in office in AD 128.

❻ Triumphal arch. Today all that is left of this arch near the Siq are niches with the remains of statues that decorated the point where the springers of the arch were constructed. The arch collapsed in 1895.

⓵⓪ Uneishu's Tomb. This tomb in the Outer Siq received its name from an inscription discovered within that read UNEISHU, BROTHER OF SHAQI-LATH, QUEEN OF THE NABATEANS.

⓳ Urn Tomb. Named for the vaselike decoration at the top of its pediment, this tomb is supported by a series of vaults at its lower level, dubbed *al makhamah* (the law court) by the locals for some long-forgotten reason; the upper level was called *a-sijn* (the prison). The Byzantine Christian inhabitants of Petra turned the Urn Tomb into a church in AD 446, as an inscription found within bears witness.

Another Good Walk

The path to the Nabatean shrine known as the **High Place of Sacrifice** ⑪ branches off from the main path through the city between the end of Facade Street and the theater. On a flat protrusion below the high place are two **obelisks** ⑫ carved from the mountain. The curving path continues past the **Lion Monument** ⑬, a fountain. About 400 yards later you'll see the tomb known as the **Garden Temple** ⑭. A short distance ahead lies the **Roman Soldier's Tomb** ⑮, an eclectic creation. Farther along is the **Renaissance Tomb** ⑯, named for its graceful facade, and the **Broken Pediment Tomb** ⑰. The relatively easy-to-follow path continues through Wadi Farasa and ends at the monument known as Pharaoh's Column, not far from the Colonnaded Street; you can also continue on to the museum.

The hike to the High Place of Sacrifice takes approximately three hours from the beginning of the ascent to the museum and its restaurant. To ascend to the High Place and then return to the main street of antiquities takes about 1½ hours.

Sights to See

⑰ Broken Pediment Tomb. This tomb is characterized by the broken-off gable of its roof, supported by four pilasters topped with capitals in the unique Nabatean style.

⑭ Garden Temple. To the right, above this tomb that also served as a temple, a wall closes off a cleft in the rock. It acted as a dam for water that reached it from a small spring south of the village of Wadi Musa. Two more water channels reached this point, bringing runoff from the area of the High Place of Sacrifice.

★ **⑪ High Place of Sacrifice.** An ancient flight of stairs renewed in recent years by the Jordanian Department of Antiquities leads to the top of Jabal Madhbah, the Mount of the Altar. True to its name, at its peak is a rectangular court surrounded on three sides by benches in the triclinium style of the Roman dining room. There is a raised block of stone in the center of the court, on which the priest may have stood. To the west are two altars accessed by steps, with a channel running in front, into which the blood of the sacrificial animal may have pooled. The existence of a triclinium may indicate that one of the rituals performed involved a ceremonial meal. The site's strategic value, overlooking the main thoroughfare of the city, is clear. A small jumble of ruined walls near the High Place of Sacrifice may have served the Nabateans as a fort.

⑬ Lion Monument. Surface runoff fed this fountain via a channel that led to the lion's mouth, from which water once streamed.

⑫ Obelisks. These two 20-foot-tall obelisks are examples of a common method of representing deities in the ancient Near East. Some scholars believe these to be representations of Dushara and al-Uzza. Others believe they are simply the remains of quarrying activity.

⑯ Renaissance Tomb. This tomb bears a resemblance to the Tomb of Sextius Florentinus (☞ A Good Walk, *above*) in the main part of the city. It may have been created around the same time, the first third of the 1st century AD.

⑮ Roman Soldier's Tomb. The figure in the niche of the tomb's facade is dressed in typical Roman military garb, while the friezes and capitals appear to have elements more typical of Nabatean architectural style before the Roman annexation. Directly opposite the Roman Soldier's Tomb is a triclinium; the rubble in between must once have been a courtyard connecting the two edifices.

Side Trip to Little Petra

3 km (2 mi) north of the village of Wadi Musa.

Little Petra was the area's main commercial center in Nabatean times. To reach this site, leave Petra and drive north, passing through Wadi Musa and continuing along the narrow blacktop. You will soon see a collection of ruins on a rocky outcropping on the left side of the road. This is all that remains of the **Crusader castle of al-Wu'eira,** built by Baldwin I in 1100, the first Crusader fortification east of the Jordan River. It was one of several strategic castles that protected the Crusader kingdom on its sensitive eastern flank. The castle also ensured the Crusaders revenue from the major trade route from Cairo to Damascus.

In 1189, al-Wu'eira was the last Crusader fortress east of the Jordan to surrender to the Muslim warrior Saladin.

Next you will come to the village of **Umm Saihun,** whose inhabitants are Bdhoul Bedouin, the main tribe of the Petra region. A 15-minute drive north will lead you to **al Beidha.** The name, Arabic for "the white," is for the color of the sandstone formations along the way. Excavations have uncovered the remains of an 11,000-year-old settlement from the Neolithic era. Findings show that the people who lived here were hunter-gatherers, but they also farmed and traded. Thousands of years after that culture became extinct, the Nabateans took over the same site and built agricultural terraces, remains of which can still be seen.

When you come to a T junction, take a left onto a dirt road. You will soon arrive at **Siq al-Barid.** This cleft in the rock will remind you of the Siq at Petra. It is much shorter and the sun does not penetrate it, hence the meaning of its Arabic name "the cold cleft." Walking through this passage, you will arrive at Little Petra. This, rather than the city of Petra itself, was the staging area for the thousands of camels that would have arrived with each caravan. In Little Petra's rock-cut courtyard, merchants conducted their business. Evidence shows they did not neglect the pleasures of life; one room constructed off the courtyard is a dining room, the ceiling of which was once richly painted. A theater was also discovered. ⊠ *Charge is included in Petra entrance fee.* ☉ *Daily, dawn to dusk. A guard will ask to see your pass.*

Lodging

$$$$ 🛏 **Petra Movenpick Hotel.** This attractive new (1996) hotel is very close to the entrance to the city of Petra and makes a comfortable, convenient base with plenty of facilities. ⊠ *Box 5315, Amman, Jordan 11183,* ☏ *03/337111 or 800/344-6835 in the U.S.,* FAX *03/337112. 156 rooms with bath, 27 suites. 2 restaurants, snack bar, minibars, no-smoking rooms, pool, sauna, exercise room, library. AE, DC, MC, V.*

$$$ 🛏 **Petra Forum.** On the outskirts of the village of Wadi Musa, the Forum is at the entrance to Petra. The Aretas restaurant serves Middle Eastern and European food and will prepare box lunches. The hotel has a souvenir shop. There are two rooms accessible for people who use wheelchairs. ⊠ *Box 30, Wadi Musa,* ☏ *03/336266,* FAX *03/336977. 147 rooms with bath. Restaurant, pool, car rental. AE, D, MC,V.*

$$$ 🛏 **Taybet Zeman.** Nine km (5½ mi) from Petra, on the outskirts of the town of Taybeh, this unique hotel is constructed in the style of a Bedouin village and has a spectacular view of the mountains of Edom. The central courtyard has a spice garden. The excellent hotel restaurant mixes eastern and western favorites; its buffet, about $25 per person, is worth a trip. ⊠ *Box 2, Wadi Musa,* ☏ *03/339111,* FAX *03/339101. 106 rooms with bath. Restaurant, sauna. AE, D, MC, V.*

$$ 🛏 **Kings Way Inn.** This establishment is in the village of Wadi Musa, 4 km (2½ mi) from Petra, across from the Ein Musa Spring. ⊠ *Box 71, Wadi Musa,* ☏ *03/336797,* FAX *03/336796. 81 rooms with bath. AE, D, MC, V.*

$$ 🛏 **Petra Palace.** A new hotel, the Palace is 250 yards from the entrance to Petra. The rate includes breakfast. ⊠ *Box 70, Wadi Musa,* ☏ *03/336723,* FAX *03/336724. 83 rooms with bath. Restaurant, bar, pool. MC, V.*

$$ 🛏 **Petra Rest House.** This option is close to the entrance to the site. *Wadi Musa,* ☏ *03/336011,* FAX *03/336014. 72 rooms with bath. Restaurant. MC, V.*

$$ \text{\$\$} \quad \textbf{⊞ Treasury Hotel.} $$

$$ ⊞ **Treasury Hotel.** This hotel is by the traffic circle at the center of the nearby village of Wadi Musa. ⊠ *Box 5, Wadi Musa.* ☎ *03/336221. 72 rooms with bath. MC, V.*

$ ⊞ **Amra Hotel.** A budget option, the Amra is in the center of Wadi Musa. ⊠ *Box 124, Wadi Musa,* ☎ *03/337070,* FAX *03/337071. 48 rooms with bath. No credit cards.*

$ ⊞ **Candles Hotel.** The Candles is 200 meters (660 feet) from the entrance to Petra. ⊠ *Box 149, Wadi Musa,* ☎ FAX *03/336954. 31 rooms with bath. AE, MC, V.*

Petra A to Z

Before You Go

BORDERS

The **Arava border crossing,** just north of Eilat in Israel, is open Sunday–Thursday 6:30 AM–10 PM, Friday–Saturday 8–8. The border crossing is closed on the religious holidays of Yom Kippur and Id el Fitr. There is a $16 border tax on the Israeli side.

Besides the Arava crossing, two other border crossings might be convenient under certain circumstances. The **Allenby Bridge** border crossing (four hours' drive from Petra) is about 45 minutes from Jerusalem. If you plan to enter Jordan here, you will need to obtain your visa ahead of time at the Jordanian Embassy in Tel Aviv (☞ Passports and Visas, *below*) or in your country of origin. The **Beit She'an** border crossing (five hours' drive from Petra) is approximately 40 minutes from Tiberias.

CURRENCY

The Jordanian unit of currency is the dinar, indicated by the suffix JD. The exchange rate at press time is approximately .708 JD to the U.S. dollar, .53 JD to the Canadian dollar, and 1.18 JD to the British pound.

PASSPORTS AND VISAS

A valid passport is necessary to cross the border into Jordan. Holders of non-Israeli passports can obtain their visas on the spot (unless you're crossing at the Allenby Bridge; *see* Borders, *above*) after crossing into Jordan or through the Jordanian Embassy (⊠ 14 Abba Hillel St., Tel Aviv, ☎ 03/751–7722). The cost of a visa for holders of U.S. passports is $21.

Arriving and Departing

BY BUS

There are only two buses per day from the Jordanian side of the Arava crossing to Aqaba, one at 7:30 AM and one at 8 PM; taxis are far more convenient.

BY CAR

Only cars registered to their drivers can be driven into Jordan (☞ Car Rentals *in* Contacts and Resources, *below*). No unleaded fuel is sold in Jordan.

BY TAXI

Taxis are available on the Jordanian side of the Arava border to take you into Aqaba, where you can rent a car. A shared taxi to Aqaba costs about $1.50 per person, a private taxi about $5.60.

BY PLANE

There are flights to Jordan's capital city of Amman from Ben-Gurion Airport near Tel Aviv by both El Al and Royal Jordanian airlines. Travelers must be at the airport two hours before flight time for the 15-minute flight and then drive three hours from Amman to Petra, so this option may have limited appeal.

Getting Around

BY CAR

Driving the narrow, winding Aqaba–Petra Highway is an experience. Remember to stay well to the right, with the thought in mind that the driver coming from the opposite direction may not be so inclined.

Contacts and Resources

CAR RENTALS

The **Petra Travel and Tourism Company** (☞ Guided Tours, *below*) is the local agent for Hertz, Avis, and other local companies. Reserving in advance makes it possible to have the car waiting for you at the Arava border crossing; otherwise, you pick up and drop off the car at the agency's offices in Aqaba.

GUIDED TOURS

A number of operators have tours to Petra that you can reserve in advance; they're a good option if you want to see the highlights without having to worry about logistics.

Galilee Tours (✉ 42 Ben Yehuda St., Tel Aviv, ☎ 03/525−2888, FAX 03/525−2999; ✉ Neptune Hotel, Eilat, ☎ 07/633−5145, FAX 07/633−5121) has a two-day tour to Wadi Rum (including a Jeep tour of its beautiful sandstone landscapes) and Petra, with an overnight in Petra. The price is $219 per person, including entrance fees, horses in Petra, and Jeeps in Wadi Rum.

Neot Hakikar (✉ 67 Ben Yehuda St., Tel Aviv, ☎ 03/522−8161, FAX 03/522−1020; ✉ Khan Amiel Center, Eilat, ☎ 07/633−0426) has a two-day trip to Petra, including a stop at Wadi Rum for a Jeep tour. The fee of $169 does not include the entrance fee to Petra.

Petra Travel and Tourism Company (✉ Headquarters at the Aqaba Gulf Hotel, Box 1312, Aqaba, Jordan, ☎ 03/316636, FAX 03/318246) offers a full-day guided tour of Petra with a driver-guide for $70 per day. You can also hire a private guide to join your car for $35−$50 per day, depending on the season.

MEDICAL CARE

There is a doctor at the **clinic** in the tourist compound near the Petra Forum Hotel at the entrance to Petra. The closest **hospital** is in Ma'an (☎ 03/332222), about 40 km (25 mi) away.

TELEPHONES

When dialing from Israel, dial 00−962 and the area code 3 before numbers in Petra; for Amman, use 00−962 and the area code 6. When dialing within Jordan, add a zero (0) before the area code. The international country code for Jordan is 962.

VISITOR INFORMATION

Petra has a **visitor center** (☎ 03/336020).

10 Chronology and Further Reading

ISRAEL AT A GLANCE: A CHRONOLOGY

By Mike
Rogoff

As the only land bridge between Africa and Asia, Israel has been a thoroughfare through the ages, a situation that made it desirable to foreign powers and often turned it into a battleground. In addition, Israel's position between the desert and the Mediterranean Sea has determined not only its climate and economy but also the character of those who conquered it and settled there.

The country was once called Canaan, then the Land of Israel (in Hebrew, Eretz Yisrael, then Israel. Later, the name Israel came to represent just the northern Israelite kingdom, including Samaria and Galilee, while the southern kingdom was called Judah. Judah became the Greek "Judea," first applied only to a small part of the country centered around Jerusalem but later to a much larger territory. After the Bar Kochba Revolt (2nd century AD), the Roman emperor Hadrian changed the name Judea to Palaestina (after the long-gone Philistines) in order to dissociate the country from its Jewish identity. Palestine later became the name of this tiny district in the huge medieval Muslim empires. To Christians it was always the Holy Land; to Jews, Eretz Yisrael. The use of the name Israel in the following chronology does not always imply any specific set of borders, past or present, but the country as a whole, the ancient Land of Israel.

Prehistoric Israel

ca. 1.2 million years ago Earliest known human habitation in Israel (Lower Paleolithic Period), at Ubeidiya in Jordan Valley.

ca. 7800 The establishment of Jericho (Neolithic Pre-Pottery Period), the oldest walled town ever found.

Canaanite Period (Bronze Age) ca. 3200 BC–1250 BC

ca. 3200–2150 Writing is developed in Mesopotamia; beginning of recorded history. Early Canaanite/Bronze Age in Israel. Major cities are built: Jerusalem, Megiddo, and Hazor.

ca. 2150–1550 Age of the Patriarchs: Abraham, Isaac, and Jacob. Middle Canaanite/Bronze Age.

ca. 1550–1250 Time of Hebrews' enslavement in Egypt. Decline of Egyptian power. Moses leads Hebrews in exodus from Egypt. Late Canaanite/Bronze Age: Israel divided into city-kingdoms.

ca. 1290 The Hebrews—the "Children of Israel"—receive the Torah (the Law) at Mt. Sinai. The nation of Israel is formed, the basis of its religion established, and its relationship with the one God defined. Forty years of desert wandering separate the nation from its Promised Land.

First Temple—Old Testament Period (Iron Age) ca. 1250 BC–586 BC

ca. 1250 Moses dies within sight of the Promised Land. Joshua leads the nation across the Jordan River and embarks on the conquest of Canaan, beginning with Jericho.

ca. 1200–1025 Period of the Judges (e.g., Deborah, Gideon, Samson), charismatic regional leaders.

ca. 1150 The Philistines invade from the west and establish a league of five city-states. Israelites appeal to the prophet Samuel for a king.

1025 Saul, of humble origin, is the first King of Israel.

1006 Saul and three sons, including Jonathan, are killed fighting the Philistines. David rules Judah.

1000 David conquers Jerusalem, a Jebusite enclave, and makes it the national capital of unified Israel. Having brought the sacred Ark of the Covenant to Jerusalem, he establishes the city as the new religious center.

968 Solomon becomes king, consolidates David's kingdom, and in 950 builds the First Temple to the Lord, in Jerusalem.

928 Division of the monarchy after death of Solomon. The northern Tribes of Israel, under Jeroboam, break away to form the Kingdom of Israel. The southern Tribes, now known as the Kingdom of Judah, with its capital at Jerusalem, are ruled by Rehoboam, Solomon's weak son.

ca. 865 Ahab rules as King of Israel (871–851) and Jehosophat as King of Judah (867–843). Peace between the two kingdoms. Ahab's wife, Jezebel, reintroduces pagan idol-worship.

721 Kingdom of Israel destroyed by the Assyrians (now the region's superpower) and exile of its population (the "Ten Lost Tribes.") Kingdom of Judah comes under the Assyrian yoke.

701 Hezekiah, King of Judah, revolts against Assyria. Assyrians lay siege to Jerusalem. With new fortifications, a superb water system, and the inspiration of the prophet Isaiah, the city withstands the siege.

609 Josiah, last great king of Judah (640–609) and important religious reformer, is killed trying to block Egyptian advance. Jeremiah prophesies national catastrophe.

586 Assyrians defeated by new power, the Babylonians, whose king, Nebuchadnezzar, conquers Judah and destroys Jerusalem and the First Temple. Of those who survive, large numbers are exiled to the "rivers of Babylon."

Second Temple Period, 538 BC–AD 70

Although during this period the Babylonians are defeated, the Temple in Jerusalem is rebuilt, and the sacrificial rites are restored, the Land of Israel must share its preeminence with important Jewish centers in Babylon, Egypt, and elsewhere. From the 3rd century BC on, deep divisions appear within the Jewish nation over theological issues and the seductive Hellenistic culture, introduced to the region by Alexander the Great. The Sadducee group, which draws its strength from the upper classes, takes a literal, Bible-based view and is willing to accommodate elements of Hellenism. The Pharisees, a Jewish group of the common people, add the Oral Law (the unwritten rabbinic interpretation of the Torah) to the authority of the Scriptures. They reject accommodation with the pagan world and give rise to spin-off groups like the ascetic Essenes and the militant Zealots.

538 Cyrus, King of Persia, conquers Babylon and allows the Jewish exiles to return home. In Jerusalem, the returnees rebuild the Temple (completed ca. 516). In Babylon, the synagogue, a communal place of assembly with an emphasis on the reading of the Bible and (eventually) on prayer, develops.

445 Nehemiah, a Jewish nobleman, is sent by the Persian king with the authority to rebuild Jerusalem's walls and rule the district.

333 Persian Empire is defeated by Alexander the Great, and the entire Near East comes under Hellenistic sway.

323 Death of Alexander and struggle for control of his empire. Ptolemy rules in Egypt; Seleucus in Syria and Mesopotamia.

301 Ptolemy establishes control over Judea (as Judah is now called) and Samaria and the Galilee (an area once known as Israel), to the north of it. Egypt's now Greek-speaking Jewish population burgeons. The Bible is translated into Greek and called the Septuagint.

198 The Syrian Seleucids defeat the Egyptian Ptolemies at Banias, the headwaters of the Jordan, annex Judea, and establish good relations with the Jewish community.

167 The Seleucid king Antiochus IV outlaws all Jewish religious practices. Beginning of the Maccabean Revolt.

165 After four decisive victories over Hellenistic armies, Judah the Maccabee (Judas Maccabeus) enters the desecrated Temple in Jerusalem, purifying and rededicating it.

142 Simon, brother of Judah the Maccabee, achieves independence for Judea and establishes the Hasmonean dynasty.

63 Pompey, the Roman general, enters the country to settle a civil war between the last Hasmonean princes and annexes it as a Roman province.

48 The influential royal counselor Antipater, a Jewish convert, appoints his sons, among them Herod, to key administrative positions.

40 Mark Antony appoints Herod as king of the Jews.

37 After fighting his way through the country, Herod claims his throne in Jerusalem. Hated by the Jews, he seeks to legitimize his reign by marrying a Hasmonean princess (whom he later murders).

31 Antony is defeated by Octavian, now the emperor Caesar Augustus. Herod pays homage to Augustus in Rome and is confirmed in his titles and territories, then rebuilds the Second Temple in Jerusalem on a grand scale, winning great esteem.

ca. 5 Birth of Jesus in Bethlehem.

4 Death of Herod, called by history "the Great." His kingdom is divided among three sons: Archelaus rules in Jerusalem (and is exiled 10 years later, replaced by the direct Roman rule of Judea by procurators based in Caesarea); Herod Antipas rules the Galilee and Perea (east of the Jordan River); and Philip controls Golan, Bashan, and the sources of the Jordan River.

ca. AD 27 Beginning of Jesus' Galilean ministry. He calls the disciples, heals and performs miracles, teaches, and preaches, mostly around the Sea of Galilee.

ca. 29 Jesus and his disciples celebrate Passover in Jerusalem. Arrest, trial, and crucifixion of Jesus by the Romans on orders of the Roman governor, Pontius Pilate. For the Romans, the claim of Jesus as the Messiah (Hebrew for "the anointed one"), with its implication of kingship, is tantamount to high treason. The New Testament relates that Jesus' death and resurrection were divinely determined, an expiation for the sins of humanity. Identification with this event as the way to personal salvation becomes the basis for the community of faith that is Christianity.

66 Start of Great Revolt against Roman oppression. Jews briefly reassert their political independence.

67 Galilee falls to the Romans. The Jewish commander defects to the enemy. Romanizing his name to Josephus Flavius, he follows the Roman campaigns, eventually recording them in *The Jewish War*.

69 Before the fall of Jerusalem, the sage Yochanan Ben Zakkai leaves the city, settling with his disciples in the town of Yavneh in the coastal plain, by grant of Roman general and caesar-elect Vespasian.

70 Jerusalem, torn by internal faction fighting, falls to the Roman general Titus after long siege. The Second Temple is destroyed. Slaughter and slavery of Jews follow. The revolt is officially at an end.

73 The last Jewish stronghold, at Masada, falls. Its defenders take their own lives rather than surrender. With the destruction of Jerusalem and the Temple, Yavneh becomes the seat of the Sanhedrin, the Jewish High Court. Its sages find religious responses to the new reality of Judaism without the Temple, and the spiritual and legal authority of Yavneh is established.

Late Roman and Byzantine Period, 73–640

132 When the Roman emperor Hadrian threatens to rebuild Jerusalem as a pagan city, another Jewish revolt breaks out, led by Bar Kochba and supported by Rabbi Akiva. Secret preparations and a strong unified command lead to spectacular initial successes.

135 Death of Bar Kochba. The revolt is brutally suppressed, but only after severe Roman losses. Hadrian plows over Jerusalem and builds in its place Aelia Capitolina, a pagan city off-limits to Jews; the name of the country is changed to Palaestina, and Jewish religious practice is outlawed. The Sanhedrin relocates to the Lower Galilee.

ca. 200 At Zippori or Sepphoris, in the Galilee, Judah the Nasi (patriarch), spiritual and political head of the Jewish community, compiles the Mishnah, the summary of the Oral Law, which is the basis of Jewish jurisprudence. Period of peace and prosperity under the tolerant Severan emperors.

325 Emperor Constantine the Great makes Christianity the imperial religion and eventually converts to the faith. His mother, Helena, comes to the Holy Land in 326 and initiates the building of major churches—the Holy Sepulcher in Jerusalem and the Nativity in Bethlehem.

330 Constantine transfers his capital from Rome to Byzantium, now renamed Constantinople. Beginning of the Byzantine Period. Judaism is on the defensive.

351 Jewish revolt, primarily in the Galilee, against the Roman ruler Gallus is brutally suppressed.

361 Emperor Julian the Apostate (r. 361–363) tries to reintroduce pagan cults.

ca. 400 Final codification of the so-called Jerusalem Talmud, the result of years of rabbinic elaboration of the Mishnah. (The Babylonian Talmud, codified a century later, is regarded as more authoritative.)

527–565 Reign of Emperor Justinian. Many important churches built or rebuilt, among them the present Church of the Nativity in Bethlehem. Vibrant Jewish community despite persecution.

614 Persian invasion, with destruction of churches and monasteries.

622 Muhammad's "flight" (*hejira*) from Mecca to Medina in Arabia; beginnings of Islam.

628 Persians defeated and Byzantine rule restored in Israel.

632 Death of Muhammad. His followers, ruled by a series of caliphs, burst out of Arabia and create a Muslim empire that within a century would extend from India to Spain.

636 Arab invasion of the country, and in 638, the fall of Byzantine Jerusalem to the caliph Omar (r. 634–644).

Medieval Period, 640–1516

691 Caliph Abd al-Malik builds the Dome of the Rock in Jerusalem.

1099 Sworn to wrest Christian holy places from Muslim control, the European armies of the First Crusade reach the Holy Land. Jerusalem is taken, and most of its population, Muslim and Jew alike, is massacred.

1100 Establishment of the Latin Kingdom of Jerusalem, with Baldwin I at its head. Chronic shortage of manpower puts the burden of defense on the monastic orders—the Hospitallers and Templars, for example—who build castles (among them Belvoir, in the Lower Galilee, and the underground quarter in Akko).

1110 Most coastal cities in Crusader hands.

1187 Crusader armies decimated by the Arab ruler Saladin. Crusaders expelled from the country.

1191 The Third Crusade arrives, led by Richard the Lionhearted of England and Philip II (Augustus) of France. The Latin Kingdom of Jerusalem never regains its former size and glory—and except for a very brief time, the holy city itself—and the Crusaders content themselves with the coast from Tyre to Jaffa and the Galilee. Acre (Akko) becomes the royal capital.

1228 The Crusaders gain Jerusalem by treaty but lose the city again in 1244.

1250 The militant Mamluk class seizes power in Egypt. The Crusade of King Louis IX (St. Louis) against Egypt fails. He is captured but comes to the Holy Land after his release.

1260 The Mamluks check the Mongol invasion at Ayn Jalout (Ein Harod), in the Jezreel Valley.

1265 Muslim reconquest of the land begins under the Mamluk sultan Baybars.

1291 Fall of Akko and end of Crusader kingdom. Commerce and trade decline with destruction of coastal cities. Beginning of period of outstanding architecture, especially in Jerusalem's Temple Mount (Haram esh-Sharif) and Muslim Quarter and in the Cave of Machpelah in Hebron.

1492 Expulsion of the Jewish community from Spain. Many of these Sephardic Jews later immigrate to Israel.

The Modern Period, 1516–Present

1516 Mamluk armies defeated in Syria by the Ottoman Turks, who extend control over the land of Israel (Palestine) as well. Jewish community throughout the country grows. Zfat (Safed) is center of Kabbalah.

1520–1566 Suleiman the Magnificent reigns. His many projects include rebuilding Jerusalem's walls.

1700 Large numbers of Ashkenazi (Eastern European) Jews arrive.

1799 Invasion by Napoléon Bonaparte founders at Akko.

1832 Egyptian nationalists under Muhammad Ali and Ibrahim Pasha take control of Israel. They are expelled in 1840 with the help of European nations.

1853 The Crimean War breaks out in Europe against the background of conflict between Catholic France and Orthodox Russia over the custody of holy places in Israel.

1882 First Aliyah (wave of Jewish immigration), mostly idealistic Eastern Europeans. Baron Edmond de Rothschild establishes new villages and wineries in the coastal plain and the Galilee.

1897 First World Zionist Conference, organized by Theodore Herzl in Basel, Switzerland, gives great impetus to the idea of a "Jewish national home."

1906 The Second Aliyah, or wave of immigration, of young Jewish idealists from Russia and Poland, including David Ben-Gurion, who would become Israel's first prime minister.

1909 Tel Aviv founded. Degania, the first kibbutz, established on the southern shore of the Sea of Galilee.

1917 British government issues Balfour Declaration expressing support for a "Jewish national home" in Palestine. General Edmund Allenby captures Jerusalem.

1918 Ottoman Turkey, which had sided with Germany during World War I, abandons Palestine.

1920–1939 As Arab nationalism rises in the post-Ottoman Middle East, tensions increase between Jews and Arabs in Palestine, peaking in the massacres of Jews in 1920, 1929, and 1936. Jewish militias form to counter the violence. Substantial immigration of European Jews, who come with growing urgency, as Nazis take power in Germany.

1921 Transjordan is separated from Palestine.

1922 The newly formed League of Nations confirms the Mandate entrusting the rule of Palestine to Great Britain and incorporating the text of the Balfour Declaration.

1939 British Government issues white paper restricting Jewish immigration to Israel and Jewish purchase of land there in an attempt to secure Arab goodwill in the coming war. In World War II, Jews enlist on Allied side. "We shall fight the war as if there were no white paper," said Palestinian Jewish leader David Ben-Gurion, "but we shall fight the white paper as if there were no war."

1945 End of World War II, in which one-third of Jewish people were annihilated by the Nazis. When British policy does not change, underground movements challenge British authority. Illegal immigrants, many of them Holocaust survivors, are brought in on ships; many don't get through British blockade. Clashes with Arabs increase.

1947 United Nations Special Commission on Palestine recommends plan to partition the country into a Jewish state and an Arab state (three disconnected territorial segments in each) and to internationalize

Jerusalem and Bethlehem. Jewish euphoria, Arab rejection. Beginning of Israel's War of Independence. Discovery of the first Dead Sea Scrolls at Qumran.

1948   May 14: Last British forces depart, ending British Mandate. David Ben-Gurion declares Israel an independent state. The new state survives invasion by the armies of seven Arab countries.

1949   End of fighting in January. UN-supervised cease-fire agreements signed. Transjordan annexes the West Bank (of the Jordan River) and East Jerusalem, which it captured in the war, and changes the country's name to the Hashemite Kingdom of Jordan. Egypt annexes the Gaza Strip along the southern Mediterranean coast. Palestinian Arabs who fled during the conflict are housed in refugee camps in neighboring countries; those who remain behind become citizens of Israel. First elections to the Knesset, Israel's parliament. David Ben-Gurion is elected prime minister; Dr. Chaim Weizmann, first president.

1949–1952   Israel absorbs great numbers of Jewish refugees, trebling its Jewish population by the end of the decade.

1950   The Knesset enacts the Law of Return, giving any Jew the right to Israeli citizenship.

1956   Sinai Campaign, in which British, French, and Israeli forces oppose Egyptian nationalization of the Suez Canal. Fedayeen terrorist attacks from Egyptian-controlled Gaza Strip become less frequent, but sporadic Syrian shelling of Israeli villages below the Golan Heights is a major security issue into the 1960s.

1964   Formation of the Palestine Liberation Organization (PLO). Seeks independent state for Palestinians and refuses to recognize the legitimacy of the state of Israel.

1967   June: Outbreak of Six-Day War. Egypt, Jordan, and Syria are routed; Israel occupies the Sinai Peninsula, Gaza Strip, West Bank, East Jerusalem, and the Golan Heights and finds itself in control of almost 1 million Palestinian Arabs. Some Jewish settlements are established in the West Bank and Golan Heights.

1973   Egypt and Syria attack Israel on the holiest Jewish holiday, the Day of Atonement (hence, the name Yom Kippur War). Israel beats off the invasion but is sobered.

1974–1975   Signing of Disengagement Agreement on the Golan with Syria and the Interim Agreement with Egypt.

1976   Dramatic Israeli commando raid frees Air France passengers taken hostage in Entebbe, Uganda, by Palestinian hijackers.

1977   Menachem Begin's Likud Party comes to power in May, ending almost four decades of Labor domination of Israeli politics. Egyptian President Anwar Sadat visits Israel.

1978   Camp David Accords give direction to Egypt-Israel peace talks and produce guidelines for a solution to the Palestinian problem.

1979   Israel-Egypt peace agreement signed.

1980   Israeli prime minister Menachem Begin and Egyptian president Anwar Sadat share the Nobel Peace Prize.

1982   Israeli forces cross into southern Lebanon in pursuit of Palestinians shelling civilian settlements in Israel. This escalates into the Lebanon War (1982–85), with unprecedented opposition from Israelis.

1987 A road accident in the Gaza Strip triggers the beginning of the *intifada,* sustained Palestinian Arab street violence, demonstrations, strikes, and sporadic terrorist activity.

1989–1992 Israel absorbs over 500,000 Soviet Jewish immigrants.

1991 Persian Gulf War; Israel under constant attack but restrained from retaliating. June: 14,500 Ethiopian Jews airlifted to Israel. December: Peace talks in Madrid between Israel and Jordan, Syria, Lebanon, and the Palestinians.

1992 In June the Labor Party under Yitzhak Rabin, vowing to step up the peace process and halt Israeli "political" settlements in West Bank, is voted in after 15 years out of office.

1993–1994 The Oslo Accords provide for mutual recognition of Israel and PLO, as well as Palestinian autonomy in the Gaza Strip and Jericho. Nobel Peace Prize shared by Yitzhak Rabin, Shimon Peres, and Yasir Arafat.

1995 Prime minister Yitzhak Rabin assassinated in November by an Israeli, a tragic climax to a year of rancorous national debate on the "territory for peace" concept. Six more Palestinian Arab West Bank cities are given autonomy.

1996 Early elections in May are colored by internal security issues as a result of bus bombings months earlier. New law for direct election of prime minister brings Likud's Binyamin Netanyahu to power by a margin of less than 1%. Contrary to expectations, the major parties lose much strength, with the religious parties—now powerful partners in the new, far more conservative government—the big winners. An advanced Israeli communications satellite is successfully launched.

FURTHER READING

History and Biography

If you haven't opened the Bible in a while, this is a good time to review biblical narratives; better yet, bring it along on your trip. For a modern look at the Bible, take a look at *Genesis and the Big Bang*, by Gerald Schroeder (Bantam). *Heritage, Civilization and the Jews*, by Abba Eban (Steimatzky), is a pictorial survey illustrating 5,000 years of Jewish civilization. *Jews, God and History*, by Max I. Dimont (Signet) is an old but very readable history of the Jewish people (and very portable for traveling). Karen Armstrong's *Jerusalem: One City, Three Faiths* (Alfred A. Knopf) traces the city's physical history and spiritual meaning from its beginning to the present day. *Understanding the Dead Sea Scrolls*, edited by Hershel Shanks (Random House) is a selection of essays by leading scholars; it provides numerous insights into that important discovery. Last, but far from least, is Flavius Josephus's *The Jewish War*. The Jewish commander who defected to the Romans during the Great Revolt wrote a still-fascinating account of the Roman campaigns.

To better understand some of the leading players in Israel's modern history, try: *The Life of Moshe Dayan*, by Robert Slater (St. Martin's Press); *Ben-Gurion*, by Shabtai Teveth (Houghton Mifflin); *The Revolt*, by Menachem Begin (Steimatzky), the former prime minister's account of the fighting unit he headed; and *My Life*, by Golda Meir (Weidenfeld and Nicolson). *O Jerusalem*, by Larry Collins and Dominique Lapierre (Simon and Schuster), is a dramatic account of the establishment of the Israeli state.

The Book of Our Heritage, by Eliayahv Kitov (Feldheim), is a superb guide to Jewish holidays and traditions.

Fiction and Poetry

Exodus, a novel by Leon Uris (Doubleday), deals with the founding of the State of Israel. *The Source,* by James Michener (Fawcett), is the novelist's vivid look at Israel's early history. *Closing the Sea,* by Yehudit Katzir (Harcourt, Brace, Jovanovich), is a book of short stories set in Israel. *The Black Box,* by Amos Oz (Flamingo), is a modern love story. *Saturday Morning Murder,* by Batya Gur (Harper Collins), is a psychological mystery. Among the works of poet Yehuda Amichai is *Poems of Jerusalem.* Other contemporary Israeli writers worth looking out for are A. B. Yehoshua, Meir Shalev, David Grossman, and Irit Linor.

Modern Israel

To Jerusalem and Back, by Saul Bellow (Avon), conveys the flavor of modern Israeli life through the impressions of the Nobel Prize–winning author. *In the Land of Israel,* by Amos Oz (Chatto and Windus), is a series of articles depicting various settlements and towns and conversations with local people. In *Arab and Jew* (Times Books), David K. Shipler, a former *New York Times* correspondent, takes a contemporary look at the relationship. *Intifada,* by Zeev Schiff and Ehud Yaari (Touchstone), gives background and analysis of the Arab unrest in the late 1980s and early '90s. In *My Enemy, Myself* (Penguin), Yoram Binur, a journalist, imagines himself a Palestinian. Thomas Friedman looks at modern events and politics in the Middle East in *From Beirut to Jerusalem* (Farrar, Straus & Giroux). And try *Jerusalem, City of Mirrors,* by Amos Elon (Fontana), and *Safed, the Mystical City,* by David Rossoff (Feldheim Publishers).

INDEX

Index

NOTES

Fodor's Travel Publications

Available at bookstores everywhere, or call 1–800–533–6478, 24 hours a day.

Gold Guides

U.S.

Alaska

Arizona

Boston

California

Cape Cod, Martha's Vineyard, Nantucket

The Carolinas & the Georgia Coast

Chicago

Colorado

Florida

Hawai'i

Las Vegas, Reno, Tahoe

Los Angeles

Maine, Vermont, New Hampshire

Maui & Lāna'i

Miami & the Keys

New England

New Orleans

New York City

Pacific North Coast

Philadelphia & the Pennsylvania Dutch Country

The Rockies

San Diego

San Francisco

Santa Fe, Taos, Albuquerque

Seattle & Vancouver

The South

U.S. & British Virgin Islands

USA

Virginia & Maryland

Washington, D.C.

Foreign

Australia

Austria

The Bahamas

Belize & Guatemala

Bermuda

Canada

Cancún, Cozumel, Yucatán Peninsula

Caribbean

China

Costa Rica

Cuba

The Czech Republic & Slovakia

Eastern & Central Europe

Europe

Florence, Tuscany & Umbria

France

Germany

Great Britain

Greece

Hong Kong

India

Ireland

Israel

Italy

Japan

London

Madrid & Barcelona

Mexico

Montréal & Québec City

Moscow, St. Petersburg, Kiev

The Netherlands, Belgium & Luxembourg

New Zealand

Norway

Nova Scotia, New Brunswick, Prince Edward Island

Paris

Portugal

Provence & the Riviera

Scandinavia

Scotland

Singapore

South Africa

South America

Southeast Asia

Spain

Sweden

Switzerland

Thailand

Tokyo

Toronto

Turkey

Vienna & the Danube

Fodor's Special-Interest Guides

Alaska Ports of Call

Caribbean Ports of Call

The Complete Guide to America's National Parks

Family Adventures

Fodor's Gay Guide to the USA

Halliday's New England Food Explorer

Halliday's New Orleans Food Explorer

Healthy Escapes

Ballpark Vacations

Kodak Guide to Shooting Great Travel Pictures

Nights to Imagine

Rock & Roll Traveler USA

Sunday in New York

Sunday in San Francisco

Walt Disney World, Universal Studios and Orlando

Walt Disney World for Adults

Wendy Perrin's Secrets Every Smart Traveler Should Know

Where Should We Take the Kids? California

Where Should We Take the Kids? Northeast

Worldwide Cruises and Ports of Call

Affordables
Caribbean
Europe
Florida
France
Germany
Great Britain
Italy
London
Paris

Bed & Breakfasts and Country Inns
America
California
The Mid-Atlantic
New England
The Pacific Northwest
The South
The Southwest
The Upper Great Lakes

The Berkeley Guides
California
Central America
Eastern Europe
Europe
France
Germany & Austria
Great Britain & Ireland
Italy
London
Mexico
New York City
Pacific Northwest & Alaska
Paris
San Francisco

Compass American Guides
Alaska
Arizona
Boston
Canada
Chicago
Colorado
Hawaii
Idaho
Hollywood
Las Vegas
Maine
Manhattan
Minnesota
Montana
New Mexico
New Orleans
Oregon
Pacific Northwest
San Francisco
Santa Fe
South Carolina
South Dakota
Southwest
Texas
Utah
Virginia
Washington
Wine Country
Wisconsin
Wyoming

Citypacks
Atlanta
Berlin
Chicago
Hong Kong
London
Los Angeles
Montréal
New York City
Paris
Prague
Rome
San Francisco
Tokyo
Washington, D.C.

Fodor's Español
Caribe Occidental
Caribe Oriental
Gran Bretaña
Londres
Paris

Exploring Guides
Australia
Boston & New England
Britain
California
Canada
Caribbean
China
Costa Rica
Egypt
Florence & Tuscany
Florida
France
Germany
Greek Islands
Hawai'i
Ireland
Israel
Italy
Japan
London
Mexico
Moscow & St. Petersburg
New York City
Paris
Prague
Provence
Rome
San Francisco
Scotland
Singapore & Malaysia
South Africa
Spain
Thailand
Turkey
Venice

Fodor's Flashmaps
Boston
New York
San Francisco
Washington, D.C.

Fodor's Gay Guides
Los Angeles & Southern California
Pacific Northwest
San Francisco and the Bay Area
USA

Fodor's Pocket Guides
Acapulco
Atlanta
Barbados
Budapest
Jamaica
London
New York City
Paris
Prague
Puerto Rico
Rome
San Francisco
Washington, D.C.

Mobil Travel Guides
America's Best Hotels & Restaurants
California & the West
Frequent Traveler's Guide to Major Cities
Great Lakes
Mid-Atlantic
Northeast
Northwest & Great Plains
Southeast
Southwest & South Central

Rivages Guides
Bed and Breakfasts of Character and Charm in France
Hotels and Country Inns of Character and Charm in France
Hotels and Country Inns of Character and Charm in Italy
Hotels and Country Inns of Character and Charm in Paris
Hotels and Country Inns of Character and Charm in Portugal
Hotels and Country Inns of Character and Charm in Spain

Short Escapes
Britain
France
New England
Near New York City

Fodor's Sports
Golf Digest's Places to Play
Skiing USA
USA Today The Complete Four Sport Stadium Guide

Fodor's Vacation Planners
Great American Learning Vacations
Great American Sports & Adventure Vacations
Great American Vacations
Great American Vacations for Travelers with Disabilities
National Parks and Seashores of the East
National Parks of the West

WHEREVER YOU TRAVEL, *H*ELP IS NEVER FAR AWAY.

From planning your trip to providing travel assistance along the way, American Express® Travel Service Offices are always there to help.

Israel

American Express Travel Service
40 Jaffa Street
Jerusalem
2/623-1710

American Express Travel Service
112 Hayarkon Street
Tel Aviv
3/524-2211

Travel

http://www.americanexpress.com/travel